Elizabeth Jolley Hicks and
George Armstrong Hicks, circa 1880
Fox and Symon carte de visite.
Courtesy International Society, Daughters of Utah Pioneers.

KING
in t
WE

The Mormons and th

Will Bagley,

VOLU

Playing with Shadows

Voices of Dissent in the Mormon West

Edited by
Polly Aird, Jeff Nichols, and Will Bagley

THE ARTHUR H. CLARK COMPANY
An imprint of the University of Oklahoma Press
Norman, Oklahoma
2011

Library of Congress Cataloging-in-Publication Data
Playing with shadows : voices of dissent in the Mormon West / edited by Polly Aird, Jeff Nichols, and Will Bagley.
p. cm. — (Kingdom in the West : the Mormons and the American frontier ; v. 13)
Includes bibliographical references and index.
ISBN 978-0-87062-380-6 (hardcover : alk. paper) — ISBN 978-0-87062-403-2 (special limited edition : alk. paper) 1. Church of Jesus Christ of Latter-day Saints—Controversial literature. 2. Mormon Church—Controversial literature. 3. Church of Jesus Christ of Latter-Day Saints—West (U.S.)—History—19th century. 4. Mormon Church—West (U.S.)—History—19th century. 5. West (U.S.)—Church history—19th century. I. Aird, Polly. II. Nichols, Jeffrey D. III. Bagley, Will, 1950–
BX8645.P53 2011
289.3092'279—dc23
2011018347

The paper in this book meets the guidelines for permanence and durability of the Committee on Production Guidelines for Book Longevity of the Council on Library Resources, Inc. ∞

Published by the University of Oklahoma Press, Norman, Publishing Division of the University.
Manufactured in the U.S.A.

1 2 3 4 5 6 7 8 9 10

I feel to say to Jew and to Gentile, Let this people alone in these valleys of the mountains, or you will find that which you are not looking for. . . . The time has come that Israel shall be redeemed, and they never shall be trampled under foot again. Now is the time; Joseph told us, before he was killed, the set time to favor Zion had come. I want you to hear, Bishops, what I am about to tell you. Kick these men out of your wards. If you want to apostatize, apostatize, and behave yourselves. You shall not disturb my peace, nor the peace of this people. If you want to go to California, go, . . . but disturb not this community, or else you will find judgment is laid to the line. Do not court persecution, for, remember, you are not playing with shadows, but it is the voice and the hand of the Almighty you are trying to play with, and you will find yourselves mistaken if you think to the contrary.

Brigham Young, warning the followers of Mormon prophet Gladden Bishop, 27 March 1853, Journal of Discourses, *1:84*

Every successful revolution puts on in time the robes of the tyrant it has deposed.

Barbara Tuchman, Stilwell and the American Experience in China, *185*

Contents

Illustrations

Preface

"The role of traitor is not one which in any wise brings credit to the performer, either from one side or the other," wrote H. H. Bancroft (or perhaps his friend and collaborator, LDS apostle Franklin D. Richards). "However great the service he may render us, we cannot but feel that he is false-hearted and vile. Many of the apostates, though they may not have written books, declare that they joined the sect only to learn their secrets and then expose them. These are the most contemptible of all."[1] This denunciation captures the passions that engulfed the thousands who joined and later abandoned the Church of Jesus Christ of Latter-day Saints, popularly known as the Mormons, during its tumultuous early years in the mid-nineteenth century. In my own youth, I recall singing about how "traitors and tyrants now fight him in vain" in the stirring hymn "Praise to the Man," the tribute to the faith's founding martyr, Joseph Smith, the hero whom death could not conquer again. The epic stories I heard repeated so often as a child, along with a complicated family history thoroughly entangled with the trails, trials, and tribulations of early Mormonism, had much to do with my enduring fascination with the past. But I inherited more of the skeptical temperament of my American ancestors, who left their faith in Mormonism at the territorial border of Utah, than of the believing nature of my faithful forebears from the English Midlands. My own faith did not survive its youthful encounter with *Letters from the Earth,* Mark Twain's send-up of nineteenth-century fundamentalism.

Encounters with the remarkable narratives that now make up this volume convinced Polly Aird, Jeff Nichols, and me that a proper documentary history of the Mormon West deserved a volume dedicated to the full spectrum of dissent, ranging from the private complaints of the publicly faithful to the

[1]Bancroft, *History of Utah,* 150.

perspectives of the outsiders, dissidents, and rebels whom Brigham Young thrashed so often and so soundly. In repeated sermons the plainspoken prophet denounced the nasty, sneaking, lying, deceitful, disgraced, and damned apostates. "If there is a despicable character on the face of the earth, it is an apostate from this Church," he told a Salt Lake congregation in the summer of 1867. "He is a traitor who has deceived his best friends, betrayed his trust, and forfeited every principle of honor that God placed within him. . . . They have forfeited their heaven, sold their birthright, and betrayed their friends." Even the devil had no use for such characters, the Mormon prophet argued.[2]

I have long thought better of the many men and women who found themselves disillusioned by the dynamics of frontier Mormonism. When we began assembling sources to represent them, I expected the collection would testify to the honesty and sincerity of these authors and provide powerful evidence of the accuracy of their stories.

As we discussed what to include in this volume, we considered narratives by John Ahmanson, Aaron DeWitt, Stephen Forsdick, Frederick Gardiner, John Pierce Hawley, Henry Hoth, John Hyde, Catherine Lewis, Frederick Loba, Thomas Ambrose Poulter, and Fanny Stenhouse. For two reasons, none of these accounts appear in this collection: first, technology has made many of them easily accessible on the Internet. Second, the sheer size of its four major narratives limited this volume's scope, although newspaper articles and other texts provide a sample of the broad range of dissenting perspectives.

The narratives presented here posed an implicit challenge to my original narrow vision for this volume, which I initially saw as a defense and vindication of dissenting viewpoints. As we worked with this material, the volume's interpretive lens expanded from an attempt to restore legitimacy to these stories to a more complicated and illuminating interpretation of the role of dissent and disillusion in a remarkable movement. Their complexity forced a reevaluation of the light that these peoples' stories shed on Mormon history and revealed the need for a more nuanced vocabulary to describe the shades of resistance. George Armstrong Hicks's personal history, written shortly after the death of Brigham Young, is a testament to the courage and moral conviction of a very brave man who dared to speak out even when his life was threatened. Charles Derry's autobiography exemplifies the story of the poor, newly arrived foreign immigrant who was powerless in pioneer Utah.

[2] 30 June 1867, *Journal of Discourses,* 12:94.

The tale told by Ann Gordge—the only woman in the group—is clearly the oddest of these critical documents. Despite her obvious fabrications, an authentic voice emerges of an obscure, penniless young female immigrant convert, one of the relatively few such personal testaments that have survived. Salt Lake police official Brigham Young Hampton's plaintive journal/autobiography provides insights into the mindset of a latter-day Danite who acted as one of theocratic Mormonism's enforcers—and whose prison terms and financial sacrifices set him at odds with the church's leaders after they made the necessary adjustments to win statehood for Utah.

An odd defensiveness still characterizes the "faithful" version of Mormon history, which occasionally borders on paranoia: the mildest critical analysis is often condemned as yet another example of the faith's long-sanctified history of persecution. To this day, the religion's protectors paint the motives of those who do not subscribe to their faith-promoting version of history as suspect. Among defenders of the faith, firsthand critical commentaries on Mormon theocracy can be dismissed as prejudicial and thus ignored. This is true even if these sources describe the reality of life in Utah Territory much more accurately than the fairy-tale history so tediously defended in Apostle Orson F. Whitney's *History of Utah* and more competently argued in B. H. Roberts's official chronicles. At times it seems that any scholar not thumping a tub for the restored Gospel is untrustworthy and relegated to an enemies' list dating all the way back to the 1830s.

Recent scholarship has broadened historical perspectives on the long tradition of dissent within Mormonism. As a young man preparing for a mission, Allen D. Roberts noticed the "extraordinary incidence of apostasy in the church" even during Joseph Smith's time. Roberts discovered that Smith excommunicated all the counselors in the First Presidency, the faith's highest-ranking leaders, except for his brother Hyrum. Nine of the first nineteen apostles were also excommunicated, while Orson Pratt and Orson Hyde suffered temporary expulsions that barred them from succeeding Brigham Young. "Thus eleven of the nineteen apostles, Smith's closest associates, were either excommunicated, disfellowshipped, or 'rejected,'" Roberts observed.[3]

Joseph Smith's sudden martyrdom was the defining moment in the story of his new religious movement. The founding prophet's death froze his rapidly

[3]Roberts, "Profile of Apostasy," 143–44. For a contemporary collection of eighteen interviews with influential but inactive Mormons, see Ure, *Leaving the Fold.*

evolving theology in place. The event galvanized his followers, provided a rallying point for the faithful, and instilled a sense of mission—along with an enduring, vengeful bitterness—in the faith's new leaders. The apostles blamed the murder on "tyrants," mostly Illinois politicians, and especially on the "traitors" they held most responsible for Smith's assassination, as the church's historians still do. The faithful saw the murder as a manifestation of the pending apocalypse. Within a year the Apostleship proclaimed that, now that the holy priesthood held "the keys," the Kingdom of God "has come: as has been predicted by ancient prophets, and prayed for in all ages." The faith's next three presidents sought to complete "the work of Joseph" by forging a united and sanctified people while defending them from the enemies determined to destroy Mormonism and the Latter-day Saints. In this light, Brigham Young was a religious revolutionary with real enemies, not a peacemaker with a persecution complex. For three decades he sought by any means necessary to prepare his people for salvation and demolish anyone who stood in the way. To create a religious utopia in the Rocky Mountains, Young demanded harmony, which required absolute loyalty and unquestioned obedience. Such a grand goal and such an intense commitment to achieving it naturally inspired disillusion, dissent, and desertion. Small wonder that overland travelers met hundreds of eastbound Saints who were "heartily sick of Brigham Young and his religion" and who complained that "Mormonism in England and in Salt Lake are two different isms."[4]

In 1989 Richard L. Saunders asked a set of perceptive rhetorical questions: "What role can dissent play in a social order that is centered on divine revelation? Does enlisting in the Church mean surrendering theological free agency; then again, if Divinity is guiding the church, how can conflict or dissent be countenanced?" This volume suggests that frontier Mormonism feared dissent as much as it valued unity. Perhaps the new religion's violent and persecuted past precluded a more benign reaction. Saunders wondered, "How does an authoritarian religious system fit into a larger socio-religious culture that is founded on the tolerance of disagreement, a constitutionally established 'agreement to disagree'?"[5] Not well, if the fifty-year battle to rule Utah is any indication.

The narratives in this volume raise difficult questions that require answers. What attracted people to this very American faith? How did the repeated

[4]Pratt, *Proclamation*, 1; Case, Laramie to Oregon, Bancroft Library.

[5]Saunders, "Francis Gladden Bishop," 57.

cycles of conversion and abandonment impact this new religious movement? Why did the faith's early leaders react so harshly against those they denounced as apostates? What was the level of dissatisfaction among the population of Utah Territory? How did the faithful account for the lack of faith that even LDS leaders guessed afflicted more than half the population of Utah Territory? And why, despite the slings and arrows that doubters endured, did so many dissidents ultimately retain their belief in Joseph the Seer and remain so loyal and devoted to the dynamic and compelling society they helped create?

This study seeks to shed light on these questions. The entirely remarkable nature of this material and its richness proved astonishing, a feeling I hope our readers share. Of the thousands of LDS documents and life narratives I have surveyed over many years, four of the ten most challenging, compelling, and complex appear here for the first time. By any standard, these voices of dissent merit a respected place in the Mormon past.

Will Bagley
Salt Lake City, April 2010

Acknowledgments

Many dedicated professionals and institutions have assisted us throughout this project, including the staff of the Library-Archives of the Historical Department of the Church of Jesus Christ of Latter-day Saints, who are unfailingly courteous and helpful. We are grateful as well to the experts in Special Collections/Western Americana at the University of Utah's Marriott Library, especially Walter Jones and Gregory C. Thompson. Thanks also to the dedicated professionals at Yale University's Beinecke Rare Book and Manuscript Library; the Utah State Historical Society; the Western Reading Room of the Denver Public Library; the Idaho State Historical Society; the Montana State Historical Society; the William H. Kohrs Museum in Deer Lodge, Montana; the LDS Family History Library; the Harold B. Lee Library of Brigham Young University; and the team at the Huntington Library, notably Peter Blodgett. Members of the John D. Lee Family Association were helpful and generous, especially Verne Lee, as well as Lee descendants Lorraine Manderscheid and Gena Raban.

A quick glance at the footnotes demonstrates how much we relied on Juanita Brooks's courageous work. As Polly Aird wrote, we are "constantly amazed by what she accomplished, the felicity with which she wrote, and the depth of her research."

We are indebted to a host of friends and historians. Waldo Perkins, M.D., alerted Polly to a story that illustrated George A. Hicks's kindness to others, an account we would otherwise have missed. In searching out some of Hicks's most obscure references, Louisa Rose proved to be a tireless and imaginative researcher. Michael Marquardt graciously shared his vast knowledge of the Mormon past, especially his research on Jesse Thompson Hartley. We are pleased to present this distinguished scholar's study of Hartley's murder as the keepsake for the limited edition of this volume.

We have had the support of several institutions. Jeff Nichols benefited greatly from two Gore Individual Summer Grants, thanks to the Gore Family Foundation and Westminster College. Professor Nichols also thanks the Charles Redd Center for a John Topham and Susan Redd Butler Faculty Research Award. Several of his colleagues at Westminster College, including Jeffrey M. McCarthy and Douglas Wright, read portions of the manuscript and offered insightful criticism. Folklorist David Stanley was particularly helpful. The journalist Christopher Ketcham read the introductions to the study's four major life stories and offered valuable advice. Nichols's substantial contributions to this project would have been impossible without his research assistant, Sherrie Bakelar. Will Bagley is grateful to the Beinecke Library at Yale University, the Utah Humanities Council, and the Tanner Humanities and Wallace Stegner centers at the University of Utah and Chevron Corporation, whose sponsorship of grants and fellowships made his work possible.

Although it is one of the great life histories to emerge from frontier Utah, none of the state's many archives contained a copy of George A. Hicks's history when former LDS assistant church historian Davis Bitton published an article on him in Summer 2000.[1] Through descendant Dawn Nodzu, Will Bagley obtained a copy of the Hicks manuscript from the estate of J. Will Lewis, who died in 1999. Polly Aird transcribed the holographic copy, and her edition is published here courtesy of Hicks descendent Robert J. Huber of Bountiful, Utah.

The Ann Gordge manuscripts are published courtesy of BYU Library's Special Collections and Ms. Sharen Moon, who generously shared her story of the manuscript's provenance. The Brigham Young Hampton manuscript is published courtesy of the Library-Archives of the Historical Department of the LDS Church.

Despite our many debts, any errors are, of course, the editors' responsibility. Finally, Jeff Nichols would like to thank, as always, Cheryl Henley for her love and support, and Will Bagley must express his undying gratitude to Laura Bayer.

[1]Bitton, "'I'd Rather Have Some Roasting Ears,'" 196–222. This strange article marks the only concerted assault on the character of a Utah pioneer ever to appear in the *Utah Historical Quarterly*.

Editorial Procedures

This collection of narratives and documents attempts to faithfully represent the original records in a readable format. With the following exceptions, these transcriptions preserve the grammar, spelling, and diction of the originals. We have capitalized the first letters of sentences and of personal names and added periods to the ends of sentences; where the case used in the manuscript is ambiguous, we follow standard capitalization. Abbreviations A.M. and P.M. are set in small caps. Where a writer used commas in the place of periods, we converted them to periods, but otherwise we maintained the punctuation of the original. Brackets enclose added letters, missing words, and conjectural readings. We use [*sic*] sparingly. [Blank] indicates a blank space, while other bracketed comments, such as [*tear*], note physical defects in the manuscript. We set off interlined insertions in brackets and place them in their logical location in the text. Underlined text is italicized, while significant crossed out text is rendered as ~~strikethroughs~~.

Manuscripts found in the Library-Archives of the Historical Department of the Church of Jesus Christ of Latter-day Saints are identified as "LDS Library" or "LDS Archives" as appropriate. The Journal History of the church, a daily scrapbook of Mormon history consisting of journals, minutes, letters, and articles that Andrew Jenson extracted (and expurgated) from church records beginning in 1906, can be found at the LDS Library and is cited as Journal History. "Romney Typescript" refers to transcriptions that church secretary Edyth Romney made for Leonard Arrington's Mormon History Trust, and which were sometimes provided to us with or in place of the original documents. Items cited as History of the Church are from the LDS church historian's office, commonly known as the Manuscript History of the Church. Quotations cited in this volume are from Richard E.

Turley, ed., *Selected Collections from the Archives of the Church*. The L. Tom Perry Special Collections at Brigham Young University's Harold B. Lee Library is cited as "BYU Library." In addition to citations of John Doyle Lee's published diaries, the original diaries are cited as: Lee, Papers, diary number, date, page. Diary entries from the edited versions are cited as: Cleland and Brooks, eds., *A Mormon Chronicle*, volume number: diary number, date, page. References to the editors' supplementary materials are cited as: Cleland and Brooks, eds., *A Mormon Chronicle*, volume number: page.

The material is organized into chapters, sections, and documents. Each document contains an abbreviated heading identifying the source and its location. Where available, page/column information in newspaper articles is expressed, for example, as 2/3 in headings and footnotes. The bibliography contains a complete listing of all the books, articles, newspapers, journals, and manuscripts referenced in the footnotes, which are designed to identify the source as briefly but clearly as possible. Manuscript citations appear in roman type without quotation marks. Quoted material from the sources reproduced in this volume is often not footnoted.

We have eliminated repeated words (such as "that that") and occasionally changed paragraph breaks to facilitate reading. We have not provided sources for commonly known biographical detail that come from standard LDS biographical references, notably Andrew Jenson's *Latter-day Saint Biographical Encyclopedia* and genealogical websites, particularly Ancestry.com.

The distinct nature of the life stories that make up most of this volume posed special challenges that required individual solutions. We have adapted the above general rules to the singular nature of each narrative. For example, George A. Hicks was a literate and insightful writer, and we have edited his recollection lightly and annotated it heavily, identifying most of the people he names. Hicks and Charles Derry divided their memoirs into chapters and parts, to which we added titles drawn from their texts. B. Y. Hampton's style is equally direct, but his diary references hundreds of people, so we have limited the number of biographical footnotes to figures critical to understanding the text.

Two known holographic variants of Ann Gordge's autobiography survive. One (the "BYU variant") is held at BYU Library. The library purchased the eighty-six-page manuscript from Betty A. Riley of Hemet, California, in 1987. Archivists indicate the family obtained it by unknown means before

1913.[1] Descendants of a Salt Lake City policeman to whom Ann reportedly gave the copy in 1914 own a second copy identified as the "Bishop variant." The manuscripts are in different hands, and it is impossible to determine if Ann Gordge wrote either herself. The former owner of the Bishop variant wrote that "arthritis forced Ann to dictate some of the final pages," and the variant's last eight pages are indeed in a different, smoother hand.[2] The content of both drafts is very similar, with the mostly minor exceptions explained in footnoted references to the BYU or Bishop variant. It is difficult to determine which version is older, or if one represents a copy of the other; it seems likely that both are copies of a now-lost original. The editors used material from both to create the text presented here, following the series' standard policies and the following specific rules:

- We incorporate text when one variant provides substantial material missing from the other. For difficult passages, we used the clearest and most legible variant.
- Spelling, grammar, diction, and capitalization are from one or the other variant (that is, if a word is misspelled in this edited version, it was misspelled in both variants).
- We identify significant marginal notes as: [*marginal note*: This occurred in 1851.]
- We have cut or summarized material of minor interest, amounting to less than 10 percent of the original content. Ellipses identify these emendations.

Purists might rightfully complain that such processed text is much "cleaner" than either variant. It is, but the manuscripts provide access to the unedited text. Since neither variant appears to be the original, enough of Ann's editorial idiosyncrasies remain to provide a clear idea of her style.

For all of its problems, Ann Gordge's memoir is an example of how a historical document that plays fast and loose with fact and fiction can still be an exceptionally revealing source. Other narratives have similar problems, notably Marietta Coray Smith's tale in Green, ed., *Fifteen Years Among the Mormons.* Although Ann's tales show how reality can be twisted, exaggerated, and used to hammer an enemy, carefully investigating, documenting, and qualifying her narrative reveals a life story that has definite historical and social value.

---

[1] Register of the Ann Gordge Lee Autobiography, BYU Library.

[2] Bishop, Introduction, 2.

The text of Brigham Young Hampton's journal is based on the holographic original found in a numbered ledger book at the Library-Archives of the Historical Department of the LDS church. His spelling and grammar are notably eccentric, but his meaning is usually clear, so editorial additions and corrections have been minimal. We added periods after dates and commas to long lists of names and, where necessary, slightly modified punctuation and standardized dates to avoid ambiguity. Ellipsis points indicate deleted material—again less than 10 percent of the total—mostly lists of Hampton's visitors and the presents they brought him during his jail terms. The first sixty-six pages of the ledger, containing genealogical information and capsule histories of Hampton's ancestors, are omitted, but a few citations to the material use the following format: Hampton, Papers, page number.

Each editor has assumed primary responsibility for introducing and editing his or her sources, with Polly Aird handling George A. Hicks's lively memoir and Will Bagley editing Charles Derry's moving account of life among Brigham's minions. Jeff Nichols has taken us down Ann Gordge's historical rabbit hole on a tour of her blood-drenched wonderland and through the thickets of Brigham Young Hampton's only slightly less strange account of his life as a Utah lawman and lawbreaker. Each editor has reviewed each piece and made contributions that make this work a true collaboration.

Introduction

Tracing a Shadow
Dissent and Resistance in the Mormon West

The word "apostate" does not appear in the Bible; the term derives from the Greek *apostasia*, which Herodotus and Thucydides used to describe a political defection or revolt. Eventually spiritual leaders applied the word to marginalize those who had forsaken their cause, belief, or faith. Since at least the reign of Julian the Apostate, Edward Gibbon noted, religious advocates have used the word to fix "a stain of infamy" on their opponents—dissenters who often found themselves "overwhelmed with a torrent of pious invectives."[1]

Among the Latter-day Saints, the term quickly became an epithet. In December 1832 a Joseph Smith revelation described "the great persecutor of the church, the apostate, the whore, even Babylon, that maketh all nations to drink of her cup, in whose hearts the enemy, even Satan, sitteth to reign."[2] Ironically, Smith's church was composed almost entirely of "apostates" who had abandoned one belief system or another to join his new religious movement. In today's Mormon culture, historian Allen Roberts noted, "an apostate is one to pity, fear, and shun for opposing the church and contaminating the Saints; a person to excommunicate."[3] This study takes a broader view of the phenomenon and seeks to understand, rather than demonize or lionize, those who became disillusioned with frontier Mormonism.

Yet the concept of apostasy is so central to Mormon theology that the

[1]Gibbon, *Decline and Fall of the Roman Empire*, 524.

[2]*Doctrine and Covenants*, 86:3. Hereafter cited as *D&C*.

[3]Roberts, "Profile of Apostasy," 143.

word is impossible to avoid. "Latter-day Saints believe that apostasy occurs whenever an individual or community rejects the revelations and ordinances of God, changes the gospel of Jesus Christ, or rebels against the commandments of God, thereby losing the blessings of the Holy Ghost and of divine authority," historian Todd Compton observed in a church-sponsored reference. Mormon theology requires "a historical 'great apostasy' and subsequent loss of authority beginning in the New Testament" to justify the need for Joseph Smith's "Restoration" of the plain and simple truths of early Christianity. Even Mormon scholars have a hard time finding such a transition in the historical record, but the conviction that the Almighty withdrew from human affairs sometime before the fall of Rome is essential to their belief system. The doctrine also brands all other Christian denominations as apostate. Mormons, Compton notes, "do not view these events judgmentally."[4] The sermons collected in the youthful religion's *Journal of Discourses* often give a distinctly different impression, but both perspectives show how tightly apostasies great and small are woven into the fabric of the LDS faith.

"For it must needs be," says *The Book of Mormon*, "that there is an opposition in all things."[5] Making sense of the narratives that make up this volume requires a basic understanding of the nature of the intense opposition that early Mormonism seemed to conjure spontaneously from the soil of the young American Republic. Any assessment of the religion's long history of conflict must look closely at how profoundly its traumatic early years influenced the attitudes Latter-day Saints carried west. A thoughtful appraisal requires reexamining the faith's celebrated mythology of persecuted innocence, which paints Mormonism's early trials as a painful story of unwarranted abuse and hostility, with angry mobs destroying benevolent communities of believers. It must examine how the faithful explained why so many lost their faith.

Dissent played a central role throughout Mormonism's first quarter-century, contributing to the culture's enduring sense of victimization and betrayal that generated an enduring body of critical exposés and heartfelt recollections. This overview ends with a watershed event: the Utah War, a convenient boundary between this introduction and the Afterword, which examines how dissent in Utah Territory evolved.

---

[4]Ludlow, ed., *Encyclopedia of Mormonism*, 4:56–58.

[5]Nephi 2:11.

Gyasticutus Unchained: Frederic Lockley

Frederic E. Lockley, an eloquent and fair-minded newcomer to Utah Territory, became a reluctant warrior when he found himself dropped into the middle of America's long conflict with Mormon theocracy during Brigham Young's last years. Lockley experienced the conditions that so factionalized Mormon country and provides a singular perspective on the problematic "apostates in Zion" he met between 1873 and 1883.

The self-educated son of a London butcher who had read most of the English classics, Lockley migrated to the United States in 1848 at age 24. He chased opportunity from "New York to New Orleans, to Cleveland and Chicago, and back to New York," where he proofread *Frank Leslie's Illustrated Newspaper* and freelanced for Horace Greeley's *New York Tribune*. When the Civil War came, the recently naturalized Lockley joined the Union army as a private in 1862 and fought with the Army of the Potomac at Fredericksburg, Cold Harbor, Petersburg, and Reams Station, completing his service as a lieutenant in the Seventh New York Heavy Artillery.[6]

Afflicted with a bad case of western fever, Lockley moved his growing family from Ohio to Kansas in 1869. He spent the rest of his days as a journalist and editor, wandering the American West from Leavenworth to Indian Territory to Oregon and back to Kansas, finally settling in Missoula, Montana, where he died at age 81 in 1905. Lockley wrote sympathetically about American Indians, "praising many native qualities and defending the tribes against white injustice," John M. Coward observed. Reflecting his sympathies, Lockley signed his work "Okmulgee," "Indian," and "Viator." His encounters with Indians taught him an enduring lesson: "prejudice is an immense force to overcome."[7]

A seductive business opportunity—an operating newspaper for the taking—rather than a desire to launch a crusade inspired Lockley and fellow Kansas newspapermen George F. Prescott, A.N. "Gus" Hamilton, William Taylor, and James R. Schupbach to purchase the *Salt Lake Tribune* in November 1873. "Border Ruffians"—a reference to the thugs who made Bleeding Kansas bleed before the Civil War—became the brand that Latter-day Saint

[6]Rankin, "Type and Stereotype: Frederic E. Lockley," 61, 64, 67; Lockley, *History of the Columbia River Valley*, 2:178.

[7]Rankin, "Type and Stereotype," 61, 64, 67; and Coward, *The Newspaper Indian*, 199–200. For more on Lockley's perspective on native peoples, see Rankin, "Savage Journalists," 102–11.

critics tried to burn into the newsmen's hides even though they were in no way sympathetic with those "who sought by illegal and violent means to determine the domestic institutions of Kansas Territory."[8]

Lockley and Hamilton handled the paper's editorial chores, while Prescott managed the *Tribune*'s business. The partners arrived four years after the transcontinental railroad shattered the barrier that had long insulated the remote territory from the outside world. The U.S. Army had occupied the heights above Salt Lake for more than a decade, and its soldiers had opened Utah's treasure house of phenomenal mineral wealth. New forces energized an era of dynamic change in Utah Territory's long-moribund rural economy. With it came a feeling of independence for prominent Salt Lake businessmen Henry W. Lawrence, John Chislett, William S. Godbe, and the brothers Frederick and Samuel Sharp Walker—all dissident Mormons—and they launched a newspaper, the *Mormon Tribune*. "The paper they brought out was an opera bouffe affair," Lockley observed. "Today it would be spiritualistics, to-morrow violently anti-Mormon, the next day, perhaps, running foul of Christian orthodoxy; the tone of the paper lacked definite purpose and coherency, it was everything by turns and nothing long."

As the new business manager, Prescott had already spent a month in Salt Lake and described the lay of the land to Lockley: "A senseless fight is being waged here between the elect of God and the unconverted, with which we have no concern. I came here to make an honest living, and, I suppose, the object of your coming is the same; such being the case, a Mormon dollar in the office till is as good as a gentile dollar." Lockley would "encounter all kinds of crazy bugs coming here to ventilate their grievances, but pay no heed to such," Prescott warned. "Our business is to publish a clean, newsy sheet every morning, that will be readable to saint and sinner."

Lockley appreciated Prescott's advice, but having served the Union cause and seen much bloodshed, he felt that his partner's "convictions were somewhat nebulous." Like many of his fellow Republicans, Lockley regarded Mormon polygamy as an insult to American principles. Yet however passionate Lockley may have felt about the purity of the home, it was the faith's theocracy and not its marriage customs that aroused his opposition.

In writing the *Tribune*'s editorials, Lockley soon had excellent volunteer help: handcart veteran John Chislett, "a fluent and easy writer," submitted

---

[8]Blackmar, ed., *Kansas*, 2:207.

frequent articles, while William Godbe provided advice. Journalist T. B. H. Stenhouse "was unstinted in his aid." All these men had been prominent and successful Latter day Saints, and all were now at bitter odds with Brigham Young.[9]

As Lockley learned, his divided audience was hard to please. The non-Mormon patrons, mostly merchants and "rough and ready miners, wanted a fearless, outspoken organ; they had no patience with the arrogance and assumption of the Mormon priesthood, and a home thrust at their pretensions was a joy and delight." The lapsed Latter-day Saints proved more difficult to suit. "These revolting sectaries had suffered unspeakably and long, and for years they had been waiting for a newspaper man to arise who durst assert his rights, and tell those bogus apostles and false priests that their evil was not good." Despite this, these apostates were oddly, almost instinctively, defensive. They would "rail against the hierarchy that has oppressed them, and condemn the practices they find debasing and injurious in the religious system taught," Lockley recalled, but "if a gentile voice is raised in condemnation of a system they find intolerable, their *amour propre* is hurt and they rise against your championship."

> And yet these apostates, which form a considerable element of the Utah population, are more intense in their hatred of the organization they have revolted from than the average outsider. A stranger visits Zion, looks into the doings and expoundings that prevail, approves what he regards as useful and rejects what strikes him as wrong. But in this exercise of judgments he doesn't grow furiously mad. There are all sorts of people in the world and many kinds of religions; but the manner of people and the nature of the religion then under examination are not to his liking. The offended Mormon has more at stake. The prophet Joseph Smith he has accepted as a restorer of the rejected human race, and now he is awakened to the fact that he is the victim of a gross delusion; he vacates or is expelled from the fold, and he feels himself an alien from society. All the purposes of life seem to him jangled, out of tune and harsh. People in such a frame of mind came to the *Tribune* office or sent in their recriminations, their tongues and their pens being steeped in gall.[10]

To the *Tribune*'s new management, "it seemed as if we had invaded an enclosed Bedlam. Disaffected saints visited the office to condemn our manner

[9]Lockley, Recollections, 2–4.

[10]Ibid., 4–5.

of running the paper and to teach us the right way." Prescott printed a cautionary placard and tacked it to Lockley's desk: "Don't tell the editor how to run his paper; let the poor devil find it out himself."

> I got along smoothly for two or three weeks, my new made friends doing most of the writing, and I sedulous in rasping off the asperities, mindful of the caution I had received from the counting room. But this halcyon time broke into a storm. And it was fortunate for the interests of the paper that a change came. Patrons of the *Tribune* who had heard that Kansans had taken hold of it, were scanning its columns daily for a refreshing display of the vehemence of that Free State sentiment, which was said to have hastened the war. But to their disappointment they found its utterances cautious and unaggressive. Some of the more impulsive would come to the office and express their dissatisfaction. But Prescott stood them off in his plausible manner, and would tell in mysterious terms of a great gyasticutus he had in reserve waiting to be unchained.[11]

"The much-celebrated *Gyasticutus Americanus*," Lockley explained, was "a large but elusive four-legged beast whose evolution in the Rocky Mountains led the legs on one side of its body to grow longer than those on the other, an adaptation that facilitated walking on steep hillsides." The editor sought to avoid confronting the beast. "I always endeavored to preserve a serene temper; to avoid boisterous talk; and was ever watchful to escape degenerating into a newspaper scold." But when he began investigating city government under Mayor Daniel H. Wells and its "family way of mixing up accounts [so] characteristic of the sons of the covenant," Lockley inevitably met the gyasticutus face to face, finding himself entangled in the passions that wracked Utah Territory.[12]

One evening Lockley accompanied a veteran reporter to a city council meeting. Apparently fearful of entering the city hall, the man finally said, "Those city police who watch you so narrowly are murderers and former thugs. Their hands are red with blood." Lockley laughed off his warning, conceding "they are *toughs*, [but] they'll not blood atone you or me."[13] Blood atonement of prominent outsiders had fallen out of fashion in Brigham Young's last years, but after challenging Mormon polygamy, theocracy, and political corruption for five years, Lockley would come "to fear walking

[11]Ibid., 5.
[12]Ibid., 5–6.
[13]Ibid., 6.

the boardwalks of Salt Lake City," one historian concluded. The editor's "concern for his safety was borne out in 1878 when he was jumped by a mob as he left his office. With his attackers using brass knuckles, Lockley was beaten senseless."[14]

This fearless journalist "found his greatest challenge, his greatest ambition, and perhaps his greatest failure" in Utah. "He would attack the Mormons relentlessly, driving the resolute faithful into ever stronger defenses and alienating others willing to compromise."[15] When he died in Missoula in 1906, Frederic Lockley considered himself a failure. His entertaining recollection of his years in Utah ends abruptly in 1877: perhaps his brutal encounter with Salt Lake's Latter-day Danites was too painful to remember. Lockley and others who did battle over the future of Utah Territory found compromise impossible. His experience sets the stage for the conflicts and events that others in this volume found themselves confronting.

Cyclical Diaspora: The Mormon Sojourn to Missouri

From Parley P. Pratt in the 1830s to Thomas J. Alexander in the twenty-first century, LDS historians have passionately and persuasively recounted their new religious movement's sad tale of persecution and endurance. This story is deeply embedded in modern Mormon identity and discourse: "Violations of religious liberty, persecution, the denial of many civil rights and even death were the lot of Latter-day Saints from even before the founding of the church, extending, at least, nearly a century later," wrote the editor of the church-owned *Deseret News* as 2009 drew to a close. "The Latter-day Saints were driven from New York to Ohio to Missouri and to Illinois, eventually fleeing to Utah."[16] Even after a thousand-mile exodus to the barren wastes of the Great Basin on their quest for religious freedom, the story goes, these beleaguered pilgrims could find no rest. To this day, Mormon historians use the faith's long history of suffering to help explain the mindset that led to the atrocity at Mountain Meadows. A popular Utah history textbook told how on 24 July 1857, exactly ten years to the day after he first saw the Salt Lake

[14]Verdoia, "Genesis of a Newspaper War," 64.

[15]Rankin, "Type and Stereotype," 69.

[16]Joseph Cannon, "Mormons Are Entitled to Defend Their Freedom of Religion," *Deseret News*, 18 October 2009.

Valley, Brigham Young learned that a U.S. Army was marching to Utah. The Pioneer Day celebration "ended quickly as old concerns and memories of persecution in New York, Ohio, Missouri, and Illinois loomed . . . Young believed the army was bent on destroying the religious community."[17]

This tale is inspiring as legend but problematic as history. Ironically, in a modern culture distinguished for its patriotism and devotion to conservative social values, the Mormons' woeful narrative directly challenges America's image as a bastion of tolerance and religious liberty. The story of Mormon persecution that begins with being "driven" from New York and Ohio misrepresents the reasons their communities voluntarily moved west. This sanctified tradition of victimization ignores the central role that disillusioned believers played in the religion's failure to establish an enduring presence in western New York or northern Ohio: Even Brigham Young recalled he left Kirtland in December 1837 "in consequence of the fury of the mob, and the spirit that prevailed in the apostates, who threatened to destroy me."[18] Dissenters continued to play a major part in later disastrous confrontations in Missouri and Illinois that did lead to hatred and forced relocation, a point not lost on the faith's early leaders. "What has been the starting point of all your afflictions?" Brigham Young asked veterans of this "persecution and sorrow" among a Utah congregation in 1853. "They began with apostates in your midst; these disaffected spirits caused others to come in, worse than they, who would run out and bring in all the devils they possibly could. That has been the starting point and grand cause of all our difficulties, every time we were driven."[19]

Jesus said, "A prophet is not without honor, save in his own country." This was certainly true of Joseph Smith, Jr. Raised in one of the most scorched regions in the famous "burnt-over district" of religious revivals in western New York, the young seer had to contend with his controversial past as a professional treasure hunter. Entire books are devoted to defending his reputation in New York, but the local press greeted his translation of the ancient golden plates with skepticism and mockery. Only a handful of religious enthusiasts accepted his purported history of the origins of America's Indians—a fallen band of Israelites he called the Lamanites.

---

[17]Holzapfel and Myers, *The Utah Journey*, 152–53.

[18]Bancroft, *History of Utah*, 195–96n7.

[19]27 March 1853, *Journal of Discourses*, 1:81.

In December 1830 Joseph the Seer issued a revelation in which the Lord told his followers, "it is expedient in me that they should assemble together in Ohio," where Mormon missionaries had converted Sidney Rigdon, who had been a prominent follower of Baptist reformer Alexander Campbell, and enlisted entire Disciples of Christ congregations. A month later a conference in Fayette, New York, instructed the faithful "that ye should go to Ohio: and there I will give unto you the law." The revelation darkly warned: "the enemy in the secret chambers, seeketh your lives."[20] Already, a few early converts in New York had their doubts about who had issued such revelations. Some members "would not receive the above as the word of the Lord: but [said] that Joseph had invented it himself to deceive the people that in the end he might get gain," reported John Whitmer, the church's first official historian.[21]

As a product of his times, Joseph Smith was as likely as the next youth to fall under the spell of the West that infected a host of young Americans for generations—and he was not the first who was happy to leave behind a controversial reputation. Smith relocated the religion's headquarters to Kirtland, Ohio, partly to unite with the faith's largest concentration of believers, but also to leave trouble behind in New York. Even before the move, the young prophet had revealed a more remote destination for his flock: Independence, Missouri, site of the Garden of Eden. Six months after he established what was first called the Church of Christ, President Smith revealed that the Lord wanted missionaries to "go unto the Lamanites and preach my gospel unto them," where "the city Zion" would be built "on the borders by the Lamanites."[22] In October 1830 Peter Whitmer, Oliver Cowdery, Parley P. Pratt, and Ziba Peterson headed to Missouri to carry out this commandment.

The mission to Indian Territory failed to make a single convert, but in July 1831 the young prophet visited Independence and issued a revelation identifying the rough frontier border town as the "center place" for the city of Zion, the "land of promise" where the Saints would build the New Jerusalem and greet the return of Christ.[23] Ezra Booth, an early convert, accompanied Joseph Smith on the trip west. "When I embraced Mormonism, I conscientiously believed it to be of God. The impressions of my mind were deep and powerful, and my feelings were exerted to a degree to which

[20]Marquardt, *The Joseph Smith Revelations*, 83–89, 142–44.
[21]Westergren, ed., *From Historian to Dissident*, 6–7, 11–12.
[22]*D&C*, 38:28.
[23]Marquardt, *The Joseph Smith Revelations*, 83–89, 142–44.

I had been a stranger. Like a ghost, it haunted me by night and day," he reported. But the failures of Smith's prophesies during the journey "excited a suspicion that some things were not right."

Booth's seven letters to a Ravenna, Ohio, newspaper about how he became disillusioned with the faith and its founder made him one of its first and most important defectors. "I now know Mormonism to be a delusion," Booth wrote, and he described his escape from its "magic charm of delusion and falsehood" that had led him to sacrifice "my time and property to build up a system of delusion, almost unparalleled in the annals of the world."[24] Like many future dissenters, he turned official rhetoric back onto LDS leaders: " 'You are a liar, you are a child of the Devil, you are an enemy to all righteousness, the spirit of the Devil is in you,' and the like, is dealt out profusely against an obstinate opponent, and especially, one whom they are pleased to nickname apostate," Booth said, quoting Sidney Rigdon's denunciation of Alexander Campbell.[25]

Booth described "the Wonders of Mormonism" that had initially led many of his fellow converts to be "carried away in the spirit." They imagined "themselves addressing a congregation of their red brethren" and "would harangue their assembly, until they had convinced and converted them." Such enthusiasts "assumed the visage of the savage, and so nearly imitated him, not only in language, but in gestures and actions, that it seemed the soul and body were completely metamorphosed into the Indian." Very quickly, Mormon leaders came to regard such charismatic phenomenon as the work of the devil. As would happen time and again, such changes in policy prompted defections: "Most of those who were the principal actors, have since apostatized," Booth wrote, and such charismatic works were "unanimously discarded by the church."[26]

Ezra Booth was the first of many disillusioned Saints whose writings provided material for hundreds of articles, pamphlets, and books denouncing the new faith. He was only "one of many to drop away." Richard Bushman estimated that during Smith's lifetime more than one-fifth of all priesthood holders were formally "cut-off" or abandoned the faith, while many others simply left. "The people most exercised about Mormons were disaffected former

---

[24]"Letter 1," Ezra Booth to Ira Eddy, 12 September 1831, *Ohio Star*, 13 October 1831, 3.

[25]"Letter 7," Booth to Edward Partridge, 20 September 1831, *Ohio Star*, 24 November 1831, 3.

[26]"Letter 3," Booth to Eddy, 24 October 1831, in *Ohio Star*, 27 October 1831, 3.

adherents and near neighbors," Bushman observed.[27] Apostle George A. Smith recalled the "spirit of apostacy" was little known in Kirtland until this time, "but when these men apostatized they became more violent, more cruel, and manifested a greater spirit of persecution than any other enemies."[28]

One of Booth's converts, Symonds Ryder, departed when his commission to preach the Mormon gospel misspelled his name.[29] One Saturday night in March 1832, Ryder led a drunken assault on Smith and Rigdon at Hiram, Ohio. The mob included Campbellites, Methodists, and Baptists, with "twelve or fifteen being apostate Mormons."[30] Awakened in the middle of the night as he tended an adopted child who had the measles, Joseph Smith recalled he "found myself going out of the door, in the hands of about a dozen men." He "made a desperate struggle" and flattened one of his assailants with a powerful kick, but the mob strangled the young prophet until he passed out. When he came to, Smith "saw Elder Rigdon stretched out on the ground" and supposed he was dead. According to some accounts, the gang had brought a doctor to emasculate Smith, but they settled on tar and feathers. Smith said the men "tried to force a vial into my mouth, and broke it in my teeth." Satiated, the prophet's molesters left him conscious but badly beaten. With the help of his wife and friends, Smith scraped off the tar and appeared the next morning at a church service attended by Ryder and his gang. "With my flesh all scarified and defaced, I preached to the congregation as usual," the undaunted young visionary recalled, "and in the afternoon of the same day baptized three individuals."[31]

Smith's adopted son died five day's later, and "these circumstances exposed the life of the child," Mormon chronicles claimed. According to George A. Smith, "the whole of this persecution was got up through the influence of those apostates."[32] Ryder's attack provided a foundation to include the Buckeye state among the places where Latter-day Saints suffered unwarranted abuse, but as Fawn Brodie noted, "This was the first and the last act of violence against the Mormons in Ohio."[33]

[27]Bushman, *Joseph Smith, Rough Stone Rolling*, 170, 399.

[28]15 November 1864, *Journal of Discourses*, 11:4–5.

[29]Brodie, *No Man Knows My History*, 118.

[30]Bancroft, *History of Utah*, 46.

[31]Smith, *History of the Church*, 1:263–64; and Walker, Turley, and Leonard, *Massacre at Mountain Meadows*, 8.

[32]15 November 1864, *Journal of Discourses*, 11:6.

[33]Brodie, *No Man Knows My History*, 120.

Increasing internal conflicts among the church's leaders proved even more costly. Parley P. Pratt's brother Orson and their fellow apostle, Luke S. Johnson, filed charges against Smith for lying, extortion, and "speaking disrespectfully, against the brethren, behind their backs." Grandison Newell formed alliances with disgruntled Mormons and charged the prophet with trying to murder him. In June 1837 excommunicated printer Solomon Denton testified that Smith had asked him to assassinate Newell, and Apostle Orson Hyde swore that "Smith seemed much excited and declared that Newell should be put out of the way, or where the crows could not find him."[34]

Smith survived repeated waves of rebellion, notably in 1834 after the disastrous failure of "Zion's Camp," a proto-military march across the Midwest that failed to reclaim lost Mormon land in Missouri. The stress of building the faith's first temple at Kirtland was accompanied by charges that the young prophet carried on a "dirty, nasty, filthy affair" with his teenage housekeeper, Fanny Alger. An avalanche of lawsuits from aggrieved apostates and neighbors contributed to a growing crisis. After Joseph Smith's catastrophic venture into the Kirtland Safety Society Anti-Banking Company, the faith abandoned its Kirtland headquarters. In the wake of the disaster Heber C. Kimball recalled, "there were not twenty persons on earth that would declare that Joseph Smith was a prophet of God." Six of his twelve apostles openly rebelled: even the stalwart Parley P. Pratt threatened to sue Smith.[35]

"While he was fending off apostates, Joseph looked beyond Kirtland to a broader field," Richard Bushman wrote. Smith's "leave-taking in January was precipitous." After excommunicating a long list of his closest comrades to deflect their call to return to "the old order," on the night of 12 January 1838 Smith and Rigdon abandoned Kirtland "on horseback to escape mob violence." The prophet said he fled "the spirit of apostate mobocracy, which continued to rage and grow hotter and hotter." Smith left his wife and family to follow in a wagon and never again returned to Kirtland.[36] When the church's press burned immediately after the prophet's departure, Warren Parrish, Smith's disillusioned private secretary, charged him with setting the fire to fulfill a prophecy. He considered Smith and Rigdon "confirmed

[34]Bushman, *Joseph Smith, Rough Stone Rolling*, 323, 337.

[35]Brodie, *No Man Knows My History*, 202–204.

[36]Bancroft, *History of Utah*, 59n99.

Infidels, who have not the fear of God before their eyes," Parrish wrote. "They lie by revelation, swindle by revelation, cheat and defraud by revelation, run away by revelation, and if they do not mend their ways, I fear they will at last be damned by revelation."[37]

The abandonment of Ohio established a pattern familiar in LDS history. Dissenters "accused the leaders of the church with bad management, selfishness, seeking for riches, honor, and dominion, tyrannizing over the people, and striving constantly after power and property," wrote the disillusioned John Corrill, one of the faith's earliest converts and its third church historian. In response, "the leaders of the Church accused the dissenters with dishonesty, want of faith, and righteousness, wicked in their intentions, guilty of crimes, such as stealing, lying, encouraging the making of counterfeit money, etc.; and this strife or opposition arose to a great height, so that, instead of pulling together as brethren; they tried every way in their power, seemingly, to destroy each other."[38]

By March 1838 the young prophet and his family had reached Far West, Missouri, the "land of their inheritance" where "a new City of Zion was on its way to completion. Within a year, all would be lost."[39]

Cast Out and Trodden Under: Betrayal and Persecution in Missouri

Now on the border of the United States and Indian country, Joseph Smith and his followers expected to build the New Jerusalem in Jackson County, Missouri, and usher in the Second Coming. Ezra Booth described Independence in 1831 as "a new Town, containing a courthouse built of brick, two or three merchant stores, and fifteen or twenty dwelling houses, built mostly of logs hewed on both sides." Located "on a handsome rise of ground" about three miles from the Missouri River, the frontier settlement was only "twelve miles east of the dividing line between the U.S. and the Indian Reserve." Independence soon became an even more dynamic "place of general rendezvous" for the commerce of the plains, and the early Mormon settlers found themselves surrounded by entrepreneurs and speculators vying for Santa Fe trade. The animosities that the colorful, fast-growing frontier town felt for this strange

[37]Brodie, *No Man Knows My History*, 207.

[38]Corrill, *A Brief History*, 27.

[39]Bushman, *Joseph Smith, Rough Stone Rolling*, 340–43.

religious group erupted in November 1833 when vigilantes drove the Mormons out of Jackson County. Neighboring Clay County became the gathering place for the Saints for the next three years, but late in 1836 they moved again, this time to the newly formed Caldwell County in northern Missouri. Here they founded the town of Far West and laid the cornerstones of a temple.

Over the next two years in Missouri, some ten thousand Latter-day Saints participated in the most dramatic scenes in the Mormon epic of persecution, and none of them were imaginary. However much early Mormons felt they were being persecuted for righteousness's sake, their cultural deafness meant they were hardly innocent victims of the violence they provoked in Missouri and later in Illinois. When it came time to steal hogs and pillage farmsteads, the Mormons usually gave as good as they got.

Once again, apostates played a central role in the conflict and its bitter outcome. "Dissenters proved most troublesome," historian Stephen C. LeSueur observed, "not because they stirred up hatred from without, but because they generated contentions, doubting, and disobedience within."[40] Shortly after Joseph Smith arrived in Missouri, he had to deal with the lingering effects of the Kirtland debacle, so church authorities excommunicated David Whitmer, William W. Phelps, and John Whitmer (the old stalwarts who made up the Missouri stake presidency); former apostle Oliver Cowdery; and three current apostles, brothers Luke S. and Lyman E. Johnson and William E. McLellin.[41] On 17 June 1838 Sidney Rigdon expanded on the text: "If the salt have lost its savour, it is thenceforth good for nothing, but to be cast out and trodden under the feet of men." Rigdon did not name names, "yet it was plainly understood that he meant that dissenters, or those who had denied the faith, ought to be cast out and literally trodden under foot," recalled John Corrill.[42]

At the same time, Dr. Sampson Avard organized a band of Mormon regulators that "assumed the name of 'The Daughter of Zion,' and afterwards were called 'Danites,'" among other colorful names.[43] Both the reality

[40] LeSueur, *The 1838 Mormon War in Missouri*, 37–38.

[41] Ludlow, ed., *Encyclopedia of Mormonism*, 2:927–32.

[42] Corrill, *A Brief History*, 30.

[43] The Danites or Avenging Angels were a secret society created to protect LDS authorities in the late 1830s; John D. Lee was a member. Most scholars agree they disbanded in 1839, but contemporaries continued to credit the Danites with violent acts for decades. See Brooks, *John Doyle Lee*, 32–33; Quinn, *The Mormon Hierarchy: Extensions of Power*, 241–61; Schindler, *Orrin Porter Rockwell*, 278, 352–62; and Hartley, *My Best for the Kingdom*, 41–80.

and legend seem destined to haunt the religion forever, and the battle over where Danite fantasy begins and Avenging Angel fact ends persists. "Some historians have claimed that Joseph Smith and the rest of the First Presidency were unaware of the Danite Organization," Michael Quinn observed, "but documentary evidence shows otherwise." The faith's leaders were only marginally involved, Corrill suggested, but members of the "Big Fan" swore "that they would kill any person, if the Presidency would say it was the will of God." After they abandoned the faith, Danite veterans Avard, Reed Peck, John Cleminson, William W. Phelps, and George M. Hinkle described Mormon vigilante operations in detail.[44]

Civil war followed. At the "Battle" of Crooked River, Mormon forces commanded by "Captain Fearnot," Apostle David Patton, routed a state militia company from Ray County. Patton died in the attack, becoming the faith's first martyr, while his men killed a Missourian and wounded six others. In response, Gov. Lilburn Boggs ordered out more troops, including those who attacked the Mormon settlement at Hauns Mill on 30 October 1838. The Hauns Mill massacre was the worst atrocity of the conflict: with seventeen dead, it remains the most grievous act of violence ever carried out against the Latter-day Saints. Boggs issued Missouri Executive Order 44, his infamous "extermination order" that decreed that, having made war upon the people of his state, "the Mormons must be treated as enemies, and must be exterminated or driven from the State if necessary for the public peace—their outrages are beyond all description." In the face of overwhelming force, Joseph Smith capitulated, agreeing that the Mormons would surrender their weapons, forfeit their property to pay for damages, and leave the state immediately.[45]

District judge Austin A. King held a court of inquiry into the first Mormon War in November 1838. The court indicted the Smith brothers, Rigdon, Lyman Wight, Alexander McCrae, and Caleb Baldwin for treason and locked them up. During the long winter, faithful Saints abandoned Missouri, many finding a welcome across the Mississippi River in Illinois, while perhaps half the members simply abandoned Mormonism. During the four bitter months he spent in Liberty Jail, Joseph Smith demonstrated his finest qualities, enduring the miserable conditions and abuse with courage and dignity.

[44]Ibid., 32; and Quinn, *The Mormon Hierarchy: Origins of Power*, 93–98, 333, 543.

[45]Moore, *Bones in the Well*, 21. Two of the wounded later died.

In April 1839 Missouri officials allowed the Smiths and other prisoners to escape while on their way to trial with the implicit understanding that they would leave the state. By month's end, the resilient prophet found refuge at Quincy, Illinois, where he could "again enjoy the society of my friends and brethren, whom I love, and to whom I feel united in bonds that are stronger than death; and in a state where I believe the laws are respected, and whose citizens are humane and charitable."[46]

Do Not Betray Heaven: Conflict and Martyrdom in Illinois

Joseph Smith once again rose phoenix-like from the ashes and turned the Missouri debacle into a public-relations triumph. "I knew my innocence as well as that of the Saints, and that we had done nothing to deserve such treatment from the hands of our oppressors," he proclaimed upon reaching Illinois. Across the country, Americans sympathized with the displaced refuges, denounced Missouri's deplorable conduct, and sent aid to the Mormons. Smith reorganized the twelve apostles and dispatched them to England to seek converts, just as Britain entered a period of religious ferment that inspired thousands to respond enthusiastically to the American evangelists. He sent them off in July 1839 with the warning that in all their trials, troubles, temptations, afflictions, bonds, imprisonments, and death, "see to it, that you do not betray heaven; that you do not betray Jesus Christ; that you do not betray the brethren." Beware of apostasy "lest innocent blood be found upon your skirts, and you go down to hell," he cautioned. "All other sins are not to be compared to sinning against the Holy Ghost, and proving a traitor to the brethren."[47]

Politicians, merchants, and land speculators in Illinois extended a warm welcome to Joseph Smith and his desperate followers, who bought large tracts of land surrounding a lovely Mississippi port named Commerce. Smith founded the town Nauvoo, the City Beautiful, and eventually annexed Commerce. Draining the malarial swamps, he subdivided the land, opened a store, and launched the five most remarkable years of his extraordinary career. It also began an idyllic and romanticized epoch in Mormon history,

[46]Smith, *History of the Church*, 3:328.

[47]Ibid., 3:329, 385.

igniting an explosion of theological innovation that led to Joseph Smith's murder eighteen months before his fortieth birthday. Once again, "traitors and tyrants" played a central role in the disaster.

President Smith's troubles in Illinois had their roots in his commingling of politics and religion. He enlisted valuable allies who helped play local political interests against each other. One surprising result of the strategy was persuading the state legislature to grant the city an expansive charter, which the prophet used to rule Nauvoo as a virtual city-state. Smith assembled the Nauvoo Legion, soon to be half the size of the U.S. Army, and become the city's mayor, newspaper editor, judge, chief booster, and foremost innkeeper. Smith quietly abandoned the communalism practiced in Missouri, commanding the faithful to gather to his new utopia and prophesying in the name of the Lord that Nauvoo "shall become the greatest city in the whole world."[48] After appointing himself America's first lieutenant general since George Washington, in the spring of 1844 General Smith organized fifty-three of his most loyal associates as a super-secret "Living Constitution," better known as the Council of Fifty, as the "government of God" whose princes and priests would rule the Earth in the Last Days.

Meanwhile, the Mormon prophet feared "the ungrateful treachery of assassins." Smith felt his life was "more in danger from some little dough-head of a fool in this city than from all my numerous and inveterate enemies abroad," he said. "I am exposed to far greater danger from traitors among ourselves than from enemies without." Judas was one of Christ's apostles, he observed, "and we have a Judas in our midst."[49]

At the same time, "Joseph the Seer," as Wilford Woodruff called him, began doing "the works of Abraham," secretly organizing a Holy Order he used to seal himself to dozens of women under "the new and eternal covenant" of plural marriage. In May 1842 Smith initiated a restored version of Solomon's temple rites in the upstairs room of his store, but he eventually intended to perform them in the magnificent limestone temple rising on a bluff overlooking the Mississippi. The prophet began a burst of theological innovation involving baptism for the dead, an evolving deity, and an eternal progression to godhood that defied traditional Christian beliefs. Whether Joseph Smith "did not lust for women so much as he lusted for

[48]Ehat and Cook, *The Words of Joseph Smith*, 417.

[49]Smith, *History of the Church*, 6:152.

kin," as Richard Bushman proposed, or was caught in a reckless pathology of compulsion and grandiosity, defies a definitive answer. Whatever Smith's motives, his actions promoted neither peace with his Illinois neighbors nor harmony among his flock. Most Nauvoo Saints knew nothing about the "secret things" that Emma Smith, the prophet's only legal wife, said "cost Joseph and Hyrum their lives." These clandestine doctrines revealed to a trusted few inspired a host of controversial rites and theories—the Second Anointing, spiritual adoption to create a vast kinship network, the Curse of Ham, polygamy, Adam as God, and blood atonement—beliefs that compel and repel Smith's followers to this very day.[50]

A basic element in the enduring success of the religious revolution that Joseph Smith created was his ability to attract and win the undying loyalty of thousands of decent, honest, hard-working men and women of high moral character. At the same time, he had a distinct affection for and formed close alliances with some of the most notorious scoundrels along the Mississippi, notably Dr. John Cook Bennett; Council of Fifty member Edward Bonney, the frontier "detective" and author of *Banditti of the Prairies*; and counterfeiter Joseph H. Jackson. Only Bennett actually joined the faith, but Smith almost immediately promoted him to the rank of general and appointed him "Assistant President of the Church." After Bennett's sexual adventures became an embarrassment, he was excommunicated in 1842. He published a series of newspaper reports that soon appeared in book form as "An exposé of Joe Smith and Mormonism," which provided detailed accounts of the origins of polygamy.

Events in Nauvoo cascaded to a terrible resolution in the spring of 1844. Joseph Smith admitted that he occasionally tested the virtue of the wives of Nauvoo, but trouble boiled over when he propositioned the spouse of Dr. William Law of the church's First Presidency. After a secret council excommunicated him, Law and his brother Wilson launched the *Nauvoo Expositor*, a newspaper whose avowed intent was to expose Joseph Smith as a fallen prophet. In its first issue the *Expositor* detailed and denounced polygamy and Smith's "political schemes and intrigue." The editors pledged, "We will *not* acknowledge any man as king or lawgiver to the church" and promised to "tell the whole tale" of Smith's political plans.

There would be no more editions of the *Expositor*. The newspaper's revelations were too dangerous to ignore, since many of them were true. The

[50]Bushman, *Joseph Smith*, 440; and Quinn, *The Mormon Hierarchy: Origins of Power*, 170.

Nauvoo city council accused the editors of seduction, pandering, counterfeiting, and thievery. Mayor Smith ordered the press destroyed as a public nuisance that offended local moral standards. Warned that his press was about to be destroyed, William Law wrote, "I could not even suspect men of being such fools." Nauvoo Legionnaires marched to the *Expositor* office, wrecked the press, pied the type, and burned the remaining papers.[51]

Resentment of Mormon power had long simmered in Illinois, but when the prophet mobilized the Nauvoo Legion, hostility exploded into hysteria. "Such excitement I never witnessed in my life," a state militia officer recalled. "We all felt the time had come where either the Mormon or the old citizens had to leave." The *Warsaw Signal* proclaimed, "War and extermination is inevitable!" The act violated the constitution and was "a gross outrage upon the laws and liberties of the people," Illinois governor Thomas Ford complained. At Carthage, the county seat, William Law swore out a complaint against Joseph Smith for destroying his property and inciting a riot. A magistrate issued a warrant for Smith's arrest, and Smith and his brother Hyrum were jailed for the vandalism. On 27 June 1844 a mob stormed Carthage Jail and, after a short gunfight, assassinated the Smith brothers and wounded Apostle John Taylor.[52]

Joseph Smith's murder became Mormonism's defining event. The "Prophet and Seer of the Lord" had done more than any other man, "save Jesus only, for the salvation of men in this world," proclaimed John Taylor's tribute, later canonized as scripture. His death "left a fame and name that cannot be slain. He lived great, and he died great," having "sealed his mission and his works with his own blood." The brothers were innocent of any crime "and were only confined in jail by the conspiracy of traitors and wicked men," Taylor wrote.[53] To this day, the religion's historians blame Smith's murder on "William and Wilson Law, whose action led directly to the martyrdom of Joseph and Hyrum Smith."[54]

After much confusion and contention over who should lead the faith, the Twelve Apostles and their dynamic president, Brigham Young, won the support of most church members. The Saints never forgot Smith's murder and the conflicts that drove them from Illinois. For decades, Mormon leaders

[51]Roberts, *A Comprehensive History*, 2:236–37, 243; Cook, *William Law*, 55.

[52]Hallwas and Launius, *Cultures in Conflict*, 30–31.

[53]*D&C*, 135:3–7.

[54]Bitton, "'I'd Rather Have Some Roasting Ears,'" 218; Arrington and Bitton, *The Mormon Experience*, 59.

openly expressed their contempt for the American government and its failure to protect their property and defend their religious rights. They blamed their troubles on turncoats and politicians. Every official Joseph Smith confided in, Heber C. Kimball said in 1857, "turned traitor to him, and were the very men that took his life, aided by the apostates that left this Church; and I know it, and so do you." The beloved prophet "never trusted in one of them but what they betrayed him; and I wish to God I had taken some of their lives when I had a chance: they were blacklegs, whoremongers, murderers, liars, sorcerers, and rascals; and you may take many of the leading men of the United States Government, and they are not one whit better."[55]

Joseph Smith's martyrdom reinforced early Mormonism's defining elements: the movement's sense of mission and commitment to unity. Dissenters among the Saints seldom invoked doctrinal conflicts. Instead, their narratives describe political, economic, and personal conflicts, often spurred on by revulsion at the self-serving actions of the rigid Mormon hierarchy and its increasing reliance on intimidation and fear. Ultimately these differences represent a rejection of the movement's mission and authority. As Richard Saunders observed, "Dissent created a social crack in filial unity, which Brigham Young saw as the real casualty of conflict. It could be fatal to the church"—a point precisely understood and exploited by those whom the frontier prophet denounced as enemies of the Mormon people. If Young's actions often seemed paranoid, it is beyond dispute that he and his followers had real, resourceful, and relentless enemies who were as dedicated to destroying Utah's "theodemocracy" as the early Saints were devoted to building the Kingdom of God. "The polarity of differing views—common to most Western cultures of the time, not just the Mormons—was one reason Young and others could insist on such a clear line of inclusion and exclusion," Saunders noted.[56]

Many predicted Mormonism would not survive the demise of its founder. This underestimated the talent and devotion Smith had attracted to his movement. Not only did the main branch of the faith survive under Brigham Young, but some years later Joseph Smith III accepted the leadership of the Reorganized Church of Latter Day Saints, now known as the Community of Christ. Many other men also stepped forward to claim "the mantle of the

[55] 23 August 1857, *Journal of Discourses*, 5:178.

[56] Saunders, reader's comments in editor's possession, *Playing with Shadows*, August 2010, 3–4.

prophet." Nicknames characterize more than a dozen splinters that derive inspiration from Joseph Smith's Restoration, including Whitmerites, Strangites, Wightites, Hedrickites, Rigdonites, Bickertonites, Cutlerites, Gladdenites, Morrisites, Gibsonites, Godbeites, Baneemyites, and Conjespresites.

The temple lot in Independence, Missouri, the center place of Zion, is an excellent spot to contemplate Joseph Smith's legacy.[57] Here in August 1831 the prophet laid the northeast cornerstone of the temple to which all the Saints believe Christ will return. A modest whitewashed frame building, the headquarters of Granville Hedrick's Church of Christ (Temple Lot), now occupies a corner of the property, which it has owned since at least 1877. North of the temple lot stands the Stone Church, a Community of Christ congregation, while to the east is the site's most remarkable structure, the faith's temple. Gyo Obata designed its three-hundred-foot-tall stainless-steel spire to evoke the shell of a chambered nautilus. Unlike LDS temples that conduct endowment, sealing, and baptism ordinances, the Independence temple serves as a place of worship and education. Its chapel opens onto a Japanese meditation garden, site of a daily prayer for peace. South of the temple lot stands the Auditorium, the Community of Christ's grimly gothic Hagia Sophia, which serves as a conference center and office building. Nearby is the Children's Peace Pavilion. Kitty-corner from the temple lot, the Independence Visitor Center represents Utah's LDS church. Farther down Lexington Avenue is the Remnant Church, led by Frederick Neils Larsen, a descendant of Joseph Smith. It is one of dozens if not hundreds of independent branches of the founding prophet's Restoration of Christianity.

That a farm boy from upstate New York inspired such widespread and diverse devotion is astonishing.

Whatever one makes of Joseph Smith's colorful life, the scope of his achievement and his lasting impact are undeniable. A product and prophet of his time and birthplace, "a transcendent cross between Huck Finn and Ahab," Smith distilled the elements fermenting on the borders of the young republic—revivalism, transcendentalism, romanticism, spiritualism, and impending social and sexual revolutions—into a thoroughly American religion.[58] His achievements as a translator of lost scripture (or frontier folk-novelist), builder of temples, founder of cities, commander of cohorts, and

57 Smith, *History of the Church*, 2:254.

58 Barnes, "Joseph Smith: Lost and Found," 148.

frontier entrepreneur are impressive enough, but they pale when compared with his audacity as a theological revolutionary. Equally remarkable was his ability to captivate thousands of men and women: he inspired a devotion that is apparent even in those who concluded his successors were fallen prophets.

Mormonism did not survive Joseph Smith's death unscathed: once again, the youthful religion witnessed a massive exodus of the disillusioned. Brigham Young and the Twelve Apostles won the allegiance of only a slight majority of Latter-day Saints. By 1848 "almost one-half of the membership, along with apostles John Page, William Smith, and Lyman Wight, had rejected the leadership of the Twelve."[59]

A cynic viewing the boom and bust cycles that characterized the early LDS church's alternating explosive growth and crisis-driven collapse might conclude that Mormonism resembles a revolving door, with almost—but not quite—as many people going out as coming in. A broader view must factor in the movement's remarkable resilience, notably its ability to weather controversy, scandal, and outright disaster to emerge stronger and more resolute than ever. A sociologist's research for the LDS church discovered that some 75 percent of all Mormons leave the faith for some time during their adult years, while about 68 percent of those who leave eventually return.[60] Perhaps the varied viewpoints presented in this volume reflect a normal, even healthy, aspect of any growing religion.

Poisonous Contaminous Influence: Dissent amidst the Mormon Exodus

Brigham Young arrived in the Salt Lake Valley on 24 July 1847 determined to create a sanctuary, "Independent of all," where "no officer of the United States should ever dictate him . . . or he would hang them on a gibbet as a warning to others." From what George A. Smith called "the House of the Lord being established on the tops of the Mountains," Young planned to prepare the Kingdom of God for its return to Missouri and proclaimed his desire "to lead forth the armies of Israel to execute the judgments & justice on the persecuting Gentiles."[61] Circumstances compelled Young to return

[59]Johnson, *Polygamy on the Pedernales*, 35.

[60]Roberts, "Profile of Apostasy," 161.

[61]Bagley, ed., *Pioneer Camp of the Saints*, 28 July 1847, 244.

east to lead the rest of his flock west from Winter Quarters in 1848. In early September he met the main companies of the 1847 Mormon migration at South Pass, where he selected a Stake High Council to govern Great Salt Lake City until his return and named patriarch John Smith, Joseph Smith's uncle, to lead the fledgling community.[62]

Not long after Young's departure, a few Saints began trying to flee the new Zion. In October the High Council reported "that Bros. Wm. Weeks, Hazen Kimball, [Adolphus] Babcock and Wm. Gardiner, with their families and teams, started for Goodyear's without our knowledge or consent," referring to mountaineer Miles Goodyear's outpost at today's Ogden, Utah. The council wrote a brief letter "requesting them to return to this place immediately," and dispatched it by Brother John Van Cott, "our marshall," to insure its delivery. Van Cott had them pledge to return as soon as possible. "The dissidents took their time about returning, and made no bones about their displeasure," wrote Dale L. Morgan. "Eventually all left the valley." The High Council reported, "Their minds are somewhat embittered, and we shall do all we can to save them," ending with a crossed-out sentence: "~~It is one item of our faith to prevent any apostate going giving out from us and mingling with our enemies~~." Marshal Van Cott reported that William Weeks, the architect of the Nauvoo Temple, and his companions had all made harsh remarks and "did not like so much bondage." If it were in Weeks's power, Babcock told the high council on 26 December 1847, "he would destroy every Mormon on earth."[63]

Van Cott's policing failed to stop those who were determined to leave Salt Lake. At a special High Council meeting in December 1847, "Parley P. Pratt spoke at some length on the dissaffected spirits in the Valley," and "it was decided that the marshall should stop those who were about starting for California." The council assigned Pratt and Henry G. Sherwood "to inform Mr. Miles Goodyear why Samuel Brown, Elijah Shockley and son and Samuel Shepherd and son were stopped." Having been foiled on the road to the north, others tried to leave in the opposite direction. Van Cott "reported that he took Thos. Williams, Chas. Shumway, and Ephriam K. Hanks, and went as far south as the last large creek in the valley and turned back the five

[62]Bagley, ed., *Pioneer Camp of the Saints*, 244, 279, 345.

[63]Korns and Morgan, eds., *West from Fort Bridger*, 277; High Council to Brigham Young, 14 October 1847; and Salt Lake High Council Minutes, 11 October 1847, LDS Archives.

persons sent for; they made no opposition." Their determination paid off: "The persons turned back reported themselves to Pres. [John] Smith and were permitted by him to go on to California with Mr. Goodyear."[64] Years later, Lydia Shepherd Davidson recalled that her family "arrived in Salt Lake the forepart of September. That winter my father and another half-brother went to California with an old man who lived among the Indians."[65]

These clumsy official attempts to stop people from leaving the Mormon refuge shortly after they reached it are slightly comical, but such incidents reveal how challenging frontier Mormonism found internal conflict. The few dissenters identified in the records of 1847 represent a very slim slice of the two or three thousand Latter-day Saints who spent a hungry winter in Salt Lake. "We came on with great peace and harmony; arrived at the valley the middle of September, got timber, built us houses, made us comfortable through the Winter, sowed wheat that is now fit to harvest. The land is good enough and is to me desirable, but the society of the Saints of the Most High is more desirable," Isaac Rogers told his son. "Nothing but peace, union and tranquillity reigns in our midst." Not everyone who left for California that season abandoned Mormonism: at least two men went to San Francisco on business.[66] But coupled with the natural shock of moving from green and fertile lands to the arid Great Basin, the discovery of gold on the American River in January 1848 meant "California fever" would become an enduring problem for the faith.

Heading west in 1848, Brigham Young learned that the overland road ran in two directions: a few Saints had no interest in trying to make the desert blossom as a rose. Near Ash Hollow, Richard Ballantyne "observed 6 waggons on the south side of the River with which are some families returning from the Salt Lake Valley, because as they say, their provisions gave out and they were not able to stay."[67] Hosea Stout described them as "a company of traders and Mormon Apostates who were returning to the States with their families."[68] Camp chronicler Thomas Bullock reported "James Field, Sears, Stodham & Waters from the Valley" were camped "with Mr. Rashiaw an Indian trader." They were going back with their families "to get a fit out

[64]Ibid., 26, 28 December 1847.

[65]Shepherd to Daughters, 13 July 1926, in Carter, ed., *Our Pioneer Heritage,* 4:488–90.

[66]Rogers to Rogers, 11 July 1848, LDS Archives.

[67]Ballantyne, Journal, 8 July 1848.

[68]Brooks, ed., *On the Mormon Frontier,* 317–18n79.

(hem) for the Pacific," they claimed, but Bullock was obviously skeptical. The men gave "contradictory reports." Eating wild roots had poisoned one of Salt Lake's first five bishops, Jacob Foutz, on 14 February 1848, an indication of the raw settlement's desperate straits. They seemed "to stagger because a good man (Bishop Foutz) should die & [they] are afraid nothing can be made there," Bullock wrote.[69] John D. Lee was even harder on these "16 souls or gizards," who included William Sears, David Stidham, Loved Meeks, and Benjamin McBride. Their "Poisnous contamious [*sic*] influence of apostate Mormons reached within our camp." Lee complained.[70]

An Immense Swarm of Back Outs and Hoards of Apostates

At the beginning of the 1849 gold rush, travelers seldom reported meeting disillusioned Latter-day Saints returning to the Midwest. Instead, Mormons of all sorts—prosperous and poor, green converts and old stalwarts, the faithful and the fainthearted—disappeared over the Sierra Nevada, never to return to Utah. During the 1850s, as economic conditions declined across the region, life in Utah Territory grew much worse due to locusts, drought, and a communal system that valued church ranking more than individual initiative. Each year westbound wagon trains encountered larger groups of dissenters, until hundreds abandoned Zion every year. Defectors had a wide range of motives: "an immense swarm of back outs have arrived from the Vallies, and they now feel awful bad, and are making feeble attempts to cleanse their stomachs from the effects of living all winter on raw squash," George A. Smith reported from St. Louis in 1856. Jonathan Grimshaw told Smith "he has nothing to say against the Church or its authorities, but not knowing whether Mormonism was true or not, he thought Utah was too hard a place to live in."[71] The next spring's tithing receipts fell off in St. Louis, Apostle Erastus Snow complained, due to "the influence of hoards of Apostates" who had returned from Utah the previous fall.[72]

Heading to California in 1856, J. Robert Brown met many disillusioned

[69]Bullock, Journal, 8 July 1848. "Mr. Rashiaw" was John Richard, who guided the Mississippi Saints to Pueblo in 1846.

[70]Cleland and Brooks, eds., *A Mormon Chronicle*, 1:52–53.

[71]Smith to Brigham Young, 12 November 1856, Brigham Young Collection, LDS Archives.

[72]Snow to Brigham Young, 14 March 1857, Brigham Young Collection, LDS Archives.

Saints on the California Trail both east and west of Salt Lake. On the way, Brown ran into Bill Hickman, "a most foul and bloody murderer, but one would never suspect it from his appearance." In Echo Canyon, he found a Mormon and his little son who "were making their escape from Salt Lake. They also told many hard things of these L.D.S." In June, Brown recorded this moving encounter with a "back out":

> An old man passed us going toward the States; he had a small bundle and a gun. Some of the boys in going after water found him camped alone. When they told us of it, we sent them down to bring up the old man to camp with us; which he did without much persuasion. He said he was a reformed Mormon, and had escaped the clutches of the Mormons, and was making his way to the States. He was a man about 69 years of age; said he traveled all the way on foot from Salt Lake since April 4th. He was a man of deep, extensive reading, and used the most glowing and eloquent language in his description of the scenes, times, manners, customs, and crimes of these "latter-day devils," (saints?) especially the leaders. Every word he uttered bore the impress of truth. Poor man, he had been duped and led away from his family and friends in England, to live, or rather die, in the great American wilderness. He said he had seen so much, that he hated the name of religion, and sometimes almost believed there was no God! He told us many interesting stories, and the reason he camped by himself was that he had been repulsed and driven out of an emigrant camp during a hard snow storm, and had resolved not to intrude any more. He kept us awake until 11 o'clock. He said his name was Isaac Lamb.

At Salt Lake grasshoppers and drought had shut the temple workshops. Brown departed with a party who were all strong Mormons, but "most of these families are escaping from Salt Lake to California." Near City of Rocks, he met "a noted thief, a Mormon named Eph Pierson," leading a string of seventeen horses and mules. "Clark Roberts, David Finley, Alfred Harvey, and Mr. [William] Beers, went out on the road to see him, and they said Eph would not live a week after he got to Salt Lake, as he had been pardoned twice, and Brigham never pardoned a third time. Clark said President Young detested a thief and a liar," Brown noted. "Clark is a Mormon—the rest are not." Finley told him "many interesting things concerning the Mormons as we came along today. He says he and Alf [Harvey] have been cut off from the church, and have escaped with their lives only from that cursed community" after finally "giving them the slip." Like many visitors to the Mormon West, J. Robert Brown was not impressed. "The more I see and know of these 'Latter Day Saints,'" he wrote, "the more I am convinced the whole thing is a piece of Tomfoolery."[73]

Their Blood Will Surely Be Spilled: Fear, Reformation, and Violence

During the turbulent years leading up to the Utah War, what the Chinese call "the mandate of Heaven" did not smile upon Brigham Young and his frontier theocracy. A series of natural and man-made disasters—drought, pestilence, famine, bungled industrial enterprises, the burning of desperately needed timber and firewood by the Utes, and the handcart catastrophe—hinted that the Lord was not pleased with modern Israel. After a two-year famine, in September 1856 Mormon leaders unleashed a torrent of violent rhetoric, blaming their hard-pressed flock's lack of faith, wicked conduct, and failure to become a sanctified people as the cause of all their troubles.

Speaking in the name of Israel's God in September 1856, Jedediah Grant denounced the people's many sins: backsliding, apostasy, filthiness, lying, swearing, lust, and "everything that is evil before the God of Israel." Patience had ended: "We have been trying long enough with this people," Brigham's Hammer warned, "and I go in for letting the sword of the almighty be unsheathed not only in word, but in deed." To the same congregation, Brigham Young espoused a doctrine called "atonement by the shedding of blood," for there were sins that could not "receive forgiveness in this world, or in that which is to come" unless sinners volunteered "to have their blood spilt upon the ground, that the smoke thereof might ascend to heaven as an offering for their sins."[74] The next February, the prophet asked if they loved their brothers and sisters "when they have committed a sin that cannot be atoned for without the shedding of their blood? Will you love that man or woman well enough to shed their blood? That is what Jesus Christ meant." He went on: "This is loving our neighbour as ourselves; if he needs help, help him; and if he wants salvation and it is necessary to spill his blood on the earth in order that he may be saved, spill it."[75]

Blood atonement, as this "strong doctrine" became known, was only one feature of what is called the Mormon Reformation, arguably the most

[73] Brown, *Journal of a Trip*, 12, 34, 73, 77, 83–84, 91.
[74] 21 September 1856, *Journal of Discourses*, 4:50–51, 53.
[75] 8 February 1857, *Journal of Discourses*, 4:220.

disturbing period in the young faith's controversial history—and the most violent revival in the religious history of the American West.[76] Some prefer to discount any connection between the overheated rhetoric streaming from Salt Lake and the bloodshed that followed, but examples of such bloody threats are many and undeniable. "The best way to sanctify ourselves, and please God our heavenly Father in these days, is to rid ourselves of every thief, and sanctify the people from every vile character," Apostle Orson Hyde preached in 1853. "It would have a tendency to place a terror on those who leave these parts, that may prove their salvation when they see the heads of thieves taken off, or shot down before the public."[77] (Ironically, Apostle Orson F. Whitney later linked frontier Utah's "time of terror" to the arrival of the U.S. Army in 1858.[78]) In a sermon with the title, "Limits of Forbearance—Apostates," Heber C. Kimball said he had no doubt that hundreds would defect to the enemy. "I wish they would this fall; it might save us much trouble; and if men turn traitors to God and His servants, their blood will surely be spilled, or else they will be damned."[79]

The narratives in this volume paint a harrowing picture of the Reformation. "The wildest bombast was preached as the Gospel of Christ," George A. Hicks recalled. The church would be purified and "undesirable people" removed. There was "some good gospel doctrine advanced," but months of such bombast "had its effect on the people." Part of that effect was fear bordering on terror: Hicks said that "a spirit of secret murder stalked abroad among the people," and "unknown assassins" (unknown at least to the general public) murdered many "undesirables."[80] Some Saints became afraid to speak freely for fear of being killed. Charles Derry, "not anxious to have the Danites lurking in my path," held his peace. Others described a general climate of fear: "Times continued to grow still darker and more gloomy," said Frederick Loba. "Persons disappeared—no one knew where; murder was openly advised in the public meetings; houses were pulled down

---

[76]The existence and extent of blood atonement, shedding the blood of certain accused sinners or criminals, remains controversial. Church leaders repudiated the doctrine in the so-called Manifesto of the Apostles in 1889. Alexander, *Things in Heaven and Earth*, 182–85, 257–59; and Gardner, "Mormonism and Capital Punishment." D. Michael Quinn argues that murder or castration was ordered for a variety of transgressions, especially during the Reformation of 1856–57. Quinn, *The Mormon Hierarchy: Origins of Power*, 94, 112–13, and *The Mormon Hierarchy: Extensions of Power*, 246, 250–55.

[77]Hyde, "An Address," 9 April 1853, *Journal of Discourses*, 1:73.

[78]Whitney, *History of Utah*, 1:723.

[79]16 August 1857, *Journal of Discourses*, 4:375.

[80]Hicks, History of Spanish Fork, 13–14.

at night, and persons whose faith in Mormonism was suspected were searched in the hope of finding evidence against them."[81]

John Chatterly, a devoted loyalist, recalled the "insane (I called it) religious fanaticism" that demanded the Saints "be free of any intercourse with the Gentile world" and "wait for our Redeemer." Some of Chatterly's Iron County neighbors "formed a secret Committee, called 'Danites,' or 'distroying angels.'" Two of them warned him "to look out for myself, as I was doomed, as it was concluded by a majority in one of their meetings, that I must be put out of the way; and knew too much, and was much opposed to their hellish murderous conduct. From that time on, I dare not go out at night, or go alone far from town." Chatterly "was very cautious in my general conduct. I could tell you of single instances of quietly starting fellows off to California, that never got very far from town, but not any use to repeat such things, as much of that game was going on all over the Territory in the Fall of 1856 and the Spring of 1857."[82] As a resident of Cedar City, Chatterly saw the consequences of this festival of religious excess after John D. Lee and fellow zealots treacherously slaughtered more than 120 men, women, and children at Mountain Meadows.

Mormon historians have long attempted to accentuate the positive results of the Reformation. "Perhaps a majority of Saints," three prominent scholars proposed, "believing themselves in spiritual jeopardy, searched their souls and bettered their lives" by attending more church meetings and paying more tithing.[83] The movement "had as much to do with the lofty expectations of Church leaders as with the spiritual complacency," proposed Mormon scholar Paul H. Peterson. Critics and apologists may have made too much of the Reformation, which "was on the whole more structured and restrained than has often been believed," and "the major impact was of short duration and only moderate consequence."[84] The movement "markedly raised" the "spiritual tone of the entire Mormon commonwealth," concluded Gustive O. Larson, quoting Utah historian Andrew Neff. But even Larson described a ritual murder at Cedar City reported by "reputable eyewitnesses" where the offender "went to his unconsecrated grave in full confidence of salvation through the shedding of his blood."[85]

---

[81]"Utah and the Mormons," *New York Times*, 1 May 1858, 4.

[82]Turley and Walker, eds., *Mountain Meadows Massacre*, 283–84.

[83]Walker, Turley, and Leonard, *Massacre at Mountain Meadows*, 25.

[84]Ludlow, ed., *The Encyclopedia of Mormonism*, 4:1197.

[85]Larson, "The Mormon Reformation," 62n39.

Leonard J. Arrington argued that Brigham Young's "Minute Men"—Arrington's term for the "nonofficial Mormon vigilante group sometimes referred to as Danites or Destroying Angels"—were an overblown myth: that they were "anything more than a group willing to undertake arduous labors for their governor and church president has never been demonstrated."[86] Recent scholarship has met this challenge, tracing several crimes directly back to Governor Young. The Mountain Meadows massacre was the most extreme example of Mormon frontier violence, but it was not an isolated incident. The Reformation year of 1857 alone saw the ambush at Santa Clara in February, the Parrish-Potter murders of March, the murder of Richard Yates in October, and the slaughter of the Aiken party in November. The first two assaults have been traced to letters Brigham Young sent to bishops, and the others were in one way or another tied to church operations.[87] This raises an interesting question: virtually every one of these crimes was a botched operation, so how many disappearances and blood atonements were carried off without anyone being the wiser?

Defining the extent of religious violence in the Mormon West is a perilous task: numbering its victims is hopeless. John Hanson Beadle estimated 577 died during "the three years of blood and terror" following 1856, including 300 handcart casualties and 70 teamsters whom he claimed were executed during the Utah War. Even deducting these numbers, "the average of actual crime still remains very great," Beadle observed.[88] The standard rebuttal is that crime was rare on the Utah frontier: the occasional "isolated acts of violence that occurred in areas where Latter-day Saints lived were typical of that period in the history of the American West," as Lowell Snow argued, and they certainly "were not instances of Church-sanctioned blood Atonement."[89] The highly respected William P. MacKinnon investigated oft-repeated claims that the Utah War was "a bloodless but costly confrontation" that "spilled no blood." MacKinnon demolished this myth: "the Utah War produced about the same number of total fatalities—approximately 150—as the contemporaneous carnage in 'bleeding Kansas,' " he concluded.[90]

[86]Arrington, *Brigham Young*, 250.

[87]For accounts of these murders, see MacKinnon, *At Sword's Point*, chapter 12; Aird, *Mormon Convert*, chapters 12–15; Parshall, " 'Pursue, Retake & Punish' "; Aird, " 'You Nasty Apostates' "; and Bigler, "The Aiken Party Executions."

[88]Beadle, *Polygamy*, 192.

[89]Ludlow, ed., *The Encyclopedia of Mormonism*, 1:131.

[90]MacKinnon, " 'Lonely Bones,' " 123–24, 176.

The best guestimate of the number of victims of Mormon religious fervor lies somewhere between the decimation described in popular potboilers and the none-to-a-handful acknowledged in apologist accounts. More dispassionate analyses such as MacKinnon's indicate the number, while unknowable, would be in the hundreds.

The level of violence, at least during the excesses that accompanied the Reformation, was sufficient to create a climate of fear and intimidation and impose what President James Buchanan called "a strange system of terrorism" on the people of Utah Territory.[91] Mormon dissidents such as William Hill and Aaron DeWitt spoke of "hundreds" who kept silent rather than have their throats cut or who feared being "murdered in cold blood, and robbed to satisfy the avaricious cravings of as foul a man and as false a Prophet as ever disgraced this sin stained earth."[92] It did not require a bloodbath to instill a healthy respect for characters such as Orrin Porter Rockwell, who once repeatedly interrupted a speech by U.S. vice president Schuyler Colfax with a drunken boast: "I never killed anyone who didn't need killing."[93] A few dramatic public murders and mysterious disappearances did the job. Howard Egan shot a man who had impregnated his wife in full view of a wagon train in 1851 and escaped punishment via an extra-legal argument based on "Mountain Common Law." After that, it was hard to ignore Major Egan's "counsel."[94] And when Bill Hickman turned up as sheriff, prosecuting attorney, and tax collector in Green River County in 1854, even the grizzled veterans of the fur trade obligingly handed over their school taxes to their new Mormon overlords. Small wonder Utah Territory struck so many visitors as positively bucolic.

Recent studies have argued that Utah's violence was merely another manifestation of a broader, regional pathology.[95] However turbulent the times, trying to hide the orange of Mormon violence in the apple basket of American western violence is dishonest. The question LDS historians steadfastly avoid asking is: "What made Utah's violence *different*?" Two singularities stand out: Mormon violence was fundamentally religious violence, and Utah Territory's most powerful authorities sanctioned acts of brutality ranging

[91]Bigler and Bagley, *The Mormon Rebellion*, xi.

[92]Simmonds, "Aaron Dewitt." Hill's statement is in the Afterword.

[93]Schindler, *Orrin Porter Rockwell*, 343n31.

[94]Homer, "The Judiciary and the Common Law," 100.

[95]Walker, Turley, and Leonard, *Massacre at Mountain Meadows*, xiii–iv, 7–8.

from castration to murder. Historians will no doubt debate for generations whether Brigham Young created and enforced a "culture of violence" in territorial Utah, but the impact of Mormon autocracy described in this volume speaks for itself.[96] As Wallace Stegner observed, "it would be bad history to pretend that there were no holy murders in Utah and along the trails to California, that there was no saving of the souls of sinners by the shedding of their blood during the 'blood atonement' revival of 1856, that there were no mysterious disappearances of apostates and offensive Gentiles."[97]

Get Away If You Can: Warmer Climes

The Reformation separated the wheat of the Mormon faithful from the chaff of their less zealous neighbors, but in the process it spread as much fear and disillusion as it did righteousness. "There is a very Poor Spirit of mormonism in the Place," one of Brigham Young's informants in the new settlement at Beaver complained. Even Loren W. Babbitt, the stake president and probate judge, could not "Stand the Reformation and not being able to Stand the fire on Thursday last he left for the warmer Climes of the South." There were others, Ephraim Tomkinson reported, "who look on the Church as a System of agrandizement."[98]

By spring 1857 dissension was rapidly thinning Mormon ranks, the *Sacramento Union* reported, and "many of them have already left for the Atlantic States." "One half of the population would leave, and will do so if the Government sends a sufficient force to protect them."[99] The "hoards" of eastbound apostates had grown to about one thousand souls, not counting the people who fled west to California and Oregon, despite a host of obstacles Mormon authorities raised to prevent such defections. Frontier newspapers gave their reasons.[100]

---

[96]D. Michael Quinn described "a culture of violence" in territorial Utah, especially during the 1850s and 1860s. Quinn provides evidence that church officials sanctioned similar acts of violence against opponents until 1890. See Quinn, *The Mormon Hierarchy: Extensions of Power*, 241–61.

[97]Stegner, *Mormon Country*, 96.

[98]Ephraim Tomkinson to Brigham Young, 2 November 1856, LDS Archives. Babbitt fled to California, apparently after learning that Indians had killed his brother Almon, the territorial secretary of state.

[99]"Important from Utah," *Otsego (New York) Gazette and Examiner*, 20 August 1857, quoting *Sacramento Union*.

[100]An emigrant train of one hundred souls, including a large number of women and children, arrived at Lawrence, Kansas, on 26 July 1857. Its members left Utah "partly to escape from the relentless tyranny of the Brigham Young oligarchy, and partly to improve their pecuniary affairs." They reported "great dissatisfaction among the Saints" and estimated "about a thousand persons abandoned Utah at the same time. Several trains departed for the States, and nearly four hundred started for Oregon." "Mormonism—Disgusted 'Saints,'" *New York Times*, 5 August 1857, 2.

Root, Hog, or Die: Ephraim, Sanpete Valley, 1858
Mounted Rifleman Joseph Heger of the U.S. Army passed through the ramshackle village of Ephraim, Utah, in Sanpete Valley as he marched from Camp Floyd to Fort Union in New Mexico. His 23 July 1858 sketch shows the livestock and homes, irrigation ditch, and fort typical of Mormon frontier settlements. *Courtesy Yale Collection of Western Americana, Beinecke Rare Book and Manuscript Library.*

"Returning Mormons," *Omaha Nebraskan*, 8 July 1857, 2/5.

A train, consisting of about one hundred persons with twenty wagons, passed through this place on Friday last, on their return from Utah to the States. They formed part of a company of two hundred persons and forty teams; but some distance back the remainder took the road for Leavenworth. They left Salt Lake about the 20th of April, and were on the road a little over two months. They bore the appearance of people who have seen much trouble and privation—being reduced in body and dejected in mind. A more pitiable set of persons we never beheld. They rejoiced that they had at last reached a land where they could once more live at their ease.

The account of their experience in Utah was touching in the extreme.—In the narration of what they endured, they seem to approach the subject with reluctance and feelings of horror in calling to mind their sufferings, but in the course of their remarks they would inevitably become animated, and break out in expressions of indignation at the cruelties and oppression which they had endured. They declared the whole system to be a grand scheme of robbery and sensuality, on the part of those in authority. It is not by direct compulsion, they stated, that the property of their fellows is taken, but by

Handcarts Crossing the Plains

The handcart disasters of 1856 disillusioned many Latter-day Saints. "There was no God to help them," recalled George A. Hicks. This engraving, which appeared in *Ballou's Pictorial Drawing-Room Companion* 20 September 1856, is one of the few contemporary images of Mormon handcarts. *Courtesy Rick Grunder.*

means of religious enthusiasm. This is inspired by the promise of great spiritual rewards, and by setting before them the example of scripture characters; that as Job received an increase above all his former possessions, so should they, by their self-sacrificing, reap an increased reward of both spiritual and temporal possessions. After all their property was exhausted, then the policy of their rulers would change, and their conduct would be such as to say, "Get away if you can." If any should become dissatisfied and desire to leave, they were publicly denounced and the whole church forbidden to purchase any property they might wish to dispose of. From that day they would be subjected to the insults of the entire community, if not [in] absolute danger of their lives. One person stated that in order to get away he had to sell his farm, clandestinely at that, for sixty dollars. They reported that one man went out with three thousand dollars, and was returning in the train with his team only, and had not enough to eat. Another who had a farm worth there seven thousand dollars, sold it for thirty-five dollars. A man by the name of George Brooks, (if we recollect aright,) who had considerable grain and goods stored in his house, on incurring the displeasure of the elders, had the sides of his house literally stove in, and his property all carried off, he only escaping with his life.

When the train first approached, we inquired whether they were from California or Utah. An old man who was standing near replied, "We are from Beautiful Zion."

"What is your opinion of Zion," we inquired.

His reply was, "I went once in search of Zion, but will never go again till I know where it is to be found. It is the worst Zion that I ever set my foot into."

We inquired concerning the handcart trains, and the true reason of employing them. They said it was the greatest piece of cruelty that was ever perpetrated; that it was at times horrible to behold the condition of those who arrived in that way; that frequently their hands and feet were frozen, and their limbs, from the effects of fatigue and exposure, swollen to more than twice their natural size; that sometimes when they were no longer [able] to pull their carts, the women and children were loaded in with the baggage, and proceeded thus until they fell down from sheer exhaustion; and that after arriving in this condition, they would die off like "rotten sheep," as they expressed it. They stated that one reason for forming hand[cart] trains was that those who came in this way, on becoming dissatisfied would have no ready means of returning, and that those in authority curse the emigrant trains which pass through on their way to the Pacific, as they afford means for dissatisfied persons to escape.

In speaking with one quite intelligent young man, he stated that he had been there for nearly four years, and that the reason he did not leave sooner was because he hoped it would get better. He remarked that if he should meet a train going through he would do all that he could to persuade them not to go; but if they persisted he could only leave them to find out by sad experience. The company report that four or five hundred men were going to leave this spring, and are probably on the road by this time.—*Plattsmouth Jeffersonian.*

Innocence, Virtue, and Truth: Mormons Explain Apostasy

Apostle William Smith's newspaper, the *New-York Prophet,* asked a rhetorical question in 1845: why not respond "to the slanders and abuses which are heaped upon the saints by apostates, murderers, and their accomplices and those who apologize for murder?" The Saints stood accused "of stealing, robbery, bogus making, polygamy, adultery, and all other crimes. Why do they not reply to these gross charges?" The editorial tried "to answer the inquiry once for all."

First, the church had neither the time nor the means "to reply to such a constant flood of foul and malicious falsehoods as are continually poured forth in torrents upon the heads of the Saints." Second, those who published such falsehoods "did not want the truth, but would sooner have a lie," since their express purpose was to "murder all the men, women and children of the Saints . . . by working upon the credulity of a prejudiced world." Third, those who loved the truth and hated lies would "readily see the corrupt, unfeeling, cruel, partial, unjust, envious and hateful spirit which is breathed forth and manifested in such publications." They would know by common sense that a large community gathered "from all classes, countries and ranks of life, would have more conscience, more moral virtue than to be guilty of such crimes as were charged against the Saints." Lastly, the *Prophet* kept its silence on these subjects to "remind the public that all our actions, precepts, doctrines, principles and publications are a direct reply to these slanderous abuses. They all speak with a voice of thunder, that we, as a people, aim at innocence, virtue and truth," while "the publications of our enemies" were clearly aimed "at murder and destruction."[101]

Twelve years after their exodus to the Great Basin began, isolation sharpened the Saints' conviction that they were being persecuted for their righteousness sake. "Have not we felt the rod?" Heber C. Kimball asked two days after learning that the U.S. Army was marching to Utah.

> Yes; and God says judgment shall come, and it shall commence at the house of God first, and then it will come upon those that have rebelled in the house of God; and of all the suffering that ever fell upon men and women will fall upon the apostates. They have got to pay all the debt of the trouble that they have brought upon the innocent from the days of Joseph to this day, and they cannot get rid of it.[102]

During that heated summer of 1857, Apostle John Taylor showed the same contempt for deserters shortly after returning to Utah. "We have met on the road a great many apostates. I do not want to say much about them. If they can be happy, all right; but they do not exhibit it," he said. "When a man deserts from the Gospel, from the ordinances, from the Priesthood and its authority, from the revelations of the Spirit of God, from the spirit of prophecy, from that sweet, calm influence that broods over the upright man in all his acts, he loses the blessing of God, and falls back into error."[103] These characters were in such bad repute that they faced rejection even in Babylon.

Devout Mormons had many explanations for why so many lost their faith. A favorite was that the devil got them or, as one Mormon historian

---

[101]"The Apostates and Murderers," *New-York Prophet*, 22 February 1845, 1:40.

[102]26 July 1857, *Journal of Discourses*, 5:94.

[103]9 August 1857, Journal of Discourses, 5:115.

put it more elegantly, "misconduct had deadened them to the Spirit."[104] Two of the mainstays were that these fallen stalwarts were not stalwart enough or could not endure the endemic poverty that plagued Utah. "There were murmurings in our camp life," English convert Robert Aveson wrote of his trip across the plains in 1866. "It was an experience our immigrants had never passed through before, and the hardships they endured caused many to become cold in the faith." Aveson's train "met quite a number of discontented and dissatisfied members of our Church returning in wagon loads from the fearful valleys of Utah, to find, what appeared to them more lucrative fields of industry somewhere back in the eastern states, or in other parts of the world." Aveson credited the shock of leaving industrialized Europe "and then coming to a new country and finding it in such a crude state—over 1,000 miles from a railroad, such a change as this was the main cause of their discontentment and change of mind in regard to the gospel they had espoused."[105]

Not surprisingly, many explanations had faith-promoting elements, especially as time went on. One night in 1859, handcart pioneer William Atkin recalled, "a company of those apostates camped near us" who had "some very hard stories about Utah and the Mormons." He found "one man who was quite reasonable in his conversation." He had spent two years in Utah, having arrived with a wife and family to feed and not a dollar. "He had worked for Brigham Young but was now on his way back. Although they said we could not make a living there, during the two years of his sojourn in the valleys he had provided for his family and now had a wagon and a yoke of oxen and provision enough to carry him and his family back over a 1000 miles journey." Atkin asked if he had ever known that the gospel was true, and the man "said yes and he had that testimony yet. I told him to be sure and not speak against the Lord nor his people, and also be sure not to forget to pray and to keep that testimony always; and the day would come when he would return again to Zion." Almost four decades later, Atkin said he saw the man in Salt Lake City, "and he told me my words had been the cause of his coming back as he had kept them continually on his mind."[106]

[104]Walker, *Wayward Saints*, 166.

[105]Robert Aveson, "Reminiscences of the Long Journey from England to 'The Valley' in the Sixties," *Deseret Evening News*, 3 January 1920, sec. 4, p. 6.

[106]"Story of William Atkin, taken from an old newspaper," [*St. George Union*, May–November 1896], in Carter, *Heart Throbs of the West*, 6:385–86.

Dissent Is Never Simple

As such examples made clear to loyal Latter-day Saints, apostasy was a very bad thing. Yet the nature of Mormon faith forsaken was never simple, and those who question or leave cannot be dismissed with an easy "You are either for us or against us." This volume can feature only a few of the diverse voices in the vast literature of Mormon dissent. At one end of the spectrum is George A. Hicks, a loyal believer who wanted his religion to live up to the truth he saw in it. When it did not, he spoke out. His autobiography shows how compelling a figure the prophet Joseph Smith was and still is. Charles Derry likewise believed in the Restoration. He denounced Brigham Young but still loved Smith and eventually joined the Reorganized church. Ann Gordge presents a difficult story in which it is often impossible to distinguish reality from imagination. Nevertheless, her writing contains enough convincing detail about John D. Lee, her family, her neighbors, and her working life to make it an authentic and valuable document in the social history of southern Utah. She gives us a unique look inside the John D. Lee family, showing the enormous disruption that conversion and gathering to Utah caused, as well as the cost of marriage at a very young age to a much older man with multiple wives. Finally, she also shows the difficulties that an unmarried woman faced in trying to earn a living in the West.

That most unlikely dissenter, B.Y. Hampton, moved from serving as loyal bodyguard for Brigham Young and policeman to suffering a loss of faith in his religion's leaders, if not his devotion to the cause. Hampton, who was too young to have known Joseph Smith, remained fiercely loyal to Brother Brigham's rugged frontier brand of Mormonism and its devotion to building the Kingdom of God in defiance of all the powers of Babylon. He described with visceral vividness the battle for Utah from 1860 to 1890, a radical, desperate, violent, bitter, and high-stakes conflict in which both sides inflicted horrific blows on the other.

These perspectives should not be dismissed automatically, for they capture a picture of a dynamic religious movement transforming and adapting to stress and changing times. All of these narratives illustrate the wide variety of dissent and add new insights into church authority, polygamy, violence, doctrine, and everyday life in the Mormon West. The stories they tell, and the honest, brave, and decent people who told them, deserve to be remembered.

Chapter 1

George Armstrong Hicks
A Life among the Poor of Utah

George Armstrong Hicks (1835–1926) described his autobiography as a history of himself "containing the principle events of a life among the poor of Utah and the 'Saints' generally." Although often desperately poor and buffeted by circumstances beyond his control, Hicks was an insightful man who did not hesitate to express his opinions about his world and its leaders. In this he differed from many Mormons in the 1850s to 1870s, who generally accepted the church's authority over them—or at least did not question its word in their personal writings, much less in letters to the church president, Brigham Young, or the newspaper.

Besides being outspoken, George A. Hicks had a talent for describing characters he knew with Dickensian color, such as the strange "Pegleg Parker" and "Rattlesnake Dick," who married one of John D. Lee's daughters. He did not neglect less palatable people, either, such as A. W. Collins, who boasted in graphic detail of his cruel treatment of slaves in Mississippi. A keen observer of human nature, especially people's foibles, Hicks also singled out those who showed great kindness to others. The vigor of his voice alone makes this autobiography valuable. Hicks was no ordinary man: blessed with a remarkable memory for people and events, he had a gift for language evidenced in his writings (if not in his spelling) and in his ability as an Indian interpreter. His ideas and reactions leave the reader with much to ponder. For example, he wrote about the "happy days of Utah" when the Saints were truly "a band of brethren" and apostasy was unknown. He also wrote about the Mormon Reformation when "our peace was destroyed by the pre[a]ching of that most accursed of all cursed doctrines, . . . namely 'blood atonement.' "

George A. Hicks, circa 1892

This portrait of a genteel George A. Hicks may have been taken when he ran for justice of the peace in Spanish Fork. He won the election but, as usual, annoyed people with his outspokenness. William Creer accused him of having written letters published in the *San Francisco Chronicle* "exposing the Mountain Meadow massacre." Hicks, who had not written the letters, petitioned the Utah legislature to pass a bill to protect people from defamation of character. *Courtesy International Society, Daughters of Utah Pioneers.*

Hicks's early life is that of a classic Mormon pioneer. Born in Ontario in 1835, George was three when his parents emigrated. The Hickses lived in Nauvoo from late 1839 until 1846, when they left with the main body of the faithful after the murder of Joseph Smith. For the next six years, the family lived in Iowa, working to save enough to travel to Utah. Finally, in 1852 they set out. Soon after arriving in Utah, they moved to Palmyra in Utah County. Here George, not quite eighteen, met sixteen-year-old Elizabeth Jolley, and in 1853 they were married. George took part in the Walker War against the Ute Indians that same year.

In 1856 Brigham Young instituted a cheaper method of "gathering" new migrants to Utah.[1] They were now to pull supplies for the three-month trip in handcarts, replacing the usual wagons pulled by oxen. Of the five handcart companies that first year, two started from the Missouri River too late in the season to avoid blizzards on the high plains in present-day Wyoming. As a result, between 202 and 267 of the emigrants died, and the survivors were barely alive and badly frostbitten.[2] This tragedy, Hicks said, "revolutionized" his mind: despite the handcart convert's piety, "there was no God to help them." The universe, Hicks concluded, "is governed by laws immutable and unchangeable."

Despite the excesses of the Reformation and the handcart disaster, Hicks was still a believer. An elder in the senior Melchizedek priesthood, in April 1857 Hicks became a Seventy, a still-higher priesthood office.[3] That summer the Mormons heard that the U.S. Army was marching on Utah, bringing a civilian to replace Brigham Young as territorial governor and to reassert control in Utah, as the leaders of the church were increasingly declaring their independence from the federal government. The news did not frighten the people, Hicks wrote, for the event marked the beginning of the last days before Christ would come in power and glory. Hicks joined the Nauvoo Legion, the Utah territorial militia, to fight the U.S. Army and was made a lieutenant of a platoon, but he never saw action.[4]

[1]After baptism, gathering to Utah was the most important tenet of the LDS church in the mid-nineteenth century. Mormons believed that only in Utah would members be safe from the destruction that would sweep over "Babylon" in the millennium.

[2]These estimates, based on known fatalities, are low: deaths due to the 1856 handcart disaster "probably exceeded three hundred." Bagley, "'One Long Funeral March,'" 108–109.

[3]Record of Fiftieth Quorum of Seventies, 4–5. Seventies, a Melchizedek priesthood office, were called to preach the Gospel and serve as missionaries.

[4]Utah County Military District, rolls for 20 April, 15 June, and 15 July 1857.

CAROLINE HICKS MOORE
Born in Nauvoo, Caroline Hicks Moore (1844–1878) was age 13 during the Reformation, when church leaders campaigned for men to take more wives. She was persuaded to marry Albert K. Thurber of the Spanish Fork bishopric in the Endowment House at Salt Lake City. After the sealing ceremony, she locked Thurber out of the bedroom. Her older brother George and a friend, John Moore, helped her escape out a window. In October 1860 she married John Moore and bore eight children before dying in childbirth in 1878. *Courtesy International Society, Daughters of Utah Pioneers.*

As the army was about to enter the Salt Lake Valley, President Young ordered those living in Salt Lake City and northward to move south, leaving the main Mormon settlements deserted. The immense disruption of the population caused by this edict was made worse by its timing in the midst of the planting season. But Hicks, who lived in central Utah and thus did not have to move, saw the army's coming as a good thing. Once the army started building Camp Floyd west of Utah Lake, which would be its headquarters in Utah until the start of the Civil War, the people were offered work and were paid well, enabling the poor to buy clothes and other necessities they otherwise had no way to obtain.

In 1861 George and Betsy, with their four young children, moved four miles south to Pond Town (today's Salem). There they hoped to receive a "recommend" from the bishop, Betsy's father, so that they might receive their endowments and be sealed in the Endowment House in Salt Lake City.[5] George had angered the polygamist bishop in Spanish Fork, Albert King Thurber. During the Reformation, George's sister, thirteen-year-old Caroline, had been pressured into marrying Thurber. George with a friend stopped

[5]To receive the sacred rites requires a recommend from the local bishop stating the individual is a worthy member. The endowment teaches the plan of salvation; sealing binds a family together for eternity. Until the 1880s ordinances took place in the Endowment House in Salt Lake City.

Albert King Thurber
Born in Providence, Rhode Island, forty-niner Albert King Thurber (1826–1888) converted to Mormonism in September 1849 on his way to California and won Brigham Young's admiration after serving as a gold missionary. He had five children with Agnes Brockbank and eleven children with Thurza Melvina Berry, but A.K. Thurber's courtship and brief marriage to George A. Hicks's sister Caroline was not a success. *Courtesy Utah State Historical Society.*

the marriage from being consummated and then helped her obtain a divorce. Naturally, Hicks was convinced Thurber would deny him a recommend. But before asking Betsy's father for one, George and Betsy, along with her parents and other siblings, were called in the fall of 1862 to the Cotton Mission in southern Utah. At the October 1861 church conference, President Young, determined to make Zion self-sufficient, designated some three hundred families to move to southern Utah and grow cotton.[6] He added two hundred more a year later, greatly increasing the population of Utah's "Dixie."

With the start of their trip south in late November 1862, George and Betsy would be tried almost beyond endurance for more than fifteen years. Their slow, tedious journey southward was abruptly halted at Black Ridge near the border of Kane County, where they were swallowed up in a ferocious blizzard that lasted four days. Finally arriving in the settlement of Washington, they found such "a sickly and barren land" that Hicks contemplated running away "from my bondage like a slave from his master," but he was prevented by his duty to Betsy and their four young children, who ranged in age from one and a half to eight years old.

[6]Besides missions to foreign countries, church members could be sent on domestic missions to build the Kingdom of God.

In the spring, George set to work to plant cotton on rented acres. It was here that he became acquainted with several former slave owners from Mississippi who had been sent south to Utah's Dixie because of their familiarity with growing cotton. These Southerners sympathized with the Confederacy: Hicks knew only one other Union man besides himself. He had procured a city lot but had not the wherewithal to build anything more than an Indian-style brush "wickiup," and it was in this humble home that Betsy delivered their fifth child. Desperate to feed his family, Hicks went to the larger town of St. George to apply to Apostle Erastus Snow to do any kind of labor in exchange for flour. After hearing his request, Snow said he could not feed everyone and summarily walked out of the room, leaving Hicks to his own reflections.

Snow, the leader of the Cotton Mission, had instructed the settlers to plant all the land they could in cotton and sugar cane and promised that church members living farther north would come and be eager to trade flour and other food for their products. His prediction failed, and the cotton missionaries were left to starve. The next year Snow, now more fully aware of their plight, instructed them to grow wheat and corn as well as cotton. By this time the people lacked clothing and shoes as well as food: the family did its best, but Hicks often went bare-footed to his fields.

Remarkably, in spite of a year and a half of struggling in Washington, Hicks could see humor in their situation. A talented songwriter, poet, and storyteller, Hicks composed a lament, "Once I Lived in Cottonwood," which he sang to the delight of others. It soon became a popular ballad and is still sung today. Some days' laughter was the only food they had:

> Oh, once I lived in Cottonwood and owned a little farm,[7]
> But I was called to Dixie, which did me much alarm;
> To raise the cane and cotton, I right away must go;
> But the reason why they called on me, I'm sure I do not know.
>
> I yoked old Jim and Bolly up all for to make a start,
> To leave my house and garden, it almost broke my heart.
> We moved along quite slowly and often looked behind,
> For the sand and rocks of Dixie kept running through my mind.
>
> At length we reached the Black Ridge where I broke my wagon down,
> I could not find a carpenter so far from any town,

[7]Although Hicks never lived there, many of the first cotton missionaries came from Cottonwood, one of the loveliest spots in the Salt Lake Valley.

So with a clumsy cedar pole I fixed an awkward slide;
My wagon pulled so heavy then that Betsy could not ride.

While Betsy was a'walking, I told her to take care,
When all upon a sudden she struck a pricklypear.
Then she began to blubber out as loud as she could bawl,
"If I was back in Cottonwood, I would not come at all!"

When we reached the Sandy, we could not move at all,
For poor old Jim and Bolly began to puff and loll.
I whipped and swore a little but could not make the route,
For myself, the team, and Betsy, were all of us give out.

Next we got to Washington, where we stayed a little while
To see if April showers would make the verdure smile.
But, oh, I was mistaken and so I went away,
For the red hills of November looked just the same in May.

I feel so weak and hungry now, there's nothing here to cheer
Except prophetic sermons which we very often hear.
They will hand them out by dozens and prove them by the book—
I'd rather have some roasting ears to stay at home and cook.

I feel so weak and hungry now, I think I'm nearly dead;
'Tis seven weeks next Sunday since I have tasted bread.
Of carrot tops and lucerne greens we have enough to eat—
But I'd like to change that diet off for buck-wheat cakes and meat.

I brought this old coat with me about two years ago,
And how I'll get another one, I'm sure I do not know.
May providence protect me against the cold and wet;
I think myself and Betsy, these times will not forget.

My shirt is dyed with wild dockroot, with greasewood for a set;
I fear the colors all will fade when once it does get wet.
They said we would raise madder, and indigo so blue,
But that turned out a humbug, the story was not true.

The hot winds whirl around me and take away my breath;
I've had the chills and fever till I'm nearly shook to death.
"All earthly tribulations are but a moment here;
And, oh, if I prove faithful, a righteous crown I'll wear."

My wagons's sold for sorghum seed to make a little bread;
And poor old Jim and Bolly long ago are dead.
There's only me and Betsy left to hoe the cotton-tree;
May Heaven help the Dixie-ite wherever he may be!

The Cotton Mission was a failure. Although it was possible to grow cotton in Utah's Dixie, the region was too far from markets to be economical. At the end of the Civil War, the price of cotton dropped and spelled the end of the mission. President Young tried to bolster their efforts by moving a cotton and then a woolen factory south, but they never proved the success Young had envisioned. Many families gave up on the mission, as they could not make enough to support themselves. In the spring of 1864 George and Betsy joined those who had left and moved some thirty-five miles north to New Harmony, usually called just Harmony. George was so famished as he drove the wagon out of Washington that he tried "the experiment of the philosopher": sucking a coin to see if it would alleviate his hunger pangs. It didn't.

Life in Harmony proved equally precarious. Borrowing cornmeal to feed the family, Hicks cleared land, constructed a wickiup, planted crops, and hired himself out for labor. But the few in town who wanted labor offered only half the usual rate of pay. The Hickses' only cow died after being "poisoned" (possibly from bovine anthrax or loco weed), and then, while cooking, Betsy accidentally set the wickiup on fire. None of them were hurt, but they lost their few possessions. George took jobs at any pay, grubbing oak brush, chopping pickets and stakes, and making adobes. The Hicks family stayed primarily in Harmony until 1870. But the small farm proved only large enough to starve on, and finally they moved to Hamilton's Fort. There George taught school and was superintendent of the Sabbath school.

Hicks devoted a full chapter in his autobiography to John D. Lee, who also lived in Harmony and who caused the greatest crisis of faith in George's life. Lee was a polygamist and prosperous farmer, an adopted son of Brigham Young and perpetrator of the Mountain Meadows massacre.[8] The 1857 massacre of 120 Arkansas emigrants at a nearby alpine oasis on the California Trail, where they had been preparing to start across the Mojave Desert, had taken place seven years before the Hicks family moved to Harmony. By 1861 virtually every massacre participant except for Lee had fled the area.[9] Hicks was upset and confused about why Lee—one of the main instigators of the atrocity—was not only free but still a leader of the Harmony branch of the

[8]Adoption in that period established spiritual and temporal family bonds between unrelated people.
[9]Brooks, *Emma Lee*, 37.

church who was frequently called upon to preach and remained on intimate terms with President Young.[10] What could this mean? Did the head of the church condone the massacre? If he did not, why was he shielding Lee? And why did Young and his retinue on their annual winter trips to St. George almost always stop for the night at Lee's house to be royally entertained?

The arrival of the Cotton Mission colonists "had a profound effect upon Lee's personal fortunes. Most of the new settlers were not familiar with the fervor that had characterized the period of the Mountain Meadows Massacre and looked upon the murder of the emigrants with unmitigated horror," Robert Cleland and Juanita Brooks wrote to explain the reaction to Lee's continued high standing. "Accordingly, though taking no immediate steps to ostracize Lee, they assumed a decidedly cool attitude toward him." Such feelings surfaced overtly just before George and Betsy arrived in Harmony, when general dissatisfaction led to a meeting on 5 March 1864 "for the purpose of settling their difficulties resulting in a better state of feeling. Pres. Lee tendered his resignation as President of the Branch, which was accepted." James H. Imlay was appointed his successor.[11]

Hicks's feelings of distress grew less than a year after moving to Harmony, when Brigham Young came to Harmony to visit Lee, his old friend and adopted son. Hicks was not alone: "Whisperings about the massacre continued; the stories became more numerous and highly colored." Neighbors showed their disapproval of Lee in many ways—"turning their cattle into his grain fields, interfering with his water ditches, and making snide remarks to his wives or children."[12] In November 1866, according to Lee's diary, Hicks was one of ten men who turned their animals into Lee's cornfield.[13]

Hicks took heart a month later when President Young denounced Utah's past crimes, including the massacre. Referring to the October 1866 murder of Dr. John King Robinson, the Mormon leader said he wanted "the Saints to know how I feel about all such dastardly transactions." Some atrocities were "too horrible for me to contemplate," he asserted, naming the Hauns

[10]A branch is the smallest unit of the church. In this case, Harmony belonged to Cedar City Ward.

[11]Cleland and Brooks, eds., *A Mormon Chronicle*, 2:4, 8–9. In March 1855 Thomas D. Brown, a missionary to the southern Indians, reluctantly listed Lee's offensive behaviors, which, he concluded, "militate against the harmony of Harmony." Brooks, *Journal of the Southern Indian Mission*, 117–19.

[12]Brooks, *John Doyle Lee*, 277.

[13]Cleland and Brooks, eds., *A Mormon Chronicle*, 2:32.

Mill massacre, the murder of the Smith brothers, the Mountain Meadows massacre, and Robinson's murder. "I cannot think that there are beings upon the earth who have any claim to the sentiments and feelings which dwell in the breasts of civilized men who could be guilty of such atrocities; and it is hard to suppose that even savages would be capable of performing such inhuman acts. To call a physician out of his bed in the night under the pretext of needing his services, and then brutally kill him in the dark, is horrible." Robinson's murder was indeed horrific, but Young's habitually violent rhetoric undercut his self-proclaimed sensitivity: a New York newspaper quoted him saying he "was sorry that the doctor had been killed, for he wanted him to live and die in the ditch like a dog." The crime baffled him, Young claimed, but he made one thing clear: "If any man, woman or child that ever lived has said that Brigham Young ever counseled them to commit crime of any description, they are liars in the face of heaven."[14]

Hicks was ecstatic when the sermon appeared in the *Deseret News,* reading it again and again as he debated whether "Brother Brigham" was innocent or in favor of Lee's appalling crime. Hicks carried the newspaper clipping in his pocket and read it to anyone who would listen. During the spring of 1867, Hicks visited his parents at Spanish Fork and there learned a song written about the massacre when American soldiers traveled to southern Utah in 1859.[15] The ballad delighted Hicks, and upon his return to Harmony many people came to his house to hear him decry "the bloody massacre" and denounce the "wicked band" disguised "in Indian colors all wrapped in shame."[16]

---

[14]Using the 1862 Homestead and Preemption acts, non-Mormon Dr. John King Robinson had sought to claim land near Warm Springs just north of Salt Lake City to build a hospital. The territorial supreme court ruled against his claim, but Robinson's attempt appears to have incurred the wrath of church leaders who wanted to keep non-Mormons from owning land. On the night of 22 October 1866 Dr. Robinson was called out to attend to a man whose leg, he was told, had been smashed in an accident. Shortly after he left the house, a shot rang out. In addition to the fatal shot to the head, Robinson was found slashed by an ax or bowie knife and had other cuts and stabs. The wounds were estimated to have been inflicted by six or more men. No one was convicted of the murder. Bigler, *Forgotten Kingdom,* 247–53. Young's sermon was given on 23 December 1866 and published as "Remarks," *Deseret News,* 9 January 1867, 2–3. For Young's comments, see "Talk with Brigham Young," *New York Evening Post,* 7 November 1867, in Baskin, *Reminiscences of Early Utah,* 28.

[15]Second Dragoons captain Reuben P. Campbell left Camp Floyd with a detachment in April 1859. He met a column in southern Utah under First Dragoons major James H. Carleton, who had come from Fort Tejon, California. Both had orders to investigate reports of the massacre and Indian depredations on the Santa Clara River. Bigler and Bagley, eds., *Innocent Blood,* 204–13.

[16]Several variations of this song are available on the Internet. See also Cheney, *Mormon Songs from the Rocky Mountains,* 200–205.

Although warned to stop, Hicks continued to read the article and sing the song because he wanted "the people to believe that the sixth commandment ['Thou shalt not kill'] should be obeyed."[17] He quoted Mormon scripture: "if any persons among you shall kill they shall be delivered up and dealt with according to the laws of the land." He also referred to what is now the *Doctrine and Covenants*: "We believe that the commission of crime should be punished according to the nature of the offense; that murder, treason, robbery, theft, and the breach of the general peace, in all respects, should be punished according to their criminality and their tendency to evil among men, by the laws of that government."[18]

The ballad had a "sweet minor tune," Hicks said, and soon he was invited to sing it far and wide. It caught the ear of Harmony's young folks and soon everyone knew the song. It was not just delight in annoying John D. Lee that motivated him. Rather, Hicks had become something like an Old Testament prophet: speaking the truth even when it made others uncomfortable, warning of the need to obey God's law, seeking to turn the church back to the Lord, and having a fire in his belly that drove him to keep crying for justice even when threatened.

Threatened he was. Former Nauvoo policeman and Mormon Battalion veteran James Pace, an adopted son of John D. Lee, threatened to take Hicks's life if that is what it would take to get him to stop. Hicks went on singing in spite of Pace's warnings. According to Hicks, Pace and Lee concocted a plan to get rid of him: Pace would invite George to a dance, someone would ask him to sing the massacre song, "and if I did sing it, which I was sure to do, Lee, Pace and some of Lee's boys were to take me out and 'lay me aside.'" One of Pace's wives alerted him to the plan: Hicks went to the dance but carried a revolver inside his shirt and held his tongue.

In September 1867 John D. Lee, about to go to Salt Lake to marry more wives, asked the bishop of the newly formed Harmony Ward for a recommend saying he was a worthy member. The bishop was Wilson Daniel Pace, nephew of James Pace and soon to be Lee's son-in-law.[19] The idea that the church would recognize Lee as a faithful member drove Hicks to despair.

[17]Hicks to Brigham Young, 4 December 1868, in Bigler and Bagley, eds., *Innocent Blood*, 265.

[18]*D&C*, 42:78–79 and 134:8.

[19]Wilson Daniel Pace (1831–1899) was born in Tennessee, lived in Nauvoo, and at age 15 accompanied the Mormon Battalion as a servant to Lt. Andrew Lytle. Pace served as Hicks's bishop at New Harmony. Washington County Obituary, *Deseret News*, 6 November 1899, 7.

He wrote a letter to President Young on 11 October 1867 asking him to pardon his presumption but saying he knew of no other way "of Geting the information which I desire." Hicks told the prophet his December 1866 sermon denouncing the Mountain Meadows massacre had generated considerable talk, but "John D. Lee has said publick and Privatly that you did not mean what you said but Mearly said it to blind the eyes of the Jentiles and to Satisfy a few individuals." Hicks asked the church leader to please write and tell him his real intentions: "If you are in favor of the Mountain meadows massacre I would like to know it if you are," for Hicks had "allways believed that you are opposed to the sheding of human-blood." Lee was still in full fellowship and frequently preached "much to [the] anoyance of Good men." Pleading for help, Hicks quoted scripture: "Thes[e] things causes me some trouble of mind and a few words from you will dispose of all my dark fears."[20]

The letter never reached Brigham Young, and Lee got his recommend.[21] But Lee received a letter in April 1868 purporting to be from a Major Burt at Camp Douglas, on the edge of Salt Lake City, saying he was coming after Lee for his part in the massacre. Lee believed it was fictitious, as it was the third such letter he had received and it lacked the usual postmarks.[22] Lee's feisty English-born wife, Emma Batchelor Lee, accused Hicks and Mormon Battalion veteran John Lawson of fabricating the letter. Not one to mince words, Emma added that George "was a poor sneaking, pusylanimous Pup & always Medling with other men's Matter & that he had better sing low & keep out of her Path or she would put a load of salt in his Backsides." Hicks charged her with "unChristianlike conduct" before Wilson D. Pace's bishop's court. Hicks had provoked Emma by "a train of abuse," Lee testified. We have only Lee's account of these events from his diary, which repeatedly denies his role in the massacre: "This Hicks was a Traitor," Lee complained bitterly, "& Pointed out all the Brethrn who he thought had been at Mountain Meadow when Indians killed them to the Gentiles."[23]

---

[20]Bigler and Bagley, eds., *Innocent Blood*, 264.

[21]Cleland and Brooks, eds., *A Mormon Chronicle*, 2:87

[22]A Brevet Major A.S. Burt was stationed at Fort Bridger during this time and occasionally visited Camp Douglas. "Arrivals at the Revere House," *Union Vedette*, 8 April 1867, 3; "A Visitor," *Union Vedette*, 10 April 1867.

[23]Brooks, *John Doyle Lee*, 280–81; Cleland and Brooks, eds., *A Mormon Chronicle*, 2:100–101.

Bishop Pace ruled that Emma and George should both be rebaptized and that John D. Lee and George should "make friends."[24] Lee claimed he agreed to meet Hicks "2½ of the way but he refused." With regard to Emma having to be rebaptized, "It was rather hard to require a woman to be rebaptised for resenting abuse & defending her Husband against the insults & abuse of [a] Traitor," Lee wrote. Nevertheless, he advised her to submit. Ever-spirited Emma asked for the privilege of choosing the man to baptize her, which the bishop granted. "I am much obliged," she said, "I demand Baptism at your hands, seeing that you are so inconsiderate as to require a woman to be immersed when the water is full of snow & Ice & that too for defending the rights of her husband." She felt the bishop should pay a penalty "for making such a descision & perhaps if your back side gets wet in Ice water you will be more careful how you decide again." The bishop demurred, saying he had to go to Kanarra, and thus the matter was dropped. "Hicks stood out to the last & defyed all the authority," Lee concluded.[25]

John D. Lee's description rings true: when Hicks believed justice was on his side, he refused to compromise. It seems unlikely he had a hand in fabricating the letters: outraged citizens from Camp Douglas to Harmony felt Lee should be punished. Hicks was open and forthright about his activities, good and bad, but he never mentioned the letters.

The next fall Hicks continued his campaign against Lee, who remained confident of his position with Young. As Hicks later concluded, Lee understood his relations with the prophet better than he did. Now, over a year since his first letter to President Young, the indignant Hicks once more took up his pen.

George A. Hicks to President Brigham Young,
4 December 1868 to 21 January 1869, LDS Archives.

Dear brother, I hope you will pardon my presumption in writeing this letter to you, but you and you alone can give me enny peas of mind on the matter which rests with such might upon my mind tha[t] it is destroying my peace. On the 23d day of Dec 1866 you preached a sermon which was afterwards published in the "Deseret News" for Jan 8th 1867 in cou[r]se of your remarks you spoke of the Mountain Meadows Massacre. You classed it along with the Martyrdom of Joseph Smith and Hyrum Smith. Now I was

---

[24] Rebaptism was common among nineteenth-century Mormons.

[25] Cleland and Brooks, eds., *A Mormon Chronicle*, 2:101–102.

highly delighted to see it in print for I always had condemed that horable afair as being eaquiled in history only by such deeds as you compare it with: I felt in hopes that the perpitrators of that bloody deed would soon be punished for their crimes or [if] they were not punished, their names would be stricken from the Church books. I carried the paper containing your sermon in my pocket and I read it to a great many people. Afterwards [I] learned a song, descriptive of that murder which a gre[a]t many people came to my house to hear. In the Course of time my conduct made some excitement. I was persuaded to desist or rather advised but I continued to read and quote your remarks and to sing the song and at length I was gently warned that my course of conduct would be punished if I continued. I took the revelations and the scripture generaly, in fact, for my guides at last but I find my self deserted. Reasone[ing] done no good, scripture done no good. I have been insulted in the public streets by some of John D. Lee's family only for encourageing the people to believe that the sixth commandment should be obeyed and that those who break it should be punished according to the law of the Lord (see Doc & Cov sec XIII 21 paragraph [now *D&C* 42:78–79] also Ibid sec 110 and the 8th paragraph [now *D&C* 134:8]). John D. Lee has said in public *and I have heard him* that you did not mean what you said about the Mountain Meadows Massacre but that you said it to *blind* the eyes of the gentiles and to satisfy a few individuals like myself. He is not generaly believed, however I heard one man say he believe[d] it. As for myself I scorned the idea at first but now I hardly know what to think, doubts and fears beginning to rise in my mind in relation to the matter, in short, my peace of mind is almost gone.

I wrote you once before on the subject but John Willis the P[ost] Master of Kannarah detained my letter and gave it to John D. and [?] Lee after keeping it for a long time on public exhibition at the post office. I went to get it and *got nothing but insults for my trouble.* I have been a member of the church for over twenty five years—in fact the first thing that I remember was my father starting for Far west and from that time up to the present I have lived with the Latterday Saints.

I often ask my self the question "Can it be possible that the Church whose destiny I have so long followed through sufering privation and sorrow, to gain an exaltation not only fellowships a Company of men *whose hands have been stained with the blood of innocent women and children* but the gospel of Him who said 'Thou shalt do no murder' (see Mathew XIX Chap 18 verse)?"

Some who pretend to be my friends advise me to pray to the Lord in relation to the matter. I have done so many a time but the bloody scene passes before my mind day and night. The fact stands upon our History 'that the perpetrators are *still unpunished*' and have priveliges that I have not. If I was to venture to ask an action on your part it would be that John D. Lee if he is not punished for murder that he be deprived of a standing in the Church and then he can say what he pleases at his own option and not at the expense of the Church. No one knows the Contents of this letter but my self I have writen it with the best of feelings towards you and all good men hopeing you will give me such words of Consideration as will be for my best good.

I remain your brother in the gospel of peace,
George A. Hicks

P.S. If you should condesend to answer direct to Harmony Washin co UT[26]

Eighteen days later, Brigham Young replied to Hicks. The answer shocked the recipient.

Brigham Young to George A. Hicks,
16 February 1869, LDS Archives.

Dear Brother, I received your letter reciting a tale of grievances at which I am not a little surprised.

What would be the judgment of any reasonable being after reading your letter, since you say, "The bloody scene passes before you day and night," and "it rests with such weight upon your mind" &c, why, that you yourself must have been a participator in the horrible deed. If this is correct, one can readily imagine why "it rests with such weight upon your mind," and "why you cannot sleep at nights"; the surprise would be that you could. In such a case, if you want a remedy—rope round the neck taken with a jerk would be very salutary.

There are courts of law and officers in the Territory, appeal to them, they would be happy to attend to your case.

If you are innocent you give yourself a great deal of foolish trouble. I would ask, why do not all the Latter-day Saints feel as you do? Simply because it does not concern them. As to your faith being shaken. If the Gospel was true before the "Mountain Meadow Massacre," neither that nor any other event that may transpire can make it false.

When Gov. Cumming was here, I pledged myself to lend him every assistance in my power, in men and means to thoroughly investigate that matter, but he declined to take any action. This offer I have made time and again, but it has never been accepted. Yet I have neither doubt nor fear on my mind but the perpetrators of that tragedy will meet their reward. God will judge this matter and on that assurance I rest perfectly satisfied.

---

[26]See also Bigler and Bagley, eds., *Innocent Blood*, 265–66.

If you are innocent, you may safely do the same; if you are guilty, better try the remedy.

Yours in the Gospel, Brigham Young.[27]

Why did Brigham Young answer in such a callous way? Was he shielding Lee, his adopted son? Had Lee told him about being harassed in New Harmony? Did Young, having made up his mind that he would not expel Lee from the church, simply want to stun and silence Hicks? Was Young tired of the whole matter and just wanted it to go away? Of all the letters Young wrote, this must rank among the cruelest. The response stung and baffled Hicks but led him to the only logical conclusion: John D. Lee did indeed know more about his relations with President Young than Hicks did.

Less than three months after answering Hicks, Young took his annual tour south. In Washington, Young refused accommodation at the bishop's house and instead stayed with Lee. The next morning, the local band greeted the prophet before he ate the sumptuous breakfast that Lee's wives had spent the previous night preparing. According to Lee's diary, throngs came to hear Young preach. In the afternoon Lee escorted the Mormon leader to St. George, and when he turned to go home, Brigham Young blessed him.[28]

The organizers of Harmony's Fourth of July program in 1869 provoked Lee when they "unwisely appointed Geo. Hicks orator of the Day, Much to the anoyance of the Bishop & many others who love order & Brigham & the Kingdom & this Hick[s] was an apostate & but a short time Previous Stated that Brigham Young was led by Green backs & not by the Spirit of the Lord."[29] It is not surprising that Bishop Wilson D. Pace, soon to become Lee's son-in-law, sided with Lee—and Hicks probably did say something about Young and greenbacks, for his autobiography contains a similar statement: "It is my opinion that Brigham Young sen[ior] worshiped no God but gold."

The tide was turning against Lee. Others besides Harmony residents

---

[27]Quoted in Bigler and Bagley, eds., *Innocent Blood*, 266–67. Why did Young fail to investigate the massacre after learning of it in September 1857? He was head of the church, ex-officio governor (his replacement, Alfred Cumming, had not yet reached Utah), commander of the territorial militia, and superintendent of Indian Affairs. His claim that he offered Governor Cumming "every assistance in my power" is disingenuous. In an interview in 1876, Cumming said, "God Almighty couldn't convict the butchers unless Brigham Young was willing." Cumming was a "decent but inept man [who] lacked the courage to pursue the case." Bagley, *Blood of the Prophets*, 245. For Young's micromanagement of the militia, see MacKinnon, *At Sword's Point*, 320–21.

[28]Cleland and Brooks, eds., *A Mormon Chronicle*, 2:113–15.

[29]Ibid., 2:122–23.

questioned why Lee was still free and a member of the church. With pressure mounting, in September 1870 President Young advised Lee to pack up and move farther south. Realizing he would need to build a new house before winter set in, Lee sold his farm in Harmony and left within two weeks. But it was not enough. On 8 October 1870, thirteen years after the massacre, Young finally excommunicated Lee.[30]

With this stone in his shoe finally removed, Hicks's anger subsided. In the next three or four years, Hicks lived at Hamilton's Fort and then for a time at Mount Carmel in Long Valley south of Orderville, near where his father-in-law Henry Bryant Manning Jolley had settled.[31] But Hicks's equanimity was shattered in April 1874 when Lee returned from Lonely Dell, his hideout at an isolated Colorado River ferry crossing, to meet Brigham Young, who was returning from his annual visit to southern Utah. Hicks went to Kanarra to hear Young preach and saw Lee riding beside the president's carriage in the old companionable way.[32] In a spate of fury the next day, Hicks dashed off a letter signed "Bosco" to the *Salt Lake Tribune*:

> Hamilton's Fort, April 8, 1874. Your correspondent arrived here in time to meet the beloved Brigham, who is heading for the northern provinces in the Kingdom, followed by a retinue of lick spittles. Here he tarried for the purpose of exhibiting Old Euchre, a game he and George A. Smith have been hatching in St. George during this past winter. Brigham and his Priesthood hold the winning hand, and will fleece the honest Saints of the last rag on their backs. After his arrival, the Saints gathered them together and listened to the following harangue on euchre:

What followed appears to be close to a verbatim sermon by Brigham Young on building the temple at St. George; buying Jackson County, Missouri; the Order of Enoch (the United Order, an attempt to establish enterprises and a community on the principles of unity and equality); and joining the United Order. "Such is the chaff that people are caught with," Bosco complained. As the meeting ended, Young and George A. Smith "asked God to bless all those who had joined the 'holy' Order. Perhaps he thought those who kept out were smart enough to take care of themselves." Hicks then returned to a familiar theme:

---

[30]Cleland and Brooks, eds., *A Mormon Chronicle*, 2:135–36; and Brooks, *John Doyle Lee*, 293–94.

[31]Jolley, *Jolley Family Book*, 500.

[32]Cleland and Brooks, eds., *A Mormon Chronicle*, 2:333–38, 342n43; Brooks, *John Doyle Lee*, 332–34.

> John D. Lee came to Kanarah with Brigham. He told a friend while there that the President had sent word to him to take charge of the ferry on the Colorado, and he was doing so. Lee had come to see the Profit, and never was used better by him in his life. The Profit asked him to come with him to get instructions for the future welfare of the people. Lee was very sorry he could not accompany Brigham further on this mission and said he had been looking for the Order of Enoch for the last thirty years, and was very thankful it was now being preached. He looks very bad, is fast fading and seems quite nervous and watchful. I saw him myself, riding by the side Brigham's carriage. "Birds of a feather," etc. Bosco.[33]

The days of speaking like an Old Testament prophet were over. After receiving the intimidating letter from Young, Hicks apparently gave up any struggle to believe Young was truly a prophet. Watching the president of the church fraternize with John D. Lee even after Lee's excommunication, Hicks could no longer restrain his spring-loaded, pent-up anger. Suspecting Hicks wrote the *Tribune* letter, Bishop Henry Lunt of Cedar City questioned him, and when he did not deny writing it, Lunt "immediately cut off" Hicks without a hearing.[34] Such disrespect—calling Brigham Young "the Profit" and the church leaders traveling with him his "lick spittles," and accusing them of fleecing the faithful—could not be tolerated.

The next August Hicks went to see Mountain Meadows for himself, which he described in a letter to the editor of the *Salt Lake Tribune*. After a general description of the site and a brief recounting of the massacre, he turned to the monument to the victims:

> The monument, or grave, . . . is a pile of loose stones, twenty seven feet long and nine feet wide. The ground where they camped appears to have been once well set with grass, which has since died from being used as a sheep pasture, and the roads are fast decaying. A deep wash is formed by the rain floods, and by the small creek that murmurs along the bottom of the wash. The monument is within six feet of the bank, which is from twelve to fifteen feet high. By the natural courses of the floods, the monument will soon fall into the wash, and from thence the dust of the sleepers will soon mingle with the lands of the Colorado.

Hicks ended his description with a call to build a new monument: "It is the duty of all lovers of justice to contribute something toward erecting a more

[33]"Brigham's Last Swindle," *Salt Lake Tribune*, 16 April 1874, 4.

[34]Hicks, "Some Startling Facts," *Salt Lake Tribune*, 21 August 1874, 2/3.

suitable monument to mark the place where poor victims of fanaticism are reposing."[35]

The outrage of seventeen years having passed without the perpetrators of the massacre being brought to justice and the unfairness of not receiving a hearing before being excommunicated rankled. Within a week after his article about Mountain Meadows, Hicks related "a few facts" in a lengthy letter to the *Salt Lake Tribune* written from Hamilton's Fort. He began by quoting the *Deseret News* report that at a public meeting in Cedar City on 26 April 1874, "George A. Hicks, of Hamilton's Fort, was cut off the Church of Jesus Christ of Latter-day Saints, for apostacy."[36]

GEORGE A. HICKS, 12 AUGUST 1874, "SOME STARTLING FACTS," *SALT LAKE TRIBUNE*, 21 AUGUST 1874, 2/2–3.

The above is a very brief and unpretentious paragraph, which a business man might never notice—a paragraph which my friends who are still of the Mormon faith, would feel sad as they read it, and my enemies would perhaps rejoice at my downfall, and then it would be utterly forgotten. Not so with myself. In the notice of my excommunication, the readers only hear one side of the case, "apostasy." I shall endeavor to give the other side.

Of the forty years of my life, thirty have been spent in the Mormon Church. I, with my father's family, was expelled from Nauvoo. I thought it very cruel at the time, and still think so in fact. I have shared the joys and sorrows, the victories and defeats of the Church for thirty years.

I came to Utah in 1852, strong in the faith of Mormonism. I have seen the church when it was full of Christian charity and brotherly love. In 1850 [1856], came what is called the Reformation, which swept over the country like a tornado. It was then for the first time I heard the doctrine of Blood Atonement.[37] Leading men in the church would say if you should find your father or your mother, your sister or your brother dead by the wayside, say nothing about it, but pass on about your own business.[38] The wildest fanaticism prevailed everywhere. Secret deaths began to be quite common. If we heard of a secret murder in San Pete or Cache Valley, we knew the work of

[35]"Bosco," "Mountain Meadows. A Visit to the Site of the Massacre," *Salt Lake Tribune*, 15 August 1874, 4.

[36]"Local and other Matters," *Deseret News*, 27 May 1874, 1/1.

[37]Taught by church leaders during the Reformation, it held that sins such as murder, adultery, and apostasy were so egregious that, to atone for them, one must have one's blood spilled on the ground as an offering to God. Slitting the throat was the usual method and sign of blood atonement.

[38]Peter McAuslan heard Bishop Alonzo Hazeltine Raleigh of the Nineteenth Ward preach almost the same words on 3 December 1856: "When that time comes and is at hand you may see the dead Bodys of your Fathers, your Brothers, or your nearest, dearest relatives and friends lying upon the Streets, and if you should pass by, say not a word to anybody, nither ask the cause, just conduct yourself as if nothing had happened. All is right, it was done by athority." Aird, *Mormon Convert*, 169.

the Lord was progressing. I was then a citizen of Spanish Fork City, and be it said to the honor of that place, no one has ever been killed by any priestly assassin inside of its borders.

In the year 1857, while Johns[t]on's army was on the plains, a company of emigrants came to Utah. I saw them pass through Spanish Fork; they were quiet and orderly.[39] They traveled on to the south and stopped on the bottom between Spanish Fork and Payson to rest their teams, and in a week or two continued their journey. The next news I heard of them was they had all been killed by the Indians. It was afterwards whispered that white men and Indians together, led by one John D. Lee, had done the deed, but nothing definite was known to the public. In the Autumn of 1853 [1862], I, with my family, was "called" on a mission to Washington County to raise cotton. In Washington I was told that many of the men there had been to Sebastapol. "Sebastapol," said I, "what do you mean?" "Oh, the Mountain Meadows—but don't say that I told you," said my cautious informer. I noticed that all these men were in full fellowship in the church and some of them were the loudest preachers and could bear strong testimony of the work.[40]

I thought I would be able to break down their influence in society, as soon as I got a little acquainted. I staid at Washington one year and a half and then removed to Harmony. That settlement was the residence at that time, of John D. Lee, and he was the presiding elder of that branch of the church. Surely, thought I, Brigham Young does not know that Lee is the man who led the Indians and whitemen who murdered a train of Christian white people?

Lee is a Kentuckian.[41] He is an eloquent preacher of Mormonism, and has been very successful in making converts.

When I had been at Harmony one year, Brigham Young came to Harmony, passed through it, and drove up to the residence of John D. Lee! From that time my confidence in Brigham began to wane. Could it be possible that the Prophet of God could find no better men to associate with than John D. Lee[?] Then I tried to argue the circumstance from my mind, by saying it was not my business to say where the servants of God should stop, or whom they should stop with.

Time passed on until the murder of Dr. J. K. Robinson. Soon after that event, Brigham Young preached a sermon in Salt Lake City, in which he used the following language: "There are some things which I cannot bear to contemplate, the hounds will [Hauns Mill] massacre; the Mountain Meadows massacre, and the murder of Dr. Robinson are atrocities of this sort.

---

[39]Hicks's autobiography identified the emigrants as the Dukes train, which followed the Fancher party. Although not slaughtered at Mountain Meadows, the Dukes train ran into plenty of trouble with the Mormons and barely made it to southern California.

[40]British and French forces laid siege for eleven months to Sebastopol in 1854–1855 during the Crimean War. The Russians finally burned the ruined city and withdrew. In Utah, Sebastapol became a code word for Mountain Meadows. See Bigler and Bagley, eds., *Innocent Blood*, 242.

[41]Lee was actually born in Illinois.

These," said he, "I cannot bear to think about; but let the united brethren keep their oaths and covenants."

That last remark is significant. The sermon containing that extract, was published in the Deseret News. I read it, and re-read it; my mind, which had wavered between two opinions—one in favor of Brigham Young's innocence, and the other against it. Brother Brigham is all right, I said, and is not in favor of Lee and crime.

The people of Harmony had got tired of Lee, and had put another man in his place to preside over them, but Lee was still allowed to preach two or three times a month. In one meeting I raised an objection, and noted Brigham Young's sermon against Lee, and thought to silence him in public. Lee, who understood his "relations" with the Prophet better than I did, promptly informed me that I did not know Brother Brigham as well as he did; he (Bro. Brigham) did not mean what he had said in his sermon. He had talked that way to blind the eyes of the Gentiles, and to satisfy disaffected individuals, such as I was. I felt indignant in the highest degree that the character of the servant of God should be traduced by a man whose hand I believed to be stained with innocent blood.

I immediately informed Brigham Young by letter, of Lee's slanderous statements, recommending that Lee be cut off from the Church. I waited for an answer; it came promptly to hand. The Prophet, did not thank me for the information I had given him, but on the contrary, he pretended to think that I had taken a part in the Mountain Meadows affair, and on that conclusion, advised me to take a dose of rope around my neck "with a jerk." That little bit of prophetic advice I did not obey. From that time forth. I have believed that Lee is better acquainted with the Prophet than I am.

To the honest believing Mormon, these statements of mine will seem incredible, but they are nevertheless true. I do not wish to do Brigham Young any physical harm, but I will say to all men who read this article, that if I had only been a pious murderer I might have rode "cheek by jowl" with the Prophet as Lee has done, and been in good standing in the Church.

On the seventh day of April 1874, I saw John D. Lee by the side of Brigham Young's carriage, and reported the same to The Tribune. I was suspected of so doing. Bishop Henry Lunt of Cedar City, questioned me on the subject. I did not deny the fact, and was immediately cut off without even a hearing of any kind.

A few more words, and I will close. I was a member of the Mormon Church for nearly thirty years, and never had a charge of any kind brought against me. I have no faith in any of the religions of the day, but like Madam De Stael, I have loved God, my country, and liberty. The reader must judge whether I have or have not had just grounds for apostacy.

Respectfully,
Geo. A. Hicks

Long after his separation "from the dominant church of Utah," Hicks complained that he was ill-treated, his character was maligned, and his business was interfered with so "that it was with difficulty that I was able to support my family."[42] Hicks did not retaliate against his Mormon neighbors, as evidenced by his treatment of DeLaun Mills Cox, who recalled living in Orderville, just north of Mount Carmel, where Hicks resided in 1875. Cox broke his leg in a logging accident and wore a splint. "One day George Hicks the only gentile in town rode by and saw him busy at work with his injured leg stretched straight out on the ground—gave him $2.00 worth of stuff to be charged to his account and he also got others to donate to the amount of $8.00," Cox told an interviewer. "Although Mr. Hicks was not a praying man he was remembered that night when the Cox family offered their evening devotion."[43]

John D. Lee was executed for his part in the Mountain Meadows massacre in March 1877. Six months later, on 29 August President Brigham Young died. Hicks's two nemeses were gone. On 9 September, eleven days after Young's death, Hicks sought a new start, asking the *Deseret News,* "Please publish the following card—To All Latter-day Saints":

> Inasmuch as I was cut off the Church of Jesus Christ of Latter-day Saints on the 28th of April, 1873 [26 April 1874], at Cedar City, for apostacy, and published in the Deseret News as such, and I have said and written many hard things about the people, and authorities of the Church, I hereby confess my errors and acknowledge my follies, and ask forgiveness of all Saints who have been offended by my writings and sayings, for I desire to be restored to the fellowship of Saints, and to be forgiven of my heavenly Father. Geo. A. Hicks.[44]

George A. Hicks was apparently restored to church membership within a year or two. About 1878 his family abandoned southern Utah and returned to Utah County. A year later they settled in Thistle Valley near the headwaters of Spanish Fork River, next door to George's brother, Samuel Moroni Hicks, and his family.[45] During the next three years, Hicks adjusted to his new situation and set about writing the story of his life.

---

[42]"House of Representatives," unidentified newspaper clipping dated 9 February 1894, in the Hicks Scrapbook, LDS Archives.

[43]Cox, History, LDS Archives. Waldo Perkins, M.D., located this account.

[44]"Local and other Matters," *Deseret News,* 26 September 1877, 12.

[45]Hicks's diary entries at the end of his autobiography; 1880 United States Census, Thistle Valley, Utah Co., Utah, roll T9-1338, 51.

Family Record and History of Geo. A. Hicks Containing the Principle Events of a Life Among the Poor of Utah & the "Saints" Generally. Written by himself [1878–1880].

"Let not ambition mock their useful toil,
Their homely joys, and destiny obscure;
Nor grandeur hear with a disdainful smile
The short and simple annals of the poor." —Gray[1]

Chapter I. Honest Sons of Toil: The Hicks Family

I purpose [propose] writing a history of my life. It is my priviliege to do so if I choose and I have so chosen. I am at the present time of a little more than 43 years of age and have been more than 25 years in Utah and I know her history. I have passed through many trials with the poor of the people of Utah. I have seen the gro[w]th and progress of the territory and I have taken a part, though not in a public capacity, in her developement. It is a common custom to write a history of the great in the land; not so with my self. I am one of the toilers, one of the hewers of wood and drawers of water. My sympathies are with the poor of the land. It is the honest sons of toil who build up a country—who have to struggle against poverty and privation. I have not the least doubt that with Him who rules above, the poor are the chosen of the Earth, for this Gosple was preached to them.

I was born on the 14th day of January in the year A.D. 1835. I was born in the provence of Upper Canada in the county of Ontario at a little town called by the "Chipoway" name of Singuacoosia or Little Pine Tree.[2] My father's name is George Barton Hicks; he is a native of Ireland from the county Fermanach [Fermanagh] in the north of that country. He was born on the 15th day of Dec. 1809. His people were brought up to the Methodists church. He left his native land at the age of 17 years and with his father, mother, brothers and sister settled in Canada, all of whom became members of the "Mormon" Church and came to Nauvoo, where my grand father died

[1] Thomas Gray, "Elegy Written in a Country Graveyard," 1750.

[2] Upper Canada was an old name for southern Ontario. The Hicks farm was near Toronto.

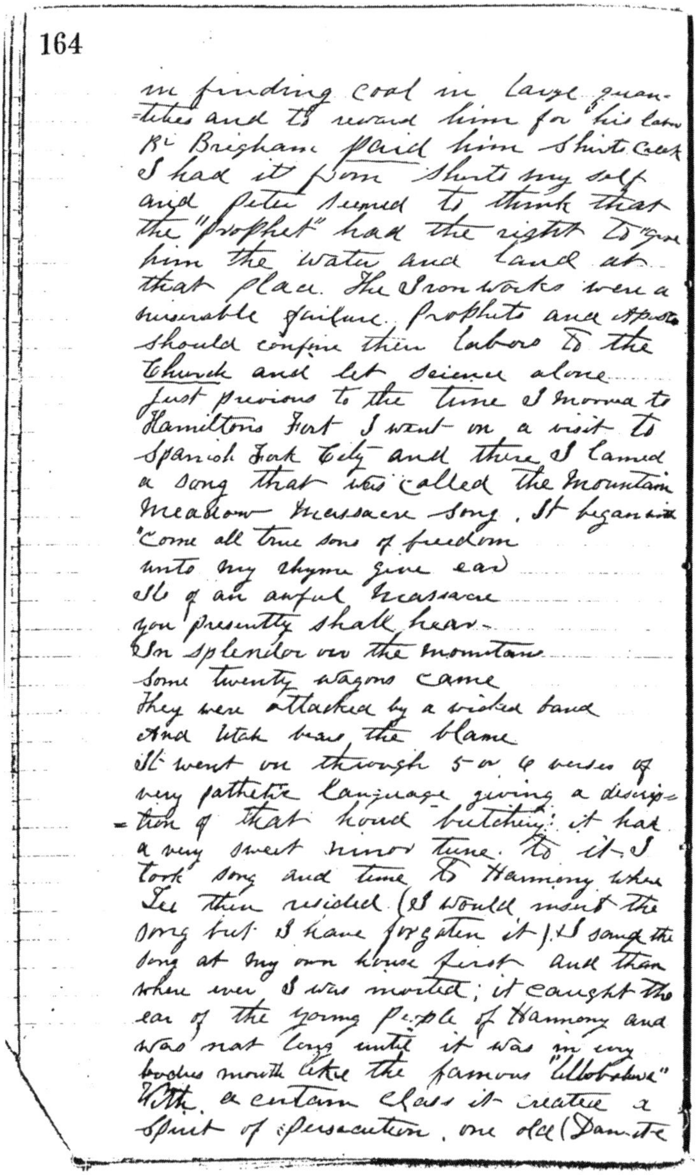

164

in finding coal in large quan-
-tities and to reward him for his labo
Br Brigham paid him Shirts Creek
I had it from Shirts my self
and Peter seemed to think that
the "Prophet" had the right to give
him the water and land at
that place. The Iron works were a
miserable failure. Prophets and Apost
should confine their labors to the
Church and let science alone
Just previous to the time I moved to
Hamiltons Fort I went on a visit to
Spanish Fork City and there I learned
a song that was called the Mountain
Meadow Massacre Song. It began with
"Come all true sons of freedom
unto my rhyme give ear
It is of an awful massacre
you presently shall hear.
In splendor over the mountains
Some twenty wagons came
They were attacked by a wicked band
And Utah bears the blame
It went on through 5 or 6 verses of
very pathetic language giving a discrip-
-tion of that horrid butchery: it had
a very sweet minor tune to it. I
took song and tune to Harmony where
Lee then resided (I would insert the
song but I have forgoten it) I sang the
song at my own house first and then
where ever I was invited; it caught the
ear of the young people of Harmony and
was not long until it was in every
bodies mouth like the famous "[illegible]"
With a certain class it created a
Spirit of persecution. one old (Danite)

Hicks Manuscript

A page from the manuscript of George A. Hicks's "Family Record and History." Although his spelling is sometimes creative, his penmanship is clear and the writing lucid. The manuscript is 167 pages long, plus an extra page of journal notations from 1879, similar, no doubt, to those he kept earlier (see mention of which on page 169) that enabled him to be so exact in regard to names, dates, and events in his autobiography.

at the ripe age of 74 years. Soon after the d[e]ath of my grand father, my father's brothers, 4 in number, became tired of "Mormonism," left Nauvoo and took my grand mother with them to the State of Wisconsin, where my grand mother lived to be 84 years of age when she died.

My mother's name was Martha Ann Wilson. She was born in Doublin [Dublin] City, Ireland, on the 5th day of March A.D. 1815, and at the age of 2½ years in connection with her father's family, she crossed the Atlantic Ocean and came to reside in Canada in the City of Toronto. My grand father's name was James Wilson. He was a Methodist preacher of some celebrity and a most bitter and determined enimy to Mormonism. My mother had one brother and one sister. Her brother's name was James. He became a man of some distinction and was at least once returned to the Canada Parliament.[3] I have, in my possession, some letters which he wrote to my mother. Judging by these letters, I concluded he was a man of fine attainments. He also adhears to the Methodist religion. My mother recieved a good education—better than the average of women. She, in her prime, was a woman of intellect, independent and spirited, somewhat proud of her family origin.

In the year 1833, my father and mother became acquainted and on the 20th day of March, 1834, they were joined together in the bonds of "holy matrimony" according to the rites of the Presbyterian Church. I was the first fruit of that union. I have two brothers and four sisters. My eldest brother's name is James Wilson, named for my mother's brother. He was born on the 9th day of Dec. 1836. My brother James W. went to California from Utah in the year A.D. 1854, and I know not whether he be living or dead as we have not heard of him since '58. The absence of my brother James W. has been the cause of great grief to my mother. Although he has been absent for 22 years, my mother continues to mourn his absence and to hope for his return. Should my brother James be still living, he is certainly guilty of the sin of ingratitude. No child should stay away from parents without writing at least once each year. We have often heard vague statements that my brother James W. was living in this or that place in California, but the most reliable report that we have heard is that he was killed at a place called Kern River or Kaysville [probably Kernville]. It is said he was killed by mystake. I believe the report to be true for he was in the habit of writing ev[e]ry month and he suddenly sto[p]ped.[4]

[3]James Wilson represented Norfolk North as a Progressive Conservative Party member of the first Parliament of Ontario, which sat from 1867 until 1871.

[4]No James Hicks born in Canada about 1836 appears in either the 1860 or 1870 U.S. census in California.

My second brother's name is Samuel Moroni. He was born in the City of Buffalo, New York, on board a steam boat, we having just crossed Lake Earie after leaving Can[ada] and on our way to Jackson County, Mo., to gather with the Later Day Saints. He was born on the 14th day of November, A.D. 1838. I have 4 sisters. The eldest Jane was born in Nauvoo, Ill. on the 30th day of Oct. 1841. We came to Nauvoo in 1839. She was a beautiful and bright little girl. I thought no boy ever had a sister so sweet and good as my sister. She was inteligent beyond her years, but like many bright children she died young. She died on the 2nd day of March 1844 in the City of Nauvoo at the age of two years and four months. The loss of my sister was a terable blow to our family. Although more than 30 years have passed, I continue to feel her loss and to mourn her as one whose place never can be filled, but I hope to meet her on the other side of the "beautiful river."

My second sister was born at Nauvoo, Ill., on the 1st day of March 1844. Her name was Caroline. She lived to be the mother of 8 children. She died in child bed with her 9th child at Spanish Fork City, Utah Co., Utah Ter. on the 9th day of May 1878. She was a woman beloved by all who knew her. My third sister's name is Martha Ann. She was born in a small tow[n] on the north side of the Desmoin [Des Moines] River in the state of Iowa. She was born in the town of Bonapart[e] on the 3 day of Jan 1847 soon after the people were expelled from Nauvoo. The name of my 4th and last sister: Rachel Emeline. She was born in Potawatamie Co., Iowa, on the 11th day of July 1849.[5]

My mother's children are all married except my brother James, and he may be if living. It is with some degree of pride that I chronicle the fact that [none] of my relations on either side have ever been tried for or convicted of any crime whatever, but on the contrary they were generaly noted for their habits of peace and industry. Although they have generaly been numbered with the poor, they have lived by their own labor in obedience to the law of the land. Before closing this chapter, I feel it my duty as well as my privliege to say in behalf of my old parents that they have done their best to bring their children up in the ways of honesty and industry, and have always taught us to believe in Mormonism as the true and only gospel of Christ.

For my father I will say I never knew him to be guilty of anything bordering on dishonesty, or to use any profane language or to speak evil against

[5]Caroline married John Moore in Spanish Fork, Utah, in 1860; Martha Ann married Richard Murray in Salt Lake City in 1868; and Rachel Emeline married Peter Fenton Boyack in Salt Lake City in 1869.

the leaders of the Mormon Church. We have been driven from our home in Nauvoo. We have often found it a difficult matter to get bread, but my parents have borne their trials with great pati[e]nce and their trust has always been in Him whose duty it is to guard his children on Earth. Now when they are old, they have a comfortable home. Though they are not rich, they have enough to keep the "wolf from their door," and are, it is to be hope[d], far beyond the power of mobs to drive them from their homes in these valleys of peace and plenty for the industrious.

Correction: On the first page I said my father's sister came to Nauvoo; this is a mystak, she never came—a slip of the pen.

Chapter II. A First Class Salvation: The Hicks Family Joins the Restoration

On the 6th day of Aprile A.D. 1830, the Church of Jesus Christ was organized with 6 members. Joseph Smith had declared to the world that an holy Angel had visited him and had given him dispensation of the gospel and that all old religions were of no avail and all mankind must repent of their sins and become members of the new church or they never coul[d] get a first class salvation.

In the early part of the year 1837, just seven years after the organization of the new church, my father and mother were living quietly in the back woods on their farm when a strange man came to their settlement, came and told them the "glad news" that he was an autherized preacher of the gospel of Christ. He taught the people that God had spoken from the Heavens that these (those) were the laterdays and that the God of Heaven was about to set up His kingdom as spoken of by Daniel the prophet.[1]

The name of the strange man was Theodore Turley.[2] He spoke with great eloquence and power. He told the people they should know for them selves, if they would ask God, whether the doctrine he taught was from Heaven or of men. He created a perfect furore in the neighborhood. Many believed the new doctrine and among the number were my father and mother. In the

[1] Daniel 2:44; 7:13–27.

[2] One of the first converts to Mormonism, Theodore Turley (1800–1872) built the first house in Nauvoo and was a clockmaker, gunsmith, and "armourer general" of the Nauvoo Legion. Brooks, *On the Mormon Frontier*, 1:5n7. A federal court indicted Turley for counterfeiting in 1845.

month of July A.D. 1837, they gave up the religion of their forefathers and were baptized into the Church of Jesus Christ of Laterday Saints.[3]

It was not long until they were fully satisfied that this new religion was realy from Heaven. My mother recieved the gift of tongues, [and] other spiritual gifts were made manifest in the small branch of the church which had been established there. My mother had at that time but two children, my brother James W. and myself. We had the whooping coug[h] very badly. The elders of the church were sent for and hands were laid upon us and we were healed immediately.

My father became a very active member of the church. He was very zealous in finding ways and mean[s] wherby the gospel might be peched [preached] in his own and the adjoining neighborhoods. At length, A. W. Babbit[t] came to our neighborhood.[4] He was a man of great intellectual abilities. Mormonism was the one and only theme of his mind. He came to my father's [house] to reside. He was very successful in spreading the new faith, and many were added to the church "such as were fit to be saved."

I am satisfied that the new beginners in the Mormon Church were as full of faith in the tenates [tenets] of thier new faith as were the followers of Jesus and the Apostles. They were full of love that the "world" was not in possession of. The sick were healed, they spoke with new tongues. Devils were cast out, and to the early members in Canada, it was no more nor no less than the restoration of the gospel of Christ. So believed my father and mother and they believe it still. Although 40 years have passed away, they have never faltered in their belief that Mormonism is the true and only gospel by which the human family can be saved and brought back into the presence of God.

It was not long untill Joseph Smith, the prophet and founder of the new faith, came to Canada in person and in a powerful manner bore testimony that God had sent an Angel and that the Angel had given him the Book of Mormon.[5] He had translated it by the power of God. He preached in a barn, the property of William Law woh [who] afterwards became a leading member of the church.

---

[3]Hicks would have been two years old when they converted, so he must have learned this early history from his parents.

[4]Almon W. Babbitt (1813–1856) was a member of Zion's Camp and in 1835 became a member of the First Quorum of Seventy. Brooks, *On the Mormon Frontier*, 1:30n58.

[5]Joseph Smith started for Canada on 27 July 1837 and returned to Kirtland in late August. Jenson, comp., *Church Chronology*, 13.

New theories of all kinds generally find opposers in proportion to its adherents. So it was then. Many of our old neighbors who were of the same faith as my parents turned against them and became bitter enemies. Although I have never heard that any resorted to violence, yet they would not speak to them if by chance they met, nor would they be seen in their company for any consideration.

Humanity is weak, but the weakness of turning against our neighbors is the most inconsistent of all, when we have no other reason, only that our neighbor has changed his mode of worshiping the "unknown God." I have felt sorrow because friends whom I loved have become alienated to the religion that I was taught to believe in, but I never felt any malace in consequence of such change of sentiment, "as man's a man for a' that."[6] I know that honest men may have an[d] hold different opinions on the same subject. Then why should they quarrel about theories of religion when it is absilutely impossable to know what the future reward of any religion will be a hundred or a thousand years hence, for, it is not given to ordinary mortals to know but very little of the future. "Who knoweth that the spirit of the beast goeth downward and the spirit of man upward" as Solomon has it.[7]

It may be of some interest to the curious to know that Turley and Babbit both apostatized from the Mormon Church long enough before thier death.[8]

After baptism and other of the "first prin[ci]ples" of the gosple had been obeyed by my parents, the "gathering" was preached. The head quarters of the Mormon Church at that time was in Jackson Co., Mo.[9] The "elders" taught the new converts it was their duty to gather up to Zion; the indignation of the Almighty was soon to be poured out on the nations of the Earth. My parents with the rest believed it was their duty to sell their possessions and go to the new Zion and live with the people of God. They got all things in readiness as soon as convenient and in the year A.D. 1838 they, in connexion

[6]From Robert Burns's poem "A Man's a Man for A' That" on the equality of humankind.

[7]"Who knoweth the spirit of man that goeth upward, and the spirit of the beast that goeth downward to the earth?" Ecclesiastes 3:21.

[8]Turley was cut off for apostasy on 14 June 1870 in Beaver, Utah: "Special to the Deseret News," *Deseret News*, 29 June 1870, 1. Babbitt was disfellowshipped twice, briefly in 1840 and again in October 1841, for teaching unorthodox doctrine but was again reinstated. Cheyenne Indians killed Babbitt, then Utah Territory's secretary of state, on 7 September 1856, prompting Brigham Young to comment, "*He undertook to quarrel with me, but soon afterwards was killed by Indians.* He lived like a fool, and died like a fool." Roberts, *Devil's Gate*, 175, emphasis in original.

[9]In 1838 Joseph Smith moved LDS church headquarters from Kirtland to Far West, Caldwell County, Missouri, the new gathering place.

with others who had joined the church, started for Jackson Co., bidding farewell to Canada for ever.

I have a distinct recolection of our family bidding adieu to our home in Canada and starting for the Far West. It was certainly a great undertaking, not as to distance, certainly, but their confidence must have been great or they never could have undertaken so great and self sacrafising an act to lay all, as it were, upon the altar of their faith and go not knowing "whither they went." About the time my parents started for the new Zion in the state of Mosouri, trouble began betwixt the Mormons and the people of Jackson Co., and my parents stoped in the state of Pensylvania at a little village called George Town in Mercer Co., where we stayed one summer. To assist in making a living, my mother opened a small confectionary shop. Saints must live as well as sinners. My father had no opertunity to work at his trad[e] (a weaver). We stayed there one summer when it was agreed upon that the Mormons should leave the state of Mosouri and go to Illinois.

During our stay in George Tow[n], Pa., I went [to] my first day to school. I had to go by a lumber yard, and on my first afternoon, a man lay drunk. As I passed by, he roused up and with an oath staggered toward me. I was badly frightened and ran away as fast as I could. At the close of school that evening I went home another way. I never could be induced to go to that school any more. It may be that the fright I got at the time has been the cause in part of my extream antipathy agains[t] drunkenness and the use of alcoholic stimulants generaly. If there is any thing that is more disgusting than a drunken man or woman, I have failed to see it thus far in life.

At the end of a year, the saints had agreed to leave the state of Mosouri and word was sent out to all to gather up to another Zion. My parents changed their course and soon were on their way in obedience to the call of their prophet Joseph Smith.

Chapter III.
A Hard Place for the Poor: Nauvoo

The great Mississippi River is the dividing line betwixt Illinois and Iowa, [with] Illinois on the east and Iowa on the west. Both of these states at that time were very sparsely inhabited. In the county of Hancock in the state of Ill's. on the east bank of the river there was a small frontier village called at that time by the very significant name of Commerce. In this little village the Mormon exiles from Mosouri were instructed to locate. There was an abundence of land and timber besides great opertunities for trade—in fact, the facilaties were such that the hand of industry would soon mak[e] us rich. In November in the year 1839, my parents reached the town of Commerce.[1] I remember it well. Houses were few in number and these were scattered around among the timber. The country was hilly and, to my young mind, any thing but homelike. My father set to work to prepare winter quarters. A rude log cabin was soon constructed without floor or window for this winter, which I remember to have been severe, but we were acustomed to severe winters in our old home in Canada.

When the winter was over, the name of our new home was changed. The village of Commerce became the City of Nauvoo. People began to flock in from all parts of the world, lots were taken in all parts of the city. My father got a lot near to our log cabbin. He built a log house on it. We soon had plenty of neighbors all around us and the place began to be quite home-like. Orchard[s] were planted, fine buildings were erected, "the waste howling wilderness"[2] of a few years before was transformed by the magic touch of industry into a "fruitful field." However, there was one or two drawbacks. Nauvoo became very sickly, "chills and fevere" were abundant, and the people had little or no capital, or if they had, it was not thought a safe place to invest what they did have.[3]

It is a well-known fact that no place can long survive the want of cash capital. Nauvoo soon became a hard place for the poor to make a living in.[4] My parents were of the poore. There was an abundance of corn and other grain raised there by those who had farms, but there was no market for it; ten cents per bushel was all corn was worth in "store pay" at that. It was almost impossable to get clothing. The poor were very destitute. Many were driven to extreams to clothe their families, althoug[h] food was abundant.

The school system in an early day in Nauvoo was far from being perfect, at least in the district where my parents resided. It is true Mrs. Southworth

[1]The Hicks family apparently traveled in a seven-wagon company of Canadian Saints from Mercer County, Pennsylvania, led by William Law. Hicks was not quite five when they reached Nauvoo in the first week of November 1839. Cook, *William Law*, 3.

[2]Deuteronomy 32:10.

[3]Malaria was endemic and widespread along the Mississippi River bottomlands, and Nauvoo had a high incidence of it. Flanders, *Nauvoo*, 53, 53n69.

[4]Flanders, *Nauvoo*, 144–78, described the precarious nature of Nauvoo's economy.

keep school near by and Sister Beebee in another place not far off. Miss Emeline Hase in an other.[5] If children went to the (very imperfect) schools, they must be paid. How could a weaver farmer who worked on a brick yard for an irresponsable company (the Mormons have been very fortunate in starting impossable companies) pay school bills or any other bills? My mother, though highly capable, did not teach school in public, but she taught her own children. Ignorance is the bane of society. My mother [k]new this and she taught me and her other children lessons at her knee. I have no recollection when I could not read, although my education is very limited. I feell in duty bound to say that my mother labered hard to give me a good English education. She not only taught me to read and spell, but she taught me to believe in the new faith and why it was necessary to believe in it.

We had in our house the Bible, the Book of Mormon, and P.P. Pratt's "Voice of Warning."[6] My mother enjoined it strictly upon me to read the Book of Mormon through and promised me as a reward that I should have the book as my own property. I undertook the task. I soon got interested in the wars betwixt the Nephites and Lamanites, but before I got through, the book fell into a tub of soap suds and was spoiled so I did not read it through.

I was fond of reading in the "Voice of Warning." I think it is one of the finest religious book[s] I ever read. It is a great pity that it is not true. I read that part which speaks of the "little stone that was cut out of the mountain without hands." This stone smote the Image on the toes and ground it to dust and the dust was blown away "like the chaff of the summer threshing floor" (see Daniel chapter 2, 40 to 46 verses).[7] I asked my mother when these things should take place. She told me that the "little stone" is the Mormon Church and that the time for breaking the "Image" is now—in a few years. That was the faith of the whole Mormon Church, and my parents were not to blame for believing it. Over thirty years have passed and come and yet the "Image" is still standing and the "stone" showing signs of decay. (The Josephites are a fragment of the "stone.")[8]

---

[5]Mary Byington Southworth (1811–1898), her husband Chester, and four children traveled to Utah with the Hicks family in 1852. Emeline Hase is probably Emeline Bigler Hess (1823–1862). Sister Beebee or Beebe is unidentified.

[6]First published in New York in 1837, Pratt's *Voice of Warning* became the most influential Mormon missionary tract of the nineteenth century.

[7]Actually Daniel 2:34–35. See also *D&C*, 65:2.

[8]Known as "Josephites" in Utah, members of the Reorganized Church of Jesus Christ of Latter Day Saints rejected polygamy and temple rituals. They believed church authority passed to the descendents of Joseph Smith.

My parents were obliged by necesity to leave Nauvoo in order to make a living. William Law was a wealthy man who had joined the Mormons at the same time and place that my parents did. Law had purchased a large body of land near to the City of Nauvoo.[9] My father, being acquainted with Law in Canada, was imployed to take charge of one of his farms. We then moved onto the farm. I think this was in the year 1842. Law had much of his land sown to hemp, which grew in great abundence, but it was a loss to the Laws, for there was two brothers of them, Wilson and William. I know their hemp was put up in large stacks on their farm and it remained there after the Laws left Nauvoo. I think the hemp was destroyed by fire. It's a well known fact in this history of Nauvoo that the Mormons became the bit[t]erest enemies to the Laws, and I have ev[e]ry reason to believe that they were unjustly persecuted and their property wantonly destroyed.[10] My uncle John Hicks, my father's eldest brother, was a kind of mechanical genious. He with much labor and expense had constructed a machine for breaking hemp for the Laws. I saw the machine standing and I saw its remains after it was burned to the ground. I believe the hemp stacks were destroyed at the same time.

I have a perfect recolection when the doctrine of plural marriage came out. I shall devote a good portion of my "space and time" to giving a description of its private workings in society. It was practiced secretly, and the girls that "went into it" were called spiritual wives, and for short were called "spirituals," and were looked upon by many as not being the best of characters. The young and unmarried men were in fear of falling in love with any of the young girls for fear she might be a "spiritual." It was said you could know them by the way they wore long sunbonnets that hid their faces. They seemed to feel above the "common herd" of the Saints.

The ceremony by which these secret marriage[s] were performed was called "sealing." It was said to be performed under the cover of night in uper rooms of houses prepared for the purpose. It was said that a girl thus "sealed" might, if she choose and opertunity offerred, marry any yo[u]ng man she choose. Marriage was supposed to be for time only and the obligation would terminate at death, but "sealing" was for eternity, and parties

[9]William and Wilson Law bought land in the upper part of Nauvoo and 580 acres of farmland east of the city. Cook, *William Law*, 21n63.

[10]William Law (1809–1892) became second counselor to Joseph Smith in 1841. He came to believe that Smith corrupted the faith with false doctrines such as the plurality of gods and wives. Smith excommunicated him in April 1844. Cook, *William Law*, 21–30.

thus joined would hold the relationship of husband and wife in the next world. I am well acquainted with one woman by the name of Julia Parks who became the "spiritual wife" of Dimic[k] B. Huntington in Nauvoo. A young man by the name of Wm. Lindsey courted and married her, never in the least suspecting that she was the "spiritual" of anyone. After several children were born, Julia confessed that she was the spiritual wife of Huntington. Most men would have turned her adrift. Not so with William; he frankley forgave her. In the fall of 1852 when they came to Utah, Brigham Young gave Julia a "bill" of divorce and then she was sealed to Br. Lindsey for time and all eternity.[11] Other instances might be mentioned if necessary.

Chapter IV.
The Highest Glory:
Polygamy and the Death of the Prophet

I have heard some of the "Josephites" say that pollyggamy was not in the Mormon Church until after the death of the Prophet. I know that pollyggamy was in the church previous to his death. One of P. P. Pratt's wives made it her hom[e] at my father's house and I know that the apostle Pratt came and visited her several times. The name of this woman was Elizabeth Brewerton [Brotherton] and I know Pratt had several other wives beside[s] her, for I have been to his house and saw them and knew them well.[1] If poliggamy had been confined to having young girls "seal[e]d" [to] men who were allready married, there perhaps never would have been as much cause for complaint as there was. [But] men of influence began to "covet" their neighbors' wives. It was said that even the Prophet Joseph, like good (!) David of old, had had the wives of a number of leading men "sealed" to him, and it was said that among the number was the wife of William Law, at least it was so whispered around among the people and I believe the report to be

[11]According to Zina Huntington, Julia Parks (1824–1913) married William B. Lindsay (1821–1889) on 19 February 1845, at the home of Zina's brother, Dimick B. Huntington. The couple had eight children. Hicks traveled to Utah with the Lindsays and so knew them well. There is no record of Brigham Young granting Julia a divorce, but she and William Lindsay were sealed on 16 October 1852, about ten days after they arrived in Salt Lake City and after they had had three children. Beecher, "All Things Move in Order in the City," 285–320; Randall Dixon, emails to Polly Aird, 4 and 8 April 2008.

[1]Pratt's first wife died in Kirtland, Ohio, in 1837. He then married Mary Ann Frost. Elizabeth Brotherton (1817–1897) became his first plural wife in 1843. In 1844 Pratt married three more women and in 1845 married one more. He wed another one in 1846 and two more in 1847, followed by two more in Utah. Pratt, *Autobiography of Parley P. Pratt*, 429–31.

true.[2] I am of the opinion that if Law had been properly treated he never would have left the Mormon Church. I once heard my mother say that she saw the Prophet and William Law's wife out carriage riding to gather [gether] when Law was absent from home. Although there was nothing criminal in a church member taking a rid[e] with the "head" of the church, I think in all probability that Law's wife was sealed to the prophet.[3] To the "uninspired" such things seem unlawful.

Men not high in standing in the church were no better than the leaders were reported to be. [A man] would go to his neighbor's house when the husband was absent and teach the new doctrine. There was one man by the name of Thos. Foy that was very active in promulgating the "glorious principle."[4] He would step into a neighbor's house and he would say in the most solemn manner, "Sister, I am an high priest," and then he would begin and tell the sister that a great and glorious principle had been revealed through the Prophet Joseph and that there would be a chance now for all good sisters to be exalted to the highest glory. Then he would perhaps ask the good sister what order of priesthood her husban[d] held. If she said he was an elder or anything below a high priest, this good man would shake his head mournfully and say, "Sister, an elder never can exalt you to that degree of glory that you are worthy of. You had better seek an high priest," and then he would mournfully retire. Be it said to the credit of the sisters, he became a laughing stock in the part of town where he lived.

I know that P.P. Pratt would not scruple to ask a brother's wife to be sealed to him. Pratt was fond of the oposite sex. I know that polyggamy has caused more disunion in the church than all other causes. I also know that it has the same claim upon our belief that baptism for the dead or any of the new dispensation ideas. I have not the least doubt that polyggamy was the cause of the death of Joseph and Hyrum Smith. It was the "rock" that the church came near splitting upon in the days of Nauvoo. It is and always was disagreable to the female members of the Church.

Although I have seen its workings since it had a beginning in the Church,

---

[2]Smith was sealed to eleven married women who were living with their husbands. Compton, *In Sacred Loneliness*, 15.

[3]Several early sources suggest Jane Silverthorne Law was, in fact, sealed to Smith. Cook, *William Law*, 25n84. On 1 October 1843 Joseph Smith initiated Jane and three other women into the Holy Order, or Quorum of the Anointed, but there is no definitive evidence that she became his plural wife. See Compton, *In Sacred Loneliness*, 254, 633–34.

[4]Probably Thomas Burke Foy (1802–1870).

I have never yet known a woman in it that I believe to be contented and happy. I, as an individual, have no particular objections to pollygamy. I know the laws of nature allow the practice of it, and if people of mature judgement wish to practice it, I have no objections. But I do not believe that wives in any number will increas[e] any man's chances of salvation. I do not believe that either Jesus or Paul were ever married (I believe they will both be saved), and neither do I believe that "many wives" is any hinderance to a man's exaltation hereafter. I believe that a Christian man may have many wives or he may have no wife, and yet he will get just as good a glory as the man who has one or many. I believe such things should be left free for people to use their own judgement on them. I never have had any spiritual testimony as to the truth or falsity of polyggamy. I know it dose not bring the peace of mind that accompany the other parts of the gospel.

I remember a piece of poetry that appeared in the Nauvoo Expositor—a paper which was started in Nauvoo by the apostates which [who] broke off because of polyggamy. It was writen by Wilson Law and was entitled the "Buckeye's Lamantation for Want of More Wives":[5]

> "I have got but one lone wife
> And I can get no more.
> The doctrine is you can't be saved
> Unless you have half a score."[6]

Again from the same piece:

> "Joe at snaring beats them all
> And at the rest doth laugh
> For widows poor and orphaned girl
> He can ensnare with chaff.
> He sets his snare around for all
> And very seldom fails
> To catch some thoughtless Partridges,
> Snowbirds or Night-engales."[7]

---

[5]The poem was first published in the *Warsaw Message*, 7 February 1844, 1, and then in the *Warsaw Signal* on 25 April 1844, 3, not the *Nauvoo Expositor*. Although originally thought to be by one of the Law brothers, Francis Higbee was the likely author. See Bergera, "Buckeye's Laments," 350–51, 358–74.

[6]The poem's first verse actually reads: "For I have but *One lone wife*/And can obtain no more/And the doctrine is, I can't be saved/Unless I've *half a score*!"

[7]The actual text reads: "But Jo[e] at snaring beats them all/And at the rest does laugh;/For *widows* poor, and *orphan girls*,/He can ensnare with *chaff*./He sets his snares around for all,—/And very seldom fails/To catch some thoughtless PARTRIDGES,/SNOW-birds or KNIGHT-ingales!"

The "Joe" signified the prophet and the "Partidges" were the daughters of a woman by that name. The Snow birds signified the poetess Eliza R. Snow, and the Night-engales were understood to be some of the daughters of the widow Night [Knight] whom it was said were the "spiritual" wives of Joseph Smith, as were all those mentioned in the poem.[8] I quote the afore from memory, I having learned the piece in childhood out of the newspaper.

I remember that the *Nauvoo Expositor* was declared to be a public nuisance by the mayor and city council of Nauvoo (Joseph Smith was mayor at the time). It was destroyed and the press and fixtures were totally demolished. I have been at the office many a time, both before and after it (the paper) was destroyed. I, in company with other boys, have gathered tipe [type] that were thrown into the street by the police of Nauvoo. This act of violence was not to be tolerated in free America. The press must be free, and instead of scattering the apostate element of Nauvoo, the act had a tendency to increase the numbers of the oposition. Law and Fosters, et al., were the proprietors of the paper, and they ap[p]lied to the civil authoraties of Carthage, Ill. Joseph and Hyrum Smith and other leading men of Nauvoo were taken to Carthage and lodged in jail and there held to answer for the destruction of the "Expositor." While they were there, an armed mob came upon them and in a cruel and brutal manner the Smiths were murdered, and I have no doubt by those who were the supporters of the press which had been destroyed.[9] There was wrong on both sides. The press is and was at that time free, being responsable for all dammages of charactor. It was certainly a very wicked and unlawful act on the part of the injured Laws and Fosters to murder prisners while in jail.[10] The Smiths were killed on June 27 A.D. 1844.

I have seen Joseph Smith and heard him preach.[11] I believe he, in the beginning of his career, was all that he claimed to be—a prophet, seer and revelator, but being mortal, he could not bear success. I have heard good and truthful men say that Joseph Smith ocationaly [occasionally] was seen

[8]The Partridges were sisters Emily Dow Partridge and Eliza Maria Partridge; the Night-engales were actually only the widow Martha McBride Knight.

[9]William Law swore out a complaint against Joseph Smith for destroying his property and inciting a riot at Carthage, the county seat. The magistrate issued a warrant for Smith's arrest, and the *Warsaw Signal* issued inflammatory articles that roused the citizens of Hancock County. Hallwas and Launius, *Cultures in Conflict*, 30–31.

[10]There is no evidence that the Laws or Fosters played any part in the mob that killed the Smiths.

[11]At Joseph Smith's death, Hicks was nine years old.

drunk.[12] It must have been strange and very ludicrous sight to wittnes a prophet of the Lord staggering home on Saturday afternoon and on Sunday go and preach an eloquent sermon on human depravity. The Prophet was realy an eloquent preacher of the gosple. Noah and Lot both drank wine, but it was certainly no credit to either of them or any of their children after them who make a practice of drinking to excess.

One peculiarity about the Mormon religion that I never could understan[d] fully and that is why is the church so near the U.S. government in administering its laws. We have bishops who are a kind of civil magistrates and the High Councils are the District Courts and a general conferences is the same as the Supreme Court.[13]

There is still an other "mystery of the Kingdom" that I fail to comprehend and that is the strong desire among our church leaders for military glory or rather military office. Joseph Smith was a lieutenant general and many of the other leaders held some military office in the Nauvoo Legion. I never read of General Peter or Colonel Paul or Major Luke, but on the contrary, Jesus and the Apostles taught the people to "beat their swords into plow shears and their spears into pruning hooks" and "he that takes to the sword shall perish by the sword." To sum the whole matter, I think that the Mormon leaders were at first faithful and honest, but as they became successful, they began to be lifted up in the pride of their own hearts and to forget God.

On the first page I made a brief statement that my father's brothers "got tired of Mormonism and left Nauvoo." I purpose now to tell why John, the eldest, went away. The cause was as follows: My father's brother Samuel was hired to William Law and one day he drove Law's carriage to meeting on the Sabbath day. There were two young women in the carriage who were on a visit at Law's house. My uncle placed the carriage behind the stand

[12]Joseph Smith enjoyed drinking socially. He installed a bar in the main room of the Mansion House, his combined home and hotel, with Porter Rockwell serving as bartender. According to Joseph Smith III, when his mother returned from a St. Louis shopping expedition and found the bar, she told her husband that it was her or the bar. He took it out. Of the several people who saw Smith drunk, one was definitely known by Hicks: "I only saw him drunk once. I found Joseph and Hyrum at a place where they kept quantities of wine," William Law reportedly said in an 1887 interview. "I remember that Joseph drank heavily, and that I talked to Hyrum, begging him to take his brother away, but that was the only time I saw the prophet drunk." Petersen, *Hearts Made Glad*, 169–70, 205.

[13]The Nauvoo city charter incorporated Joseph Smith's theocratic ideas, including a government independent of the state with its own municipal court system and militia. Besides being prophet and president of the church, Smith became mayor, head of the city council, chief justice of the municipal court, and lieutenant general of the Nauvoo Legion. Flanders, *Nauvoo*, chapter 4.

(for the meeting was held in the open air) where the young ladies could here [hear] the sp[e]aker without leaving the carriage. Dimic[k] B. Huntington was at that time acting as city marshal. He took it into his head to move the carriage back and he did so. My uncle took the carriage back where it stood. Huntington came along and orde[re]d my uncle to take it back and leave it where he (Huntington) had placed it, when an altrecation ensued when Huntington raised his cane to strike my uncle Samuel on the head. My uncle John was nearby and caught the cane and prevented the blow from fallin[g] on his brother's head. John Hicks was at that time president of all the elders in the church.[14] He was tried before the mayer and fined ten dollars for resi[s]ting an officer of the peace. He was also tried before the Elders Quorum. Although but six voted against him and one of them was Huntington, he was turned over to the general conferance, and when he was absent, his case was brought up. Hyrum Smith said he thought it would be right and proper to wait until Br. Hicks would have time to come home, and he had no doubt that all would be made right between the breathren, but Joseph Smith was presiding and he put the motion and my uncle was condemned with out being heard. I say "condemned"—he was cut off from the church before a public conference and that too contrary to the church law.[15] John Hicks was a spirited man and understood his own rights as a man and church member. After he was cut off, Josep[h] Smith came to my father in person and requested him to go to his brother John and ask him to come back into the church. My father told him it was of no use: "John," he said, "was too proud spirited to yeald to any such proceedings." John was a leading spirit in the family and all the brothers except my father eventualy followed him away from the church, although Samuel did not go until after the rest were gone. He moved to Camp Creek and had his house burned by the "gentiles" at the time that other Mormons had their houses burned in the settlements near Nauvoo.[16] I learned the particulars of my uncle leaving the church from my father since writing the first chapter of this book.

[14]He was so named in *D&C*, 124:137.

[15]General Conference minutes, 3 October 1841: "President Brigham Young presented an appeal from the decision of the Elders' quorum on a charge made against Elder John A. Hicks by Dimick B. Huntington for a breach of the ordinances of the city, for falsehood and schismatical conversation. After hearing the testimony in the case it was voted that Elder John A. Hicks be cut off from the Church." Joseph Smith signed the minutes. Smith, *History of the Church*, 4:428.

[16]This occurred in September 1845. Leonard, *Nauvoo*, 525.

At the death of Joseph Smith, Brigham Young took the leadership of the church. I have heard my father say that he was present at the time when it is said that the mantle of Joseph fell upon Brigham Young. I believe it. I believe the spirit of Joseph took possession of the body of Brigham and spoke to the people throug[h] him.[17] Brigham was the man to take the lead. "The blood of the martyrs is the seed of the church."[18] The killing of the Smiths was the means of adding many thousands to the church, but we ware not long allowed to live in peace.

It is my opinion that many dishonest men were among the Mormon people. I have heard many a "good old saint" boast that he had stolen "bear meet" and "sweet oil" (honey & pork) from the Mosourians, and no doubt if the people belonging to the church had have been strictly honest, we could have been living at our old homes in the States. I know that I have heard men boast here in Utah of their dishonest acts at Nauvoo.[19] I heard one old man at Orderville in Kane Co., Utah, boast that he had killed a dozen head of cattle and that he knew they were all stolen from the gentiles. The name of this good man was Braff.[20] It is such characters [who] brought trouble on those who were honestly disposed, and all had to suffer for the sins of the dishonest. I know there were many men in Nauvoo of whom it was said they had been thieves in Mosouri and one man of the name of John Taylor (not him who succeeded B. Young to the presidency of the church). He, it was said, had been in prison in Mosouri for stealin[g] from the gentiles. I know that he was called "Mosouri John" (he apostatized here in Utah).

It is my firm belief that many men who would be strictly honest in dealing with their breathren of the church would not scruple to steal from those who did not belong to the church. I have heard old men say by way of apology that the people of Mosouri hassled [?] the saints and the saints had to steal or starve. I know that my father always found work among those who

---

[17]Several people believed Brigham Young was "transfigured" in a meeting on 8 August 1844, which convinced them that Young was the chosen leader. For contemporary accounts, see Allen, " 'We Were Willing Because We Were Obliged To,' " 8–9. For a thorough analysis, see Van Wagoner, "The Making of a Mormon Myth," 1–24.

[18]Tertullian, *Apologeticus*, chapter 50.

[19]Thievery by Mormons of goods belonging to non-Mormons in Hancock County is described in documents in Hallwas and Launius, *Cultures in Conflict*, 67, 70–77. See also Godfrey, "Crime and Punishment in Mormon Nauvoo"; and Shepard, "Stealing at Mormon Nauvoo."

[20]George Washington Braffit (also Brafitt, Braffet, Braff) (circa 1801–1887). Born in New York, Braffit came to Utah in 1849. He was called to the Iron Mission, Iron County, in southern Utah in December 1850. Kane County is adjacent to Iron County. Shirts and Shirts, *A Trial Furnace*, 110, 426.

were not members of the church and get his pay for it. There is no apology; honest industry was allways rewarde[d] where ever I have lived. The people of the wes[t] welcomed the Menonites to this country and no doubt would have done the same to Mormons. I know, however, there were many honest God-fearing people in Nauvoo.

There is one thing which I have read in the history of Joseph Smith which I believe to be a falshood. In the *Juvenile Instructor,* the history says that O. P. Rockwell did not shoot Gov. Boggs of Mosouri. I know that it was commonly talked among the people of Nauvoo that Rockwell did shoot Boggs, and the reason he was not killed was because Rockwell put [only] two balls in the gun and that he shot him throug[h] a glass window.[21] Rockwell died while under inditement for many murders.[22] It always has been a mystery to me why such characters a[s] O. P. Rockwell, Bill Hickman, and men of that ilk have always been tolerated in the Mormon Church.

Chapter V.
Cheerfull in Our Exile: Mormon Diaspora

After the death of Joseph Smith, the people of Nauvoo were allowed to live in peace and the Temple which had been started some years before was pushed forwar[d] very rapidly. My father had left Law's farm and had rented a piece of land belonging to one James Moffit, a Roman Catholic—a fine man and a good neighbor. Here we raised [an] abundence of the necessaries of life. [We] were living at this place when trouble again broke out betwixt the Mormons and the citizens of Hancock County, Ill. When my uncle Samuel's house was burned at Camp Creek by the "gentiles," he came to our place and we had plenty of corn to do both families.

One circumstance I remember well. My uncle had a large fat hog in a stable about 100 yards from the house where we lived. One dark night some parties came and stole his hog that had been fattened on corn that my father had given him, he having lost his own at the time his house was burned. The next day my father and uncle tracked the parties to Nauvoo, but they did not

[21]Whether Rockwell tried to kill Boggs is an open question, but Hicks reflects the conviction of most Nauvoo residents that he did. In gold rush California, Rockwell was much admired by his fellow Mormons for shooting the governor. Schindler, *Orrin Porter Rockwell,* 67–73.

[22]Rockwell was indicted in September 1877 for killing John Aiken in 1857. Rockwell died 9 June 1878, before his case came to trial. For details, see Bigler, "The Aiken Party Executions," 457–76.

recover the pork. We also had many of our chickens stolen at that place (two miles away [outside Nauvoo]). I presume that many in Nauvoo thought that because that [*sic*] my father's folks had most of them left the church and we were living on land that belonged to a gentile, we were no better than apostates and it was no harm to rob us before we followed the Laws to Wisconsin. My uncle did not remain long after the hog was stolen (who can blame him).

The difficulties between the Mormons and the gentiles increase[d] daily and a treaty was made between them, and the Mormons, good and bad, agreed to leave Nauvoo and hunt a new home in the West beyond the great Mississippi River. I think it was cruel on the part of the "gentiles" and I think unnecessary on the part of the Saints. I am quite sure that if the principles of justice and righteousness had have been acted upon by both parties, it would have been better for all. If the Mormons had have punished offenders among themselves and [had] used due diligence to assist the officers of the law to catch all who were trangressor[s] against the law, we might have been living in Hancock County today and have been at peace with all mankin[d], but it was otherwise to be.

We left Nauvoo in A.D. 1846. There were a great many Germans came in to buy out the sett[l]ers. I remember that my father sold two good log houses, and one of them was filled with unthrashed wheat, for the paltry sum of four dollars. It was all he could [get] and that was more than some got for better places than ours. He took the money and we gave up our home. It was an humble one, it is true, but it was our own and all we had. (I say here that my father had not sold his place in Nauvoo during all the moves we had made, although he might have done so to advantage financialy.) We had no wagon of our own and but one yoke of cattle. My father got the use of a wagon from Br. Whitford Wilson, and we crosed the "big river" and went not knowing whither we went "into a strange land among strangers."[1]

As I look back upon those scenes, I think we must have been inspired with something more than common zeal—there was, it seems, a power behind the scene invisable to us that proted [prodded] us to "go," and, to use one of the sayings of Geo. A. Smith, "we went cheerfully when we were obliged to."[2] There was a vast territory in the West that was waiting [for] the hand

[1]Whitford G. Wilson (1799–1863) was born in Vermont, went to Utah in 1850, and died in Farmington.

[2]Nauvoo resident Martha Pane Jones Thomas recalled hearing Mormon apostle George A. Smith saying, "We were willing because we were obliged to" about leaving Nauvoo. Allen, "'We Were Willing Because We Were Obliged To,'" 18.

of industry to bring it into usefulness, and Providence had decreed that we, the Mormon exiles who could not live in peace with [the] people of Mossouri and Illinois, must go and build up—shall I say an empire? No, we must be purified in the wilderness, we must live alone and learn to live on our own resources, and to prepare the way for the spread of the great republic of the West. We did not realize the greatness of our mission at that time, but as the panoramma of years have rolled by, these things have been made manifest. The individual must be blind indeed who cannot see that there has been a power that has guided the destiny of the Mormon people. We had a work to do and it seems as though it is done.

We stoped at a small town on the beautiful Desmoin [Des Moines] River in the state of Iowa. There were quite a number of families who had left Nauvoo at the same time. This town was 35 miles from Nauvoo. Here my father, and also the other men, found plenty of work and were well paid for their labor, for the harvest came on soon after our arrival and the farmers were willing to give employment to all that were willing to labor.

There was a number [of] wealthy men in that neighborhood by the name of Meeks.[3] These men were very kind to the retreating Mormons. They done a great amount of business—lumbering, farming, etc. They were said to be infidels in belief, although there were many Methodists in Bonapart[e] (for that was the name of the town) who seemed to be sincere in their religion. It was there I first heard groaning at a religious meeting (the Methodists groan when they have religion).

My father was attacked by *c[h]olera morbus* while in the harvest field. He was brought home and we called a physician, one Dr. Wyman (he too was an infidel). He came and gave medicine to my father. He watched by his bed side until the disease took a turn. The usual price that Dr. Wyman asked was one dollar pr. visit. He came to see my father seven times. When my father recovered, he aske[d] the doctor what was the amount of his fee. He looked my father in the face and then replied, "Hicks, if you will haul me a d—nd good load of wood, I will be satisfied." Dr. Wyman perhaps thought he was an infidel, but I think he was a Christian, for he "visited the sick" and "did unto others as he would have had them do unto him." His heart was warm and kind. He knew how to sympathize with the poor and

[3]William Meek founded Bonaparte, Iowa, and with his sons had a flour mill, sawmill, and farm and forest lands in late 1846 when the Mormon refugees arrived. Van Buren County Historical Society, comp., *History of Bonaparte*, 2–3.

he felt it was his duty to administer to their sufferings.[4] I am sorry there is not more such "infidels" in the world.

I once thought that infidelity consisted of hatred toward Christ and his opinions, but I find I was wrong. I have met many men who were open and avowed infidels whose hearts were full of kindness and love for the human race, who were always willing to lend a helping hand to those who were in need of help. Most men are partial to their own church or creed and are generaly circumscribed by the tenets of their o[w]n church, while the infidel is free to take and except [accept] the good that he finds where ever he finds it. Many men think them selves Christian that are utterly destitute of all Christian atributes.

When we left Nauvoo, my father had agreed to send me back to help Br. Wilson to move.[5] I was sent in company of a man by the name of White who was going back to help some of his friends, but before we reached Nauvoo, Br. White met his friends and he turned back and I went on alone. I got a chance to cross the [Mississippi] river and I went to our old hom[e] of a few weeks previous, but oh, how changed! Since I had left, the mob, for that was what we called our enemies, had marched in and there had been a battle there.[6] Not in the part of the town where we had lived, but the whole place looke[d] dead and deserted. The part of the town where my parents had lived was built mostly of log houses. These houses had been taken down and moved a way. The chimneys were standing here and there like lon[e]ly monuments of fallen greatness. The fences were all gone, the gardens where once bloomed fruit trees and flowers were grown up to a kind of weed that was called "dog fennell." Fine orchards were turned out, as it were, to the commons. The streets where happy children had played were silent and deserted. I went from place to place, but found no friendly voice to welcome me. I burst into tears for I felt as though I was alone in the world.[7]

I went to the house of Br. Wilson (a brick [house]) and there I saw signs of life. I ventured to the door yard and rap[p]ed at the door. I heard

---

[4]Dr. R.H. Wyman (1817–1881 or 1887) was born in Oswego, New York, educated at Middlebury College, Vermont, and graduated from medical school at the University of Pennsylvania in 1843. He moved to Iowa in 1846. Fairchild, "History of Medicine in Iowa." One wonders why his father did not call on church elders to lay hands on him, the usual Mormon practice.

[5]Probably Whitford G. Wilson, who lent George's father a wagon.

[6]From 12 to 16 September 1846 an armed mob battled the smaller Mormon "Spartan Band." The treaty that followed the "Battle of Nauvoo" allowed the remaining Mormons to evacuate the city in peace.

[7]Hicks was eleven years old.

an unknown tongue within. I knocked again and again. I heard the strange words. Then the door was opened and a stranger stood before me. My friends were gone and I had missed them on the way. I knew by the dress and general appearance that these people who stood before me were Germans. I aske[d] about my friends and was answered "nix for stay," or something that I took to be that. I turned sorrowfully away. I was about to start back to the river when a boy came along. I ventured to speak to him and to my delight he understood what I said. I learned from him that my friend Wilson had left Nauvoo two or thre[e] days previous. This is no idle romance, but facts as I saw them. I went back, recrossed the river, and made my way home as best I could. Soon after my return, I took the pleuresy in my side and suffered severly, but at length recovered.

There were not less than ten or twelve Mormon families wintered in the town of Bonapart[e] the first winter after leaving Nauvoo. Generally two families ocupied one house. We did not pretend to hold religious worsh[ip] of any kind, but we spent the long winter evening[s] in visiting each other's houses and chatting, singing songs, and the like, for we were cheerfull in our exile.

One circumstance I well remember which hapened at my father's house one evening. Brother and Sister Wilcox came over to spend the evening with us and while there Br. Wilcox began to mimic the Methodists, shouting glory and clapping his hands in jist [jest] when suddenly the "spirit" took possession of him and he began to cry and shout in real earnest. He was some time before he got control of himself. He had once been a Methodist and he knew the feeling as soon as it came. Samuel Wilcox was never known to make light of the Methodists afterwards.[8]

Before the Saints left Nauvoo, the faithful had been throug[h] the temple and had recieved thier indowments. This intitled them to wear wahat [*sic*] are called "garments." These areticles of dress were considered sacred, and the promise was that the "garments" when worn should be a protection or shield to the body of the wearer, and the promise was that not even bullets should pass through them. I give the above as a preface to a number of circumstance[s] which hapened at Bonapart[e], and I know them to be true for they transpired while we were living there and I was at that time well acquainted with the parties.

[8]Samuel Allen Wilcox (1819–1898) and Martha Parker Wilcox (1820–1912) were married in Ontario, Canada. They had four children in Nauvoo and a fifth in Bonaparte in February 1847.

In one house in Bonaparte, there lived two families who had been neighbors of ours in Nauvoo. The name of one of these families was Ainscough and the other was Tillford.[9] A boy by the name of Jonny Tillford who was very fond [of] shooting with a pistle, which he owned. One day he was car[e]lessly handling the pistle in the house when it was accidently discharged. The ball from it struck Mrs. Aianscough on the back. The ball went throug[h] her outsid[e] clothing, but stoped when it struck her "garments" and she was not hurt in the least. I know the pistle was a good one. I have many a time shot a hole through an inch board with it. Again, Samuel Wilcox was hewing timber with a broad axe. He struck a glancing blow with the axe. It turned and struck him on the shinbone, cutting through his pants and sock and then stoped against his "garment" leg, without doing him any injury father than a slight bruise.

One more instance I shall mention. A Mormon whose name I have forgotten had a quarrel with a mercha[n]t by the name of Holland. He drew a dirk knife and struck the Mormon neare the navil. The dirk was one of those that opened like a common pocket knife and fastened with a catch. It passed through the outer clothing of the Mormon and struck his "garments" and turned. It went half shut and cut a severe gash in Holland's hand while the Mormon was not hurt in the least. I mention these things because I know them to be true and was well acquainte[d] with the parties at the time. They might have been acidents, but they nevertheless hapened.

Chapter VI.
A Trying Ordeal: Gathering to Utah

In the month of June A.D. 1847, the people that belonged to the Mormon Church concluded to "gather up to head quarters" at Council Bluffs, Iowa, and my father and family in connection with the rest of the Mormons gathered our effects [to]gather and started, and in a few weeks we came to the east bank of the Mosouri River, where we found the Saints had an abundance of corn and buck wheat and seemed as happy as though they

[9]William Ainscough (1818–1893) and Mary Clark Ainscough (1817–1885). He was from England, she from Pennsylvania. They married in Nauvoo in 1843. John Telford (1802–1896) and Jane Telford (1795–1886), first cousins, were both born in Ulster, Ireland. Their son John was born in Ontario in 1832, making him fourteen at the time of this story.

had never been driven from their homes. They seemed to "take joyfully the spoiling of their goods."[1]

Our family did not stay long at that place. We went to a place called Bullock's Grove to spend the winter.[2] We lived in a log house in the woods where there was no schools or meetings, but ocationally [occasionally] the young people met for dances or pleasure. This was a great place for priarie chickens, and during the winter I killed many of them by catching them in traps. This place belonged to one Clark Hubbard. It was about 6 miles e.n. [northeast] of O. Hide's [Orson Hyde's] place [Hyde Park] and during that winter my father made [fence] rails for Elder Hide an[d] took them to him. It was at this home where I became aquainted with many men who have distinguished themselves, among the number were Isaac Bullock and his brother Kimball.[3] Although our home in the woods was far removed from society, yet we were comparatively happy for we had good health.

In the spring of '48, our family moved to a home of our own, which was situated about 1½ mile[s] north of Kanesville where we made our selves a good home. We built a log cabbin and fenced and cleared a small farm where we raised an abundence of corn, potatoes, and buck wheat, but this place, althoug[h] surrounded by hills, was very unhealthy for myself. I generaly had fever and ague about 6 months in each year beginning about harvest time, and [it] lasted untill Christmas.

At this place we lived among our old neighbors from Nauvoo and many was the social gatherin[gs] at our house, and the long winter months wer[e] passed in dancing and relegious exercises, for the Later-day Saints were full of brotherly love and faith in the future triump[h]ing of the gospel dispensation. During the 5 years that we lived at this place, I went part of two winters to school. I was 16 years of age during the first term, and while going, I got the measels and lost nearly half the term (3 months being a term). The name of the

[1]Hebrews 10:34; Lectures on Faith, 6:2.

[2]Bullock's Grove, named for Benjamin Kimball Bullock, was a few miles southeast of Kanesville (later Council Bluffs) in Pottawattamie County.

[3]Isaac Bullock (1824–1891) and his brother Benjamin Kimball Bullock (1821–1901), sons of Benjamin and Dorothy Kimball Bullock, were born in New Hampshire. Isaac led a company of Saints across the plains in 1852. In 1853 he was appointed captain of the second group of missionaries to Green River. He returned to Provo in 1857 and opened the Bullock Hotel. In 1863 he left for a mission in England and was called in 1877 as president of the High Priests Quorum. Benjamin Kimball, called Kimball, came across the plains with his brother. He served three terms as mayor of Provo from 1855 to 1860 and as city councilman in 1864 and 1865.

teacher was Jonathan C. Wright, who has distinguished himself as a legislator in Utah.[4] The next and last winter we stopped in Iowa, I went part of a term of school to a man by the name of Henry Emery. He was an English man by birth, but was a fine man and took great pains with me to bring me forward.[5]

One thing I remember is this: There was a "gold" excitement broke out in Potawatamie Co., and many dug for the precious metals. This was done in the most secret manner posable. I do not know of any being found.[6]

During the winter of 1851–2, the Saints were preparing with all their energies to moove [*sic*] to Utah in the spring following. Two of the apostles, O. Hyde and E. T. Benson, were very active in stimulating the people to gather up to Zion.[7]

During the time we lived in this part of Iowa, I read the "Life of David Crockett." It was the most interesting [book] I have ever read. My father bought a great many books of romance for me to read when I was sick so that I might be able to pass the terms of sickness through which I had to pass.

In the spring of 1850, I remember the emigrants to California were very numerous and grain came up almost to fabulous prices. Corn was $3.00 per bushel and wheat $2.50. The usual price of corn was .25 and wheat .50, but the demand was so great that corn was brought from Mosouri.

While we lived in Potawatime Co., I remember O. Hyde got a code of laws for the goverment of the people, and by one of these laws, it became the duty of the people to deliver all persons to the authoraties from Mo. for stealing. But Brigham Young was gone to Utah at the time, and when he returned, he (B. Y.) was very angry and raved and threw down the paper containing the law and stamped with his foot and swore by the Eternal God that if any man from Miosouri should lay his hand [on] his sholder and say "you are my prisner," "So help me God, I will kill him." I never heard any

[4]Jonathan Calkins Wright (1808–1880) was marshal of Nauvoo and a member of the city council when the Illinois legislature annulled the Nauvoo Charter. In Utah he served in twenty-two sessions of the legislature.

[5]Henry Emery (1825–1881) was from Yorkshire, England. He, his wife, and father traveled with the Hicks family to Utah in 1852. Emery, "Journal of Henry 'Harry' Emery."

[6]California gold fever proved highly contagious. Nelson Whipple reported something that looked like gold found in the bluffs west of Kanesville. Apostle Orson Hyde, church leader in Iowa, "went over to the place with some others and saw it and dedicated it to the Lord. . . . The stuff turned out to be entirely worthless." Bennett, *Mormons at the Missouri*, 222.

[7]Orson Hyde made overland trips to Utah and back in 1850, 1851, and 1852, the year he moved his family to Salt Lake. In 1851 Apostle Ezra T. Benson left Salt Lake for Iowa to "gather up the Saints," returning in August 1852.

man go on as he did, and on my way home, I asked my father if it was not wrong for a man in the pulpit to take the name of God in vain.[8]

There is no doubt in my mind that if O. Hyde had have had his way, there would have been less stealing among the "Saints," but O. Hyde did not have his way. I remember one man was whip[p]ed sever[e]ly for stealing from one of his breathren, which was considered wrong by many. The name of the man that was apointed to do the whipping was James Craygan and was called "Marshall" Craygan ever afterward.[9]

Early in the spring of 1852, my father began to busy himself in preparing for our journey to the "Valley." We sold our home for a "song" and on the 5th day of June, 1852, we bade adieu to our home where we had toiled for 5 years preparing for the journey. We had one ox team and a couple of cows, but we had great faith. We believed we were the chosen of God—that it was our duty to gather out of Babylon while the judgements of God should pass over the nation, and in part it has been so, for the great rebellion in the U. S. [the Civil War], which has cost the nation so much blo[o]d an[d] treasure, has "passed over" the country. I think I am safe in saying that Utah has suffered the least of any state or territory in the union by the war. It would be very hard for me to believe that the gathering of the Mormon people was all the work of chance and fanaticism. "There is a divinity. . ." (Shak[espeare])[10]

We were organized into companies of 50 wagons with a captain over us. Then we were again organized into tens with a captain overe [*sic*] each ten wagons. The name of our captain of 50 was [John B.] Walker, and the [company] number was 14th. The Capt. of our ten was John Myres.[11] On the last

[8]At Winter Quarters on 14 May 1848, shortly before Brigham Young returned to Salt Lake City, he "called upon the Lord to bless this place for the good of the saints and curse every Jentile who should attempt to settle here, with sickness, rotenness and death, also to course [curse] the land of Missouri that it might sease to bring forth Grain or fruit of any kind to its inhabitants, and that they might be cursed [with] Sickness, rotenness and death; that their flesh might consume away on their bones and their blood be turned into Maggots, and that their torments never sease, but increase until they leave the land and it be blessed for the possession of the Saints," Mary Richards wrote in her diary. Ward, ed., *Winter Quarters*, 216–17.

[9]On 17 January 1848 James Termain (Tremain), who had stolen a horse from a Brother Allen, was tried before "Bishops Millar [George Miller] and [William G.] Perkins." After examining witnesses, they found him guilty and sentenced him "to receive 39 lashes on his bare back . . . under the hands of the marshal, James Cragun." Journal History, 17 January 1848, 1. James Cragun (1814–1887) was sustained as a marshal on 25 December 1847 in Kanesville, Iowa. Harwell, ed., *Manuscript History of Brigham Young*, 81.

[10]From Shakespeare's *Hamlet*, act 5: "There is a divinity that shapes our ends."

[11]John B. Walker captained the fourteenth wagon train in 1852. John Myers (1814–1900) traveled with his wife, Sarah Dickson Myers, and toddler daughter.

day of June, we crossed the Mo. River at Winter Quarters and bid farewell to the United States.[12] We had not gone far on our journey when the c[h]olera broke out in our company and 13 died of that malignant disease. My brother [Samuel] Moroni was the first to take the disease, but recovered. It was sad to part with loved ones and leave them forever on the lon[e]ly plains to return to "dust." I remember one woman, strong and healthy at the Loup Fork of the Platte River who did a big washing of clothes and the next day died with the colera and was buried.

I remember one woman, the wife of one Joseph Robertson, who got frightened and believed she was taking the colera. Her husband believed it was fear that caused his wife's sickness. He forced her to get out of the wagon and walk about. He forbid her under penalty of a "good flogging" to go to bed any more that day. She recovered immediately.[13] We hurried along as fast as our ox teams could be made to travil, so that we could get out of the stricken district. Our company was the 14 in number and I believe there were 22 in all.[14] The way side was marked by graves—more frequent than mile stones in the old [eastern] States.

Apostle Ezra T. Benson came along and told us that it was our duty to laugh and dance and make merry, as much as we could. I often saw the ordine[n]ce of laying on hands tried to no purpose. It was generaly young people and women that died on the plains. I remember helping to bury one woman on the plains who was still warm. We had no coffins, but used the bark off the cotton wood tree when it could be obtained.

Our road lay on the north side of the Platt[e] R[iver] until we reached Fort Laramie. Then we crossed over to the south side. We saw many large herds of buffalos and killed many of them. I killed one myself. We saw many of the Sioux Indians who were very peacable. When we reached a higher altitude, the colera disappeared from our midst. After we got throug[h] the Black Hills [just west of Fort Laramie], we divided up into smaller companies for [to find] feed for our teams.

The feelings of the company was generaly good, but we had one little "difficulty," which grew out of a love affair in one of the "tens" of our company.

---

[12]They were still within the United States but were in Indian country, which became Nebraska Territory in 1854.

[13]Probably Joseph Robinson, 24, and his wife, Elizabeth Hobson, 22, both from England and married in St. Louis in 1852.

[14]Twenty-one companies left Kanesville in 1852. *Deseret News 1989–1990 Church Almanac*, 176–77.

There was a young and beautiful girl of about 17 years of age. A young man in our company, a gentile by the name of James Mathews, was pay[ing] his address to her and she was coquetting with him. Another young man in our [company] by the name of Samuel Curtis asked the girl to go to a dance with him (the place selected for the dance was perhaps a few hundred yards from the camp).[15] She refused, which was her right of course, but she afterwards went with Mathews. Curtis made some light remark which soon reached the ears of Mathews. Mathews was of a fiery temper and threatened the life of Curtis if he did not recall his words and exposed a dagger, whiche, said he, would take the life of Curtis as soon as oportunity offered. It was told Curtis that Mathews threatened his life. One night some time afterwards, Mathews was in the act of leading the Columbia Williams[16] out to dance when Curtis steped up to him, forbid him to dance, saying at the same time, "You have threatened my life and you shall not dance." The two young [men] steped asid[e] and the matter was peaceably and amicably settled between them. The next day, out side parties were giving theire opinion as we rested at noon when one Stewart Dixon expressed the opinion that Mathews got off to[o] easy.[17] Some one of the friend[s] of Mathews took up the saying and in a few moments not less than 25 men and half-grown boys were menacing each other and making loud threats of what they would do.

There was a young man—a cripple in one leg—by the name of "Jet" Sherman who was very abusive in his language toward Curtis.[18] Curtis at last became exasperated at the abuse and stepped up to Sherman and with his open hand, hit him a slap on the cheek. Sherman struck at Curtis with his crutch but did not hit him. Then there was a general rushing together of the parties from both sides, but no more blows followed. A man by the name of Davis McOlney—a man of resolute courage and good sense—seeing the course things were taking, jumped upon a wagon tongue and in a short and eloquent speech in which he told them how folish [foolish] they were ac[t]ing and warned they were in an Indian country—that union was necessary for self protection.[19] All parties slunk off to their wagons and there was no more

[15]Samuel Thomas Curtis (1834–1917) from Chautauqua County, New York, was seventeen.

[16]Harriet Columbia Williams (1838–1917), called Columbia, was fourteen, not seventeen, at the time of this affair. She married Reuben Augustus McBride in 1855 in Salt Lake City. See Rogers, ed., East Millard Pioneers.

[17]Charles Stewart Dickson (1827–1911), born in Ontario, Canada, married in Iowa in 1849.

[18]Probably Samuel S. Sherman (1839–1871), born in New Jersey.

[19]Davis McOlney (1797–1867), born in Vermont, had been a policeman in Nauvoo. He was fifty-five in 1852.

public demonstrations, but some were not satisfied and a council was held by the captains of "tens" where some of these thought Mathews ought to be put out of the way (i.e., killed) for threatening the life of a Saint. One Daniel M. Burbanks plead for Mathews and he was spared.[20] Nothing further disturbed the peace of our company, and in closing the chapter, I will say that crossing the plains with ox teams is a trying ordeal—one requiring great patience and fortitude. My health, which had not been good for years, vastly improved and for the first autumn in seven years I did not have the chills and fever.

Chapter VII.
The Happy Days of Utah

On the 3rd day of October 1852, we arrived at Great Salt Lake City all in good health but very much worn by our long and weary journey of 1,030 miles.[1] We were within two days of being 4 months from the time we left our home in Potawatami Co., Iowa, until we reached the end of our journey, and rest was sweet. We were met at one of the public squares by old friends and kindly welcomed. One friend, Jonathan Parkar by name, invited our whole ten to his house in one of the lower wards where he had a large and splendid garden of choice vegitables.[2] He invited us in an[d] bid us help ourselves to such as we liked best, and be assured we feasted on the fine potatoes, squashes, and cabbages. This was certainly brotherly.

Utah had been settled but 5 years before we came in, and Salt Lake City was a mear [mere] village at that time, but the Saints had done wonders considering their circumstances. They had plenty of the common necesaries of life. Wheat was worth $2.00 pr. bushel and flour $6.00 pr. 100 lbs. My father had brought 400 lbs of salaratus from the alkali lakes on the plains and this he sold for .25 cts. pr. pound in flour and vegitables.[3]

One little circumstance I feel disposed to mention. One day I saw a young woman in a crowd to whom I very much wished to speak, but was

[20] Daniel Mark Burbank (1814–1894) was traveling with his wife and four young children.

[1] Hicks was seventeen when the family arrived in Utah.

[2] Jonathan Parker (1817–1889) lived in Nauvoo at the same time as the Hicks family. Parker emigrated with his family to Utah in 1848.

[3] Saleratus is a leavening agent consisting of potassium or sodium bicarbonate. Common on the trail west of today's Casper, Wyoming, many Saints collected it at a large alkali "pan" near Independence Rock called Saleratus Lake. It was unusual that Hicks's father collected such a large amount, since by that point teams were worn down and people often cast off treasured possessions to lighten the load.

prevented and I tried to watch her home, but failed to keep track of her. On returning to camp, I got lost and wandered until midnight in the fields. (Moral: Beware of young ladies!)

On the 6th day of the month [October], I went to the general conference and heard much good preaching and rejoicing in the gospel. I heard Prest. Brigham Young boast at this time that he was worth $80,000. He told us what fine abilities he had for making money.[4] I was somewhat surprised to hear him, for I had known him to be a poor man in Nauvoo and I know it was said of him that he had to be helped from Winter Quarters[5] and how could a man in that short space of 5 years accumulate the vast sum of $80,000 without the benefit of trade, at the same time situated 1000 miles from any commercial center?[6] It is no mystery at the present time. The $80,000 was tithing that he had filched from his honest but ignorant followers, and at his death the mystery of his (B. Young's) money making was explained.[7] I am aware that the ability to accumulate wealth is a great gift of nature, but I do not consider it the *ne plus ultra* of all Christian virtues.

Polygamy, which had been a secret practice in the states, was now made public, and instead of women who were thus married being called "spirituals," they were honored by the title of "wife." Brother Jones, who was much married, spoke with pride of his "second wife," his "sixth wife" or his "first wife." I think I am safe in venturing the opinion that plural marriage was not as repulsive here in Utah as it was in the states.

---

[4]Brigham Young's boasting does not appear in the edited records of the fall conference. "Minutes of the General Conference," 5 October 1852, *Millennial Star*, 5 March 1853, 152.

[5]Young received part of the Mormon Battalion's pay, which helped the Mormons survive at Winter Quarters and outfit the move west. The Mormon Battalion was an all-Mormon volunteer army unit formed during the Mexican-American War. The battalion marched about two thousand miles from Council Bluffs, Iowa, to San Diego and helped secure the borders of the U.S. Southwest.

[6]Young had several sources for income: from tolls at ferries on the North Platte, Green, Weber, and Bear rivers; from Mormon Battalion veterans paying tithing on gold mined in California; from men sent to California to pan for gold; and from cattle driven to California to sell. In addition, he also made money from tolls in City Creek Canyon where Salt Lake residents obtained their firewood and from a host of businesses, including sawmills, tanneries, distilleries, and overland freighting.

[7]Hicks wrote his autobiography a year after President Young's death in 1877 as executors tried to settle his estate. As trustee-in-trust, Young had mingled his personal and church finances. According to Arrington, Young and other church authorities "drew on the tithing resources of the church, and at a later date repaid part or all of the obligation in money, property, or services" as needed. The ability "to draw, almost at will, on church as well as his own funds, was a great advantage to Brigham Young and was certainly one of the reasons for his worldly success." George Q. Cannon wrote in January 1878, "It is felt that the funds of the Church have been used with a freedom not warranted by the authority which he [Young] held." Arrington, "The Settlement of the Brigham Young Estate," 1, 4n13, 7.

The people of this country I found were healthyer and I believe happier than they were in Iowa. We ware realy a band of breathren and it was the way of all to treat each other as brothers and sisters, for apostasy was not known in the midst of the Saints as it is now.

Our family camped in the "Big Field" near Salt Lake City for 3 weeks resting our teames and recruiting ourselves.[8] While there we heard of Utah Co. and concluded to go there and get new homes and "grow up with the country." We moved camp and in a few days reached what was at that time called Palmyra. There were good opertunaties to take up land which only needed the magic touch of industry to make good farms and plentiful homes. The water had been taken out of the Spanish Fork River that same spring, but only a small stream. There was a few families living there, and among the number was Stephen Markham, [one] of the prominent friends of Joseph Smith, the Mormon prophet.[9] Br. Markham and two or three others had raised a little wheat.

My father drove our team down by the Spanish Fork River and we camped there, for at that time there was plenty of timber growing on the river bottom. There we found H. B. M. Jolley and family camped. Br. Jolley and family were our neighbors at Nauvoo.[10] Among his family was a daughter, tall and graceful with bright black eyes, fair face and long dark hair. She had an intel[l]igent look. She was but a few months past 15 years of age. She was my ideal of what a young girl should be—modest and retiring. I was soon introduced to her and I found her all I had believed her to be.

An intimacy began which in a few months ripened into love. I took her to all or nearly all "parties" and balls in Palmyra during the winter of 1852–3, and in the following spring, on the 24 day of March, Elizabeth T. M. Jolley became my wife.[11] The marriage ceremony was performed by one Silas

---

[8]The Big Field was more than five thousand acres south of Great Salt Lake City reserved for farming. Residents could apply for five or ten acres in addition to their one-and-a-quarter-acre lots in the city.

[9]A New Yorker who was baptized in 1837, Stephen Markham (1800–1878) was one of the last visitors to Joseph Smith the day he was killed and an officer in Brigham Young's 1847 Pioneer Company. He served as bishop of Palmyra, Utah, and as a colonel in the Nauvoo Legion during the Walker War.

[10]Born in North Carolina and called Bryant or H. B. M., Henry Bryant Manning Jolley (1813–1896) was living in Tennessee in 1842 when he converted to Mormonism. With his family he moved to Nauvoo, where he and his wife were endowed in 1846. Jolley led a party of some 340 emigrants across the plains in 1852. Near Fort Laramie, a fight almost broke out between Jolley and Lewis Barney. Barney and others left Jolley's company and continued to Utah independently. Barney, *One Side by Himself*, 132–35.

[11]Several contributions to Familysearch.org give her name as Elizabeth Temperance Worthy Ann Jolley, but the photograph of her marriage certificate and Hicks's autobiography give her middle initial as "M." Jolley, *Jolley Family Book*, 495.

Hillman, a Justice of the Peace. The wedding was at the home of my wife's father. Twenty five years have passed and my wife still lives and our love is young and fresh, and I am proud to say I have not yet had any cause to regret my choice of a wife. I have ever found her fa[i]thful, careful, industrious, and sympathetic, an indulgent mother, and a loving companion. We never have not [*sic*] been sealed and probably never will be. I never have had but one wife and have no desire to get any more. My wife is the second daughter of H. B. M. and Brit[t]anna Jolley. She is one of a large family. During the first winter at Palm[y]ra, I went to school a short time to Silas Hillman, and her who afterward became my wife attended the same school, and I fear there was more love making than studying of books, for young lovers make bad students of books.[12]

During the winter of 1852 & 3, my father and I threshed Stephen Markham's wheat for him with flails for the tenth bushel.[13] In the fall of 1852, many of the Saints who had crossed the plains that summer came to Palmyra and took up land, and during the winter we lived in what was called "dugouts." These were made by digging a celler or hole in the ground and putting a roof of willows and earth over it and then making a fireplace insid[e]. These "dugouts" were very warm. I remember the first winter in Utah was very severe. I think I [have] not seen one like it since. The old settlers had built a school house before we came there.[14] This was used for the purposes of meeting house, school house, and dancing hall. Dancing was at that time and always has been our chief amus[e]ment, although we ocationaly [occasionally] varied the monotony by having a theatrical performance. I must say I have seen some excellent stage playing at that early day.[15]

I purpose to describe an old time dance such as we had on special ocations. The time of the year is Christmas. A select committee are chosen by the people to make the necessary ar[r]angements some time before hand, and a general invitation is given out at the Sunday meeting. Then for a few

[12]Nevertheless, Hicks "was a student in the school of Mr. Hillman, and graduated at the end of the first quarter with 'high honors' being able to read in the Testament or the Book of Mormon without making many mistakes in the pronunciation of words, with a very limited knowledge of arithmetic, and none whatever of grammar or history." Of the three teachers in Spanish Fork, Silas Hillman, A. K. Thurber, and "a man named Cook," Hillman was the most competent. Hicks, History of Spanish Fork, 4.

[13]That is, George and his father kept every tenth bushel they threshed as pay.

[14]Hicks described the schoolhouse as "a plain four-square building" of adobe. Hicks, History of Spanish Fork, 3.

[15]For the vibrant cultural life of Utah's pioneers, see Walker and Dant, eds., *Nearly Everything Imaginable.*

days, all is *stir* and bustle. Young men engage their *girls* to go with them to the dance, for every boy or young man must take a girl. Calico dresses are brought out and put under repairs or perhaps linsey or "flannen" dresses are "turned" and old white shirts are brought out and starched in good style.[16] Women council together in regard to what they shal[l] wear and how they shall wear it. Then comes the preparing of food—baking pies, frying cakes, and getting up knicknacks for the ocation. At length the happy day arives and is we[l]comed by plenty of noise and burning of powder.

Early in the day, a few young men and youn[g] women are chosen to go and put the school-meeting house in order for the festivities. The house is thoroughly cleaned and decorated with boughs of evergreens and festoon of paper flowers. The seats are all taken out but a few, and these are aranged round the house next [to] the wall so as to make as much room as possable for dancing. Then an elevated seat is made at one end of the hall for the music, then a good fire is built. The house [is] locked up for the rest of the day and those who have been busy in preparing the hall go and prepar[e] themselves for the night's enjoyment.

Early in the evening—about 6 o'clock—the house is opened and the people begin to gather in from all parts of the town—old and young, the richest and the poor, small and great turn out without reserve. Friends meet friends and neighbors greet at the place of gathering, and this interim is spent in social chat until it is time to begin the dance. The music, generaly two violin players, take the elevated seat at one end of the hall. Then the bishop or presiding church officer call[s] the assembly to order. When all talking ceases [and] when a brief statement of the cause of gathering is made, then the dance is opened by prayer either by the bishop or some one that he selects. Many of these pray[e]rs are quite eloquent. The blessing of God is asked for all present and absent belonging to us. Then our Father is asked to let a spirit of peace and good order be with us to keep us from all harm.

After prayer, the co[m]mittee proceed[s] to let the male members draw numbers which have been prepared for the ocation. These are mad[e] of small bits of white paper with figures marked on them. These are put into a hat general[l]y and are drawn out permicously [promiscuously], the manage[r] men being careful to make the numbers tally to the number of those who

[16]Linsey is a fabric woven with linen or cotton; when woven with wool it was known as linsey-woolsey. Flannen clothes were made of flannel.

wish to draw. After the drawing is over, a floor manager is chosen to call the numbers and keep order. Then for a short time there is talk and noise and whispering. When the manager takes his position, [he] call[s] the at[t]ention of the aud[i]ance and makes a brief speech and requests all present to keep good order. Then he begins and calls the numbers from one to four or to eight as house room will permit. When the floor is full or when all the quadrilles that the hall will admit of are formed, someone is selected to "call off" and the word "ready" is given. The music strikes up a quadrille tune. These are tunes of 4 parts or 2 parts played twice over 4/4 time. The "caller" gives the word and the ball is opened for the night. A good caller is [a] very important personage and much depends on him whither the dance is orderly or disorderly. It is generaly rulable to give each set two "changes" when [after which] they take their seats, and the floor is again filled and so the time is put in with an ocation[al] waltz or contra dance. When the dancers begin to tire, someone is called on for a song or perhaps a resitation [recitation]. I have heard some splendid songs both comic and sentimental at our dances.

General[ly] about midnight, the picknic which has been left at the house nearest the hall is brought in and all take a recess while the good things are hande[d] round and all partake of the homely viands and laugh and be [as] happy as possable. After refreshments, the numbers were given to the "women folks" when dancing is again resumed and kept up with about the same spirit often untill day break, when the assembly was dismissed by prayer and all went home happy. Many a love affair has had its beginning at one of the social parties.

Ye rich and great of the earth who meet in the gilded halls of pride, who robe your selves in satin and point lace, who pride your selves in the richness of your apperal, I venture to say you never were half as happy as us poor Mormons were at one of our social dances.

Those were the happy days of Utah. These were the days before our peace was destroyed by the pre[a]ching of that most accursed of all cursed doctrines [that] was preached in Utah by that arch fiend Brigham Young, namely "blood atonement." These days were before Utah was stained with human blood from one end to the other, these days were before that most horable of all the horable deeds was committed—the Mountain Meadows Massacre.

If our dances were well attended, so were our religious meetings—particularly the prayer meetings. These were held on Thursday and Sunday evenings when all were allowed to speak and "bear their testimony" to the truth of the gospel as revealed in these last days, and many a man and woman I have heard say they knew this church to be the work of God, for God had revealed it to them. I have often heard them speak with "new tounges" and prophecy of things that would yet come to pass. The church was full of the "first love," and the spirit which had prom[p]ted them to leave their homes was not yet dead.[17]

I remember once hearing Geo. A. Smith talk in the old school house at Palmyra. He was speaking sweet words of incouragement to the Saints of Palmyra. Said he, "Eye hath not seen nor ear heard, neither hath it entered into the heart of man the greatness that is in store for the citizens of Palmyra." I was glad. I thanked God that we had an inspired priesthood that could tell us the future while the gentiles had to grovel in darkness. But alas, the delusion has passed away and the future "greatness" came suddenly to a full stop, and all who had paid attention to the "inspired" ravings of the "man of God" had the "satisfaction" of losing all there [their] buildings, for water began to raise [rise] in the cellars of the houses and we must moove and lose nearly two years' work.[18] I lost a house that cost me $300 in hard labor and I never lived in it an hour. Cedar City [in] Iron County has been twice mooved by the bab[b]ling of the same "inspired" fool, but so it was.[19] The Saints in those days were poor in this world's goods, but they were full of hope for the future and faith in the gospel which they had received, and when we mad[e] a moove, there was a united effort.

During our first winter at Palmyra, we were set apart as a branch of the church and Stephen Markham was ap[p]ointed bishop and the branch was soon afterward put in working order. I remember a man coming there by the name of Josep[h] G. Hovey, an old Nauvoo Saint and pr[e]aching strange doctrines. He tried to get the people to confess their fa[u]lts in public

---

[17]Such charismatic events were common in early Mormonism but are not today.

[18]Apostle George A. Smith laid out Palmyra in 1852, but in February 1856 President Young advised the families living there to move one and a half miles from the low, swampy site to higher ground in Spanish Fork. Irrigation had caused alkali salt to rise in the soil and destroy the crops in the Palmyra area. About four hundred people moved. Allred, *Spanish Fork*, 12–17.

[19]Cedar City was first located in 1851 by George A. Smith on the north bank of Coal Creek. Because the town was vulnerable to Indian attack from the hill, it was moved south early in 1853. Two years later Brigham Young recommended moving the city out of the flood plain to the present site.

meeting, but the people counted him a fool and rejected his teaching. He was an eastern man and in speech he left out the letter "r" and I remember hearing him say he was the "little stone cuttah" and he was not come on a "Tom fool's and [errand]." He made some noise but no converts. He went to Payson and proceeded in pursuading one Rowe to confes[s] to sheep stealing.[20]

Chapter VIII.
A Blaze of War: Conflict with the Utes

The spring of 1853 came on early in the month of March and the people of Palmyra set to work in real earnest fencing land, grubbing griswood [greasewood], and making preperations for extensive farming. In the meantime, seed had to be obtained, but the peop[le] had no money to buy [seed] grain with, so a meeting was cal[l]ed and Br. Stephen Markham took his own money and all he could borrow, himself becoming responsable for the whole amount. Teams were sent off and seed was brought in to the place and distributed among the people so that all might have some to sow on their ground. It is seldom that I have seen such unselfish manifestations among men as in the case just mentioned above. The man that will thus sacrafice his own for the use of his needy fellows deserve[s] something more than a mear [mere] name in history—he deserves to live in the hearts of all honest men that know him and I presume he will never be forgot[t]en.[1]

When our crops were put in, the next thing of importance was to make a dam and get out the water for ir[r]igating the crops. The old settlers had taken out a small stream in the year '52, but this stream was too small to supply the demand and a new ditch had to be made. Some of the old settlers expressed themselves that we might have the use of their dam for nothing, but they were not willing to help make a new ditch, and thereby a feeling of antipathy sprang up betwixt the old and new settlers which bid to become great, but fortunately the dam belonging to the old settlers went [washed] away and then all hands turned out and built two new ones before

[20]Probably Delaware-born Conderset Rowe (1823–1904), who was living in Payson with his wife and four children. President Young described Hovey as "a blacksmith, carpenter, stone cutter, wood chopper; or anything else within his power, the particular channel of his operations depending entirely upon counsel." 24 February 1856, *Journal of Discourses*, 3:236.

[1]In his Stephen Markham Biographical Sketch, Hicks repeated this story and added that Markham "waited until after harvest for his pay."

they got one to stay, and by this time, it was the first of July before we got the water out and some of the [crops] had to be watered to bring it up, but notwithstanding the latenes[s] of the season, our wheat got ripe and we had an abundant harvest and I know it.

During the summer while we were busy about our crops, Brigham Young came to our place and preached at night in the old school house. He upbraided us for not forting in. Said he, "You [are] standing in the light of Christ." To me the expression was an ambiguity and so remains to this day. He then began to talk about an Indian that had been killed—one Squash Head—at Springville. He said that such things ought to be kept secret.[2] "Why," said he, "I can carry mollases in my pocket and no body would know it."—"I," he went on, "would put the molasses in to a bottle and cork it up tight and then I think it would stay there." He then warned us that the Indians were dangerous, that we would be glad to build forts for self-protection. "Even now," said he, "they are looking over the mountains at you and before long they will pounce upon you before you are aware of it, and you will be obliged to fort up for safety." I heard him myself. Of all the prophecies that I ever have heard him utter, this is the only one that I ever knew to be filled. I think it must have been an accidental hit.[3]

However, we were busy at work on our damn in the Spanish Fork River and all was peace, no one even thinking of danger when a war suddenly broke out between us and the Utah Indians. The trouble began at Springville in Utah County, 6 miles north of Spanish Fork City. The trouble had a very small beginning—an Indian by the name of Sower Socketts [Shower-o-sho-a-kats or Shower-Ocats] was whipping his squaw at the house of one Joseph Kelley, a citizen of that place. There hapened to be a man by the name of James Ivy stopping at the house of Kelley. He told the Indian to stop whipping the woman. The Indian refused and Ivy struck the Indian over the head with a gun and knocked him down, but did not kill him. This

[2]Squash-head, Tintic, and a few other Utes stole livestock, made threats, and complained of Mormon settlers taking their hunting and fishing lands. In February 1856, after an outbreak known as the Tintic War, a posse wounded Tintic and killed several other Indians. They captured Squash-head, and while he was held prisoner in the house of Springville bishop Aaron Johnson, his throat was slit from ear to ear on 5 March 1856. Guards claimed Squash-head committed suicide with a table knife while eating breakfast, but others "darkly hinted" that a white person had "done the bloody dead." Peterson, *Utah's Black Hawk War*, 73.

[3]Hicks conflated two Brigham Young visits. The "fort up" lecture one was on 24 April 1853, three years before Squash-head was killed.

unfortunate event happened on the 19th day of July, 1853.[4] The Indians were at that time a strong tribe. They immediately sprang to arms and a blaze of war flashed over the country, the Indians going to the mountains to prey on the stock belonging to the people.

The whites were suddenly brought together and forts were laid out in all the settlements and we were obliged to stand guard to protect ourselves from sudden attacks. We were very illy prepared for war. Many of us were destitute of firearms and [we] being an agricultural people, the Indians were muc[h] better prepared for war than we were, but they were cowardly or they might have swept the country with all ease, that is, the southern part of the territory.

About the 20th of July a man by the name of Alexander Keel was placed on picket guard near Payson City.[5] An Indian by the name of Wahwoona cre[pt]ed onto him in the night, shot him through the breast, killing him on the spot. (The Indian afterwards boasted of the killing of Keel after peace was made.) Keel was a good man and left a large family. The news was brought to Palmyra that same night, and the people of Payson asked us to send help for they believed they were in great danger of a sudden attack. The people of Palmyra had organized into two companies, one of cavelry and one of infantry. W. W. Willis was captain of the cavelry and John P. Chidester was captain of the infantry.[6] A number of men were chose[n] to go to Payson in the night and also I was one of the number and Capt. Chidester took command and we marched off in the darkness. We reached Payson in safety, and the body of Keel had been brought in and I saw it lying in state.

[4]Hicks is essentially correct. The incident took place on 17 July 1853 at the home of James Ivie, who precipitated both the Walker War and the Tintic War in 1856. Mrs. Ivie and the Indian woman were bargaining over a trade of trout for flour. The Indian man, perhaps her husband, allegedly beat her for not making a good trade. Ivie knocked him out, another Indian, and then the woman as each attacked him. Springville resident Joseph Kelly saw the incident and tried to revive the Indians. The first, mortally wounded, was taken to Wakara, leader of the Northern Ute bands, who was camped close by. Angry over encroachment on Ute land and attempts to stop his lucrative slave trade, Wakara launched the guerilla campaign known as the Walker War. Peterson, *Utah's Black Hawk War*, 64–67; and George McKenzie, Statement, in Gottfredson, *Indian Depredations in Utah*, 43–46.

[5]Actually 18 July 1853. Born in Tennessee, Alexander Keele (or Keel) (1822–1853) married Minerva Dixon in 1841. He came to Utah from Nauvoo between 1850 and 1852. He had five children.

[6]William Wesley Willis (1811–1872) was born in Illinois and was a lieutenant in the Mormon Battalion. John Peck Chidester (1831–1897), son of John Madison Chidester, was born in Michigan and was with his parents in Zion's Camp in 1834. He joined the LDS church in 1840 and came to Utah in 1850, married in Salt Lake City in 1851, and was living in Palmyra in 1852. He became a captain in the Nauvoo Legion and fought in the Walker War.

It was a sad sight to me, it being the first person that I had ever seen that had been killed by gun shot.

The next morning after we went up into Petetenete [Peteetneet] Kanyon and [there we] had a chance to v[i]ew the Indians going over the hill from a saw mill that was in the kanyon. There was a family living at the mill—one John Bellows and family—and some lumbermen who were bringing logs to the mill. An Indian came with in shooting distance and shot twice at the people, but did not hit any of them. We ware to[o] close on the tracks of the Indians for them to take time to come and kill the people at the mill. When we found the people at the mill were safe, we gave up the pursuit of the Indians.

Our company was then ordered to Manti in Sanpete Co. I was bearfooted at the time, but I wen[t] anyway. We went in wagons in the night as far as Nephi. On our way, there was an accident—a gun was discharged and the ball struck one of the team horses in the hip, but did very little harm. We went on to Manti the next day and found the people all safe, & a number of our troops went into the mountains, found a few Indians, and dispatched them in a summary manner. The next day some of us went to Allred Settlement.[7] They [We] were thanked for the kind offer, but were told that they did not need any help, but were strong enough for self protection. This was by "Uncle Jimmy Allred." In three days after, the Indians came and drove off nearly all their cattle.[8]

While at Manti one of the soldiers stole some horse shoes and was tried by a court marshal and proved guilty. He was sentenced to have two quarts of cold water po[u]red down his shirt sleeve for three mornings in succession, he holding up his arm as high as possable, and this was to be done in [the] presence of all the assembled troops. I saw him brought out and the water poured down his sleeve. I have forgotten his name. This kind of punnishment caused a great deal of mirth among the "boys" of the camp and was not very bad on the thief for it was July.

We did not stop long at Manti until we were ordered home. Two circumstances on our way home I shall relate. We stop[p]ed to "noon" at a spring

---

[7]James Allred founded the settlement later known as Spring City about fifteen miles north of Manti in Sanpete Valley at a spring the Utes had used for years. That the Mormons now claimed it further angered the Indians.

[8]The settlers had been slow to build a fort. With no place to protect their stock, the Indians drove off over two hundred head of cattle and horses on 28 July 1853. According to Orson Whitney, President Young was irritated that the settlers had failed to build a fort as he had counseled and told Daniel H. Wells to write to them and say, "Inasmuch as you have no oxen and cows to trouble you, you can go to harvesting and take care of yourselves." Christy, "The Walker War," 403–407; and Whitney, *History of Utah*, 1:520.

in the north end of Sanpete Valley. We found a prairie chicken and not les[s] than 50 shots were fired at the chicken before it was killed. We then mooved on to Willow Creek where Mona now stands and there we had a liv[e]ly time wrestling, jumping, and other athletic sports with any amount of noise, but in our boistrous enjoyment, the guns which were fired at the chicken were forgotten. In the night the Indians came and fired on the men that were out guarding the horses but did not hit any of them. Shots were exchanged on both sides. Both parties rushed for their horses, but the white men were successful and their horses were all brought safe into camp while the Indians retreated. Then there came a time for loadin[g] guns in "hot haste" and the greatest confusion prevailed in camp. It is my opinion that 25 Indians could have put our whole camp to flight and have killed half of us, but the Indians were cowardly.[9]

The next morning a detachment of men was sent up to the mouth of the kanyon, but no Indians were to be found. We then marched home all safe and sound. While we ware gone, some Indians came down (3 in number) at night. Two men were on picket guard and saw them come past, but dare[d] not fire at them. The names of those men were Wm. Sommerville and Thomas McFate. [The latter] was about 18 years of age, but Sommerville was a man of [with] a family. The Indians came in and got a few head of cattle that were outside the corall and were driving them off when a man by the name of Charles Price, who had been a British soldier in his youth and a little boy whos[e] name I have forgotten ran after the Indians and got back the cattle. The Indians shot at him and wounded him in the knee, but that made no difference to the old man. He fired at the Indians who ran away in great fright. The boy ran back to the fort and left the brave old soldier the sole victor to hobble in as best he could. The gunshot in the old hero's knee made him lame for life.[10]

Another circumstance occur[r]ed that summer which I shall note. Two men went to Manti to take an express [message]—John W. Berry and [Clark] Roberts—and on their return at Santaquin, they were fired on by the Indians and were both wounded, Roberts in the shoulder and Berry in the wrist.[11]

---

[9]Neither Mormon frontier militias nor Utah's Indians were particularly valiant warriors, but they were not necessarily cowardly. Both sides used tactics designed to minimize their losses.

[10]William Somerville (1817–1878) was from Scotland. At the time of the Walker War, he had two wives and four children. Thomas William McFate (1833–1906) was born in Pennsylvania. He was nineteen at the time of this event. Charles Price (1800–1873) later owned a sawmill on Salt Creek, now Nephi.

[11]Tennessean John William Berry (1822–1890) came to Utah in 1849 and moved to Palmyra with A.K. Thurber. Berry served as Bishop Butler's first counselor.

Berry's wound bled profusely and he began to feel faint as they rode along at full speed, the Indians, four in number, following as fast as their horses could carry them. Roberts, whose left arm was powerless, was cool and brave. He would turn and ride back toward the Indians, raise his gun as best he could, while Berry rode on as fast as his weak condition would permit. The Indians, who are cowards from instinct, kept out of rang[e] of the gun of Roberts. It was six miles to Payson, which place they reached where they were properly cared for. There is no doubt that both of these men owe their lives to the cool bravery of Roberts.[12]

I must mention one rather ludicrous circumstance that transpired during the summer of the Indian war. Zeebe [Zebedee] Coltrin, who was at that time a lietennant, he was on duty one night.[13] There was an old fanning mill standing out in a lot near the fort. Z. Coltrin saw it and believing it to be an Indian, fired at it and then ran to the fort and gave the alarm that he had seen an Indian.[14] A few men marched out and captured the mill.

There was one young man, Ber[r]y Jolley by name. One night at guard mount was [while] standing in "file," he threw his foot around his gun in a very car[e]less manner and fired his gun off and shot himself in the eye brow. He fell to the ground. The ball had knocked the arch that was over his eye off completely. A small portion of his brain came out. He was carried to his own house and a physician was sent for. The wound was sewed up, the wound partial[l]y healed, but the eye was gone. The ac[c]ident injured the young man's intellect. There was a constant running sore over his eye hole. At length he had fits. He lived for eight years. He married two wives and died soon after he took the last wife, leaving several small children.[15]

There is one other circumstance I will mention which shows what man will attempt when clothed with a little brief authority. A man by the name of Luke under took to travail [travel] from Manti to Salt Creek where Nephi

[12]Berry and Roberts were dispatched from Manti on 23 July 1853 with a message to President Young about the killing of Alexander Keele. For participant John W. Berry's account, see Gottfredson, *Indian Depredations*, 47–48.

[13]New Yorker Zebedee Coltrin (1804–1867) was an early convert, a member of Zion's Camp, and ordained a Seventy by Joseph Smith. He came to Utah in 1847 with the Pioneer Company. Coltrin's first wife died in Kirtland; he married again and in Nauvoo married twice more (one ended in divorce). In Utah he married a fourth wife in February 1857 during the Reformation, but she later divorced him. Cook, *Nauvoo Marriages*, 97; Launius, *Zion's Camp*, 164.

[14]A fanning mill is a square or rectangular box with a crank handle used to clean grains before planting.

[15]This was Pelic Berry Jolley (1834–1862), a cousin of Hicks's wife Betsy, who was from Tennessee. He married two sisters, Sarah and Eliza Knight.

City now stands. The Indians came upon [him] and killed him [and] mutilated his body in the most brutal manner. He was found by some parties from Salt Creek.[16] Word was sent to the various settlements as far north as Provo and a small detatchment of men were called on from the different settlements to go and carry the sad inteligence to the people of Manti and the other settlements in Sanpete Valley.

In Palmyra at that time there was living a young man (the son and only support of a widowed mother) by the name of Charles McKinley.[17] He was the owner of a fine team of horses and when the word came that Luke had been killed, he was ready to start for Salt Lake City. A man by the name of Wesley W. Willis (one of the Mormon Battalion) had been chosen captain of one of the companies. Willis sent an orderly to young McKinley and demanded one of his teams to go to Sanpete on express. McKinley was a young man that had never shrank a duty of any kind, but this time he refused to let the horse go. It was just roll call in the morning. A file of men were sent to the home of McKinley and he was brought out on to the parad[e] ground. Willis asked him if he refused to give up his horse. The young man told Willis his circumstances and in a mild but firm manner, refused to give up his horse. Willis ordered him taken and tied up for insubordination. A strong and brutal man by the name of John Mott took hold of McKinley and felled him to the ground where he was held until handcuffs were brought and put on him. It happened that one "Duff" Potter was present who did not belong to our place. [He] attempted to shoot young Mc., but was prevented.[18]

[16]William Luke, William Reed, James Nelson, and Thomas Clark of Manti were murdered on 1 October 1853 near Salt Creek Canyon while traveling to Salt Lake City with two wagons of wheat. Indians allegedly attacked them at dawn and then mutilated the bodies. Christy, "The Walker War," 411–12. In August 2006 workers excavating a foundation in Nephi unearthed the skeletons of seven Utah Indians, victims of an act of vengeance ordered by Sanpete Stake president Isaac Morley the day after the Luke murders. Martha Spence Heywood felt "this barbarous circumstance" would not have happened had her husband, federal marshal Joseph L. Heywood, accompanied them. The natives, "looking for protection and bread," were summarily "shot down without one minute's notice." See Myrna Trauntvein, "Native American Remains Reveal Evidence of Being Executed," *Nephi Times-News*, 7 June 2007, 1; and Brooks, ed., *Not by Bread Alone*, 1 January 1854, 97.

[17]Charles Dixon McKinlay (1833–1894) of New Brunswick, Canada, came to Utah in 1852 with his mother, Elizabeth Dixon McKinlay, and several siblings. He never married and was the support for his mother. By 1880 Charley was living with his brother George Edward McKinlay and his family in California.

[18]Three and a half years later, Springville resident Gardiner "Duff" Potter, on the instructions of Bishop Aaron Johnson, became involved in a plot to kill William Parrish and his two sons as they attempted to leave for California after losing their faith. Mistaken for one of the sons, Potter was also killed. For details of the Parrish-Potter murders, see Bigler, *Forgotten Kingdom*, 131–32; Aird, "'You Nasty Apostates,'" 173–91; Aird, *Mormon Convert*, 174–77.

McKinley was put under guard and marched around inside the fort. I saw him and [my] sympathies were with poor "Charley," but I could do nothing for him. His horse was taken and he was forced to submit.

The same day, Willis was assisting to build [a] fort wall, and in a conversation with the brave Z. Coltrin, I heard Willis say, "If I had had my holster pistles [pistols] with me, I should have killed him," meaning McKinley. I then said, "Captain Willis, how would you have felt if you had have killed that poor widow's son?" "I," said the brute, "would have felt first rate."[19] "Charley" was, in a few days after the return of his horse, allowed to go on his business trip to S[alt] Lake. Had not a large majority of the people sympatized with the man McKinley, he would have fared worse to say the least.

There was during the summer of the war a man by the name of Joseph Outhouse. He had at one time in his life been a member of the Mormon Church, but had given it up and become an infidel, but he was well respected for his uprightness and general good character. He was an efficient soldier. He, in the spring before the war, began a crop of wheat which was suffering for water. It happened that a crowed [crowd] were talking about the great necessity for rain when Outhouse made the remark that if the Mormon God would send a good rain, he would give Him ten bushels of wheat in the fall. It so happened that the sky was overcast. The same evening and during the night that followed, it began to rain copiously and did not stop until the fields were thoroughly saturated. Tru[e] to his promise, at threshing time he took ten bushels of wheat and put it in the tithing office, telling the bishop it was for God Almighty, to pay for the rain which He had sent him when his wheat was suffering for water in the spring, and Bishop Markham took the wheat and gave Outhouse credit on the books. Outhouse soon went to California.[20]

During the summer of the Indian war, a man by the name of Ferna Tindall, who was once a citizen of Palmyra, was killed at Summit Creek in a field

[19]"The worst report was given of [Willis] being ill to his men," recalled Mormon Battalion veteran John Steele. Leading a detachment to Colorado, Lieutenant Willis crossed the Sangre de Cristo Range in mid-winter. Joseph Skeen said Willis "would threaten to cut their Damned throats and scalp them and to cut them to pieces if they would not keep up when they ware not able to scarcely to walk." Other diaries were equally critical. Bigler and Bagley, *Army of Israel*, 286–95.

[20]Joseph Outhouse (1820–1873) married Charity Holdaway at Nauvoo in February 1846. He captained the fourth company in 1852 but resigned as leader shortly after starting. He left Utah with his wife and her family sometime before 1856, for their only son John was born in California that year. In the 1860 census he is listed as a miner in Sacramento County and in the 1870 census as a farmer in San Luis Obispo County. Nauvoo Temple Records; 1860 U.S. Census, Cosumnes, Sacramento, California, roll M653-63, 405; 1870 U.S. Census, Morro, San Luis Obispo, California, roll M593-87, 286.

LAND OF GOSHEN, 1858

In July 1858 Mounted Rifleman Joseph Heger of the U.S. Army sketched Goshen, a hardscrabble Mormon village about twenty miles southwest of the Hicks family home in Palmyra, Utah. *Courtesy Yale Collection of Western Americana, Beinecke Rare Book and Manuscript Library.*

while at work tending his crop, and after peace was made, an Indian wore his hat into the Palmyra fort and I saw him.[21] At harvest time the Indians came and set fire to a house up on the bottom near the mouth of Spanish Fork Kanyon. The house was the property of Wilson D. Pace. The[y] also killed a number of geese belon[ing] to the Paces.

About 50 men went from Palmyra and trailed the Indians across the bottom and into the brush, but the Indians were gone, but we found out the direction the[y] travailed [traveled] and the trail was followed and the Indians were eventualy found in Goshen Valley where a number of them were killed. They were about to surrender when Col. Stephen Markham came up and ordered the men to fire on the Indians after the most of them had come out of [the] cane that they were hiding in. This act was considdered by many that were ther[e] to be very unjust on the part of Col. Markham. Had it not been for this impetuosity, the Indians could have all been (i.e., those that were

[21]His name is given variously as Furney Tindale (1821–1853) and Firney Tindrell, but his friend Albert Jones gave it as Fernee L. Tindrell. This event took place on 14 October 1853. See Jones's description of the killing in Gottfredson, *Indian Depredations*, 78–82. See also "Indian Difficulties," *Deseret News*, 29 October 1853, 2; and Christy, "The Walker War," 413.

there) brought in without killing any of them. Long after peace was made, the Indians would speak of this act and they always considered it an act of treachery.[22] I was not in this "battle." I was bearfooted and had to go to Salt Lake City and take produce and sell it before I could get a pair of shoes, and while I was gone, this engagement happened. No Mormons were killed.

We were put to great inconvenience by having to stand guard at least two nights out of every week and work in the day time. We made dobies [adobe bricks] and tended our farms. Evy [every] thing had to be done by a force strong enough to defend us against an at[t]ack of the Indians. I remember one circumstance in which I presume a few persons came near losing some of our number: We were in Payson Kanyon drawing logs to a saw mill. We ware about ten or twe[l]ve in force and were at the time I speak of, "mending" the road above the mill. One of our number was on guard a short distance from us, but was som[e]what neglectful of duty. One of these that were at work—a man by the name of Durfey—began to find fa[u]lt with the guard, saying we might all be killed and the guard would not know it. Durfey and the sentinel had some words about the matter. Durfey was then placed on guard.[23] He took his position forty or fifty yards from us on an eminence where he could both see and hear. He came back in a few minutes to where we were at work. He lo[o]ked pale and excited, telling us he heard Indians above us in the Kanyon. We instantly picked up our guns and started up to where he had heard the sound. The Indians no doubt were watching us, for they turned and fled. We came to their tracks. There were but two of them. One had waded the creek and then walked a log that hapened to lie in his way and his tracks were still wet when we came up to them. We tracke[d]

---

[22]John W. Berry recalled "another expedition" on 26 September 1853: "We came to an Indian camp just at day break and took the savages by surprise. As they begged for peace, we told them if they would give up their arms and go to the settlements, we would not hurt them." The militia "dallied with them for some time, as they did not like to give up their arms, that being the last thing an Indian will part with." Colonel Markham gave the Indians five minutes to surrender and then "gave the order for our company to attack. The Indians returned the fire very lively for some time, but our men pressed them so hard that they soon silenced the firing." Those "not killed retreated into a cane swamp" on Utah Lake and escaped. "Casualties on our side were small, considering the smartness of fire of the Indians." Bishop Charles Hancock "was slightly wounded in the head, and one horse shot in the hip." The Indians in the swamp dragged their dead into the cane: "consequently we could not tell how many were killed." Gottfredson, *Indian Depredations*, 50–51. The killings apparently prompted the murder and mutilation of William Luke and three men on 1 October 1853. Christy, "The Walker War," 411.

[23]Born in Ontario, Canada, Royal Durfee or Durfey (1811–1879) converted in 1836 and emigrated from Iowa to Utah in 1852 with his family. They first settled in Palmyra and moved to Pond Town in 1856. He and his wife Lydia Abell Durfey spent the rest of their lives in Salem, Utah.

them into the brush and left them, returning to our work on the road. We were not brought into contact with the Indians any more in the kanyon. It is my opinion that the change of guard was the means of saving at least two of our lives. Had not the Indians been cowards from instinct, many more would have been killed. The Utahs [Utes] were like wolves, only killing the whites when the[y] were assured there own lives were safe.

All earth[l]y things have an end, [and] so it was with the "Walker War," for that is the name by which that war is known in history. The war chief of the Utahs at that time was called Wahker, which signifies "yellow" in English. Early in the winter of 1853 & 4, p[e]ace was made betwe[e]n the Mormons and Utahs, and the Indians agreed to "behave."

I remember well when the first Indians came into the fort at Palmyra. There were three in number. Th[e]y went to the house of Stephen Markham (Col. Markham). I was sent for to act as inturpriter and I went. The Indians were very shy, but at last told their business—that they wanted to be friends with the whites. One old Indian was very spirited in showing the advantages of peace. He took a pipe, filled it with tobacco and "taminump."[24] He lighted the pipe, then held it above his head and in a low guttu[r]al language, offered a kind of prayer to his god. I could not understand all the prayer. The pipe was then passed round and both white men and Indians smoked "p[e]ace." Markham then gave the Indians two guns he had taken at Goshen. The Indians left in peace.[25]

Chapter IX.
A Shower of Grasshoppers: Palmyra Abandoned

After the I[n]dian war was over for that season, we citizens of Palmyra were granted a city charter and a board of officers were elected, consisting of a

[24]"Tahmunump" is a Uintah word referring to tobacco. Thanks to Louisa Rose of Seattle and Venita K. Taveapont of the Ute Language Program for their research.

[25]After the fighting ended, several Utes asked Markham to return their arms. Hicks acted as Numbod's interpreter at that meeting, where the Utes agreed not to take part in another war "but be at peace with the Mormon people," Hicks recalled. Colonel Markham returned their firearms: "A few of us smoked the pipe of peace with the Indians. At the close of the Pow Wow an Indian raised his hands and closed his eyes and offered a prayer of thanks to God asking Him to bless the treaty which we had made, so I know that Indian believed in a Supreme being who could answer prayer. The Indians took their arms and went their way." Hicks, Stephen Markham Biographical Sketch. For a discussion of Brigham Young's policy of defense and conciliation with the Indians, see Christy, " 'Open Hand and Mailed Fist,' " 216–35.

mayor, four aldermen, and nine councillors. John M. Chidester, an old Nauvoo Saint, was the first mayor.[1] I do not remember the names of all the city council.

It was here in Palmyra that I became acquainted [with] one Mr. [Jesse Thompson] Hartley, a "Gentile," the same one that Bill Hickman says he killed by "church orders." Mr. Hartley was a gentleman and scholar. He taught a school in Palmyra and gave general satisfaction. He married a young woman at Provo, Polly Bulloch by name, [whom] I was acquainted with in Iowa. Why he was killed I never knew.[2]

It was in the days of Palmyra when our (B. Young's) legislature held their first session at Fillmore. I remember when they were pas[s]ing through our city—W. W. Phelps was with them—one of our citizens, John W. Berry by name, asked Phelps why he was going, meaning to joke him. But Phelps who was a good joker replied that Br. Brigham was going to Fillmore to make laws and he (Phelps) was goin[g] along to *laugh*. That "joke" was founded on fact. It was a truism, for Brigham Young had power to pass any measure he saw fit. He was pupet king and sole law giver of the Mormon world. By his "council" [*sic*] any man might or might not be sent to the legislature—and no member dare to oppose any measure that the prophet saw fit to have brought forward. In fact, our Territorial elections and the working of our legislature did not come up to the standered [*sic*] of good farces. We no doubt would not have been called on to vote, but such things were necessary to legalize the will of our "Prophet" here in America. But as Jane Taylor has it, "there is an end to all earthly greatness," and so those days are gone to oblivion, never to return, I hope.[3]

Although peace was declared, we did not stop building forts. Although we had been taught that the Lamanite[s] (Indians) were the Lord's battle ax and that they would fight the battles of the Saints, it seemed that the Devil generaly got the handle in his own hands and turned the edge the wrong way, which was construed by our leaders to [into] a whip to scourge us into obedience to the will of God (Brigham Young).

After the Indian war was over, we went to work with new diligence to

[1]John Madison Chidester (1809–1893), born in New York and baptized in 1832, was a member of Zion's Camp in 1834 who later settled in Nauvoo. When the Mormons evacuated Nauvoo, Chidester ferried them across the Mississippi River. He came to Utah in 1851. "Death of John M. Chidester," *Deseret News*, September 16, 1893, 31.

[2]Hicks knew the Bullocks, not Hartley, in Iowa. Hicks probably read Hickman's confession, *Brigham's Destroying Angel*, published in 1872, which described Jesse Thompson Hartley's murder. H. Michael Marquardt's keepsake for this volume's limited edition analyzes Hartley's murder.

[3]English poet Jane Taylor (1783–1824) is best known for "Twinkle, Twinkle Little Star."

build our fort so that we would be prepared for the next out break. We built a house for an old Indian Chief by the name of Peteteneet [Peteetneet]. He was a good old man and always favored peace.[4]

There is one fact I will mention which does not speak very well for the morals of our church, which allows such actions and holds the parties in fellowship. In the town of Palmyra, there was a poor man and his wife came there to make them a home. They had joined the Mormon Church in Wales and had gathered to this modern Zion. The woman was barren. She had recieved a patriarchal blessin[g] in the states from some Mormon patriarch. In this blessing, Sister Hugh[e]s (the man's name being Morgan Hugh[e]s) was promised that she would become a mother if faithful. This good sister believed that it was brother Hugh[e]s that was to blame for her not having *children*. She complained against him. She told her troubles to one Wm. Pace, a man of some note, an American. He was the acting bishop of what was at that time called the Upper Settlement.[5] Pace proposed to take the woman. He allready had one wife and a large family of children. Sister Hugh[e]s left her husband and was sealed by Geo. A. Smith to Bp. Pace at his own house. Although twenty-two years have passed and Pace has been dead a number of years, Sister Hughes is still barren, while Morgan Hughes, who took to himself another wif[e] some two years after his first left, is now the father of a numerous family and is a well respected member of society—so much for patriarchal blessings.[6] I am well known to the above circumstances and am well a[c]quainted with all the parties connected there with.

---

[4]Hicks told how a number of young Indians crowded up to the large table being spread at a Palmyra Pioneer Day celebration, "getting in the way of the waiters and no doubt preparing to help themselves to the victuals when they were put on the table." Special policeman Robert McKell "ordered the young Indians to get out of the way. One of them refused to go, so McKell gave him a light push and shook his club over the Indian's head, but did not strike him." The Utes "strung their bows instantly and prepared to battle. None of us were armed and the Indians would have had a very easy time in killing a lot of us." From the speaker's platform tribal leader Peteetneet ordered his men "to stand back and keep out of the way or he would have them all flogged. He was their chief and they obeyed him, knowing what would follow in case of disobedience. I was present and saw the whole performance. The Indians gave us no further trouble that day," Hicks said. Peteetneet's "home was on the Spanish Fork River and on the Utah Lake at the mouth of the river." Hicks, History of Spanish Fork, 11.

[5]William Franklin Pace (1806–1876) was born in Georgia but grew up in Tennessee, where he married in 1828. He was baptized in 1841 and soon moved with his family to Nauvoo where he became a policeman. The Paces traveled to Utah in the Brigham Young company of 1848. He was bishop of Palmyra from 1851 to 1853, and then of Spanish Fork from 1853 to 1856. In 1862 he was called on the Cotton Mission but settled instead in New Harmony.

[6]Morgan Hughes (1824–1890) came to Utah from Wales in 1852 with his wife Margaret Evans (1825–1912). Margaret Evans married William Pace (1806–1876) in April 1853. Morgan married his second wife, Hannah David, also from Wales, the next December. Hannah proceeded to have thirteen children. William Pace's first wife, Margaret Nichols, had already produced twelve children, but Margaret Evans remained childless.

Myself and two others were chosen in Palmyra to preside over the lesser priesthood. I did my best to magnify my office and calling in the church and was ordained an Elder before I was 21 years of age. I was not as active an Elder as I had been a priest. I dreaded to attend quorum meetings for fear I should be asked to speak, for speaking in public was a great task.[7]

In the spring of 1854, we had put in a very large crop of all kinds of field products and about the middle of July there came a shower of grasshoppers on our crops, but wheat and other small grain was to[o] far advanced for them to do it much harm, but corn and other green crops suffered more or less. The "hoppers" were new to us. We knew nothing of their nature and supposed that when winter should come they would die and that would be the end of them. We had plenty of wheat and were quite indifferent as to what became of the hoppers. The winter came on as usual and the hoppers were forgotten, and when spring came again [in 1855], we started as usual to plow and sow, but the visitors of the autumn before had deposited their eggs in millions and when the [sun] began to warm our grain into life, the eggs began to hatch out and the young "hoppers," which were no larger than half a grain of wheat, began to eat our young grain as it came out of the ground. Although we saw that they were liter[al]ly devouring our crops, we all believed it would spring up again as soon as they passed away, but alas, we were doomed to suffer disap[p]ointment. The grain which was eaten died, [did] not grow, and the ground was left perfectly bare. If we had have known the nature of the insects, we could have saved much of our grain, but we were ignorant and had to suffer. There were a few fought them off and saved their crops.[8]

---

[7]The LDS church has two priesthoods. The Aaronic or lesser priesthood is now for boys, but in the mid-nineteenth century was almost exclusively for men. It has three ranks: deacon, teacher, and priest. The Melchizedek or higher priesthood has elders, high priests, patriarchs, Seventies, and apostles. Older boys, like Hicks, sometimes received ordinations to the office of priest (the term used for only the Aaronic rank), but as a general rule this did not occur until the church-wide announcement in 1877. Priesthood groups or quorums in Hicks's day met once a month at best and, lacking formal lessons to teach, the meetings were basically testimony meetings. Hicks would thus have felt an obligation in an elders quorum to take his turn standing up and speaking to the group. In early Palmyra the priests probably did not have regular meetings unless perhaps a block teacher meeting to go over assignments. Hartley, "From Men to Boys: LDS Aaronic Priesthood Offices"; William G. Hartley, emails to Polly Aird, 10 February 2011.

[8]These were not actually grasshoppers but the now-extinct Rocky Mountain locust, *Melanoplus spretus*. In an outbreak, prevailing winds carried them from the Rocky Mountains to wherever they found food, especially crops. They swept across the land, denuding fields and leaving thousands of eggs to hatch the next year. Upon emerging in the spring, the nymphs gathered in bands and, after developing wings, began to swarm, rising in immense, glittering clouds. Locusts usually ate young grains, but when they arrived well into the growing season in July 1854, they attacked corn, not normally a favored crop. The greatest outbreak of locusts the Mormons ever experienced was in 1855. Lockwood, *Locust*, 9, 21–30.

I presume that the p[e]ople of Spanish Fork lost not less than 800 acres of grain, one half of it at least might could have been saved. If it were asked where was our prophet that he did not tell us how to fight the hoppers, the answer is his inspiration did not lead to any thing useful, but he told us that the grasshoppers were the Lord's army and that God's judgements must commence at the house of God and we believed him correct.[9] The blind lead the blind and we all fall into the ditch together.

The hoppers ate all that was green on the Spanish [Fork] River bottom except some large box elder trees, and on the benches neare the river, there was not a green thing to be seen. About the 10th of June [1855], the "hoppers" began to shed their skins and to fly and by the first of July they had disappeared, leaving desolation and naked fields behind them. Although we generaly had enough potatoes and the like to live upon through the winter at Palmyra, yet many in the Territory suffered for bread.[10] Our situation was precarious to say the least. It was a thousand miles to where we could get supplies. There was no rail road communication in those days, and if there were, we had no money to send off and buy. Many of us suffered for bread the following spring for those who had a sirplus put it up to fablous prices. I will say for one, however—a man by the name of Filo Allen who hap[p]ened to have a surplus sold his flour for six cts. pr. pound when he could have had two or three times that amount just for the asking. A man by the name of John H. Redd sold his for 10 cts, but must have gold. A man by the name of Stewart at Springville sold wheat at five dollars pr. bushel in gold.[11] I do not know of any starving to death.

[9]Two excerpts convey Young's teachings: "You now see one of His armies passing through here, sweeping everything before them. Has He nothing to do with these grasshoppers that are destroying our crops? Yes, as he has with every thing else on the earth. Has He anything to do with the locusts in Egypt? Yes." 3 June 1855, *Journal of Discourses*, 2:308. Young felt the chastisement was "from the hand of the Lord" but considered the crop failures "one of the greatest blessings that could be bestowed upon us," since it was "a prelude, forerunner, or testifier, that afflictions will come upon us, unless we humble ourselves before our God." 8 October 1855, *Journal of Discourses*, 3:116–17.

[10]Hicks later wrote, "We lived on fish, weeds, and milk. There was one weed known as lambsquarter, that was our main support." Commonly called pig-weed, it made "a pretty fair article of food for a few meals" but became monotonous as a steady diet. Local settlers relied heavily on fish from Utah Lake and its tributaries. Hicks, History of Spanish Fork, 9.

[11]Philo Allen (1818–1909) of Connecticut lived in Nauvoo before trekking to Utah in 1849. John H. Redd (1799–1858) came from Tennessee with his wife and six slaves. He became a counselor to Bishop Stephen Markham of Palmyra in 1851. Redd owned a sawmill on the Spanish Fork River that Indians burned during the Walker War. Allred, *Spanish Fork*, 11; Hartley, *My Best for the Kingdom*, 258, 261. Stewart may be John M. Stewart, a counselor to the bishop and a justice of the peace in Springville. J. M. Stewart to the editor, *Valley Tan*, 24 August 1859, 2.

In the year 1855 in the spring, the gover[n]ment of the U. S. established an Indian reservation on the Spanish Fork River on the south side of the river. This "farm" was a great benefit to the poor, hungry Mormons, for it gave employment to many and they were enabled to earn a little money to purchase bread for their families. I feel in duty bound to say for Dr. Garland Hurt—a Virginian—he was a gentleman and a scholar, he was a prom[p]t pay master, and a staunch Democrat in politics, although he was very much apposed to the Mormon faith.[12]

One thing I perhaps shoul[d] have said before—During the time the hoppers were eating our crops, our spiritual advisors got up a sort of religious revival among the people. The[y] told us the "hoppers" were the Lord's army and He had sent them to punish His people for their wickedness. We were told to go and be baptized for the remission of our sins and if we would only repent, the Lord's army would be stayed. We tryed the experiment generaly, but it made no change in the *nature* of the "hoppers." They continued to devour the same after we were baptized as they did before. It is a fact that ignorance and superstition go hand in hand, and those who depend upon God to do work that which they themselves can do have to suffer for the neglect of their own duty. Whether from ignorance or otherwise, prayer had no visable effect on the "Lord's army." If we had turned out in full force and fought them, we might have saved the most part of our grain as we have done since when the "Lord's army" have visited us. Ignorance tho[u] art a great curse! Thou art an evil ruler. Thou art the mother of most of our woes and thy twin sister superstition is the mother of all the rest. We should beware of both.

The industry of the Mormon pe[o]ple is proverbial. We had labored at Palmyra for a little over three years when our prophet Brigham came and told us that our city was in the wrong place. It should have been built on the bench at the mouth of Spanish Fork Kanyon, and in the cou[r]se of his remarks, he said he wished the Utah Lake would raise [*sic*] so high that it would wash the Palmyra Fort away—"not," continued he, "that I want anyone drowned, but this (aluding to Palmyra) is no place for a city." I doubt whether these remarks have a parallel in history. The City of Palmyra was located

[12]Named U.S. Indian agent in September 1854, Garland Hurt arrived in Utah in February 1855. He established several Indian farms, including one on the west bank of the Spanish Fork River. Initially 640 acres, it was enlarged the next April to 12,380 acres. For his life and efforts to help the Indians, see Bigler, "Garland Hurt," 149–70.

by Geo. A. Smith, and we went to work in full faith under his instructions and we labored hard for three years before our leader found out we were in the wrong place. He [Young] had at least visited us twice before and if he knew we were wrong, why had he not told us before we had wasted so much time and labor, for we had little else to lose. The truth is he did not know and when the blunder was apparent instead of saying there had been a blunder, like most tyrants he threw the blame on the people and not on the priesthood where it belonged.[13]

The present beautiful cite [site] of Spanish Fork City is where our city should have been in the first place, but the "inspired" idiots who stood at the head of the uninspired did not think so and the consequence is that thousands of dollars worth of labor was thrown away. I lost two houses, one of which I had just built at a cost of about $300.00 in labor. I did not even live in it an hour, no, not at all.

In the spring of 1856 the people of Palmyra were told to moove up to Spanish Fork City. Although I was much apposed to breaking up my home which I had labored so hard to make, I and my family was the first to moove up. It was no use to stay when the people were gone. In fact, Palmyra never was a suitable location for a city and we only did in mooving that which shoul[d] have been done at first. There was about 80 families in Palmyra or from 400 to 500 persons who lost their labor for from two to three years by following those "inspired" "pro[p]hets, seers and revelators."

I well remember one circumstance which I think almost eaquals oriental tyranny. Once at a [militia] "training" on the public square north of the Palmyra fort, I was there and saw what I am going to write. Geo. A. Smith was there, one of the people from of [*sic*] the upper settlement, John H. Redd by name, walked up to Br. "Geo. A." and said something in an under tone that I could not hear. "No," replied the man of God in a loud voice, "you cannot." This inspired leader then turned half around and in the same loud tone of voice continued, "Br. Redd, the course you are taking is the last remains of an ill-spent, worn out Gentile life." Br. Redd was a man of sense and education. He was also a man of good financial abilaties. He turned a way in seeming sorrow with a down cast look. I made inquiry

[13]After completing the Palmyra fort, the settlers dug a ditch inside the walls and "turned water in at the North-east corner of the fort," Hicks recalled. The ditch made the ground south of the fort "quite moist near the surface rendering the land unfit for building ground, and as time passed, the moisture increased." Hicks, History of Spanish Fork, 10–11.

into the matter and I learned that Br. Redd went and asked Br. "Geo A." in behalf of himself and those who owned land at the upper settlement for the privalege of building a fort on the present cite [site] of Spanish Fork City. The people afterwards got permission from Prest. B. Young and they built a fort in the upper part of the city. I will say for Brigham Young, he was a better financier than Geo. A. Smith.[14]

It is certainly not very strange that people who were led by such men should be poor. I feel in duty bound to relate one more circumstance in relation to John H. Redd. He at the time of the Indian war housed his potatoes at his vacated home, and some of the Palmyra Saints stole a wagon load and brought them to Palmyra. Mr. Redd followed the track of the wagon to the insid[e] of our fort but did not find his potatoes. A few years afterwards, A.K. Thurber's wife, a sister of John W. Berry, told one of my sisters that A.K. Thurber, her husband, and her brother John W. [Berry] had stolen Mr. Redd's pottatoes. A.K. Thurber afterwards became a "great man" in Utah.[15] He went many years to the legislature, but there is not the least doubt in my mind but A.K. Thurber and John W. Berry stole John H. Redd's potatoes [and] used them to feed their famalies. I am quite sure that if the people generaly had have known who stole Mr. Redd's potatoes, they would have informed him and have assisted him to gain his lost property. I do not beli[e]ve that Thurber made his living generaly by stealing, but there was a feeling against the people of the upper "settlement."[16]

As for John W. Berry, he is a good neighbor, but I have no faith in his honesty. I know that a few of the poor and hungry people of Spanish Fork built a bridge across the Spanish Fork River and after it had been built a year or two, the County Court of Utah Co. appropriated three hundred

[14]"Mr. Redd was a man of feeling and high moral sentiments, a man of education, of means and influence among his own people before joining the Mormon Church," Hicks elaborated. Influential leaders whose farms were on the river bottom met and selected H.B.M. Jolley, J.B. Hawks, and John H. Redd "to take the matter up to President Brigham Young," with Redd as spokesman. He "laid the matter before the President showing the advantages it would be to the landowners on the upper river bottom." Young listened closely and told them to "go and build your fort," which "was a victory for the right; a victory which decided the fate of Palmyra. The men came home rejoicing." Hicks, History of Spanish Fork, 11–12.

[15]Born in Rhode Island, Albert King Thurber (1826–1888) came to Utah on his way to California and was one of the few forty-niners to join the Saints. An early settler of Palmyra, Thurber served as bishop of Spanish Fork after John L. Butler's death in 1859, as mayor of Spanish Fork for eight years, as a brigadier-general in the Nauvoo Legion, and as a territorial legislator for seventeen terms. For Thurber's account of his experiences as a gold missionary, see Owens, ed., *Gold Rush Saints*, 268–74.

[16]Redd lived in the upper settlement that became Spanish Fork. The communities took issue with cattle trampling crops. Tullidge, "History of Spanish Fork" (April 1884): 142.

dollars to pay for the bridge, and John W. Berry was "middle man" between the people that built the bri[d]ge and the court. John kept the money and we that did the work lost our pay. I lost $12.00, but such is life.[17]

Chapter X.
When the Wicked Rule: The Reformation

I shall in this chapter ende[a]ver to give a short history of what is known as the Reformation. I know nothing as incorrectly named as that "manifestation," for in truth that is all it was. It began in the autumn of 1855 [1856] at the October conferance by one J. M. Grant, a counsellor to B. Young, and from thence it spread to all the settlements in the Territory and was the cause of a great deal of evil and no doubt some little good.[1] It began, I presume, like most religious revivals—like the Moody & Sankey movements of the present time.[2] There seems to be in all human beings a kind of reverance for the unknown and now and then an individual makes his (or her) appearance and by a kind of magnetic power, the dormant feelings in regard to religion is operated upon, and in ignorant communaties like we were at that time, the masses are made to move in any direction the leaders choose to move them.

When men of virtuous minds—men of intellect—are leading in great movements, then good is accomplished, but when men who are ignorant and vindictive are by circumstances brought into the lead and the masses give way to the dictatorship of such men as our leaders were at that [time], then the country or nation must suffer. For "when the wicked rule, the people mourn."[3] Here in Utah at that time we had but one sentiment and that one was unqualified obedience to our leaders, for we believed them to be at that

[17]The residents of Palmyra greatly expanded the population of Spanish Fork. A timber bridge was built across the river that took a week's labor and cost twelve hundred dollars. "Trip to Iron County," *Deseret News*, 1 July 1857, 5. "The settlers built the county bridge by donations." Tullidge, "History of Spanish Fork" (April 1884): 142.

[1]When the Reformation began is open to debate. March 1856 brought vindictive, violent language from Young and his counselors, but most date it to early September 1856, when Young launched a full program of reform. In October, Young appointed "home missionaries" to call the people to repentance. Peterson, *The Mormon Reformation*, 15–23.

[2]Dwight Lyman Moody (1837–1899) held enormous revivals in 1875 and 1876, starting a great religious awakening that blazed across the northern United States. More than two million Americans of all Protestant affiliations attended his meetings in Brooklyn, Philadelphia, New York City, and Chicago. Ira D. Sankey (1840–1908), known as "The Sweet Singer of Methodism," wrote gospel hymns and sang them at Moody's revivals.

[3]Proverbs 29:2; *D&C* 98:9.

time the mouth pieces of Jehovah. No man in the last century has had as good an opertunity to build up a good and virtuous community as Brigham Young has had. For many years he was the sole dictator of all classes of society. At the beginning and during the first stages of the Reformation, the people of Utah believed as he did, thought as he thought, and wept or smiled when he smiled. When he said Adam was the god of this world, the people believed it or pretended to believe it. In all mat[t]ers he was the sun of our systim. Many of the people of Utah were supersticious in the extream. I have seen a few of those who were once follow[er]s of Father Miller and had long been looking for the "true church."[4] Ignorance and superstition generaly go hand in hand and we were at that time afflicted with both.

J.M. Grant at the conferance struck the keynote of the pe[o]ple's feeling. He told us we were the Kingdom of God—that God had brought His people out from the nations of the Earth while the scourges should pass over the nations (the Rebelion in the southern states was just culminating at that time), and we, His chosen people, were fast asleep. It was our duty to wake up and prune the Lord's vin[e]yard, to realize our positions that before long we would be the head and not the tail—the wicked Gentiles would soon all be destroyed and we the Saints should inherit the Earth. We had always been taught that the "Earth is the Lord's and the fullness there off [*sic*]," and that he had and would provide for his Saints.[5] Brigham Young (who no doubt lived and died an atheist)[6] saw in the Reformation a grand opertunity for to get more power and to crush out all vestage of free thought and selfhood. [He] put himself at the head of the movement giving it a double force. He put a class of men in the field that he knew would do exactly as he told them, men who had become known by their fanatical obedience to the will of the "prophet."

Having given the foregoing general out line of society at that time, I shall now confine my self more particularly to Spanish Fork City. I well remember

---

[4]A product of New York's Burned-Over District, Baptist literalist William Miller (1782–1849) declared in about 1833 that, based on the prophecies of Daniel, the Second Advent of Jesus would take place in or before 1843. At least fifty thousand, perhaps many more, awaited the Second Coming. After the Great Disappointment of 22 October 1844 when Christ did not reappear, many of his followers joined groups such as the Shakers. The remnant Millerites eventually became the Advent Christian Church and the Seventh-day Adventist Church. Hicks had probably seen Millerites in Nauvoo. John Taylor wrote in the *Times and Seasons* in March 1844 that "proselytes of Miller are also holding forth in this city, as well as in all the principle cities of the west." See Underwood, *The Millenarian World of Early Mormonism*, 119–20.

[5]Psalm 24:1.

[6]Hicks explains later why he believed Young must have been an atheist.

when the first Reformation missionaries came to Spanish Fork City. They gave out an appointment for a meeting, but I had some work in the field and did not attend, but on my way home in the evening, I stoped at the house of a neighbor and was told of the wonderful preaching. "Anything new?" I asked. "Yes, all new," said my informant. I was then told that there was to be a meeting that night.[7]

I went to the meeting. It was held in the open air inside of our fort. The meeting was largely attended. The first speaker was John Young, a brother to Prest. Brigham Young. He quoted from the 25th chapter of Mathew, 6th verse. At midnight there was a cry made, "Behold the bridegroom cometh," etc. etc. The speaker thought it was about midnight with the Saints. He thought they had no oil in their lamp[s], that they were all asleep and that the bride groom would soon come and who among you are prepared to meet him? He handled the subject in an earnest and exciting manner. I noticed that he seemed more interested and interesting than I had ever known him before. He held the congr[eg]ation as it were spell bound. I felt my self giving way to his influence. After he closed, J. V. Long, a man of schollarly attainments, arose and in a very eloquent manner "bore testimony to the truth of" Br. Young's preaching.[8]

By this time the congregation were completely under [their] control. The meeting was then given over to the people and a general invitation was given to all who wished to speak. Although it was getting late, the congrigation did not seem the least tired. The first one of the audience that arose was a young man by the name of K. T. Butler, a son of Bishop J. L. Butler who I shall speak of farther on.[9] Although young Butler was not a man of good morals, yet he spoke in a very forcible manner such as I never had heard of him or in fact any young man speak. I saw and felt there was an "inspiration"

[7]As Jedediah M. Grant toured northern Utah preaching the Reformation, John Young, the eldest brother of Brigham Young, set off south with home missionaries John V. Long, Daniel D. Hunt, and Joseph G. Hovey. They reached Spanish Fork on 27 September 1856. For three days they held three meetings a day. "Minutes of a Quarterly Conference Held in Spanish Fork City," *Deseret News*, 22 October 1856, 2.

[8]English convert John Varah Long (1826–1869) began recording Mormon sermons in Pittman shorthand in April 1852. Until his excommunication in June 1866, Long worked for the *Deseret News*, served as a clerk for Brigham Young, and frequently reported on Young's travels. "Long had become too fond of liquor and wine and having attended so many private meetings and conferences," Juanita Brooks speculated, "could not be trusted to be discreet in his talk." Brooks, *On the Mormon Frontier*, 723n25.

[9]Kentuckian John L. Butler (1808–1860) joined the LDS faith in 1835, became a Danite in Missouri, served as a bodyguard to Joseph Smith, and entered polygamy in Nauvoo. He and his families came to Utah in 1852, and he was bishop of Spanish Fork from 1856 until his death in 1860. Kenion Taylor Butler (1831–1886) was his oldest son.

about him that was not common. He ended by declaring that he knew this is the Kingdom of God.

The next speaker was a woman by the name of Sarah Broomhead. She, as it hap[p]ened, was said to be at that time making to[o] familiar with the young man she afterwards married. She was at that time a widow with one child and I know not whether her husband was living or dead.[10] She arose and began to speak in tongues. This was the first time I had heard anyone spake in tongues in a public meetin[g] in Utah. She was followed by a good man—a Welsh man by the name of David Davis who gave the interpretation of her toungue.[11]

I was the next speaker. Although I had been raised in the Mormon Church, I never had spoken to a general audience. I felt an irresistable power which I could scarce control impeling me to arise and say something. I yelled and a power which was new to me took possession of my speaking organs and spoke as it were through me and I listened like the rest of the people present. My heart and feelings under went a change. I was filled with love for the whole human race. I felt like a new being, my mind was filled with a kind of confused light. I saw as it were "through a glass darkley."[12] I could see beauties in the "Gospel" that I had never seen before. I felt as thoug[h] it was not only a duty but a priviliege to serve God. I felt as though my sins were all blot[t]ed out of the Book of Remembrance. I was quite sure that Mormonism was true, and I thought I could convince all the world of the truth of our religion, and I longed for a chance to tell the "glad news" to others. I am very bashful by nature, but when under the influence I forgot all bashfulness: "perfect love casteth out all fear."[13]

I presume in giving a description of my feelings, I give the feelings of a large majority of new converts to religion, and I am quite sure that all

---

[10]English convert Benjamin Broomhead (1825–1855) died in St. Louis in June 1855, leaving his wife, Sarah Jarvis Broomhead (1826–1904), to cross the plains with an infant and a three-year-old. Sarah married William Banks at Spanish Fork in early December 1856, about two months after this September evening, when Hicks felt she was "making too familiar" with Banks.

[11]David Thomas Davis (1819–1905) is believed to have come to Utah in 1856 in a wagon company.

[12]1 Corinthians 13:12.

[13]1 John 4:18; Moroni 8:16. On the evening of 28 September a clerk described what took place: "Br. Hunt gave liberty for the brethren and sisters to free their minds, as they should be dictated by the Spirit. Many bore testimony, and the Spirit of God was in our midst." The next morning Hunt said, "he felt as though angels were in our midst." At the end of the third day, "the brethren and sisters had liberty to free their minds, which they did by pouring forth the fullness of their souls for the great manifestations of the power of God." "Minutes," *Deseret News*, 22 October 1856, 2.

those who were honestly brought under the "influence" felt as I did. I have no doubt thatt [*sic*] all converts to all "Christian" denominations feel as we felt. There was at that time living at Spanish Fork a man by the name of Moses T. Shepherd who had been a Methodist.[14] I talked with him about our meetings and about the good "spirit" that we all recieved. Br. Shepherd said it was just like getting religion at a Methodist meeting, only at our meeting we did not shout but the feeling was the same, and I believe he was right. I think there is a strong similarity between all religious revivals. Although nearly a quarter of a century has passed, I am still at a loss to know from what source the power comes: Is it of man or is of God or is [it] the influence of unseen spirits who are around us and are ever ready to make themselves *felt*? Mormons say it is the power of the Holy Ghost, Spiritualists say it [is] spirits, the Methodists say it [is] "grace." Alas, alas! How little we [know] about "the way to be saved."

Some 20 years after the Reformation I read a number of Mr. Moodey's sermons and I acknow[l]edge they made some impression on my mind and in a small degree produced the same feelings, and if I had have heard Moody as I did [John] Young, perhaps I might have been "converted." I am only human. I think a particular kind of argument when brought to bear on a certain class of minds will produced an effect in spite of us. When we hear argument sufficiently potent, we are bound to yield and we cannot help our selves. There fore it is our duty to carefully weigh all ideas in the balance of *Reason* before we adopt them, and [if] your mature judgement is fully convinced, then it [*sic*] and not until then does it become our duty to adopt any new idea.

I think that Spiritualism is the foundation of all religions.[15] I think that man has made the distinction in all churches. I think that priests are the cause of the hatred which exists between "Christians." When men of brutal dispositions get into power in the church, they worship a brutal god and they teach a brutal faith, and when a community beli[e]ve in an infalible

[14]Born in Ohio, Moses Trader Shepherd (1820–1866) served in the Mormon Battalion and settled in Palmyra in 1852.

[15]Like Mormonism, modern spiritualism began in upstate New York and claimed direct revelation from beyond our material world. Horace Greeley; Robert Dale Owen, son of the social reformer; and Senator Nathaniel P. Tallmadge became adherents and the movement claimed millions of followers in the 1870s. Spiritualism seemed to offer empirical proofs of life after death and immortality; it incorporated faith healing, the bestowal of the Holy Spirit through the laying on of hands, and belief in spiritual communication between minds. For Mormons who became spiritualists and connections between the two movements, see Walker, *Wayward Saints*, and Hazen, *The Village Enlightenment in America*.

priesthood, and believe that a class of men stand betwe[e]n them and salvation, although they may know full well that the priesthood has forsaken the gospel, the majority are loth to say so and for fear of offending God, they will let the most overt acts pass for a time in silance untill some leading sp[i]rit shall arise to awaken the sleeping public.

After the first out burst of the Reformation, we held meeting[s] without any one from Salt Lake City to take the lead. Bp. John L. Butler soon became a very active man in awakening the people to the importance of taking a part in the Reformation. He choose a number of men whome he called teachers. The men were called togather night after night and were taught "in the true light of the Gospel." After the "bishops" [were] through, they were sufficiently "awake." They were sent round to hold meetings at private houses. Four of the men were placed over four districts of the city and were called "ward bishops." There names were as follows: Levi N. Harmon of the first ward. Levi was a good man and no fanatic, but a sincere Saint. The name of the "bishop" of the 2nd ward was Chas. A. Davis. He was from the state of Massachusetts and was very fanatical. The name of the 3d bishop was Henry Garfield. He was from England and was a very good man, but somewhat inthusiastic. The name of the 4th ward bishop was S.R. Wells. He was from London. He was a man of some education and a good deal of common sense.[16]

In connection with the four l[e]ading teachers, there was a number of other teachers called into the "field" to assist in waking up the people.[17] I will give the names of a few of the most fanatical of these men: James G. Higginson, Edmond Ellis, and John P. Chidester.[18] These three were very fond of telling the people to wake up. Higgi[n]son and Ellis were at that

[16]Levi N. Harmon (1829–1874), born in Pennsylvania, settled in Palmyra in 1852 and married in 1854. Charles A. Davis (1810–1897) came to Palmyra in the fall of 1851. In 1853 he was made the town's postmaster and later also held the position for Spanish Fork. English converts Henry H. Garfield (1826–1888) and his wife arrived in Utah and settled in Palmyra in 1852, where he took a plural wife. Born in London, Stephen Robert Wells (1822–1889) married an English woman in Kanesville, Iowa. He emigrated to Utah in 1851 and settled in Palmyra, where he took an English second wife in 1857. That same year, in Spanish Fork, he played the part of Heber C. Kimball in a play called "Priestcraft in Danger." A polygamist, he had two English wives and six children when he moved to St. George. For the play, see Huff, *Memories that Live*, 398.

[17]At this time teachers held the Aaronic priesthood and were mature, capable men who functioned as the bishop's right hand, checking the spiritual and temporal welfare of each family in the ward and acting as peace officers to mediate disputes.

[18]Englishman James Greenwood Higginson (1833–1902) married his American wife in Spanish Fork in 1856 and served in the handcart rescue. Agricultural laborer Edmond Ellis was born in 1832 in Devon, England. Baptized in 1854, he came to Utah in 1855. With his wife and two young children, he left Mormonism for California in 1859.

time ignorant young men. They were English men and each had a broad accent. We often held meetings at private homes, and here these "teachers" would come to preside and give those that were considdered to be in the dark proper instructions. Higginson would say "Wack oop, you hin the dark! Why don't you 'ave the *spurit* of God like Br. Hellis and oi?" It was quite a common thing for these two young fools to tell old and tried members of the church that they were on the broad road to Hell and command them in the most authoritative maner to "wack oop" and repent of their sins.

It was in those fanatical days that Brigham Young put forth the idea that Adam was the god of this world, that he was the head of the human race and naturaly had the right to [be] a god unto his own children. We were taught that by obedience we might *all* become gods and have thrones and dominions, and the Gentiles were to be our servants in the next world if not in this.[19] It was surprising how eagerly those fanatics grasped the idea: We ware all gods in embryo. Adam is a god, "the pro[p]het says so and that is enough for me," the teachers would say. Adam who was once a man had become a god, we his children by followin[g] in his footsteps may also become gods. The idea was carried still farther than this, for some believed that Prest. Young was very near to being a god at present. Charles A. Davis at a meeting one night in my hearing said when talking on the god subject that "father Adam was the great god of this world. He (Adam) was Jesus Christ's god, and Jesus is Br. Joseph Smith's god, and Br. Joseph is Brother Brigham's god and Br. Brigham is Bishop John L. Butler's god, and John L. Butler is your god. Do you hear it breathren?" said he with all the seeming confidence of an early Saint.[20] There were perhaps not more than half the people who believed these teachings, but people dare not get up and dispute them, for who knows who is god or where he dwel[l]s.

There was one part of our faith that [was] more particularly put in practice than any of the rest, and that was polygamy. That, with some of our teachers, was the most prominent point of their faith. The young girls of

[19]Brigham Young began preaching his Adam-God doctrine in April 1852 and again at fall conference in October 1854. He said that Adam had come from another planet and brought Eve, one of his wives, with him, and that Adam was the same as God and the father of Jesus Christ, a doctrine since abandoned. Collier, comp., *The Teachings of President Brigham Young*, 71–98, 343–74.

[20]In a similar vein, Heber C. Kimball said on 10 April 1852: "Some have said that I was very presumptuous to say that Brother Brigham was my god and savior—Brother Joseph was his god—the one that gave Joseph the Keys of the Kingdom was his god, which was Peter. Jesus Christ was his god and the God and father of Jesus Christ was Adam." Collier, comp., *The Teachings of President Brigham Young*, 95.

Spanish Fork were fairley besieged by men old enough to be their fathers. The young women from 13 to 16 years of age were many of them sealed to men three times their own age. The girls were told that if any faithful man made them an offer of marriage, it was their imperative duty to except [accept] the offer. An old and tried man in the gospel [was] more capable of giving a high degree of glory than a young and untried man. Zebbedee Coltrin was very active in preaching this doctrine. I have heard it said that during the two years while the "Reformation" was raging that there were 1500 marriages in Utah and that the year after, there were 1700 divorces given by B. Young to dissatisfied parties. How much truth there is in the answer I am unable to say. I presume it is not far from correct to say that perhaps not more than one in ten of these plural marriages which were solemnized in the Reformation remained in that state for more than one year and many of them only a few months.[21]

Although our prophet told the women that his "bills" of divorce were of no value, he was not slow in giving them to any one who had the money to pay for them. Ten dollars was the price paid for each divorce. I know that to be the price for I acted as agent for one of my own sisters who was inveigled into a plural marriage.[22] This was a very lucrative business for our prophet, seer, and revelator to be ingaged in. He must have made from $500 to $10,000 out of the business.[23] O for shame that men will suffer the love of gold to cankir their souls that the[y] will take advantage of the ignorant to get gain. Can it be possable that anyone who believes that a time is coming when they shall be rewarded for their good acts and punished for their bad ones would thus rob their ignorant followers? Certainly not Brigham Young; [he] must have been an atheist.

---

[21]As plural marriages were not recorded, subsequent divorces cannot be tracked accurately. One study showed that in 1856–57, plural marriages rose 65 percent over any other two-year period. Brigham Young granted 1,645 divorces during his presidency. Of twenty-six plural wives married at Manti during the Reformation, ten later divorced, seven of them within five years. Ivins, "Notes on Mormon Polygamy"; Quinn, ed., *The New Mormon History*, 171–72, 181; Daynes, *More Wives Than One*, 165–66.

[22]This was Caroline Hicks (1844–1878), who married A. K. Thurber on 21 March 1857, in the Salt Lake City Endowment House during the Reformation marriage frenzy when she had just turned thirteen. Returning from the sealing ceremony, Caroline locked Thurber out of the bedroom. Along with John Moore, Hicks helped her escape, and the three rode back to Salt Lake City to get the sealing canceled. In 1860 she married Moore and eventually had eight children. See Lewis, Caroline Hicks.

[23]Hicks is correct: $10.00 per divorce was the fee Young usually charged. Hardy, *Doing the Works of Abraham*, 180. If Young granted 1,645 divorces (see note above) and the fee remained the same, he would have made $16,450.

In our little city of Spanish Fork, there were but three girls who stood out against the "old men." I will give their names: Lucilla Beck, Jane Buchannan, and Polly Ann Dorrity. I think they deserve a name in history for their moral courage and good sense. Polly Ann Dorrity was a cousin of my wife's and I am well known to what she had to endure to remain single. She had no less than five married men at the same time offering her salvation, and among the number was the president of the branch, J. W. Berry, who came very nea[r] taking her off [as] her father favored this suit. One day after the time was set for them to go to Salt Lake City to go through the Endowment House, Polly Ann came in to the room where her father was and bursting into tears declared that if she was forced to marry John W. Berry, she would destroy her own life. This declaration reached her father's sympathy. Her father was not a bad man, only blinded by fanaticism. Br. Berry was informed of the change of mind and took back some presents he had given her.[24]

Johnathan McKee, one of the teachers, was doing his utmost to get the same girl. Johnathan had a wife and a large family. He was determined to obtain her hand. He went so far as to say that an Angel of the Lord had visited him and told him it was his duty to take Polly Ann and it was her duty if she wished to be saved to mar[r]y him. The girl's mother believed the story and urged her to obey, but her father thought the Angel should have visited him or his daughter and Br. McKee failed in gaining his object. Johnathan McKee is now a firm "Josephite" notwithstanding he had an holy Angel point out his duty. He must have willfully lied about the Angel to make a point and to gratify his lustful nature.[25]

One feature of the Reformation was that we were particularly fond of fighting our enemies, the Gentiles. I well remember Br. Johnathan McKee making the following remark: "I want to be prepared to fight our enemies and when I do go to fight them, I would rather go full of the spirit of God, without arms, than to go destitute of that spirit with a sword in each hand and a cannon on [at] my back." Johnathan was a fair specimin of our fighting men in church,

[24]Anna Lucilla Beck (1838–1918) married John Wesley Snell (1834–1911) in March 1857; Eliza Jane Buchanan (1836–1922) married James Greenwood Higginson in January 1856; and Mary "Polly" Ann Dorrity (1840–1866) married Albert Gay (1833–1916) in 1866. None married men more than seven years older than they. John W. Berry was eighteen years older than Polly Ann Dorrity.

[25]In 1856 Pennsylvanian Jonathan McKee (1821–1895) had five children. He and his wife emigrated from Iowa to Utah in 1852 and returned to Iowa about 1864, where he joined the Reorganized Church of Jesus Christ of Latter Day Saints.

and we had many such. Religious fanaticism intensifies the passions of men and carries them off in what ever direction their inclinations lead them.

It was during the Reformation that that horable doctrine known as "blood atonement" was first preached in Utah. John Young, the same one man that started the Reformation in Spanish Fork, I heard him preach the first Reformation sermon. He said there were hypocrites in Zion and that were not fit to live and the time had come that their blood would have to be shed to save them and, he continued, "If you sho[u]ld find your fathers or your mothers by the way side with their throats cut, go on about your own business and say nothing about it, for it would be all right. Zion must be purified."

George A. Smith preached the same doctrine at Payson, but I did not hear him. A.K. Thurber, the first councillor of J. L. Butler, often gave us a blood atonement sermon and I have heard him. I believe that Heber C. Kimbal was the first to preach blood atonement in Salt Lake City.[26] This preaching soon began to have an effect throughout the country and many were the victims that fell by the hand of the destroyer, but not one in Spanish Fork City.[27] My wife and myself both saw the blood of the Parishes at Springville two days after the murder. Those were truly peralous times such as only fanatics [k]now how to bring on a country.

Chapter XI.
Light and Darkness: Religious Life in Spanish Fork

In this chapter I will try to give a faithful description of one of our evening meetings. These meetings were generaly held at private houses and sometimes at the ward s[c]hool houses. The neighbors would generaly gather at the largest house—from 50 to 75 persons. Then if there was none of the "teachers" present, some one else having the high priesthood would be chosen to presid[e].

---

[26]As not all sermons were published, one cannot say definitively who preached the doctrine first. On 2 March 1856, Brigham Young and Jedediah Grant and, to a lesser extent, Heber C. Kimball all preached blood atonement. *Journal of Discourses*, 3:221–36.

[27]Hicks is referring to a number of known murders besides the attempt to kill drifters John G. Ambrose and Thomas W. Betts in February 1857 on the Santa Clara River: in March 1857, William and Beason Parrish outside Springville; in September 1857, the Mountain Meadows massacre; in October 1857, Richard E. Yates in Echo Canyon; in November 1857, six members of the Aiken party; in January 1858, Henry Forbes in Springville; in April 1858, Henry Jones and his mother, she in Payson, he on the road between Payson and Pond Town. MacKinnon, "'Lonely Bones'"; and Aird, Letter to the editor, vi–vii.

We always sang a hymn, generaly Eliza R. Snow's hymn w[h]ich is called "O My Father," or some appropriate hymn. After singing, the "president" or some one that he would call upon would offer prayer. These pray[e]rs were generaly about the same. The president of the church and his council were always held up to Devine notice as being worthy objects of His special care, then came the twelve apostles who were immediately associated with them, then all those who were preaching the gospel in foreign lands. These ware particularly commend[ed] to the "kind care and keeping of Jehovah." Then the sick and the afflicted "among thy people, Oh Lord." Then the praye[r] became more general and finally the present congregation was brought to the notice of [the] Deity. Then came the Amen.

After pray[e]rs, we then sang a second hymn. Then the presiding officer would arise and make a few remarks, something like the following: "Brethren and sisters," (he always began in that way), "I feel thankfull for the priviliege of standing before you and bearing my testimony. I know this is the Kingdom of God, set up in these the last days (see Hebrews 1 chap. 1st & 2nd verses), no more to be thrown down nor given to an other people (Daniel 2:44 vs.). I feel it is a duty to live my religion and do as I am told. In fact, living our religion consists in doing as we are told by the authoraties that are placed over us by the Almighty." Then God was again asked to bless us all.

Then the meeting was given into the hands of the congregation with the priviliege to anyone to speak that wished, both men and women. *Then meeting began*. Br. John Boyce, if he was present, was always ready to say something.[1] Br. Boyce was very inthusiastic—was always full of the spirit (he was left-handed in gestures). He was much edified by the remarks of Br. Chidester or Br. McKee or any other brother who had spoken. Br. Boyce was very fond of speaking in tongues. These tongues are almost beyond my power to describe. While I believe in the spiritual gift of tongues as it is often spoken of in the New Testiment, Br. Boyce made him self rediculous with his tounges. I have often seen and heard him. I saw him one night get up to speak. His eyes looked wild and starring. He seemed to be under a high degree of excitement when he began to give utterence to a stream of (to me) uninte[ll]ig[i]ble sounds, not unlike what any unknown tongue might sound

[1]Born in Ontario, John Boice or Boyce (1814–1886) married in Kirtland in 1840 after his first wife and a son had died and was endowed in Nauvoo. He came to Utah in 1852 with his new wife and at least five children, settling in Palmyra.

to an ear not familiar to it. His whole body was subject to the most violent gesture. He had not spoken but a very short time when he began to jump sideways very rapidly, firs[t] to the right and then to left in rapid succession, at the same time extending both his hands in the same direction and snapping his thumbs and fingers. His movements were very rapid. He then began to dance or rather to jump up and down very rapidly, then he began to talk and gesticulate as if he were talking to people in a circle around him. After the elap[s]e of about 15 minutes, he sat down seemmingly exhausted.

Br. Zebadee Coltrin got up immediately to give an interpritation to Br. Boyce's maneuvering. He told us that Br. Boyce was giving us a spiritual imitation of the Laplanders and if any of us were to see a Laplander under the influence of the spirit of God, he would act just as we had seen Br. Boyce act. Br. Coltrin's interpritation gave entire satisfaction to all present. I believe there is no end to the theories of religion and it is posable that Br. Coltrin may be right in his theory. My opinion is that Br. Boyce was undere the influence of some delusive spirit.

There were quite a number of other persons who made a practice of talking in tounges at our evening meetings. Among these was a sister Bonner, a Welsh woman with quite a large family.[2] I well remember her tounges. I heard it so often that I think I could speak it quite fluently at the present time. It was like this: "Tickrevisee, tickreviso," never varying the three vowel sounds "i," "e," and "o." At times she would occupy ten minutes in repeating theses [*sic*] two words or sentences. At times she would vary the monotony of the "tounge" by speaking it fast or slow as ocation [occasion] required, and at other times I have heard her emphasize the first syllable, giving it the sound "tee-ee-eek," but always ended with "reviso." I have heard her sing the same thing many times and give the interpretation which was about as monotinous as the tounge. It was generaly something like this: "The Lord is well pleased with His people for they are striving to keep His commandments, they are building up His kingdom in these the last days, and He will bless them," etc. I doubt whether there was a single individual in Spanish Fork who believed that Sister Boner's tongue was any thing but a humbug of Sister B.'s own invention, although it passed for genuine at the meetings.

It was at these meetings where the breathren bore their testimony to the truth of Mormonism. Many a brother and sister I have heard, when standing

[2]This may be Ann Boner or Bonner, born about 1806. In the 1860 census she and husband, William, a carpenter, were living in Fairfield, Utah, with two nearly grown children, all born in Wales.

up in these meetings, say they knew that Joseph Smith was a prophet of God and that Brigham Young was his legal successor. A testimony was like this generaly: "I know this is the Kingdom of God for the spirit of God has revealed it to me. I know it for myself and not for another." I have been at a Methodist class [camp] meeting and I think there is a great similarity between the two meetings. The Methodist groans instead of speaking in tounges.

My opinion is this about speaking in tounges: I believe it is a spiritual manifestation. I believe that the spirit of some one who has departed this life takes possession of the speaker and speaks through them. I never have spoken in tongues, but I have given the interpritation and I know there is a power or a sp[i]rit connected with it. I felt after hearing the "toungue," I felt a strong desire to arise and speak to which I yealded and I did so. When I had commenced to speak, I lost all control of myself and became a listener as the "spirit gave me utterance," and when the spirit had said what it had to say, I was left to exercise my own will and to wonder at the manifestation. I presume the gift of toungues is the same as the interpritation. We know it is a power, but what is it we know not. To me it is a strong proof of the truth of the spiritual gifts spoken of in the second chapter of the Acts of the Apostles.

I will relate a case of healing the sick by laying on of hands at one of these meetings. I was present and know of what I write. The meeting was at my father's house. A man by the name of Thomas McKee, a brother to Joh[n] athan, had been in a poor state of health for about thre[e] months, but was not entirley bedfast.[3] He was bar[e]ly able to go out to these meetings when they were held neare to his own house. One night he asked the Elders to lay hands on him and pray for him, which they did as follows: The Elde[r]s formed a circle around him and one of them prayed and rebuked the disease in the name of Jesus Christ. In a few minutes, after they had concluded the cerimony, Br. McKee got up and told the congregation that he was healed and he went forth in sound health and he remained in good health long after wards. I know him well.

I think we do not understand the principle by which the sick are healed. I think it is more than likely it is the laying on of the hands that heals the sick and not the pray[e]rs. I on[c]e had a spiritualist lay hands on me for a head ache and was heal[e]d immediately. I believe that any numbere of

[3]David Thomas McKee (1817–1875) was born in Pennsylvania, married in Illinois in 1841, and emigrated west in 1853 with his wife and four children, two of whom were born in Council Bluffs. The next child was born in Palmyra in 1854. Thomas remained in the LDS faith.

healthy persons who were united in their faith might benefit the sick by laying on hands. I am of the opinion that the reason the Methodists and other denominations do not heal the sick is because they have not the faith to try to do it. A Mormon elder will tell you that it is the power of the Holy Priesthood by which the sick are healed. If that is the case, why did not Jesus or the apostles in his time make some mention of the priesthood as a healing power? But they did not do so and after Jesus was taken away, they did not call in the aid of any "Holy Priesthood." See Acts 4 ch[apter] 10 vs. [verse]; 9 ch, 17 vs; 39 & 40th, same chap[ter] [i.e., Acts 4:10 and 9:17, 39–40]. It is evident that the priesthood idea has been taken from the Jews and the heathen nations around them. Jesus denounced the priests of the Jews in the powerful language and in my opinion, all men who claim any pri[e]sthood from God are nothing but impostures [impostors].[4]

Like all public excitement, the Reformation had its time of existance, and time, the cure of all evils, has swept it away and but very little remains excep[t]ing a history of the evil deeds of those that were in power in the Church. I am quite sure that the "Reformation" left the church in Utah in a worse situation by far than it found it. Our history was at that time but little stained with blood, but now with the single exception of Spanish Fork City, I do not know a city that had an existence in Utah that has not shed the blood of from one to many victims, and although times have changed and the fanatical rule of the priesthood is in a measure broken, it will be many generations before the blood staine[d] spots will be effaced from [the] character of the Mormon Church.

There are many in this country who are anxious for the priesthood to rule supreme in the land. God forbid. The return of pr[i]estly rule in Utah would no doubt bring back all the atendant evils that afflict all pr[i]est-ruled countries. There must exist two parties, for one party that is wholy ameanable to itself—is its own judge and jury—is sure to carry out its own will and to cover up it[s] own faults, while the ignor[ant] in society are kept in awe of the priest whow they [thus] stand[s] between them and God. There are two principles in all nature: male and female, cold and hot, light and darkness, good and evil, and even positive and negative electricity, and it is right and proper that there should be two parties in religion as well as politics, for one will watch the other and keep them from many crimes that otherwise

[4]Hicks wrote this when he was estranged from the LDS church. He had been ordained a Seventy, a Melchizedek priesthood office, in April 1857 at Spanish Fork. Record of Fiftieth Quorum of Seventies, 4–5.

would be commited. I think that education and an exchange of ideas is all that can change fanatics into good and reasonable citizens.

I will relate one circumstance that I know to have transpired in Spanish Fork City. [There was] a man by the name of James A. Riley who had a dificulty with one of the brethren which resulted in a bishop's trial before John L. Butler of Spanish Fork in which Riley was disfelowshipe[d] from the church.[5] Riley asked for the papers containing the minits [minutes] of the trial. Butler told Riley to come the next Saturday and he could have the papers. Riley wished to take an appeal to the High Council. I hapened to be present at the time and heard Riley ask for the papers. When Riley came, Bp. Butler had prepared a hawthorn stick ab[o]ut the size of a small walking cane, and when Riley came, Butler gave him a severe floging over the back and sholders, wearing the stick to a boom at the end. Butler was a very large and strong man, and Riley was rather above the average for size and strength, but he made no attempt to defend himself against the at[t]acks of Butler. Riley was no doubt afraid it would cost him his life if he would have resisted the bishop, which no doubt would have been the case in those times of fanatical rule.

When the bishop was questioned as to why he did so, he replied that God had given him a revelation and had commanded him to give Riley a floging when he came for the minits of the trial. He (Butler) had went in secret prayer befor[e] God and had asked Him what he should do with Riley, and it was made known to him what to do, and he had only carried out the will of God in the matter. Riley prefered a charge against Butler before the High Council at Provo and Butler was summoned to answer, whi[ch] he did and plead the revelation as a justification of his act, but the High Council did not except [accept] that as sufficient grounds for such an act and decided that Bp. Butler was "a little to[o] fast" and that (Butler) he shoul[d] come home and make a public confession before the assembled people of Spanish Fork City, which he did in my hearing.[6]

A.K. Thurber, the first councillor of Bp. Butler, felt himself "in duty bound" to confess also in public, which he also did. He stated that the bishop had *asked him* what he should do with Riley, and he had told the

[5]James Anderson Riley was born in Tennessee in 1826 and baptized in 1848. In 1859 he and his family left Utah for California.

[6]"The High Council of Provo, sat in the City Hall, . . . on a charge against Bp. Butler for whipping with a stick, a man named Riley, who had made considerable trouble in the branch and possessed a murmuring disposition. The Council decided that the Bp. was too fast." Church Historian's Office Journal, 24 April 1858, 21:3.

bishop he (Thurber) thought a good floging would do Riley the most good of any thing, and if he had done any thing wrong, he wanted the people to forgive him. They were both forgiven. Thus passed off the glory of the bp's [bishop's] revelation. This hapened in 1857, I believe.[7]

Chapter XII.
Fanaticism Bears Sway: The Utah War

It was in the winter of 1856 & 7 that we first heard that there was hostile preperation being mad[e] by the government of the United States against the people of Utah and that an army was all ready to march in the spring for Utah. We as a people were not frightened by the news. We put our trust in God and believed we were His people and He was able to take care of His Saints. However we made preperations by organizing a "standing army" and drilling them for se[r]vice.[1] We beli[e]ved the time was at ha[n]d that "one man should chase a thousand and two should put ten thousand to flight."[2] We believed it was our duty to do all we were able to do and God would do the rest and we were full of f[a]ith that the set time had come to favor Zion.

About that time, all the cities of Utah, except Spanish Fork, made and published a sort of manife[s]to or declaration of their intentions, the most of them quoting the well known phrase "our lives, our fortunes, and our sacred honor," showing a willingness to stand by each other under all circumstances. Why Spanish Fork was silent, I never knew, for I know the people there was as willing as and [any] of them to defend their homes and fire-sides against a common enimy.[3]

I remember when a company started for Echo Kanyon to keep back the "mob" that many were forbidden the priviliege of going, for some must stay at home. I for one, though very anxious to go out, was not permited to go because others were in better circumstances to fit them selves out. I furnished a gun and amunition to go. As the company started away, we all gave three cheers for God and liberty. We were at that time a God-trusting

---

[7]Actually spring 1858.

[1]Brigham Young first proposed creating a standing army in October 1857.

[2]On 8 October 1857 Young assured the Saints, "I know that ten men, such as I could name and select, could stop" the U.S. Army. "I count five such men equal to twenty-five thousand, and believe that two of them could put ten thousand to flight." *Journal of Discourses*, 5:339–40.

[3]Spanish Fork, nevertheless, had its unit of the Nauvoo Legion, in which Hicks served as a lieutenant. Utah County Military District, rolls for 20 April, 15 June, and 15 July 1857.

people and all our leaders at that tim[e] taught us to believe that we could keep the whole world out of the mountains.

In the summer of 1857, I saw the Dukes Company pass through Spanish Fork City on its way to California. They were well fit[t]ed out with good wagons and teames. They were quiet and orderly, as far as I know, although I have since heard many evil things against them. They were the same that was so cruely murdered at Mountain Meadows.[4] I went to them and tried to sell them flour and potatoes, but was told that they did not need any supplies. I have often heard it said that this company could not purchase provisions in any of the settlements as they passed through. I know the statement to be false.[5] I shall at some future time devote a chapter to the Mountain Meadows Massacre.

In the winter of 1857 & 8, the U.S. army were kept at bay all winter at Fort Bridger. We thought it was kept there by Divine providence, but at the present time, I do not beli[e]ve the government ever intend[ed] to harm the people of Utah, but I think the [that] President James Buchannan, who was a Democrat, wished to have the army of the United States mooved away so that the south might prepare for going out of the union.[6]

There was alway[s] some dificult[i]es among the people, a few of which I shall mention. A man by the name of Thomas Job was teaching a class—the science of astrology.[7] The most fanatical among us said astrology was of the Devil and should be put down. I noticed the most ignorant became somewhat divided on the subject. The fanatics brought plenty of scripture to maintain their position. A man by the name of John A. Lewis was the worst.[8] A man by the name of Mires [Myers], a Pennsylvani[a] Dutch man,

---

[4]The Fancher party, traveling a few days ahead of the Dukes company, were killed at Mountain Meadows. Governor Young's 10 September 1857 directive to stake president Isaac C. Haight not to meddle with emigrants probably saved the Dukes train from a similar fate. Bagley, *Blood of the Prophets*, 164–68.

[5]Late in July 1857 church leaders ordered people to prepare for war and not sell a single kernel of grain to outsiders. In August George A. Smith toured southern settlements, distributing letters from Young to the bishops giving the same orders. Nevertheless, some people in Provo reportedly ignored the order. MacKinnon, *At Sword's Point*, 231–36; Walker, Turley, and Leonard, *Massacre at Mountain Meadows*, 108–109.

[6]For a discussion of this theory, see Furniss, *The Mormon Conflict*, 71–72.

[7]Welshman Thomas Job (1812–1890), baptized in 1851, came to Utah in 1854 and settled in Salt Lake City, where he taught and published articles questioning Newton's theory of planetary orbits (*Deseret News*, 25 and 30 January, 8 February 1855). Orson Pratt wrote a response in the *Deseret News* of 8 February 1855. Job and his family moved to Springville in 1858 and then to Spanish Fork in 1860, where again he taught classes in astrology. He later joined the Reorganized church. Many converts returned east, but Job became president of Utah's RLDS branches. Brimley, *Book of Thomas Job*.

[8]Former Methodist minister, rock mason, dock builder, and merchant John A. Lewis (1814–1887) traveled from Wales in 1854 on the same ship, the *Golconda*, as Thomas Job. In Utah he helped found Brigham City and later moved to Spanish Fork.

was another. He was a presiden[t] of "Seventies."[9] James Thompson, an other president of "Seventies," was very vehement in his denunciations.[10] Wm. W. Riley, a man of so[me] talents as a preacher, was always ready to prove that all the astrologers were children of the Devil.[11] A man by the name of James Allen—a Seventy—was visited by "teachers" [of the Seventies Quorum] and the[y] told him he must stop practicing the art of astrology, for Br. Thompson had said so. (Thompson was scarcely able to read or write.) Allen told the teachers that Br. Thompson was not a competent judge of astrology. I was present in the Quorum when the teachers brought in their report of what Allen has said concerning Br. Thompson. Wm. R. Riley took the floor and made [a] "flaming speech" against Allen and astrology. He said Br. Thompson held the Holy Priesthood and that was superior to every thing else, and a man clothed upon wi[th] the spirit and power of his calling was competen[t] to judge of all mateters [*sic*]. A motion was made to cut Allen of[f] from the quorum for practicing the art of astrology. My self and two other young man [men] tried to save him, but we could not and he was cut off and subsequently cut of[f] from the church. Alle[n] was a scholar and a gentleman, sociable, inteligent, temperate, and peacibly disposed toward all men and had a wife and two or three children.[12]

Soon after Allen was cut off, a young man—Thomas Robertson by name, and a Scotch man by birth—was bro't up before the Quorum for studying

---

[9]Born in York County, Pennsylvania, George Myers (or Mayer) (1805–1896) converted to Mormonism in 1843. In the summer after the death of Joseph and Hyrum Smith in 1844, he moved to Nauvoo, where he was made a policeman to guard the temple and Brigham Young and his counselors. He was also ordained a Seventy and then a senior president of the Thirty-second Quorum of Seventy. After being driven from Nauvoo with the other Mormons in 1846, he and his family went to Winter Quarters, where George made saddles. In 1848 George, his wife Ann Yost Myers, and six children traveled to Utah and settled in Salt Lake City. In 1852 he was called on a mission to Switzerland and Germany. George married a plural wife in 1856 and eventually moved with her to Spanish Fork, where he had a second large family.

[10]New Yorker James Lewis Thompson (1818–1891) converted to Mormonism in 1833 and joined Zion's Camp in 1834. He lived in Kirtland, married at Nauvoo, and then moved to Council Bluffs, Iowa. A member of the Mormon Battalion, he settled in Palmyra in 1852 and was elected a city councilor in Spanish Fork in 1861. Thompson must have been ordained a president of the Seventies between 1858 and early 1861.

[11]An older brother of James Anderson Riley, William Wommack Riley (1813–1899) was born at Nashville, Tennessee. He converted to Mormonism in 1839 and served as a captain in the Nauvoo Legion. With his two wives and child, he emigrated to Utah and settled at Palmyra in 1852. He was called on a mission to Las Vegas, where on 19 October 1856 he "preached upon the devilish power and influence that had been used by some men from the rise of the Church until the present." On 16 November 1856 Riley "gave a lengthy discourse upon the power unclean spirits had over the minds of men on earth." Youngberg, ed., *Conquerors of the West*, 4:2210–12; Jenson, comp., "History of Las Vegas Mission," 249, 254.

[12]James Allen and his wife Elizabeth were from England. In Utah they had three daughters. The family left Utah and by 1860 were living in St. Joseph, Missouri, where Allen taught school. 1860 United States Census, St. Joseph, Buchanan, Missouri, roll M653-609, 264.

astrology.[13] He was a bla[c]ksmith by trade and a very useful member of society. Thomas and myself were great friends, and I often had the privilege of reading his books and from them I learned that astrology instead of being based on the "Devil" as the opponents said of it, I found that it was based on the works of God, for we read in the scriptures that "God created the Heavens and the Earth." Astrology pretends to foretell events that are to come upon the Earth by the movements of the Heavenly bodies. I took up the idea from this that if God had created the Heavens and the Earth and had given them their seasons, then God and not the "Devil" was the author of astrology.

Wm. Creer, a young man of good abilaties, joined withe me.[14] He took up the character of Robertson and his moral right to s[t]udy anything he chose as long as he did not violate any of his moral obligations to society. We car[r]ied our point and for once the intolerance and bigotry [of] the priests did not succeed. Thomas Robertson is still a firm member of the church and also a useful member of society, althoug[h] he has of his own free will given up the art of astrology.

I was aquainted with a young man in the city of Spanish Fork by the name of John McKinly.[15] John was highly educated, although self-taught. He was considered an "eccentric." John and my self were intimate although he was no Mormon. I was sorry for him and often told him he should join the church. John believed all churches to be fanatical organizations. I well remember once talking with him concerning the soldiers coming into Utah and the Mormons going to war with them. John scouted [mocked] the idea. Said he, "In all parobability [*sic*] it will all blow over without any fighting on either side." I pitied his ignorance, but John was the only man in the cit[y] that entertained correct views on the subject.[16]

Although our leaders often told us that the soldiers never would come in to Salt Lake Valley, yet they did come in and after they were in we were told that they never should pass the "Point of the Mountain" which seperates

[13]Thomas Robertson (1825–1887) was born in Scotland and came to Utah with his five brothers: Charles, William, John, James, and Alexander.

[14]British convert William Creer (1836–1900) came to Utah in 1855 or 1856. In 1858 he married in Spanish Fork, where he remained the rest of his life.

[15]John Dixon McKinlay was born around 1829 in New Brunswick, Canada. He was the brother of Charles Dixon McKinlay, a widow's son who was harassed during the Walker War by Wesley W. Willis. John came to Utah in 1849, and Charles and his mother, Elizabeth, came in 1852. By 1880 Charles was living north of Napa, California.

[16]The Utah War involved no battles, but it was not bloodless: the Mountain Meadows massacre alone killed some 120 men, women, and children. Henry Forbes was murdered at Springville in 1858, perhaps to prevent him reporting on the disarray of Mormon forces to the army.

Utah Valley from Salt Lake Valley.[17] They did pass, however, and built Camp Floyd and a great benefit they proved to be, for we were very destitute and they gave us employmen[t] and paid us well. They purchased our surplus produce and gave us gold in exchang[e]. In fact I do not know what the poor of the country would have done for the common necessaries of life if the army had not have come to Utah. We cut wood for them, we made dobies [adobe bricks], we took lumber to them, and many took their families and lived near Camp Floyd so eager were we to get gains.

Although it is true, I am ashamed to say that some of the women of this country became prostitutes and quite a number of young girls married sold[i]ers and when the camp mooved were left behind. One woman, a Mrs. Leah, a woman of some refinement and education, was taken over to camp by her husband Charl[e]s Leah to sing on the stage. She was a very excellent singer. Mrs. Leah never came back, but left her husband and married an Irish soldier and went with him when the camp mooved away. Leah, her husband, got another wife and has raised a large family.[18]

Another woman by the name of Mercy Tuckett, the wife of Henry Tuckett, ran away with a stroling player called Dick White and left a number of small children. She went to Carson City. She fail[e]d as an actress there and died soon after leaving an infant child which Tuckett, her husband, went and got.[19] I beli[e]ve women to be less virtuous than men and more fickel.

In the year 1855 Bri[g]ham Young conceived the idea of bringing the people, that is the new converts, to the Mormon faith into this territory with hand

---

[17]Similar statements confirm that Brigham Young promised the army would never enter the Salt Lake Valley: "You may query will the soldiers be really permitted to enter Salt Lake Valley? *No! they will not!!!*" Brigham Young to H.S. Eldredge, 8 August 1857, Brigham Young Collection. "Fixed my detirmination not to let any troops enter this territory. And unless the Government assumes a more pacific attitude to, declare emigration by overland route Stopt, And make every preparation to give the U.S. a Sound drubbing I do not feel to be imposed upon any more." Cooley, ed., *Diary of Brigham Young*, 11 August 1857, 58.

[18]Charles Wagner Leah (1820–1908), born in England, remarried Dorothy Chisholm in 1861 and had eight children. His first wife, Margaret, was a teacher in 1857 at Spanish Fork before marrying an unidentified soldier. Allred, *Spanish Fork*, 19.

[19]Mercy Ellen Westwood (1833–1863) married Henry Tuckett (1831–1923) in St. Louis in 1852 before emigrating to Utah. Both English, they had three children when church authorities called Mercy to perform in Salt Lake. Her brother organized a dramatic company that toured Camp Floyd, where Mercy quickly became popular. Pregnant, she left Tuckett and moved to Nevada with her brothers, David and Phillip Moss Westwood, their families, and her youngest child, Phillip. Eveline Mercy Tuckett was born in Virginia City in 1860 and was raised by Phillip Westwood and his wife. In 1862 in Folsom, California, Mercy married former sergeant Richard C. White, who had organized Camp Floyd's Military Dramatic Association. She died in 1863 soon after the birth of their first child, who also died. Godfrey, "Housewives, Hussies, and Heroines," 170–71; Moorman, *Camp Floyd and the Mormons*, 88–89; "Editor of the Valley Tan," *Valley Tan*, 28 September 1859, 2.

carts.[20] The poor and ignoran[t] converts from the Brittish Isles were so anxious to come to Zion that they gladly excepted [accepted] the perveage [privilege] of coming in that way. One company, Captain Martin's Co., did not start untill the 1st of October.[21] Their leaders prophesized that the Lord would turn the storms to the right ha[n]d and to the left and that they shou[l]d be brought through the mountains like the children of Isriel were brought through the Red Sea. One Cyrus Wheelock was very full of the spirit of prophecy.[22]

The suffering of that company beggars description. Twenty percent died of cold and hunger, one out of ev[e]ry five persons.[23] Some were crippled for life and all would have perished perhaps had not the people of Utah sent them help. I remmember well our leaders telling us that we were to say nothing about the hand cart failure, for if we did, God would curse us for so doing.[24] The reason they threatened was no doubt that they wished to hide their own blunders and *ignorance* of nature's laws. Other companies suffered, but none so bad. It was said that they were kept there in order to make money out of them. I think B. Young wished to try an experiment on human indurance and he did. The scheme was soon abandoned and the emigrants were brought with ox teams until the R.R. [railroad] was built.[25]

---

[20]Brigham Young first mentioned using handcarts in the General Epistle of October 1851. In September 1855, he wrote to F.D. Richards, European Mission president, outlining plans to use handcarts in 1856. Hafen and Hafen, *Handcarts to Zion*, 29–31.

[21]The handcart company led by Edward Martin left Florence, Nebraska, on 25 August 1856. On October 1, the party was still on the North Platte River and had not yet reached Chimney Rock. Turner, *Emigrating Journals*, 105, 113.

[22]Willie company veteran John Chislett wrote, "The emigrants were entirely ignorant of the country and climate—simple, honest, eager to go to 'Zion' at once, and obedient as little children to the 'servants of God.' . . . They [the elders] prophesied in the name of God that we should get through in safety. Were we not God's people, and would he not protect us? Even the elements he would arrange for our good." Stenhouse, *Rocky Mountain Saints*, 316–17. Returning British missionary Cyrus H. Wheelock prophesied the party would come through safely. Bangerter and Bangerter, *Tragedy and Triumph*, 77–78. The phrase "on their right hand and on their left," as Hicks suggests, comes from the story of God parting the Red Sea: "the waters were a wall unto them on their right hand, and on their left" (Exodus 14:22). The phrase appears frequently in *The Book of Mormon* and *Doctrine and Covenants*.

[23]At least one out of four died in the Martin company: between 135 and 150 of the 576 people. Hafen and Hafen, *Handcarts to Zion*, 193. For more recent assessments, see Bagley, "'One Long Funeral March,'" 108–109.

[24]On 2 November 1856 Brigham Young preached, "If any man or woman complains of me or of my Counselors, in regard to the lateness of some of this season's immigration, let the curse of God be on them and blast their substance with mildew and destruction, until their names are forgotten from the earth." Ibid., 94.

[25]Young sent missionaries from Utah east in April 1857 with handcarts to prove the method was practical. Two westbound handcart trains crossed the plains that summer. In 1859 one and in 1860 two final handcart companies reached Utah. The LDS church launched the "down and back" scheme in 1861, with wagons from Utah sent to Florence, Nebraska Territory, to bring back converts and freight. For the travails of the last handcart companies, see Bagley, "'One Long Funeral March,'" 100–106.

The failure of the hand carts or the deaths and sufferings of the Saints in those companies has been the means of completely revolution[i]zing my mind. At that time I beli[e]ved that the universe was governed by the will of a Supreme Being and that he kept the whole human family under his eye, as it were, and meted out to all acording to there need, as a good father would do for his children, and that "the righteous were neve[r] forsaken." The poor hand cart companies called upon God twice ev[e]ry day; they sang psalms to his praise as they traveled along. They hoped, they trusted in him, but all in vain. They no doubt read in the Bible how Jehovah had brought the Isrielites through the wilderness and fed them on man[n]a and he would do so for them. There was no God to help them and all that were not physicaly strong enough to bear the hardships of that journey perished by the way, and those that could endure the journey came through. I do not beli[e]ve that "God" will ever have a better opertunity to help poor suffering humanity than then. The truth is the universe is governed by laws immutable and unchangeable. I have read many books writen by "Christian" authors in which they have tried to prove that nature's laws have been suspended for the Christians' special benefit, but I have never known a single instance of divine interposition contrary to known laws of the universe. People say I am an infidel. Perhaps. I have facts and reason to sustain my position while those who oppose my opinions in these matters have only faith and falsehoods to sustain them. These I call fanatics.

The army of the United States that were kep[t] out at Fort Bridger all winter came cursing and profaning the name of God and none of them died of want. Why? Because they were clothed and fed, or in other words, their bodaly wants were prepared for and they did not need to call on any god to help them for they could help them selves in spite of prayers, for the Saints of Utah offered many prayers to God to put a hook in there [the soldiers'] jaws and to turn them away from us.

It is our duty to learn the laws of nature and obey them, for if we do not, we are building on uncertainties and sooner or later we will come to grief. I know that many of the leading men of Utah have changed as well as myself and have more faith in the laws of nature than they have in any god. The most of this class of infidels call the laws of nature the laws of God. Of late years there has been more said and taught on this subject by our leading men, and many of our most inteligent and best educated young men are very sceptical as to their belief in a god. And no doubt that in a few more years, infidelity will become a leading quality of Utah minds.

Where fanaticism bears sway in a community as it did in Utah in 1857, it is well that people should have a change of sentiment. I would prefer Ingersoll's radical ideas to some of those we had in Utah just previous to the army coming in here.[26] As I have said before, we need two parties for perfect safety. I will say that with all my infidelity, I have never lost faith in a glorious world beyond the grave where there is no death, but I do not beli[e]ve in any resurection of the body, but I believe in the immortality of the soul and in eternal progression. I also beli[e]ve in future rewards and punishments. I believe that a time will come when we will all be judged acording to the deeds done in the body and that we will be classified acording to our inteligence.

I shall here mention one incident which perhaps should have been put down before; that is an attempt to keep Dr. Garland Hurt, the United States government Indian agent from escaping and going out to meet the army that was coming in here.[27] It is my opinion that one great reason why the people of Utah were not willing to let him get out [of Utah] was he would tell how weak we were and he would probably act as a guide to the army and lead them in here. I remember I was at that time what was called a captain of a ten with rank of second lieut. in the Mormon "Legion."[28]

One afternoon the malitia [*sic*] of Spanish Fork was ordered out onto the public square and from thence to proceed to the Indian farm west of

---

[26]Robert Green Ingersoll (1833–1899) was an Illinois lawyer, politician, orator, freethinker, and agnostic. He commanded the 11th Illinois Cavalry at the Battle of Shiloh and later served as attorney general of Illinois. He entertained radical ideas on slavery, women's suffrage, and the separation of church and state. In his scrapbook, Hicks pasted a quotation from Ingersoll, which he labeled "Beautiful Thoughts": "The idea of immortality, that like a sea has ebbed and flowed, in the human heart with its countless waves of hope and fear beating against the shores and rocks of time and fate, was not born of any book, nor of any creed, nor of any religion. It was born of human affection and will continue to ebb and flow beneath the mists and clouds and darkness as long as love kissed the lips of death." Ingersoll, from his lecture "The Ghosts."

[27]A Virginian, Garland Hurt (1819–1903) studied medicine and served in the Kentucky state legislature. President Franklin Pierce commissioned him as an Indian agent in Utah Territory in 1854. By September 1857 Hurt was the only non-Mormon federal official still in Utah. After the Mountain Meadows massacre—which, as Indian agent, he quickly learned about as the Mormons were laying blame on the Paiutes—and the imposition of martial law on 15 September, Hurt realized he was in danger. The Utes helped him escape across the Uinta Mountains. Hurt joined the army on the Sweetwater River near South Pass in today's Wyoming.

[28]Utah County Military District, rolls for 20 April, 15 June, and 15 July 1857.

the city. We started. We were poorly armed and while we were crossing the Spanish Fork River bottom a halt was called and the brethren *were told to arm themselves* with *clubs*. Those who had no guns did so and there were not a few (mostly Danish men). We then marched on to the bench about half way from the Spanish Fork bridge where we were met by men from other settlements. We were about four hundred strong. A man by the name of John S. Fullmer—an old Mormon—was colonel and had command.[29] We had a number [of] majors among whom were A.K. Thurber and John L. Butler, the bp. [bishop] of Spanish Fork City. Our col[onel] called the majors to one side and held a consultation which lasted for more than an hour while the men were standing in rank.

During this time about 250 Indians made there appearence between us and the Indian farm house. They uttered yells of defiance and daring us to come on. They were all well mounted and some of them rode within fifty yards of us yelling and whooping in the most terrific manner. Our officers still stood in consultation while we of the rank and file stood like a flock of sheep. Presently we saw a horseman coming from the south at full speed. He came up. It was a man by the name of Wm. Maxwell.[30] He brought the startling inteligence that Dr. Hurt had gone some hours before. Our bird had flown. He was well mounted on a large iron-grey horse and had an escort of Indians with him and was safe out of our reach. I think we might have taken him but for our officers. I am glad we did not get him, for more than likely he would have been killed if we had. There is no doubt but the Indians were sent to keep us back while their Dr. made good his escape, and we were out-generaled that time. The "battle ax of the Lord," as the Indians are called, were at that time, as they generally are, were the fr[i]ends of the Lord's enamies.[31]

Soon after Maxwell came up, we saw an Indian aproaching holding a

---

[29]John Solomon Fullmer (1807–1883), born in Pennsylvania and baptized in 1839 at Nauvoo by Joseph Smith, was private secretary to the prophet and visited Carthage Jail the day before the murder of the Smith brothers. The Fullmer family crossed the plains in 1848. After returning from a mission to England, he moved to Springville with three wives. Fullmer was temporarily in command because Aaron Johnson was in Salt Lake City.

[30]William Bailey Maxwell (1821–1895) was born in Illinois and baptized in Nauvoo about 1845. A Mormon Battalion veteran and Nauvoo Legion captain during the Utah War, he helped colonize Santaquin, just south of Payson, in 1856.

[31]Mormons believed that the Indians would side with them in a conflict with the U.S. government and be "the battle ax of the Lord" against their enemies. Bagley, *Blood of the Prophets*, 26.

paper in his hand which fluttered in the wind. He came up and gave the paper to Col. Fullmer who read it to us. It was a statement writen by Dr. Hurt to Bp. J. L. Butler stating that he deemed it advisable to leave the Indian Farm for a while. Said he, "If I should again be permmited to come back and teach the poor and ignorant Indians the arts of peace and civilization." What an absurdity, I thought. He gave Bp. Butler full charge of the Indian farm with instructions to manage it as he saw fit. That was a wise stroke of policy. Hurt doubtless though[t] that Bp. Butler would take care of the place from selfish motives. The farm was at that time a valuable piece of property. I have been told that the *Democrats* wasted $25,000 on that farm.[32]

We were, soon after the reading the Dr.['s] note, ordered to return home. Just as we were ready to start, H. B. M. Jolley, my father-in-law, came ov[e]r a hill near us, he not knowing any thing about why we were there, having started out in the morning to hunt stock on the range. An Indian who was near him fired at him but did not hit him. This was the only shot fired. It was then near sunset. A shout was raise[d] that an Indian shot at Jolley. This threwe [*sic*] the whole of us into confusion. Most of us were on foot, but H. B. M. Jolley was on horse back. We all ran for home as hard as we could and the farther we ran, the faster we flew in the most perfect confusion down the hill and across the Spanish Fork bridge. Jolley by this time was among the foot men who were hindmost. We were followed by a few Indians hooting and yelling, "Squaws!" "Cowards!" &c. &c. We all got safe home.

There were many people—myself among the number—who beli[e]ve that there was a previous agreement between Bp. Butler, Col. Fullmer, and Dr. Hurt to the effect that Hurt was to leave the country in peace, and perhaps they were well paid for keeping us back untill Hurt was fairly gone.[33] All this hapened just previous to the army coming in to our territory. As soon as the army was bar[e]ly in, Hurt came back and took possession of the Indian Farm and proceeded to "teach the Indians the arts of peace" and ev[er]y thing went on as though nothing had hapened.

---

[32]Hicks, a staunch Republican, referred to the Democratic administration of James Buchanan from 1857 to 1861. How Hicks came up with twenty-five thousand dollars being wasted on the Indian farm is unclear. After 1865 the Utes were removed to a reservation in Uinta Valley. For the Indian farms, see Beeton, "Teach Them to Till the Soil," 299–320.

[33]William G. Hartley concluded Butler did not help Hurt escape, but that he could have done more "to prevent the escape also seems evident." To prevent the possible killing of a federal agent, perhaps "Butler did not act vigorously when Hurt made his escape." Hartley, *My Best for the Kingdom*, 322.

Chapter XIII.
Little Tyrants: Pond Town

In the spring of 1861, I with my family left Spanish Fork and mooved to Pond Town (now called Salem) in Utah Co. That moove has prooved the most unfortunate to my temporal welfare. It has been the means of keeping me in poverty. It has been the means of me losing confidence in many people with whom I have had dealings, and in a great measure it has been the means of destroying my peace of mind for life here below. My reasons for going were these: My wife and I had never been through [the] Indowment, nor had we been seal[e]d to each other. Bp. J. L. Butler was dead at Spanish Fork and A. K. Thurber had taken his place. He [Thurber] had *seduced* my sister in to a polygamous marriag[e] with him and she had gotten a bill of divorce from him. I had assisted her in getting it and of course I had incured the displeasure of Bp. Thurber, and no private man can get through the Endowment House without a recommend from his bishop and to get such a recommend from Bp. Thurber I would be obliged to submit to *his* terms and I consi[d]ered that to[o] humiliating for a man of any spirit.

My father-in-law was bishop of Pond Town and to him I went, but I did never ask him for a reccommend although I well knew that I could have had one for the asking, for in those day[s] I was strong in the faith and believed these things to be more necessary than all else, and I know honest ignorant people who still beli[e]ve that Endowment House ceremonies are of more importance than good homes or any worldly goods.

Pond Town, although a small place, was full of difficult and evil feeling one toward another. The great cause of this internal trouble lay between one Royal Durfey and Bp. Jolley. In the spring of 1860, the Pond Town ward had hired Alma Durfey, a son of Royal Durfey, to drive a team back to the Mousouri River to bring in a load of the poor Saints and had agreed to pay him $100 in labor and produce. Some of the people did not comply with their portion of the contract and Durfey laid all the blame on Bp. Jolley, although he had paid more than a proportionate share as he had agreed to do.

When I came to Pond Tow[n], Durfey was all paid up but $34.00. I, being of a religious turn of mind, was not long there until I was chosen to be a ward teacher, and it became my duty to visit the members of the ward and to enquire into all matters of faith and fellow[ship] of the members of the ward.

I and my partner, a brother teacher, went to visit Durfey and he soon began to speak very hard thing[s] agains[t] Bp. Jolley for not paying him for his son's services. I asked him if the bishop had agreed to pay it all himself. "No," he replied, "but he might make the people pay up." "How much is due you?" I asked. "$34," he replied. We told him we would see about it and try and stir the people up to pay him. Durfey then began to rail agains[t] Bp. Jolley, sayin[g] he was a thief and he could prove it. He said th[e]re were other thieves in Pond Town and he could prove that also, and so he went on as long as we would listen to him. We asked him to tell who else were thieves beside the bishop and he said Bob Moncur had stolen one of his, Durfey's, logs in the kanyon, describing the log to be a red pine log that lay on top of the "Jump Off" hill in Loafer Kanyon. I asked him if that was his log (I having seen the [log] laying there. It had been cut before I went to Pond Town). He said it was and Bob had stolen it, "the damned thief."

We left Durfe[y]'s house and went on our business and in the cou[r]se of time, we went and made a report to the bishop and to Robert Moncur.[1] Both of the men were the very soul of honor and we knew it. Rob't Moncur, as soon as he heard what Durfey had said about him, he went dow[n] to see him and in a very mild manner ask[ed] him if he had said he (Moncur) had stolen his log. "Yes, you did," said Durfey, "and there is the log," said he, pointing to the mill yard which was near by. "Did you cut that log?" sa[i]d Moncur quite colley [cooly]. Alma, who was sitting by, jumped up and siad [*sic*], "Yes, and you da—nd thieving s–n of a b–ch stole it." "You are an infernal liar," said Moncur, at the same time making a spring toward Durfe[y] junior. Durfey senior got in be twixt the two young men. "Let the d–m son a of b–ch come," said Alma, but the words were not out of his mo[u]th until Moncur had planted a blow on his cheek which sent him reeling to the ground. Moncur was a small man but very active. Durfey sen[ior] clinched Moncur, but in an instant Moncur had him down and was on top of him and had planted a number of settlers in his face and no doubt would have beaten him to a jelley had no one interfered.[2]

Alma was satisfied with what he had got and did not come "to time" any more.[3] Myself and my brother teacher who had acompanied Moncur to assist in settling the difficulty did all we could to sepperate Durfey and Moncur. I

[1]Born in Dundee, Scotland, and "small of stature," Robert Moncur (1839–1932) converted to Mormonism with his mother and stepfather in 1848. They came to Utah in 1852 and settled in Palmyra, where he worked for H. B. M. Jolley. In 1860 he married Jolley's daughter Frances, a younger sister of Hicks's wife Elizabeth. Youngberg, ed., *Conquerors of the West*, 3:1690.

[2]"Settler" is slang for a knockdown blow.

[3]In boxing, "to come to time" means to resume the contest at the end of an interval when "time" is called.

caught hold of Moncur and was pulling him off when one of the bystanders (Jake Cloward) took hold of me and jerked me to one side, saying "Let them fight, for Durfey has needed a licking for a long time." By this time most of the people in the town were there and some one, I don't know who, took Moncur off of Durfe[y]. Durfey then took up a large stone saying, "By God, I'l[l] finish him." He made an atempt to strike Moncur, but the stone was wrested from him by one of the by standers. Durfey then took up a chaire [*sic*] which hapened to be near and made an attempt to strike with it, but was also prevented. The crowd soon after dispersed and Moncur with them.

I presume the whole of the above disturbance did not occupy more than from ten to fifteen minutes time from beginning to the end, but small fountains make mighty rivers and little beginning[s] some times bring about years of sorrow or joy, and I think the sequel of this will prove my assertion to the satisfaction of all who may chance to read these imperfectly writen pages.

My self and my brother teacher made a report of our attemp[t] to settle the dificulty. A meeting was called soon afterward and the Durfeys were invited to attend, which they did. We discussed the matter in regard to paying Durfey the remaining $34.00. Uriah Curtis, a councillor to the bishop, said he had been to see Br. Durfey and had offered him som[e] good molasses on the donation that the people had agreed to pay him.[4] Durfey said he did not want any donations to keep up his table. In fact, he would not take molasses any way. Uriah Curtis said it made him think of a man he once knew who had his house burned and his neighbors thought it was their duty to give him som[e]thing of what ever they had to spare. Rye was the most abundant with one old man and he took a sack full over to the unfortunate man and offered to give it to him. "I won't have it," said the unfortunate, "*I am done taking rye*." That appeared to be the way with Br. Durfey. He is done taking molasses. The people present burst into a loud laugh. Alma Durfey sprang to his feet and started toward Uriah Curtis, sliping up his shirt sleeves as though he would fight Br. Curtis (who was an old man). One present laid his hand on Alma's shoulder and stoped him. I made a motion that Alma be cut off the church for disorderly conduct. The motion was carried and the meeting broke up in confusion soon after wards to no purpose.

[4]Born in New York and baptized in 1831, Uriah Curtis (1805–1863) moved to Jackson County, Missouri, in 1832. He lived Nauvoo and in 1848 was listed as branch president of Big Pigeon near Council Bluffs. In 1852 he led a company to Utah of some 365 persons, including his two wives and their children. He took two more wives, the last in 1860.

In a few days afterwards, Bp. Jolley went over to Spring City, Sanpete Co., to see Elder Orson Hyde (one of the Twelve Apostles) and lay the matter before him and get his advice in the matter. Bp. Jolley came back and brought a letter from Hyde to the people of Pond Town, telling them to pay Br. Durfey and to try and settle their difficulties and live in peace. Bp. Jolley was instructed to read this letter in a public meeting on the followin[g] Sunday, which he did. Hyde told Bp. Jolley he would be at Pond Town on his way to the October Conference and if the matter was not then settled, he would give it a hearing as he went by.

During the interium [*sic*], a few who had not paid up their subscribed portion of the $34.00 busied themselves about paying up. Durfey also made great preparations to entertain his friend Hyde when he should arrive, on the second of October.[5] He (Durfey) went and bought a bottle of whiskey, and on his way home he showed the bottle to his son-in-law, K. T. Butler, and an other young man by the name of G. W. Sevey at the same time, telling them that "This 'ere licker is for Daddy Hyde."[6] On the morning of Oct. third, Durfey killed a sheep so that he might have som[e]thing to eat as well as drink. He ceartainly [*sic*] was apprised of the coming of Elder Hyde, for about 3 o'clock Hyde in company with two others drove up to Durfies house and were welcomed by his family.

A meeting of the people of the ward was called at "early candle-light," and although nearly 19 years have elap[s]ed since that, to me, memorible third of October, [1862], I cannot think or write about it without a feeling of indignation. As soon as the meeting was called to order, the choir sang. The choir was a poor one but it did as well as could be expected from such a choir. The sounds hardly ceased before Elder Hyde began to abuse us for not singing better. The poet Gray speaks of the "little tyrants of the field."[7] Hyde was one of the "little tyrants" of the church. After the meeting was opened, Elder Hyde asked Bp. Jolley if he had read his (Hydes') letter to the people of Pond Town. Durfey answered he (Jolley) had not read it. The Bp. replied he had. "All of it?" asked Hyde. "Yes, all of it," said the bishop.

[5]Whether Durfey was actually a friend of Hyde is not known. Hicks may have meant that Durfey intended to "buy" his friendship.

[6]K. T. Butler was married to Olive Artemeshy Durfey, Royal's daughter. George Washington Sevy (or Sevey) (1832–1902) fell ill in Great Salt Lake City on his way to California in 1849. He converted and married Bishop Butler's daughter Phoebe Melinda. A polygamist, Sevy moved first to Panguitch, Utah, and then to Juarez, Mexico, where he became the first bishop.

[7]From Thomas Gray's *Elegy Written in a Country Churchyard*.

"I never heard it," said Durfey. The truth was Durfey never atended the ward meetings and he did not know what was done there. Durfey was one of those "fair day" Saints who make a point to be agreeable to the high dignataries of the church, but always falied [failed] to perform any of the common duties of the church.

Hyde then aske[d] Durfey if he had gotten his pay. Durfey said he had not. Elder Hyde then arose and let his passion loose. His face was flushed, his eyes wore the expression of the most intense anger and with a savage leer he turned toward the bishop and asked "How is this?" The bishop offered to explain. "Shut your mouth," said Hyde, "The Spirit of God has made the whole matter known to me before I came here." Then Hyde turned his savage glance toward the congregation and began to abuse us for being contract breakers, for not paying Br. Durfey as we had agred to do. Again the bishop asked to be heard. Then Hyde turned upon him with all the savage vindictiveness of a southern overseer [of slaves] and ordered him to keep his mouth shut or he (Hyde) would cut him of[f] from the church and "disorganize the ward in five minutes."

If Hyd[e] had been abusive before, he now raged. He raised the floodgates of his evil nature and we poor slaves had to submit to his scorpion lash. He said Pond Town was a rendesvous for thieves and the bishop knew it. Bp. Jolley said he did not know it. "You do know it and you will hide in the brush and cower before them." "I might cower before the bullet of a cursed thief, but no other way." Bp. Jolley said [continued] in [a] very mild manner that if there was any such work, he knew nothing of it. "Shut your mo[u]th," said Hyde and then waved his hand violently, saying as he did so, "The first man that rises to contend, I will cut him of[f] from the church and take the priesthood from him." Hyde then went on with his abuse untill he seemed to be satisfied, no one daring to open his mouth on peril of his standing in the church, poor slaves that we were.

Bishop Jolley was not afraid of any physical foe, but like most of the pe[o]ple of Utah at that time, he was afraid of the priesthood. We believed at that time they stood between us and our soul's salvation and that they held the keys that opened the gates of Heaven. Oh, Superstition, thou art a cruel master. Thou makest thy votaries to bow into the dust and so thou has always chained thy victims to the pillar of faith and scourged them with a whip of scorpions. But than[k]s to reason and progress, I have lost all regard for every thing of a priestly name and nature. I believe that all priesthoods to be a relic of ancient superstition and ignorance.[8]

As soon as Elder Hyde's torrent of abuse had som[e]what subsided, Bishop Jolley said if he was permited, he would have the clerk of the branch read the names of those who had agreed to pay a portion of the donation to Durfey. Elder Hyde gave his consent. He doubtless thought that by so doing he would have an opertunity for individual chastisement. The clerk proceeded to call the names with the amount subscribed by each individual. Each man answered to his name and said "Paid" if he had paid, or "Not paid" if he had not paid. All had paid but two, and one of these had offered to pay his part in molasses which Durfey refused to take. Both of these men had only promised the sum of three dollars or one dollar fifty each, one of whom had offered to pay Durfey in mollasas, but he wanted wheat. The contract made with Durfey was that he was to have his pay in produce and labor. At the calling then of the last name, the clerk remarked that this makes the thirty-four dollars.

Hyde seemed to be astonished for a moment. . . . (I have known others to *judge* matters by the "Spirit of God" and I have never know[n] them to be right.) Hyde turned toward Durfey and asked him, "How is this Br. Durfey? You say you have not had your pay when the people testify they have paid you?"[9] Durfey put the end of his tongue out of his mouth, then began to scratch his head, as was his custom. At length he replied. He said, "When the folks found out you were comin', the[y] began to hustle around for fear you'd lick 'em." For a short time Hyde seemed to be astonished. He doubtless [k]new by this time that he was in the wrong, but he had claimed to have had the matter revealed to him by the Spirit of God and that Spirit had lied, that is, Hyde had lied in saying he had had a revelation. Elder Hyde said perhaps he had been to[o] fast. "Let my words be as the wind," said he. "But if it is as Br. Durfey says that you have but recently paid him, you deserved them."

---

[8]During the 1870s and 1880s, the "Common Sense" ideas of the Scottish Enlightenment—that reason was the only reliable path to knowledge and understanding, and that belief must be based on empirical evidence—spread across the land. Scientific discoveries in evolution, genetics, microbiology, and the relationship between the nervous system and human behavior reinforced these ideas, as did the practical applications of magnetism, electricity, the telegraph, and the propagation of light. See Hazen, *The Village Enlightenment in America.*

[9]Here Hicks's manuscript essentially repeats a paragraph, which has been cut.

If the aincent [ancient] apostles were anything like Apostle Hyde, I am not surprised that they met the fate they did. The matter concerning the saw log [was] then brought up and Hyde asked, "What had become of the log?" "It is sawed up," said Durfey. "Sawed up, is it," said Hyde in an angry tone. Robert Moncur spoke and said he could prove that Thos. Keel cut the log and he (Moncur) had permission to take it.[10] "They can prove any thing over there," said Durfey. G. W. Hickman, a respectable citizen, had seen Keell cutting the tree and was there ready to testify to the fact.[11] Elder Hyde would not hear a word of evidence. He arose to his feet. "I have a way of disposing of such matters. May the curse of Almighty God rest upon the person or persons that are to blame in the matter." And he continued vehemently, "I say the curse of God *shall* rest upon him."

What a blessing it is the [that] finite man do[e]s not have the power to control the curses of omnipotence. It is bad enough when priests once had control of the block, the faggot, and the halter, and could at pleasure *fulfill* any curse that they in their vindictiveness might pronounce against a defenceless offender.

Durfey had been cut off from the church for general disorderly conduct. He had said the bishop was a thief. Hyde asked what the bishop had stolen. "He stole one of my tree tops," said Durfey. Bp. Jolley had been on the mountain and had hauled down some tree top[s] for firewood. These tree tops were left by lumbermen who had been log[g]ing at the saw mills in Peteteneet [Peteetneet] Kanyon. There were perhaps thousands of these to[ps] and they were not claimed by any one in particular after the trunk of the trees were taken away. Bp. Jolley said he could prove that there were any amount of tree tops where he had got his load from. "They can prove any thing over there," said Durfey pointing to the part of the house where the Bp. and some of his friends were sitting. "Hold on, Br. Durfey," said Hyde. He then proposed that they let the tree top go to the Devil and let that matter drop.

Hyde then asked if Durfey made a practice of getting drunk. A number present made answer that they had heard him sware [swear]. "Is he the only one that will sware in Pond Town?" said Hyde. "However he is the only one

[10] Thomas Henry Keele (or Keel) (1829–1914), brother of the Alexander Keele who was killed in the Walker War, married the older sister of Hicks's wife.

[11] George Washington Hickman (1825–1893) was a younger brother of the notorious William Adams "Bill" Hickman. G. W. Hickman, in contrast, was a sober man who had studied medicine.

on trial tonight," he remarked. Hyde then asked Durfey if he paid his tithing. "Yes," said he. "He does not," said the bishop, "and my book will show that he does not." Stephen Markham happened to be present. He asked to speak. Hyde looked at him for a short time. "Yes, you may speak. You may speak, Br. Markham, you *do not* live here." Mr. Markham arose and said that he once presided over a ward where Br. Durfey lived and he would not then pay his tithing. Then Hyde told Durfey he had better pay his tithing, seeming to believe the testimony of Br. Markham. Hyde then called on Hamilton, one of his companions, to speak. Hamilton was from Sanpete Co.[12] He said that it seemed to him as though all parties had seceded from the gospel. Hyd[e] then called on Bp. Bradley, saying, "Let Bishop Bradley speak, for he is a wise and a good bishop." (My notes do not say to which settlement he belonged.)[13] Whether he was too dull to comprehend the nature of the case or not, I can't tell, but his remarks had no bearing.

Hyde then asked if Br. Durfey was a good neighbor. Two men by the name of Curtis (Moses and Lyman) answered and said he was a good and a peac[e]able neighbor. "Yes," said Elder Hyde. "Let Brs. Moses and Lyman testify." Then they in turns testified that Durfey was a good and pecable [peaceable] man. Wm. Teeples spoke and said, "If you would hear some evidence on the other side, you would see the matter in a different light."[14] "Shut your mouth," said Hyde, which Teeples did. What was the cause of the Curtises testifying to a falsehood I can not tell, unless they wished to gain favor with Apostle Hyde. I know they both testified falseley, for I knew Royal Durfey and lived near to him in Iowa an[d] I knew him to be an habitual drunkard, a profane swarer, a notorious liar, and one of the most disagreeable neighbors I ever knew, always in difficulty with some one. I do not think that Durfey would scruple at any thing short of murder to carry his point. He died a miserable death beli[e]ving all men to be his enamies after havin[g] lost his eyesigh[t] and reason.[15]

[12]This is probably Madison D. Hamilton (sometimes Hambleton) (1811–1869), who founded Mount Pleasant, Sanpete County, in 1852.

[13]This is George Washington Bradley (1813–1891), bishop of the new settlement of Moroni. "San Pete County Correspondence," *Deseret News*, 27 July 1859, 2.

[14]William Randolph Teeples (1834–1883) was born in Michigan and was a blacksmith by trade. He lived in Nauvoo as a child and came to Utah in 1848 with his parents.

[15]The 1860 census showed Durfey as illiterate. He died of "apoplexy"—a cerebral stroke—at age 69. U.S. Federal Census Mortality Schedules Index (listed as "Regal" Durfey and dying in 1880), Ancestry.com.

After the Curtises sat down, Hyde said for Br. Durfey to come down to the pond in the morning and he would baptize him just to honor the priesthood of the Bp. [bishop] and he wanted Bp. Jolley to come and be a wittness. Also wanted a few others to come. Hyde then went [on] to say that Br. Durfey had his failings, but he was a man of integrity. Hyde then turned to Alma Durfey. Aske[d] if he had not been cut off the church for fighting. Som[e] one siad [said] he was disfelowshiped for sliping his sleeves up to fight Uriah Curtis. His mother said that was only a way he had. Hyde then restored Alman [*sic*] without baptism. Hyde then said, "Alma," in the mildest manner possable, "God bless you. You have been to gather the poor and you shall be blest."[16] The contrast was great betwixt the way he talked to young Moncur and young Durfey. The meeting then closed and wickedness had triumphed over honesty, truth, and virtue.

The next morning Elder Hyde baptized Durfey as he agreed to do the night befor[e]. I went and saw it done. Hyde said to Bp. Jolley in hearing [of all] that he (Hyde) had left his barrel at Br. Durfey's for the brethren to fill with molasses, and if the breathren would fill it for him, he would probably be a little sweeter the next time he came along. (He was willing to take molasses if Durfey was not.) The people did not fill his barrel, although molas[s]es was raised in great abundance at that place. One man, Marion Haws by name, said he would not give Hyde any molasses if it would save his (Hyde's) life.

Hyde and Durfey are both dead. If I was a Christian, I should believe in the Christian's hell, and if I had the hope of a Christian, I should hope Hyde and Durfey were both in hell together, but I have no such "hope" or belief. However, let God's will be done in the matter. If He sends them there, I shall not object. Hyde and company went on to conference and the matter passed in to history.

The people of Pond Town got up a petition asking Prest. Young to give the matter a rehearing, but the matter was never over hauled, although G. A. Smith and A.K. Thurber came and asked Durfey a few *questions* privately, but did not openly investigate the matter. They did not for Hyde was above them in the church. As soon as conference was over, we got the astounding inteligence that Bp. Jolley and all his family connextions were called on a mission to southern Utah—to Washington Co.—to raise cotton. That *call*

[16]Hyde was referring to his "down and back" wagon trip to transport new members from Florence, Nebraska Territory.

meant something. It meant that we were to be banished from our homes, or if we did not respond to the *call* we would lose our standing in the church and become a hiss among our neighbors and be for evere debased of all the *blessings* and privileges of the church. At one time England sent her convicts to Bondsman's Land; Russia sends hers to Siberia, but Utah—or the church at that time—sent hers to the cotton farm of southern Utah. She now sends her derelict sons to labor on the wastes of Arizona.

Chapter XIV. The Red Hills of November: The Cotton Mission

We, the sons and sons-in-law of Bp. Jolley, were notified that we had been called on a mission at a general conference of the whole church and it was our duty to prepare to obey the servants of the Lord and to go that same fall if we wished to do right.[1] Durfey was overjoyed. He boasted that he had sent off one gang of his enemies and more would be sent if they did not look out.[2] Such was and always has been the power of priestly gover[n]ment over its dupes and ignorant followers.

We offered our property for sale, that is our land, and soon found buyers, but not to any great advantage. I had but very little to sell and sold that for ab[o]ut half I had paid for it in the Spring before. We all fitted up, and late in November [1862] we started on our journey south, I with a heavy heart. We mooved along slowly, driving cattle and sheep with us. Nothing of any importance happened untill we reached the "Black Ridge," a reef of volcanic rock on the border of Kane County.[3] We camped for the night and a storm came up from the north just as we stoped for the night. The wind blew a perfect gale. A blinding snow storm came with the wind. We turned our stock out among some cedars standing near. The snow fell to the depth of two feet and drift[d] around our wagons. We were but poorly

[1]In October 1861 President Young called three hundred men to southern Utah to grow cotton to reduce Utah's dependence on imports. After the 1862 fall conference, he called another two hundred to the Cotton Mission, including the extended Jolley family. Journal History, 19 October 1862, 5.

[2]Heber C. Kimball met with those called for the mission and insisted church leaders "had selected good men—not one sent to get rid of him. . . . God is inspiring this mission." Journal History, 19 October 1862, 7.

[3]This road "for sheer roughness and teeth-rattling cruelty could scarcely be equaled anywhere in Dixie or, for that matter, in all Utah Territory." Larson and Larson, eds., *Diary of Charles Lowell Walker*, 2:582n48.

clad and not atal prepared for such exposure.[4] I was never out in such a storm. After the snow ceased, the wind blew a gale for four days and nights without ceasing. No one knows how we suffered. On the fifth day some of the people of Harmony hapened to find out we were there. [They] came and asked us to moove up there, 4 miles from where we were camped. Bp. would not go, althoug[h] I tried hard to persuade him to do so. He was our leader and we would not leave him. Our mission was to raise cotton and if we went to Harmony, that we could not do.[5] Bp. Jolley believed in carrying out instructions to the very letter.

After the storm was over, our teames were all gone and were not found untill the eighth day when by chance I found them, and we mooved on to the Grape Vine Spring where we spent our Christmas. Although we had just passed through such a severe storm, the weather was bright and warm. There we found other pilgrims camped and among them were John W. Berry and his brother William. We lay over one day and then mooved on to Washington where we found the apple trees had not lost all their leaves.[6] The ground was dry and dirty for the late storm had not reached there, and we were at the end of our journey in a sickly and barren land with very little to go upon. I will say had it not been for leaving my wife and little children, I should have ran away from my bondage like a slave from his master. I often thought of doing so, but duty prevented me so doing.[7]

I shall now devote a page or two to giving a description of Washin[g]ton. The bishop, whose name was Covington, had been a Mississippi slave driver.[8] He could scarcely read or write but was a strong Mormon and had two wives and a numerous family. He was a strong Rebel sympathizer and rejoiced when ever he heard of a Southern victory.[9] His first councillor was called

---

[4]The family consisted of George, Betsy, and their four young boys—George W., Henry B., Moroni, and Robert.

[5]The Cotton Mission was to grow cotton on land watered by the Rio Virgin and Santa Clara rivers and their tributaries. Harmony was north of that area.

[6]The town of Washington, in Washington County, is six miles east of St. George.

[7]Called to the Cotton Mission at the same time as Hicks, Charles Lowell Walker arrived in St. George a week or so before Hicks reached Washington. The scene did not impress Walker: "To look on the country it [is a] dry, parched, barren waste with here and there a green spot on the margin of the streams. Very windy, dusty, blowing nearly all the time." Larson and Larson, eds., *Diary of Charles Lowell Walker,* 1:241.

[8]Born in North Carolina, Robert Dockery Covington (1815–1902) moved with his wife and his parents to Mississippi where they had a large cotton plantation and many slaves. Baptized in 1843, he moved to Nauvoo in 1845 and came to Utah in the pioneer company of 1847. He was bishop of Washington Ward from 1858 to 1869.

[9]The Civil War had started the year before.

A. W. Collins. He also had been a Southern slave driver.[10] He used to often entertain his hearers at places where people were gathered for public work, such as dam building or ditch making, by narrating acts of cruelty which he had committed in whipping slaves while on plantations in the South.

I will relate two of his acts of which he used to boast when in his best humor. One "nigger" man had been disobedient and he had had him tied up and he had whiped him till he thought it was enough. He had him turned lose. When he [the slave] made some thereat [*sic*] when he had the "nigger" tied up again and that time he determined to conquer him if he kille[d] him. He whiped him on the bare back, but the "nigger" was stubborn and would not beg. He whiped him till he fainted. Then he untied him and "brought him to" by putting salt on his back. "You bet your life that will fetch a nigger to in a hurry," he would say. He had him put in the cotton house and next morning he was *dead*.

Another of his exploits was his experience among the female slaves. One plantation where he had "overseed" there was quite a lot of nigger women and grown girls. He had had sexual intercourse with all but one, and that one was married to a young man. "I had tried her several times," he would say, ["]and she always refused, but that only made me the more determined. One day I put a lot of them to clean the crab grass out in a patch of corn. I went over after a while to see how they were doing when I found the nigger gal and her man sit[t]ing down betwixt two corn rows. I had my cow hide in my hand—I always carried it. She was looking [at] the nigger's head. Now was my time. I gave the nigger two or three licks with the whip and told him to go to work. The gal began to beg for him. The nigger jumped to work. I marched the gal off to a little grove and told her she must either give up to me or I would 'lick' her nearly to death. She gave up and I licked a sapling and she hollered."[11] Such had been his character and such his occupation when the "Gospel" found him in the Southern States. He was the owner of some property and a man of rather industrious habbits.

---

[10]Albert Washington Collins (1814–1873) was born in Georgia. The lives of the Collins and Covington families were interconnected: Collins married Susan N. Thomas, whose mother was a Covington, and Covington married Susan Thomas Collins's sister Elizabeth Ann Thomas. Both families had cotton plantations near the now-extinct town of Summerville, Mississippi. In 1846 the families moved to Winter Quarters and traveled to Utah in the Edward Hunter company in 1847.

[11]Overseers on the Deep South's cotton plantations treated their slaves brutally compared to those in border states such as Missouri and Kentucky. Mark Twain's *Pudd'nhead Wilson* memorably describes the terror slaves felt when threatened with being "sold down the river."

The second councillor of the bishop was named Robert Lloyd. He was from Texas. He had killed a man and then fled the country and became a Mormon. He was a man of some education. He was assessor and collector for the county of Washington and made his living mostly by his offices, for he was also pound keeper.[12] He was an inexorable creature on the poore both in taxes and pound bills.[13] He was a man that always had money and I have known him to buy wheat of [from] the poor to pay [their] taxes, postage, etc., for 50¢ pr. bushel when the price among the people (in trade) was $2.00.

With such a bishop and such a pair of councillors, one may imagine what kind of church government we had in Washington. The probate judge lived at Washington at that time.[14] His name was James D. McCullough. He was a gentleman and schollar. His wife was a lady of refinement and education. They were Tennesseans but had joined the Mormon Church in Texas.[15]

John D. Lee had two wives there and a portion of the time he lived there himself. I shall speak of him farther on as I got a[c]quainted with him and his family.[16]

The old settlers of Washington were all southerners and southern sympathizers. There were but two Union men in Washington—myself and an old friend from Nauvoo by the name of John P. Chidester. There were a number of men there who had taken a part in the Mountain Meadows Massacre, which was at that time called the Sebastopool affair. All of the[m] held a good standing in the church.

My self and my wife's brother-in-law, Robert Moncur by name, took a job of building [a] stone wall for "Uncle" Sam Adair, a fine old man who had once been a "hard-shell" Baptist preacher.[17] He was a good old man and paid us as

---

[12]Tennessean Robert Lewis Lloyd (1822–1892) joined the LDS church at age 17. He moved to near present-day Fort Worth, Texas, and married there. He and his wife arrived in Utah in 1854, and in March 1857 they were among the first ten families called to Washington County, where he became assessor and tax collector in 1862. No information has been found on his having killed someone, presumably in Tennessee.

[13]Stray animals were kept in the local pound until owners paid a "pound bill" to redeem them.

[14]Mormons completely controlled the probate courts at this time. Firmage and Mangrum, *Zion in the Courts*, 219.

[15]Born and married in Tennessee James Dillard McCullough (1827–1873) joined the LDS church in 1852 and came to Utah in 1856. He was appointed Washington County's first justice of the peace and in 1859 replaced John D. Lee as probate judge, an office he held until 1870.

[16]In this period John D. Lee had eight wives.

[17]Samuel Jefferson Adair (1806–1889) was born in South Carolina, but his family moved to Tennessee, Alabama, and Mississippi, where he was listed as "Christian" clergy or "Minister of the Gospel" between 1841 and 1845. He converted to the LDS faith in 1845, moving to Nauvoo and then to Iowa, where his wife and three sons died at Mount Pisgah. The surviving family came to Utah in 1852 and lived at Payson in 1857, when Samuel was called to lead the Cotton Mission with Robert D. Covington.

he agreed to do. During the winter when I was at Washington, a number of us started a dramatic company and gave a number of entertainments. I won considderable celebrity by playing "Steenie" in the "Rose of Etric Vale."[18]

In the spring [1863], I rented a few acres of land from A. W. Collins and planted it in cotton. During the latter part [of] that summer we sufered many privations. I had taken up a city lot but had neither time nor means to build a house so I built a brush wickiup like an Indian and we lived in it. One of our children—James W.—was born there. I well remember going over to St. George to see Erastus Snow to ask him for the *prialiege* [privilege] of working in his garden or doing any kind of labor for a little flour.[19] I had been told that the Danes of San Pete Co. had presented him a wagon load [of flour].[20] Snow treated me with the utmost contempt, telling me he could not feed ev[e]ry body, getting up and going out of the room in the most indignant manner, [and] leaving me to my reflections.[21] From that day to the present, I have entertained a distaste for that apostle and always expect to.

I well remember the first Spring [1863] that I lived in Washington that Apostle Snow came over from St. George to Washington to give us our instructions as to the kind of crops we should put in and the amount of each kind. He told us to put in all the [sugar] cane and cotton we could possably manage, for said he, "The breathren in the north will be very glad to b[u]y your cotton and molasses and pay you a good price for it." We followed the "voice and instructions" of this "inspired" fool and the consequence was that when fall came around, we had a cirplus [surplus] of cotton and mollases and a very poor market for either. There were a few men came in from the northern settlements to exchange flour and potatoes for cotton and

---

[18]"Wandering Steenie" was a major part in comedian Thomas J. Lynch's drama in two acts, *The Rose of Ettrick Vale, or, The Bridal of the Borders.* First written in 1825, the play was popular in Great Britain, Australia, and New Zealand as well as the United States. It was performed at Cedar City in the 1860s. Arrington and Bitton, *The Mormon Experience*, 219.

[19]Several verses of "Once I Lived in Cottonwood" refer to the scarcity of food: "I feel so weak and hungry now, there's nothing here to cheer/Except prophetic sermons which we very often hear."

[20]Apostle Erastus Snow (1818–1888) served as president of the Scandinavian Mission from 1850 to 1852. Sent to southern Utah in 1861 to oversee the Cotton Mission, Snow lived in St. George. The region suffered a major food shortage in 1863 and 1864 when a lengthy drought and flash floods on the Virgin River and its tributaries washed out the dams. Farther north in Sanpete County in central Utah, nearly a quarter of the residents were Danes. They probably responded to an appeal from Snow for flour. Arrington, *Great Basin Kingdom*, 216–19.

[21]At the April 1864 conference, Erastus Snow told the assembly that there were "over a thousand persons in St. George, one-half of whom would have to leave unless something was done to relieve the mission and help the poor man to continue his labors." Ibid., 219.

molasses. One hundred pounds of flour was worth sixteen of cotton. Cotton was worth .50 cts pr pound and molasses $1.00 per galon. It cost 16 lbs of cotton or 8 galons of molasses to buy one hundred pounds of flour. It was about all that myself and two little boys could do to pick cotton enough to make 16 pounds of gin[n]ed cotton in one day, and when we had furnished a scanty supply for the winter, we had nothing left to buy clothing with.[22] My wife did her best to clothe us by carding and spinning by hand, but the demand being so much greater than the suply that we soon became very destitute for clothing.[23] Shoes were out of the question. Many a day I went to the field bear-footed.[24]

Prest. B. Young came down to see us and spoke comforting words to us. He told us he was going to build a cotton factory and he would take our cotton and make it into cloth for ev[e]ry fifth yard.[25] We felt incouraged and we bour our toil with more patience. I heard Brigham make the promise in public at St. George.[26] In the mean time the poor were slowly starving.

We lived through until the next spring [1864] when the same Apostle Snow came over to give us our anuell [annual] instructions. (I think there is no set of men except lightning rod agents and commercial drummers that have the cheek of Mormon apostles.) I well remember how he talked to [us]. He began by telling us that last spring the Spirit of Wisdom had dictated him to tell us to plant all the cotton and cane we could manage, (he had a habbit of smacking his lips together), but this year (smack, smack), "the Sprit of Wisdom (smack, smack) seems to dictate us to instruct you to put in all the

[22]The two oldest Hicks boys were then nine and six years old.

[23]Several verses from Hicks's "Once I Lived in Cottonwood" touch on the scarcity of clothing.

[24]On his way to St. George in 1861, cotton missionary Robert Gardner (1819–1906) met old neighbors as he passed through Washington and found their appearance discouraging: "nearly all of them had the fever and ague or chills as they called it in this country. They had worked hard and had wore out their clothes and had replaced them from the cotton they had raised on their own lots and farms which their women had carded, spun and wove by hand. Colored with weeds, men's shirts, women's dresses and sunbonnets were all made of the same piece; and their clothes and their faces were of the same color, being a kind of blue as most everyone had the chills. This tried me more than anything I have seen in my Mormon experience. Thinking that my wives and children, from the nature of the climate, would have to look as sickly as those now around me." Gardner, Biography and Journal, 49 (punctuation and spelling corrected).

[25]The settlers paid for the factory services by giving it every fifth yard.

[26]President Young bought the water rights to Mill Creek in 1864 to power a cotton factory. On 5 May 1865 he wrote to Erastus Snow asking him to look for a suitable site for the factory along that creek. On 18 September 1865 Young bought the land on which to erect a factory while visiting St. George. He intended to move the machinery of an existing mill in Parley's Canyon near Salt Lake to Washington when the factory was built. Larson, *Red Hills of November*, 184; Journal History, 17 September, 2; and 18 September 1865, 1.

Apostle Erastus Snow
Born in Vermont, Erastus Fairbanks Snow joined the Mormons in 1833. When Brigham Young lost a telescope in 1847 while chasing cattle in Snow's charge, Young gave him a "regular built dressing," saying Snow "would not go out of his road one rod, he is so lazy." Snow went on to become one of the first two men to enter Salt Lake Valley and an apostle in 1849. Sent south in 1861, Snow was the Cotton Mission's spiritual leader when George A. Hicks asked him for a little flour. The apostle responded "with the utmost contempt, telling me he could not feed ev[e]ry body." Snow died of diabetes at Salt Lake City in 1888. *Courtesy Utah State Historical Society.*

wheat and corn you can (smack)."[27] The truth is Snow was ignorant of the real wants of the people and he tried to conceal his ignorance behind the "spirit of inspiration." One thing which I noticed, there were a few men who acted a wiser part and raised grain and those who had a surplus sold it to men that were frieghting goods from California for there own price to feed there teams on, while we poor—who had followed the instructions of the "Spirit of Wisdom"—had to suffer for bread.

As soon as I could do it, I left Washington and mooved to Harmony where I underwent many hard ships and privation[s] which I shall try to describe in my next chapter.[28] About the time I left Washington, Prest. B.

[27]Novelist Maurine Whipple, basing her description on church magazine articles and "local memory," wrote of Snow's "characteristic writhing of his lips back from his teeth and the following smack which prefaced most of his slow, quiet speech." Whipple, *The Giant Joshua*, preface, 57.

[28]After the Civil War, the price of cotton dropped nationally. Many cotton missionaries, finding it impossible to make a living, left. Nearby mining towns at Pioche, Nevada, and Silver Reef, Utah, provided a new market for wine, molasses, and dried fruit, so many of the remaining settlers stopped growing cotton to raise cash crops "under circumstances almost unbelievably adverse," Leonard Arrington observed. "It seemed to the colonists as though all earth and hell had conspired to render the Cotton Mission a failure. Year after year, calamity after calamity forced the colonists to their knees." Alkali soil, floods, *(continued)*

THE COTTON FACTORY

The Cotton factory on Mill Creek near Washington, Utah, produced cloth for the Cotton Mission. George A. and Elizabeth Hicks attended the opening celebration of the first floor, built of red sandstone and timber, on 24 July 1866. Machinery arrived from Salt Lake City in 1867, and a second story and attic were added in 1870. In spite of initial success and great hopes among the people who earned a salary there, competition from the South and high production costs in an arid desert led farmers in Utah's "Dixie" to turn to more lucrative crops. The factory limped along until 1904. Restored by Norma Cannizzaro in the 1980s, it is now the Star Nursery. The Washington County Historical Society attests that the factory "is now a center of all that is good in Washington City." Historic American Building Survey, Delos H. Smith, Photographer. *Courtesy Library of Congress.*

Young began to build his cotton factory. The people had great hopes of better times when that should start up. By and by the bui[l]ding was completed and a grand ball was given in honor of the ocation [occasion]. My wife and I were invited and we went a distance of 30 miles. The factory at length had

droughts, locust and cricket infestations, malaria, and "backbreaking toil under a broiling sun" made many give up and leave, and "those who remained frequently had cause to doubt the wisdom of their call." Arrington, *Great Basin Kingdom,* 221. See also Larson, *"I Was Called to Dixie,"* 192, 205; and Topping, *Leonard J. Arrington,* 90–91.

the machinery put in motion and it began to produce a pretty fair quality of cotton yarn, but our Prophet, Seer, and Revelator had made the discovery that he could not afford to take the people's cotton as he had agreed to do and card and spin and weave it into cloth for the fifth yard, but he would buy their cotton and sell them yarn. He would pay .40 cts pr. pound for gin[n]ed cotton and he would sell them yarn for $10.00 pr. bund[le] of 5 pounds (or for the remarkable low price of two dollars pr. pound) or 5 pound[s] of cotton would buy one pound of yarn. He also produced a very inferior quality of cotton "factory" which was sold for .50 cts. pr. yard. This cloth woul[d] not in any way compare with the "factory" that is now brought in to this country and sold for 10 cts pr. yard.[29] The yarn was twisted to[o] hard and in weaving it did not beat up close but was very open.

The opening of the factory was hailed with delight, for it afforded a better opurtunity to get clothing than making it by hand. Besides it gave employment to a number of people, and the spinning wheel and the hand looms were laid aside and a better day dawned on the people, for a small income is much bet[t]er than no income. The factory was not long running before machinery for making wollen [*sic*] goods was put in and the making of cotton fabrics were stoped.[30] Although many were disappointed by the course of Prest. B. Young, the factory proved a great benefit to the poor of Washington County. The factory was in time sold out in shares which never paid any dividen[d], the profits being consumed in paying interest on money that Prest. B. Young advanced the managers to get a supply of materials to carry on the business, which never was a success.[31]

Before closing this chapter, I feel it my duty to record a number of circumstances which I [k]new to transpire in Washington before I left there. While I was living there, an *election* was held for the choosing [of] territorial and county officers. I know that I saw and heard a number of men at the polls give in names of men and *vote them* who were not there and very probably

[29]"Factory" meant unbleached muslin cloth made in a factory instead of by hand.

[30]President Young told the southern Saints on 1 May 1869 that if they raised wool as well as cotton, he would move his woolen factory down from the north. Larson, *Red Hills of November*, 190.

[31]The cotton factory began operations in 1867, but nearly always lacked enough money to buy raw materials and pay the employees and mechanics. Brigham Young encouraged the local people to buy shares and make it a cooperative company. They established Zion's Cooperative Rio Virgen Manufacturing Company in 1871 and agreed to pay Young forty-four thousand dollars for his investment, to be paid with interest in annual payments. The business was a failure and shareholders did not receive dividends. Larson, *"I Was Called to Dixie,"* 195–99, 202, 203–234; Larson, *Red Hills of November*, 193; Arrington, *Great Basin Kingdom*, 219–20, 318–19.

there were no such men in existence. I heard one leading men [*sic*] at the polls say it made no difference as we all voted the same way.[32]

Again—I once went to the post office to enquire for letters. I was told by Mrs. Crawford, the wife of the P.M. [postmaster] that the mail had not come in that week. "Is it not due?" said I. "Yes," said Mrs. Crawford, "it was due yesterday. I have h[e]ard from it—it will be here in a few days. Br. Snow sent his molasses mill rol[l]ers up to Parrowan to get them turned and as soon as Br. Wilcox gets them done, the mail will come." I said, "Oh." It was then that the priesthood ruled us.

I had hired to work for a man by the name of Thos. Adair—one of the hero(s) of the Mountain Meadow Massacre, as I afterwards learned—to work for one month.[33] The work was getting the water out of South Ash Creek to be applied in the town of Bellevew.[34] I was to have 20 bush[els] of wheat for my month's work. I done my month's work. Part of the time I stayed alone and lived on bread baked in the ashes and molasses. Adair gave me an order for 20 bushels of wheat on [a] man by the name of "Jimmy" Williamson at Pahragoona [Paragonah] in Iron Co. I went and presented my order, but Williamson would [not] let me have any wheat. I sent Adair word and wa[i]ted 8 days for him to come and get my wheat. He did not come and I went home without it. I sued Adair and got judgement for $60.00. I had a jury of 6 men. They divided the [court] cost between Adair and myself. The cost was $15.00. I paid my share by hauling manure for the judge (McCulloch). I asked the judge how the cost came to so much. He informed me that he had filed the complaint and the answer and that should have been done by the parties or there [their] attorneys and he had allowed himself $8.00 for that. Adair had nothing that could be taken by law, so I was $7.50 poorer than when I went to law.[35] I then concluded to try Adair in the church. He thought a great

[32]The fortifying of the voter rolls was no doubt related to the efforts by the church leadership in 1862 to qualify for statehood.

[33]A brother of "Uncle Sam" Adair who had hired Hicks and Moncur when they first arrived in Washington, Thomas Jefferson Adair (1814–1890) was born in Indiana. His family converted to Mormonism in 1844 or 1845. They moved to Mount Pisgah, Iowa, with the Saints, and there Thomas's wife and two of his children died. In 1850 he remarried and migrated to Utah in 1852. The Adairs were living in Payson in 1857 when they were called to the Cotton Mission. Hicks facetiously referred to Thomas as a "hero" of the Mountain Meadows massacre, but he has confused him with his brother George Washington Adair, a participant.

[34]In 1925 Bellvue (or Bellview) was renamed Pintura. Located on Ash Creek, it lies between Cedar City and St. George.

[35]That is, half the court fee.

deal of his standing in the church. He would not suffer the case to come to a trial, but paid me the wheat. I got the 20 bush[els], but it cost me $85.00 [?] before I did so, beside[s] any amount of vexation an[d] disappointment.

One circumstance I had forgotten. When I first mooved to Washington, I was told that Bp. Covington had taken a young man up for stealing peaches and fined him 85 dollars and had taken a city lot from [him] to pay the fine. While I was there he took up and fined a man by the name of Follett 5 dollars for letting his oxen get in the field. The bishop held his court on Sunday afternoon. All this he claimed he had the right to d[o] by his authority in the priesthood. It so happened that O[rson] Pratt, the apostle, preached in St. George the same day on the power and authority of the priesthood, and in the course of his remarks, he said that the priesthood would never have authority to deprive men of liberty or property but only to deal with them in their fellowship in the c[h]urch.[36]

While I was living at Washington, when Prest. B. Young published his famous decree that men should be cut off from the church for not paying tithing, and I believe that Walker Bros. of Salt Lake City were the first to [be] cut off and they have prospered ever since and are now millionaires.[37]

Before I close this chapter, I will try to give [a] description of a strange character. His name was Parker. He called himself Doctor Parker. He claimed to know all that was known on Earth. I once heard him say that he had recie'd [received] the keys of know[l]edge from Jos. Smith, the prophet. The people of Washington believed him to be in possession of the power of witchcraft. He was called Pegleg Parker because he had at some period of his life lost one of his legs and had a wooden one which when he walked made a creaking noise, and at the end of e[a]ch step, the leg made a peculiar snap[p]ing noise as though there was a wooden spring which flew in and

[36]*D&C*, 134:10 asserted that religious societies had a right to deal with their members' disorderly conduct according to their rules and regulations, "provided that such dealings be for fellowship and good standing." Religious societies lacked "authority to try men on the right of property or life, to take from them this world's goods, or put them in jeopardy of either life or limb, or to inflict any physical punishment upon them. They can only excommunicate them from their society, and withdraw from them their fellowship."

[37]Hicks probably referred to September 1868 when President Young said the people should not spend a single cent with merchants who did not tithe. Walker Brothers, run by apostate Mormons, was initially greatly affected, especially as Young was developing his ideas for cooperative merchandizing, which resulted in the establishment of the Zion's Co-operative Mercantile Institution (ZCMI). The development of mining in Utah saved Walker Brothers and other non-Mormon merchants. See Arrington, *Great Basin Kingdom*, 296–99, 306–307, 496n61.

out of place.[38] This noise might be heard for ten to fifteen rods of[f] as he walked the streets. He allways carried two canes to assist him in walking, one of which was armed at the lower end by having a kind of tommahawk put on to it. This, he said, he carried to defend himself against dogs, which alwa[y]s came out at him because of the peculiar noise he made in walking. His clothes were always shabby and dirty and on his head he wore a kind of hood with a curtain around the back part of his head. This hood was similar to those I have seen on the head of priests in Bible pictures. The hood was generaly made of red flannel but was always filthy and dirty looking. Parker was tall and slender with sharp visage and small piercing eyes. He was very quick spoken with a coars[e], huskey voice. He was the father of a large family whom he supported by begging from door to door. He came there after I did. He had a large boney woman for a wife that always carried a sheath knife at her waist and used tobaco.

Parker always did the begging. He generaly went around in the forenoon of the day when the men were about [their work]. The women were all afraid of him and would give the last bit of brea[d] in [the] house before they would gain his ill will. He allways had a tail [tale] of misfortune to tell [of] poverty and loss. A large majority of the people believed he had power to curse and to bring evil to anyone he chose to afflict. He could bewitch the cows, he could kill oxen by witchcraft, he could afflict the infant in the cradle or the father at the plow. In short, he could do any thing his Satanic Majesty could do and it was believed by some that Parker and the Devil often used to meet each other and hold consultations. When the poor werer [*sic*] starving, Parker had plenty.

I well rem[em]ber him coming in to my house to beg. When he came in, I happened to be in. "How do you do, how do you do," said he. I offered him a seat which he took. He then asked my name, when and where I was born. I told him. Then he wanted to know the hour. I told him "9 o'clock."

---

[38]Samuel Parker, born about 1795 in New Hampshire, and his wife, Mary Elizabeth Gifford Parker, crossed the plains in the Brigham Young company in 1848 and settled in Salt Lake City. The 1850 census places the Parkers in Salt Lake with Samuel listed as a teacher. John H. Woodbury recalled going to school on West Temple and Fifth South. "A man named Parker was the teacher. 'Pegleg' Parker we boys called him." By the 1860 census Samuel, Mary, and five young children were living in Goshen, Cedar County. The date of his death is unknown; neither he nor his family appear in the 1870 census. Mary Parker was murdered in April 1880 in Rockville, Washington County. "She was the widow of Samuel Parker, a lame man, known by some as Doctor Parker," the *Deseret News* wrote. "She was a strange woman and sometimes disagreeable in her manners, but was always true to the work of God. After she lived with Parker she was called a witch by many, who were foolish enough to believe it." "More of the Parker Murder," *Deseret News*, 9 June 1880, 8.

"Well, well," said the old man. "You ought to be a man that knowes enough to take care of your self." He then began his tale of woe. I was not afraid of him, but I gave him a few potatoes for we had no bread nor any thing to make it of. He blessed me and mine for *ever* and departed. He neve[r] came back for he [k]new who had bread and who had none.

Him and family lived in one room of a house belonging to one of my friends. I was once in there in my friend's room when Parker and his family were preparing for family prayers. Lee, Johnny Lee, was the name of my friend. He was fond of a joke. I listened while Parker prayed. His pray[e]r was long and earnest. I never can forget the closing parigraphs of that prayer. "O Lord," he went on, "Bless me and mine. Bless the hair of my head and my toe nails, the oil in my joints and the marrow in my bones, my good leg and my stump. Reveal ev[e]rything to me that ever has been revealed, can be revealed, or will be revealed. Give me as many wives as Solomon had—seven hundred and fifty—and two of them right away. In the name of Jesus, Amen." "Give me a drink of water and I will go to work," said the old man in the same breath. I think the old man was nearer a lunatic than a (male) witch. He afterward visited a milk ranch at Pinto Creek in Iron Co. and drank so much cheese whey that he died and ev[e]ry body was glad.

I will now close this chapter by bidding good-by[e] to Washington, and on the 27[th] day of Apr. we left there with out sellin[g] my property and on the 30[th] day of Apr 18[64] we reached Harmony,[39] but had nothing for supper the night before but milk and no money to buy any thing with although there was plenty to sell there.

Chapter XV.
Poor Devil: Life at Harmony

On the first day of May [1864] I took up a piece of land on Ash Cre[e]k two miles below Harmony, and the same day I trim[m]ed up a number of small ash trees and prepared to build a brush wickiup to live in. My father-in-law had mooved there before I did. He was well off, but he is a man that believes in every body helping themselves. I went up to Harmony and borrowed a little corn meal of Wm. Pace, Uncle Billy as he was called. He was a close dealer but was not destitute of sympathy for the poor. I had known him

[39]Fort Harmony was abandoned in 1862 after a severe rainstorm demolished it. New Harmony—generally called Harmony—where Hicks moved, was built several miles upstream on Ash Creek.

and family before they came there. Mr. Pace was well to do in the world. He had been sent to Washington Co. to raise cotton, he being a Southern man, but had stoped at Harmony, had taken up a farm, and had plenty while I, poor Devil, had went on my mission as I was told by the priesthood and had nothing to eat. I will remark here that Mr. Pace was well of[f] before he came here and I was not.

John D. Lee was at that time president of the Harmony Branch of the church.[1] Wm. and James Pace, his brother, were the adopted sons of John D. and they had been invited to settle there by Lee.[2] One of my old Spanish Fork neighbors by the name of Stephen R. Wells had been sent to St. George on a mission the year before. Br. Wells had been the owner of a good farm at Spanish Fork and had plenty, but he had now become reduced to almost [a] starving point. He came to Harmony to hunt work. He wanted bread for his family. He would work for the Paces or anyone els[e] for what ever the[y] had a mind to pay him. William Pace had a family of grown up sons, two of whom lived at Harmony, Willson D. and Harvey A.[3] These "boys" were well to do, particularly Wils, as the eldest was called, but he was a remorseless wretch. The wail of the hungry made no impresion on him, but Harvey A. was kind, generous, and noble-spirited.

It so happened that the people of Harmony concluded to build in the form of a town on a piece of unbroken ground. The ground was covered with oak brush. Br. Wells went and offered to grub brush for Wils P[ace]. Wils offered him one half bushel of corn pr. day to grub oak brush. Wells had no alternative. He had children at home that were starving and he accepted the proposal. Corn was worth $4.50 pr. bushel, Wils said, and if

---

[1]Lee, still a prominent churchman and speaker, resigned as branch president of Harmony on 5 March 1864, a month before the Hicks family arrived, "because of much dissatisfaction among the people toward him. Elder James H. Imlay was selected and set apart to succeed him as President." Shirts and Shirts, *A Trial Furnace*, 407. The Harmony Branch at that time belonged to Bishop Henry Lunt's Cedar City Ward.

[2]The "law of adoption" was a temple rite that sealed a person to a leader to establish temporal and spiritual family ties. It was never widely practiced and is no longer part of the LDS faith. James Pace (1811–1888), born in Tennessee, was the brother of William Franklin Pace. An 1839 convert, he moved to Nauvoo, where Joseph Smith made him a policeman in 1843. He served in the Mormon Battalion and moved his family to Utah in 1850. After living twenty years in New Harmony and Washington, Utah, he spent the rest of his life in southern Arizona. Pace, Autobiography.

[3]Wilson Daniel Pace (1831–1899) and Harvey Alexander Pace (1833–1917) were born in Tennessee. Wilson went west to California as servant to Lt. Andrew Lytle in the Mormon Battalion (he was fifteen), while Harvey came to Utah with the rest of the family in 1848. A veteran of the Walker War of 1853, Harvey was called on the Cotton Mission in 1861 and settled in New Harmony. Wilson moved south where he became New Harmony's bishop in 1867. The next year he married John D. Lee's daughter Elizabeth.

a man got two dollars pr day and board he did well. Pace said Br. Brigham had said that when bread stuff went up, labor should not go up also. That is about the only quotation I ever heard him make from the prophet. The usual price for a day's labor was one bushel of corn or wheat. The reason I have been so particular in relating the above circumstance is because that it became the price of labor and the poor must work for that or starve. I will say right here that Harvey Pace never paid less that [than] one bushel pr. day, but he hired very little work done.

I was then in the prime of life and was used to labor. I was counted rather extra with an ax. I set to work with a will to chop fencing and to clearing my land. I fenced, cleared, and put in about 4 acres to corn, potatoes, sorghum, and garden stuff. I would go and work for the Paces when I was out of bread and then for myself. It took me about h[a]lf my time to get bread for my family. We had milk (my father-in-law had plen[t]y of cows). My last and only cow got poisoned and died there.[4] During that summer I got a land war[r]ant from the gover[n]ment for the services in the Walker War in 1853. I sold it for $85.00 in cash. It called for 160 acres of land and was just as good in a U.S. land office as $200.00, but I had to sell it or starve.[5] I had offered Pratt Pace 8 cts. pr. pound for some corn shorts only fit for pig feed.[6] I offered him labor, but he refused me, but when I got my money I went and got the shorts and it was used as food in my family.

I will here say that on my way up to Harmony, I tried the experiment of the philosopher. I put a piece of silver coin into my mouth to see if it would have any affect on the pangs of hunger that were gnawing at my vitals, but I found it had no effect whatever.[7] I bought some corn from Wils Pace, enough to keep me untill nearly fall, but I got out and for three weeks and four days, lived without bread, but we had plenty of "garden stuff." My corn got ripe. I cut it and hauled it in to a corral. I had taken the Harmony sheep to herd. One of my dicey [?] friends had sent one of his cows up to our place. One

[4]Possibly from bovine anthrax or locoweed.

[5]Under the Pension Act of 1832, Hicks was allowed 160 acres of bounty land and, having filed an application, he was awarded a land warrant. Most veterans sold or exchanged their warrants. Walker War veteran Harvey A. Pace also received a warrant for 160 acres.

[6]Parley Pratt Pace (1844–1882) was a younger brother of Wilson and Harvey Pace.

[7]No source for this story has been found. Classics scholar Radcliffe Edmonds of Bryn Mawr College does not believe this anecdote has classical antecedents. Edmonds, email to Polly Aird, 5 November 2008. Perhaps this is a variation of sucking a smooth stone to alleviate thirst, a folk remedy in arid areas. For example, see Clark, *Travel and Adventure*, 53.

night this breechy cow [one that could breach a fence] broke through my fence and let in the sheep herd and when I arose in the morning, my corn was all wasted. I did not kill the cow.

That same fall my wife set fire to our brush wickiup and burned it down. This, of course, was acidental. We lost considerable of our scanty household goods. I then built a cedar log house and made it quite comfortable with out floor or window. Winter came on cold and severe. We had a large family of small children. I went up and hired out to Uncle Billy Pace for ½ bushel corn and board per day when the weather was suitable to work. I was choping cedar picket to[o]. These pickets were of such a size that 25 of them would made a load for a yoke of oxen and wagon. I also cut two stakes to each of these pickets I cut, never less than 50 pickets and 100 stakes and often more. I remember one day cutting 75 pickets and 150 stakes. I was consciencious [conscientious] and believed it my duty to do a fair day's work although I knew I was only getting half pay.

During that winter my brother S. M. [Samuel Moroni Hicks] came down to see the southern country. He came to visit me and saw our destitute circumstances. He made a traid [trade] with Pratt Pace and got ten bushel[s] of corn and gave it to me that helped me out till after crop planting time.

I remark here that during the harvest before, I could not get to work a single day for any of the farmers. The Paces joined together and done their own work. Grain was high and they would work night and day rather than hire. If I had an enemy that I wanted to punish, I should, if I had [the] power, give him a large family, send him to Harmony, and *compel* him to work for Wils Pace, and Wils should have the privilege of paying what ever he (Pace) thought to be right.

The next spring I mooved up to Harmony and sol[d] out my place to Br. Josep[h] L. Heywood for some cows. I thought I could do better by day wages and so I did. I took a job of making adobies [adobe bricks] for Lemuel H. Redd.[8] I took my wife's brother-in-law with me, Robert Moncur. Redd was to let us have a beef ox to kill in the fall the [that] he said had a touch of the big jaw [lockjaw] but not enough to hurt him any. The ox was off on a ranch get[ting] fat. The herds man had told him that the ox was

[8]North Carolinian Lemuel Hardison Redd (1836–1910) grew up in Tennessee, where John D. Lee converted his parents and the Pace family in 1842. Two of his sisters married Pace brothers and he married Keziah Jane Butler, daughter of John L. Butler. The Redd, Pace, and Butler families were from the South and all lived in Spanish Fork before moving to Harmony.

getting very fat. We took Redd's word for it. We were to have our board while making the dobies.

I will now relate one circumstance that one day while we were at dinner, the butter on the table gave out and "Lem" told his daughter to go down [to the] cellar and get some more butter. His wife, who by the way is a daughter of Bp. John L. Butler, spoke up and said no, butter was worth 40 cts. pr. pound. The girl stoped, but Lemuel made her go and get the butter while Kizziah, for that was here [*sic*] name, done some severe grumbling.

Robert Moncur never came back any mor[e] for his meals, but I was not so easily daunted. The board was part of our wages and it proved [to] be about all that was wort[h] any thing, for in the fall, when we got our beef ox, he was so poor that he was nearly worthless and if it had not have been for our extream want, we never would have eaten the meet [meat], but hunger is a refiner of the human apetite.

Br. Lemuel H. Redd is a good Mormon, has three wives sealed to him, and has pas[s]ed through all the Endowment House honors, but he has never paid Bob Moncur and I for making his dobies and probably never will. Kizziah, his wife, was a good match for him. Once when one of Moncur's children went to Redd's for some beef that Redd was owing him, after the child had gotten the beef and had started home, it suddenly [came] to Kizziah that there might be some fat about the meet. She told the child to stop and let her look at the meet. She found a smal[l] piece of fat and began to cut it off. "Don't," said Lem. "I will," said she, "for that grease will make soap. Now go," said she to the child.

I was living at Harmony when Prest. Lincoln was assas[s]inated. I well remember Lem Redd quoting the words of [John Wilkes] Booth, the assassion: "Sic semper tyranis," and rejoicing because the president was killed.[9] Redd was a southern man as also were the Paces and John D. Lee.

I was living at Harmoney when Prest. B. Young started cooperation in all branches of business that he could. It is my opinion that tithing was the sole cause of cooperation in Utah. As it was, people paid an individual tithing, but if they put their property into a cooperation, then he (B. Young) would be more likely to get a true tithing.[10] I was living at Harmoney when

[9]"Sic semper tyrannis" is Latin for "Thus, ever [or always] to tyrants."

[10]As Andrew Karl Larson wrote, placing livestock into cooperative herds "guaranteed both care of the stock and profits from them; furthermore it permitted the long arm of the church to keep in close touch with this important industry and to exercise a large measure of control over its operations," since local LDS leaders invariably dominated the cooperative boards. "*I Was Called to Dixie*," 237.

Cedar City started their coop sheep herd, which afterwards became note[d] as a profitable investment.[11] About three or four years after it started, the directors thought best to improve the stock of their sheep. The Cotswold was at that time recommended. The directors asked the advice of Prest. Young as to whether he considered the Cotswold the best kind of sheep to introduce. An idea flashed into the mind of that brilliant financier. Cotswold were the best, said the prophet, and he had them to *sell* cheap for cash. Of course these fanatical Cedarites would patronise "President Young." They bought fifty head of bucks at sixty dollars pr. head. I presume the people of Cedar were at that time like myself—totally ignorant of what a Cotswold sheep was like. In two years after they found out. They had made a great mistake in buying these bucks from Prest. Young and their wool clip had greatly diminished, but the Prophet had profited by their loss. I have often seen the Cedar sheep herd and I do not bel[i]eve there was any Cotswold blood in any of the bucks sold them by that "man of God." I was told the above by one of the directors of the herd. The "Cotswolds" and all their male progeny [were] soon destroyed and other blood infused.[12] It is my opinion that Brigham Young sen[ior] worshiped no God but gold, that he would sacrific[e] friends, honor, fame, and ev[e]ry thing over which he had any control for to increase his earthly wealth.

Chapter XVI.
The Character of John D. Lee

In this chapter I shall endever to describe the character of John D. Lee and family. Lee was a stout heavy set man of fair complexion, rather corpulant. He had a low forehead on a short, thick neck. He was a man of industrious

[11]Cedar City formed a cooperative sheep herd in 1870. By the fall of 1874, the herd numbered ten thousand head and the cooperative was "paying a handsome dividend." "Correspondence," *Deseret News*, 1 April 1874, 7; "Our Country Correspondence," *Deseret News*, 29 November 1874, 11.

[12]During the fall of 1873, the Cedar City sheep board bought six Cotswold bucks for six hundred dollars. A year's experience convinced most that the breed was not adapted to local conditions. "The wool is not so saleable, and a flock of three thousand Cotswold sheep will eat and destroy more range than six thousand Merinos," a major consideration in arid, impoverished Iron County. The mixed Cotswold ewes lacked the mothering skills of the Merinos: during lambing "they are more wild and scary, requiring great care and cautiousness from the herdsman, or else they will drop their lambs and run away." Scotia, "Correspondence," *Deseret News*, 1 March 1876, 10. Where the sheep board bought the Cotswold bucks is not known. Perhaps they asked Brigham Young's advice when he passed through Cedar City about 12 December 1873.

habbits. He was a good farmer and stock raiser. He was the owner (by squatter's right) of a large and valuable farm. He was quite an orator in the pulpit, but was not reliable in his scriptural quotations. If he wanted to make a point, he had no hesatancy in *making* scripture to prove his point. I presume he got into the habbit of it by preaching to a lot of ignorant families by the name of Wolsey that had settled around him at Harmony at an early day.[1]

I well remember Lee preaching on the principle of people defending themselves against there enamies. He quoted from the New Testament where Jesus had *commande[d]* Peter to draw h[i]s sword and fight the servants of the High Priests. (See Mat. 26 chap, ver[se] 51 and 52. See also John 18th chap, 10 and 11 verses.) After meeting was out, I step[p]ed up to Lee and told him there was no such scripture as he had quoted and I would prove it. Lee folded his arms in a dignifide manner, saying he would be pleased to learn from wiser men. I steped over the street home and got the Bible and showed Lee where Jesus had forbidden the use of the sword. Lee was for the moment non-plussed. He went home and the next day I saw him and he was prepared for the ocation [occasion]. He had not had a revalation, as was his custom, but he remembered that Br. Joseph had told him that Jesus had so taught. Of course that was a clincher I could not dispute.

Lee was once chosen orator of the day for the 24th of July [Pioneer Day 1869] and in the course of his remarks, he was telling us how the Mormon Battalion had passed through so many dangers and trials and how the Lord had sent His angels to watch over them.[2] When Lee had worked *himself* up to a sufficient pitch, he began to discribe a particularly narrow escape that the Battalion had passed through. It was like this: The Mexicans were laying in ambush watching the approach of the "weary and worn out soldiers," but God put it into the heart of their leader to turn aside and go another way. The Battalion passed in saf[e]ty. Then the enemy who had been disappointed of his prey undertook to follow the trail of the Battalion, but the Lord had covered up their *trail*. Then Lee turned up his eyes, extended both his hands in the air, with tears coursing down his cheeks, asked the question, "Why

[1]Joseph Hyrum Woolsey (1828–1886) married Lucinda Jameson Woolsey at Council Bluffs in 1846. The 1860 census locates them in Payson, Utah County, and by 1870 they were living in Cedar City with five children. The parents could read but not write. None of the children, including one age 12 and another 13, could read or write. 1870 U.S. Census, Cedar City, Iron, Utah Territory, Roll M593-1610, 263.

[2]Lee was selected orator of the day on 24 July 1869 "to represent the Pioneers. I spoke 1 hour & give good satisfaction. Bp. W.D. Pace [represented] the M[ormon]. Battalion. All went off well." Cleland and Brooks, eds., *A Mormon Chronicle*, 2:123.

was the Lord Almighty so mindful of that handful of men wandering in the desert? It was because they put trus[t] in that Arm that could not be broken." Perhaps I was wanting in appreciation of Lee's eloquence, but it had the effect to make me laugh.

Lee sat down amidst the applause of his audie[n]ce. Bp. Wilson D. Pace took the platform as next speaker. He said that if any thing such as Br. Lee had been talking about had ever hap[p]aned, he had never heard of it before, and he was one of the Battalion. Pace continued that he presumed that Br. Lee was al[l]uding to a time that the Battalion were traveling on a road that led to the copper mines in Mexico from California. This road was a plain wagon road, "as plain as the road from here to Kannarrah [Kanarra]," said the bishop, "and I could see it for more than ten miles. This road led to[o] much to the south to suit our commander, and he turned of[f] to the west of it. In a few days we heard," said Pace, "that some Mexicans were laying in ambush for us." Lee was completely discomfit[t]ed. Oh cruel deed, Pace, to spoil the effect of that marvelous escape! Lee was not in the Battalion. I have since read Tyler's history of the Mormon Battalion and I fail to find anything for a foundation for Lee to build on.[3]

I have been told that Lee would go to where men were assembled and play the evesdroper [eavesdropper] and in a day or two would make known what he had heard and say the Lord had revealed it to him. I myself have heard [him] say that he has seen holy angels and conversed with them.[4] Lee was a swindler in dealing, a liar in conversation, and a low sensual brute of a man. He has been the husband of 19 wives, although he had but eight when I knew him.[5] He was undoubtedly a hypocrite in religion. His house was a great stoping place for "Gentile" strag[g]lers, and if rumer [rumor] is to [be] credited, his house was but little better than a house of ill fame. His wives were in the habbit to twitting each other of their *little foibles* and once while

[3]Tyler, *A Concise History of the Mormon Battalion*. Tyler had been a sergeant of Company C. Church president John Taylor, who succeeded Brigham Young, encouraged Tyler to write this heroic religious epic, which George Q. Cannon edited with a heavy hand.

[4]In March 1855 Indian missionary Thomas D. Brown found that Lee had an "abundance of dreams, vision and revelations, from which he instructs, reproves & governs; telling most of them in public meetings, saying his position as leader of this people demands that he should have such close association with the heavens, but some of the people say that they know his most important revelations are those he overhears listening as an eavesdropper. He listened behind a fence to Brors P. Shirts & Wm. Young who were talking of his immeasurable selfishness, and he repeated it next meeting as having read it from a sheet let down from the heavens before his eyes, this caused much ill feeling among the brethren, for he was seen listening by a third party." Brooks, *Journal of the Southern Indian Mission*, 118.

[5]Hicks is correct about the number of Lee's wives. See Brooks, *John Doyle Lee*, 378.

I lived at Harmony, his wives made general confession to Lee and to each other for having had sexual intercourse with Richard Darling (Rattle-snake Dick, as he was called). This man was a deserter from Camp Douglass. Lee preached Mormonism to [him]. He was baptized into the church and married one of Lee's daughters, lived with her for six months, then stol[e] a horse, a revolver, and a suit of clothes, and then ran away while Lee was gone to S. L. City to have more wives sealed to him. I well remember Lee came home without getting the wives. He seemed much depres[s]ed, for he had prophecied that Darling would become a great man in the Kingdom of God.[6]

My reasons for being so particular in describing Lee and his family are these: I wish to show the kind of society that was good enough for our Prophet, Seer, and Revelator to honor (!) with his company when making his ann[u]al tours through his kingdom. I was living at Harmony one spring when Prest. Young and company were making a visit to southern Utah when our prophet manifested his brotherly affection for Lee by going to his house, him and his train of tithing-eaters staying with him all night.[7] There were other men at Harmony who were more able to entertain our president and were very much disappointed by not having the priviliege of entertaining him, but they were plain, honest men and had not distinguished themselves by sheading innocent blood like "Br. Lee" had done at Mountain Meadows.

[6]Born in Kentucky about 1840, John Richard Darling was mustered in as a private in the First Battalion of the Nevada Cavalry based at Fort Churchill. In the fall of 1864 his company was sent to Camp Douglas. He married John D. Lee's daughter in the spring of 1866. Although Lee's diaries do not cover this period, Lee's last wife, Ann Gordge, and Hicks, under the pseudonym "Bosco," in a letter to the editor of the *Salt Lake Tribune*, identify her as Nancy, daughter of Rachel Andora Woolsey Lee. Gordge described Darling as a good fiddler who had to join the LDS church to marry Lee's daughter. In mid-May 1866 Darling and his bride left Utah and set out for Virginia City, Nevada, by stagecoach. During the trip he robbed a female passenger of her watch and money, and Darling was later accused of several robberies around Virginia City. Imprisoned, he insisted he was innocent. In May 1867 John D. Lee claimed he received twenty-five dollars from a man who had bought a horse "that Dick Darling stole from me and sold to him." On 1 May 1868 the Utah Southern Mission conference cut off Darling "for unfaithful conduct." Darling married saloonkeeper Jessie M. Case in October 1871 at Virginia City, but two months later he was again accused of robbery and imprisoned. He was murdered after a dispute with another outlaw while working as a brakeman on the Carson and Colorado Railroad. His moniker "Rattlesnake Dick" was copied from that of Richard Barter, an outlaw who terrorized Sierra Nevada mining towns during the late 1850s. A newspaper article at the time of Darling's death described him as "a great bluffer." See Ann Gordge's account of Darling in this volume and 1880 U.S. Census, State Prison, Carson City, Ormsby, Nevada, Roll T9-759, 87; Bosco, "Lee's Eccentricities," *Salt Lake Tribune*, 10 January 1875, 4; "A Bad Man Gone," *Daily Nevada State Journal* (Reno), 25 August 1883, 3; Cleland and Brooks, eds., *A Mormon Chronicle*, 2:71; Journal History, 3 May 1868, 6; Ancestry.com Civil War databases; Long, *The Saints and the Union*, 241; Convis and Convis, *Outlaw Tales of Nevada*, 27–36.

[7]This was most likely September 1864: "Though [James H.] Imlay was the highest town official, Brigham Young and some fifteen carriage loads of his company apparently traveled far across the fields to find accommodations in the Lee household." Cleland and Brooks, eds., *A Mormon Chronicle*, 2:9.

Excuse me, kind reader, for dweling so long on the subject of Lee—a few more words and I will dismiss the subject for the present. Brigham Young [knew about] the part Lee had taken in that horable [horrible] slaughter of innosint [innocent] men, women, and children, for in Lee's first trial, he [Young] gave evidence that Lee had writen to him asking his (Young's) advice in the matter.[8] Brigham had Lee cut off from the church, but not untill he (P[res]. Y[oung].) began to see that he was losing his own influence in the church by not doing it,[9] and then poor Lee was made a sacrafice for the sins of many that had been too fast to follow the council of their leaders and had lost all sence of honesty. (My letter to B.Y. on next page.)

When Lee was getting his recommend to get another wife, I for one did all I could to prevent it.[10] I hear[d] Lee say at one time that Br. Brigham Young was a friend to him and upheld him in all he had done. Prest. [Young] once said in a public sermon that the Mountain Meadows Massacre was too horable for him to contemplate, calasing [classing] it with the Haun's Mill massacre.[11] I, after that was made public, did all I could against Lee in the church to try and prevent him from preaching, etc. Lee in a public meeting in Harmony in my hearing got up and said Br. Brigham did not mean what he had said, but had given utterance to such sentiments to satisfy disaffected

[8]Rather than testify at Lee's first trial, which was held in Beaver, Utah, in 1875, President Young submitted a deposition in which he acknowledged receiving about 10 September 1857 "a communication from Isaac C. Haight or any other person of Cedar City, concerning a company of emigrants called the Arkansas company." He had "made diligent search for it but cannot find it," Young claimed. Brooks, *Mountain Meadows Massacre*, 287.

[9]Brigham Young and his large entourage visited Mountain Meadows in May 1861. On returning north, Lee treated the company to a "sumptuous dinner." Juanita Brooks wrote, "It would seem that cordial relations still existed between Lee and the president up to this time, although the former had lost prestige among his neighbors." More evidence came out until "sentiment from within the church became so strong that by 1870 the leaders were forced to formally excommunicate Isaac C. Haight and John D. Lee for their part in it [the massacre]." Brooks, *Mountain Meadows Massacre*, 183–87. Lee was finally excommunicated on 8 October 1870.

[10]Lee received a temple "recommend" stating he was a worthy individual in full fellowship with the LDS church from Bishop Wilson D. Pace on 15 September 1867. Lee started for Salt Lake City a month later and at Fillmore picked up a young woman, Jane Woolsey, who had told him she wished to marry him. Lee planned to be sealed to her in Salt Lake, but her behavior made Lee change his mind. Cleland and Brooks, eds., *A Mormon Chronicle*, 2:75–76, 87–90. Jane, the daughter of Thomas (1805–1897) and Mary Burrell Woolsey (1813–1858), was born in 1851 at Mount Pisgah, Iowa, and was sixteen at this time. She married George W. Robinson about 1872.

[11]"There are transactions that are too horrible for me to contemplate. The massacre at Haun's mill, and that of Joseph and Hyrum Smith, and the Mountain Meadows massacre and the murder of Dr. Robinson are of this character," Young said in the Salt Lake Tabernacle on 23 December 1866. "I cannot think that there are beings upon the earth who have any claim to the sentiments and feelings which dwell in the breasts of civilized men who could be guilty of such atrocities." "Remarks," *Deseret News*, 9 January 1867, 2–3.

individuals such as I was and to blind the eyes of gentiles, but the prophet was his friend. He had sat under the drip[p]ings of the sanctuary and knew that the prophet was his friend. I [did not] beli[e]ve Lee was correct in his opinion. I did not believe Lee for one moment. I thought his statement a base slander against a true servant of God.

I was indignant against Lee and in my over flow of zeal, I wrote a letter informing the president of Lee's statement, asking him to cut Lee off from the church for slandering him. The President replied to my letter. My poor pen fails me to describe my feelings as I read its contents. The prop[h]et did not thank me for my information, but on the contrary he informed me that the Mountain Meadows massacre was none of my business. He said to me that any one reading my letter to him would conclud[e] that I myself had taken a part in the massacre and if so, he would advise to take a dose of *rope* around my neck "with a jerk."[12] Of course I did not take his prescription for I had not taken "any part." That letter settled my mind. I have always beli[e]ved since then that Lee was correct in his statement.

I have lived to see Lee convicted and heard [the] sentence of death pronounced against him. Daniel H. Wells testify [testified] against him, but it has not changed my belief.[13] I think that Brigham Young gave the council [counsel] that caused that slaughter. The country has undergone a great change of sentiment since then. All the perticapants [participants] in that murder have fled the country or are dead. Even Brigham is dead and his name is not honored now as it was in his life time. His children have quarreled about his ill-gotten gains. Lee's family are scattered from place to place.

In concluding this chapter, I will [mention] that my father-in-law bought an orchard at Washington and my wife and some of my children went down to dry peaches, caught the fever and ague.[14] My wife came near dying. She was four months not abble to cook a meal's victuals. She will never get over the effects of that spell of sickness. I was compeled to stay at home and take care of her and our small children. I became reduced to the most extream

[12]Hicks wrote two letters to Young, the second after the postmaster handed his earlier, shorter one over to John D. Lee. See the introduction to Hicks's autobiography for these letters and Young's 16 February 1869 reply.

[13]Convicted of murder on 20 September 1876, Lee was executed on 23 March 1877, almost twenty years after the massacre. Daniel H. Wells was second counselor to President Young. Judge Jacob Boreman excluded Wells's testimony, its "irrelevancy being apparent & manifest," but concluded it "let the jury see that the church was on the side of the prosecution." Arrington, "Crusade against Theocracy," 43.

[14]Malaria.

poverty. No one knows the affliction of poverty unless they have tried it. I look on poverty as one of the greatest curses that honest humanity is afflicted with. I am aware that riches often prove a curse to the foolish, but poverty is no blessing to the wise. I have often thought of Pope's line, "If some honored lord but own[s] the lines, How the wit brightens, how the sense refines."[15] A man that is poor though he be a very Solon is not as "good" as a rich fool.[16] I considder the first duty of all to fortify themselves against the grim monster poverty by laying up treasures on Earth, not for the sole priveliege of hording wealth but for the conveniences that wealth affords. I think the grass grows the best on the rich man's lawn.

Poverty is the cloud of genius, it is the curse of ambition, it is a benefit only to drunkards and other fools, while nothing can be accomplished without the aid of money or means. The young man that has no regard for wealth and its proper use has som[e]thing to learn. I think that if parents when old would try and be worth about $150,000, their children wou[ld] be more obedient to them.

Chapter XVII.
A Spirit of Persecution: Hamilton's Fort

During the summer of 1867 I went to a place called Hamilton's Fort to work in the ha[r]vest field and while there, I made the acquaintance of a man by the name of Peter Fife. He at that time owned one half [of] the cultivated land at that place. Fife was a Scot[c]hman, an old Mormon, one of the Mormon Battalion, and was a man that made great pretention to religion.[1] He was an excellent farmer an[d] owned a splendi[d] farm. He was a man well advanced in life—over 60 years of age but hardy and quite active for one of his age. His wife was a most excellent woman. I think she possesed all the Christian qualities.

"Peter" took quite a liking to me for I was at that time an expert binder

[15]"But let a lord once own the happy lines/How the wit brightens! how the style refines!" From *An Essay on Criticism* by Alexander Pope (1688–1744).

[16]Solon (ca. 638–558 B.C.E.) was an Athenian lawmaker, poet, and statesman.

[1]Named for John Hamilton, Sr., Hamilton's Fort was four miles south of Cedar City. Peter Muir Fife (1806–1873) was born just south of Edinburgh, Scotland. He was baptized in 1840 when missionaries first arrived in Scotland and immigrated to Nauvoo a year later, after his first wife died. Fife joined the Mormon Battalion in July 1846 and, after his discharge, traveled with other veterans in 1848 over the Spanish Trail to Utah. At Great Salt Lake City in 1849 he married again and was sent to Iron County in 1850. The first settlers of Hamilton Fort were Peter Shirts, John Hamilton, Sr., and Fife. "Obituary," *Deseret News*, 20 August 1873, 7; Hafen and Hafen, *Journals of Forty-Niners*, 141, 145–46, 163, 222.

in the harvest. I was not long there before Peter offered to rent me his farm. I took the offer with great thankfulness, for I was tired of the prices paid for labor at Harmony. As soon as threshing was over, I began to plow and kept at it until I had all the land plowed that I wanted for grain. I esteemed it a great privilege to be a tiller of his ground. Mr. Fife furnished seed, plows, [and] one yoke of oxen, and I one. In the spring following [1868] I mooved there and I and my small boys set to work in earnest to try and raise a good crop, which we did, of wheat, barley, corn, and potatoes.[2] I got the promise of his farm for another year.

Peter Fife was one of those strange freaks of nature called a kleptomaniac. He would steal to gratify the love of stealing. He would steal a small whip from one of my boys and the next day perhaps his daughter would bring it back. He would steal ropes, larietts, bridals or any thing that a traveler who camped near his home chanced to leave laying around loose. In the fall when we were hauling wheat, I caught him gathering the loose grain around my stack of wheat in the night when I went [out] before bed time. At another time my wife caught him stealing our corn that was laying in a pile husked on the ground. He ran off and left his sack with corn in it. Now Fife was rich and I was poor. He made great pretentions to religion and paid his tithing punctualy and to all outward appearencences [*sic*] was full of faith toward God.

The stream of water that was used here for irrigation was called Shirts Creek. It was so named in honor of an old pioneer by the name of Peter Shirts. When Cedar City was first settled, iron ore was found in great abundance and the church (B. Young) concluded to erect iron works at Cedar City, but there was no stone coal, at least none had been discovered.[3] Prest. B. Young offered a reward of one thousand dollars to any one that would discover a coal mine within a radius of 20 miles of Cedar City.[4] Peter Shirts started in search and was not many days in finding coal in large quantities, and to reward him for his labor, Br. Brigham *paid* him Shirts Creek.[5] I had

[2]In the spring of 1868, Hicks's boys were George W., just fourteen; Henry B., eleven; Moroni, nine; and Robert, seven.

[3]"Stone" coal is probably bituminous coal. Shirts and Shirts, *A Trial Furnace*, 395.

[4]Facing a chronic firewood shortage, in 1854 the third session of the territorial legislature sought other resources. The legislative assembly offered one thousand dollars "as a reward to any resident of this Territory who will open a good coal-mine not less than eighteen inches thick, within forty miles of Great Salt Lake City, in any accessible position, and that can be profitably worked." The act specified that "the Governor shall control said coal mine until further provided for by law." "Acts and Resolutions," *Deseret News*, 19 January 1854, 3.

[5]Shirts Creek was named for Peter Shirts, but whether it was his reward for discovering coal near Cedar City is unknown. Shirts and Shirts, *A Trial Furnace*, 48, 234, 265–66, 351, 378.

it from Shirts my self and Peter seemed to think that the "prophet" had the right to give him the water and land at that place. The iron works were a miserable failure.[6] Prophets and apostles should confine their labors to the *church* and let science alone.

Just previous to the time I mooved to Hamilton's Fort, I went on a visit to Spanish Fork City and there I learned a song that was called the "Mountain Meadow Massacre" song. It began with,

> Come all true sons of freedom
> Unto my rhyme give ear
> It's of an awful massacre
> You presently shall hear.
> In splendor on the mountains
> Some twenty wagons came.
> They were attacked by a wicked band
> And Utah bears the blame.

It went on through 5 or 6 verses of very pathetic language giving a description of that horid butchery. It had a very sweet minor tune to it. I took song and tune to Harmony where Lee then resided. (I would insert the song but I have forgoten it.)[7] I sang the song at my own house first and then where ever I was invited. It caught the ear of the young people of Harmony and [it] was not long until it was in ev[e]ry bodies mouth like the famous "Lillobolera" [Lillibullero].[8]

With a certain class it created a spirit of persecution. One old (Dan-ite), James Pace by name, said I ought to be stoped from singing the song if it took

---

[6]George A. Smith led the Iron Mission that started south in December 1850 with about 120 men, many British converts with some knowledge of iron manufacturing. They eventually built a blast furnace at today's Cedar City and produced low-grade iron in September 1852. A succession of problems doomed the operation: the furnace was too close to the creek on ground too soft to support its weight, Coal Creek flooded frequently, the ore was six miles up the canyon, the furnace lining of clay and sandstone liquefied at lower temperatures than required for smelting, and the coal was unsuitable for making coke. In addition, the men had to build houses and grow food to feed themselves, which was hampered by drought and locusts. Without currency, the mission could only pay employees with credit on the company store, which never had enough goods. Over half of the missionaries, including the leaders, participated in the Mountain Meadows massacre, and the mission closed in October 1858. See Shirts and Shirts, *A Trial Furnace*.

[7]A U.S. soldier or soldiers apparently wrote this ballad. Maj. James H. Carleton and companies of the First Dragoons escorted Paymaster Henry Prince north from Fort Tejon in California to Utah in April 1859. On the Santa Clara River, Carleton met some three hundred men from Camp Floyd under Capt. Reuben Campbell. Both officers had orders to investigate reports of the Mountain Meadows massacre. For his report see Carleton, *Mountain Meadows Massacre*.

[8]"Lillibullero" was an oft-sung satire on the Confederacy from the Civil War era whose tune had Irish roots from the seventeenth century. Thanks to Louisa Rose for deciphering this word and knowing the tune.

my life. It was stiring up an ill feeling against "Br." Lee. I did not stop but gave out word that I would sing it to all grown up people that would come to my hous[e] free and to children for half price. Many came. James Pace was an adopted son of J. D. Lee. Pace and Lee formed a plan to stop the singing of the song. It was this: Pace was to make a dance and invite me to it and Lee was to be there. Some one was [to] ask me to sing the song and if I did sing it, which I was sure to do, Lee, Pace and some of Lee's boys were to take me out and "lay me aside." I am not trying to make a hero of my self. Pace droped a hint of what was going to be done with me before one of his wives and she sent me word by one of Pace's daughters. I went to the dance for a while in the first part of the evening, but I had a good Colt "Navy" [revolver] in my bosom. Pace was there and he came grinning and smiling up to me in the most friendly manner. He was a man that well knew how to "smile and smile and be a villain."[9] I did not stay long. I have no desire to become a "martyr for the truth['s] sake." Pace afterward told one of his confidents that it was on the end of his tong[u]e more than fifty times to ask Br. Brigham when he was with him if it would not be best to lay me aside. But I still live and so does Pace and laying people aside is intirely out of fashion now.

I must say a word or two in favor of Father and Mother Hamilton of Hamilton's Fort. They were fine old people. They were Irish by birth and I being of that decent, I was the old man's mouth piece on od[d] ocations [occasions].[10] The place was named for him and he was spiritual adviser. It was there I first taught a small school.[11] I was supt. of the Sabbath school and was assisted by Sister Fife, and I will say for her, she was an excellent teacher and did all she could for the children to make Christian impressions on the[i]r young minds. She hass passed away, I presume to a better world where she can probably realize her anticipations.

John Hamilton, a son of Father and Mother Hamilton, was a despicable

[9]From Shakespeare's *Hamlet*, act 1, scene 5.

[10]Born in County Down, Ireland, John Hamilton, Sr. (1807–1890), and his wife, Mary Creighton Hamilton (1807–1890), were baptized into the LDS faith in November 1840 and endowed in Nauvoo in January 1846. The 1850 U.S. census placed them with two sons in Great Salt Lake City. They soon moved south to establish Hamilton's Fort, where they spent the rest of their lives.

[11]Pasted in Hicks's scrapbook is a circular piece of lined copybook paper with a sawtooth edge and small circles cut inside the circumference. It reads in unsure lettering, "Hamiltons Feb 5, 1874, The rose is read, the vilet Blue. I like to Learn to read & I like my School Master H[icks]." It is signed Mary L. Jane Hamilt[on]. Mary Lovina Jane Hamilton was born 11 April 1867 in Heber City, Wasatch County, to the Hamilton's son and daughter-in-law, John and Mary McDonald Hamilton. Mary was not quite seven when she made this card. Hicks, Scrapbook, LDS Archives.

wretch.[12] He went to S. Lake City and got possesion of the town cite [site] of Hamiltons Fort and a part of our land. He refused to deed to the lawful owner and the balance that he did let us have, he mad[e] us pay double price for it.[13]

In the little town of Hamilton's Fort, there was a man by the name of John Middleton who came in with the handcart company who by industry and economy has grown rich. He is a good man and worthy [of] the esteem of all who know him.[14] I bel[i]eve riches to be the effect of law and exersion [*sic*], although I have known many who have toiled long and earnestly who have never become rich, although I have not known any to become so without exertion.

Perhaps one of the most unfortunate mooves of my life was to go back to Harmony, but we do not always know just what is best for us to do. I bought a small piece of land which was only enough to starve on. "Poverty is no crime," but it is very inconvenient to be poor, at least I have found it so.[15] I did not stay long at Harmony, but moved back to Hamilton's Fort again and rented a farm from John Middliton, but there being a very dry summer, I had a very light harvest. I took a load of shelled corn to Panaca in Meadow Valley, 12 m[iles] from Pioche. I broke the axel out of my wagon within 11 miles of the town and had to go in and hire a wagon to get my load in to town. I paid $12.00 for getting the wagon repaired to a man named Proctor.[16] When I got my load in town, there was no sale for it. I stored my grain, sent the team and wagon home, and went to work for a man by the name of Joshua Fielding choping cord wood for $1.00 pr. cord.[17] I took a

[12]John Hamilton, Jr. (1834–1917), sailed with his parents and brother to New Orleans in 1843. The family settled at Nauvoo and crossed the plains in 1850. In Springville, Utah, John, Jr., met and married Mary McDonald (1838–1899), also from Ireland. They moved to Parowan and then to Heber City, where their daughter Mary Lovina Jane was born. In 1868 they returned to Hamilton Fort, but in 1891 moved back to Heber. Mortimer, ed., *How Beautiful Upon the Mountains*, 869–70.

[13]On 7 September 1872 in Salt Lake City, John Hamilton, Jr., was granted a land patent from the U.S. Land Office. "Local and Other Matters," *Deseret News*, 9 October 1872, 9. Hamilton was living at Hamilton Fort, so it appears this is when he took possession of the town site Hicks described.

[14]Englishman John Middleton (1840–1895) came to Utah with his parents at age 16 in the Martin Handcart Company of 1856. A short biography attributes his economy and desire for plenty to suffering from extreme hunger in the disaster. Known as a man of "broad human sympathies" who would help anyone in need, Middleton became a successful livestock breeder. "John Middleton," 49–50.

[15]The great Russian dramatist Alexander Ostrovsky (1823–1886) wrote the comedy "Poverty Is No Crime" in 1854.

[16]Born in Lancashire, England, William Proctor (1839–1878) traveled to Utah with his family in 1852.

[17]Another Lancashire native, Joshua Fielding (1837–1909) came to Utah with his parents and siblings in 1854.

contract of 100 cords and hired a young man from Iowa, Wm. Ball by name, paying him $1.50 pr. cord. Ball earned $9.00 more than I. Panaca was a small town at the time, perhaps not more than 400 or 500 inhabitants. I sold my corn through the [end of autobiography].

[Four diary entries, covering fourteen months and written "for future reference," follow, describing the damming of Benny Creek to irrigate Hicks's benchland. Such notes, as Hicks mentions on page 169, were undoubtedly used in writing his autobiography.]

Apostate Dog: The Last Years of George A. Hicks

George and Betsy had endured sixteen years of hardship and trouble in southern Utah, and their move north began a new phase of their lives, with Hicks writing his autobiography between 1878 and 1880. At the same time, he became increasingly involved in civic affairs, working once more for the cause of justice, this time for his neighbors, the sixteen or so families in Thistle Valley, Utah County.

Utah Territory now had two political parties, the Liberal Party and the church's People's Party. To register the residents of Thistle Valley in 1882, the Utah County registrar selected a deputy who belonged to the Liberal Party, lived in Springville, and was a stranger to the community, where all the residents belonged to the People's Party. Insulting the faithful Mormons, the deputy set up his "office" in a saloon near the railroad but fifteen miles from Thistle Valley and outside the precinct boundaries. All who wished to register must come to the saloon during the day and a half he would be there, the deputy insisted.

Hicks, who lived closest to the railroad line, and other residents proposed a compromise. The residents would assemble at Hick's house and send a buggy for the deputy so he could come halfway—eight miles—to register them. Many of them had to travel some seven miles to reach Hicks's house. After they assembled and sent the buggy, the deputy refused to accept the ride. Instead he rode his horse to Hicks's house and demanded to know "what in hell they wanted." George explained the situation, but he would not budge. The residents must come to his "office" in the saloon. In the end, only about half the eligible voters made the trip, and several did not reach home again before midnight.

"It was by a mere accident that the people of Thistle Valley heard of a deputy being appointed," Hicks wrote to a Provo newspaper. By chance someone had read the notice "posted at Mr. Dallin's saloon on which it was stated that the people of Thistle Valley precinct must come there if they wished to register." He told how Thistle Valley residents met at his house and sent for the deputy:

> When he arrived he attempted to excuse himself for not having formally notified the people of the time and place of registering, by saying that he had sent the notice to a precinct in another county. I offered to take the gentleman back to the saloon for his papers (he having stated that he had left them there), and, also, offered any required accommodation that a reasonable man could ask during the time he would be engaged in the registration. I also made him a promise to return him to the saloon in time for the train, so that he could fill all his other appointments farther up the canyon without any inconvenience or expense to himself. The gentleman refused my offers, and so a portion of the people were compelled to travel a distance of fifteen miles to suit the whim of this official upstart, and quite a number, as was correctly stated in your issue of Sept. 27th, declined to travel so far and to such a place as he had selected for his office. It is only just to infer that the privilege of the franchise was too dear at the price set upon it by this ignorant upstart.[1]

The episode illustrates George's willingness to fight for justice whether religious or secular, and his sympathy for the People's Party suggests he was once more among the church faithful. Within four years, Hicks had moved his family to Clinton, now Birdseye, in Spanish Fork Canyon. As Utah struggled to win statehood and resolve the conflict over polygamy, Hicks "wrote to the Bishop [G. D. Snell] at Spanish Fork and suggested that the people give up polygamy," his daughter Frances recalled. "The reply from the Bishop was to cut him off the Church without a hearing."[2] In November 1886 Hicks printed a broadside to advertise his play, *Celestial Marriage*, "a drama in five acts, a domestic tragedy designed for the stage."[3] No known copy of the play survives, but the title suggests Hicks was on another campaign to rid the church of a troublesome issue.

---

[1]Geo. A. Hicks, Thistle Valley, 10 October 1882, in "A Blast from Thistle Valley," *Territorial Enquirer* (Provo), 14 October 1882, Journal History, 10 October 1882, 9.

[2]Hicks and Lewis, Life History of George A. Hicks, 13. In February 1887 Congress passed the more severe Edmunds-Tucker Act. In April 1887 Bishop Snell was arrested for "unlawful cohabitation," fined two hundred dollars plus fifty dollars in court costs, and imprisoned for six months. Larson, ed., *Prisoner for Polygamy*, 141, 161n4.

[3]The broadside was stamped Clinton, Utah, 1 November 1886.

Evidence that he was again excommunicated is contradictory and debatable. Frances "Fanny" Brittanna Hicks Ellison related her father's history after his death, recalling events at least forty years old. In 1894, about ten years after the polygamy letter affair, Hicks recalled being cut off in Cedar City but did not mention a second excommunication. In the early 1920s Hicks said he had been out of the church for some thirty-eight years, thus referring to the second excommunication.[4] The discrepancy comes, perhaps, from Hicks being unsure whether he had been truly cut off a second time in about 1884.

The Hicks family moved to Spanish Fork in 1890. Two years later, Hicks ran for justice of the peace, and in 1894 he recalled that since moving to Utah County, he had served as justice of the peace, "postmaster, deputy registrar, school trustee, pound-keeper and I now am one of the executive committee of the Republican League of Utah Territory."[5] His public-spiritedness is evident, but he continued to annoy people, including William Creer, an attorney and former mayor of Spanish Fork. According to Hicks, during the 1892 election, Creer, a Democrat, had "said on the public streets of Spanish Fork City that I had written a letter or series of letters to the San Francisco Chronicle, exposing the Mountain Meadow massacre, and that these letters and others of the same character, written by apostate Mormons, were the direct cause of the assassination of the Mormon elders Gibbs and Berry in Tennessee."[6] Former Spanish Fork residents John H. Gibbs and William S. Berry had been murdered while serving missions in Tennessee in 1884, but there is no evidence Hicks ever wrote to newspapers outside Utah in an attempt to expose or hurt the Mormon faith.

Hicks went immediately to the district court at Provo looking for redress, but the prosecuting attorney told him there were no laws on the books for defamation of character. Hicks petitioned the Utah House of Representatives to pass a bill that "will punish such offenses and protect the character of the citizen against the vicious innuendoes of fanatics, pettifoggers or unscrupulous demagogues." His case was not an isolated one: "to my certain knowledge there are a number of citizens of southern Utah who

[4]Hicks to Bishop Ralph D. Morgan, Hicks Scrapbook, LDS Archives.

[5]Republican ticket for 1892 city election and "House of Representatives," Hicks Scrapbook, LDS Archives.

[6]Ibid. During the 1850s William Creer had been a friend of Hicks; both had once defended Thomas Job's right to study astrology.

would be benefited by the enactment of such laws." Hicks's petition was tabled indefinitely.[7]

Others honored George A. Hicks for his passionate defense of what he saw as right and just. After Utah finally became a state in 1896, Hicks was chosen as the speaker at Spanish Fork's celebration.[8] A few years later, he received a letter under the letterhead "State of Utah, Supreme Court." Although the signature is illegible, it was undoubtedly from William M. McCarty, chief justice from 1906 to 1908.

> Your letter of the 22nd Inst. was duly received. I was pleased to hear from you; also to get the information contained in your letter. I was only a small boy during those strenuous times, but I have a very vivid recollection of you, Frank Woolley and Orson Pratt, known as "Young Orson Pratt."[9] Since receiving your letter I will now add one more to the list. You gentlemen and father, as I remember it, were the only Union men in that section of the country. I had gotten the impression that Judge [John Foy] Ch[i]dester's father at that time resided in Eagle's Valley, Nevada, and came to Washington [County] later on; but am pleased that you have set me right on this as I very frequently, in speaking of you and other pioneers of the Dixie country, refer to you as one of the very few who in spirit and deed were true republicans. In talking matters over with Judge [Alfred] Saxey I took occasion to refer to you and the courage you showed in facing public opinion and standing up for the Union during those exciting times. Judge Chidester often speaks of you with great pride, and from what I have heard him say respecting his early political training and associations in the Dixie country I am justified in believing that you had much to do with starting him off right.[10]

The chief justice invited Hicks to visit him in Salt Lake. McCarty was born in 1859 in Alpine, Utah County, and had grown up in the Cotton Mission. Poor and struggling like the Hicks family, the McCartys moved to Summit Creek in Iron County in 1868, where they raised corn and hogs to sell to Nevada mining camps. His father left the church in 1872 because, according to his son, "he did not approve of the defiant attitude of the church toward the Government." Self-taught in the law, McCarty joined the bar in 1887 and soon became assistant U.S. attorney in southern Utah's Second District. Like Hicks, he was a Republican. Although estranged from Mormonism, he

[7]"House of Representatives," Hicks Scrapbook, LDS Archives.

[8]Celebration of Statehood Day, Spanish Fork, 6 January 1896, printed program, Hicks Scrapbook, LDS Archives.

[9]Pratt and Franklin B. Woolley, sons of prominent Mormons, were noted southern Utah dissenters. Indians allegedly murdered Woolley on the Mojave Desert in March 1869.

[10]McCarty to Hicks, 26 October 1907, Utah State Archives, "Supreme Court," Agency History #868.

was respected and popular among the faithful for his fairness, honesty, and devotion to justice during his three terms as Utah's chief justice.[11]

As Hicks celebrated his eighty-second birthday in 1917, his thoughts turned toward reconciliation with the church. He had thought of it earlier in the 1890s but changed his mind, as he explained to the bishop of Spanish Fork's Third Ward about 1922.

Hicks to My Dear Friend, Bishop Ralph D. Morgan,
Undated Typescript, Hicks Scrapbook, LDS Archives.

While Marinus Larsen was Bishop of the Third Ward I made application to come back into the Church. He favored my comming and said he would help me all he could.

I propose telling you how, and why I changed my mind. I went into the Sabbath School Bible Class to see how I would be treated. John Moore was leading the class. The subject, for consideration, was the raising of Lazaus [*sic*] (See St. John Eleventh Chapter—and eleventh verse). I said "ma[y]be he was not dead; consider the eleventh verse."

John Moore snapped at me in a most savage manner, "I'll considder what I please Sir." I said no more. I had a point to make. The next Sunday was the Land of Palestine to be considered. I prepared myself for the subject but when it came to my turn I was not allowed to speak.

John Moore was still presiding. I was the only one in the class that was prepared to give a fair description of that country. That class had no use for me and from that time to the present I have had no use for that Sabbath School.

I immediately charnged [*sic*] my mind. I have been out of the Church for about Thirty Eight Years. Bishop G. D. Snell cut me off for taking a stand against Polygamy in favor of National Law.

John Moore again. I was taken sick with Nervous Prost[r]ation. My son Robert sent to Salt Lake City and bought me a quart bottle of Port Wine. That wine was put into John Moore's hands to send to me in Spanish Fork Canyon. John did not send the wine to me, no sir but drank it himself.

What right had I to a bottle of wine? "An apostate Dog" from his stand point, when a faithful High Priest had a lip for it.

I had one equal privilege. Giving a dollar once or twice a year, for the Church, that was all. I always gave it.

Your friend, [George A. Hicks][12]

---

[11] Alley, "Utah Supreme Court Justice William M. McCarty," 373, 375–80, 383.

[12] These events happened in 1893 or 1894, as Marinus Larsen was bishop of Spanish Fork's Third Ward from December 1891 to 1903, but John Moore was on a mission to England from April 1891 to 1893. Moore was George's brother-in-law, married to his sister Caroline, who had died in 1878. Hicks's excommunication apparently led to the falling out.

JOHN MOORE
Born in Derbyshire, England, John Moore (1838–1920) came to Utah in 1853 with his uncles and was baptized in 1854 at age 16. Moore married Caroline Hicks in 1860. Moore held many public offices in Spanish Fork, including alderman, city councilman, and recorder, and served as a county judge for six years. During the 1890s when George A. Hicks returned to Spanish Fork, the two men had a falling out, apparently because Hicks had been excommunicated. Moore was a widower for more than forty years. *Courtesy International Society, Daughters of Utah Pioneers.*

The incident illustrates Hicks's continued feistiness when he felt he had been unjustly treated. He pursued rebaptism again in June 1917, and won the support of Bishop George Hales of the Third Ward, but nothing came of it, perhaps because the stake high council refused its approval.[13] George and Betsy celebrated their sixty-fifth anniversary in March 1918, and three years later, in 1921, a sixty-eighth: They were said to be the oldest known couple in Utah.[14] When Elizabeth Jolley died at age 84 in January 1922, her husband wrote a tribute that was engraved on her gravestone:

> She was a virtuous, loving wife
> Who kept her home with prudent care.
> To usefulness, she gave her life
> And was respected everywhere.[15]

His daughter Fanny came to live with him.[16] Now without his beloved wife with whom he had shared so much, Hicks again took up the issue of

[13] J. S. Page, Jr., to George A. Hicks, 7 June 1917, Hicks Scrapbook, LDS Archives.

[14] "Mr. and Mrs. Hicks Married Three Score and Five Years," *Deseret News*, 30 March 1918, in Journal History, 24 March 1918, 3; "Spanish Fork Couple Celebrate Their Sixty Eighth Wedding Anniversary," *Deseret News*, 26 March 1921, in Journal History, 24 March 1921, 3–4.

[15] Jolley, *Jolley Family Book*, 501.

[16] Frances Brittanna Hicks married John Ellison in 1889 and had eight children. John died in 1918.

rebaptism. What the Stake High Council discovered five years earlier in its search for his records is not known, but Hicks "was always concerned about the question as to whether he was actually excommunicated from the Church. He was a staunch Republican all his life and a great admirer of Senator Reed Smoot, so he had Senator Smoot go into the records to find out, but they were unable to find any official record that he had ever been excommunicated."[17] James A. Boyack finally rebaptized George A. Hicks at Spanish Fork on 5 May 1923, and Marinus Larsen confirmed and re-ordained him a Seventy the next day.[18] Six weeks later George traveled to Salt Lake City at the request of Apostle Reed Smoot, so the senator could "gladly attend to the business that I was asked by the Presidency to attend to for you." At the Hotel Utah on 25 June 1923, Smoot noted later that day, "As per instructions of the First Presidency of the Church I have this day reconfirmed on George A. Hicks all his former blessings together with the restoration to him of the position of seventy in the Church of Jesus Christ of Latter Day Saints."[19]

Once again reconciled with the church whose leaders had caused him such anguish, George was sealed to Betsy for time and all eternity on their seventieth wedding anniversary in the Salt Lake Temple.[20] A little over a year later, John H. Hayes ordained him a high priest. So late in life, Hicks was back in full fellowship and finally sealed to his devoted wife after the call to the Cotton Mission had delayed the couple's hopes for the ordinance for sixty-three years.

Old age brought other joys. Over the years Hicks helped veterans of the Walker and Black Hawk Indian wars obtain pensions. Distinguished educators, including Edward Rowe of Brigham Young University and Frederick Pack of the University of Utah, asked him to speak about pioneer days, while surgeon George Middleton, chief of staff at LDS Hospital, visited him "seeking historical facts." Hicks had been Middleton's first teacher in Iron County.[21]

Another pleasure of Hicks's declining years was attending reunions of veterans of the Indian wars. He wrote "The March of Peace," which Rees D.

---

[17] Jolley, *Jolley Family Book*, 501.

[18] Ibid.; "Passing Events," *Improvement Era* 26 (June 1923).

[19] Reed Smoot to George A. Hicks, 22 June 1923; Reed Smoot to Joseph Reece, president of the Nebo Stake, 25 June 1923; both letters in Hicks Scrapbook, LDS Archives.

[20] Jolley, *Jolley Family Book*, 500.

[21] Hicks and Lewis, comp., Life History of George A. Hicks, 15.

James set to music for the reunion held before James died in 1917. Hicks's scrapbook includes a printed booklet of songs for the 1922 Spanish Fork encampment, including one unattributed song that he probably composed. Photographs show he attended the 1923 encampment. His "March of Peace" captures the sentiment of those events:

> Dear Comrades, we have met again
> To pass the time away—
> To shake each other by the hand
> And hear the music play,
> To talk about those dreadful days,
> When Indian wars were rife,
> And Walker and his thieving band
> Were out for Mormon life.
>
> Chorus:
> But now those dreadful days are gone
> Oh may they ever cease;
> Now comrades come and join with us
> In the march of peace.
>
> 'Twas out in Sanpete's pleasant vale
> Where many a comrade fell
> While fighting for his friends and home,
> And those he loved so well;
> But now the Indians are at rest,
> No more we hear their cries
> For we together live in peace
> Beneath our mountain skies.
>
> Dear comrades we are growing old,
> Our locks are turning gray;
> And by the common lot of all
> We soon must pass away,
> To meet again in that bright land,
> Where troubles are no more,
> And live an everlasting life
> With those we loved of yore.[22]

Hicks moved to Salt Lake City with Fanny in 1925. "While living in Salt Lake City, every day if the weather permitted he would take a walk," she recalled. "On his last walk, he became ill and afraid that he might become

[22]"The March of Peace," printed page in Hicks Scrapbook, LDS Archives.

George A. Hicks Reminisces

George A. Hicks (*left*) reminiscing with another veteran, probably John W. Turner, about the Walker War of 1853, in which the Utes sought to protect their lucrative trade in captives and stop Mormon encroachment on their land. Hicks, just eighteen, took an active part, learning the Ute language and serving as an interpreter during the peace negotiations. Hicks helped many veterans of the Walker and Black Hawk wars obtain pensions. Hicks was a great raconteur, and educators at Brigham Young University and the University of Utah sought him out to speak about pioneer days. *Courtesy George Edward Anderson Collection, Perry Special Collections, Harold B. Lee Library, Brigham Young University.*

OLD COMRADES UNITE, SPRINGVILLE, 1923

George A. Hicks (*second row, third from left*) at age 88 was among the oldest Indian Wars veterans who reunited near Springville, Utah, in July 1923. Hicks wrote songs for such occasions, including "The March of Peace," whose chorus begins: "But now those dreadful days are gone/Oh may they ever cease;/Now comrades come and join with us/In the march of peace." *Courtesy George Edward Anderson Collection, Perry Special Collections, Harold B. Lee Library, Brigham Young University.*

unconscious or die before reaching home, and being a stranger in Salt Lake City, no one would know him so he sat down and wrote his name and address on a piece of paper and placed it in his pocket showing his mind [was] clear and elert and ever thotful of others."[23]

George Armstrong Hicks died on 30 June 1926 at age 91. He had lived a remarkably full life. His fresh, colorful, and unorthodox autobiography portrays his neighbors not as perfect Saints but as flawed human beings, and he took delight in describing them. His memoirs and the scattered records of his later life paint a picture of a bright, outspoken, and brave man who would not let injustices pass without trying to correct them. When faced with the choice of remaining silent for the sake of unity and peace or in deference to authority, or speaking out when he perceived a wrong, Hicks could be counted on to choose the harder path. His actions raised the ire of many powerful men but, like a biblical prophet, Hicks was proved right in the end: John D. Lee was finally cut off from the church and executed for his crimes, and Mormonism gave up polygamy and Utah became a state.

George Armstrong Hicks pasted the poems of his later years in his scrapbook. The title of "The Light" comes from Jesus: "I am the Light of the world." Its last verse captures the faith that seemed always to illuminate his life and struggles: it is a fitting end to the story of the life of this kind, courageous, and decent pioneer:

> When I shall draw my latest breath
> And render back this clay,
> Be with me Lord in hours of death
> To teach my soul the way.
> Then waft me by thou boundless love
> To an immortal sphere,
> Where I may dwell with Saints above
> One endless peaceful year.[24]

---

[23]Hicks and Lewis, comp., Life History of George A. Hicks, 12.

[24]This is the later of two versions of this poem in the Hicks Scrapbook, LDS Archives.

Charles Derry

The stars and stripes adorning the frame of this portrait of Charles Derry suggest it may have been taken about April 1865, when Joseph Smith III called him to serve on the Council of Twelve Apostles of the Reorganized Church of Jesus Christ of Latter Day Saints, where he was known as the "Apostle of Purity." *Courtesy Community of Christ Archives.*

Chapter 2

Charles Derry
The Distant Feeling That Seemed to Pervade the Very Atmosphere

As Charles Derry's impassioned narrative of his years in Utah reveals, Mormon history, like all history, traditionally tells the story of the rich, powerful, and successful, not the stories of the poor, powerless, and obscure. Derry's "unvarnished but thrillingly interesting" memoir takes a decidedly different view of territorial history than the heroic narratives that have long dominated the subject. Derry provides a compelling and moving look at life under Utah's frontier theocracy from the bottom up.

Charles Derry, born in 1826 just north of Birmingham, England, joined the Baptists at age 19 and converted to Mormonism in 1847. Trained as a blacksmith, he soon gave up manual labor and set out to preach the Restored Gospel: "During the six years of my ministry I had labored in the counties of Stafford, Warwick, Salop, Worcester, Gloucester, Flint, Montgomery, and transiently in Nottingham, Derby, Yorkshire, Lancashire, and in London. And the close of my labors found me as penniless as when I first started out." Elder Derry married Ann (or perhaps Angelina) Stokes at Saint John's Church in Staffordshire, England, in 1849. His bride "realized that hers was destined to be a life of sacrifice, and self-denial," Derry recalled. "She had rejected fairer offers than mine, believing that it was God's will that she should unite with me, let the sacrifice be what it might." The birth of Alice Amelia in June 1851 and George Nephi in August 1852 blessed the marriage.

With a great desire to "gather to Zion," Derry was released from his office as president of the Lincolnshire conference. As he had no means to pay for the journey to Utah, the Lincolnshire conference contributed half the fare and the LDS church's Perpetual Emigrating Fund, a program to lend money to poor but faithful Mormons, loaned the other half. An unsolicited fourteen pounds from his brother-in-law and three pounds from his brother George helped to outfit the Derry family for the journey.

Along with 393 fellow Latter-day Saints, including fifty-nine Waldensian converts from Switzerland and Italy, the Derrys sailed from Liverpool on 12 March 1854 aboard the *John M. Wood*. After several deaths during the fifty-one-day voyage, the storm-tossed company arrived in New Orleans, where they boarded steamboats for the trip to Saint Louis.[1]

Here the family's trials began. Placed in quarantine on an island in the Mississippi, "we saw the terrible effects of cholera." Many of the pilgrims would be "well and cheerful at six o'clock of a morning, and before noon they would be carried to the grave."[2] Derry applied dry flour to treat the "erysipelas in his limbs" that now afflicted George Nephi. It seemed to help, "but some other ailment came upon him, and he lost his appetite." The toddler "lingered in sickness until he arrived in Utah," but Derry's wife and cousin were not so fortunate.[3]

Besides writing many hymns and more than two hundred poems, Charles Derry kept detailed journals for forty-seven years, which the Reorganized Church of Jesus Christ of Latter Day Saints published as an autobiography in the early twentieth century.[4] The selection reprinted here tells of his five hard years living under "the 'big bugs,' as some called the leaders" of Brigham Young's kingdom.

As with all the other voices in this book, Charles Derry speaks from a distinct perspective. The narrative of his ordeal in Utah paints a portrait of a theocratic oligarchy, whose leaders used and abused public works laborers, tithing house receipts, and their expansive judicial, legislative, and military power. He shows how Brigham Young used Perpetual Emigrating Fund debts to manipulate the population and control dissidents. Derry expounded on this later in his autobiography, noting that an emigrant was told it would be

---

[1]Derry, "Autobiography of Elder Charles Derry," 260–62, 268–69. The statistics in this paragraph have been corrected from Derry's "Autobiography." See Aird, *Mormon Convert*, 100–101, 104, 112.

[2]For a fuller account of the cholera that raged along the Mississippi River in 1854, see ibid., chapter 8.

[3]Derry, "Autobiography," 269–70.

[4]The excerpts included here are from the *Journal of History* series "Autobiography of Elder Charles Derry," which is available on GoogleBooks. Derry's memoir was republished in 1997 as *Autobiography of Elder Charles Derry: The Apostle of Purity*.

an easy matter to repay their loans in Utah, where instead he found himself destitute "of every comfort of life, with a debt upon his hands that will cost him years of labor to get rid of."[5] During the mid-1850s Utah's impoverished, cashless economy meant recent settlers had no way to pay off their debts, which, as Derry noted, compounded at 10 percent annually.

For all his admirable traits, Charles Derry could be a hard man to like, as Norma Derry Hiles wrote in a recollection of her great-uncle. In later life Derry's simplistic and narrow views of right and wrong led him to refuse to administer to a woman dying of cancer because she had left the faith, and he confidently explained away the deaths of two young twin sisters "because they went to dances and parties."[6] In his own way, the Apostle of Purity became as much a fanatic as the Brighamites he reviled, but nevertheless he had learned some compassion during his sojourn in Utah, for he always defended the freedom of his church's members to think and speak their minds.

His harsh morality and later devotion to the Restoration color much of Derry's perspective, but his story conveys the man's fundamental integrity. The account of his Utah experiences is accurate and his insights into men and events enlightening. Among the most revealing of Derry's character sketches is his portrait of Tennessean John Brown (1820–1897). Brown stands in the front rank of Mormon frontiersman: he led a company of nineteen wagons known as the "Mississippi Saints" to Fort Laramie in 1846 before learning that Brigham Young had changed plans and delayed the LDS exodus to the West for a year. Brown took the party south to winter at Fort Pueblo on the Arkansas River and then traveled to Winter Quarters in time to lead the 1847 "Camp of Israel" as a captain of ten. Brown subsequently served as a missionary, explorer, Nauvoo Legion colonel, overland captain, legislator, mayor, and emigration agent. Derry reports that while acting as secretary to the presiding bishop, the office that still manages the financial affairs of the Corporation of the President, Brown confided to him that he knew Mormonism was a humbug, but as long as he received a good salary he would stay. It is surprising confession from a legendary stalwart, but John Brown would not be the first, nor the last, unbeliever who remained inside the Mormon fold for a variety of reasons, ranging from finance to family to a simple desire to keep the peace.

---

[5] Derry, *Autobiography*, 513–14.

[6] Hiles, "Charles Derry," 22–29.

Charles Derry, "Autobiography," *Journal of History* 1:3 (July 1908): 270–91.

Part I. Root, Hog, or Die

Many deaths occurred on this [Missouri River steamboat] trip, which rendered it a sad and weary journey. My cousin, William Littley, met us there with an ox-team, and took us to the general camp-ground, Westport [Kansas City]. Here we remained about three months, the cholera daily thinning our ranks. At length we were divided into numbers of ten to each wagon, and started on our overland journey of thirteen hundred miles, through a desolate wilderness, and over wild and rugged mountains, to the Great Salt Lake Valley. There were thirty-six wagons.

Our journey hitherto had been far from pleasant; but here were trials of a different nature. To use a Yankee phrase we were "green," our cattle unbroken, and we had never seen an ox yoked up. I had seen them harnessed like a horse in England, but that was a rare sight. But to catch wild cattle, yoke them up, and hitch them to a wagon and drive them through rivers, swamps, over sand-ridges and mountains, was not a pleasant task to those who were to the manor born, and to us it was a terrible task; but it was "root, hog, or die," and we chose to live. Some died with the terrible worry and fatigue, among the rest my cousin William Littley, who with his family was in our ten, passed away in a few days after our starting overland.[7] Our little boy still lingered, growing weaker every day. And one day after traveling several weeks my wife suggested after arriving in camp that night and seeing the children safe in bed, that we should take a walk as she had something to tell me. We did so, and then she revealed to me her forebodings, first saying, "Charles, you never deceived me in your life. But I feel I have not always done my duty by you, and I want you to forgive me wherein I have lacked." I assured her she had never failed in her duty to me, she had always been faithful and true, and I could not ask her to do more, and if anything was lacking it was on my part. She then told me she was strongly impressed that she could not live to reach our destination. I tried to dispel

[7]The Mormon Pioneer Overland Travel website suggests the Derry family traveled with the Darwin Richardson Company, which left Westport on 17 June and arrived at Salt Lake on 30 September 1854. The site gives the date of Littley's death as 24 June 1854.

those fears, but in vain. I sat down upon a grassy knoll and took her upon my knee and tried to comfort her. I then arose and laid my hands upon her head and prayed God to rebuke the destroyer and to spare her life, that she might train her little ones in the fear of God, as she earnestly desired; but, strange to say, from that hour she became ill, and lingered for several weeks, growing more feeble every day. One day she sat in the wagon looking at her little babes, and big tears rolled down her pale cheeks and her heart throbbed with anguish as she saw that she must soon leave them forever. Those tears caught the eye of little Alice, and in an instant she sprang into her mother's arms and sobbed upon her bosom, and mother and child wept together as mother afterward told me. She, like her little boy, had no appetite, and our food being sad bread and fat bacon, such as I could prepare with my own hands, was not calculated to entice her appetite at all.

There was a man in the company who had two wagons well loaded with provisions and just his own family and a servant-girl to care for. Being a blacksmith I had shod this man's cattle on the journey without charge. Wife told me one morning that she thought she could drink a cup of coffee.[8] I had none to give her; but I went to this man and asked him if he would kindly give her a cup of coffee. He refused the little kindness. I returned with a sad heart to wife and told of his refusal. She did not complain but tried to comfort me. Three weeks from that day his servant-girl brought a mug of coffee for the wife, who was now too weak to help herself in any way. I asked this servant-girl to hold [my] wife as she tried to sit up on the bed. I then turned around to give her the coffee, when my heel caught the vessel and knocked it over, and that moment the spirit of my wife departed, and I was left alone with my two sweet, motherless babes, and one of them apparently at the point of death. Only those who have passed through the terrible ordeal can judge of my grief. Neither pen nor tongue can describe it. My hopes were blasted. The only being on earth except my mother, who had sympathized with me in my trials, and given comfort and cheer to me in life's dark hours, had passed away. A little while prior to her departure she spoke of some one being near to her bed. Was it God's angel sent to bear her blessed spirit away? She was indeed an heir of salvation. I was satisfied

[8]Coffee and tea are regularly found on provision lists of Mormon overland companies, for the Word of Wisdom, which advised abstaining from hot drinks, was not yet binding. Arrington, *Great Basin Kingdom*, 250.

she was in her right mind, but I was not permitted to see any person there. The day of her departure was the seventh day of September, 1854. The place of her departure was called "Ice Springs," on the Rocky Mountains, and in about two hours from her death, she was buried from my sight, only a piece of board to mark the spot where lay her loved remains.[9] Five short years had spanned our married life. She had borne me two sweet babes, upon whom must be concentrated all my love and care, next to God and his cause. True and constant through life, faithful even unto death, she has passed to the paradise of God, to await the glorious resurrection, when I trust mother, husband, and babes will greet each other, where separation is not known, pain is not felt, and privation and grief have no place.

Life did not seem worth living; but my motherless babes absorbed my care. I must live for them. I clasped them convulsively to my heart, and dedicated them and myself anew to God. I sought guidance from his hand, that I might fill my obligations to them and my God in carrying out our united purpose to train them up in righteousness. It seemed as though a mother's love had entered my heart. I determined to watch over them with jealous care, nor would I enter into any condition that would render their young lives a burden. But how unqualified was I to act in this capacity and perform the tender offices of a mother, and such a mother as she had been! And if I could not, who could? Surely not a stranger! Hence, feeling the weight of my burden, I went to my Father in whom I had trusted hitherto, and asked him to direct events for my children's good.

Part II.
The Grasshopper Raid

On the 30th of September, 1854, we landed in Salt Lake Valley, being eight months since we left our home, and seven months of travel from Liverpool, by sea, rivers, and land. If possible I felt still more lonely than ever. No kindred spirit to comfort me, no home; no means of support, for I was penniless; and six years in the [LDS] ministry had disqualified me for hard manual labor; and my scholarship did not warrant me in seeking clerical employment. Enfeebled by sickness and the care of my children, one of

[9]Noted as a source of perennial subterranean ice, Ice Spring or Ice Slough was a well-known trail landmark located nine and a half miles east of today's Sweetwater Station, Wyoming.

whom seemed ready to die and the other far from well, was it any wonder my spirits were broken? Add to this the distant feeling that seemed to pervade the very atmosphere. Brethren and sisters seemed more distant than strangers, and if they noticed one at all, it seemed only for the purpose of getting what clothing one might have, that our straightened condition would compel us to dispose of, for which they would offer us pumpkins, squash, and potatoes, but rarely any flour, meat, butter, or other valuable necessities. And they wanted our clothing for a trifle, while they charged exorbitantly for their commodities.

Some would come around pretending great friendship, and caution us against some others whom they declared would take advantage of us, while they themselves were seeking to do the same thing. I confess this shook my faith in humanity, but not in the gospel. It was a cold, dark picture, not inspiring to a heart already crushed and bleeding.

But there was one who will always be remembered, a Bro. George Snow, from Birmingham, England, who had seen my name in the list of emigrants and whom years before I had been the means of bringing into the church.[10] He was looking for me in the camp and heard my voice in a tent. He knew it and came in and invited me with him to his home with my little ones. I was welcomed to their humble fare, nor did they seek reward. Sr. [Sister] Snow was kind and tried to care for my little ones. George was a noble-hearted man, but I regret to say that he had sunk to the level of a drunkard, and, worse still, he was by no means alone.[11]

Some may doubt the picture I have presented, in view of the fact that travelers have extolled the hospitality of those people in the mountains; but I have lived long enough to know that there is a great difference between poor, moneyless emigrants from whom no gain can be expected, and those who go there laden with the good things of life, and from whom great gains are expected. Besides there is great desire to secure a good name and soften down the prejudice of the world, who have been led to hold them in bad repute. However, whatever conclusion may be drawn, I know, and

[10]George Barnfield Snow (1826–1890) came to Utah in 1852 with his wife, Emma Brooks, in the Perpetual Emigrating Fund's James McGaw company. In 1880 he was working as a well digger in Salt Lake City. Powell, *James McGaw*, 116.

[11]The Great Salt Lake City Council passed an ordinance in 1851 declaring the distilleries and breweries in the valley a nuisance. Even when the population was almost entirely Mormon, many drank. See Sanders, "A Thirst in the Desert," 1.

so do thousands of others of that time, that my presentation is a just one. But in that picture I only saw the weakness of humanity. The gospel I had obeyed and preached was still as dear as ever to my heart. Nor would I cast the reflection that all with whom I came in contact had fallen so low as to allow the spirit of greed to govern their conduct.

But to return. Having shared the hospitality of Bro. Snow and wife for about two weeks, I was kindly invited to take my children to a widow Newman's, where I could leave my children while I went to labor for their support, I stopping with them at nights.[12] The first employment I obtained was serving mason, which tested every muscle and bone of my emaciated frame. The next was digging potatoes on shares, whereby I was enabled to lay up a good winter supply of those tubers. In the meantime, feeling the great need of a companion, I sought unto God, remembering the lesson taught at my grandmother's table, that he might guide me in the choice of a wife. I wanted a mother for my children. Women were plentiful, and my record was known, but not every woman can be a mother to other children than her own. I wanted a mother for my babes and I asked God to give me such an one.

One day while engaged in digging potatoes, I looked eastward and saw a train of emigrants just emerging from Emigration Canyon and winding its serpentine way over the bench. The thought came to mind to go and look for a wife. I flung down my hoe and started. I met the train and went into camp with them on one of the public squares of the city. Many were in the train that I had known in my former fields of labor, but as yet I had seen none into whose care I could trust my babes. But while talking to a young woman from the Lincolnshire conference, another young woman of fair complexion and a lovable face passed by me. I caught a glance of her soft blue eyes and instantly the thought flashed to my mind that she would be my wife. I turned to the young woman I was conversing with and said, "Jane, do you see that lassie yonder? That lassie is going to be my wife!"

Jane made the welkin ring with her laughter. I followed the fair-haired damsel to her wagon, and without further ceremony I said, "Sister, my name is Charles Derry; I have been in this valley three weeks. My wife lies on

[12] Mary Ann Jackson Newman (1810–1886), widow of William Newman, came to Utah from England with her three children in the Claudius V. Spencer party in 1853. See Tanner, Autobiographical Sketches, 1–2.

yonder mountains, having been dead seven weeks. I have two little children, one is sick. I have no home at present. I am a blacksmith by trade, and I hope to be able to make a living. If under these conditions you will consent to be my wife and a mother to my children, I will be a husband to you in every sense of the word!"

Not a very enticing picture surely! It was then the custom for men both old and young to rush to meet the trains to select young maidens for the harems of those already married, and for the foundation of a harem for those not married. Wives, too, would be prominent in their solicitations for plural wives to their husbands; hence to some it would seem that my chances of success were very slim, since all the inducement I had to offer was my poverty. My tongue had never been prostituted to flattery. It was a square deal I wanted. The happiness of my children was at stake. I could not afford to make a false move. Others sought her hand with wealth to offer, but God was working for me. I had rested my case in his hands. I had proved him true before; he would not fail me now. The answer came, which was one of the sweetest sounds my ears ever heard. It was the distinctly rounded monosyllable, "Yes," though uttered with due maidenly modesty, yet with firmness that told me it was the utterance of the heart.

I believe it was within three days from that time that I roused up [acting] Bishop Cummings [Andrew Cunningham] of the fifteenth ward to pronounce the sentence that we were husband and wife. I took her to my lodgings, introduced my children to her, and as she kissed my little girl and took my darling babe, George, a perfect skeleton, on her knee, I saw a big tear from her eye on his pale and emaciated cheek. It seemed like the refreshing dews of heaven upon the perishing flower, and from that moment the child revived. He had found a mother's care. This was on the night of the 28th of October, 1854, that we were united in the sacred bonds *to be each other's, husband and wife, to keep ourselves for each other and from all others during our lives.* Over forty-seven years have rolled away since that day, and that bond remains unbroken, not a thread of it shattered; and the continued love of my children for their mother is an irrefutable evidence that she has been to them a mother indeed. Thus I have twice proved the wisdom of my aunt's determination to seek unto God for guidance in the choice of a companion, if she had her time again. I have instructed the young to make Him their friend and guide, giving them my own experience as evidence that he will not treat with disdain their trust and confidence in him. Here is another evidence added to the many I have received that God hears and answers prayers relating to our temporal as well as to our spiritual necessities, when we seek him aright.

My wife's maiden name was Eliza Herbert, youngest daughter of John and Mary Herbert. Her mother died when Eliza was three years old, hence she was deprived of a mother's care. But her father was good and kind to his children. He accepted the gospel, and also came to this land with his two daughters, Jane, four years older than Eliza, and Eliza. He died in coming up the river between St. Louis and Kansas City. Thus the two girls were left alone. Eliza was now twenty-three years of age.[13]

Directly after our marriage I rented a small adobe room belonging to Hugh Hilton, secured a little home, made furniture, and secured a job on the public works, the wages nominally two dollars per day, to be paid out of the tithing house in such things as were brought in, and at the price determined by the authorities.[14] Such a thing as money was not seen by us, except, I believe, two dollars and fifty cents that I received, with which I bought half a pound of tea and some sugar, for which latter article I paid twenty-five cents per pound, and this was all the tea and sugar we had during the four years and a half that we remained in Utah. We were not allowed the luxuries of sugar, tea, or coffee, etc. Flour, potatoes, and other vegetables, were dealt out to us only to a limited degree, and those I would have to pack about two miles, and I had to go about three miles to my work. Butter and meat were articles that the poor could seldom obtain. They were great luxuries; but the leaders, and those in the practice of polygamy, devoured these things. It was very rarely that I had anything but dry bread to eat during the time that I worked on the public works. But I was thankful, and used to dip my bread in the clear mountain stream, and I can truly say I never murmured. I realized I was in a new country, and being used to hardships, it did not seem so hard for me.

[13]According to Community of Christ records, Eliza Herbert Derry was born in Castle-Eaton, England, on 3 August 1831 and died on 31 May 1907. She apparently traveled to Utah with Thomas S. Williams's freight train, which brought twelve poor families numbering sixty-eight people from Westport under Captain Aaron Farr. The train arrived in Great Salt Lake City about 23 October 1854. See the description of the company at the Mormon Pioneer Overland Travel website.

[14]Born at Bolton, England, in 1821, Hilton joined the LDS church in 1840 and migrated to Utah in 1852. He settled in Salt Lake before moving to Lehi in 1858. Called to the Cotton Mission in 1861, he suffered alongside the other cotton missionaries. Eventually in "Virgen City," he prospered and "was a friend to those in need; good father and kind husband, and a firm believer in the gospel of Jesus Christ." After a long illness, Hilton died of asthma on 19 September 1873. "Died," *Deseret News Weekly*, 8 October 1873, 5:576.

CHARLES AND ELIZA DERRY, CIRCA 1857
Charles Derry lost his first wife while crossing the plains in 1854; Eliza Herbert accepted the offer of this impoverished, heartbroken man "to be my wife and a mother to my children" upon meeting him. Like many other British converts who dreamed of joining the community of believers in Zion, he was disappointed with the "cold, dark picture" he encountered in Utah's rough frontier theodemocracy. *Courtesy Community of Christ Archives.*

Besides, I was willing to make any sacrifice for the building up of "Zion," for as yet I had not learned to distrust the leaders, or question the divinity of their teachings. I believed, then as now, that "sacrifice brings forth the blessings of heaven," and I had gone there to assist in building up the kingdom of God. But as stubborn facts developed I was enabled to see the difference between the service of God, and the impositions of aspiring and ambitious men, and my ardor began to cool, and especially when after working some time on the public works. I was sent in connection with several other men to drive a herd of cattle belonging to the church up to Cache Valley, and there get hay to feed them with during the winter; for it happened during the time I was there, which was near a month, it being near one hundred miles north of Salt Lake City, my wife had to go to the tithing office for the weekly allowance for the family, and there she saw that only the "big bugs," as some called the leaders, could obtain such articles as butter, meat, eggs, etc.[15] For their wives could obtain whatever they asked for, but *she* must be content with a little flour and such vegetables as she could carry home; and to cap the climax, when she went to church on the Sunday, she heard Heber C. Kimball preaching about the men on the public works grumbling because they could get nothing but dry bread to eat. Then, in the vehemence of his pious (?) zeal he said, "Damn it! dip it in City Creek and wet it; there is no need to eat dry bread as long as there is plenty of water in City Creek."

This was one feather too much; it strained the "camel's back." So that when I returned home, she begged of me to quit working on the public works, for she did not want to be treated as a pauper when she went to receive what was her just due, earned by her husband's honest toil. I complied with her wish. She also told me that he insulted the "working men's" wives who had applied for that which their husbands had earned, by telling them in his vulgar and abusive manner to "go home and mend their draggled tailed skirts and not be hanging about the tithing office to see what they could get."[16] I settled up with the authorities and they brought me in debt to the sum of forty-three dollars. I had kept a strict account of all we had received, and they were really in debt to me to the amount of thirty dollars, making

[15]English convert John Hyde, Jr., described how church leaders took advantage of the public works laborers paid with tithing funds: "as the authorities are engaged on public duty, they have the first selection, the tithing clerks posting an open account between them and the Lord." The system practiced the most glaring favoritism in how it distributed goods, pretending "to pay very large wages to artizans, and salaries to the clerks, but charge equally exorbitantly for articles paid; and while the leading clerks, etc., have an abundance, the poor artizan is half starved, half clad, wretchedly housed, almost insulted on applying for any thing." Hyde, *Mormonism*, 38.

[16]"Where are many women spending their time? Around the Tithing Office, idling from morning until night, spending their time for naught," Heber C. Kimball preached on 21 December 1856. "What are you lounging about there for, with your dresses and petticoats, looking as though they were sadly in want of soap and repairing? You know that I have said that the women who go about with the lower edges of their clothes draggled into strings and fragments, are the women who rule their husbands; they are so constantly making snaps and flirts, like a whip lash." *Journal of Discourses*, 4:144.

the sum seventy-three dollars which they were robbing me of. I demanded an investigation, item by item, of what they had charged against me, and I found they had charged me with articles we had never had, such as silks, groceries, and luxuries which we were utter strangers to. But they held the debt against me. I am satisfied they or some of their employees as clerks had obtained them, and charged them to me. Many poor men found themselves in the same condition, but we were powerless to obtain redress.[17] Our eyes began to open as to the spirit that actuated our leaders, and I examined more deeply into matters than before. The more I examined the more corruption I found, even with those who claimed to be the living oracles of God to the church. The fruit of the tree was bitter.

But the principles of the gospel which I obeyed were true. They were in perfect harmony with the scriptures; in fact, they were the pure word of God. And here was the enigma which my poor mind could not solve: How could wicked, ambitious, aspiring men, receive such light upon God's word as to be able to weave a system of religion so in harmony with Holy Writ that not a flaw could be found, not even a single point upon which a valid objection could be hung? I refer to the gospel as taught by Joseph Smith, before polygamy had thrust its lecherous head into view. The learning of the world for seventeen centuries had been trying to evolve from the Holy Scriptures a system that should unite all grades and classes of men in one common faith, but had only succeeded in widening the gulf that separated them, and had covered the earth with seas of blood, and made the heavens lurid with the flames that devoured the martyrs. But *this system so long as its adherents remained true to its precepts,* was fast opening the eyes of men to the one universal truth revealed in and through Christ; and binding them together in one common brotherhood, and this was the stamp of its divinity. No other system under heaven bears that stamp, not even in this the twentieth century. The truth is that all professors of every shade of religion are fast becoming ashamed of their manmade creeds, and are struggling to free themselves from them; but like Pilgrim in the slough of despond, the more they struggle the deeper they sink in the quagmire of confusion. It was the blessed result of that truth on my heart and mind—that truth which

[17]John Hyde wrote in the same vein: "By some singular system of bookkeeping, although these unfortunate men [laborers on the public works] are never half paid, they are always found to *be in debt,* should they wish to leave." Emphasis in original. John Hyde, Jr., "Salt Lake and Its Rulers," *Harper's Weekly* 1 (11 July 1857): 442.

these men had taught me, and which I had been so wonderfully blessed in teaching, and had beheld its blessed effects upon others who had obeyed it at my hands, that caused me to hesitate, when I thought of turning away, and seeking rest for my wearied soul elsewhere. Hence I sought to content myself, and honor those principles which I knew to be true, in my own life, and let those I had no evidence of alone.

But it was difficult to live in the midst of corruption and keep from taint. And if it was difficult for me how would it be for my little children, if they had to be reared under its influences, mingle with other children that were trained from the cradle in its corruption and fed with its poison?

I struggled on under adverse circumstances, but the longer I stayed the more I became painfully aware that I had made a mistake in supposing I could raise my children under righteous influences, where such a system obtained as that which here had been attached to the gospel under the deceptive name of "celestial marriage." It is true they boasted of purity, but the very atmosphere was impregnated with lust. Groups of men could be seen at street-corners and public places, with their eyes fixed upon every female that passed, and more especially the young women, and from the lips of these men would fall some filthy, lewd expression, such as could only spring from a lecherous heart. Nor was the sacred desk which had been professedly consecrated to the gospel of purity free from this accursed taint. It, too, was desecrated to the spreading and encouraging of this system of lust called "celestial marriage," with all its filthy tendencies.

In the month of October, 1855, I removed with my family to Ogden, and rented a board cabin, the boards of which were nailed straight up and down. The boards had shrunk; and as there was nothing but the boards and scantling which formed the framework, we could see between them, and hence it was a very cold place. But it was the best we could do, and we were glad to get it for five dollars per month. Another family rented one room, which made it easier for us to pay the rent, they paying half.

We now began to feel the terrible effects of the drouth and the grasshopper raid. There was no work to be had. Almost every vestige of vegetation was destroyed in most parts of the territory. Some were fortunate in raising parts of a crop, and I had laid in some wheat by working for such farmers as had been thus fortunate, but not sufficient to carry us through the winter. Common laborers' wages ranged from one dollar and a half to two dollars per day, when crops were plentiful; but now it was almost impossible to find work at any price. I offered to work at fifty cents per day and take my pay in provisions. Many others sought the same privilege, but in vain. Many farmers had been blessed in the past with good crops, and had stored them up and now charged famine prices for what they had. The tithing had brought in a good supply to the tithing store, year after year; but this was only available to those who had control, and such as were dependent upon them, and also to such employees as were considered necessary in the public works. Of course all the leading men had farms of their own, from which their families were amply supplied, and if they lacked, they could draw from the tithing store.

Money or clothing were the only commodities that would buy breadstuffs, as both of these articles were very scarce. Clothing, brought there by the store-keeper, was very costly. Most of the emigrants from other countries brought a supply for themselves and families, and in many instances their clothing served to furnish them with bread. But there were many emigrants who had barely enough money to pay for their passage to the mountains, hence, when they arrived they found themselves not only destitute of money, but scant of clothing; such was my fate.[18] It is true I had furnished my wife and children with clothing, and I had an extra suit; but I was in a new country, where wearing-apparel was very scarce, and always loving to see my family and myself neatly clad we clung to it as long as we could without perishing for food. But necessity drove us to dispose of it to the best advantage we could. We will notice this hereafter. It was almost impossible to buy breadstuffs on credit, and if you could a note had to be given drawing ten per cent interest, thus thrusting the poor down lower and lower. Understanding from the law of God that one purpose of the tithing was for the relief of the poor, I went to James Browning, then bishop of Ogden, to get some provisions from the tithing house.[19] He told me they had no more than what would supply the tithing hands. But he finally told me there were potatoes and squash that

[18]John Fell Squires, who arrived from England with his family in 1853, wrote of the period when he was twelve years old: "Times were hared [*sic*] in those days and it taxed the ability of the average parent to russtle enough food and clothes to keep boddy and soul togather. We were hungry most of the time and very poorley clad. The childrens clothes consisted mostely of patch work like Joseph's coat of many colors, so that we resembled a panorama of crazy quilts then on dress parade, but we were all in the fashion of the times." Squires, Autobiographical Sketch, 5.

[19]Territorial assemblyman James G. Browning replaced Isaac Clark as bishop and postmaster of Ogden on 8 April 1854 after Clark's death. See "History of Weber County," *Tullidge's Quarterly Magazine* 4:2 (July 1883): 602.

were frozen in the tithing house cellar that I might have for taking home. I gladly availed myself of this privilege and packed them home. They were hard as rocks, and I found they had been thawed and frozen again, until every bit of nourishment was destroyed out of them. But we gladly ate them, and then tried to eat the peelings, but they were so bitter and nauseous that we thought if we could live with those in our stomachs we could live without them, and we threw them away.

Here I must relate the kindness of an English lady, whom I had known in England by the name of Fletcher, but here had married a man by the name of Wadley. She had learned of our condition, and her husband, at her request, sent me word that I could have some potatoes. I tarried not on the order of my going, but went, and they kindly let me have three bushels of potatoes and some meat, for which I paid them in work the next spring. I shall never forget their kindness.

These hardships we considered a natural consequence. The country was new, and the havoc wrought by the drouth and grasshoppers was unavoidable. Our faith in God and his truth remained unshaken, but the dealings of some who professed to be Christ's ministers had shattered our confidence in them. We still hoped the tree was not rotten from head to foot, and we hung on, hoping for better things. I must give an instance of the generosity of a leading man in Ogden. He was wealthy and had several wives. He had also an abundance of cattle. But the pastures were destroyed, and the crops had been devoured. He saw no way of wintering his cattle. But he knew of hundreds of men destitute of provisions, and being a thoroughbred Yankee, he hit upon a plan to save further loss to himself, as some of the cattle had already died of starvation, and he knew the others would die, and so these he slaughtered and sold the meat, such as it was, at ten cents per pound, to poor men, they being obligated to pay for it in work the coming spring; and that labor was exacted at the time when those men should be earning money for their then present needs.

Another rich man, one of the numerous fathers-in-law of President [Lorin] Farr, among other stock had a cow that was so poor that when she lay down she could not get up without help.[20] He had called on myself and a man

[20]Lorin Farr (1820–1909) was born in Vermont and baptized at age 11. His family moved to Kirtland and eventually to Nauvoo. He came to Utah in 1847 and was called as president of the newly formed Weber Stake in 1851.

named [James?] Goff several times to assist him in getting it up; but it died. Then he generously offered us the cow if we would skin it and give him the skin. This we gladly assented to. We skinned the animal, gave him the skin, and divided the bones between us. I took my part home, salted it down in a barrel, and wife cooked some; but there was no meat on the bones, it was skin and froth, not a star of grease about it. Besides, it was very bitter to the taste, and unwholesome, affording no nourishment, and we concluded, as we had done with the frozen potatoes and squash, that if we could live with that we could better live without it. So lest my neighbors should see me throw it away and think me wasteful, one night after dark I rolled the barrel outside of the city wall and emptied its contents into a ditch of water out of which the mud composing the wall was dug.

That winter I saw cattle stagger toward the brush which they had stripped of every leaf and twig, and fall down dead; such was the extremity to which many were reduced in the fall and winter of 1855.

When the spring of 1856 came we still lived and were thankful; but we had to wait till crops were raised before we could expect to satisfy our hunger sufficiently. We concluded we could no longer pay rent, so we moved up to the foot of the mountains. There I made a dug out, covered it with brush, dug up a garden-patch, my wife aiding in my work, for she was an helpmeet indeed, and securing a few seeds we planted a few onions and other vegetables; but we could not afford to plant potatoes, so what few we obtained we peeled, planting the peelings but eating the potatoes. I also rented a piece of ground in the big field south of Ogden City and about three miles from our dugout. Having no team I hired my plowing done, and put in my corn with a hoe and tended it with the same. I raised twenty-eight dollars worth of stuff for my share and the team work cost me thirty-eight, for which I had to pay in work. I had paid for the teaming before hand and had to wait until late fall before I could get my crop in, hence the small crop.

During most of this time we had nothing but bran and weeds and sego roots which I dug up out of the prairie, and hence I was very weak. If I went away from home and did not return as wife expected she would start to hunt for me, fearing I would fall down and could not get up again. Such was the condition to which I was reduced. Wife and children stood it better than I did. One day I met President Farr and requested him to give me some work. He told me he would give me a job ditching, for which he would give me one dollar and fifty cents per day, one fourth of which was to be in breadstuffs, and the other three fourths was to be allowed on my tithing. To this I agreed, and as I had a neighbor in a similar condition to myself I asked Farr if he would not employ him also. He told me to bring him along. The next morning, having walked over two miles, I got to Farr's house about seven o'clock, just as he was riding out of his yard on horseback. He said, "Heigh, Bro. Derry, you are late this morning!" I told him I had to get my breakfast before I came. He replied, "I have had mine two hours ago." "Very likely," I said, "but I had to dig mine out of the ground before wife could cook it, and yours was all ready to cook." "Why," he said, "have you no flour?" "No, sir." "Well," he replied, "if that is the case I must let you have some to-night." That night he gave me twelve pounds of graham flour, and my wife and children were made happy. We continued our work until the third day. Mr. Farr looked over our work and complained that we had not done enough. I did not reply. I had done all I could, and his words hurt me, but I could not speak. The next day he returned. I was prepared to speak now. I said, "President Farr, yesterday you complained that we had not done sufficient work for you. I want you to understand that my conscience is not made of such stuff as to allow me to do any less work for you than I would do for myself. If you will give me twenty-five pounds for these four days' work, we will cry quits; and if I do you any more work I will give you satisfaction." Farr replied in a confused manner. "Bro. Derry, I am perfectly satisfied with your work. It was the other man I had reference to, not you." I gave him to understand he made no distinction and I would quit with the evening. I did so, and never would work for Farr any more. He charged six dollars per hundred pounds for the graham flour. He had a mill of his own and was wealthy. Remember, I only received one fourth of my wages, the remainder was accredited to me as tithing which did not benefit me.

Bishop Erastus Bingham treated me worse.[21] It seemed to me that the leading men were set upon crushing out what manhood there was in the people by their oppressions, and at the same time, the burden of their teaching was, "obedience to counsel," "follow your leaders," "do as you are told," "heed

[21]Born in Vermont in 1798, Bingham joined the LDS church in 1833 and followed its fortunes from Kirtland to Far West to Nauvoo and Council Bluffs. He came to Utah in 1847. His grazing permit in the Oquirrh Mountains gave his name to Bingham Canyon, future site of the Kennecott copper mine. After settling at Ogden in 1850, Bingham served as a bishop, legislator, and councilman. His five wives bore him ten children before his death in 1882. See Bingham et al., *Sketch of the Life of Erastus Bingham.*

the counsel of the living oracles," "paying tithing," "building the temple," "celestial marriage," which latter I finally concluded was infernal lust.[22]

It was very rare that a gospel sermon was heard. And when the lesser officers visited the members, the above was the burden of their message with the overshadowing question, "What do you think of President Young? Do you uphold him as the prophet of God?" These two questions were the tests of our spirituality and worthiness as members. They were scarcely second to the tithing question. But those who could bear the test of this three-fold shibboleth were considered worthy of exaltation, hence entitled to as many wives as they chose.

But the spirit of rebellion had seized upon me. I determined to be a free man, and do my own thinking, let the consequences be what they may.[23] And for the first time I rebelled in spirit; but I kept a still tongue and minded my own business, so that I was not suspected of harboring what they termed a spirit of apostasy; and when the visiting officers came around, and inquired my feeling toward President Young, I told them truthfully, that I was satisfied with him; but had they pressed the matter closer and inquired in what way I was satisfied, I should have emphatically told them I was satisfied that he was no prophet of God. But as they were satisfied with my answer I saw no necessity of revealing my true feelings, and thereby incurring the wrath of the authorities. I had heard that a "still tongue made a wise head," but I believed that a *wise head would keep a still tongue.* I was not anxious to have the Danites lurking in my path.

It was about this time that Bishop Bingham thought that as I had not received my endowments I had better receive them. I had had no thought of applying for them, but as he now suggested it I made no opposition. He wrote out a recommendation, in, as near as I can remember, these words: "President Brigham Young: Bro. Charles Derry is worthy to receive all the blessings his heart desires. Yours in Christ, Erastus Bingham." I took the paper home;

[22]Peter McAuslan, who sailed with Derry on the *John M. Wood* in 1854, wrote, "The Doctrin of doing as you are told, whither it appears to you to be right or rong [wrong], was most strongly urged the last year or two that I was thare, so much so that I could not believe it, and of course I found out that I could not be consistently a Mormon." Aird, *Mormon Convert,* 279. In one of the many examples of church leaders preaching obedience, Heber C. Kimball on 8 November 1857 exhorted, "Learn to do as you are told . . . if you are told by your leader to do a thing, do it. None of your business whether it is right or wrong." *Journal of Discourses,* 6:32.

[23]McAuslan shared the same spirit when he quoted Shakespeare's *Julius Caesar*: "I'de rather be a dog and bay at the moon then give up my right to do my own thinking and become a Slave to such base Authority." Aird, *Mormon Convert,* 191.

and after wife and I retired to bed I made known to her what I had received from the bishop. I did not tell her in the day lest other ears should hear my views. After telling her of the recommendation, I told her I did not want to receive any endowments. She inquired why. I told her I had been brought in contact with many who had received them, and as there were always some who were anxious to tell all they knew, and as I was a good listener, I was willing to hear; and, from their declared experience, I concluded there were oaths to take that I could not conscientiously subscribe to, and I should be under the necessity of refusing, which refusal would be likely to bring down their wrath upon me. This little revelation filled her with surprise and she wept bitterly. My wife was a very conscientious woman, she believed the gospel with all her heart, and never thought of deception in those from whose hands she had received it. Nor had she had the opportunities to see and learn what I had seen and learned; hence she was not prepared to suspect wrong in the teachings and practices of these "living oracles." But she had every confidence in her husband, and accepted my views. Some might wonder why I had not told her of these things. My reasons were these. I loved her and did not desire to cause her any unnecessary sorrow. I had every confidence in her abiding love for me, but there was danger in her making my views known to her sister, who was a radical Brighamite, but a good woman. She would not do this with a view to betray me, but in her innocence and confidence she might drop such words as might lead to suspicion that something was wrong, hence I kept my own fears and doubts burning in my own breast until the proper time when I could divulge them with safety. Suffice it to say, I never sought for any endowment, but burned or otherwise destroyed the recommendation from the bishop, and bided my time. Wife was perfectly satisfied to risk our gaining eternal life without our endowment.

I said above, Bishop Erastus Bingham treated me worse than Farr. During the year 1856 we suffered keenly from the famine; so much so that for six weeks we had nothing but bran and such edible weeds and roots as we could gather from the prairies. I once obtained through the kindness of a more fortunate neighbor, some corn meal siftings; that was all they could spare. We tried to eat them, but we could not cook them in any way so as to eat them. I went to Sanford Bingham, a son of the bishop, hearing that he had a steer to sell, to try to make some kind of bargain by which we could obtain some meat. I had a valuable coat and vest, worth then thirty dollars. This was the last of the wearing apparel I had to spare. They had not been worn, though I had bought them in England and were tailor made and of excellent quality. Mr. Bingham wanted for his two-year-old steer the coat and vest and three thousand adobes, the price of which was ten dollars per thousand, making the steer to cost me sixty dollars. I must either accept the offer or starve, with my family, as at this time the crop of 1856 was not matured. I agreed to his demand, gave him my coat and vest, and as soon thereafter as I could make the adobes, I did, and as they were to be delivered on my adobe yard, I notified him that they were ready; but for some reason he did not haul them away. But we killed the steer and it furnished us food for quite a while, for we rarely obtained anything but bran or sego roots and weeds to eat with it. He allowed the adobes to remain on the yard all the winter and many were greatly damaged.

In the spring and summer of 1857, I still followed the occupation of adobe making, and also rented a small piece of land and put in a small crop, and as I was going home from my adobe yard one night I was summoned to be at Bishop [Chauncey W.] West's, then a colonel of the Nauvoo militia, with gun, ammunition and blankets ready to march to the mountains by nine o'clock that night, the cause for which I will state hereafter. I obeyed the summons, was out in the mountains three months, reaching my family at or about Christmas. While being mustered out, Bishop [Erastus] Bingham came to me in the ranks and demanded that as soon as possible I should make three thousand more adobes, as the others were ruined. I told him that was his son's lookout, not mine. He insisted that I must make them. I told him I would not submit to such injustice, and did not. But after some time he learned that a certain brother was owing me twenty-five dollars. He secured that and thus robbed me of my just due. I had already paid sixty dollars for the steer, and the bishop's last grab made it eighty-five. It was useless for me to seek redress. However, all these things served to open my eyes a little wider and led me nearer to the solution of the problem as to what spirit actuated those men who claimed to be the Lord's anointed. But among the rank and file there were evidences of true and genuine Christianity, which I am pleased to record. Prior to obtaining the above steer, as I have before stated, we were compelled to live on bran and sego roots, the latter being a very delicious little root that bore a beautiful flower, but they were very small, and not plentiful, hence it required considerable time to hunt them up, and it required quite a number to make a meal.[24]

[24]In recognition of the significance of the bulbous perennial in the pioneer diet, the sego lily became Utah's state flower.

One morning I was going to my adobe yard which was two miles from my cave. Away in the distance I saw before me something lying on the ground, and I saw a man on horseback ride by it, and as he came to the object he stopped for an instant and looked down at it but rode on without getting off his horse. I walked on until I came to it and found it was a small sack, and to my joy I found it was full of barley cakes. With a glad heart I picked it up and returned to my family with the prize. Wife divided it up among us all, and it made us a delicious meal. Alice Amelia, seeing her mother give to each their portion, said, "Mother, you will give us more when you get it, won't you?" That was the nearest a murmur that was heard in my family in those trying scenes.

Another time I was traveling the same road to my work. I met a man with a wagon load of provisions, flour, graham, and bran. I requested the man to give me some bran, as I did not expect to get flour any more. He refused, saying he wanted it for his hogs. In words which I confess were more forcible than polite I told him my wife and children were dearer to me than his hogs could be to him, and I must have some bran, and would pay him for it in work, as I had nothing else to offer. He then told me to roll off a sack of bran. I did so, and asked him how much I must pay for it. He replied: "Bring me the sack back; that is all." I thanked him and packed that bran two miles to my family, and never did man pack a nugget of gold home with greater joy than I packed that sack of bran; and I returned the sack to its owner, Captain James Brown.[25]

About the time that the above circumstance occurred, an Englishman named William Pidcock came to our place, having heard of our condition, and brought us some flour and sugar.[26] He told my wife that he had seen me in the city, that I was sick and very weak, and he was sure that we needed help, and he had gone among his neighbors and had begged the flour for us, and he had brought what he could, hoping to find me at home; but as I had not returned wife felt alarmed lest I might have fallen down and could not get home. She started down toward the city and saw me slowly wending

[25]This is a surprisingly sympathetic story about the colorful James Brown (1801–1863), who as captain of the Mormon Battalion's Company C commanded the detachments sent to winter on the Arkansas River in 1846. British adventurer George Ruxton described him as "'Cap'en Brown'—a hard featured, black-coated man of five-and-forty, correctly got up in his black continuations, and white handkerchief around his neck, a costume seldom seen at the foot of the Rocky Mountains." His men considered Brown a tyrant, and one wife complained of having "to stand and here the insults of an unfeeling Man." Sent to collect the detachment's pay in California in 1847, Brown used the money to purchase Miles Goodyear's fort. Ogden's first name was Browns Fort. See Bagley, *Frontiersman*, 43n52, 118–20.

[26]Blacksmith and a merchant William Hazelgrove Pidcock (1832–1906) migrated from England the same year as Derry. At this time he and his wife Hannah had two young children.

my way homeward, and she assisted me home. Neither the kindness of Bro. Pidcock, nor the tender solicitude of my faithful companion will ever be forgotten by me. Wife and children endured those privations better than I did. Perhaps it was because I had the burden of supporting them on my mind, and my efforts to obtain work.

I have no desire to create the impression that the mass of the people of Utah were bad. On the contrary, I am satisfied there were many God-fearing people, who had made great sacrifices for the truth; but like myself they had been blinded by their leaders, and were led into error through their sincere belief that those men were truly inspired of God, hence they did not question their teachings.[27]

Charles Derry, "Autobiography."
Journal of History 1:4 (October 1908): 423–38.

Part III. Brigham's Minions

From subsequent events it appears that Brigham had received information that the United States Government was about to send an army to enforce the law of the land with respect to polygamy; and knowing that not one fourth of the men in the territory had gone into its practice, and fearing those who had not would not be sufficiently interested in defending those who had indulged in it, he saw the necessity of bringing all under the bonds of this "cable chain," and hence introduced a so-called "reformation," the leading feature of which was "celestial marriage."[28] He made a great noise about the wickedness of the people, and their neglect to keep this celestial law, which he claimed was the fullness of the gospel. In order to bring about this reformation he called out a great number of missionaries and had them to renew their covenants by being baptized again. Then he armed them with a long catechism, or a list of questions covering every sin in the catalogue of crimes, to be put to every member of the church, old and young, in their several homes. In addition to this they were to hold public meetings, in which they were to urge the necessity of renewing their covenants and also

[27]Peter McAuslan wrote, "I do know that there are many just as good men as I would wish to ascocaite with whose expearience in Mormonizm has made them Stronger in the Faith. And I must say that my feelings are very Charityable towards them as a people, that is to those who are honest in the faith." Aird, *Mormon Convert*, 280.

[28]Plural marriage was advocated especially forcefully after Jedediah Grant's death in December 1856. Aird, *Mormon Convert*, 179.

the necessity of obeying the law of celestial marriage. The questions must be put to each one, and answers must be given in the most solemn manner and a clean breast made by the ones catechized by these inquisitors. No matter how great or small their sins, each individual must be rebaptized. The heaviest curses were held over their heads if they kept anything back in their confessions. However, they were granted the privilege of private examinations if desired. This was simply a ruse to bring the people more directly under the control of Brigham Young.

This inquisition had a terrible effect upon the minds of some, especially females.[29] Some were reported as driven to insanity. The inquisitors came to my place, and questioned me in the presence of my wife, as I had nothing to keep secret from her. Then they gave her the privilege of a private examination, but she told them she had done nothing that she would be ashamed for her husband to know. Bishop Bingham then turned to me and asked me if my wife was not a good woman? I replied, "Bishop, I don't want her to be any better lest she should go up, and I left alone." The large mouth of the bishop spread out to indefinite proportions and he and his fellow inquisitor left us, to seek after other sinners.

Public meetings were called specially for the sisters, in which these men showed the magnitude of the awful crime of preventing their husbands from obeying this great law of "enlargement"; showing that it was their duty to seek out other women for their husbands. In these meetings, married women were called upon to stand up. Then the polygamic ones must stand up. Next all the unmarried females from fourteen and upward were to stand up, these, if expressing their dissent from polygamy, as well as all the married ones who did not believe in it, were held up to ridicule and told they could not be exalted in the kingdom of God. Thus many were led to embrace this God-dishonoring doctrine who in their hearts abhorred it. The man with only one wife was given to understand that he never could be exalted to the celestial kingdom of God, but must be content with a lesser glory.

It was a common thing to see a blooming young girl adorning the shriveled and withered person of some old man, old enough to be her grandfather, who already had a number of concubines. It was indeed comical to see him

[29]Englishwoman Hannah Tapfield King wrote, "The people shrunk, shivered, wept, [and] groaned like whipped children. They were told to get up in meeting and confess their sins. They did so 'till it was sickening, and brought disease. . . . Never shall I forget the darkness, desolation, *and horror* of those times!" Emphasis in original. King, Journals, 142–43.

introduce her as "wife number —," but alas! when these poor foolish girls learned what it was to occupy a fraction only of a divided heart, and that heart incapable of a pure and devoted love, many found that the marriage bed was a bed of thorns, a gridiron of burning hate, fanned by the flames of envy and jealousy, deadly as the fires of hell and ofttimes resulted in demands for divorce, as testified by Brigham Young when he made his public boast that the demand for divorces kept him supplied with pin money. When he also declared that at a given time he would set every woman free from her husband, his own among the number, but when the time came, it is presumed that he feared the women would leave himself and colleagues in polygamy in the lurch, hence he never carried out his threat.[30]

Another object of the "reformation" seemed to be to discover who were the doubters as to his claim to divine calling as prophet and president of the church of Christ. This object was manifest when we saw the anxiety of the inquisitors to know in what light we regarded President Young. Woe betide the man who dared to express a doubt as to his claim to divine calling as prophet or president of the church of Christ. He was a marked man. If he was a laboring man he would lose his employment. If a business man his trade would fall off, and these were the least evils he might expect. I was in a meeting called by Lorenzo [Lorin] Farr and others of this inquisition, when every man was called upon to covenant that he would not hear any speak disrespectfully of President Young. And they were told it was their duty to knock such a man down. They were further told that no man would be permitted to leave the Territory, and if they attempted to leave, they must leave their property and their wives and children behind them.[31] I leave it to common sense to judge how far such men, who were stripped of all that was dear to them, would be permitted to go.

Brigham's minions were always ready to complete their fiendish work. I think it was in 1857 or 1858, that Henry Jarvis and his wife were waylaid in one of the streets in Salt Lake City one night on their returning home from a visit,

[30]Fanny Stenhouse described the "pin money" boast in "*Tell It All*," 390. On 21 September 1856 Brigham Young announced he would give Mormon women two weeks "to make up their minds whether they would stay with their Husbands or be liberated." Young revised his offer at conference on 6 October and set "certain conditions": women must "appear forthwith at my office & give good & sufficient reasons" for him to grant a divorce, and they must "marry men that will not have but one wife." See Bigler, *Forgotten Kingdom*, 126.

[31]"The moment a person decides to leave this people, he is cut off from every object that is durable for time and eternity," Brigham Young preached on 17 August 1856. "Every possession and object of affection will be taken from those who forsake the truth, and their identity and existence will eventually cease." *Journal of Discourses*, 4:31–32.

by a band of these cutthroats and stripped of their clothing and their bodies besmeared with human excrement, and their mouths filled with the same.[32] This man Jarvis was an Englishman, and had spent years of labor in the mission field in England; but after emigrating to Salt Lake Valley his eyes had become open as to the true status of things. In the bitterness of his disappointment he had given vent to his feelings in words not complimentary to the authorities in Utah, and at the crook of Brigham's finger, the Danites visited this filthy, degrading, and fiendish vengeance upon the poor man and his wife.[33]

Does the religion of Jesus Christ justify such devilish work? Does it stand in need of such diabolical defense? From such my soul turns away in utter disgust. Is it any wonder that thousands lost all respect for men who could sanction such damning deeds, to say nothing of those ordering them to be done? I know whereof I speak. I know that polygamy, blood atonement, and their oppressing system of tithing, together with the necessity of honoring the "file leaders"—more appropriately, vile leaders—as the Lord's anointed, were the burden of their teaching.

In all this I maintained as discreet a silence as I could, realizing my head was in the lion's mouth. Once I was taken to task by a priest in one of the wards in Salt Lake City, as to what I thought of President Young. I answered, "I believe he is a man like us."

"Don't you believe he is a prophet?"

"No. If I did I should believe that he lied when he declared he was no prophet."

"Well, but he is and I know it."

"You and he for it, but I am inclined to believe him rather than you," I replied, "and he declares he is not a prophet."[34]

---

[32]A similar attack was made on T. B. H. and Fanny Stenhouse. Stenhouse, *"Tell It All,"* 580. See page 367n89 herein.

[33]On 16 November 1856, Heber C. Kimball moved "that Henry J. Jarvis, Thomas S. Williams, Lorin W. Babbitt and those who went with said Babbitt to California be cut from the Church of Jesus Christ of Latter Day Saints for their wickedness, their slandering and their meanness." All present assented. *Deseret News,* 26 November 1856, 298/4. Henry John Jarvis (1822–1878) and his wife Caroline Rowling Jarvis emigrated from England in 1854, the same season as Derry. On 14 January 1857 Hosea Stout described a similar assault: "Last night Jarvis House was broken into and his family drove out, the House set on fire in two or three places and he beaten and drove off and hell played generally." Brooks, ed., *On the Mormon Frontier,* 618. By the 1860 census, the Jarvis family was living in Iowa. Young's crooked finger was fraught with meaning, as T. B. H. Stenhouse pointed out: "It was no idle threat when he [Young] said: 'Apostates, or men who never made any profession of religion, had better be careful how they come here, lest I should bend my little finger.'" Stenhouse, *Rocky Mountain Saints,* 277.

[34]Brigham Young repeatedly acknowledged he was not a prophet like Joseph Smith. See, for example, a sermon given on 26 July 1857, *Journal of Discourses* 5:77.

One of the threats made by Brigham was that if they did not obey the law now given, they would be brought under the Mosaic law. I had taken but little interest in the so-called "reformation," except to observe its effect upon others, and in a few months it was a thing of the past.

I recollect one little incident in one of the missionary meetings in Ogden City. A man named George Bellamy bore his testimony to the truth as revealed of God in these last days, and made some reference to President Young without throwing discredit upon him, or unfavorably reflecting upon his claims; in fact the authorities present rather considered his testimony as being in favor of Brigham's claims. When he closed, Captain Brown, counselor to the president of the stake, arose and very fervently declared, "That ar man has got the Spirit of God, that ar man has I could feel it at my finger ends." The fact was Bellamy had delivered that little speech to cover up his tracks and blind them as to his real intentions, for in a few days from that time he had slipped away, on his way back to the States, and the next time I saw him he was in St. Louis. So much for the power of discernment possessed by Counselor Brown. I believe Brother Bellamy presided for a time over the St. Louis Branch of the Reorganized Church.[35]

I have made reference to an expedition to the mountains in which I was compelled to take part. I will now dwell upon it more fully. As before stated, strong intimations had been received by President Young that the United States Government was contemplating sending an army to place a new governor over the Territory and enforce the laws of the nation therein. For the purpose of blocking this intention of the Government, Brigham had ordered that every able-bodied man should be enrolled in the Nauvoo Militia and undergo a system of drilling in the use of firearms, and they were accordingly drilled, myself among the number.

On the 24th day of July, 1857, while Brigham Young and a select party were celebrating the tenth anniversary of the entrance of the pioneers into Salt Lake Valley in Big Cottonwood Canyon, a messenger arrived and reported that General Harney with two thousand infantry and a proportionate number of artillery and cavalry was ordered to Utah.[36] This news aroused the ire of Brigham and he recalled to their minds that ten years ago when they entered

[35]When Elder George Bellamy, a man of "strong impulses," died at St. Louis on 1 April 1872 at the age of fifty-four, the Reorganization lost "a most efficient man, in the warfare of truth against error." Bellamy left a wife and child behind. See *True Latter Day Saints' Herald*, 1 and 15 May 1872, 263, 318.

[36]Gen. William S. Harney, known as "Mad Bear" to the Sioux and "Squaw Killer" among the Mormons, was reassigned from the Utah Expedition to deal with "Bleeding Kansas." Albert Sidney Johnston took command of the expedition at Fort Leavenworth in September 1857.

Salt Lake Valley, he declared that if the United States would let us alone ten years we would ask no odds of them, meaning, of course, that we would be independent of the United States.[37] He said now they were independent and would never again be subject to the United States Government. Heber C. Kimball delivered himself in a similar strain, also others of the leading men, and they talked very loudly about "Buck and Bright" being no longer yoked up together. "Buck" represented the Government under Buchanan, and "Bright" Utah under the rule of Brigham. He further declared that the United States army should never enter those valleys, but they should melt away as the dew before the sun. All this in the name of Almighty God.[38]

From this time the drilling of the militia went on more vigorously than ever, and on the 15th day of September Brigham declared the territory under martial law, and at the same time large numbers of armed militia were ordered to Echo Canyon and other points, to prevent the soldiers from coming in. As before stated, on the 19th day of September as I was going home from my work I was ordered to be at Colonel West's office by nine o'clock that night, it being now about seven o'clock in the evening. Bitter as the pill was, I had to swallow it or be treated as an enemy. I responded with great reluctance after dedicating my family and myself to God. I was mustered in with the rest of the men and about three o'clock the next morning was on the march to the mountains. Only those who have passed through the ordeal can tell my feelings at leaving all that was dear to me on earth to engage in a war in which I had no interest whatever. I had to furnish my own outfit, which consisted of an old musket and some bedding. I determined to shed no blood, and I am thankful we were never brought into conditions that demanded it. While in Echo Canyon our business was to fortify the canyon, dig trenches, pile rocks on the steep sides of the canyon, and throw up breastworks.

After being in the mountains three weeks we were ordered back to Ogden, and permitted to sleep one night in our homes. The next day we were ordered to March Valley, where we expected to meet a portion of the enemy, but they were not there and I was glad.[39] After staying there a week we were ordered back to Echo, and went into Camp until about three days before Christmas,

[37]See Bagley, *Blood of the Prophets,* 80.

[38]"We commenced last Sunday to declare that we are a free people, and we will be free from this day henceforth and for ever," Heber C. Kimball preached on 6 September 1857. "The bow-pin has dropped out of old Bright's bow, and the bow has dropped out, and the yoke is now on old Buck-anan's neck." *Journal of Discourses,* 5:217.

[39]"March Valley" is probably the Malad Valley in southern Idaho. The Nauvoo Legion scouted the Malad in the fall of 1857, fearing that the army would enter Utah via Soda Springs and the Bear River.

at which time we were ordered home, and I rejoiced to know that I had never been ordered to fire a gun. I reached home on Christmas Eve and right royal was the welcome I received from wife and children. Wife had harvested the corn and potatoes and had moved into a warmer cabin that I had bought prior to being mustered into the "army." Scouts were left in the mountains to harrass the Government troops and destroy the supply-trains. In the meantime Brigham claimed to have a revelation from God commanding the raising of a standing army of two thousand men. Accordingly an inventory of every man's property was taken, and a tax levied upon the same to furnish every necessity for the equipment and maintenance of the army, which was to consist of cavalry. If one person could fit out one or more men he had to do it. If it required twenty men to fit out one, they must do it. The poorest had to do according to their means, for the Prophet Brigham said, "The Lord required it." The means were raised, the men equipped, but perhaps Uncle Sam's icy fetters were broken and the mountains of snow had melted and Brother Brigham saw the fiery determination in Uncle Sam's eye to enter those valleys if he had to wade through the blood of Brigham's hosts; for Brigham declared the Lord accepted the sacrifice and the standing army was disbanded. But Brigham's lord forgot to return the poor man's cow, or horse, etc., now that they were no longer needed. Perhaps Brigham needed them.[40]

The next move on the docket was in the spring of 1858, when an order from Brigham was issued that every man, woman, and child north of Utah County must abandon their homes and remove into the southern part of the Territory under the penalty of having their houses burned over their heads; "Leaving only a few men in every settlement to apply the torch in case the troops on their arrival should prove to be hostile." So the *Juvenile Instructor* puts it, but the understanding was, they must be burned *if the soldiers came in*. Brigham declared he knew of a portion of the Territory where that people could hide up for twenty years and the United States could not find

[40]On 17 October 1857 Brigham Young proposed selecting some two thousand "of the right kind of men, have them provided with excellent rifles, and let them furnished themselves with good bows and plenty of arrows, and learn to be as adept in their use as in sharpshooting with the Rifle, and organize them into a standing army to be most—or all—the time on duty in the field, and so appointed on the different feasable [*sic*] approaches to our Territory as circumstances may from time to time require, and each Ward supporting so many families, so that our solders can be perfectly free." He suggested stationing about one hundred men on the southern route to California, another hundred to the north "to watch for Oregonians," some two hundred on the Humboldt River, "and the remainder to watch the different eastern routes, the latter so placing their stores and rendezvous that they can operate together or apart." Young believed "2000 men of the right stripe can prevent all the armies of the world from coming here." MacKinnon, *At Sword's Point*, 272, 360–61. For more on this unique American military unit, see Bigler and Bagley, *The Mormon Rebellion*, 270–75.

them.[41] I removed my family as far south as Battle Creek [Pleasant Grove, Utah County]. I went on to Provo and worked, making a road in Provo Canyon. Here I earned forty dollars in ten days, but it was in "Deseret scrip." I quickly turned my scrip into a cow, and I had hardly got the cow to my family before the "Deseret scrip" was all called in, being now worthless. Brigham's pretended hiding-place could not be found by his explorers, and the United States army came into the valley, June 26, 1858, and as they came in they designated their twelve pieces of artillery as the "twelve apostles." The new governor, Alfred Cumming, took his place, issued a proclamation for the citizens to return to their homes, and counseled obedience to the law of the land.[42]

I and my family did not return to Ogden City. I moved as far north as City Bountiful and rented a log cabin on the bottoms. Mr. James Lemon, a "Gentile," let me have a team to fetch my family.[43] I then obtained work and earned our winter's bread. Mr. Lemon let me have seventy-five pounds of beef to be paid for in work in the spring, and I appreciated his kindness. I now concluded I would get a team, though I had no money to pay for it, and one morning I said to my wife, "I am going to try to get me a team."

"Why, Charles," she replied, "you have got no money."

I told her I must have one and would, at least, try. Some way I felt confident I should be successful, but I knew not how or where; but I went up into the settlement and made inquiries where I could get a yoke of cattle. I met Thomas Roberts and inquired of him. He told me Bishop William Smith, of Centerville, had just purchased a large herd of cattle that had just crossed the plains, hauling a train of merchandise.[44] He said he had bought them for forty

[41]The best account of the search for this hiding place is Stott, *Search for Sanctuary*.

[42]For more on the Deseret script's "shinplasters" and the "Move South," see Bigler and Bagley, *The Mormon Rebellion*, 274–75, 294–96, 301, 315, 320, 326.

[43]This may be James William Lemmon (1827–1908), whose name appears on Mormon mining records in California. He apparently traveled with Mormon Battalion veterans to Utah, where he appeared on Salt Lake property lists and was "rebaptized" in Great Salt Lake City in November 1848. A second possibility is James Abbott Lemmon (1815–1882), who came to Utah with his family in the William McPherson company in 1851, settled in Sanpete County, and died in Rockville, near today's Zion National Park. See the Mormon Pioneer Overland Travel website. One of these men was probably the "Brother" James Lemmon whom Brigham Young's business agent, Horace Eldredge, said started for Utah in 1859 "with a train of 17 wagons loaded with assorted merchandise" consisting of staple goods "selected expressly for that market," including "Groceries nails Glass Paints, Oil Hard ware Dye stuffs &c." See Eldredge to Young, 20 June 1859, Brigham Young Collection, LDS Archives.

[44]Born in Canada, William Reed Smith (1826–1894) joined the LDS church in 1841 and moved to Nauvoo, where he suffered so badly from malaria that he relocated in Stark County, Illinois. Smith came to Utah in 1849 and prospered driving cattle to and trading in California. Appointed bishop at Centerville in 1855, he also served as a probate judge, legislator, and as president of the Davis Stake. See "Gone to Rest," *Davis County Clipper*, 18 January 1894, 1/4.

or forty-five dollars per yoke. Bishop Smith was a stranger to me; I had heard him preach once, but had never spoken to him. He knew nothing of me, but I determined to see him. I went right up to his place at Centerville. He was not at home, but one of his wives told me he was down in the pasture looking after his new herd. I found him with his cattle in his large pasture. I told him who I was and my business. He told me to look out a yoke that would suit me. I did so. I then told him I had no money, but I had a cow worth thirty dollars, and if I got the cattle I intended to haul wood from the mountains to Salt Lake City and bring him the money as I obtained it. I asked him the price. He said, "You can have them for ninety dollars if paid now, but if not, on the following terms: I will take the cow at your price, and if you pay the remainder in one month they will be ninety-three dollars; in two months, ninety-five dollars; if I wait three months they will be one hundred dollars, and if they are not paid for then I will take them back and charge you for the use of them." It was a big undertaking, but I had found it impossible to make a decent living without a team, and I determined to take the cattle, I said, "You will want my note?" He replied, "Your face looks honest enough without any note."

I took the cattle home and brought him the cow with which he was well satisfied. I then managed to get a second-hand wagon, and hauled wood from the mountains to Salt Lake City and sold it for cash; and I brought him the money as I received it until I had paid all but ten dollars within the first month. Then my hay gave out. I could not buy any for love nor money. The army was paying twenty-five dollars per ton for it, and the farmers took theirs there and received the ready cash. In the meantime I had told my wife's brother-in-law that it was my intention to leave in the spring. He communicated the information to the bishop of the ward in which we were living, John Stoker. Bishop Stoker came to see me and inquired if I was intending to leave the Territory. I told him I was. He expressed great surprise, and inquired my reasons. I told him I had no interest there. He remarked, "You are one of the last men that I should think of leaving the Territory." He then said, "You are owing the church one hundred and thirteen dollars." I replied, "According to your books I am owing the church one hundred and twenty dollars." He looked at his book and said, "You are right, I must take your cattle and wagon as payment."[45] He

[45]John Stoker (1817–1881) joined the Mormons in 1836 and came to Utah in 1848 as a captain of fifty in the Brigham Young Company. Appointed bishop of Bountiful's North Mill Creek Ward in 1851, he married three women, fathered sixteen children, and in 1877 became a patriarch before his death from paralysis. His action with Derry typifies the way LDS authorities used Perpetual Emigrating Fund debts to control dissenters.

never inquired if I could pay it; it seemed as though he thought I could not get away without a team, which was true, nor could I have paid it all that time.

I have already stated in a former chapter that the church offered to furnish half of our fare to Utah. This was my indebtedness. I had not been able to repay that, as I landed in Utah without a cent, and the following years the crops were mostly destroyed. Then came the "Mormon War," and after this the great move southward, and with all these hindrances, it had been a hard matter to live at all, without paying a debt which in strict justice I did not owe. I had spent six years in preaching the gospel without remuneration, and had come to Utah in obedience to the counsel of the authorities. Still it was my intention to pay the debt.

He took my cattle and wagon-gears, leaving the bed for us to sleep in, as we had had no bedstead since we moved to the south. I now determined to see President Young, and try to get my team back. I went to the city and sought admission to the president, but was hindered from entering by an armed policeman who was pacing to and fro before the entrance.[46] I then went to a friend's house, wrote a note, handed that to the policeman, and requested him to deliver it to Brigham Young. In that note I told him plainly but respectfully of my labors in the missionary field, my coming there in obedience to counsel, the church offering to furnish half the cost of my emigration, my landing there without a cent; I reminded him of the grasshopper raid and the famine in consequence, then of my compulsory service in the "Mormon War," and afterward the general move southward in obedience to his order in 1858, and requested him to order the return of my cattle and wagon, without which I was crippled in my efforts to leave in the spring, to say nothing of paying that debt. When he read the note he ordered the policeman to send me into the office. I entered. He demanded in rather a peremptory tone, "Are you the man who wrote that note?"

"Yes, sir."

"What are your reasons for leaving?"

---

[46]In the wake of the Utah War, Brigham Young retreated from public view and seldom met with outsiders except when personally armed and heavily guarded. Overland emigrants often commented on the Mormon leader's odd behavior: "Brigham Young has a whole square to himself which is surrounded by a high stone wall 10 ft high on the corner," John S. Wilson noted in July 1859. "At the entrance gate there is a constant watch so that no one can gain admittance except by permission. Brigham Young is hardly ever seen except on Sunday and when he does go out he is accompanied by 30 or 40 of the faithful as a guard not from the Gentiles as they call those not mormans but from some of the erring brethren who have been expelled from the church." Wilson, Overland Journey, 12 July 1859, 49–50.

"I have no interest here."

"What, don't you believe Mormonism?"

"No, sir, nor any other ism."

"Aha, I knew you could not believe any other ism."

"Here," Heber Kimball interjected rather contemptuously. "You were a Methodist, wasn't you?"

"No, sir."

Then Brigham told me that I had labored long and endured many privations for this work, and assured me if I would remain and be faithful I should not lose my reward.

I replied, "President Young, if you will forgive that debt you may take all the reward."

He answered he could not, but he would arrange it so that I could have my cattle to work with. He then told me of judgments that were coming on the earth; among the rest there would be a seven-year famine in the United States and two years here, commencing with the next year, and I would be glad to come back.

I replied, "President Young, I have gone through one year's famine here, and I would rather risk seven years of famine in the States than one year here." There ended our colloquy. However, he gave me a note to deliver to Bishop Hunter, the head bishop, authorizing him to order Bishop Stoker to let me have my cattle and wagon.[47] But from the fact that Bishop Stoker paid no attention to it, I was satisfied secret orders were given countermanding that order. I knew Bishop Stoker dared not disobey counsel. Brigham did give me a certificate afterward, declaring that I had made proper settlement with the church and was not to be molested on my journey eastward. This was to prevent the Danites from interfering with us. It was midwinter when they took my cattle, and as I had sold all the wood that I had hauled to pay for the cattle, I was now left to pack what wood we burned from a willow patch on the bottoms.

I was owing ten dollars on the cattle, but I had a yearling heifer which I sold for sixteen dollars and I paid Bishop Smith his ten dollars, so that now I was free from all financial demands, except for the beef we were eating and that I paid in work in the spring of 1859 as per agreement. I now bent every energy to get my family safe away to the Eastern States. My wife was

[47]Edward Hunter was presiding bishop in 1859.

questioned by the ward authorities as to her willingness to go with me, and to find out if I was using any undue influence to get her away. Offers were made to her by her relatives as inducements to stay. But she told them her mind was fixed,—where I went she would go, and in the language of Ruth to Naomi, she told me, "Where you go I will go, your people shall be my people and your God my God." My cup of joy was full; she seemed dearer to me now than ever. I cared nothing for obstacles that lay in my way, and we united our efforts to accomplish our deliverance.

When I had straightened matters up with Mr. Lemon, who had kindly waited, we removed to Salt Lake City as soon as we could after spring opened. There I secured work at gardening for two dollars per day to be paid in flour. Wife helped wonderfully by her economy, and we made a raise of sixty dollars by selling our flour. With this and twenty dollars loaned me by Brother Robert Holt, who also was intending to leave, I bought a yoke of cattle.[48] But prior to our removal to the city with my family I had met another John Brown who was secretary to the head bishop—Hunter. He, Brown, had learned that I was going to leave and inquired my reason. I gave it as I had given it to others. He took my arm and requested me to take a walk with him. I did so. He then said, "Charlie, there is but one difference between you and me, you are going and I am going to stay. I am satisfied this thing is a humbug, but I am getting a good salary, and as long as I can do that I shall stay." He then said, "If you will pledge your word and honor not to disclose who told you, I will tell you of a man who is going to leave, and is rich, and will have several teams, and I think he will give you a chance to drive one of his teams and permit your family to go with you." He gave me the name and address. I visited the man named at his house. I told him I wished to have a private interview with him. He invited me into a private room. There I made known my errand. He affected to be very indignant, and demanded to know who had told me such a story as that he was going to leave. I told him I had given my pledge of honor not to divulge the name of my informant, and I would not. He went on to say he was well satisfied with Utah, that his means were invested in real estate there, and there was no reason for his leaving. I then told

[48]Born 8 February 1814, Robert Holt served for many years as president of the Manchester Conference in England. He came to Utah in 1856 as a captain in Edward Martin's disastrous handcart company. Of the 664 members of the party, the eight named Holt ranged from Joseph, age 3, to Ellen Walker Holt, age 44. See the Mormon Pioneer Overland Travel website; and Josiah Rogerson, "Martin's Handcart Company, 1856," *Salt Lake Herald*, 27 October 1907.

him I was sorry if I had been misinformed, and that being all my business our interview was at an end. His manner immediately softened, and he continued to talk, saying he was satisfied with Mormonism, it was just as good as any other ism. This last sentence gave me the key to his mind. I knew that no true Mormon could allow any such comparison of Mormonism with any other ism. He further said, "I have been a Catholic and know of the corruptions of Catholicism and its tyranny, but it is not to be compared with Mormonism for either." He then advised me to see Governor Cumming, who he thought would render me assistance by Government trains. I saw Cumming, but he refused to assist me. It is possible he thought I was a spy sent out by Brigham to lay some trap for him.[49] I received no help from either source. The above incident transpired prior to our removal to Salt Lake City.

I will here state that the gentleman Brown referred me to was William Thompson, one of the chief clerks in the tithing store, and he did leave that summer or fall. I remember hearing of him in Missouri.[50] But at times it was absolutely necessary for a man to keep his own counsel, as it was an easy matter to throw obstacles in his way and prevent him from leaving. I am satisfied my cattle and wagon had been taken from me for that purpose.[51] But such as had received their endowments were in greater danger. I had not received any, though as before stated I had been recommended for that purpose, hence I was not supposed to know the secrets of the endowment house, and hence not considered dangerous.[52]

[49]Alfred Cumming's refusal to help Derry reveals that the purported governor's great show of pretending to support the rights of anyone who wanted to leave Utah was mere puffery. Englishman Frederick Gardiner (1832–1903) also wanted to leave under Cumming's protection. He was included in the group of some two hundred who left, but was twice called back from their camp at the edge of the city to Brigham Young's office. The first time Young tried to dissuade him, and the second time was to force him to pay a debt owed by his father. Although his father insisted the debt was his own, Gardiner paid it so that he could leave. Aird, "'You Nasty Apostates,'" 133–34, 144–45.

[50]Scotsman William McMillan Thompson (1821–1890) immigrated to Nauvoo and came to Utah in 1848 as clerk of the Heber C. Kimball company: on the trek he kept the semi-literate apostle's journal. After leaving Utah, Thompson settled in Leavenworth County, Kansas. See McCall, A Biography of Joseph Smith Thompson. He left behind a second wife, Emma M. Burdett, a handcart veteran he married in 1856.

[51]Thomas Poulter (1817–1892), who sailed from Liverpool with Derry, in preparing to leave for California wrote, "I gave my brother all my winter's food, pig and all, for I could not sell a thing at Bountiful without the Bishop hearing of it and he had often preached that the destroying angels would not save all such who wanted to leave Utah." Aird, "'You Nasty Apostates,'" 169.

[52]Many believed that those who had received their endowments and thus knew "the mysteries" of Mormonism were at greater peril if they wanted to leave Utah. Englishman Stephen Forsdick (1835–1927) wrote, "At that time, the Temple had not been built, but all the secret work was done in the Endowment House, with oaths and vows of secrecy. They had Destroying Angels to enforce the penalty for violating such oaths." Ibid., 170.

I have already stated that an English brother named Robert Holt had kindly loaned me the sum of twenty dollars, without note, which sum I put with the sixty dollars we had earned and saved, and I bought a yoke of cattle, and not having sufficient to buy a wagon, I obtained permission from William A. Moore, who was also leaving, to hitch my cattle with his to his wagon, and my family was to ride with his wife to the States.[53] I must here express, as well as I can, my heartfelt gratitude to these brethren for their kindness in the hour of need, and especially to Robert Holt, without whose kindly aid I could not have obtained my cattle, and hence must have remained in Utah another year. Brother Holt had also made me a pair of boots for which he credited me until I could pay him in the States.

On the third day of June, 1859, eleven families of us, in ten wagons, bade farewell to the "city of the Saints." We elected Robert Holt as captain of the company, and that night encamped on the mountain. I think it was called, "the little mountain," and either that night or the next, Ephraim Hanks and his band camped beside us. They were noted as Danites. We did not know their purpose, but we put out a guard, and every man that slept had his rifle by his side. But our camp was not molested. Indeed, we were permitted to leave the Territory without molestation.

We found the snow on the mountains very deep, and as it melted it raised the rivers and streams, which made them difficult and dangerous to cross.[54] We found the Bear River raging, and the bridge across it was rising and falling as the waves dashed against and over it. We had each family cross with their own team, while every man rendered what aid he could until every family and team was safely over. One of the little mountain streams, I forget its name, was raging like a mighty river. I guided our team by jumping into the stream, grabbing the yoke of the near ox, and by word and pulling of the animal, I guided them to the landing place, but it was a dangerous undertaking, as I had never swam a foot in my life, the cattle were swimming, and it looked as though we would be drowned. But thank God we all kept our

[53]William A. Moore, the superintendent of the poor in Neversink, New York, became a Mormon missionary as early as 1841. On 6 August 1844 he gave the benediction at an LDS conference held in Easton, Pennsylvania. See John Conway, "Mormons Left Their Legacy in Neversink," *Times Herald-Record (Middletown, New York)*, 20 February 2002; and *Times and Seasons*, 5:646–47. Moore was later active in the Reorganized faith.

[54]*San Francisco Herald*, 12 May 1859, 3; 8 June 1859, 3; 14 June 1859, 2; and *Valley Tan*, 22 March 1859, 2; 12 April 1859, 2; and 24 May 1859, 2. Both newspapers reported heavy snows, a late spring, and flooding.

self-control, and all got safely across the raging stream. We arrived safely at the Sweet Water, where we met a number of gold hunters who had started for Pike's Peak, but were now on the way for California.[55] Brother Holt found they had a wagon for sale, having lost some of their cattle. He bought the wagon for twenty-five dollars and then came to me and told me to hitch my cattle to the wagon, and put my family therein, and then we could ride more comfortably to the States. This was a great accommodation to us and we gladly availed ourselves of it. Our trip across the plains was as pleasant as it could be under the circumstances. Nothing transpired to cause us to look back with regret to the salt land. Our provisions became scarce, but this was the result of our feeding Indians and emigrants whom we met on the way. About fifty miles east of Fort Laramie we met a train of hand-carts on their way to Utah. They were nearly destitute of food, and presented a sorry sight. We shared what we had with them and they were grateful.[56]

The Apostle of Purity

Derry left Utah in June 1859 with ten other families and "squatted on a piece of land on Maple Creek" at Fontenelle, Nebraska, near his brother George, "whom my letters had prevented going further west." For a time he abandoned religion entirely. Yet despite his bitter experiences, he remained intensely connected to Joseph Smith: Derry rejoined "the Restoration" in 1861 when the founding prophet's son organized his own church. Derry, a man whose character shines through his honest prose, was called to serve in Joseph Smith III's Quorum of the Twelve as "the Apostle of Purity." Five years later Derry resigned, feeling he had not received a proper call from the Lord to that high office. He became spokesman for and one of the most intimate and trusted friends of "Young Joseph," and remained a devoted minister, traveling elder, and patriarch until his death on 16 July 1921, nine days shy of his ninety-fifth birthday.

---

[55]In 1859 would-be millionaires swarmed to Pikes Peak in the Rocky Mountains, lured by glowing reports of newfound gold. It did not take long for the fifty-niners to find that the diggings failed to live up to their superlative advertisements, and they struggled back to the states or to California. West, *The Contested Plains*, 174–77.

[56]"The diaries and reminiscences of the participants in those last five handcart parties," David Roberts wrote, "are full of the same kinds of heart-wrenching testimonies to exhaustion and near-starvation as the more oft-quoted Willie and Martin sources." *Devil's Gate*, 312–13.

Ann Gordge, circa 1890

Like so much about Ann Gordge, the date and place of this photograph are unknown, but it may have been taken about the time she wrote her autobiography. *Courtesy Eric Wadsworth.*

Chapter 3

Ann Gordge
Reality and Imagination

John Doyle Lee has not lacked for attention since he led the Mountain Meadows massacre in September 1857. The man Juanita Brooks dubbed "zealot, pioneer builder, scapegoat" has figured in popular history, scholarly monographs, fiction, and film, as well as in reissues of his own writing.[1] But the women around him, namely his nineteen wives, remain much less well known. Ann Gordge is remembered, if at all, because she became Lee's last wife. Some of those familiar with Lee family legends recall her as one of his faithless wives who refused to join him in exile, unlike the loyal Rachel and Emma.[2] Ann even abandoned her two older children to be raised by these two women, making her seem an unnatural mother as well. But Ann told her own version of her life, one that hurls accusations at Lee and the Mormons while crafting an image of herself as a strong, self-reliant woman and the heroine of a fabulous adventure tale.

Ann Gordge's vital statistics can be sketched quickly. She was born in 1849 into an Australian family of Irish and Welsh ancestry whose members converted to the Church of Jesus Christ of Latter-day Saints. Her father died (or perhaps deserted the family), and the remaining Gordges sailed to California in 1854. Ann's mother, Merab, married John Phillips, and the family moved to southern Utah in 1857, when Brigham Young called in

[1]Brooks, *John Doyle Lee*, is a full-length biography largely based on Lee's own writings. Recent titles with Lee connections include Denton, *American Massacre*; Bagley, *Blood of the Prophets*; Henrie, *Writings of John D. Lee*; Walker, Turley, and Leonard, *Massacre at Mountain Meadows*; Bagley and Bigler, *Innocent Blood*; and an updated edition of Cleland and Brooks, eds., *A Mormon Chronicle*. The film *September Dawn*, a fictionalized version of the massacre, opened in August 2007 to scathing reviews and quickly disappeared from theaters.

[2]Emma, Rachel, and Ann have received some attention. Emma Batchelor Lee is the subject of Brooks's *Emma Lee*. Judith Freeman used Rachel Lee's brief journal and Ann's memoir, among other sources, for her novel *Red Water*, in which the three wives are the main characters. Gerald Grimmett invented a Lee wife in his novel *The Ferry Woman*.

outlying Mormon settlements as the Utah Expedition approached the territory. As a member of a typical struggling farm family, Ann began doing child farm labor in the hamlets of Washington, Beaver, and Harmony. Sometime between 1862 and 1865, when Gordge was thirteen to sixteen years old, she became the nineteenth plural wife of John D. Lee, who was at least forty-eight. When Ann met him, Lee was a prominent Mormon official, farmer, rancher, and town builder, though many shunned him because of his conduct at Mountain Meadows. Ann bore Lee three children and lived the difficult life of a frontier bride in close and often rocky relationships with her sister-wives. When Lee went into exile in 1871 to avoid arrest, Gordge left him and returned to her mother's house, taking only her newborn son.

Gordge's two older children, Samuel James and Merab Emma, grew up "often feeling extra and unwanted," Juanita Brooks wrote, "always faced with the story that their mother was a bad, wicked woman who had deserted them and left the church." According to a family legend, Ann, while heavily pregnant with Albert Doyle, was trapped in a potato pit, and "two of the boys" (perhaps Lee's older sons) were so amused that the humiliated woman decided to leave the family. Brooks concluded that someone had advised Ann to forsake her excommunicated husband, who never paid her the attention she desired. When Gordge left Harmony, family history indicates she left Albert at her brother David's house in Beaver while she sought work or perhaps embarked on her adventures. Albert began living with her at age eight, but the older children saw Ann only years later.[3]

After she left Lee, Gordge worked a series of low-paying jobs, including that of domestic servant. She reportedly remarried, became a Catholic, reunited in Idaho with her adult children, and lived in and around Salt Lake City until at least 1915. One family source suggests that she died in the Tintic mining district sometime after 1915.[4]

---

[3]Quotations from Brooks, *John Doyle Lee*, 297–98; and Henrie, *Descendants of John Doyle Lee*, 777–85. John D. Lee made loving references to all three of Ann's children in letters sent from his jail cell. See, for example, John D. Lee to Rachel Lee, 24 September 1876, Beaver; John D. Lee to Rachel Lee and family, 12 October 1876, Beaver; both in Lee, Papers. Albert, age 9, appears in the 1880 census living with his maternal grandparents. United States Bureau of the Census, Tenth Census of the United States, 1880, Beaver City, Beaver County, Territory of Utah, page 18, lines 40–42.

[4]Information on Ann's post-autobiography life is from Henrie, *Descendants of John Doyle Lee*, 777–98; Cleland and Brooks, eds., *A Mormon Chronicle*, vol. 2: diary 3, 257n67; Kimball, Diary, and Bishop, Unpublished Introduction. Henrie, Cleland, and Brooks reported Gordge's undocumented marriage to a mining engineer named Frank Kennedy in 1895. Henrie reproduces a brief memoir by Merab Emma, 782–85. She writes that in "the year 1904 I made a trip to Idaho and there found my own mother and two brothers,

At some point, probably about 1890, Ann wrote (or perhaps dictated) a very different life story. In her version, she is indeed born in Australia, but mysteriously loses her father; she comes to America and immediately falls into a secretive and frightening world of thieves and murderers. She is blackmailed by threats of violence into marrying the infamous John D. Lee. In a mysterious waking dream, she observes him killing a man, and she manages a thrilling escape before she can be killed. She leads authorities to capture her villainous ex-husband and travels as a willing captive with a band of Apaches led by "Goromando"; Billy the Kid rescues her and the two have vaguely described but exciting adventures throughout the Southwest; and she goes on to overcome adversity in further sketchy adventures around the world.

This version of Ann's life, while much more exciting, is highly problematic for a historian. Ann plays fast and loose with fundamental details, and her escapades after she left Lee are especially suspect. Her story has gaps and errors: she seldom gives dates (or even years) or names, and those she does cite can often be proven wrong. Her account reads as if it were generated from an unreliable memory, with more specific places and dates as she approached the more recent events of her life. A rough formula for interpreting an Ann Gordge story might be to divide any number (especially dollars or number of victims) by ten, adjust the date by two years, and double-check all names. Ann makes no mention of her miscarriage or her three children.[5] These omissions and errors—in addition to the clearly imagined elements—have caused most scholars to steer well clear of this document. The manuscript register for the BYU variant, for example, warns that "while the work makes references to historical events, the researcher is cautioned that most of the work seems to be pure fiction."[6] But the wild accusations in Ann Gordge's autobiography often have some basis in fact. More than that, the story has value as a crude and unpolished work of imagination that both draws on and enriches the mythology of the West.

[Samuel] James and Albert" (785). Albert, with his wife and baby daughter Merab, was a farm laborer in Cassia County, Idaho, in 1900. United States Bureau of the Census, Twelfth Census of the United States, 1900, Basin Precinct, Cassia County, Idaho, Enumeration district 35, sheet 17, lines 89–91.

[5]Ann's miscarriage was recorded to have occurred on 11 March 1866. Samuel James was born on 14 March 1867, Merab (sometimes spelled Mareb) Emma was born on 12 October 1868, and Albert Doyle was born on 8 November 1870. John D. Lee, Family Geneology [*sic*], Lee, Papers. Lee also recorded Samuel James's birth in his diary. Lee, Papers, diary three, 14 March 1867, 57. Only Samuel James's birth is recorded in the New Harmony Ward Record, 280.

[6]Register of the Ann Gordge Lee Autobiography, BYU Library.

The first half of the memoir, before Ann turns to her personal tale, is dominated by stories of violence perpetrated by Mormons. Ann describes a Utah Territory ruled by coercion and murder: the massacre of an emigrant party at Mountain Meadows, miners killed for their money, Mormon men killed for leaving the church, women killed for turning down a bishop's proposal, castrations, burnings, stabbings, torture, and gang rape. Although the numbers of victims are not always specified, the body count approaches five hundred.

The scores of factual errors, many pointed out in the annotations, make the details of this recitation suspect. However, there is substance to some of Gordge's bloody stories, especially about Mountain Meadows. (Even here Ann makes a poor witness, as she was eight years old when the massacre was perpetrated and admits that she was not in Utah until after the fact.) Juanita Brooks, D. Michael Quinn, Will Bagley, Polly Aird, and other scholars have amply demonstrated that some Mormons took their leaders seriously when they talked about making apostates or adulterers atone for their sins, or when they swore to avenge the blood of the prophets by killing their persecutors. And as in any other society, some persons committed crimes for their own selfish reasons.[7]

The genuine tribulations of Ann Gordge's young life undoubtedly shaped her recollection of events. Consider again her experience, and imagine how a young girl might understand her world: she lost her father, and her mother's new faith required such all-encompassing dedication that the family had to make a long sea voyage to another continent. There her mother remarried and began bearing her new husband's children, but the family and their neighbors were uprooted again and ordered to move to Utah by a distant authority. Near the end of their arduous trek across the desert, they encountered a scene of fresh horror at Mountain Meadows: the remains of scores of men, women, and children rent by bullets, knives, clubs, and wild animals. At their camp near the massacre site the emigrants were greeted by a group of important local men, several of whom, including John D. Lee, clearly knew a good deal about the crime. The startled emigrants had arrived in their new home—a hardscrabble frontier society roiled by the Mormon Reformation and exhibiting a siege mentality as it expected war with the United States.[8]

[7]Brooks, *Mountain Meadows*; Quinn, *The Mormon Hierarchy: Extensions of Power*, 241–61; Bagley, *Blood of the Prophets*; and Aird, "'You Nasty Apostates.'"

[8]For the Reformation at Harmony and Lee's role in it, see Brooks, *John Doyle Lee*, 187–88. For a general outline of the Utah War, see Bigler, *Forgotten Kingdom*, 141–99.

The Phillips family settled in Beaver, a tiny hamlet north of Lee's homes at Harmony and Washington. Lee was clearly respected by many but feared by some, and he passed through Beaver periodically with a retinue of wives and children, preaching, laying hands on the ill or injured, and sharing meals.[9] The child Ann would have watched Lee speak with her stepfather and other adults, and she may have listened to older settlers whispering to each other while some refused to speak to him. Lee must have looked back at her, because a few years later Ann became his nineteenth wife. She was the newest member of an extended family of wives and children (some of the latter older than her), subject to all the usual human tensions and hardships plus the special burdens of polygamous relationships.[10] Lee, a notoriously sexual man, may have paid disproportionate physical attention to his newest mate.[11] He placed her at Harmony with another of his wives, and she set to work around the household and fields. Lee, who had been prosperous, began to suffer small disasters and financial reversals. His neighbors became more openly hostile toward him, and the church leaders, with whom he had been so close, now began to distance themselves.[12] Six years, at least four pregnancies, and three children after she married him, Lee left for exile in a remote location that promised little but poverty and isolation. Ann Gordge rejected that future—she was not yet twenty-three years old. Looked at in this light, Ann's colorful recitation of her early life might represent a type of trauma narrative, a garbled attempt to comprehend and convey her experiences as a way of healing her older self.[13]

While Ann's lived experience undoubtedly shaped her harsh portrayal of her world, she also possessed an active imagination, especially when it came to scenes of violence. The memoir achieves full takeoff into fancy with the story of her break with John D. Lee. Ann relates a waking dream in which she sees

[9]For examples of Lee as preacher and healer, see Brooks, *John Doyle Lee*, 258–59.

[10]The 1870 census counted John D. Lee with five wives (including Ann) and twenty-five children among five households. United States Bureau of the Census, Ninth Census of the United States, 1870, Harmony, Kane County, Territory of Utah, page 1, lines 16–40, page 2, lines 1–6.

[11]As a younger man, Lee bragged about his sexual appetite. See Bagley, *Blood of the Prophets*, 21.

[12]On Lee's success in the early 1860s, see "Prosperity," chap. in Brooks, *John Doyle Lee*, 257–68; on his reversals, see the chapters "Disaster" and "Excommunicated," 269–302. Many Mormons were appalled by the stories they heard about Mountain Meadows and shunned Lee. See George A. Hicks in this volume and Bagley, *Blood of the Prophets*, 262–63. On the LDS authorities' eventual decision to cut ties to Lee, see ibid., 268–86.

[13]For an introduction to the growing literature on trauma, see Gilmore, *The Limits of Autobiography*, and LaCapra, *Writing History, Writing Trauma*.

Lee cut the throat of an old man, then realizes she must escape before Lee "put her out of the way." The rest of her tale seems to be mostly invention, including the Indians and outlaws, but also trips to Australia (twice) and Ireland, which seem beyond her financial means. She ends with a more plausible recitation of work she performed in the mining camps of Idaho and Montana.

What can we make of this baffling document? Why did Ann write it, and what could she possibly have intended to do with it? We have little besides the memoir itself to go on, and its clues are slight. Despite the roughness of her style, Ann obviously tried to tell her life's story in approved nineteenth-century autobiographical fashion, beginning with her birth and ending with what she evidently viewed as the close of her adventures, settling in Salt Lake City in 1883. She addresses the "reader" and includes phrases like "we will now remove to," indicating that she expected others to read the memoir. Several hypotheses are conceivable. Ann, a fugitive from polygamy and a Catholic convert, might have wanted to leave testimony that would discredit the LDS church. She rehearses some of the most prevalent contemporary accusations against Mormons: secrecy, tyranny, greed, lechery, and violence. Ann believed that she remained the target of Mormon animosity decades after Lee was dead, the LDS Church had abandoned plural marriage, and Utah had become a state. In an unpublished introduction to a version of the autobiography, Lee Bishop states that in 1914, his ancestor O. L. Bishop, a Salt Lake City policeman,

> was dispatched to an old westside apartment where an elderly woman and her daughter lived. He found them virtually imprisoned and on the verge of starving to death. Officer Bishop went out and bought meat and groceries for them out of his own money. . . . The women were shunned by the usually hospitable Mormons. They would not let her son (and Lee's too) enter the apartment house. . . . Non-Mormon neighbors brought what food and coal they could afford, passing it to them through a small window that opened into the alley. Ann Gordge Lee was a pitiful sight, her life wasting away, all of this as a result of turning Lee in to the authorities.[14]

---

[14]Bishop, Unpublished Introduction. At the age of 88, O. L. Bishop's daughter executed an affidavit attesting that she had accompanied her father on such visits "a number of times." Ruth Bishop Sievers, Affidavit, Twin Falls, Idaho, 26 July 1988. One small piece of evidence arguing against this section of Ann's story (besides the absence of any evidence that she assisted in Lee's arrest) is that Mormon authority J. Golden Kimball, no friend of apostates, hired "Ann Kenny. [Kennedy?]" to help his wife with housework in 1897. She told Kimball that she had married Lee when she was thirteen, had borne ten children (another apparent exaggeration), and had traveled all over the world. See J. Golden Kimball, Diary, 13, 23 October 1897, Marriott Library.

On a more personal level, Ann may have wanted to counter the role that she played in Lee family legend of the unfaithful wife who abandoned her children. Perhaps she wrote herself into the posse that captured Lee as a sort of posthumous revenge on her notorious husband.[15]

But none of these possibilities explain the Billy the Kid and Goromando episodes. The obviously imaginative elements and exaggerations and the supposed persecution described above could indicate that Ann had difficulty separating reality from fiction. But her storytelling might have been rational and deliberate. Ann may have hoped to write a dime novel, or to sell her raw material to a latter-day Ned Buntline who could then turn it into a book. After all, she had an intimate link to one of the West's most notorious figures, a claim to fame comparable to that of Ann Eliza Webb, Brigham Young's unhappy bride.[16] Ann may have wanted to cash in on her connection by claiming to be Lee's teenaged victim, then his heroic captor. John D. Lee was already well established in Utah's and the nation's collective consciousness as a great villain, a scapegoat, or some combination of the two.[17] Adding Indians and outlaws may have seemed a sure-fire formula. Ann Gordge was working at a busy western crossroads where experience, folklore, legend, myth, and popular culture intersect. She drew from all these abundant wells to fashion her adventures in a form that she hoped her contemporaries would understand, and perhaps even pay to read.

Some definitions of terms may be useful as we examine Ann's possible source materials. First, folklore: the Utah folklorist Barre Toelken hesitates to offer a static definition but writes that folklore's "primary characteristic is that its ingredients seem to come directly from dynamic interactions among human beings in vernacular performance contexts rather than through the more rigid channels and fossilized structures of technical instruction or bureaucratized education, or through the relatively stable channels of the formally taught classical traditions."[18] Legend refers to stories that attribute

[15]Lee Bishop writes that Ann wanted "to expose John D. Lee to the world for what he really was." Unpublished Introduction, 2.

[16]Young, *Wife No. 19*. Her book includes brief versions of the Yates, Aiken, and other murders Ann described. Ned Buntline (Edward Z.C. Judson) made Buffalo Bill Cody the star of adventure stories beginning in 1869. For dime novels, see Bold, "Malaeska's Revenge," 21–42; Thomas J. Lyon, "The Literary West," in Milner et al., *The Oxford History of the American West*, 707–41.

[17]California newspapers began spreading the story of Mountain Meadows within weeks, and dozens of journalists and authors told their versions. Bagley, *Blood of the Prophets*, 188–91, 208–209, 280. Lee made his apologia through his lawyer in Bishop, ed., *Mormonism Unveiled*.

[18]Toelken, *The Dynamics of Folklore*, 32.

extraordinary feats to real people, like Parson Weems inventing the story of George Washington and the cherry tree. As for myths, the scholar Richard Slotkin defines them as "stories, drawn from history, that have acquired through usage over many generations a symbolizing function that is central to the cultural functioning of the society that produces them."[19] Popular culture includes commercial narratives produced for public consumption, such as the books, magazines, and newspapers that rapidly multiplied in America's industrializing society. An event might begin as a genuine experience, become repeated and altered as folklore, incorporate legendary elements, and over time, if it is repeated often enough via (among other avenues) the media of popular culture, it might become a myth.

Ann's autobiography is loaded with fragments of folk belief, elements that may be centuries old and whose origins are impossible to trace. For example, a terrifying experience causes a woman's hair to turn white overnight; children are born with birthmarks resulting from their parents' crimes; twin sisters die simultaneously, although they live on separate continents; and the ghosts of victims haunt their murderers.

Most of Ann's individual stories take the form of legend, as she embellished deeds of real people, such as her tale of Brigham Young's raid on his rival Kate Flint. Ann includes folkloric details to create legends about real but mysterious places, like the shafts for disposing of murder victims under Porter Rockwell's house and the Endowment House. This is not the only recurring plot device: Ann describes several scenes in which men plotting murder are overheard by someone hiding in the loft of the barn above or under the bed, or listening at the door. The eavesdropper (in one scene, Ann herself) rushes to warn the intended victim, who escapes certain death in the nick of time.[20]

Ann also draws from Mormon theology, such as when she suggests that the Moqui Indians might be descended from the Lost Tribes of Israel. She also offers the alternative theory that the Moquis might descend from a Welsh nobleman of the twelfth century, a folk belief that Wallace Stegner wrote was still prevalent among Mormons fifty years ago.[21]

---

[19]Slotkin, *Regeneration through Violence*, 16.

[20]See George A. Hicks's reports of John D. Lee's eavesdropping earlier in this volume.

[21]Mormon doctrine holds that Indians are Lamanites, or descendants of Israelites who migrated to America. Although they had fallen away from the true faith, they could (and should) be redeemed. See McConkie, *Mormon Doctrine*, s.v. "American Indians"; Arrington and Bitton, *The Mormon Experience*, 145–47; Fife and Fife, *Saints of Sage and Saddle*, 42–43; and Stegner, *Mormon Country*, 148–49.

Richard Slotkin suggests that the first distinctly Euroamerican mythology came out of the colonial Indian wars and, especially, the stories of whites held captive by Indians. The first well-known captivity narrative is "The Sovereignty and Goodness of God," published by Mary Rowlandson in 1682. American colonists used Rowlandson's story and those that followed, with their alarming undercurrents of racial and sexual chaos, to draw distinctions between civilized Europeans and savage Indians and to underscore the necessity of redeeming the wilderness. Ann's not-quite-captivity among the Apaches might draw from these stories, several of which became very popular, but her sojourn seems closer to Mary Jemison's, who was captured by Indians in 1755 and became fully transculturated. Such "willing captive" narratives contain a different and perhaps more disturbing lesson: some whites, especially women, found Indian culture and gender roles more congenial. That lesson might well apply to Ann's escape from plural marriage and Mormon tyranny.[22]

Ann's depiction of Billy the Kid draws on the powerful myth of the frontier hero. Slotkin and others have demonstrated that Daniel Boone became the first great indigenous frontier hero, through the work of John Filson, who published "The Adventures of Daniel Boon" in 1784. Filson's version of Boone's story established the model for frontier heroes to follow, some real men and others entirely fictional, like James Fenimore Cooper's "Deerslayer" and Karl May's "Old Shatterhand." This evolving myth received a boost through the burgeoning print media, at about the same time that Euroamericans in numbers began pushing west of the Mississippi. Men like Kit Carson became heroes in stories that scarcely nod to actual events but that follow the outlines of the existing myth, now in a recognizably western setting of covered wagons and maidens imperiled by Comanches or Sioux.[23]

The real take-off into mass-produced popular culture began in 1860 when publishers Beadle and Adams began issuing a series of orange-covered "dime novels." The series featured dozens of western heroes, usually some minor variant on the Boone/Deerslayer/Carson character, although markedly more

[22]Slotkin, *Regeneration through Violence*, 94–116. Captivity narratives have been the subject of several recent provocative studies, including Derounian-Stodola, Zabelle, and Levernier, *The Indian Captivity Narrative*: on Rowlandson, 94–111; on feminist implications of captivity, 44–50; on transculturated captives, 73–85. See also Ebersole, *Captured by Texts*, esp. 216–37; and the story of Eunice Williams, a transculturated captive, in Demos, *The Unredeemed Captive*.

[23]Slotkin, *Regeneration through Violence*, 20–22, 268–69; Aquila, "Introduction," 1–16; and Limerick, "Making the Most of Words," 167.

violent. Many incorporated elements of the Indian captivity narrative. Readers devoured them; some five million copies of Beadle's dime novels were reportedly sold in the first five years, and dozens of competitors appeared in the following decades.[24] Most stories follow a simple narrative arc: a brave and resourceful hero faces danger from savage Indians, or outlaws, or the elements, and he overcomes them all to accomplish his ends, which usually advance white conquest and settlement.

Ann Gordge seems to have been familiar with some formulaic scenes of these popular tales, especially those adventures that draw on the captivity narrative genre or those that put a twist on the myth by casting heroic women. *The Red Rider: Or, the White Queen of the Apaches* stars a young white woman leading Apaches in attacks on miners and Mexicans.[25] A Creole woman is chased into an Apache band in another tale.[26] Ann's descriptions of her journey with Apaches through the Southwest suggest that she may have read or heard of the Oatman sisters, captured by Yavapai raiders in 1851 and sold as slaves to Mohaves. Their story, *Life Among the Indians*, first appeared in 1857.[27]

Mormons often appeared as villains in dime novels, murdering innocents or seducing maidens. The prolific Col. Prentiss Ingraham padded his "true history" of Robert "Pony Bob" Haslam, a genuine Pony Express rider, with hair-raising brushes with "Danites," a band of Mormon assassins.[28] In what sounds like a case of life imitating art, one of Ann's characters shares a name with a dime novel hero: she describes Dick Darling, a Gentile soldier, marrying one of John D. Lee's daughters, stealing other Mormons' wives, and making off with some of Lee's best horses—audacious (if not exactly heroic) behavior. Beadle published at least two editions of *Dick Darling, the Pony Expressman.*[29]

Billy the Kid and Geronimo might seem likely candidates for the villain's role. Billy, who supposedly killed twenty-one men, one for each of his years, was featured prominently in the *Police Gazette*, especially after he broke out of prison and killed two guards in 1881. Billy's killer, Sheriff Pat Garrett, quickly published a ghostwritten version of events, one of many that

[24]Smith, *Virgin Land; The American West as Symbol and Myth*, 90–101.

[25]Bowen, *The Red Rider.*

[26]Willett, *The White Apache.*

[27]Derounian-Stodola and Levernier, *The Indian Captivity Narrative*, 122.

[28]Ingraham, *Pony Bob.* See also Allen, "The Heroic Ride in Western Popular Historical Tradition," esp. 401, where Allen describes James Haslam's ride with a message from Brigham Young about the Fancher party at Mountain Meadows as well as "Pony Bob's" 380-mile ride.

[29]Whittaker, *Dick Darling.* Unlike Ann's Darling, the novelistic Dick had little to do with Mormons and romanced Métis and Mexican girls.

appeared within months of the Kid's death later that year.[30] Stories of the wily Geronimo, the Chiricahua Apache warrior who held off enemies until 1886, appeared in national newspapers around the time Ann was writing. But Ann declines to make either her bad guy. Perhaps influenced by dime novel "social bandits" like Deadwood Dick, Ann gives us a Kid who is not a murderous thug, but rather a rescuer and perhaps a lover, and also a skilled plainsman who sought to exact vengeance for the victims of Mormon murders (although Ann neglects to tell us exactly why).[31] Her Goromando is no bloodthirsty savage, but rather he treats Ann respectfully and never threatens her with the horrors that Mary Rowlandson and her literary descendants feared. In Ann's narrative, the Indians of the Southwest are either friendly and admirably self-sufficient, or they are used as convenient scapegoats for the crimes of Mormons.

So Ann declines to make outlaws or Indians the villains that her story requires, but she gives us plenty of others: some from her personal experience, some from the folklore and legends she heard, and some evidently from written sources. Ann must have heard rumors of John D. Lee's involvement in Mountain Meadows before she married him, and despite the oath that the culprits swore never to discuss their crimes, stories of the massacre and other acts of violence circulated throughout southern Utah.[32] Ann might even have heard some versions from her husband or her sister-wives. She apparently drew on John D. Lee's written story, too. Just before his execution at Mountain Meadows in 1877, Lee and his attorney published his reputed confessions. They feature extensive accounts of Mormon crimes, some of them much like Ann's tales.

Ann may also have drawn from contemporary anti-Mormon novels and magazine articles, which often followed the plot lines established in dozens of earlier anti-Catholic, anti-Masonic, and abolitionist tracts, which in turn borrowed heavily from Indian captivity narratives. The anti-Mormon works, often in the form of purported memoir, substituted lecherous LDS bishops for Catholic priests, Masons, slave masters, or Indian bucks. One of these works reads suspiciously like Ann's story. The anonymous narrator of "Saved from the Mormons," published serially in a New York magazine in 1872, is a

[30]Utley, *Billy the Kid*, 176–200. Young Henry McCarty was himself an avid reader of dime novels and the *Police Gazette*. See Wallis, *Billy the Kid*, 86–87.

[31]On Deadwood Dick, see Bold, "Malaeska's Revenge," 26–27. On social bandits, see White, "Outlaw Gangs of the Middle Border."

[32]For the oath, see Bagley, *Blood of the Prophets*, 158; Brooks, *John Doyle Lee*, 220–21.

young English girl whose father is converted by a Mormon missionary. They emigrate to Utah, and when she turns eighteen, her father tries to make her become the eighth wife of Elder Platt. She flees for California instead and is aided by a friendly Navajo, then lives with the Moquis, an "industrious, simple, virtuous people." Eventually she makes it safely to California with the help of brave U.S. soldiers.[33]

Along with the crimes of lesser-known Mormons, Ann describes the murderous exploits of famous badmen like Bill Hickman and Orrin Porter Rockwell. Hickman and a journalist published a confession of his reputed career as a hit man for Brigham Young in 1872, and stories of Porter Rockwell's many killings circulated in Utah for years. Both Hickman and Rockwell appear as Danites in *Pony Bob, the Reckless Rider of the Rockies*.[34] Ann's most vicious character was the one she presumably knew the most about: her husband, John D. Lee. While she credits Lee with many crimes, she also recounts some positive scenes that create a fuller and more persuasive portrait. Lee stuck up for her against his other wives and bought her expensive gifts, and he sometimes defended others from unjust attacks. Ann also insists (probably following Lee's own version) that LDS leaders sacrificed him to the federal authorities as a scapegoat for the collective crime at Mountain Meadows.[35]

The Mormon reign of terror that Ann describes does not go unchallenged. While Billy and others defy Mormons, Ann casts herself as the leading heroine. She relates how hardworking and independent she is, even as a child. When she marries Lee, it is only the result of coercion and a desire to save her mother. Despite her relative youth, Ann insists that she receive her fair share of the goods and gifts that her husband distributes among his families. When Rachel tries to steal from her, Ann beats her up. She is far from the frail, deluded, innocent woman duped by a Mormon man so often portrayed in the anti-polygamy literature, but rather a tough, resilient rebel who bides her time for the vengeance to come.[36]

---

[33]"Saved from the Mormons," *The Galaxy*, quote on 830. For an example of a contemporary anti-Mormon history by a journalist who spent time in Utah, complete with brief (and unreliable) versions of the Aiken, Parrish, Yates, and Mountain Meadows murders, and other reputed crimes, see Beadle, *Life in Utah*, 177–95. On the antecedents of anti-Mormon literature, see Davis, "Some Themes of Counter-Subversion"; Arrington and Haupt, "Intolerable Zion"; and Givens, *The Viper on the Hearth*, 97–152.

[34]For folk tales about Orrin Porter Rockwell, see Larson, "Orrin Porter Rockwell," 179–90; Burt, "Ditties of Death in Deseret," 162–63.

[35]Brooks, *John Doyle Lee*, 367.

[36]On delusion, mesmerism, and coercion in anti-Mormon literature, see Givens, *The Viper on the Hearth*, 137–52.

Son of Thunder: Orrin Porter Rockwell
Orrin Porter Rockwell (1813–1878) may have become a Mormon on 6 April 1830, the day the faith was founded. His career as a devoted bodyguard for Joseph Smith and Brigham Young and his many adventures as a plainsman, saloon keeper, bogus-passer, mail contractor, guerrilla raider, and deputy marshal of Great Salt Lake City made him Mormonism's most legendary—and feared—frontiersman. When he died while awaiting trial for the 1857 Aiken murders, the *Salt Lake Tribune* said the great avenging angel had murdered fellow Saints who held dangerous secrets and a hundred or more unsuspecting travelers: "Apostates who dared to wag their tongues about the wrongs they had endured," and "mere sojourners in Zion merely to keep his hand in." Porter "had his little faults," Joseph F. Smith told the one thousand people who gathered for the old Danite's funeral, but the future prophet insisted that Rockwell's controversial life "reflected honor upon the church." *Courtesy Utah State Historical Society.*

Ann's claimed power does not flow from her maternal status; in fact, she effaces her children from her text entirely. She may have felt guilty for abandoning her two older children (although legally, Lee could have probably claimed all three). But few western heroines have children (except as the happy culmination of their adventures), let alone abandon them for someone else to raise. With few exceptions, Ann is a besieged loner. She expresses little solidarity with or affection for her sister-wives, other than sympathizing

WILLIAM ADAMS HICKMAN
Longtime Mormon stalwart William Adams "Bill" Hickman's service as an overland trader, mail contractor, lawyer, sheriff, tax collector, and road agent led Utah's legislative assembly to recommend his appointment as U.S. attorney for Utah Territory in January 1857. Hickman's autobiography dubbed him "Brigham's destroying angel," and a journalist called him a "human hyena." George A. Hicks wondered, "It always has been a mystery to me why such characters a[s] O.P. Rockwell, Bill Hickman, and men of that ilk have always been tolerated in the Mormon Church." Hickman gave federal authorities a description of the Yates murder similar to the story told by Ann Gordge. *C. W. Carter photograph, © Trustees of the British Museum.*

with Caroline for her many children and describing one homey scene with Aggatha Ann and a cup of coffee.[37] Emma and Ann lived together at Harmony, but not always in harmony. Only three weeks after Emma's twins were born, one of whom was named for Ann, John D. Lee wrote vaguely in his diary that "a very unpleasant occurence transpired between Emma B. one of the Most high Strung women of the age, who colaps with Ann G. but soon repentd & sought restitution."[38]

Instead of a motherly or sisterly persona, the self that Ann imagined demonstrates supposedly masculine attributes of strength and courage. In this she reflects the realities of challenging frontier life. Lee's diary attests to Ann's genuine pugnacity. A neighbor began cutting Lee's shade trees; by the time Lee arrived, Ann and the neighbor were "both on the ground & Ann with one hand in his hair & with the other pounding him in the face in the mean time Emma return with a New supply of hot water & then pitched into him with Ann & they both haddled him rather Ruff, his face

[37]For a discussion of the relationships among frontier women as revealed in their writing, see Margaret K. Brady, "In Her Own Words: Women's Frontier Friendships," in Stewart et al., *Worldviews and the American West,* 62–78. For a discussion of companionship in plural marriages, see Iverson, "Feminist Implications of Mormon Polygyny"; Goodson, "Plural Wives," 89–112.

[38]Lee, Papers, diary 3, 18 August 1866, 26.

ANN GORDGE AND HER CHILDREN *(standing, from left)* Albert Doyle Lee, Emma Merab Lee, and Samuel James Lee, Ann Gordge's children with John D. Lee. Ann Gordge is seated. When she left Lee, Ann took only the infant Albert with her. Rachel Lee raised Merab, while Emma Batchelor Lee raised Samuel James. According to family tradition, the children were reunited with Ann in Idaho sometime after 1900 and her reported marriage to Frank Kennedy. *Courtesy Eric Wadsworth.*

was in a gore of Blood." Lee won the ensuing court action.[39] Ann does not write of either of those events. Her descriptions of her riding prowess, her masculine disguise, her rescue of a U.S. soldier, and her adventures with outlaws and Indians may borrow from dime novel Amazons like Hurricane Nell, a crack shot who sometimes wore men's clothing, or Calamity Jane, another gun-toting, cross-dressing heroine.[40] Ann also recounts the strength and defiance of other women: a woman, forced to become a plural wife, who murdered her husband and two sister-wives; another who killed three armed attackers with an iron poker; and Mormon girls who rejected the suits of John D. Lee's sons in favor of better mates. Strong women can be villains in Ann's world, too: "old mother Shirts" accompanies her sons to Mountain Meadows and helps to murder women and children. One of Lee's daughters kills her husband and passes it off as a suicide. These stories, with their fragments of reality, may constitute Ann's literary compensation for

[39]Ibid., 29 November 1869, 129–30.

[40]See Smith, *Virgin Land*, 112–20; Cox, *The Dime Novel Companion*, 46–47; and Bold, "Malaeska's Revenge," 28–29.

EMMA BATCHELOR LEE
English convert and handcart survivor Emma Batchelor became John D. Lee's seventeenth wife in January 1858. She shared a home with Ann Gordge in 1866 and reportedly named one of her twin daughters for Ann. The two women sometimes quarreled but joined forces to beat up a trespassing neighbor. After Ann Gordge abandoned her fugitive husband, Emma raised her oldest son, Samuel James. *Courtesy Utah State Historical Society.*

the relatively powerless position of Mormon women like her: mostly young, poor, isolated, trapped in a cycle of pregnancy, child rearing, and work, and subject to the near-complete patriarchal authority of husband and church.

Ann Gordge clearly was an imaginative and selectively retentive listener and reader. She read or heard stories in many genres and combined fragments of them with some of the actual events of her life to fashion herself as a western heroine—the star of her own story—a woman who resisted tyranny, escaped bloody reprisals, and returned to take her own vengeance. She redeemed herself and justified her sacrifices when John D. Lee paid for his bloody deeds at the hands of a firing squad. Once freed from her oppressors, she could romp through the West on her own or with companions equally powerful, rebellious, and independent.

The apparent date of her writing—somewhere around 1890—may indicate her awareness of the changes occurring in Utah, as a long contest for power came to a head. The "judicial crusade" against plural marriage had jailed

MARTHA JANE CANARY, CALAMITY JANE
Like her contemporary Ann Gordge, Martha Jane Canary (1852–1903) was a mythmaker and self-created western heroine who wrote a brief, highly colored autobiography. She worked at a variety of menial jobs throughout the West and appeared in both Buffalo Bill Cody's Wild West Show and the Pan-American Exposition. She claimed to have been a scout with Gen. George A. Custer, and a persistent legend has her secretly marrying Wild Bill Hickok. *Courtesy Utah State Historical Society.*

hundreds of Mormon men and driven church leaders underground. Federal legislation disincorporated the LDS church and ordered much of its property seized. Non-Mormons won control of Salt Lake City's government for the first time. In September 1890 LDS president Wilford Woodruff issued what came to be known as his "manifesto" advising against plural marriage. By the mid-1890s Utah's unique all-Mormon and all-Gentile political parties had been disbanded and branches of the national political parties established, while the LDS church sold off many of its business enterprises and promised not to dictate to its members in political matters. As a result, the territory finally achieved statehood in 1896. The Latter-day Saints had retreated grudgingly from their grand project of establishing the Kingdom of God on earth in their time.[41] Ann Gordge's villains had been brought to heel, and she had crafted for herself a small but vital role in the morality play.

[41]On events of the 1890s, see Firmage and Mangrum, *Zion in the Courts*, 160–260; Alexander, *Mormonism in Transition*, 3–15.

Oh Utah Blush with Shame: Ann Gordge's Tales of Blood Atonement

I was born in Australia in the year 1849.[42] My father was Samuel Gordge my mother's name was Merab Hancock of London Derry Ireland. She Joined the Mormons in 1842. She was in Wales at the time, she Joined the Church under her Uncle William Williams.[43] Grandfather drove her from home because of her Joining the Church, and in 1846 she met with Father whom she married in 1847. In 1848, they emigrated to Australia, at that time there was not Mormons in Australia. After the supposed death of Father in 1853[44] the Mormans came to my Mother's House Eleven in number namely C. W. Wandell, who afterwards apostized from the Church, [C?] P Eldridge, he died and was buried in the sea the 14th day of May 1854 next William Hyde[,] Porter Dowdell, George Flemming, William H Farman and Nebuchodonsor Chemins.[45]

In 1854 she Imigrated with the Mormons to California, She left Australia the [21st?] of February 1854 and landed in San Pedro [?] 1854 with her son and daughter [?][46] from the ship to the landing [?] met Parley P. Pratt, who was

[42]Ann Gordge, Certificate of Birth, No. 2600, Births in the District of Adelaide, South Australia, issued 10 January 1975, shows a birthdate of 30 May 1849 to father Samuel Gordge, a brickmaker, and mother Mina Hancock Gordge. Birth certificate in the possession of Gena Raban; information from Marjorie Newton to Will Bagley, 3 February 1997; and Gena Raban to Jeff Nichols, 27 October 2006. John D. Lee's own Family Geneology [*sic*] cites the same birthdate, Lee, Papers; while the New Harmony Ward Record gives a 30 May 1848 birthdate for "Mary Ann Gordge," 192.

[43]Merab Hancock was baptized into the Church of England on 5 January 1820 in Wales. See Church in Wales, Parish Church, Pembroke, Dale, Bishop's Transcripts, 1799–1878, baptism no. 106, p. 14. She consistently gave Wales as her birthplace; she appears as a twenty-year-old servant in Census of Wales, 1841, Registration District Haverford West, Pembrokeshire County, Borough of Milford, Parish of Hubberston; and in the U.S. census. The British Isles were the earliest and among the most successful mission grounds for the LDS church. Arrington and Bitton, *The Mormon Experience*, 129.

[44]Burr Frost, an LDS missionary in Australia, wrote on 15 October 1853 that he "went in Search of Samuel Gorge a man who Br Dowdl had written about to me that had Left adalade about one year ago leaving his family destitute." Burr Frost, Diary, 176.

[45]John R. Murdock and Charles Wesley Wandell headed the Australasian Mission in 1851. See General Minutes of the Australasian Mission. In 1853 new mission president August Farnham worked with Absalom Porter Dowdle, William Hyde, Josiah W. Fleming, and John S. Eldredge. Farnham wrote of a "brother and sister Gorgd." Farnham, Missionary Journal, 28 May, 6 June, 14 July 1853. William Hyde left Australia on 22 March 1854 with sixty-three converts, including Merab Gordge and children Ann and David on the *Julia Ann*. William Hyde, *Private Journal*, 50–79; Dowdle, Autobiography. Burr Frost described the arrival of these Saints. Frost, Diary, 288–92. See also Newton, *Southern Cross Saints*, 26–30. C. W. Wandell lived in Beaver, Utah, in the late 1850s, but he became convinced that Brigham Young had ordered the massacre at Mountain Meadows. He investigated the crime and wrote a series of letters (signed "Argus") to the *Corinne Daily Reporter* in Corinne. See Newton, *Hero or Traitor*, 20–48; Merkley, ed., *Monuments to Courage*, 115; and Brooks, ed., *On the Mormon Frontier*, 489n30, 492, 680. John S. Eldredge survived the wreck of the *Julia Ann* on a subsequent voyage. Newton, *Southern Cross Saints*, 145–46.

[46]The *Julia Ann* arrived at San Pedro, California, on 12 June 1854. See Newton, *Southern Cross Saints*, 136.

on his way to the vessel to [go to?] Sanfrancisco to Join George Q Cannan, who at the time was Editor of the Paper, called the Mormon, Printed in San Francisco Cal.[47] After we left the ship Mother went to look after her bagage, she missed the Trunk or Chest containing family Hair Looms, consisting of a silver Tea set, with the Crest of the Dragon and Olive branches which is a Spanish design, and also a Dinner Set of same pattern, Knives, Forks spoons, desert spoons and Tea spoons to match and also a China basket filled with Gold nuget weighing in Dollars three Hundred pounds sterling and also notes on the First National Bank of San Francisco Cal. for nine Hundred pounds. The Value of the Trunk or Chest and contents thereof was twenty thousand dollars, all of which went to the Church, or in other words which was stolen by the Church. This I Know for a fact I saw them with my own eyes. In the possession of Brigham Young and they can not deney it and I also saw the same articles not latter than two weeks ago in the possession of the present Wilford Woodruff.[48]

Two years after we arrived in California my Mother married a man by the name of John Phillips in the year 1855. In two years after in the year 1857 my Mother and Step Father moved to Utah.[49] In the month of September of the above year was committed what is Known as the Mountain Medow Massacre,[50] I saw the people there after the ocurrance scattered over the

[47]Parley Parker Pratt, one of the original LDS Twelve Apostles, "met with a company of Saints from Australia, under the direction of Elder William Hyde" at San Pedro, then left ten days later for San Francisco. Pratt, *Autobiography*, 14 June 1854, 408–409. George Q. Cannon, later an LDS apostle and a member of the First Presidency, established and edited the *Western Standard*. See Ekins, ed., *Defending Zion*.

[48]Ann appears to refer to Wilford Woodruff as the "present" president of the LDS church; as Woodruff became president in April 1889 and served until his death in September 1898, the manuscript appears to date from between those years. See Alexander, *Things in Heaven and Earth*, 242–45, 330.

[49]A colony of Mormons settled at San Bernardino, California, in 1851; Brigham Young recalled them in spring 1857 and in the fall ordered all outlying Mormon settlements to relocate to Utah. Some fifty-five families moved to Beaver, likely including the Phillips (Gordge) family. See Bradley, *A History of Beaver County*, 63; and Lyman, *San Bernardino*, 371–410. Another Australian convert described the journey in early 1858; see Barton, Autobiographical sketch. The San Bernardino refugees crossed Mountain Meadows, and several confirm Gordge's description of seeing scattered remains. Bagley, *Blood of the Prophets*, 193–94. Merab and John Phillips had three children; Lee's diaries mention his Phillips in-laws in Beaver, Utah. See Cleland and Brooks, eds., *A Mormon Chronicle*, 2:250–51n25; 13 March 1867, 57; 8 June 1867, 76; 29 January 1868, 96. In 1860 a census taker found Jonathan Phillips, 49, and "Mary," 41, born in Wales; with Ann G., 11 years old (with dittoes under Wales birthplace); Daniel G., 9; and two other children, evidently Jonathan and Merab's, living in Beaver City. See United States Bureau of the Census, Eighth Census of the United States, 1860, Beaver City, Beaver County, Territory of Utah, page 124, lines 2–7.

[50]For full-length accounts of the massacre see Brooks, *Mountain Meadows Massacre*; Bagley, *Blood of the Prophets*; and Walker, Turley, and Leonard, *Massacre at Mountain Meadows*. For an influential early version, see Stenhouse, *The Rocky Mountain Saints*, 424–58. The prosecuting attorney in Lee's first trial wrote his version in Baskin, *Reminiscences of Early Utah*, 83–149.

ground butchred in the most horridable maner. ~~Little children with long dresses on their Heads put between the spokes of the Wagon wheel, and their necks broken, and mothers in the family way pregant with their bowels Riped open and babies torn from them and thrown upon the ground~~.

We camped two days at Mountain Medows, and moved South to Jacob Hamblins Ranch,[51] as we came to the Ranch the following named persons were there Isaac Height. John M. Higby. George A Smith one of the Twelve Apostles, Major John D. Lee.[52] I heard the above named men talking about the Mountain Medow affair and how the bodies of the men were muteladed, with their privates cut off and the young women and girls treated in the same or Simular manner to leave the impression that the Indians had committed this dastardly and most Revolting deed, after they got through talking, George A. Smith said the blessing of the Church be upon you. Brigham Young will be here in a few days and will divide the property, I supposed you have got it safe; and they answered yes. There were two men made their escape from the slaughter, then two Indians and one white man were sent after them, they were captured at Mohave New Mexico where they Killed them, their horses were brought back with five or six Hundred Dollars in money taken from the murdred men. Ira Hatch the white man who helped with the two Indians to capture the two men who were fleeing for their lives, Hatch wanted to Keep the money they had taken from the murdred men for his own use.[53] No, No, Said Isaac C. Height and William H. Dame[54] we want the money for Brigham when he comes, they expected him right away, but he did not come until the following Spring after the adjournment of the

[51]Jacob Hamblin established a ranch at Mountain Meadows in 1856. See Alder and Brooks, *A History of Washington County*, 31; and Hamblin, Diary, 1854–1857.

[52]During the September 1857 assault and massacre at Mountain Meadows, Isaac Haight was the LDS Cedar Stake president and a major in the Iron County Militia; Maj. John M. Higbee was one of Haight's counselors; George A. Smith was a counselor in Brigham Young's First Presidency; and Maj. John D. Lee was Indian agent ("Farmer to the Indians") at Harmony. Higbee and Lee participated in the massacre; Haight helped to plan the attack; and Bagley makes a persuasive case that Smith's defiant sermons throughout southwest Utah in the weeks prior were instrumental in inspiring the crime. See Alexander, *Utah*, 129–32; Bagley, *Blood of the Prophets*, 34–35, 83–87, 115, 118, 126–30; and Walker, Turley, and Leonard, *Massacre at Mountain Meadows*, 67–73.

[53]Ann appears to be referring to three emigrants who reportedly escaped Mountain Meadows. While the accounts vary, Mormon Indian interpreter Ira Hatch is named as a participant in most versions, all of which conclude that Mormons caught and killed the men within five days of the massacre. Bagley, *Blood of the Prophets*, 142, 160–62.

[54]Colonel William H. Dame presided over the LDS Parowan Stake in Iron County and commanded the Iron County Brigade. Seegmiller, *A History of Iron County*, 267.

Legislature. John D. Lee was a member of the Legislature from Washington County[55] when he came up as a Member he brought with him twenty two thousand dollars, money taken from the distroyed train and murdered people which Sum of Money was turned over by Mr. Lee to Brigham Young, who expressed his astonishment at receiving so small amount. There was taken from the train and Murdered people three million of dollars, the above amount was divided between Six.[56]

This Emigrant Train Massacred at Mountain Medow was from Ft. Scott Kansas and Ft. Smith; the Captain, in charge of the Train was one Charles Francher, and the Lt's name was James Doughherity.[57] As the Emigrant Train was passing through the Territory of Utah they tried to buy vegetables, but the Mormons would not to sell them anything the object was to hamper them So they could not get through. All the Mormons ahead were notified that the train was on the Road and to not to Sell them anything. The Massacre was planed in Salt Lake City by Brigham Young, and the Mountain Medows was the place agreed upon to do the work. Brigham Young wrote a letter to John D. Lee instructing him how to do the work but by all means to Keep his name in the dark, as Knowing nothing about it, and having nothing to do with the Job directly or indirectly, that thereby he would be able to help and do him more good in the hereafter. This letter was Signed by Brigham Young, Governor of the State of Deserett. The Emigrants had an Ox who died on the road, the Mormons immediately filled the flesh of the dead Ox with poison. The Indians ate of the Ox and were poisoned

[55]The legislature met in December 1857. Bagley, *Blood of the Prophets*, 185.

[56]According to most accounts, Bishop Philip Klingensmith, Haight, and Lee distributed the loot from the massacre. See Bagley, *Blood of the Prophets*, 170–87. According to Wilford Woodruff, Lee told Brigham Young on 29 September 1857 that Indians got all the property. In November Lee submitted a written report to Young repeating the story; Brooks, *Mountain Meadows*, 66–67, 140–41, 152–53. In his confession, Lee wrote that the search produced "a little money and a few watches, but there was not much money." He thought Higbee and Klingensmith kept the property. Bishop, *Mormonism Unveiled*, 244–45; see also 248–58. Lee reportedly profited from some of the party's cattle, and there are many stories about the victims' clothing, jewelry, and a reported $4,000 in cash. Bagley, *Blood of the Prophets*, 171–74. Walker, Turley, and Leonard discuss property in *Massacre at Mountain Meadows*, 216, 221–22, 251–54; they estimate cash ranging from $3,194 to $8,028 and a total value of property between $27,240 and $48,102.50.

[57]Most of the emigrants came from northwestern Arkansas and took the Cherokee Trail (which passed south of Fort Scott) until it met the Oregon-California Trail near Fort Bridger. The party was led by Alexander Fancher, who Juanita Brooks identified as Charles Fancher. Brooks, *John Doyle Lee*, 215. Alexander's son Christopher Carson was five years old at the time of the massacre; Lee informally adopted him and called him Charley. Jacob Hamblin returned him to Indian Superintendant Jacob Forney in 1859. Bagley, *Blood of the Prophets*, 56–68, 159, 215. No source lists the name "Doughherity" or anything similar. See Appendix A, "The Emigrants," in Walker, Turley, and Leonard, *Massacre at Mountain Meadows*, 243–49.

so that many of them died. This was done for the purpose of inciting and infurating the Indians against the Emigrants. They also poisoned one of the wells, one of the children took a drink of the water and died in a few minutes. The Emigrants moved from there to where they could get pure water. The Mormons would not give the lumber to make a coffin for the child. They took the lumber after which they marched on to Beaver, there they were warned not to go that road by Iron county but to Keep off more towards Nevada. Every town they went through they were hated and called all Kinds of names and treated most shamefully by a people claiming to be Christians.

When they got to Mountain Medows they correlled their train as usual. After they had everything as they thought secure all their Stock was run off by the Mormons who were constantly on their trail; when they saw the fix they were in, they went to digging trenches and throwing up breast works to defend themselves. They were unfortunately camped about fifty yards from the Spring, the Mormons all dressed like Indians and painted up like Indians on the war path and they had the train surrounded. The emigrants were correlled and could do nothing to help themselves. The water supply cut off they had not tasted water for three days. They dressed two little girls in white and sent them to get water from the Spring, when the two little Girls were within a few steps of the Spring they were shot down dead. John D. Lee, Issac Hate and William H. Dame went among the Emigrants under a flag of Truse as peace makers, and made the Emigrants believe that they could controll the Indians. The poor Emigrants were led to believe that this was their only hope, there were induced to stack their arms and march out of their intrenchments and breast works and when farely out, the men were shot down like dogs.[58] The women were all of them put into a large wagon. The driver was a Mormon he drove the wagon a short distance from where the men were murdered then here the wagon was attacked and all the women both young and old taken out of the wagon and ravished in the presence of each other, after which they were most brutally murdered and most horrably mutilated this was done to leave the impression that the

[58]Lee and William Bateman, among others, carried the flag of truce to the emigrants' camp and negotiated their surrender. Lee, Brooks, Bagley, and Walker, Turley, and Leonard agree that Haight and Dame gave or passed along orders but were not at Mountain Meadows during the massacre. Bishop, *Mormonism Unveiled*, 246; Brooks, *Mountain Meadows*, 69–96; Bagley, *Blood of the Prophets*, 140–51; Walker, Turley, and Leonard, *Massacre at Mountain Meadows*, 257.

Indians were guilty of this most cowardly and dastardly and must revolting deed. When the revolting crime was committed by white man claiming to be Christians, after those same white man had given the Emigrants every assurance that their helpless condition would be respected, this plot was gotten up by the Mormons to save their cowardly Souls from being hurt from a frightened and defenseless people.

There was one young girl made her escape from where the slaughtering was going on, in her great excitement she did not know where she was going. She met a young man on horse back, begged the young man to save her, he asked her what was the matter, she told him they were murdering all her people, this young man did not Know anything about the massacre, while they were talking up came John D. Lee. She beged the young man to save her from that man. he took hold of the girl, the young man spoke up and said Father what are you going to do, the young man proved to be Lee's oldest son.[59] Mr. Lee told him to go and mind his own business. The young man obeyed orders and left, after he was gone Lee ravished the girl and then murdered her.[60]

When the emigrants were surrounded, one man was sent to Salt Lake City for further orders from Brigham Young. The messenger ~~Kie~~ Cye Simkins was forty eight hours in making the trip to the city where he saw Mr. Young, after he got his orders he started back and was forty eight hours in making the return trip with a message from Brigham Young to hold them as prisoners, but they had already been massacred before the return of the messenger from Salt Lake City.[61] Parley P. Pratt was one of the apostles and was in Kansas at Ft. Scott and Ft. Smith for the purpose of enlightening the benighted people on Mormonism, he unfortunately for himself was murdered by the heathen gentiles. This emigrant train happened to be from the same section of the country where Pratt was Killed the Mormons were so insulted and indignant over the death or murder of Pratt, that they recked

[59]Lee's oldest son was John Alma. Brooks, *John Doyle Lee*, 379.

[60]This rape/murder story is one of many variants. See Brooks, *Mountain Meadows*, 105–106; Bagley, *Blood of the Prophets*, 151; and Walker, Turley, and Leonard, *Massacre at Mountain Meadows*, 207.

[61]All other sources identify the messenger as James Haslam, an ironworker and member of Dame's Iron County regiment. See Bagley, *Blood of the Prophets*, 127, 132; Brooks, *Mountain Meadows*, 209, 223, 243; and Walker, Turley, and Leonard, *Massacre at Mountain Meadows*, 181–82, 186, 225. One Hezekiah ("Kie"?) Simpkins (or Simkins), 21, lived on his family's Beaver City farm in 1860. United States Bureau of the Census, Eighth Census of the United States, 1860, Beaver County, Territory of Utah, page 131, line 12. See also the "Pioneer Honor Roll" in Merkley, eds., *Monuments to Courage*.

uncontroled vengence on the poor emigrants. This is supposed to be the cause of the Mountain Medow Massacre.[62]

Those six men divided the plunder equally among themselves, and then gave an equal amount towards raising twenty two thousand and dollars in cash for Brigham Young, in addition to the above he received six silver and six Gold candlesticks, two challeses one Gold and one Silver, and also two Silver and two Gold plates, together with alter clothes and alter linen. I did not know when I saw the above named articles what they were for until after I became a Catholic, then I Knew what they were for.

Come all bold sons of Freedom
unto my Rhyme give ear
It is of an awful Massacre
You presently shall hear
In splendour from the Mountains
some thirty wagons came
attacted by a wicked Band
and Utah bares the Blame
All on this Mountain Medow
this little train was seen
they fourth with correlled thier Horses
all on this Mountain Stream
Both in Indian garb and Colours
thoes bloody hounds were seen
To flock around this train
all on the Meadows Green
attacked in the morning
While they were on their way
they fourth with correlled their horses
and fought in Blood all day
To see mothers and their children
lay Rowling in their agore
[Ho?] such a bloody sight
I Know was never seen before
Until the Leader of this Band
thoese words to them did give
that if their arms they would give up

[62]Brooks and Bagley agree that Mormon outrage over Pratt's death may have helped trigger the massacre. Pratt's widow Eleanor McLean (whose first husband murdered Pratt) arrived in Salt Lake and met with Mormon leaders just before the Fancher party came through the territorial capital. Brooks, *Mountain Meadows*, 57–59; Bagley, *Blood of the Prophets*, 70–72, 80–81, 89, 98, 184, 190, 266, 269. Walker, Turley, and Leonard give the murder less weight. *Massacre at Mountain Meadows*, 30–32, 37.

They shurely would let them live
To this Request they did comply
thinking their lives to save
But their words, were broken, as the Rest
[And?] sent them to their Graves,
At once their Arms they did give up.
and started for Cedar City
But they fell on them, in Indian Style
Oh what a human pity
They melted down at one accord
Like wax before the Flames
Both men and women old an young
Oh Utah Blush with Shame
this money was divided among thoes wicked men
and Uncle Sam his bound to see this wicked matter through
For he as troop assembled all through this Utah Land
To ferret out those murders, and brake this accused Band
Both in money and in property, those murderes did abound
and this is what they were murdered for
the world as heard the sound.
By the order of the General, the deed was done you see
The Leader of this cruel Band, his name was ~~John D. Lee~~[63]
We will toutch lightly on the subject, for the Reasons are not Known
and in some future time, the case will more plainly show
This life will soon be ended, and another coming on
and the perpentrators of this deed
Will answer for their Rong[64]

After we had been in Washington County[65] one year, the Bishop Bob

[63]"Brigham" is written above the deleted name, evidently in a different hand.

[64]Folklorist Austin Fife analyzed five similar variants of this ballad and suggested a soldier might have been composed it. Fife, "A Ballad of the Mountain Meadows Massacre." J. Barre Toelken discussed another variant in "The Ballad of the 'Mountain Meadows Massacre.'" See also Burt, "Murder Ballads of Mormondom."

[65]George A. Smith and Ezra T. Benson named Iron County in 1850 as they attempted to establish an iron industry in southern Utah. John D. Lee was clerk of the Iron Mission. They built their first settlement, later named Parowan, on Center Creek in spring 1851. See Brooks, ed., *Journal of the Southern Indian Mission*, ix–xi. In 1852 Washington County was created; it extended across the entire southern tier of the territory. Kane County was carved out of the eastern two-thirds of Washington in 1870; by 1896, the final arrangement of Beaver, Iron, and Washington counties from north to south in far southwestern Utah was set. John D. Lee, Elisha H. Groves, and others established the first settlement in what became Washington County at Harmony in 1850 on Ash Creek; it became the county seat in 1852 and headquarters of the Southern Indian Mission. Washington City was established in 1857 and made the seat in 1859. Lee was LDS branch president at Harmony. See Seegmiller, *Iron County*, 44–64; Larson, *"I Was Called to Dixie"*; Cleland and Brooks, eds., *A Mormon Chronicle*, 2:3–9; and George A. Hicks's account in this volume.

Covington[66] came to my step Fathers house and told him to get ready and go to Salt Lake City for the purpose of going through the Endowment House to get washed and annointed with Sallad Oil, known as Olive Oil in the church.[67] While the Bishop was with my Father talking, I was hid under the bed the Bishop says to my step Father where is Annie, my Father answered She is with her mother up to Woodards. Well if she is away I will tell you what we want. There is a young boy here in the Town, he is not a good Mormon and we want him put out of the way. My Father answered him No, that he would have nothing at all to do with it, the Bishop told my step Father that in case he would not do as requested he would not give him a certificate to go through the Endowment House. While they were still in the house, Amasy M. Lyman, Charles C. Rich and George A. Smith[68] and Amasy says to my step Father well John have you been to Salt Lake yet, my Father answered No, what is the reason, you have been here two years and have not gone yet. My step Father answered that he could not get his certificate because he would not destroy the young man's life as requested by the Bishop, Amasy said they did not want murdering done and he gave my step Father a certificate to go to Salt Lake City, after they all left except my step Father and the Bishop and a man by the name of Slade,[69] the Bishop Says to him that Boy has got to be put out of the way, and so it was arranged that the boy was to be disposed of at 12 o'clock that night, after they left the house, I sliped out and went down to Uncle Buck Smithtons, and I said Uncle Buck where is Johnnie he said that he was in the house, what is

---

[66]Robert D. Covington was Washington's long-time LDS bishop; see the discussion in the George A. Hicks section of this volume. Harrison Pierce baptized Ann Gordge on 6 June 1858 in Washington. John D. Lee, Family Geneology [*sic*], Lee Papers. Harrison Pearce was one of Bishop Covington's counselors. See Larson, *Red Hills of November*, 224, 256. On Covington, see also Alder and Brooks, *A History of Washington County*, 9–29; Larson, *Red Hills of November*, passim; and Brooks, History of Washington County. For Covington's dealings with John D. Lee, see Cleland and Brooks, eds., *A Mormon Chronicle*, vol. 1, passim.

[67]Mormons performed sacred ordinances in the Endowment House from 1855 until November 1889. See Alexander, *Things in Heaven and Earth*, 177.

[68]LDS apostles Amasa Lyman, Charles C. Rich, and George A. Smith were in southern Utah in July–August 1858 and questioned Lee and others about the massacre. See Brooks, *John Doyle Lee*, 241–42. Lyman and Rich had established the Mormon colony in San Bernardino; Lyman's journal noted that he saw "nearly the last of the San Bernardino emigration" arriving in Utah territory. Lyman, Journal, 4 February 1858, 17. Lyman was also in Washington in March–May 1858. Ibid., 23–39.

[69]Perhaps "Jef" (Jefferson) Slade, whom John D. Lee hired in August 1859 in Washington. Cleland and Brooks, eds., *A Mormon Chronicle*, 26 August 1859, 1:218. Lee also knew the William Slades, father and son. See, for example, Cleland and Brooks, eds., *A Mormon Chronicle*, 21 May 1858 and 17 September 1859, 1:164, 219. Lee claimed both were present at Mountain Meadows; Bishop, *Mormonism Unveiled*, 228; and both are listed in Walker, Turley, and Leonard, *Massacre at Mountain Meadows*, 262.

the matter I told him that the Bishop was going to Kill Johnnie that night at 12 o'clock and that he had better leave to save his life.[70] And they came that night at 12 o'clock the hour agreed upon. The Bishop and two others, Conington, Slade and John Hawley,[71] and they called Mr. Smithton out and asked him where is your notorious Son: Smithton answered he is in Nevada by this time thanks to a friend. . . .

John D. Lee came down from Harmoney with three of his wives, he also brought with him three children one of whom was taken out of the Mountain Medow Massacre.[72] One Sunday morning after Mr. Lee came down myself and the *children* were sitting on the grass, Emma one of the wives of Mr. Lee came out to where we were siting. She was dressed in a rich Moreantique silk dress Leghorn hat trimmed in black and Pink ribbon heavy Gold Bracelets, Gold Watch and chain, and heavy Gold Ear Rings and the little girl who was rescued from the Mountain Massacre Slaughter Saw her She Said She has got my mothers dress on. John D. Lee who was Siting close by heard the childs remark, he got up walked over to where the Child was Siting reached down took the child by the head and bent her head back and cut her throat from ear to ear then threw her body in a well close by, this I Saw with my own eyes.[73]

There was a very nice young man by the name of Anderson, he worked on Heber C Kimbills[74] Farm, he was engaged to one of the most beautiful, most elegant young ladies in the neighborhood. She and her lover Anderson were secretly married but this interfered with the arrangements of the Bishop who wanted the young Lady for one of his wives. But the young

[70]William "Buck" Smithson was a San Bernardino settler recalled in 1857; he settled in Washington. Larson, *"I Was Called To Dixie,"* 71.

[71]John Hawley lived in Pine Valley, Washington County, in 1870. United States Bureau of the Census, Ninth Census of the United States, 1870, Washington County, Territory of Utah, page 1, line 12. Hawley confronted John D. Lee about Mountain Meadows. Bagley, *Blood of the Prophets*, 262; Walker, Turley, and Leonard, *Massacre at Mountain Meadows*, 258.

[72]John D. Lee married nineteen women and fathered sixty-four children over the course of his life. While married to Ann Gordge from about 1865 to 1872, he cohabited with his first wife Aggatha Ann Woolsey, Sarah Caroline Williams (called Caroline), Rachel Andora Woolsey (Aggatha's sister), Mary Vance Young (called Polly), Lavina Young (Mary Vance's sister), Mary Leah Groves, Emma Batchelor, and Terressa Morse Chamberlain. See Brooks, *John Doyle Lee*, 379–84. Lee's household at Harmony in 1858 included Aggatha, Caroline, Rachel, Mary, Emma, and Terressa. Lee was frequently in Washington City from late 1858 on, and he settled wives Polly and Lavina there. Brooks, *John Doyle Lee*, 245–46.

[73]Juanita Brooks noted the many variants of this story with different child victims. Brooks, *Mountain Meadows*, 103–104.

[74]Heber C. Kimball was first counselor to Brigham Young.

man loved the young Lady with all his heart, he would not give her up. She fully reciprocated the young man's affection and would not hear [to?] Such a thing as giving up her lover and in reality her husband, when they found they could not reason him out of his resolution, they called a meeting to dispose of his case, . . . after they got through with the secret meeting they sent for the young Man and the young Lady as a last effort, to Know if he Still resisted in his resolution and he answered yes until death. They then told the young Lady to go home, he wanted to go with her but they would not let him. After she had gone, they took and bound him hands and feet and blindfolded, he wanted to know what they were going to do with him they told him that he would soon see, they took down his pants and castrated him then and there this was on Saturday and hanging his privates on a nail and on Sunday at the public Service the privates of the young man hanging on the nail was pointed out to every one in the meeting I suppose as a warning to be careful and not cross the designs or wishes of the Bishop. With all the young man's misfortunes the young Lady never forsook him and they are now living together as man and wife in Nevada.[75]

A Negro called Sambo with a wife and four children, he was well fixed he had a good team and a few cows and some money, the Mormons followed the Negro family and robbed them of everything they had. Then the Mormon Danites burned them alive after robbing them. Some Gentiles going through to California passed the place soon after the Negro was burned. They saw that the dirt was fresh and recently disturbed and were some what curious to Know what it was done for and in digging down into the Soft dirt, to See, after a Spade or two they come upon the body of one of the children who was yet alive but died in about twelve hours after being exhumed, the bodies of the Father and Mother was yet warm they had been but a short time in the ground.

A Mr. John Anderson lived in a Small town called Canara he had his wife and children and also a neice living with him. He did not want to marry his neice but cohabited with her and she had a child by him. The Teacher of the

[75]John D. Lee wrote that castration "was the favorite revenge of old, worn-out members of the Priesthood, who wanted young women sealed to them, and found that the girl preferred some handsome young man. The old priests generally got the girls, and many a young man was unsexed for refusing to give up his sweetheart at the request of an old and failing, but still sensual apostle or member of the Priesthood." Bishop, *Mormonism Unveiled*, 284–85. The bishop of Manti, Warren Snow, carried out this punishment against Thomas Lewis. Bishop, *Mormonism Unveiled* 285–86; Young, *Wife No. 19*, 280–82; and Bigler, *Forgotten Kingdom*, 132.

Mormon Church had him cited before them for the offence of cohabiting with his neice, and they told him he could not marry her, but that he must have nothing more to do with her, that if he did he would have to answer with blood attonement which he did in two years afterwards. The Bishop came to him and said well Anderson are you ready and Anderson answered yes. Give me three hours, he took and washed himself all over with Sweet oil, after which he dressed himself in a suit of new garments belonging to the Church after which he was clothed in a white robe covering the first garment also belonging to the Church with white cap on his head, they then took him about a mile out of Town where they had a newly dug grave; where they cut his throat from ear to ear, but it appears that this ceremony must be accomplished without getting a drop of blood on the white robes covering the victims person, the blood had to run on the ground to save his soul, showing that he was regarded as a very clever man, and the Church was going to do all in its power to make his passage to the dark and Misterious River as pleasant as possible, this being a part of this cerimony it has to be performed at the hours of 12 o'clock at night in accordance to the rules of the Mormon religion, they then put him in a coffin and buried him, after which they went to his house and there they found his wife and two children lying dead on the floor, but it was never Known how they came to their death, the Church got all the property which was considerable, the property being the objective point to get rid of the family.[76] No one ever lived in the house after that. The Bishop put one of his wives to live in the house, she came out screaming as though the Devil was after her and she never went back. [H]er hair was black when she went in to the house, and when she came out her hair was as white as Snow.

On September 1858 at a place called Cottonwood in Washington County a man and his wifes brother and two sisters, the wife was in the ~~family way~~ pregnant at the time the Mormons cut the women open and took the child from her while yet alive, they hung the baby by the feet on a tree, while the wife and mother was in the agonies of death, they killed the balance of the family while she was still alive that she might see, the agony and torture of

[76]According to John D. Lee, Rosmos Anderson, a Dane, married a widow and wanted to marry her daughter as well, but Bishop Philip Klingensmith wanted her, too. When Anderson and the stepdaughter confessed to adultery, hoping that would lead to permission to marry, they were rebaptized under a "covenant" that if they committed adultery again, Anderson would be killed. Klingensmith later decided that Anderson must be killed, and the victim and his wife willingly prepared for the execution. Bishop, *Mormonism Unveiled*, 282–84.

her relatives. While they were going through with their bloody work the woman pulled the mask off of one of the men, and she Knew him back East where she went to the same school with him, his name was Newcomb, who afterwards Killed himself through remorse, There was an Indian girl who saw the whole transaction, and she said that she would tell that it was not the Indians done it, that they blame the Indians for all this Kind of work, when they were not guilty, She could talk when I found her, and She told me all about it, so they murdered the poor Indian Girl who was afterwards buried by an Indian called Big Finger. . . .

In October 1858, there was a man called Harry, who worked for a man by the name of Hate, Woods, Lunt and Stewart,[77] this Harry was to get $25.00 per month with board and clothes, he worked for those parties three years saved every cent by not drawing any of his pay. There was a party of Emigrants from the States going through to California to the Gold Mines and this Harry wanted to go with them and drew all his pay amounting to about $700[78] dollars, at this time the Indians were on war path and were very troublesome. Hate, Woods, Lunt and Stewart, proposed to accompany him to the Emigrant Train, the poor fellow, poor Harry never saw the Train, for when they came to Some lonesome spot they Killed poor Harry and thereby got all their money back; afterwards Hate came up to Harmony and told Rachel one of John D. Lee's wives that he had put another man over the rim of the Basin, the Sword that he done it with was covered with the Boys blood, and he said if she said anything about it he would put her in the same fix.[79]

In 1858 the Mormons fixed up an outfit to go to the White Mountains in the southern part of this Territory, their object in going there was to intercept an Emigrant train, but I did not Know the objective point of the Mormon outfit. The Train was in charge of two brothers by the name of Egans, there was about fifteen or Twenty in the Train two or three families, the Mormons Killed the whole outfit except the Egan brothers, as they thought, but there was one young man made his escape. After they tied the

[77]George Wood, Henry Lunt, Levi Stewart, and William C. Stewart were prominent southern Utah pioneers and frequently interacted with John D. Lee. Wood and William Stewart were at Mountain Meadows. See Cleland and Brooks, eds., *A Mormon Chronicle*, passim; Brooks, *John Doyle Lee*, passim. Lunt was one of the founders of Cedar City. Prince, *Gathering in Harmony*, 196.

[78]The BYU variant of this manuscript reads nine hundred dollars, page 16.

[79]In John D. Lee's confessions, Barney Carter and another man told Rachel they had "been on a mission" to take a young Gentile "*over the rim of the basin.*" Carter showed her his bloody sword "and he said he used that to help the Gentile over the *edge*." Bishop, *Mormonism Unveiled*, 279, italics in original.

Egans to a wagon in the Train and then tortured the women and children in the most barbarous manner before putting them to death, this was done in the presence of the Egan brothers, who were lashed to the wagon. The poor brothers had no hope of mercy from such fiends after what they saw. The Mormons then took both brothers from the Wagon and then dug holes and buried them in the holes up to their Shoulders, they Kept them in this condition four or five days torturing the poor prisoners in every immaginable manner giving them Salt and water together with gaul to drink, the poor wretches beged for water, they beged for one draft of water, or from thirst we will surely die. The Mormons supposed they were and left them in the sand but one was dead, and one Survived. This boy who escaped dug the Egan brothers out of the Sand but one was dead. That night they went off and found water and then returned to the train where the Mormons had murdered the Emigrants. They found a few spades and shovels, and buried the dead as best they could, they stayed four or five days on the desert on account of a good Spring, on looking around they found two Jacks or Burroes, they took and packed what they could on the Jacks such as Blankets and food and started for the Colorado River where they struck a place called Harpers Ferry, where the Egan Brother died.[80] This boy who had made his escape from the Mormons was captured by the Apache Indians. I saw him in 1872 and he told me that he had Killed three of the Mormons that was in that outfit, he said that he hoped that he could live longer so that he could Kill the whole of them, but unfortunately he was wounded the day before in a fight defending a Mexican Rancher against the Mormon Maurauders and Navajoe Indians who were Mormons also, but if Billy the Kid lives long enough he will get the whole of them. That night the boy died and we took him fifty Miles to have him burried by a Mexican Catholic Preist.

The Mormons returned to Washington county after committing those horable Murders; where the favorites were honored by being permited to

[80]Perhaps a reference to the Aiken party, which consisted of six Californian men, including brothers John and Thomas Aiken, who came from California in October 1857 apparently intending to meet the Utah Expedition. Mormon forces arrested them as spies, and a party including Orrin Porter Rockwell was dispatched to guide the Aikens and two other men back to California. The escorts attacked the four at a camp near Nephi, killing two; two others escaped with wounds but were gunned down at Willow Creek, near today's Mona. A fifth was later murdered in northern Utah. William Hickman was allegedly among the attackers, one of whom, Sylvanus Collett, was brought to trial in 1878 but acquitted. Hickman claimed he finished off the fifth man, known to him only as "Buck." Hickman and Beadle, eds., *Brigham's Destroying Angel*, 127–30; Baskin, *Reminiscences of Early Utah*, 150–51. For the full story, see Bigler, "The Aiken Party Executions," 457–76.

receive and have a third wife, with the benediction of the Bishop. One of the party George Spencer took to himself two wives, one of the women was a Mexican and she was forced to marry him, this gave him four wives in all. The night after he married these two women, he and two of his wives, his first and last wives were murdered, and there was not a mark on them to indicate how it was done, the Mexican wife was gone, and no one Knew where, as she was the wife that was forced to marry him, It was supposed she was the wife that done the deed, as she was no where to be found, the second wife went crasy and died in a short time after the above Murders.[81]

Three gentiles were Killed in a Whiskey Distillery in Cedar City Iron County. They were Miners 49ers returning from California to their families in the East, they were murdered for their money amounting to five ~~hundred~~ thousand dollars, they were advised to turn back and go East by way of Cape Horn, as it was dangerous to go the way they contemplated, but they did not take the Kindly advice, and the result was the murder of all three, not one left to tell the tale. This Man Weston who owned the Distilary was visited by the wrath of God, it appears, for he had but one child, an only son about ten years of age, Who was taken sick the following day and never walked a step afterwards, and he is still living, his body grew but his legs never did. This Man Weston afterwards married he had four daughters by his second marriage all of whom were cripples, notwithstanding the large amount he got from the Murdered Miners, he was reduced to poverty, and then through remorse or something else he hung himself.[82]

Immediately after the above occurrence, there hapened the Massacre of Cedar City Iron County where there was thirty four Families murdered and tortured in the most cruel and barbarous manner, the children even were torn limb from limb while yet alive and the women were treated in the same manner, while the men were securely tied and permitted to look and see the torture and murder of their wives and children, and afterward the men were tortured in like manner, murdered, and cut up unto small pieces and ground up in to mince meat, all this grinding was done in a

[81]George Spencer was at Mountain Meadows but was deeply troubled by what he had done and seen. Bagley, *Blood of the Prophets*, 261.

[82]John D. Lee relates that three poor men en route to California just prior to Mountain Meadows were suspected of being U.S. Army spies. They were made to drink at the Cedar City distillery and attacked and killed by a group including John M. Higbee, John Weston (or Western), James Haslem [*sic*], and William C. Stewart. Bishop, *Mormonism Unveiled*, 273. John Weston may have been at Mountain Meadows. See Walker, Turley, and Leonard, *Massacre at Mountain Meadows*, 263.

Grist Mill. The parties guilty of this most heanous offence were a Mr. Lunt, Hate, Higby, Dame, Smith, Walker, Smith, Stewart and Hawley, they made strong efforts to bring the notorious John D. Lee into this Massacre but in that matter they failed, for John D. Lee with all his meanness and all his faults, and the Lord Knows he was as mean as a man could be, but he was not in the Cedar City Massacre, he could prove an alibi, for he at the time was a member of the Legislature, when this massacre was done, it was done for plunder, — all of which Brigham Young was the bennificiary and instigator of all the brutality, practiced on that occasion and was directed and conducted under his orders.[83]

In the Spring of 59,[84] one Joseph Wood murdered two women and three children, Mrs. Emily Combs a Widow and Miss Combs her daughter and three children all girls, the fiend Woods killed the whole family, because he thought his son was going to see them to often to suit him, he was tried for the crime and was sent to states prison for three years, his wife had twins, she washed and dressed the murdered children, the twins when born were badly marked having the appearance of being bloody all over, they died when four years old.[85] Miss Combs was shot through the hip, she crawled six miles on her hands and Knees to a friendly Indian camp where she was Kindly cared for. She lost the use of her limb entirely, this brute Wood tried to Kill the girl after he got out of prison, he was afterwards made Bishop by Brigham Young, his murdering the family proved to Brigham that he was the right Kind of timber to make a Bishop, he is living in Cedar City a great and holy man in the Mormon light.[86]

[83]Lee left for Great Salt Lake City to attend the territorial legislature in December 1857 and was back in Harmony on 5 February 1858. Brooks, *John Doyle Lee*, 227–33; Cleland and Brooks, eds., *A Mormon Chronicle*, 27 December 1857 to 5 February 1858, 1:139–48. The "Cedar City Massacre" seems to be a complete invention.

[84]In the BYU variant, "59" is struck through and "1861" added in another hand. The actual Coombs murder happened in 1862.

[85]Many Mormons held similar belief in a parent's experience resulting in prenatal marking of babies. Fife, "Birthmarks and Psychic Imprinting of Babies in Utah Folk Medicine," 121–30.

[86]Ann evidently means the murder of Olive Coombs, killed by George Wood at Cedar Fort in July 1862. Wood also wounded Coombs's daughter, Emily, age 13. Wood may have killed Coombs because she was asking about the Mountain Meadows massacre. Wood pled guilty and was sentenced to life, but in 1865 Gov. James Doty pardoned him after over two hundred of Iron County's leading citizens petitioned him. See Wray, The Story of the Second Murder in Iron County, Utah: Olive Olivia Curtis Coombs. Prominent southern Utah pioneer Christopher Arthur wrote that George Wood shot the two women because he suspected them of seducing his son Joseph. Arthur, The Autobiography of Christopher J. Arthur, 23. Joseph Wood married John D. Lee's and Rachel's daughter Helen Rachel on 30 December 1868. Cleland and Brooks, eds., *A Mormon Chronicle*, 3, 26 November 1868, 2:111; Brooks, *John Doyle Lee*, 381.

Close to Cedar city, about two miles, there is an Iron mine, they were working the mine at this time, there was nine Welch men miners who came that way and they were engaged to work in the mine, the miners had considerable money of their own, they went to work and worked about a year without drawing any pay, it was given out that they had drawn their pay and had gone on to Salt Lake City, a few days after some children were taking a walk in the neighborhood of the mine when they suddenly came upon the dead bodies of the nine Welch men, who were murdered for their money, and their years pay coming to them, the Mine was never worked after that occurence. Two Scotchmen Father and Son came along and went into the mine with intention of working the mine, the old man never came out of the mine alive, the young man succeeded in getting out with his hair turned from black to as white as Snow.[87] The old man Urey had another son John Urey who married a widow, an Irish woman from Australia by the name of O'Farrall, she had five children two daughters and three sons, she came from California to Cedar City and there She married John Urey, she had nine children by Urey all boys, after he married this women, he left the Mormon Church. After which, he was called upon by ten masked man who wanted him to come out, but the wife, a large powerfull Irish woman, being forewarned by her son who had overheard the plot to Kill his Step Father that night, so when they called for Mr. Urey, she would not let him go out, but went to the door herself with a large Iron poker in her hand, and opened the door, and asked what they wanted, and without further parley she opened fire on them with the Iron poker, right and left, with the assistance of her Son, they Killed three of the assailants that night. The family were never troubled after.[88] The three oldest boys went to California, there they became citizens of the United States, after they returned to Cedar city each one of the boys took up one hundred and sixty acres of Government land on which was situated Cedar City, after the boys received their Tittle or pattent, they made it comfortably warm for those living in Cedar City, the citizens were compelled to buy their ground from the three brothers at fabulous prices.

[87]The mines were established beginning in 1851 by the Iron Mission, which included John D. Lee; Cedar City was established in November on Coal Creek, about twenty miles southwest of Parowan. See Shirts and Shirts, *Trial Furnace*, 147–90; Brooks, *John Doyle Lee*, 153–54.

[88]Blacksmith John Urie was an early Cedar City settler, an acquaintance of Lee's and a massacre perpetrator; in 1870, the census recorded John, born in Scotland, and wife Sarah, born in Ireland, with eight children. See United States Bureau of the Census, Ninth Census of the United States, 1870, Iron County, Territory of Utah, page 20, line 9; Cleland and Brooks, eds., *A Mormon Chronicle*, 3, 7, 18 March 1867, 2:56, 58; and Walker, Turley, and Leonard, *Massacre at Mountain Meadows*, 263.

A family by the name of Jackson[89] living at Summit Creek, husband and wife with ten children, who had left the Mormon Church, and started for California. The Mormons allowed them to leave and get on the big desert, when they were followed by the Mormons a days march behind them until they got into the big desert. When they were overtaken, by the Mormons and relieved of everything they had, their Horses were ham strung so that they could not move: and there they were left to starve, they all died but three, two girls and a boy, who were picked up by some friendly Indians, one of the girls afterwards married an Indian Chief.

We will now remove to Parawan. I was working out for a lady, I worked for her about eight months, she had a baby about three months old, one night about twelve o'clock,[90] there was a loud rapping on the door, her husband got up to see what was the matter there was five men at the door, all masked, he asked them what they wanted, they told him to put on his clothes. And come with them, that they had a Job for him to do, so he put on his clothes, went and Kissed his wife and baby, and she asked him what he done that for and he told her that was the last Kiss he would give her in this life. He started off with them, those masked men with whom he went brought him back next morning with his throat cut from ear to ear, they brought him in and laid him on the bed; they were so very considerate, she took a skillet from a large fireplace in the room and placed it under his head so as to catch the blood from driping on the bed. The wife commenced to cry, and they told her to shut up or they would serve her in the same manner.[91] That night the same party came and took the body away and I suppose buried it. In about two weeks afterwards they came again, the same parties, and they disposed of her in the same manner, as they had done with her husband. When I found her and the baby, they were both dead. The family were murdered for their property. Poor families were never troubled in that way. After this happened my step Father came to Parawan and took me home to Washington County.

Afterwards Johnson's Army came to Washington County for the purpose of finding out all the facts and information possible in reference to the

[89]The BYU variant names the family Jonson, page 21.

[90]The BYU variant says three oclock, page 22.

[91]Fanny Stenhouse reported a similar story from a woman who had lived in southern Utah. Another woman came running across the fields saying that two masked men had roused her husband from bed and brought him back lifeless, laid him on the bed, took out a bake-kettle "and stood it beside the bed, in order to catch the blood that was flowing from a fearful wound in his throat. They then left the house telling me to make as little noise about it as possible or they might serve me in the same way." Stenhouse, *"Tell It All,"* 319–20.

Mountain Medow Massacre. When the Army came to Parawan there were none of the men there who had taken part in the Massacre, the Army then moved to Cedar City, there was seven of the little children that was saved from the massacre they were turned over to the Army. There the Army fared sumtuously as the Mormon women furnished them with everything they wanted such as chickens, ducks, Geese and Turkeys, and all other luxuries to be to had in the country. They left Cedar City and marched to Fort Harmoney about eighteen miles where John D. Lee lived when they got there, it proved to be the same as the former place, no men to be found, they asked the women where the men were and one of the women named Rachel one of the wives of John D. Lee told them that the men had all gone to Salt Lake City. They came to Washington, a small village in the southern part of the Territory, where there was a large cave about a mile from Town full of men. At that time I was eleven years old, and we the children carried the food to the men in the cave. Cpt Forney hid his men in the hills to watch and the Mormons supposed the Army had gone to Camp Floyd,[92] and eight or ten of them ventured out, and went back to Fort Harmoney, the Soldiers run in on them, and while the officers were eating supper and engaged in lively conversation with the women, John D. Lee and his men made their escape, and in doing so Killed four soldiers who were Standing guard, and to make the matter worse, one of the Soldiers remarked that this was a blasted country where a person could not get anything to drink. One of John D. Lee's boys told him he could get him something to drink and wanted to Know what the Soldier would give, the soldier answered that he would give him five dollars, there was a Still house close by, and the boy took him there, where the Soldiers all got beastly drunk and therefore of no earthly account. John D. Lee and his men came back and had a big dance over their victory over Uncle Sam's drunken Soldiers.[93] Brigham Young ordered that company out of the Territory. Col. Steptoe came in there place, they were met by a Mormon Battalion at the head of Echo Canyon and they Stampeded the Government Mules; the road passed through a narrow canyon and the

[92]Camp Floyd was the U.S. Army post in Cedar Valley, southwest of Salt Lake, and was established in 1858. See Moorman with Sessions, *Camp Floyd and the Mormons*, 53–57, 275.

[93]Ann seems to be referring to events of April–May 1859, when federal judge John Cradlebaugh accompanied U.S. troops to southern Utah to investigate Mountain Meadows. Lee and other culprits hid in the mountains, but no fight occurred. "Cpt. Forney" appears to confuse Capt. R.P. Campbell, commanding the U.S. forces, with Jacob Forney, the Indian superintendent charged with reclaiming the surviving Fancher party children. See Bagley, *Blood of the Prophets*, 216–18, 225–30. For Lee's fragmentary journal of this period, see Kelly, ed., *Journals of John D. Lee*, 11–16 May 1859, 203–10.

Mormon Battalion climed up the mountain and rolled large rocks down on the Soldiers as they passed the narrow defile, many of the Soldiers were wounded, but none were Killed.[94] There was another company of about fifty men, they were all distroyed, none escaped to tell of the dreadful Massacre, all their wagons and in fact everything they had was destroyed. The Elk Mountain Utes were accused of this Slaughter, in fact nearly all the crimes committed by the Mormons was laid to the Noble Red Man of the Forest.

William Hickman one of the distroying Angels, was sent to waylay Dr. Yates by Brigham Young, they had given this Dr. Yates two hundred thousand dollars for his drug Store, the Dr. Started to leave the country his destination was Oregon where his people lived. He expected to Join an Emigrant train at a place called Corinne he was to late, the train had passed two or three days before the Dr. reached Corinne. The Dr. started by himself in his bugy on the trail hoping to catch up with the Emigrant train, but he never caught up for the poor man was murdered between Corinne and Promontory about fifty miles distance from Corinne he was robbed of his money and everything he had and left for dead, but he came to himself again and was picked up by a passing Emigrant train. He lived about a week, concious at the time, and told the parties who rescued him, who robbed him and who assaulted him. This Hickman the murderer returned to Salt Lake City and went to Brigham Young to give up the money he robbed the Dr. of. Brigham Knew the amount of money the Dr. had, and he wanted it all. Hickman said no Brother Brigham you did not do the work, I done the work and will have my pay for it. Brigham then wanted Hickman to pay his Tithes out of the amount that he had taken from the Dr. Hickman paid the Tithing amounting to about twenty thousand dollars, Brigham blessed him then and told him he would have children as numerous as the Sands of the Sea, and that they would became a great nation.[95]

[94]Ann conflates unrelated events. Lt. Col. Edward J. Steptoe was the officer ordered to investigate the death of Capt. John Gunnison, who was killed in October 1853 on the Sevier River in central Utah. Pahvant Utes evidently killed Gunnison, but many people suspected Mormons. Steptoe declined an appointment as territorial governor and left for California in 1855. Bigler, *Forgotten Kingdom*, 88–92. On Gunnison and Steptoe, see Fielding, *The Unsolicited Chronicler*, 213–23. Echo Canyon is the main eastern approach to Salt Lake; the Mormons fortified it against the Utah Expedition in fall 1857. The only armed incidents were raids carried out by Mormon guerrillas upon U.S. Army supply trains. Moorman with Sessions, *Camp Floyd*, 26–30; and Bigler, *Forgotten Kingdom*, 88–90.

[95]William A. Hickman became notorious when he and J.H. Beadle published his autobiography, *Brigham's Destroying Angel*, which described committing crimes on behalf of the LDS church during the "Mormon War." Richard Yates was not a doctor (perhaps Ann confused him with other infamous murders, that of Dr. John M. Vaughn at Manti in 1851 or Dr. J. King Robinson at Salt Lake in 1866), but he was a Green River trader whom the Mormons rightly suspected of selling ammunition to (*continued*)

In the Summer of Sixty[96] at the town of Springville, a family of ten by the name of Parish were murdered all but one boy who made his escape, there was also two men driving Teams for the family were also murdered at the same time. This Massacre was led by Bishop Joseph Johnson of Springville. The murdered family were Mormons, but apostatised from the Mormon Church. The family were on their way to California to take up land, they had a daughter living there. She was married to a Mormon by the name of Shepard. The family was murdered because they left the Church, this is called blood atonement Sheding their blood to save their souls. Holy religion.[97]

My Step Father and mother moved from Washington county to a Town called Beaver, Beaver county.[98] Then commenced my hard life working in the field doing a mans work, carding, spinning and weaving, and going barefoot summer and winter and hearding cows in all Kinds of weather. The first pair of shoes I ever wore I worked for them and paid five dollars for them this was after I was eleven years old. . . .

The boy Elick Weldan was tried before what is called in the Church the Teachers Quorum, but found nothing against him, they then turned him over to the Elders who found him guilty of some misdemeanor. His case was then turned over to the Danites or in other words the distroying Angels to be delt with, according to the laws of the Church. The Danites held a meeting in an old Barn about a mile from Town. The boy with other boys (boy like) were stealing water melons and were in the old Barn, they heard the men coming, and they slipped up unto the Hay loft and hid themselves, they heard the whole plot and the whole arrangement to Kill the Weldan boy;

---

federal soldiers. Joseph A. Young, Brigham's oldest son, told him his father wanted Yates killed, Hickman claimed. The book's artwork showed Hickman killing Yates and "delivering the murdered man Yates' money to Brigham Young" (119, see also 124–26). Robert N. Baskin, an attorney who heard Hickman's confession, argued for his credibility. See Baskin, *Reminiscences of Early Utah*, 36–38. Hickman was arrested with several others for several murders but was never tried, and he was excommunicated for apostasy in 1868. See Hilton, *"Wild Bill" Hickman*; on Yates, see 77, 78, 125; on Hickman's book, 127–28. The town of Corinne, originally a northern Utah railroad construction camp where the rails crossed the Bear River, was not settled until early 1869, twelve years after Yates's murder. See Madsen, *Corinne*, 5–11.

[96]The BYU variant reads "Summer of 1861," page 25; the correct year is 1857.

[97]Ann relates a version of the 1857 Parrish-Potter murders. See Aird, "You Nasty Apostates," 173–91. Bishop Aaron Johnson of Springville was suspected of ordering the murders. Hosea Stout served as Johnson's attorney. See Brooks, ed., *On the Mormon Frontier*, 690–93. For a contemporary view (unfriendly to Mormons) of the incident, for which no one was ever brought to trial, see "Discharge of the Grand Jury," 29 March 1859, 3/3; "The Murder of the Parrishes and Potter at Springville, on Sunday night, March 14, 1857," 5 April 1859, 1/1; "The Parrish Murder," 19 April 1859, 1/1; all in the *Valley Tan*. See also Stenhouse, *Rocky Mountain Saints*, 462–69. The words "Holy religion" do not appear in the BYU variant.

[98]Settlers from Parowan founded Beaver City in April 1856. Bradley, *A History of Beaver County*, 50–53.

lots were drawn, and it fell to the lot of the boys Father (who was a Danite) to Kill his son that night; the boy hearing the whole arrangements got out of the Barn and ran home and told his mother, she told the boy they would not do it, but the boy insisted they would and told his Mother he would not leave, but would stay right there. The first word his Father said when he came home, was where is Elick, the boy's mother answered he is in bed, but you are not going to fulfil your oath here, one murder is enough he wanted to Know how she found out, she told him Elick heard it all in the Barn and came and told her, he left the house and went strait to the Danite comitte, and told them the whole matter was communicated to his wife as cases like this among their own people must be done very secretly, the case was put off for another meeting, at that meeting it was decided to Kill the whole family, except the old Lady. They came to carry out their hellish design, but the family it appears was notified of their coming, and were well prepared to give them a warm reception as soon as they made their appearance; the fight began and the result was eight of the attacking party were Killed, Just one half their number, old man Weldan is now in the Insane asylum a hopeless lunitic he is now about eighty five years old, the boy is still living in Arazona,[99] he spent a term in the States prison for poligamy.

Old Mother Shirts lived down in Canara Kane County. She was regarded as an old witch or Devil who urged her sons to go to the Mountain Medow Massacre, and she went herself to urge on her boys. She took an active part herself in murdering the women and children, She lived in Kane County many years after the Massacre, and lived an exemplary life for a woman of her disposition. She became a very prominent member of the Church, very high up, so that she was looked upon with considerable veneration. She went with one of her sons to California, and was gone three or four years, She returned to her former house in Kane County. Almost immediately after her return She was taken sick and lay sick for two years before she died. When death came it seemed that she could not die, from the horror ~~of the Spectors of the~~ departed spirits of the Mountain Medow Massacre which appeared to Surround her bed on all Sides, in the most hideous forms, and Kept her in a State of mental anxiety all the time. So they were compelled to surround the bed with blankets, to exclude the light, to enable her to pass away in comparative ease; how she crossed the dark and misterious River no one

[99]The BYU variant reads New Mexico, page 29. The elder Weldan might be Elliott Willden, one of nine men indicted for Mountain Meadows.

Knows. After she died, She had been so long sick, that she became partially decomposed so much so that she could not be washed, She was rolled up in the bed clothes she died in she was buried in about two hours after death.[100]

In Beaver city one Charles A. Booth he had one wife whom he called his cow, he was a Mormon from Calcuta India, there was a family living in Beaver city who had a little daughter about eight years old, the family made this child work in the field for this man, Booth, who took advantage of the child, when out in the lonely field and raped her, this matter was reported to his Highness the Bishop, who called a Teachers meeting to try the amorous Booth or brother, this meeting was in sitting for two days, before they came to a decision. And the teachers cut him off from the rights and privilidges of the Mormon Church for the space of one year, this was placing him on I suppose on probation.[101] When he was taken back into the Church in full fellowship, after he was baptised in the pond, Bishop Farnsworth[102] gave him a certificate to take his wife to Salt Lake City to go through the Endowment house, while they were in the city, the first thing that occured, she received a letter from her home in India, informing her that she was heiress to a large fortune but that it was so arranged, that she could not handle the principal but could use the interest for the raising of the children. While in the city they received about three thousand dollars Interest money. She in accordance to the will could not go through the Endowment house, she being of the Mahometan religion of the higher cast. She had to abandon the Mormon

[100]Probably Belana Pulsipher Shirts (sometimes written Schurtz), wife of Peter Shirts, a fellow Iron Missionary with John D. Lee. Peter's son (by another wife who died in 1849) Don Carlos Shirts married Mary Adoline, Lee's daughter by Aggatha Ann. Don Carlos (or "Carl") was part of the Mormon militia that attacked the emigrant party at Mountain Meadows. See Brooks, *Mountain Meadows*, xix; Brooks, *John Doyle Lee*, 199, 379; and Shirts and Shirts, *Trial Furnace*, passim, esp. 142. "Mother" Shirts's deathbed visions are a remarkable prefiguration of the visions that Nephi Johnson suffered decades later. See Brooks, *John Doyle Lee*, 12–15.

[101]Charles Booth, born in India of English heritage, was a steamship engineer and one of the few converts made by the East India Mission. See Britsch, "Early Latter-day Saint Missions to South and East Asia." Charles was baptized on 14 August 1853, and his wife Louisa on 22 September; Musser, Diary, 14 August 1853, 25; 22 September 1853, 60. In June 1855 he took a ship for San Francisco with Louisa and daughter Ellen (and the engineer's logbook); they lived in Beaver for decades. Booth, Journal, 1854–1855. Ann's rape story may have some truth. Booth's application for naturalization was denied because "he has not behaved as a man of good moral character." Second District Court, Minute Book Four, 347. In 1870 a census taker noted Charles, a thirty-eight-year-old farmer, and Louisa Booth, age 34, both born in "East India." United States Bureau of the Census, Ninth Census of the United States, 1870, Beaver City, Beaver County, Territory of Utah, page 3, lines 28–29.

[102]Philo T. Farnsworth was bishop of Beaver from 1856–1864 until replaced by John Murdock. Bradley, *A History of Beaver County*, 79–80.

Church to receive the money or abandon the money and go through the Endowment house, She very wisely chose the former course.

In about a year the Bishop gave him a certificate to take or seal unto himself two wives in addition to his first, one of his second wives he had sealed to him as his first wife. The first wife proper it appears was cut off from the Church because she would not go through the Endowment House, but was permitted to live with her husband, on account of the Interest money that was anually arriving which according to the religion of the Mormons would not do to let go by. The second wife a widow by the name of Limb, She buried her husband one day and the next day went with Booth as his second wife to Salt Lake City to get sealed to him, he also had with him at the time a women by the name of Hannah Evans, she was his third wife, but second in the Church. Mrs. Limb superceded the Indian wife by becoming the first wife in the Church. The India wife stood the arrangement for a couple of years. The first wife in the Church never had any children; but the second wife in the Church had children by him. The first wife in the Church left him and married another man, his second wife in the Church stayed with him and had a large family of children by him. He left his first and legal wife the East India women because she stoped his getting any more money from East India. He put his second in the same house to live with his first or legal wife. The second wife and her children, abused the first or legal wife most shamefully, So that this first and legal wife was compelled to leave him. She and her five children went to live in a house by themselves, She died in my mother's house, at the time of her death, she and been separated from her husband about ten years, during this time the Church was useing its influence to get him to force her to transfer this money to him so that he could have absolute control, he still after her death had a hold on the children. The conditions of the will were such, that the children could not draw the money without his signature, and he made each one of the children pay him one thousand dollars before he would sign the papers to enable them five in number, to get their money. The children go it after paying the Fee demanded, about a year ago the oldest boy was Killed by a horse, after the boy's funeral the old man fixed himself up and went to Salt Lake City to draw the boys money amounting to Fifty thousand dollars, and he demanded the money of the court as the legal heir of his son, but the son it appears, the day before his death, called to see an old neighbor and a very dear friend a Mrs. Philips who was sick at the time, after talking some time the old Lady turned to him and asked him, Charley have you made your will, and he answered no. She told him he had better make it as he would be a corpse tomorrow, the young man made his will that afternoon dividing everything he had, equally between his brothers and sisters, so that he left the Father out in the cold. The Judge told him he had nothing to do with the estate. The Father tried to get the money from the youngest child who was Idiotic from the cause of the treatment of the mother while bearing the Child. On the Mothers death, she appointed Judge Zane to care for and act as Guardian for the child; the old Father failed to get control of the child's money. The Judge managed that affair.[103]

Gen. Conner arrived in Salt Lake City in 1861 Brigham Young sent the General word not to cross the Jordan River but Genl. Conner paid no attention to Mr. Young at all, Brigham at the time was Governor of what they called the State of Desertette, Genl. Conner marched with his troops into the heart of the city, he marched up to the Lyon house and saluted the Governor, this was about Conference time, the Fall Conference. Brigham saw that he could not do anything with the Soldiers; he ordered his people to leave their nice Houses and fine cultivated farms and to go to Dixey that is in the South of Utah Territory. It would appear from this move that his object was to starve out the troops, and I suppose that was one object to prevent the Soldiers from foraging on the country, but he had a more important object in view, and that was to enrich himself at the expense of his own people, when he got them South, he robbed them of their fine homes and highly cultivated farms. When the poor people got to Dixey it proved to be nothing but a barren Desert with an Oasis here and there scatered over the country, where there were already a few settlers, with areable land scarsely sufficient to maintain them.[104] So the new comers suffered terrably for the

[103]The 1880 census recorded Charles Booth living with two wives: Louisa, age 43 (who emigrated with Charles from India) along with their son Charles, 23; and Hannah, 27, born in Wales. Bureau of the Census, Tenth Census of the United States, 1880, Beaver City, Beaver County, Territory of Utah, page 12, lines 18–29. In 1900 Charles was recorded living with wife Hannah and *their* son Charles, 15. Bureau of the Census, Twelfth Census, 1900, Beaver City, Beaver County, Utah, enumeration district 70, sheet 10, lines 76–86. Charles S. Zane was appointed to the federal third district court in Salt Lake City in 1884 and served as chief justice of the Utah Supreme Court. See Alexander, "Charles S. Zane, Apostle of the New Era."

[104]Ann conflates the arrival of Col. Patrick Edward Connor and his California Volunteers in 1862 with the approach of the Utah Expedition ("Johnston's Army") in 1857, when Young ordered the "move south." The stated purpose of the Utah Expedition was to replace Brigham Young with Alfred Cumming as territorial governor, although Mormons continued a "shadow government" with Brigham Young as governor of the State of Deseret. See Bigler, *Forgotten Kingdom*, 45–50, 201–219; Morgan, *The State of Deseret*. For Connor, see Madsen, *Glory Hunter*; for the arrival of his command, 65–72.

necessaries of life, at this time there was not a house in St. George, now the largest city in the South, the people were compelled to eat a grass or clover called Lucerne & carrot tops and muscal which they dug up and eat the roots and Prickly Pear leaves, and there was another root and Indian root the name of which I have now forgotten, this root they dug up dryed and ground into a Kind of meal or Flour of which they made their bread. From October to March, was the most distressing time, until the new vegatables came in.[105]

In the fall of 1861 their was one thousand Danes all Mormons, as soon as they came in the teams that brought them were from the south of Utah and Brigham ordered them all south, the Danes went south to a place eight miles south west of St George to a place called St Clare there they settled. At this time, Nevada was a Territory, after the Government Surveys were run it was found that St Clare was not in Utah, but in the State of Nevada. Brigham after he found the settlement was not in Utah, he ordered them to go to a place called Middletown between Washington and St. George but they through the advice of a Danish Lawyer, refused to obey the order of Governor Brigham Young, and would not go. Brigham charged each one five hundred dollars Emigration Fee, which they refused to pay through the advise of this same Danish Lawyer. This community were very prosperous and happy and became very wealthy and independent. Brigham being disappointed at their not obeying his orders and coming into the Territory, was determined to do them all the damage possible and hired parties to burn their city, in which the noble effort of the Governor failed, and to accuse the Noble Red Man of the Forest as the guilty parties of the dasterly outrage. . . .[106]

The Morrisite Church, a branch from the Mormon Church, headed by one John Joseph Abraham Morris and John H. Fairbank [Banks], they had formerly been Bishops. After seceding from the Mormon Church they with their followers went up to the head of Weber Canyon, there they founded a Colony, and were very quiet and peaceable to their own business. This Morris got people from all over the country or Territory and from countries

[105]See George A. Hicks's description of near-starvation in this volume, including his reference to "carrot tops and lucerne greens."

[106]Ann may be referring to an influx of Swiss immigrants, who Brigham Young sent south in 1861 to settle Santa Clara, a few miles west of St. George. Journal History, 7 October, 5 December 1861; Alder and Brooks, *A History of Washington County*, 40. For a first-person account, see Hafen, *Recollections of a Handcart Pioneer of 1860*. On Danish converts, see Mulder, *Homeward to Zion*. In 1864 settlers began a cotton mission southwest of St. George on the Muddy River. In 1866 a survey determined that the Muddy colonies were in Nevada. See Arrington, *Great Basin Kingdom*, 217, 221–22.

beyond the sea to Join his Church. They never held church in the day time, always in the night time or moon light, they never used light in the Church, the darker the object was and the impression they wished to convey that they needed no light, that they were light enough themselves. When Morris got up to preach he threw a white cloth over his head, this cloth was covered all over with Phosphorus so that he was the only object in the room to be seen by the congregation, this man Fairbanks was a fanatic, and believed in home sacrafice and sacrificed one of his own children, he took his child and dressed it in White, after which he put the child on a Snow white horse and marched behind with a drum corps for nine days, at the end of the ninth day at Sundown, he shot the child and horse himself this was his sacrifice for his own family. The services of the last Supper is held in the dark, and no woman is allowed to attend this service unless she could make her own dress from the raw material, card spin and weave. This Church went on for about three years; when Brigham Young ordered them out of the Territory, as they were interfering very materially with his business, they would not go. They made the poor old man Sick, he became indignant at their obstinacy and told them that if they would not go, that he would send them to Hell cross Lots, which he afterwards did in grand shape by murdering, sacking, burning all their property. They made a hard fight but were overpowered, no man, women or child were spared all were put to the torture, were slautered. But three who escaped to the mountains, they returned to see what was left they found the bodies of Morris and Fairbanks. They put the bodies in a wagon and watched three days, as he told that he would be Killed, but that he would rise again on the third day, but failed to materialise.[107]

This wholesale massacre was laid to the Indians as usual, one of the Mormons rode in from the Weber Canyon and told the Governor that the Indians were murdering the whites, the Governor called on Genl. Conner and his soldiers to go to the protection of the whites, Genl. Conner went and followed the Indians up Bear River, the Indians divided, part going to the Elk Mountains and a part up the Bear River, Conner followed the

[107]John Morris, a self-proclaimed prophet, gathered nearly one thousand followers to his settlement at the mouth of the Weber River between 1860 and June 1862. When a federal judge ordered the release of dissenters Morris had imprisoned, the acting territorial governor authorized the use of militia against Morris. The Nauvoo Legion, under the command of LDS leaders, fought a three-day battle in which Morris and many of his followers, including John Banks, were killed. See Bigler, *Forgotten Kingdom*, 208–17; and the Afterword of this volume.

Bear River Band[108] almost into Soda Springs. At this time the Band Stole a child from Moses Thacker now one of the Twelve Appostals, the child is still with the Indians, Conner overtook the Indians at Bear River there the Indians showed fight and shook the scalps of white women and dared him to come on, Irish gentile Son of a Bitch. The Genl. did come on and Killed the whole outfit, he did not spare one.[109]

After the fight the troops returned to Franklyn[110] in the dead of winter, in cold and enclemant weather and almost Starved to death, as the Mormons or Indians, which is the same thing made an attack and Killed some of the drivers. The supplies in the wagons the Genl. would not let his men touch it, as he feared poison. The troops marched about fifteen miles from the abandoned wagons and came to an abandoned Ranch where they got Some Potatoes and Quarter of Beef, some chickens and anything else they could utilise. From the Ranch they marched to a little town called Malad. There the Genl. Succeeded in getting transportation to Salt Lake City the Soldiers were in a bad fix, as the Governor had forbid his people from selling anything to the Soldiers. After the Soldiers got to Corrine on Box Elder they made a raid on the place and took what they wanted, the raid was made in this way they paid for everything they took, and because of their receiving pay, Brigham had them all cut off from the Church, they were not considered good Mormons, the Soldiers got along first Rate until they got to Ogden, there they got on a regular drunk and seven of them were killed, not in an open fight, but in the dark, when a soldier would be passing he would be shot down or Knocked down and brained. A complaint was made to the Governor about it and he had a few arrested, but that was all that was ever done in the matter.[111]

---

[108]The Bishop variant refers three times to the "Beaver" river.

[109]Here Ann conflates the battle against the Morrisites with Connor's campaign against the Northwestern Shoshones that culminated in the Bear River massacre of 29 January 1863. Her version of the Shoshone taunts is similar to that of an on-the-scene newspaper correspondent, who wrote that "one of the chiefs was galloping up and down the bench in front of his warriors, haranguing them and dangling his spear on which was hung a female scalp in the face of the troops, while many of the warriors sang out: 'Fours right, fours left, Come on, you California sons of b——s.'" *San Francisco Bulletin*, 20 February 1863, quoted in Madsen, *The Shoshoni Frontier and the Bear River Massacre*, 186, 258n45. The Shoshones were overwhelmingly defeated and many women and children slaughtered; Madsen estimates that 250 were killed. Ibid., 192.

[110]The Bishop variant reads "Salt Lake City," page 28.

[111]Connor's victorious troops, much injured by freezing weather and with dozens of wounded, returned south via Franklin (now in Idaho), Logan, Wellsville, Brigham City, and Ogden and were back at Camp Douglas by 4 February. Most white Utahns, including Mormons, praised the attack and gave food, shelter, and medical attention to the soldiers. Madsen, *The Shoshoni Frontier and the Bear River Massacre*, 193–96. Ann again sets events in Corinne before it was founded in 1869.

Brigham Young concluded he would try another scheme to rob the deluded people, he took contracts on the U.P.R.R. and he got his people to do all the work, for which he never paid them if at any time there was anything coming to any of them instead it was paid into the Church as tithing or the emigration fund, poor deluded fools still worked on the R.R. until the Golden Spike was driven,[112] all this time the men were working on the road, the women at home were not idle they were employed in making adobe brick to build adobe houses, they done all the work of the farm such as gathering in the crops, threshing the grain, when the Bishop would come around and take one tenth of everything the people raised even down to the chickens, the women had to spin and weave all the clothes to wear, as they were not permitted to wear what is called Store clothes, those that did not wear home made clothing were cast off from the church.[113]

This Is My Actual Experience

We will now return to the South to a place called Beaver, this is my actual experience from the year of 1861 up to the present time, in the fall of 1861 I worked hard in the harvest field for a man by the name of Walker an Irishman a Protestant, he was a noble good man, his wife was equally as good a women as he was a man, her name was Drusila, she was named after her religion, for She was a Druid in faith, She never had any children of her own, she took one of her twin Sisters children to raise, her Sisters name was Druid, Mary Orcilla Evans was the name of the child they took to raise. Mrs. Walker died, and in about six months after her death Mr. Walker received a letter from Ireland announcing the death of Mrs. Walker's Twin Sister and there is something singularly remarkable about the death as she died the same day and the same hour in Ireland that her Sister died in America.

Mr Walker married again. He married a widow by the name of Mrs Law, she was one of those strong minded woman Law by name and Law by nature. She wanted to start a religion of her own she insisted that there was

[112] The Union Pacific Railroad failed to make good on contracted payments to Young reportedly totaling nearly one million dollars. See Bain, *Empire Express*, 494–500, 532–35, 537, 541–43, 552–53, 659–60; and Arrington, *Great Basin Kingdom*, 265–70.

[113] A reference to tithing, the Mormon practice of contributing 10 percent of one's "increase" to the church and the "cooperative movement" that some Saints practiced in varied fashion from 1868 to 1884; Arrington, *Great Basin Kingdom*, 133–45 and 293–322.

seven Heavens and that they were graded from the lowest to the highest, She was to reign Queen over all, she would not allow Brigham Young not in to the lowest Heaven in fact she would have nothing to do with him at all.[114]

I worked nearly two years for Mr Walker, I never Received any money, but Mr Walker deeded me twenty acres of Land in consideration of the amount due me for my services, on which land was an oil well or Spring, the land at this time was not surveyed by the Goverment, [between lines: "my StepFather took up on Hundred and sixty acres of Land ~~wh~~ for which he got of a Paten for"] and my twenty acres happened to be in that survey. Mr Phillips did not try to beat me out of it, when he died he left it in the will to me with the condition, that my mother was to have her living off the land during her lifetime.

After quiting Mr Walker I went to work for a man by the name of Phillip Baker in the Town of Beaver I worked for him six months at two dollars per week he had no money to pay me, my folks at this time was living on a Lot belonging to Mr Baker, he turned that lot and a year old calf over to my Step Father, in payment for the time I worked for him.[115] I next worked for a woman by the name of Mrs Laud she agreed to pay me a dollar a day for spining two pounds of Wool Rolls a day, I worked for her seven days, She refused to pay me anything, She left some money on the table. Five dollars in Green Backs and, I took it, it was two dollars short of my pay, I took it considering it better that nothing. She went to my Step Father to have him make me give it up, my Step Father told her to pay me and then I would give up the money. She never paid me. . . .

I next went to work for a man by the name of Ashworth[116] my Step Father wanted to take some pigs from him for my services, but Mr Asworth said No he would not allow it, he said the I needed clothes from the skin out and his wife made the clothes for me it was hand made, the first, I Ever wore, She

[114]The 1860 census found Matthew Walker, a fifty-year-old Irish-born silversmith, living with four-year-old Urcilla, born in California. The only adult women recorded in the household are Sarah, age 15, born in England, and Ann Willsher, 37, also born in England. Bureau of the Census, Eighth Census, 1860, Beaver City, Beaver County, Territory of Utah, page 120, lines 24–27.

[115]Philip Baker is on the "Pioneer Honor Roll" in Merkley, ed., *Monuments to Courage*. In 1870 he was listed as a tanner with a wife and three children. Bureau of the Census, Ninth Census of the United States, 1870, Beaver City, Beaver County, Territory of Utah, page 2, line 17.

[116]Perhaps John or William B. Ashworth, a father and son who helped establish a carding plant near Beaver and launched the Beaver Woolen Mills in 1870. See Ashworth, Autobiography, 39, 58; Bradley, *A History of Beaver County*, 89; and Merkley, ed., *Monuments to Courage*, 90, 104.

made two dresses one Linsey and one Wool dress, they got me shoes stockings and a complete outfit for the times and scoiety in which we lived and moved. I worked next for a man by the name of Reed, I worked two months for him at the Rate of two dollars and fifty cents per week, I did not receive any pay for five years afterwards, and then I took my pay in Oats, that being the best I could do, I Received from him thirty bushels of oats for twenty dollars, I sold the Oats for Forty five dollars, I would not have got that were it not for his [brother?] and my school Teatcher who talked him into it. . . .

I . . . went to work for John D. Lee in Washington. Lee had two wives living in Washington.[117] While I was working there he sent for three Soldiers who were working for him at a place called Harmoney, their names were Dick Darling, Billy Forshey and Mat Carney they came down to build a Stone wall around a ten acre Lot, they stayed about three weeks and finished the wall, and went back to Harmoney,[118] Stayed about ten days after they left, for which I Received my pay all Right. There was a Big Ball to be at Mr Lee's House, Mr Lee went to St George and bought me the most beautiful and eligant dress I ever saw it was for me to appear in at the Ball. He got his daughter Lizzie one at the same time.[119] Thy made Lizzie's dress, but her aunt would not make mine, but took and put it in the Fire and burned it up. She was an old wretch. Mr Lee went the next day to St George and got me another dress more costly and beautiful than the former one. . . .

That night after the Ball was over. Mr Lee, his daughter Lizzie and myself immediately started for Harmoney, wher Mr Lee had another wife which was expected every day to be confined. We arived there the next night at about midnight we traveled sixty two miles from day ligh in the morning to midnight, they were not expecting us home that night, and they were having a glorious good time, had a dance and a super, the Table fairly Groaned

[117]Lee built a large stone "mansion" in Washington. Sisters Polly and Lavina Young Lee lived there. See Cleland and Brooks, eds., *A Mormon Chronicle*, 2:3. Larson says Polly and Terressa Morse lived in the "mansion." Larson, *Red Hills of November*, 25–27.

[118]Brooks describes Lee building a "stone fence" in Washington with "a crew of men" in the winter 1859–60. See Brooks, *John Doyle Lee*, 257. "Billy Forsha" appears once, giving a work reference to another man, in Cleland and Brooks, eds., *A Mormon Chronicle*, 3, 10 August 1871, 2:173. For Dick Darling, see note 120 below.

[119]Presumably Elizabeth, John's daughter with Mary Vance (Polly), born in Parowan in 1851. See Brooks, *John Doyle Lee*, 166, 382. Lee often hosted dances and other parties. See, for example, the dances on New Year's day and 4 January 1861, which Ann may have attended. Cleland and Brooks, eds., *A Mormon Chronicle*, 1 January, 6 January 1861, 1:289–90; Larson, *Red Hills of November*, 280–81; Larson, *"I Was Called to Dixie,"* 457–76; and Wilson, "Folklore of Dixie," 12–13.

with the luxaries of the Land, everything went off pleasantly. Dick Darling one of the Gentiles Soldiers was a good Fidler, and played for the party, he became facinated with one of John D Lee's daughters, by the name of Nancey, it appears that his attentions were highly appreciated, and his affections was most fully Reciprocated. In about six weeks he was married to Miss Nancy, but he had to Join the Church and be baptised before he could get Miss Nancy, Dick went through the firey Ordeal and got his girl, he lived with her from April 15th to May 15th and then skippet the Country.[120] The other boys baptised at the same time was Mat Carney, Billy Forshay and Charley St Clair.[121] Billy Forshay married a cousin of Miss Nancey. She was a splendid young Lady, he lived with his wife twenty seven years and hung himself at last, he had six children who were deaf and dumb all but one, it is supposed that he worried over the affliction and misfortune of his children that it caused him to take his own life. His oldest Child a girl, was very Beautiful and briliant and was not afflicted as the other Children, she was seven years old, when her father one day found her dead body on the Road side, a short distance from the house, someone had murdered the child no one ever found out who done the dasterdly deed.

Mat Carney one of the soldiers stayed there nearly a year after Dick got married. But got into a little trouble with one of the woman. It was Reported that he had left and gone to Salt Lake City. He was gone about five days, I was hunting for my Cow as she had strayed away, I went by an old Cave in the neighborhood, and in passing this cave I heard a groan, and went in to see what could it mean, there I found Mat Carney the soldier, laying on his back bound and gaged. I unbound him and let him loose, he was very weak from hunger and exposure. I told him to stay there until I came back and

[120]No known record of a marriage between Nancy Emily Lee and Dick Darling survives, but a letter from "Bosco," George A. Hicks, tells of "Dick Darling, or Rattlesnake Dick," a "discharged 'bummer' from Camp Douglas" who worked for John D. Lee and married Nancy but left her months later ("Lee's Eccentricities," *Salt Lake Tribune*, 10 January 1875, 4/4). In 1868 "Richard Darling" was cut off from the LDS church "for unfaithful conduct." "Conference of the Southern Mission," Journal History, 1–3 May 1868. George A. Hicks claims that Lee's wives confessed to sex with Darling (see the chapter on Hicks herein for this, as well as Darling's later criminal career).

[121]Lee hired Union veteran Charles St. Clair to teach his children at Harmony. When St. Clair fell ill, Lee laid on hands and prayed for him "though not Baptised." Lee left him in charge of the farm while he traveled to Salt Lake but, upon his return, found that St. Clair had "turnd to drinking." Lee paid him off and fired him. Cleland and Brooks, eds., *A Mormon Chronicle*, 28 March 1867, 8 December 1867, 2:61, 93. Ann may be referring to "St. Clair Forsha," whom John D. Lee baptized on the day he rebaptized Ann Gordge, 26 March 1865. New Harmony Ward Record, 192.

I would bring him something to eat, but I dare not come until dark, when it became dark, I took him a supply to eat, and a bottle of Whiskey, and I gave him five dollars in Green Backs, he left that or on the following night, and one of the finest horses in the stable was gone, but the Horse afterwards Returned back to the Range, I did not hear anything from him for fifteen years, when one day I Received a letter containing forty Dollars no writing in the letter Simply signed Mat, I think the letter came from Port Diamond Montana. While he was in the Cave bound and gaged, the parties that put him there called to see how he was getting along, he always pretended to be almost dead, Just able to breath with the gags still in his mouth. The second day after I let him loose he was gone, and the parties that put him there missed him right away, they called a meeting and examined, all the women as to what they knew about this man Mat until they came to me. I asked what they wanted. The told me they wanted to Know something about Mat. I told them I Knew nothing about him, that I heard them say that he was gone to Salt Lake City and that I supposed he was, he was bound and gaged because he was to familiar with Rachell one of John D. Lee's wives. He was gaged by two of John D. Lee's sons. Joseph and Alma Lee. This Joseph Lee married his first cousin they had seven children none of whom could walk they were all cripples from birth. Joseph was called to go on a mission to Europe, he went Lancaster England there he did not succeed, his health broke down completely, so he was compelled to come home, he brought two English women with him home. When they got to Salt Lake City, the women saw men vastly superior in general apperence and money, so Mr Joseph Lee was Ruled out in the Cold. He afterwards married his two Sisters in Law, his first wifes sisters, they had no children fortunately.

My Step Father Mr Phillips bought about thirty head of sheep from John D. Lee, for which Mr Lee was to take a mule in part payment for the sheep, but Mr Lee concluded he did not want the mule at this time I was eleven years old and was very tall for my age and considered good looking. Mr Lee would not take the mule, but said to Mr Phillips that he would let him Know in a couple of years what he wanted for the sheep. I was working for Caroline, one of Lee's wives his third at that time. I was working there when the two years was up. I was then thirteen years old when Mr J.D. Lee wrote to my Step Father and told him that he wanted me in liquadition of his indebtness to him for the sheep. My Mother fought against it, with all the power she had, when we were made of understand that if he did not yeald to the arrangements, we would both be murdered, that the Knife would be brought unto Requisition. Mother would not consent. But I consented, to save my Mothers life.

After I consented he took his first wife and myself to Salt Lake City, May the first 1862 to go through the Endowment house,[122] we started from home Kanob was the first place we stoped at, we stayed in there three days we went from there to Cedar City we stoped there overnight. Mr Lee preached there that night, the next morning we went to Parawan we stayed with a man by the name of Deckor. Mrs Deckor had been one of John D Lee's wives in the State of Illinois, before they left that state she was his second wife.[123] The next day we went Elkhorn Springs, the next day to Indian Creek; We passed through Beaver. My Mother lived in Beaver but Mr Lee would not let me go to see Mother, but he went to see her. He had a wagon and he persuaded her to come out to Indian Creek, they went back next morning in an other wagon She and my brother came out they stayed all night, before they started by brother eleven years old[124] stood up and said John D. Lee you are a Son of B. You are taking my Sister against her will, and you will Rue the day you ever done So dasterdly an act, of that be assured. After this we went to Wild Cat canyon where we stayed two or three hours, We stayed with Isaac Ripple,[125] he said to Lee you are doing a great wrong, you are taking a girl that dose not want you and the Mother is bitterly opposed to you and you

---

[122]Gordge and Lee's marriage date is elusive. No Lee diaries survive from 4 June 1861 to 22 May 1866. Cleland and Brooks, eds., *A Mormon Chronicle*, 2: 9. Lee's "Confessions" claim "the last wife I got was Ann Gordge. Brigham Young gave her to me, and I was sealed to her in Salt Lake by Heber C. Kimball. This was my nineteenth, . . . After 1861 I never asked Brigham Young for another wife." Bishop, *Mormonism Unveiled*, 289. George A. Hicks claimed Lee received a "recommend" for another wife in 1867. "After 1861" suggests a sealing date in line with Ann's claim of spring 1862, but no other evidence confirms a date this early. Lee's family genealogy lists his sealing to Ann Gordge in the Endowment House on 10 June 1865; she "Miscaried with a Daughter March 11th, 1866, about [5 or 6?] months along." Lee, Papers. Her first mention in Lee's diary is "Ann my last wife has been dropping corn & other Seeds." Lee, Papers, diary 3, 24 May 1866, 11. Gordge later refers to "the whole of the six years that I was there," which is in line with Lee's recording of a marriage that lasted from 1865 until he records her leaving Harmony in 1871. Ann's account of the trip north follows the territorial wagon road to Great Salt Lake City. See Lee's description of a similar trip in 1867 in Cleland and Brooks, eds., *A Mormon Chronicle*, 26 April to 13 May 1867, 2:67–71; and "The Utah of John D. Lee," map in Brooks, *John Doyle Lee*, 152.

[123]Nancy Bean married Lee in 1845 in Nauvoo; they had one child. She later married Zachariah Decker. See Brooks, *John Doyle Lee*, 379.

[124]Ann's brother David was born in 1851, so he would be eleven years old in 1862. See Cleland and Brooks, eds., *A Mormon Chronicle*, 2:250–51n25; Newton, *Southern Cross Saints*, 25.

[125]Isaac Riddle was an Iron Mission veteran. See "Isaac Riddle Tells his Story" in Carter, ed., *Our Pioneer Heritage*, 11:169–81; Brooks, *Journal of the Southern Indian Mission*, 2; and the "Pioneer Honor Roll" in Merkley, *Monuments to Courage*.

will Repent the day and wish that she had never been born. We then went to Cove Creek, We stayed with the Weldons[126] that night, the next morning we went to dog Valley, there we met the Bishop of Beaver, John R. Murdock. ~~The~~ Bishop said to Lee you are stealing one of my girls, Lee answered I am going to take her so Keep your mouth shut, they had a few words after which, Lee took a two gallon Jug out of the wagon and asked the Bishop to take a drink, the Bishop Replied that he did not drink with a Murderer. Lee Replied. the Kettle must not call the pot Black, and then they took a big drink, in fact four or five on the discovering of each others characters. . . .

Sims Matheny Bishop of Filmore[127] . . . had Just got himself a Bran new wife of the Latest improved fashion, the Bishop's first wife, a very elegant old Lady was [Rouded?] out by her Noble Lord and Bishop and moved out of the little house she lived in, unto a Wagon Box, to Root Hog or Die, on or about the fifteenth of May, the great soldier Dick Darling made his apperance in the neighborhood and like Galarat Soldier stole the Bishop's wife, and as his hand was in the Business, and a man with a great amount of pluck and enterprise, he concluded he would not stop with the Raid on the Bishop and continued his deperdation on the women generally, he stole Bartholomew's wife and Hunters and [scooped?] down on poor William Walsey and stole his wife. She leaving behind an infant baby in Bed for Wolsey to amuse himself with, until the Return of Sister Wolsey She Returned in a about a year afterwards. . . .

We went to Rockwells Place. He was one of the destroying Angels. Mr Rockwell had his house built on a Point of the Mountain, called Point of West Mountain underneath his house was a subterranean passage about fifteen miles long in which were shafts or wells sunk at diferent points, where many a poor man has been lured to his death in this Tunnel or passage. If appears from the number of people missing and never heard of afterwards, that the place was purposely arranged for the Business of murder and plunder. . . .[128]

---

[126]Built in 1867 in Cove Valley, about halfway between Beaver and Fillmore, Cove Fort served as a common stop for travelers. Bradley, *A History of Beaver County*, 71. Charles Willden was an early settler. Merkley, *Monuments to Courage*, 128–29.

[127]Lee's friend Sims Matheny was reportedly at Mountain Meadows. See Cleland and Brooks, eds., *A Mormon Chronicle*, 2:30 January–7 February 1867, 47–50. A warrant was issued for Matheny's arrest, but Walker, Turley, and Leonard could not confirm his participation. *Massacre at Mountain Meadows*, 393n2.

[128]An original Danite, Orrin Porter Rockwell was a bodyguard for Joseph Smith and Brigham Young. Some contemporaries credit him with dozens of murders (or, alternatively, justified killings of enemies of the LDS church). A founding member of the Council of Fifty, Rockwell was a friend of Lee and William Hickman. Quinn, *The Mormon Hierarchy: Extensions of Power*, 242. Rockwell operated the Hot Springs Brewery Hotel and stage station from 1858 or 1859 until late 1866 at the Point of the Mountain in southern Salt Lake Valley. See Schindler, *Orrin Porter Rockwell*; for his house, 9, 291, 342.

On the 9th we went to the City. We stayed with a family by the name of Heywood, we got in about 10 oclock in the morning after we got in Mr. Lee said to me you had better go down town and get what you want I went and dressed. Mrs. Haywood and myself went down to make my purchases. John D Lee wanted me to buy some dresses or presents for his other wives. But I would do nothing of the Kind. Mrs. Haywood told me that I would need things for house Keeping, and that I had better spend my money in fixing up comfortable. I bought a stove for thirty five dollars and a general House Keeping outfit. After I got through my purchases I had Just sixteen dollars left. With that I bought my mother a couple of dresses. After I got through with everything, I had nine dollars left. Mr John D Lee told me to say nothing of the amount of money he had, as he did not went to pay his Thithing as they had got enough out of him. The Church had spoken to the people at the Bank and found out the amount. When Lee went to get the Check Cashed they came in for the Thithing and Lee was compeled to tell a Lie and said the money did not belong to him, but belonged to another man.

Saturday morning we fixed to go to the Endowment House, we had to take a bath and wash clean all over and put on pure white clean clothes, about half past eight oclock we started from Mrs Haywood's for the Endowment house after we got there, we went unto a Room a long low dark Room, on each side of the Room near the wall were benches for seating purposes the center of the Room was vacant, the Room being oblong on the West End of the Room was erected a large high Desk and a man siting at the Desk Recording the names of the women and the men, the womens names were taking first than the men A. O Spencer was Church Recorder, after we got through Recording our names we went into another Room, we had to pass into this by a narrow Curtin, the men passing the curtain on the Right, and the women on the left, there was a curtian drawn through the Centere of the Room, from one end of the Room to the other, this Curtain went through the center of the Room and Reached within eighteen inches of the Walls, at each end of the curtains there was fixed Bath Tabs. After everything was arranged all the parties Striped starked naked, as naked as when they were born, the men on one side of the Curtain and the women on the other, after which our Clothes was tied up in separate Bundles and taken up stairs unto another Room, we were then introduced to the Bath Tubs. There were three women who had charge of the Bath Tubs on the female side of the Curtain, Mrs E. R Snow, Emiline Wells, and Hyram Smith's wife those ladies were of very high standing in the Mormon Church. Mrs Snow was high Priestess, Prophetess Poietess,[129] they washed us there after which they anointed us with sweet oil, after which they gave each of us a new name, my name was to be Elizabeth and all the other women were named the same. We then were put in the Garments called the Combination Garment. This Garment is marked on the Right Side with a Square on the left side with a heart accros the brest and Rent accross the bowels, indicating the penallity of an oath which will be more fully explained here after, the mark accross the Knee, was to Remind you when you Kneeled down to pray you must curse the Gentiles and the Goverment.

After we put on our Garments or Combination suit or skirt, we were required to put over this a Robe, three yards long, two widths of linen, put on the right shoulder and crossed to the left; something after the manner of the ancient Roman stile, the feet were dressed in white Stockings and white Slippers made of white bleached muslin, the head dress was a cap, hat or bonnet made of white Swiss Muslin lightly made so that the front of the head dress fell over the face acting as a veil. After we were dressed in this style or costume, they opened another room or door and passed into the Garden of Eden. There was a man and a women placed there to represent Adam and Eve: the one representing Adam was Daniel H. Wells[130] and the one representing Eve, was Mrs. Snow. This place was the most beautiful place I ever saw, there was painted on the walls and sealing all Kinds of animals, Birds and serpents and in fact everything that was supposed to be in the Garden of Eden, on one side was painted the Tree of life, and all around was painted beautiful Streams where all Kinds of Cattle and animals were supposed to quench their thirst. Everything was so beautifully gotten up that it was almost beyond my powers to explain.

After we had been in there a few minutes, Ellowean[131] came in and gave his orders to eat of all the fruit in the Garden, but the Tree of Knowledge, but of that tree they should not eat, least they should be cursed and banished and driven hence from the Garden of Eden. Ellowean left, after which his most Prescious Excellency the Devil made his appearance. This gentleman

[129]Eliza Roxcy Snow married Joseph Smith, Jr., then Brigham Young; she was widely considered the leading woman in Utah. Emmeline B. Wells was a leader in the Relief Society, longtime editor of the *Woman's Exponent*, a suffragist, and the (unhappy) plural wife of Daniel H. Wells. See Beecher, "Eliza R. Snow," 25–41, and Dushku, "Feminists," 177–97. Hyrum Smith was killed at Carthage with his brother Joseph; some of his wives remarried and came to Utah. Poll et al., eds., *Utah's History*, 109; Cook, *Nauvoo Marriages, Proxy Sealings*, 3–5.

[130]Daniel H. Wells was Brigham Young's second counselor, commander of the Nauvoo Legion, and mayor of Salt Lake from 1866 to 1874. Alexander and Allen, *Mormons and Gentiles*, 49, 91, 93, 95, 107.

[131]Evidently Elohim, a Hebrew name for God or gods. The BYU variant reads "the Lord," pages 50–51.

was dressed for the occasion, with a large red velvet cap with a large red velvet Tassel, black velvet Coat with blood red Buttons, red velvet Knee britches, red Silk Stockings, red Shoes made Something like turned up behind and before. The Tail was a long back Tail ending the shape of an Anchor and Spear, his hands and face were black giving him the appearance of having come from a very hot and Smutty country, with large feirce red eyes, he came two three times, he was very polite and moved around with exceeding gracefullness ~~was indeed the Adonas~~ he was the admiration of Mother Eve, and she asked Adam who was that most elegant gentleman. She became perfectly infatuated with his beautiful appearance, he made love to her to her exellency the Queen of Eden, and he flirted with her and charmed her so that he had her perfectly under his control, he went out and came back again with a large bunch of raisins in his hands, he walked up to the Tree of Knowledge and acted as though he was picking the fruit from off of the tree, he picked one off and gave it to Eve to eat, and she did eat and liked it, he picked an other and gave it to her and she gave it to Adam and he did eat thereof, and they then for the first time discovered their nakedness.

After they discovered their nakedness they went and hid themselves, and the Lord came in the person of Heber C. Kimble and called Adam, Adam where art though, and Adam answered Ellowean we are here, we are here, and naked and dare not show ourselves. Ellowean then showed them how to make aprons for themselves out of Fig leaves, the apron used in the Church is about one foot square, made out of white muslin and green Silk with imitation Fig leaves worked in the center and one in each corner making five leaves in all. Adam came around among the men and put an apron on each one, and Eve done the same office with women. The veil drawn over their faces, they are then driven out of the Garden of Eden into utter darkness, to earn their bread by the sweat of their brow. The room that they were driven into was completely bare with no furniture except a few common benches, this room is where we took the oath against the Goverment and avenge the blood of Joseph Smith; this oath was taken under drawn swords.[132] At the

[132]Often called the Oath of Vengeance, this vow evolved over time. Henry Lawrence, who had administered sacraments in the Endowment House from 1865 to 1869 before joining the Godbeite protest movement, testified that the "substance" of the vow was: "You each and all agree to avenge the blood of the prophets, Joseph and Hyrum, who have sealed their testimony with their blood, this you will teach this to your children and your children's children to the third and fourth generations." *Salt Lake Tribune,* 22 November 1889, 4/2. The pledge apparently was modified when the ceremony was first written down in 1876. Testimony given at the 1904 U.S. Senate reported the vow was then, "I will pray, and never cease to pray, and never cease to importune high heaven to avenge the blood of the Prophets on this nation." Buerger, *The Mysteries of Godliness,* 139–40. The oath was removed from the ceremony in 1927.

same time all the passwords, signs and grips were communecated to us and we were instructed as to the meaning of the marks on the garment, and what they called for, the mark across the bowels means that you would Suffer yourself to be disemboweled rather than reveal any sign, grip or password or anything you saw or heard in the Temple, and the mark on the left side over the heart meant to avenge the blood of Joseph Smith on the Gentiles either by fair or foul means, or have your heart taken out while yet alive, this oath was taken under a drawn Sword, the mark on the right side indicated that you had to work for your living and be industrious and faithful and prompt in paying your Tithes to the Church. The mark on the Knee indicated prayer and curses on the Goverment of the United States.[133]

We were ushered into another room up Stairs. This room up Stairs represented the grave, it is a large room with a curtain drawn across the middle of the room, the marks on the garment are also on this curtain. You touch the man on the other side on the Knee through the curtain with your Knee, then through the right hand holding the curtain he gives you the grip, and he asks what is your annointed name, you tell him, and he will tell you to raise your veil and come, then you go through on the other side, across the veil or curtain into what is called the sealing room or where you get married. In this room there is an alter something in the shape of a Coffin upholstered with red velvet, on each side are low benches upholstered in the same manner, these benches are for the purpose of Kneeling on, here you have to Kneel down when the marage ceremony is performed, there is a man on the left hand side of the alter and a women on the right hand side and Heber C. Kimbal, Brigham Young's first councelor and one of the Twelve Appostals and the man deligated to perform the marage ceremony, performed the ceremony, the ceremony is very short. He simply asks the man if he takes this woman to be his wife, and he answers yes, that ends the ceremony.[134] The women is regarded as a cipher

[133]In November 1889 a federal judge in Salt Lake City held hearings on naturalizing Mormon immigrants and heard conflicting testimony from excommunicated Mormons about whether they were made to swear oaths against the federal government. Henry Lawrence affirmed the disloyal content of the oaths; some supported him, while others denied so swearing. These hearings added to the pressure on the LDS church that resulted in the Manifesto of the Apostles disavowing blood atonement and the Woodruff Manifesto counseling against plural marriage. See Alexander, *Things in Heaven and Earth*, 254–70; Baskin, *Reminiscences of Early Utah*, 89–98.

[134]Ann's description of the Endowment House ceremony agrees in many respects with some other dissidents' versions, including John Hyde, Jr., who claimed to undergo the sealing ceremony in 1854 with E.R. Snow as Eve and W.W. Phelps as the devil. Hyde, *Mormonism*, 90–100. John Ahmanson saw the same cast; Ahmanson, *Secret History*, 133–40. For women's versions, see Stenhouse, *"Tell It All,"* 358–69; Green, *Fifteen Years Among the Mormons*, 41–49; and Young, *Wife No. 19*, 355–72.

in the contract and is asked no questions at all and is taken for granted that she must take the man for her husband wheather she likes it or not, on the principal I suppose that she ought to feel proud to get a husband under any circumstances. After we were married Mr. Kimbal Said to Mr Lee we will all rue the day you brought this women into this house, Mr Lee answering said she was young, and would in the course of time learn diferent and make a good and faithful member of the Church. Mr. Kimbal answered Mr. Lee and said, she is not at heart a Mormon or a member of the Church and never will be, you and I may not live to see it but there are others that will.

After they got through talking, I went into another room, called a dressing room for ladies and there I dressed in my former dress, the one I first appeared in at the Endowment House. Mr. Lee went into another room, called a dressing room for gentlemen where he changed, and put on the clothing he first appeared in at the Endowment House, there were some twenty couples to be married and we had to stay until all were married. On this occasion there were two young ladies present without escorts one of whom was very beautiful equal to that of Queen Mary, Queen of Scotts, the other was the most homely person you could imagine, very unattractive.

Heber Kimbal took the beautiful one into an adjoining room to talk to her as he said, he stayed with her about fifteen minutes and came out, this was repeated by nine other different persons after they were all through with their brutal conduct, the girl appeared in the door and fell dead from loss of blood, after she fell, the incarnate Devil of a Kimbal, looked with the cool indeference of a brute and said put her away and She was droped down into a hole through a trap door made for the purpose, where many a person had gone before her. She was an English Girl with a widowed mother, she had not been in the country over six months. The man representing the Devil at the Endowment was one by the name of Phelps, made the remark, what will I do with the mother, and he was answered that they would silence her which was promptly done. . . .

We . . . went to Willow Creek, Mr. Rockwells place and stayed there over night, there were two young men came in after dark, and they got up a game of cards; they all had money, the two young men had about fourteen hundred dollars. Each had a fine Team, they belonged to the Goverment, they were on their way to Camp Floyd,[135] they played cards until twelve

[135]Camp Floyd, later Fort Crittenden, was closed in 1861, before Ann claims she married Lee; perhaps she means Camp Douglas, established on the east bench of Great Salt Lake City in October 1862.

o'clock. Mr. Rockwell appeared to be the looser in the game, about Seven hundred dollars, and he accused Mr. Lee of cheating. Mr. Lee indignantly denied cheating, he then accused the two young men of cheating. Mr. Lee sided with the young men and said they did not cheat, and Mr. Rockwell said we will see, after which they went to bed. In the morning we got and breakfasted about half past five. Mr. Lee asked where the young men were, Mr. Rockwell said they were in bed and did not want to eat before ten. Mr. Lee hitched up his teams and left. I drove one of the teams, we never heard anything more of the young men until about a year afterwards when the Colonel wrote to a Soldier in the neighborhood by the name of Mat Carney; inquiring about them. This Soldier inquired of Mr. Lee about them Mr. Lee said he had seen two such men but he could not tell where. Mr. Lee told me to say nothing about where we had seen the men, and by all means to give nothing away. . . .

We went to a place called Alkli, we stayed over night. While here Brigham Young had a tragedy performed for our benifit by having Lot Hamilton, Charles Chase and George Hancock put to death for horse stealing.[136] While we were there, an old man came along by the name of Miller, he was generally Known by the name of Bogus Brigham,[137] he came up from his place to see about getting a young Girl For his wife he had his eye on one for some time, but he was Just a little to late, She had already married an apostate Mormon, he went to see the Girls Father about the matter, the Father told Mr. Miller that his children were not poligmous children, and he did not intend they should be. This remark was his death warrant. . . .

Mrs. Lee[138] was whining around for Tea. She asked me if I had any, I told her I had some for my mother. I told her if I had some cream I could make a good cup of coffee, at the Same time a Mormon woman came along with cream for sale, Mrs Lee bought the cream and I made her a royal cup of coffee, for which she never forgot me, After breakfast we went to Mr. Daltons, Mrs. Lees son in law,[139] we stayed there three or four days picking

[136]Possibly a reference to a group of horse thieves including one Lot Huntington of whom Lee wrote, although well before he married Ann. See Cleland and Brooks, eds., *A Mormon Chronicle*, 12 November 1859, 1:222–23.

[137]William Miller impersonated Brigham Young in Carthage to help Young escape arrest for counterfeiting. See Young, 23 July 1871, *Journal of Discourses*, 14:218–22. He settled in Springville and became president of Utah Stake. Brooks, ed., *On the Mormon Frontier*, 99n53.

[138]Aggatha Ann Woolsey Lee.

[139]Charles W. Dalton married Aggatha's daughter Sarah Jane; they lived in Beaver. See Brooks, *John Doyle Lee*, 379.

wool and washing. While there Dick Darling came along in the neighborhood stoping at Dr. Arnolds, he did not show up at the Daltons Ranch, this Dick Darling and two other Darlings ordered dinner, after they got dinner Darling told them to charge to John D. Lee and left and went to the city of Salt Lake. This Dick Darling was a Soldier, and was out on a short furlow, on his return to the city he stole one of the finest horses in the country from John D. Lee and gave the horse to Gel. Conner. The reader will remember that this Dick Darling was Lee's son-in law, in whom Mr. Lee had implicit confidence. Lee left Darling in charge of everything at a place called Harmony, while he was absent in the city, Darling stole fifty fine cows and sold the cows to a man by the name of Bob Patterson and pocketed the money. His wife (Lee's daughter) asked him what he was agoing to do with the money and he told her it was none of her business he left the house and went north to where the troops were located in Salt Lake. That was the last we heard of him until the month of August following, we did not see him personally, but he left a note that he was in the neighborhood and he got away with ten head of horses, the best in the place, he would have none but the best. . . .[140]

We took an early start and went to Wild Cat Canyon, where Isaac Riddle lived, we stayed there until about three o'clock in the afternoon, there I met a girl I used to Know in California, and she gave me Fitzs for marrying John D. Lee. I told her not to be alarmed, that I would make dollars and cents out of them before I got through with them, of that she could rest assured, . . . We next went to Indian Creek, we Stayed all night got up early Sunday morning and went to Beaver. We had breakfast at my mothers house, we stayed there that day, Mr. Lee preached there three times that day. The next morning we went to the River, about half a mile from Town, where we washed wool all day, we got through about four o'clock in the afternoon. We came back to town and had supper at Mothers. Mr. Lee and Mrs. Lee No. 1 went three miles up to Ashworths Carding Woolen Mill to have the wool carded into rolls, I stayed at Mothers all night and done some washing, my mother helped me. I unpacked some of my things and gave Mother the things I bought for her, the next night Tuesday they came down from the woolen mill, we eat supper at Mother's, after supper, I said Mr. Lee did you do with my rolls as I told you to do, and he said I did as far as I could.

[140]John D. Lee noted only that he got twenty-five dollars from a man in Provo for a horse that Dick Darling stole from Lee and sold to the Provo man. Cleland and Brooks, eds., *A Mormon Chronicle*, 11 May 1867, 2:71.

Why did you not do as I told you, he said Mrs. Lee wanted the gray wool, I told him I wanted the gray myself, and that I would have it, and I got it and gave half to my mother, which made Mrs. Lee furiously angry.

We left Mothers house for Harmoney, we crossed the River about two miles, we stoped at a little Town called Jacksonville to buy some vegitables, Mrs. Lee wanted me to give her everything I had in the wagon and not go any farther, and walk back to my Mothers house and stay there. John D. Lee came back to the wagon and asked me if I had any money and I told him I had, and I said Mr. Lee do you Know what Mrs. Lee wants me to do, he said no, she wants me to give her everything in the wagon and walk back to Mothers and stay there. Mr. John D. Lee became furious and classically speaking gave the old lady Hell, so she had no more to say on the subject....

While in Cedar, Mr. Lee met two of his wives Rachel and Emma they had a wagon and were eloping with two gentiles, on their way to God's Country, Mr. Lee's appearance put a stop to their progress and they turned and went with us. We left Cedar at dark for Canara[141] about twelve miles. We camped there that night, the horses gave out and we had to stop. During the night there were two men came down from the mountains and camped with us, they brought with them a man that was crushed to death, they said by falling Timbers. But come to find out, the man was murdered for his wife. She was married in two weeks afterwards to the Bishop; and in about six weeks after that, the Bishop cut her throat because she would not let him have her daughter, the daughter would not have him, arrangements were being made to put her out of the way but she was informed of what was going on by her younger brother. She braced herself up for the occasion and murdered the Bishop herself and put him out of the way, so you can see it was dimond cut dimond, she afterwards became insane.

Next morning we had quite a racket, Rachel and Emma Mr. Lee's wives No. 9 and No. 18 wanted to go through my wagon and take what they wanted. I told them they were not big enough; Mr. Lee said they should not go near my wagon, they wanted to Know from him where their share of the rolls of wool were, he told them they would get their share in time, they then wanted their share of the dishes and other goods that I had bought for myself. Mr. Lee told them they could not have anything in the wagon. If they wanted anything of the Kind they could go and get it as I had done,

[141] Cedar City and Kanarraville.

that answer raised the Devil, the result was I was in perfect Hell the whole of the six years that I was there, unless they hapened to want a favor, and then they were as good as Pie.[142]

After we got through quarreling we went on to the Town of Canara, where lived one of Mr. Lee's wives Mary Leah. Mary and her two sisters went to work and got up a very fine dinner, in the meantime Mr. Lee told me to drive my wagon into Mr. Groves[143] yard to prevent the other women from getting in it, when dinner was ready I was no where to be found, I went to Mr. Grove's and stayed, I took from my wagon some nice Nic Nacs and a few luxories I had bought in the City, we had fried chicken and with what I had bought. Mrs. Groves and her daughter Lucy and myself had a first class dinner in every respect.

After dinner Mr. Lee sent his son in charge of the wagon with three of his wives, wife No. 1, wife No 9 Rachel and Emma No 18 with positive instructions to disturb nothing in the wagon until he returned which he did not do for three days. When he did return, he found the wagon robbed of all its contents, nothing left to tell the Tale, he was somewhat astonished to find that the wagon was not gone; the wives commenced Kicking and quarling about my having so much wool, as I had no family, I did not need it. Mr. Lee asked his son Wilard[144] if he had cleaned the house as he told him, Wilard answered and said he had not touched the ~~dammed~~ darned house, this house was to be fixed up for my residence, with the assistance of Mr Lee's son and nephew I cleaned up the house and got everything in good and comfortable shape. That night his wife Caroline called to see me, and wanted to Know if she could help me. I told her no, but if she would she might make a fire put on the Tea Kettle and make some biscuits and we would have a cup of tea, and she said she would send and get a chicken. She got the chicken and a large cup of cream, we got the supper, and Just as we were about to sit down there was a rap at the door, I went to see who was there and it was Rachel and her sister Mrs. Lee, and wanted to Know how I was getting along. I told her I was not near fixed up yet, but was approximating towards it, she wanted

[142]Ronald W. Walker noted that sharing of food and furnishings among settlers was common and often necessary. See Walker, "Golden Memories," 50–53.

[143]Elisha H. Groves, co-founder with John D. Lee of Harmony in 1850. Lee married Groves's daughter Mary Leah. Cleland and Brooks, eds., *A Mormon Chronicle*, 1: passim; 3, 5 August 1866, 25; 2:249n14; Brooks, *John Doyle Lee*, 383; and Alder and Brooks, *A History of Washington County*, 16–18.

[144]John Willard Lee, a son of John D. and Aggatha Ann, a teenager at the time. Brooks, *John Doyle Lee*, 379.

Rachel to see my dishes. Mr. John D. Lee bought each of his wives a set of China Tea cups and saucers, half dozen each of China plates, the next day he divided the China ware between his wives, he hunted up the wool rolls and weighed them and divided the wool equally between his wives. My share of the wool I turned over to his wife Caroline (she had eleven children) she needed it worse than any of the others the wool I made a present to Caroline, she made me a present of six geese, Two dozen of chickens and a good milk Cow, and Mr. Lee gave me six more, making seven altogether in all. I had my own Garden and everything in that way that I needed.

After I got settled down, I went to work to divide my wool rolls to get them in shape for working, spinning and weaving. I spun my wool and weaved it into cloth, after which I went to work for Mrs. Margaret Pace,[145] I spun and weaved for her one hundred and sixty pounds, for which she paid me seventy five dollars. . . .

Rachel flamed up and was about to elope with a fellow by the name of Mat. Carney, this was Mat's second attemped in which he failed, it went very near costing him his life. Mr. Lee called a meeting on account of his wives having a devil of a big row among themselves, he called all together, women and children and he prayed and talked, it was something like a class meeting, he asked them one after another to get up and ask each others forgiveness for what they had done, and that would pray for each other, he went through with all the women and children, and made them confess whatever they had done, the women wheather they had at any time had intercourse with a gentile, and who the gentile was it was this Kind of confession that got Mat. Carney into trouble. He went through with everyone until he came to me, he asked me to get up and confess, I told him I had nothing to confess, and got up and left the room, . . .

Mr. Lee asked his wife Emma to Kill some chickens and get dinner, She said why don't you go to the other house and get dinner (meaning my place). She has hams and everything else to get up a first class dinner, and he said he would not do it, that he would not speak to that woman again for three months, and he Kept his word, . . .

The next Spring there were extensive preparations made to put in the largest crop of everything they ever raised, and they got it in all right and

[145]There were at least two "Margaret Paces" around Harmony: Margaret N. Pace, who married John Imlay, and William Pace's wife. See "New Harmony Ward Record," 282, 358. Lee, Papers, diary 3, 26 August 1866, 27.

everything looked favorable for an emence crop, when the Grass hopers came along and cleaned up everything distroyed everything that was planted except the Potatoe crop, which for Some reason they did not toutch, and the Peas they did not eat.[146]

This Season Mr. Lee's first wife died Agatha Ann[147] Mr. Lee took her death very hard, and he made a big effort to get three more wives to console him, but the lades to whom he applied respectfully declined. He took them to the city, he bought dresses of fine fabric, and other presents. They would lay on the bed with him and fondle on him, but would not marrie him, when they got to Salt Lake City the three women gave him the slip, and all three women married gentiles, his wife Rachel was with him this time, Mr. Lee's wife Emma had a sister to come over from England, she had five children, She left her husband in England because she could not live with him. She came in the fall, after she came her sister Emma had Twins girls which was considered a great event in the family.[148]

When the twins were eight months old, he took their mother Emma to the city, Emma was to intercede with her sister for Mr. Lee, which she would do in both their presence with great eloquence, but when Lee's back was turned Emma would Scortch him, burn him up to her sister for everything she could think of. She said she would not marry him then, but she let her three oldest children two boys and a girl, go home with him, if the place suited them, all right she would go, but if it did not suit her children she would not go. The children went down to see how they would like the place, the oldest boy and girl liked the place, but the youngest did not like it. John D. Lee went to the city again in the fall, and he took his wife Rachel with him and also the three children.[149]

While on the road to the city, he picked up three other young women on whom he spent considerable money. He was taking them to the city to

[146]Lee, who was a careful farmer, does not note any grasshoppers in 1866, but bad weather did harm his crops. See Cleland and Brooks, eds., *A Mormon Chronicle*, 3, 29 August 1866, 2:28.

[147]Ann was with Lee and five of his other wives at Aggatha's deathbed. See Lee, Papers, diary 3, 24 May–3 June 1866, 11–16; Brooks, *John Doyle Lee*, 274–75.

[148]On 22 July 1866 Emma gave birth to and named one of her twin girls "Ann Eliza" in honor of her sister-wife. See New Harmony Ward Record, 280; and Brooks, *John Doyle Lee*, 277. Two years later Lee built them a house at New Harmony to replace their leaky cabin. Brooks says that Lee reportedly considered marrying two more women in fall 1866, but "the girls were so giddy and giggling, so irresponsible and silly" that he decided against it; perhaps this relates to the 1867 recommend that George A. Hicks claimed Lee received. Brooks, *John Doyle Lee*, 279–80.

[149]Emma's sister Fanny Gilbert was a widow with three children; the latter spent summer 1867 with Emma (and probably Ann). Brooks, *John Doyle Lee*, 278–79.

have them sealed to him. The mother of the girls followed them, and took them away from Mr. Lee and he lost all the money he spent on the women. They went to the city in October and did not return until December, they brought back with them a demented boy whom they lost on the way. He was a nephew of his wife Emma, he was one of the children he took to the city. This sealing is done in a very simple manner, there in no cerimony about it, you are simply asked if you take this women to be your wife and you answer in the affirmative, that is all there is of it. You can be sealed to a dead man or a dead woman. This stile of sealing is for the purpose of gaining a great crown with a brilant Star to wear in that good and better land, any children born to such sealing are assigned and belong to such dead person man or woman as the case may be. A woman that is barren, can never wear a crown in the other world. She is not without her remedy, she can cure the defect by getting a lot of women sealed to her husband and can be sealed to some dead person, whom she may fancy or she could have some dead woman sealed to her husband, such as taking Queen Elizabeth or Abraham's wife Sara and sealing them to her husband. The more she gets in this way the brighter will be her crown in the good and better land, they preach about the reserection, the women that died, if the man does not raise the veil of the woman, she lays one thousand years: if the man raises the veil and finds and finds her wanting in anything she still has to remain one thousand years in probation. If the children born in the Church do not live to go through the Endowment house and be washed and annointed they are considered disembodied spirits; but if I had a child that way, I could go and be washed and annointed and relieve from the child the embaressment and place it before the proper light before God, so the child would not be lost.[150]

Mr. Lee returned home from Salt Lake City. He brought home a lot of things for the women, when got to Beaver, my mother had collected some money that was owing to me, and she bought a lot of things she thought I might need and sent them to me, she sent me ten dollars in cash, and in that letter, she enumerated the articles she had sent me. The articles came all right, before Christmas, Rachel one of Mr. Lee's wives, came down to my house, she wanted me to let her have some of the things my mother sent me, She said Mr. Lee sent her after them. I told her she told a lie. I was

[150]For a discussion of Mormon beliefs on marriage and the family, see "Marriage and Family Patterns," in Arrington and Bitton, *The Mormon Experience*, 185–205.

dressed upon the occasion, and she asked me where I was going, I told her I was going to see a lady friend of mine, Mrs. Emaly. She went home, but she came back again, I supposed she would. I got back before she returned, and hid myself in the house and watched her every movement. She unlocked my Trunk and commenced taking things out of the Trunk. When I bounced down on her, she fought like a Tiger. I was young at the time and did not care a cent for the consequences, we got into a regular fight and I bit a big piece out of her cheek, disfiguring her for life. Just as I got her out of the house Mr. John D Lee came along and asked me what was the matter, and I told him she had been in my Trunk stealing my things, and I told him to search her pockets and he would find them. He did so, and found Tea, Coffee, sugar and five dollars in money, he took it away from her and gave it back to me, he told her to go home and never come near my house again and she never did. I told Mr. Lee if she ever did that I would Kill her. Mr. Lee asked me where I got my money, I told him that my mother sent it to me in a letter, well he said your mother said nothing to me about sending you money, but did you get all things she enumerated in her letter. I told him I got everything.

Mr. Lee said he wanted me to get ready to go to Beaver, where my Mother lived. I told him I was ready at any time, and he said I want you to put your things in your Trunk and put it in the wagon, so that you will not loose anything and let Caroline take care of the house while you are gone. I hid away such as I did not want interfered with, I gave Caroline some Sugar, Tea and Coffee, my money I took with me about one hundred dollars. I raised my own Pork and Bacon from one end of the year to the other, the other women did not do that, they were always short because they were extravigant. So I Killed one pig out of fourteen, this pig I Killed for my mother, as she did not have any. Caroline got up her pigs all of them to pay for the goods that she got for her family, Rachel had a lot of pigs but while she was gone, Nancy sold all she had, but she did not get the amount of money she thought she would get, from the fact that the pigs were not in good condition and lacked in weight. So John D Lee took some of Carolines hogs and some of Emmas to pay his indebtness to Dalton, for goods that he had got from him, for his diferent families, he did not take any of my pigs, because I did not get any of the goods, and therefore I was not indebeted to him. I had plenty of everything on hand and no family.

On the 21st of December we started for mothers house. She lived in Beaver we got there on the 23rd, we suffered fearfully from the cold, after we got there, we drove to mothers first. My Step father at the time was very sick almost unto death. Mr. Lee said there was so much sickness in the family that he would not stay. He would go down to Mr. Daltons his son in law, and I told him I would not go down there, that I would stay Just where I was. I asked him if he could get my things out of the wagon, he said he could, and took out four geese, and some Ducks, and a good fat pig, the Geese and Ducks were alive. Mother Killed all the Ducks but one, she thought a hen duck, but it proved to be a drake and she called his name Jake, and he was a great pet, he would come every morning for his feed upon my mother calling him by name. My StepFather wanted to pay me for the pig, but I told him no, that the pig was a present from me to my mother. Mr. Dalton was very angry because he did not get the fat pig. Mr. Lee told him the pig belonged to Annie and not to him and that she gave the pig to her mother.

We stayed there until the 1st of February, then we went back home to Harmoney, we had not been back but a few days when Spring came on, we had an early Spring. Mr. Robert Patterson of Pioche, Nevada, came to get his pigs and some Beef Cattle for which he had contracted for, sometime before Caroline agreed to give him two Pigs. Mr. Patterson told her if she did not have the pigs, he would take the equvilent in Geese and Turkeys, so she said all right I will give you Geese and Turkeys. Rachel had nothing to give in the way of stock, not withstanding she had got several new dresses from him, Rachel wanted him to take his pay out of what he had bought from me, he said he could not do that, that he had to pay me cash for everything he got, there was no trade in it. She said it is strange, she does not buy anything, and she always appears to have plenty of everything. Well he said she does not disipate in anything, which accounts for her having plenty at all times. He got everything and went on his way, but said he would be back in September.[151]

That Summer Nancy married Eli. N. Pace,[152] that summer everything appeared to be backward. The cattle and horses died off and the storms proved disastrous, so that everything had a depressing apperence, there was not the

[151]John D. Lee noted that R. Patterson came to Harmony in February 1868 to purchase one hundred head of cattle and left merchandise to be sold on commission. Cleland and Brooks, eds., *A Mormon Chronicle*, 3, 28 February 1868, 7 March 1868, 2:98–99. Pioche was a mining district just west of the southern Utah communities.

[152]Nancy Lee married Eli Pace on 22 July 1869. New Harmony Ward Record, 358.

prosperous times that we had in former years. The Gentiles were becoming to numerous for comfort and prosperity. The winter came on, we had plenty to sell, and got good prices for everything we sold, yet notwithstanding all this; there appeared to be a Pall, a dark impenetrable cloud hanging over everyone, they did not appear to be themselves. This feeling pervaded the whole Territory. Winter passed away, nothing occurred worthy of note, until Nancy Killed her husband on the 22nd day of February, She Shot him through the heart, she took time to put a pillow under his head and the Revolver into his hand before she gave the alarm, this was done to leave the impression that it was self distruction or Suicide, there was nothing done to her under the Gentile law,[153] but under the rules of the Mormon Church she was dispossed of all her property, which she afterwards recovered under the Gentile laws.

Brigham Young would come down to see Lee often, but he would always send word ahead to get up a big dinner as he always came with a crowd of the dignataries of the Church, and would talk about the inevitable Storm that was approaching, and resolve themselves Into a committe of ways and means, how to meet it, and it was desided that all the Old Mormons and those regarded as leaders must leave and go to New Mexico, Arizona and old Mexico, and that to scatter would be the best thing to do.[154]

Mr. Patterson and Uncle John came back that fall to buy Stock, they were in the neighborhood about three months. Patterson went on with the cattle and left Uncle John behind with the Teams to follow him in two or three days. This outfit had plenty of money, Forty five or fifty thousand dollars. Uncle John hitched up about four oclock in the evening and said he would make Pinto that night. Lee said I will saddle my horse and go with you, and show you a good camping ground, and Uncle John said all right, that was the last ever seen of Uncle John alive. The woman were all at home, Emma his wife asked him if he was coming home that night and he answered yes, she said will I sit up for you, he said Yes I will be home, he came home about nine oclock, Emma, Caroline and myself were talking when he came home, he said we had better go home, that we would have prayers first, but I

[153]John D. Lee called it a suicide. Lee, Papers, diary 3, 29 January 1870, 133–34.

[154]In September 1870 Brigham Young counseled Lee to move his family to a more remote location, part of the president's campaign to distance his church from the chief suspect in the Mountain Meadows massacre. Lee wrote that Young "sent word to my wives that they were all divorced from me and could leave me, if they wished to do so." Bishop, *Mormonism Unveiled*, 266. Lee sold his New Harmony properties and moved Rachel and her children to Lower Skutumpah, a remote valley outside Kanab. News of his excommunication reached Lee within weeks. Brooks, *John Doyle Lee*, 289–302.

did not wait for prayers but went straight home, I did not go to sleep, I felt worried, I felt sure there was some dirt going on. I went to Lee's house to see what was going on and found they were all asleep. I then went back to my own house and went to bed. I still felt much troubled in mind, because I saw John D. Lee get his Buck Skin suit out, when he had that on he looked more like an Indian than a white man. I felt sure there was something wrong going on, when I saw he was agoing to disguise himself in the Indian suit. I went to bed and must have gone to sleep, for I knew nothing until next morning. When I got up I saw blood on my feet, and on the lower part of my night Shirt. Then all that happened the night before came back to me like a flash. That morning I went out to look for the cows. I ran across the dead body of Uncle John about three miles up Pinto Canyon. I also found Lee's Indian suit where he had hid it, all this I saw in my sleep, for I had followed him up the canyon in my sleep and saw Mr. Lee had a Knife in his hand I saw him Stoop and cut Uncle Johns throat from ear to ear. Mr. Lee did not see me, and did not Know that I followed him. The following morning everything that passed the night before was so vividly impressed upon my mind I could tell him every movement he made.[155]

Mr. Lee had the wagons loaded and everything ready to move out of the country after the murder of Uncle John, he took his wife Rachel and her family first into Arizona where he proposed to live, he came back for Caroline and Emma, in the meantime while he was gone I was taken sick and became delirious. While in this state I gave the murder of Uncle John and all its particulars away. Every one Knew that I Knew all about the murder. When Lee came back and found out that I had given the whole thing away Mr. Lee called a meeting for the purpose of making to put me out of the way, he called the men into the Barn to fix up the matter. William Orson Lee son of Mr. Lee[156] was at the time up in the Hay Mow and heard every word of what was said and all the arrangments to put me out of the way,

[155]Beginning with Joseph Smith, many Mormons put great stock in dreams and visions. Priesthood holders also "enjoy[ed] divinely inspired dreams, visions, and visitations." Arrington and Bitton, *The Mormon Experience*, 5–9; and Fife and Fife, *Saints of Sage*, 183, 218–19. Lee's diaries are full of dreams that he considered important. See Cleland and Brooks, eds., *A Mormon Chronicle*, passim. Juanita Brooks quotes an anonymous account describing how a few weeks after Mountain Meadows, John D. Lee told an audience at Harmony about the event, which "he represented . . . as a vision which had occurred to him some time, probably six months before." Brooks, *Mountain Meadows*, xix–xx. See also the discussion of Lee's dreams in the George A. Hicks section of this volume.

[156]William Orson was Lee's son with Martha Elizabeth Berry. He worked for his father at Harmony. See Brooks, *John Doyle Lee*, 276, 381.

and he came and told me that I must get up and leave at once, that they had everything arranged to finish me that night, he said you get ready and came to the lower part of or end of town, and I will have a wagon and team ready for you, I will walk through the water to the team to prevent their tracking me, you must get your trunk and I will take it to the team; he came about nine oclock for the Trunk and told me to come by ten oclock sure, before leaving I made a fire in the house for the purpose of burning the house down. We stayed awhile in the neighborhood and watched to see how the fire would work, we saw it all ablaze on the inside and Knew they would be looking for us. We broke for the team and started for the Stage road. We got there Just in time to catch the stage that went to Beaver, William Orson drove the team back and put the horses in the Stable before daylight, he then came to my mothers at Corn Creek.[157] My Step Father wanted to Know what I left for, I told him I did not propose to have my throt cut by any man, he told me that I might as well have my throat cut as to be hanged. I stayed there from 1869 to 1870. [158]

The Grand Jury was empanelled, the first Grand Jury of a Gentile nature ever sat there. There were indictments found against Lee, Height, Dame and Higby. Height and Dame made their escape. J.D. Lee was captured in the fall of 1870 but was out on Bail until 1876, when Lee was called up for trial I went with the possee to show them where they would find him, not in the house, but under the corn crib.[159] I was disguised in mens clothing. I was a very good rider and was mounted on a good fast horse. One of Lee's sons who was in the plot to put me out of the way, recognized me and cried out, There is the Trator catch her. I put spurs to my horse and broke for the River. With two of Lee's sons after me, I went into the River and crossed into a band of Abache Indians who opened fire on the Lee boys, which stoped their further progress.

---

[157]The BYU variant reads Indian Creek, which is located six miles north of Beaver, Utah.

[158]Lee spent Christmas 1870 in Harmony with Caroline, Emma, Terressa, and Ann and intended to bring the rest of his family south in the spring. On 20 April 1871 Emma arrived at Lower Skutumpah with Ann's older son and daughter and told Lee that Ann had taken Albert, just three months old, and gone north. Cleland and Brooks, eds., *A Mormon Chronicle*, 20 April 1871, 2:159; Brooks, *John Doyle Lee*, 297–98.

[159]A grand jury indicted nine men involved in Mountain Meadows in September 1874. Ann may be borrowing here from the story of Lee's capture on 7 November 1874, when U.S. Deputy Marshal William Stokes and his posse discovered Lee in a chicken coop outside Caroline's house in Panguitch. The first jury split along Mormon-Gentile/apostate lines. See Bagley, *Blood of the Prophets*, 287–90. Lee was released on bail in early 1876 and reported voluntarily for his second trial at Beaver in September. See Bagley, *Blood of the Prophets*, 300–301.

Lee was captured and taken to Beaver for a hearing he gave Bail in the sum of Ten thousand dollars. Brigham Young informed on Lee, he gave Lee away to save himself. Clinton Smith one of the Mountain Medow Massacre men was going to appear as a witness against Lee, but his career was cut short by being thrown down a shaft and Killed in Pioche Nevada.[160] Lee was tried in Beaver in 1876, and was sent to States prison where he was held until March 1877. He was taken out of prison and taken to Mountain Medows, where he had committed his high crime, and there he was shot dead, one of his sons claimed the body, and it was turned over to him, he was buried beside his first wife in Harmoney, he appeared to have lost all his old friends, in fact he was friend less.

The head men in the Church, went to his wife Rachel who had charge of all of Lee papers and represented to her, that Mr. had sent them for all his papers as he wanted to use them in his defence. She supposed all those men to be Lee's best friends and high dignataries of the Church, after those dignataries got possesion of the papers, they went back on Lee, they robed of the only defence he had in the world, when he found his papers were all gone, and in whoes hands they were, he exclaimed—I am lost, nothing can save me now. It was a low cowardly act on the part of those claiming to be his best friends, for they were as deep in the mire and guilt as was John D. Lee, but they all worked against him to save their own hides, he was to be the sacrafice, Orson Pratt and Daniel H. Wells were high dignataries who robed him of his defence. His wife Rachel was visiting in Brigham Youngs family, Brigham told her to leave, that they would get him out of the trouble all right, of that she could rest assured. Lee answered and was taken from Salt Lake City to Beaver there he had his trial, in the morning after the trial he was taken to to Mountain Medow, where he had committed his crime, on the same ground he was shot to death.[161]

[160]Ann probably means Philip Klingensmith (often rendered as "P.K. Smith" or "Philip Klingen Smith"), a massacre participant whose affidavit in 1871 in a Nevada court helped build the case against Lee; he testified for the prosecution at Lee's first trial. For a full biography, see Backus, *Mountain Meadows Witness.* Several rumors about his death exist: that he was killed by Mormons and his body thrown into a Sonora mine, or alternatively, that Mormons killed him and buried him near his Nevada ranch. See Bagley, *Blood of the Prophets*, 275–76, 292, 325–26; Backus, 231–35. The Sonora story is detailed in "Klingensmith: He Is Supposed to Have Been Murdered by Mormons," *Salt Lake Tribune*, 4 August 1881, 4; the article cites a letter received "in the vicinity of Pioche."

[161]For the trials and execution, see Brooks, *Mountain Meadows*, 191–210; and Bagley, *Blood of the Prophets*, 287–322. In 1877, while in jail in Beaver, Lee reportedly asked for his journals and papers to write his version of the massacre for his "Confessions," but Emma reported that three men took and burned Lee's diary with the written massacre order from Dame and Haight. Bagley, *Blood of the Prophets*, 311–12.

I was with the Apache Indians eighteen months with the Apache Indians before I made my escape. While I was with them I went to Arizona up amongst the Cliff dwelers in one of the caves we found a Skeleton about seven feet high, we also found Pots and crockery, and cooking utensils of every Kind, the floor of this cave was white marble very finely finished, as was also the four walls, which were artiscally enlaid with Gold, evendently the house of the Chief, or the head man of the Nation. We went into several caves almost as well furnished as the first excepting one about fourteen feet square, in this cave or chamber, there was a chimney, and some cooking furniture and close to the Chimney was the Skeleton of a very old women, She held in her hand a Pestal as though in the act of pounding maze in a large Stone mortar which stood directly in the front of her.[162]

We Stayed in this place about two months. There was a fine orchard in this place, it was wild, but had every appearance that at sometime in the past, no one Knows when, it had been a highly cultivated Orchard. There were growing in that Orchard Some of the finest Peaches I ever saw. After we left this place, we went to Moquite Village, this Village is not built as other Villages, the walls are built six or eight hundred feet long, there are no doors to enter, you climb up a lader and enter your room from the Top, pulling the lader after you. They have everything in good shape and order. They have water all through this village in case of Seige they would have plenty of water, the water is brought in through wooden pipes from the Rio Grande River. Those people are called Moquite.[163] Some think they are of the lost Tribe, others think they are Welsh a band of Welsh who left Wales, because they would not be ruled, by any King or Queen not of their own people. They claim that one of the Queens of England came to Wales to be confined, and that hundreds of Welsh families cursed the Queen and left and landed in this country. This is their tradition. They speak the Welsh tongue.[164] They are not warlike. They are small and light in color.

[162]The cliff dwellings of the Anasazi or Ancestral Puebloan peoples became well-known with discoveries made in the 1870s and 1880s, such as those by the photographer William Henry Jackson at Mesa Verde in 1874. See Ortiz, ed., *Southwest*, 5–7.

[163]Moqui was a contemporary term for the Hopi and was sometimes applied to other pueblo dwellers. The Hopi reservation (in north-central Arizona, well west of the Rio Grande) was often called the Moqui Reservation as late as 1923, but the Hopis find the term offensive and the federal government changed the name. See Connelly, "Hopi Social Organization," 539–63; Euler and Dobyns, *The Hopi People*. Jacob Hamblin, a Mormon missionary to many southwest Indian peoples, made the first of several trips into Hopi country in 1858. See Hamblin, Diary; Gibbons, Diaries, 1858, 1877–1878; and Carter, ed., "Ten Pioneer Autobiographies," *Our Pioneer Heritage*, 11:174–77.

[164]For an example of others exploring the Welsh Indian legend, see Calloway, *One Vast Winter Count*, 394.

They migrate every hundred years, from one place to another, they are now located in the Grand galapo mountains in Old Mexico. In game they never Kill but only Just what they want. Brigham Young sent missions among them, they would have nothing to do with them. They said they did not Know his God, he could do nothing with them.

After we left there we went to a Navahoe village, about two hundred miles on this side of the Rio Grande River. They had every thing in good shape, large farms and abundance of good stock. They lived in adobes houses, a large fine looking race of people for Indians.[165] We Stayed there about two or three weeks, during harvest, they had Grist mills, and lived very much like the whites. Brigham Young in a religious point of view could do nothing with them, he could hire them to do his murdering for him, but that is as far as he could go. The Navahoes chief wanted chief Goromando to give me up to him, chief Goromando said he would not do anything of the Kind, that I was not a captive, and that I should have the best of treatment until we got among the whites, and then I could go with my own people if I wanted to.[166]

We went about two hundred miles from the Navahoe village to the Ferry or crossing of the Rio Grande River. Chief Goromando, took twenty five of his best looking men and an equal amount of his best looking women, those he took across into old Mexico. We had to go through the San Francisco mountains, a most beautiful country, and alive with game of all Kinds, and all Kinds of wild fruit.[167] We stoped about two weeks we felt as though we could stay there forever, everything was so grand. We then broke camp and went about one hundred miles to a Catholic Monistary, we stayed there a couple of days, . . .

We went from there to Sonora, where we met some of the Apache tribe, and also some of the Comanche Indians. We stayed in Sonora from Nov until Feb, when we returned to America, by almost the same route we came. We had a rough time in getting back, the travling was bad and very mudy,

---

[165]Navajos characteristically build forked-pole and earth octagonal hogans rather than adobe structures; the latter are characteristic of the Pueblo. Iverson, *Diné,* 20–21.

[166]"Goromando" is probably Ann's rendering of "Geronimo," a di-yin, or shaman, and war leader of the Nde'indai or southernmost Chiricahua Apaches. During the period Ann claims to have been with him, Geronimo and his followers hunted and raided from southern Arizona and New Mexico into Chihuahua and Sonora. He was captured in 1877 and brought to San Carlos Reservation in Arizona, where he stayed until fleeing for Mexico in fall 1881; he surrendered for good in September 1886. See Haley, *Apaches,* 66, 281, 313–14; Aleshire, *The Fox and the Whirlwind,* esp. chap. 9; and Debo, *Geronimo.*

[167]Perhaps the San Francisco Range, on the west bank of the San Francisco River near the New Mexico–Arizona border, or the San Francisco Mountains in north-central Arizona, west of the Hopi Reservation.

and the streams all swolen and in some instances impassable. We got back finally and went to Red Cliff[168] where the band organized. We stayed at Red Cliff all Summer in the fall we started back towards Utah. We went over the same ground, when we got there the Moquites were moving for another home, we occupied the places that this tribe left.

We stayed in this place about two months, when the Apaches the tribe I was with got on the war path against the whites. The Indians went to the Colorado River, but did not cross, they went up the River to a place called Round Mountain.[169] We camped at Round Mountain a few days to make provision for the women and children before the fighting would commence. The second night after we came to Round Mountain, there was a white came among the Indians, but they did not Know he was white. This white man came and told me that I had better make my escape that night as there would be bloody work on the morrow, I said how am I to go, he said I will have a horse at the River and I will cross you over, this was about midnight when we started to cross the River. The River was very full at the time. We crossed about two miles above where John D Lee's place was located.[170]

Billy the Kid was the person was the person who crossed me over the River,[171] he took me through the San Juan country into Colorado, from Colorado, we struck New Mexico and went next to Arizona, from there we went to the Mohave country, which lies in New Mexico between Arizona and California.[172] All through the Mohave country all Kinds of wild fruit

[168]Perhaps Red Butte, just south of the Colorado River and some twenty miles west of the present Navajo Reservation in Arizona.

[169]Perhaps Round Rock, about 120 miles east of Red Butte, on today's Highway 191 just north of Canyon de Chelly.

[170]Ann evidently means Lee's ferry site at "Lonely Dell" on the Colorado, below today's Glen Canyon Dam. Lee was ordered to move from Lower Skutumpah to the Colorado River in 1871 and was officially authorized by Brigham Young to operate a ferry in 1874. See Brooks, *John Doyle Lee*, 302–33.

[171]If Ann began her time with the Apaches after escaping at Lee's capture on 7 November 1874 and spent eighteen months with them as she states, Billy the Kid helped her escape from the Apaches sometime in spring 1876. But her first reference to the Kid is dated 1872. According to Robert Utley, among the Kid's most reliable biographers, Henry McCarty would have then been between twelve and sixteen years old. His brief life of crime evidently began in September 1875 when he stole some laundry in Silver City, New Mexico. Utley writes that the next two years of Henry's life are sparsely documented, but he spent time in Apache territory and killed his first man in August 1877. McCarty started to become well-known during the Lincoln County War of 1878, and by late 1880 newspapers around the country had made Billy the Kid famous. Sheriff Pat Garrett killed him on 14 July 1881. See Utley, *Billy the Kid*, 6–10, 46–146, 198; and Wallis, *Billy the Kid*. Ann is part of a long tradition of writers filling in Henry's missing years; one newspaper even claimed that he killed a man in New York City. Weddle, *Antrim Is My Stepfather's Name*, 30.

[172]Ann may mean today's Sonoran Desert, which straddles the Arizona-California border, or the Mohave valley, in far western Arizona, just east of the Colorado River. The Mojave Desert lies to the northwest, perhaps Ann's "California desert."

grow in abundance. We left Mohave and in twenty four hours we struck the California desert, which is barren of everything, it is one hundred and sixty miles across this desert, we got about half way across, when the Kid said we would stop that this was the only place we could get water until we got on the other side. I told him I could not see any water any where, he said he could find water, there was a small bunch of Miskete brush growing near by he went to the green brush and spread it apart, and with his hands scratched away the sand and sure enough there appeared a very fine spring.

We stayed two days, we left and to Arnagoch[173] where there was plenty of fine water, we stayed there two days. In this place all Kinds of wild vegitables were growing in abundance. The Mormons Built a fort there at one time, and lived there until the Indians drove them out. They lived there but one year. We went next to a place called the Muddy.[174] There were some families living, and we stayed a week in the place, we left the Muddy and struck out to the Rio Virgin we crossed this River about eighteen times, the last time we crossed over to the Side, we went up the River about four hundred miles,[175] we crossed again on the west side, we traveled until we came to some mountains the name of the mountains I have forgotten. We struck a cave, and being curious to Know what was in it, we Started to explore the cave, we went on and on until we Struck Porter Rockwells door. The Kid said he knew where he was, I said I did to, and he observed that we had better get out of there so we went back to where we left our horses.

We stayed there until the next day when we started across the hills in the direction of the railroad. We struck the road in about fifteen miles. After we struck the road "Billy the Kid" gave me four thousand dollars and told me to take the train and go to Virginia City, Nevada, you will get as much money after you get there as you have now and may be more, but you must be very careful while you are in Ogden and not get robbed. You will have stay to stay in Ogden about ten days to fix yourself up in a genteel outfit and other things that you may need.

I went to Ogden and stayed ten days. I left on the eleventh. They charged me at the rate of fourteen dollars a week, while I was there. I went from

---

[173]Perhaps "Amargosa," the name of a seasonal stream in Death Valley. There is also a town called "Amargosa Valley" just east of the California-Nevada border, a possible stop if en route to the Virgin River.

[174]Probably the river in southeast Nevada that merges with the Virgin at the Arizona border.

[175]The BYU variant reads "about a hundred miles," page 78, which is the approximate length of the Virgin.

there to a place called Winnemuck,[176] Nevada. I stayed there four days from there I went to Virginia City, Nevada, when I got there I received twelve thousand dollars. I stayed there about one month. While there I lost five thousand dollars speculating in mining stocks. Before I left I was fortunate enough to make two thousand dollars of my loss back. From there I went to San Francisco where I stayed for sometime.

The year I left Salt Lake City Brigham Young was running a percentage hoar house in the city, he would go around every morning and collect his percentage with the regularity of clockwork. The girls did not stay in the house day times, but stayed at home with their parents until night when they would put in an appearance at the house of pleasure. One of his own daughters got into this house to try her luck. It almost broke old Brigham's heart. Kate Flint and Army follower. She came with General Conners Army and she started a first class sporting house. Brigham did not like the opposition and concluded he would break it up, as it interfered very materially with his business. So he got some Mormon girls to go to the house and become inmates of the house for the purpose of raiding the house. The girls at a certain time agreed upon were to open the doors and let Brigham's raiding force in to clean the house out. Everything was very nicely arranged, but one of Brigham's girls gave the whole plot away to Mrs Kate Flint. So Mrs Flint to counteract the plot had the house filled with soldiers from Conners Army on the night agreed upon to make the raid. When Brigham's forces made their appearance to raid the house, the doors were thrown open and in marched the raiding party, to be confronted with a house full of soldiers, who had been secreted in the house to meet the contemplated raid. The fight commenced and a bloody one it was. The raiders were surprised to meet with such unlooked for opposition, the raiders were driven out of the house badly beaten. Mrs Flint then striped all the Mormon girls off of all their clothing (she had given them the clothing) and turned them out of the house into the street. The Mormon girl who posted her about the raid she dressed up in good style and send to school to the sisters in San Francisco. Mrs Flint went down town next morning and swore out a warrant against Brigham Young and brought suit against him for one hundred and fifty thousand dollars and got judgement for that sum. And which was still more pleasing to her, she got the money by selling all the personal property of Brigham's

[176] Winnemucca, named for the famous Northern Paiute leader.

that the officers could lay their hands on, even down to his fine carriage horses.[177] Right after this occurance he was indicted for twelve murderers. He never stood trial for any of them.[178]

I went to San Francisco where I stayed two months. I then went to Los Angeles in Southern California. I stayed there four months cooking in a hotel, the Belle of the Union.[179] From there I took a ship to Sidney Australia from there I took the railroad to Melburne I stayed there about twelve days. I was trying this time to find a couple of uncles I had in the place, but I failed to find them. I went next to Port Adelade the place of my birth, here I stayed with a family by the name of Graham, they were married when I was a baby, they never had any children. While I was there Mrs Graham gave birth to twins girls.

From here I took a steamer to Belfast, Ireland where my grandmother lives. I stayed with her six months after which I went to London England and stayed about one month with an uncle. I had two uncles in that place, my father's brothers. They were very kind to me and give me considerable money, and wanted me to say with them the balance of my days. I could not stay as to me there was no country like America. The last words my Uncle Tom said to me was to beware of my cousin George, that he was trying to get this money that was coming to me.

My Uncle Tom went with me to Liverpool, where I took steamer for Sidney. I did not stay in Sidney very long this time. I took steamer for Honolulu, here I stayed a month and a half, here I took steamer for San Francisco from here I went to Kelton Utah, from Kelton I went to Idaho in

[177]Kate Flint ran a brothel in Corinne as early as 1870, then ran houses in Salt Lake City for almost two decades. Salt Lake police officers raided her brothel in 1872. Flint sued, claiming they had destroyed personal property under an improper warrant, and won damages. But there is no evidence of U.S. soldiers (except perhaps as customers) or Mormon girl spies, and the amount Flint won was thirty-four hundred dollars in a judgment against the police and city court justice, not Brigham Young. See Nichols, *Prostitution, Polygamy, and Power*, 28–30. It is perhaps noteworthy that the Salt Lake City Council voted to pay Flint only weeks after Brigham Young's death. Salt Lake City Council Minutes, Book H, 18 September 1877, 103–104. There is also a persistent legend that "Gentile Kate" bought one of Young's carriages at auction. See DeVoto, "Sin Comes to Ogden," 451–52.

[178]The third district grand jury indicted Brigham Young and others in 1872 for the Yates murder based on William Hickman's testimony. Before the cases could come to trial, the U.S. Supreme Court ruled in *Clinton v. Englebrecht* that Utah's federal grand juries had been improperly impaneled, and eighteen months' worth of cases were dismissed. See Bigler, *Forgotten Kingdom*, 289–92, 294–95; and Firmage and Mangrum, *Zion in the Courts*, 145–47, 246. See also the account of these events in the B.Y. Hampton section of this volume.

[179]Perhaps the Bella Union Hotel. *Directory of Los Angeles, 1873*, xxxiv.

June 1872. Here I stayed until March, 1873. I left this place and came back to Corinne Utah, and here I stayed with a family by the name of Monroe, where I stayed from the 21st of March until the 1st of June, 1873.[180]

My next move was to Salmon City, Idaho,[181] there I took in washing for two months. I then went across the mountains to a place called Horse Prarie. In Horse Prarie I went into Partnership with a woman who had a lot of cows. I was to milk the cows and make butter and get half of the proceeds. I stayed here about six weeks, when the woman my partner got mad about something, I do not know what. We disolved partnership, but she would not pay me a cent for the time or work I was there. She wanted to buy my riding habit. She offered me a dollar for it and my side saddle. I had a sack and a half of flour and she offered me a dollar and a half for it. At the same time flour was worth a dollar a pound. I had about twenty five pounds of tea, and about an equal quantity of coffee, sugar and other articles in proportion. The potatoes I had I gave them to a miner, a prospector by the name of Silvey. We got rid of all we did not want.[182] We had but two horses, and we packed them all they could carry.

We left for Bannock in Montana, thirty five miles from Horse Prarie.[183] We walked all the way and led our horses. We stayed outside of Bannock a few days to get some things we needed in the way of clothes. We left Bannock and went fifteen miles to a saw mill. Here we stayed over night, that night we had to keep fires all night to keep off the grisly bears as they were very bad. Our stock was very much alarmed, and very restless, so much so we had to be constantly on the watch. Next day went over into the Big Hole Bason we stayed here two days fishing and hunting.[184] We caught all the fish we wanted, and we killed eleven otters and they were as black as black could be. We packed up our traps and started for the wagon road, but we got lost

[180]Possibly Thomas Monroe, a wagonmaster, or W.H. Munro, a freighter and one-time Corinne mayor. See Madsen, *Corinne*, 46, 49–50, 95.

[181]Salmon City lies at the junction of Rock Creek and the Lemhi River, where they become the Salmon River in east-central Idaho.

[182]It is unclear which other person constitutes "we" here and through the end—Billy the Kid? Note "he killed the cows" some three pages down.

[183]Bannack, now a ghost town, is about twenty miles west of Dillon and seventy miles south of Butte on a tributary to the Beaverhead River. It was the site of Montana's first major gold strike in 1862 and the first territorial capital. Horse Prairie is just southwest of Bannack. Burlingame and Toole, *A History of Montana*, 1:124–25.

[184]The Big Hole Basin, site of a famous battle between the U.S. Army and the Nez Perce, is about twenty-five miles northwest of Bannack; Ann presumably crossed the mountains at Big Hole Pass.

and we wandered around for four or five days, making every effort to find the road. We finally found the road by seeing a band of Indians coming down the mountain side into the road.

As quick as we struck the road we knew where we were. The road was a most fearful road to travel. After we gained the apex of the mountain, we struck north down the river until we reached the Bluffs, three very large rocks off immense hight, one red, one black and one white. The Indians called the rocks the babies, the whites called them the Bluff. We stayed here all night. We were troubled during the night by the appearance of a large grisley bear in camp. Here I lost my otter skins. I went off and left them on the rocks, but I was fortunate after all, I got them back in three days, an Indian found them and brought them to me, his name was Bannock Jim. I was always afraid of him for the year before, he killed six women and five men on the Camas Prarie.[185]

After we left the rocks we went to a place called Rosses hole, on the Mullin Road or Emigrants Road. This place is the west fork of the Bitter Root River, here the Placer mining was what might be called first class at that time, but could not be worked on account of the Indians which were very bad, they were constantly on the war path.[186] We left here and crossed over the mountain to the main River of Bitter Root. If we had taken the Indian trail we need not have crossed the River at all, but we took the wagon road about sixteen miles around and thereby had to cross the river eleven times. We did not make much progress this day as the Indians were bad, and they viglants not much better,[187] and as we had to be constantly on our guard which made our movements very slow.

[185]In a violent encounter on the Great Camas Prairie near the Big Wood River on 23 June 1872, young warriors in Pagwite's band killed a herdsman and wounded two other whites, committing "premeditated murder . . . at the insistence of the medicine men," according to Fort Hall agent Johnson N. High. Pagwite, better known as Bannack Jim, went on to become a principal leader in the Ghost Dance movement at Fort Hall, where a mixed-race butcher killed him in 1891. See Smoak, *Ghost Dances and Identity*, 96, 121–24, 129, 166, 174–76, 184.

[186]Ann seems to describe crossing the Anaconda Range from Big Hole Basin to the Bitterroot Valley. Ross's Hole (named for Pacific Fur Company explorer Alexander Ross) is at the upper, or southern, end of the Bitterroot Valley; Ross's Fork is known today as the east fork of the Bitterroot River. While some prospectors continued to practice placer mining, by the 1870s it had largely given way to industrial mining. The Mullan Road, built 1858–1862, connected Fort Benton to Walla Walla. See Burlingame and Toole, *History of Montana*, 1:81–83, 124–30.

[187]Montana's best-known vigilante movement, organized to fight road agents in the gold camps, was over by the organization of the Territory of Montana in May 1864. Ibid., 2:173–75.

The next day we made Squaw Man's Ranche, his name was George W. Doolittle.[188] He was harvesting where we got there and they were very kind. to us. He gave us a house to live in, and treated us most kindly in every way. He gave us cows to milk, and before we came away he gave me a very fine horse. There was some disease among his horses and many of them died, he did not know what to do for them. One was sick and he said to me if you save that horse I will give you the other horse. I saved the horse, but I did not know at the time how I did it. I gave the horse grated potatoes and discovered that potatoes grated would have the desired effect. It cured the horses, he tryed it on two stallions he had, but let them run to long before he tried the remedy and they died.

We helped him get their harvest in, after which we started down the Bitter Root River to a place called Gurand Creek. We stayed here all winter with a man name Joe Pardee.[189] I milked cows and got half of the butter. I also worked through the harvest and thrashing for which I received forty dollars a month. Before they got through thrashing there came up a very severe storm, two men and eight horses were frozen to death, and many of the others were more or less frozen and injured from the effects of the storm. This storm lasted up to the first of December it then cleared off, and then came what they called a chinook wind which melted all the snow off the ground. We had no more winter that year, every body went to plowing and putting in their crops.

The first of March it was a little cold, but not at all serious. I went to Masula[190] ninety miles in the stage. I bought me a stove, rented me a house and started a laundry and took in washing at twenty five cents a price for handkerchiefs, twenty cents a pair for socks and fifty cents for shirts, and all other articles except dresses and white skirts, which were a dollar a piece and a half according to the trimming on them. We stayed here from March until the middle of June, the water got very low and we went to Pioneer.[191] There open a laundry at the same prices. In this place flour was very scarce. While in Massula I took considerable quantity of flour at seventy five cents

[188]The 1870 census found E. M. Doolittle, age 39, farming in the Bitterroot Valley; he had a seven-year-old son, George. Bureau of the Census, Ninth Census of the United States, 1870, Missoula County, Territory of Montana, page 7, lines 4, 6.

[189]One Joseph Pardee, age 40, farmed in the Bitterroot Valley with six laborers listed in 1870. Bureau of the Census, Ninth Census of the United States, 1870, Missoula County, Territory of Montana, page 4, line 13.

[190]Missoula, where the Bitterroot and Clark Fork rivers merge.

[191]Pioneer was between Missoula and Deer Lodge, about fifteen miles northwest from the latter.

per hundred, about two thousand pounds. This flour I had freighted up to Pioneer, there I sold my flour for seventy five dollars a hundred. Ten dollars a hundred for freight.[192]

I stayed in Pioneer from the first of June to the first of September. I gathered together all my effects and went to Deer Lodge and here I opened up a laundry at five dollars a dozen. I run this laundry about a year when some miscreant not having the fear of God before his eyes set fire to the house and burned it down, together with five thousand dollars in greenbacks I had in the house at the time. The Fashion Stables next to the house I lived in was burned at the same time together with some of the finest horses that ever came to Montana. The house I lived in was the first ever built in this place.[193] After I got burned out I got money enough and went to Helena. Then I went to Cooking in the Cosmopolitan Hotel. Here I stayed until 1876.[194]

In May of that year I went to the little Big horn within three miles of the Custer Massacre.[195] We then went to Gallitan Valley,[196] there we stayed all summer and winter. I did nothing while there. In the spring we went to Spring hill on the stage Road to keep stage station.[197] Here we stayed from March until January. We quit the station and went to live in a Cabin, we had three cows. He killed the cows and sold them to the Indians. In the Spring we went again on the Yellow stone river about two miles from the National Park. Where we took up a ranch and was getting along fairly well. We had the ranche partly fenced, when the Indians came and run us out of the place. We then went back to Bozeman and from Bozeman to Sheridan.[198] In Sheridan I started a laundry and remained until September 1879 when I was again burned out. I lost every thing. After we were burned

[192]On freighting in Montana, see Burlingame and Toole, *History of Montana*, 2:64–66.

[193]*The Deer Lodge New North-West* reported "some scoundrel made an earnest but ineffectual effort to burn Mr. D.S. Kenyon's stable the other night." "Local Brevities," 1 October 1875, 4/2.

[194]In 1883 the Cosmopolitan was described as "the only first-class hotel in Helena." Schroeder and Graff, comps., *Historic Helena*, n.p. Its proprietors bragged in 1889 that "the tables are unexcelled by any other hotel in Montana." *Ide's Helena City Directory for 1889*, 45.

[195]The Battle of the Little Bighorn occurred on 25 June 1876.

[196]The Gallatin River is one of the three forks of the Missouri; the Gallatin has a west fork that flows north from Yellowstone National Park and an east fork that flows through Bozeman, in what is generally referred to as the Gallatin Valley. By the 1860s it was a major agricultural area supplying the mining camps. Burlingame and Toole, *History of Montana*, 1:129, 291.

[197]Springhill, an early milling and orchard center and stage stop between Helena and Salt Lake City, is about fifteen miles north of Bozeman. Ibid., 2:62–63, 172.

[198]Sheridan lies some fifty miles west of Bozeman.

out we hitched up our team and started for Payette Valley, Idaho. We left Sheridan in September 1879 and moved to Payette Valley. We rented a ranche of a man by the name of Stewart. This ranched contained one hundred and sixty acres of land. We went to work and put it all in grain and potatoes. Everything looked well, the grain was heading up beautifully, the potatoes were in full bloom, in fact no crop could look more satisfactory when all at once the River rose to an unusual height, and overflowed the whole ranch and washed away every particle of the crop, left nothing but bare ground. Several other ranches suffered alike fate.[199]

We went from there over to the Boise River and stayed there all summer. I worked in this place all summer for a man by the name of Hultz, and got beat out of my money.[200] I never got a cent for my summer's work. I moved into Boise city and started a laundry. I stayed here but a short time and then moved to a place called Silver City here I stayed from 1881 to 1883.[201] I left and went to Oregon but did not tarry in Oregon. I came back to Boise City, here I stayed a short time and came back to Utah Territory, and have remained here ever since.[202]

---

[199]The Payette is a tributary of the Snake River in southwest Idaho, north of Boise City and parallel to the Boise River. By the 1870s the lower Boise and Payette valleys were productive irrigated farmlands. Arrington, *History of Idaho*, 1:473, 483.

[200]One Nathaniel Hultz farmed in Boise in 1870. Bureau of the Census, Ninth Census, 1870, Ada County, Territory of Idaho, page 26, line 38.

[201]Silver City is about fifty miles southwest of Boise. There was a mineral rush there in the 1860s. Arrington, *History of Idaho*, 1:241, 244–46, 386–87.

[202]According to Bishop family lore, Ann Gordge and her daughter "eventually escaped their predicament with the aid of her son and friendly Indians, presumably to Oregon." Bishop, Unpublished Introduction.

Brigham Young Hampton, circa 1886

Brigham Young Hampton (1836–1902) spent four decades prepared to fight "to the death in defence of God's people if Need bee" as bodyguard and law enforcement officer. *Courtesy International Society, Daughters of Utah Pioneers.*

Chapter 4

Brigham Young Hampton
Trials of Faith

Brigham Young Hampton was not a high-ranking authority in the Church of Jesus Christ of Latter-day Saints, but he played a starring role in many public dramas during the Mormon-Gentile conflict that raged from the Utah War of 1857 until the state's admission to the Union in 1896. Like other Latter-day Saints of his time and place, Hampton developed an impassioned identity that was self-consciously at odds with non-Mormons; he was eager to live his faith and defend his church. Unlike other figures in this volume, Hampton was no apostate: he remained loyal to the LDS church, despite his anger and disillusionment with some of its leaders after the death of Brigham Young. Hampton's dissent was expressed privately. His story provides an intimate look inside the struggle for power in Utah, as well as a glimpse into the domestic realities of living in plural marriage and the sacrifices both could entail.

From before his birth, Hampton's family was closely linked to Brigham Young. Young joined the LDS church in 1832; less than a year later, he married Jonathan Hampton to Julia Foster, whom Young had also courted. When Julia bore her second son, the Hamptons granted Young's request for the honor of naming the infant. Perhaps gaining a small victory, he gave the child his own name, thus "Brigham Young Hampton." For the rest of his life, if his autobiography is any indication, Hampton demonstrated unwavering loyalty and respect for the Lion of the Lord.

The Hampton family weathered the central events that dominate the legendary story of the fitful Mormon trek west, including the departure from Kirtland, Ohio; the flight from Far West, Missouri; and the mob violence in Nauvoo and Carthage, Illinois. After Jonathan's death, Julia was sealed to Brigham Young for time (that is, the lives of the spouses) and to her late husband for eternity. The family did not join the exodus to the Salt Lake Valley until 1855, where Brigham Young folded Julia into his large household, although she did not stay long.

The family had arrived in the territory at a tense and eventful time. The Mormon Reformation was about to burst forth with its spiritual fervor and defiant rhetoric. Less than two years later the U.S. Army marched on Utah threatening war. For the next three-plus decades, Mormons struggled with merchants, miners, attorneys, and journalists to control the territory.[1] The bitterness of this conflict vividly stamps the pages of Hampton's story. His diary/autobiography is full of aspersions on sinister "Gentiles" and "apostates," contrasted with defenses of the character, spirituality, and actions of Latter-day Saints. This period corresponds with Hampton's active adult life, during which he prospered modestly at several trades and started several families while serving in mid-level LDS church offices. His reputation among Mormons became that of a pious and popular Saint devoted to his church and its cause; among non-Mormons, his image was sometimes that of a latter-day thug.

Hampton fully engaged in LDS life: he underwent multiple baptisms, tithed regularly, performed temple work, and participated in meetings and prayer circles. A practitioner of plural marriage, he joined the United Order of Enoch, performed endowments for dead relatives, and stood watch at Brigham Young's deathbed. He was an eager participant in the dances, parties, and theater that enlivened Mormon society. Hampton also served a long career as a kind of utility bodyguard, detective, and foot soldier in the Mormon cause. The memories of Missouri and Illinois violence remained fresh in many Saints' minds, and they were determined to defend their Utah communities from similar threats. Hampton's friend Hosea Stout called the loose group of men who engaged as forceful defenders of Mormon interests "Be'hoys" or "Brigham's Boys." Hampton, although younger and a later arrival in Utah than other "Be'hoys," can be counted in their number.[2] At a reported six foot

[1]Histories of Utah and the Mormons spend many pages on this dramatic period. See Arrington and Bitton, *The Mormon Experience,* 161–84; Alexander, *Utah,* 126–217; and the official LDS history, Roberts, *A Comprehensive History,* vols. 5–6. Larson, *The "Americanization" of Utah for Statehood,* and Bigler, *Forgotten Kingdom,* concentrate on this period.

[2]For "Be'hoys," see Brooks, ed., *On the Mormon Frontier,* 8 March 1858, 653; Quinn, *The Mormon Hierarchy: Extensions of Power,* 242–44. Hampton was also friendly with the "Be'hoy" William H. Kimball and shared a jail cell with Stout and Kimball in 1871.

Julia Foster Hampton
Born in 1811, Julia Foster married Jonathan Hampton in Kirtland, Ohio, in 1833. Brigham Young had considered marrying her after his first wife's death and gave his name to the couple's second son. After Jonathan's death in 1844, she was sealed to Brigham Young. She moved to Utah with her children in 1855 and parted from Young sometime after 1858. Julia later lived with her children in Ogden, Nevada, and Salt Lake City. She died at her son Brigham's home in January 1891, "beloved and respected by all who knew her." *Courtesy International Society, Daughters of Utah Pioneers.*

two-and-one-half inches, he was evidently an imposing man.[3] Although once arrested for a notorious murder, Hampton was never convicted of a violent act. He rarely admits in his diary to engaging in violence, but he repeatedly states his willingness to do so and often was armed in the course of duty with various branches of Salt Lake's church-dominated police force.

Hampton served for years as a commissioned city and county enforcement officer and performed many mundane—and some dangerous—tasks. In 1870 Hampton joined most of the Salt Lake police force in abating Paul Englebrecht's saloon, a minor enforcement action that proved to loom surprisingly large. This was only one among many incidents that roiled Utah territory for the next two decades. Mormons, understandably enough, wanted to continue their exclusive control over the place where they planned to build the Kingdom of God. Non-Mormons, however, wanted at least a share of economic and political power. Until 1870 the Saints constituted the vast majority of the population, but the transcontinental railroad brought miners, merchants, lawyers, journalists, and adventurers into the territory in large numbers. As

[3] "Interesting Exhumations at Salt Lake," *Journal History*, 29 October 1869, 2–3.

MARY JANE RANDOLPH ROBINSON HAMPTON
Mary Jane Randolph Robinson was born in 1848 in England. She married B.Y. Hampton in 1870 and eventually bore ten children. B.Y. considered her the only one of his three wives who fulfilled her spousal obligations. *Courtesy International Society, Daughters of Utah Pioneers.*

commander of federal forces at Camp Douglas, Patrick Edward Connor worked hard with his allies to attract Gentiles to the territory, especially through the lure of mining. Rival institutions and power centers emerged in the capital city. The Mormons had the numbers to easily win elections for the territorial legislature and municipal governments and direct their law enforcement bodies. They controlled the local courts, including the low-level justice courts and the probate court system, and they established print organs, the *Deseret News* and *Salt Lake Herald.* Most importantly, of course, they had their well-organized religion with its powerful leadership.[4] The vastly outnumbered non-Mormons who contested for power could call on U.S. soldiers at Camp Douglas; the federally appointed governor; the judges, U.S. attorneys and marshals in the federal courts; or even the government in Washington. They expressed their views through the *Salt Lake Tribune.*

Hampton's experiences provide unique insights into this complex and often visceral struggle. Low-level clashes between church agents and their

[4]The rival legal systems are discussed throughout Firmage and Mangrum, *Zion in the Courts,* esp. chap. 9, "Mormon Law, Gentile Law."

opponents continued during most of Hampton's adult life, with him often on the scene. Until the 1880s he could be confident of the backing of LDS authorities. Church-paid attorneys, for example, fought the Englebrecht case all the way to the U.S. Supreme Court, ironically freeing Hampton from a murder charge, along with other Saints. Brigham Young himself hosted a party for the freed prisoners. But after Young's death, that kind of support seemed to vanish while the power of federal intervention waxed stronger. Hampton was jailed again for virtually all of 1886 when a scheme to entrap federal officials into a brothel backfired. Hampton was left to serve his sentence, while the other members of his "detective committee" declined to continue the prosecutions of federal officials. High LDS officials replied sympathetically to Hampton's pleas for financial help but did nothing concrete to relieve his distress. Even the *Deseret News* seemed to abandon him, neglecting to publish a petition for his pardon.

Hampton's domestic arrangements were as turbulent as his public activities. Like all Saints, he heard many exhortations to practice celestial marriage, and his mother was one of the Prophet's many wives. Hampton himself married three times. Although we have very little evidence other than his version of events, some clues can be teased out about his relationships and his wives' experiences, which reflect many of the complaints other plural wives made about the tension and unhappiness that came with sharing a husband. The dominant reality of those marriages was childbearing and raising: Hampton's first wife gave birth to five of his children, his second four, and his third ten. His first wife, Bertha, left him after only a few years of marriage; Helen was even unhappier but persisted in her marriage. Hampton's story also hints at the patriarchal power a husband enjoyed as he shuffled his wives in and out of various houses and their children between various wives.

By Hampton's lights, Mary, his third wife, was his only mate who behaved properly, standing by him throughout his legal troubles, managing his properties, and raising their many children. Despite the "judicial crusade" that was rocking the Mormon world, Hampton seems to have never been targeted for his marital relations, probably because he lived with Mary alone during the most intense period of the prosecutions. But B.Y. and Mary did expose themselves to risk, as members of the First Presidency sometimes spent nights "on the underground" in their home. Mary must have found marriage and motherhood trying, too. Undoubtedly her most terrible ordeal had nothing to do with religion or politics. One of the diphtheria epidemics that periodically swept through Utah Territory like the Angel of Death killed four of her children within three weeks during the summer of 1879.

Hampton's story combines retrospective accounts, such as his version of the persecution of the Mormons and Joseph Smith's murder, with periodic, often daily entries. The more frequent entries commence with the momentous events of July 1857, when the rank-and-file Saints learned of the approach of the Utah Expedition. Like many diarists, his industry sometimes lapsed for months, but when he had time, especially during his jail terms, the entries were more frequent and of greater length. He occasionally refers to scrapbooks that evidently do not survive. Hampton also read books and newspapers, both Mormon and secular, and cheered or disputed their contents. His story contains intriguing gaps and omissions. For example, there are no entries for most of 1866, including October, when Dr. J. King Robinson was murdered, a crime for which Hampton would be indicted. Hampton says nothing about the 1883 murder of chief of police Andrew Burt, his close friend while he was on the force, or the subsequent lynching of Burt's evident killer.[5] After closely following the anti-polygamy crusade through the late 1880s, including the death of church president John Taylor and the escheatment of LDS church property, Hampton says nothing about the climactic event of 1890, the Woodruff Manifesto that renounced the practice of polygamy. Instead, his long 1890–1891 entries are headlined "Brigham Young Trust Cos Record of their making me *ther scape goat*." Here, once again, B.Y. Hampton found himself facing prison time for running a house of prostitution. The Brigham Young Trust Company, whose officers included high-ranking officials in the LDS church, owned the building in question. Hampton became convinced that they were willing to sacrifice him to the legal authorities while they profited from illegal activities on their property and soiled the late Prophet's good name. Eventually the U.S. attorney dismissed the charge, much to Hampton's surprise.

After his near-brush with a third jail term, Hampton was clearly disillusioned. He blamed LDS leaders for tarnishing Brigham Young's legacy in pursuit of financial gain and, like many aging Latter-day stalwarts, he may have found his church's retreat from plural marriage and the Kingdom of

[5]On Robinson, see below; on the Burt murder and the lynching of Sam Joe Harvey, see Alexander and Allen, *Mormons and Gentiles*, 120.

God a bitter disappointment. As an enforcer of the Lord's justice, Hampton had outlived his usefulness. After 1890 he retreated from his public duties to concentrate on private business, including building and running a hotel. His narrative reflects the inward turn, focusing on personal temple work and his family, with occasional references to the birthdays or deaths of high LDS officials and his obvious joy over the opening of the Salt Lake Temple. His money troubles dominate the last pages.

Hampton's death in 1902 did not attract much notice in either the Mormon or Gentile-owned press. Utah was enjoying one of the periodic lulls in its rhetorical wars and, other than among his family and friends, Hampton probably seemed a relic of a past era, when the LDS faith needed stouthearted defenders. The causes he had served—protecting Zion from military invasion, sheltering the Prophet from attack, proving the moral hypocrisy of anti-polygamists—probably seemed quaint, or settled and best forgotten. The historical circumstances that produced Brigham Young Hampton's style of muscular chauvinism had passed, but his story vividly evokes his turbulent times.[6]

In Defence of God's People

I Brigham Young Hampton Son of Jonithan Hampton And Julia Foster was born in the Town of Kirtland Geouga County (now Lake County) Ohio on the 4th day of February 1836 being the eldest child of my Fathers Familey with the exception of my brother Nephi, who was born in the town of Lyon Wayne County state of Nieu York June 22d 1834.

Brigham Young converted my parents to the Principals of the Gosple and on April 15th 1833 at [blank] Babtised and Confirmed them Members in the Church of Jesus Christ of Laterday Saints. . . .[7]

Brigham Young and my Father carried on the carpenter business in Kirtland togather and both courted Miss Julia Foster my Mother at the same time as my Father commenced courting first. Brigham Young told him that he could have the first chance of poping the question and if Sister Foster did not accept him then he (Young) would try his luck in the same

---

[6]For changes in the Mormon world, see Alexander, *Mormonism in Transition*; Bigler, *Forgotten Kingdom*, 341–62; and Arrington, *Great Basin Kingdom*, 380–412.

[7]Brigham Young wrote that in Lyon, New York, he "baptized thirteen and organized a branch of the Church, among whom was a young man, Jonathan Hampton, whom I ordained a Priest and took with me." Journal History, 1 April 1833. See also Palmer and Butler, *Brigham Young*, 60–83.

direction. My Father went the same evening and Asked her hand in Marrige the request Was granted and on September 4th 1833 They were Married at [blank] Brigham Young performing the Serimony.[8]

Subsiquently while Brigham Young was traveling on a mision he caled at my parients House in Kirtland. I then being an infant without a name he requested the privilage of naming me. The request was granted and he gave me his name in full at the same time making me a presant of a pair of Red shoes.

May the 7th 1837 my Sister Sarah Cerena was born in Kirtland.

July 6th 1838. My parents in company with 515 other Saints left Kirtland for Missoura being driven from their homes and friends by Mobe violence.[9]

On the 17th of October 1838 my Sister Sarah Cerena died and was burried in Cadwell County Missouria.

Between April the 18th and 20th 1839 the Saints evacuated Far West. My Parents being again driven from their homes at the hands of a ruthless horribing Mob.[10]

Through all their persicutions destruction and loss of property and the death of their little Daughter they remained faithfull to the cause of truth and in the confidence and esteam of the Saints and all good people.

After being driven from Missouria they went to Quincy Adams County Illinois where they and most of the Saints tarried for a short time after being expeled from their houses and previous to moving to Comerce afterwards caled Nauvoo.[11]

---

[8]For Brigham Young as a carpenter in Ohio, see Arrington, *Brigham Young*, 35–36. Young's first wife died in 1832, and he did not marry again until 1834. "I Brigham Young have maried Jonathan Hampton aged 22 years and Julia Foster aged 21 years," Young noted on 4 September 1833, the date Hampton gives for his parents' sealing at the hands of Young—his first. See Diary of Brigham Young, quoted in Cook, *Nauvoo Marriages, Proxy Sealings*, 188n1.

[9]Jonathan Hampton and his father-in-law, James Foster, belonged to the Second Quorum of Seventy. Journal History, 31 December 1836, 4. Jonathan was a member of the Kirtland Safety Society Anti-Banking Company, a poorly capitalized and unchartered bank (or anti-bank) that collapsed before the panic of 1837. See Journal History, 2 January 1837, 3; Arrington, *Great Basin Kingdom*, 13–15. James Foster was one of the counsellors who led the move from Kirtland on 6 July 1838; Journal History, 13 March 1838. History of the Church, 423. "The chief difficulty in Ohio was economic," two leading LDS historians observed. Some five hundred Mormons remained, and not all left when Hyrum Smith commanded them to move to Nauvoo in 1841. See Allen and Leonard, *The Story of the Latter-day Saints*, 120, 125.

[10]Brothers James and Jonathan and cousin Robert Hampton signed a petition to Missouri governor Lilburn Boggs asking for protection from mobs. Petition of the Saints of De Witt to Governor Boggs, Journal History, 22 September 1838. Instead, Boggs issued his infamous extermination order. Bigler, *Forgotten Kingdom*, 26–27. For the moves from Kirtland and Far West, see Arrington and Bitton, *The Mormon Experience*, 44–64. Amanda Smith's vivid first-hand description of the Hauns Mill attack is reproduced in History of the Church, 72–73.

[11]Joseph Smith, Jr., renamed Commerce, a small town in Hancock County, Illinois, Nauvoo from a Hebrew word meaning "beautiful." For a history, see Leonard, *Nauvoo*; for the naming, 58–59.

In the year 1840 my parents moved to a Small town caled Fa[i]rfield in Adams County Ilinois. The Same year December 28th 1840 my brother Eaderly Foster was born. They then moved to a town called Mendoss in Hancock County Illinois.[12]

June 22d 1842. My brother Nephi was babtized and confirmed a member in the Church of Jesus Christ of Laterday Saints by Father.

February 4th 1844. I became eight years old and was baptized and confirmed a member in the Church of Jesus Christ of Laterday Saints by my Father.

June 27th 1844 Joseph and Hyrum Smith was assassinated in Carthage Jale by a masked Mob.[13]

December 16th 1844. My Sister Julia Anna was born in Mendoss Hancock County Illinoys and on the 30th of the Same month and year my Father died after an ilness of about thirty hours brought on by exposure in guarding the Prophet Joseph Smith Jr and others of the Bretheren and hard works. His remains were enterd in the Nauvoo Cemetry.[14]

In the Same year that Joseph and Hurum Smith were murdered I became eight years old and was baptised and confirmed a member in the Church my Sister Julia Ann was born and my Father died.

In the Spring of 1845 Mother and Family moved to Nauvoo and lived in a house belonging to Brigham Young. Mother recived her Endowments in the Temple at Nauvoo and was Sealed to Father for Eternity and to Brigham Young for time February 3d 1846.

[*Marginal note*: Sealed by Amasa M. Lyman Wendell Mace Witnesses Miles Romney as per record John Nicholson Recorder].[15]

September 27th 1845. The authorities of the Church made a treaty with the mob to evacuate Nauvoo the following Spring. In February 1846 the Saints began their Exidess from Nauvoo to the Rockey Mountains.

---

[12]Hampton likely meant Mendon, originally named Fairfield, in Adams County, just across the line from Hancock County.

[13]On the murder of the Smith brothers, see Leonard, *Nauvoo*, 387–98; and Hay, "The Mormon Prophet's Tragedy," 671–78.

[14]Jonathan Hampton appears in Siegfried, comp., List of Known Dead Buried in Old Mormon Cemetery Nauvoo, 3, with a death date of 30 December 1844.

[15]This was a proxy marriage, with Brigham Young standing proxy for Jonathan Hampton for time but not eternity. Julia Foster is mentioned in passing, if at all, in biographies of Brigham Young. Hirshon, *The Lion of the Lord*, 204, 219–20, lists her as both wife 32, "Julia Foster," and 66, "Mrs. Hampton." Leonard Arrington's more scholarly study does not mention Julia in his appendix of the prophet's wives. Arrington, *Brigham Young*, 420–21. Jeffery O. Johnson confirmed that Young married Julia Foster on 3 February 1846, one of Young's nineteen marriages in five weeks as the Saints hurried to perform their ceremonies in the Nauvoo Temple. Johnson, "Determining and Defining 'Wife,'" 61, 68n36; for proxy marriages, see 58.

We having no means of conveyance Brigham Young promised to Send teams to move us in two weeks from the time he left Nauvoo. In the mean time Granfather Foster came for us to gone with him to his home in Morgan County Illinoys. After waiting Seven or eight weeks for the promised teams and Granfather refusing to wait any longer we were compelled to accept his offer. We afterwards learned that the team came for us in about two weeks after we had left. Mother felt very much anoyed because she did not wait longer as She was anxious to go with the Saints.[16]

In the fall of 1847 my mother married a man by the name of Thomas Cole an Englishman being almost compeled to do so on account of having a Family of small children her Father dead and no way of suporting them.[17] Coal proved to be a mean Scoundrell we had no peace from the time of his marrige untill he left us and went to California he abused and beat my mother and her children most unmercifully.

September 23d 1848. My half Sister Vilate was born.

When I was forteen years old I left home worked on a farm for my Uncle Miles Haladay several months. I then moved in to Jacksonville boarded at a private House and cut cord wood for a living for one winter. I then learned Collar making. Afterward went to work as a Journeyman in a Harness Shop and received the Same wages as those that had learned the business. Not liking the business I learned the Degeuaratype business with a man by the name of [Riners?] and was employed in that business when I left for Utah in 1855. . . .

In the year 1852 or 3 Coal left us and went to California for which blessing God bee prased. After he had been gone some time Mother obtained a Divorce from him by due process of Law.

Some time in May 1855 Thomas Colbern and James Cace Mormon missionarys came to our house in Jacksonville Morgan Co. Ill. where we were then living being requested to do so by Pres. Brigham Young, to see if we were still in the Faith and desirous to gather with the Saints, and if so to assist us on our journey to Salt Lake City, Utah Territory, which offer we

[16]Julia's father, James Foster, was excommunicated for unclear reasons in 1844, perhaps as part of the struggle over who would succeed Joseph Smith. For Foster's appointment as a president of Seventies in September 1837, see Faulring, ed., *An American Prophet's Record*, 165; see also Quinn, *The Mormon Hierarchy: Origins of Power*, 466, 545–46, and *The Mormon Hierarchy: Extensions of Power*, 141–42. For his excommunication, see Journal History, 7 October 1844, 4.

[17]Hampton noted that James Foster died 21 December 1846. Papers, 60.

gladly accepted, and all of us that was over eight years old were babtized and rebabtized and confirmed under the hands of James Cace.[18]

June 22d 1855. We Started on our Jounrey to Salt Lake City. Some months [later?] arived in Saint Louis. Stayed there about two weeks untill the arival of other Saints from the Old Country.

The Steamboat Seronack No 2 was chartered on which we took pasage with the rest of the Saints during our passage up the Missiouria River. Many of the pasengers were atac with the Colera several died and were buried on the banks of the River in difrent placeses.[19]

Sometime in July we arived at Atchison Kansas and camped about three miles from there in what was known as Mormon Grove, the outfiting place of the Saints previous to crossing the Plains.

July 28th 1855. We Started on our Journey acros the Plains in a train known as the Church Train but mostly owned by Erastus Snow one of the twelve Apostles. Isaac Aldred Captain and James Pace assistant.[20]

On the first part of the Journey I was very sick and came near dieing and was sick the most of the Journey. We had a long and tedious Journey acrost the Plains of over one thousand Miles in Ox Teams (from Larime to Bridger the distance is about five hundred miles). The whole company ran out of provisions at Laramie and had but one pint of Flour per head per day and not any thing else to eat till we arived at Bridger, where we met teams from the valey with provisions for us (the company).

We with the portion of the Train carrying Familes arrived in Salt Lake City November 2d 1855 in the evening. The balance of the Train carrying merchandise arrived some time in December.

November 8th 1855. Mother, Nephi and I made a visit to Pres Youngs. We

[18]Julia Hampton wrote Brigham Young on 1 March 1853; he replied some months later (only the reply survives) offering assistance in migrating to Utah. See Brigham Young to Julia Hampton, 25 July 1853, in Brigham Young Office Files, letterpress copybook transcriptions, 126–27, in Turley, ed., *Selected Collections*. Thomas Colburn wrote that he and James Case rebaptized eight people at Julia Hampton's home, including her sons Brigham Y. and Edaly Foster. Journal History, 31 May 1855.

[19]Although downplayed by LDS church officials, cholera played havoc with elements of the 1855 emigration. See Andrus, "News' Correspondence," *Deseret News*, 18 July 1855, 8/1. "The cry of the dying and shrieks of the living presented nothing but the true scene, even all the horrors of death imaginable," wrote Capt. Seth Blair after more than thirty-five members of his train died at Deer Creek in Kansas Territory. See Seth M. Blair/Edward Stevenson company narrative, Mormon Pioneer Overland Travel website.

[20]The train under the command of Isaac Allred left Mormon Grove on 31 July. "Our Correspondence," *Deseret News*, 5 September 1855, 8/1–2. See also "Report of the General Immigration of Latter-day Saints, from Mormon Grove, Atchison, Kansas Territory to Utah, 1855," in History of the Church, 8 July 1855, 73.

was frindly recived and ate diner with him and Family in the Behive House. Mother and her children with the exception of my self moved in to a home in the twelft ward rented for them by Pres Young. He also furnished us with employment provisions and such other things as was needed. I remained at Pres Young's at his request as one of his Familey.

March 1856. Nephi and I were rebabtised in City Creek and Same month received our Endowments in the Endowment House Salt Lake City.

In the fore part of 1856 Pres Young Sent me to Jesse W Fox to learn the Surveying. I worked a[t] that business for Several months.[21]

In the later part of the same year Pres Young's first wifes Sister Aunt Jamima as she was caled was taken Crazy and under my charge about two months.[22]

Some time in 1856 Mother took charge of the Lyon House at Pres Young's request.[23]

October 12th 1856, I Married one Bertha King, a Divorced Wife of David Candlass [Candland] and a Daughter of Thomas King and Hannah Tapfield King. She Bertha was born in Norage England [blank] 1835. We were married in Pres Youngs office, he performing the Serimony in presence of Sister King and others.[24] We then commenced keeping house in the Seventh Ward.

February 23d 1857. I was ordained a Seventy under the hands of William Miller and Raial Borney and admited a member in the Tenth Quorum of Seventies.[25]

July 23d 1857. I and wife started up big Cottonwood Canion in company with Pres Young and many others to the lake at the head of big Cottonwood

---

[21]Jesse W. Fox later served as LDS church surveyor; his son, Jesse, Jr., was a close friend of Hampton's and also a surveyor. See Bigler, *Forgotten Kingdom*, 142–43; "Excursion to Fort Limhi," *Deseret News*, 10 June 1857, 4/4.

[22]Jemima Angell, sister of Mary Ann Angell. Ann Eliza Webb Young claimed Aunt Mima was a proxy wife who "worked until she became broken down in mind and body." See Young, *Wife No. 19*, 513.

[23]It is unclear how long Julia Foster remained Young's wife, or at the Lion House. Young biographer Stanley Hirshon claims that "several visitors to Utah repeated the complicated story of Mrs. Hampton . . . [who] refused to be sealed to Young for eternity, left him in a huff." Hirshon, *The Lion of the Lord*, 204, 219–20. A contemporary writer claimed that "some misunderstanding" caused Brigham to "cast off . . . Mrs. Hampton." Waite, *The Mormon Prophet and His Harem*, 220. Hampton writes without explanation that Julia moved to Ogden with children Nephi and Vilate in 1858. Hampton, Papers, 65. The Lion House, home to a constantly changing cast of wives and children, was completed in 1856. See Dixon, "The Beehive and Lion Houses," 124–31.

[24]Hannah Tapfield King was an English convert who became prominent in Mormon women's circles, although her husband never joined the church. Hannah was sealed to Brigham Young for eternity in 1872 but remained married to Thomas King. Johnson, "Determining and Defining 'Wife'"; Beecher, "The 'Leading Sisters.'"

[25]A Seventy, a priesthood office under the Quorum of the Twelve Apostles, has primarily missionary responsibilities. Bitton, *Historical Dictionary of Mormonism*, s.v. "Seventy."

Canion Some twenty miles from the City for the purpose of celebrating the aneversey of the arivle of the Pioneers in Salt Lake Valley on July 24th 1847. We arived at the Lake on the 24th. Canon was fired in the afternoon. Bands played and all went forth in the dance and such other amusments as was had for the occasion.

On the 25 of July 1857[26] Brother A. O. Smoot, Porter Rockwell, and Judson Stottard [and] Elias Smith arived the two latter from the states on horse back bringing the inteligence that Government (James Bucanon President) have stoped our Mail and was Sending an Armey of Two Thousand five hundred Soldiers under comand of General Harney to use us up and drive us from our homes and rob and murder us as the Mobs had done in Ohio, Missora and Illinoys.[27]

Saturday 26th Started home and arived the Same evening.

Sunday August 16th 1857. My Wife Bertha bear me a Son at 7 O clock in the morning.[28]

September 15th. Pres Young caled for fifty volunteers and wood not say what for. Every one thought as the Armey was on us that the Volunteers were wanted for Some forlorn hope or to run the gauntled in some desperate undertaking. I thought the Same and volunteered with forty two others and was accepted.[29]

Sunday Sept 20th 1857. Wife and I took our baby to the 17th Ward meating and had our son blessed and named Brigham Young under the hands of Orson Hyde, one of the twelve apstles, and Bishop Calister. Bro Hyde Mouth and gave him as good a blessing as I ever heard.[30]

---

[26]The messengers actually rode in a day earlier at about noon. See, for example, Brooks, ed., *On the Mormon Frontier,* 24 July 1857, 634. For a description of the celebration, see History of the Church, 24 July 1857, 397–400.

[27]Although the motives behind the Utah Expedition are still unclear, reports of federal territorial officials convinced Buchanan that Utah was in a state of potential rebellion. See MacKinnon, *At Sword's Point,* 99–111; and Bigler, *Forgotten Kingdom,* 141–47. Young probably knew of the army's approach for about a month and took dramatic advantage of the public announcement at the tenth anniversary of the pioneer company's arrival in the valley. Smoot was Salt Lake City's mayor; he and Stoddard were driving cattle east and had been refused the mail for Utah at Independence, Missouri. See Schindler, *Orrin Porter Rockwell,* 248–52.

[28]Hannah Tapfield King noted the birth in her journal, now at LDS Archives: "At 8 o'clock A.M. news was brought to me of the birth of my grandson, Brigham Young Hampton, being the morning on which Brother Young declared the independence of our people of the United States upon the stand in consequence of the repeated unfilial measures they had taken against us, and in the prospect of a troop of 1000 soldiers coming here with sealed orders, etc." Courtesy of David L. Bigler.

[29]The list of names, including Hampton's, appears in History of the Church, 13 September 1857, 513–14. William Knox says that all the others besides him volunteered very reluctantly, and he also thought they were going to fight the army directly. Knox, diary, 13 September–12 November 1857.

[30]Infants of Mormon families are given a name and blessing by priesthood holders at a Sunday meeting. Bitton, *Historical Dictionary of Mormonism,* s.v. "Blessing of infants."

Some time in November 1857 I with the rest of the Volunteers started for Blackfoot near Fort Hall two hundred miles north of Salt Lake City, where we arived the same month. Our instructions wer to look out for the Soldiers. We built Fort Lookout and looked out and cut hay, build dams, made ditches and planted forty or fifty acres of wheat.

After being there Sometime an Express mesenger came from Pres Young warning us to leave as the Soldiers were gowing to Foart Hall to winter (Which afterwards Prove untrue). The Same evening that we recived the message we Cached our provisions and other things that we could not hall as we only had suficient Teams to hall what provisions we needed and our beading.

About the Same time the Bretheren that was misionarys to the Indians on Salmon River were driven out by the Indians and all their provisions taken. Our Caches of Provisions proved a blessing to them and kept them from Starving.[31]

The third day after my arival at home from Fort Lookout I was caled upon to gow in Search of Indians that had been Stealing Stock from the people in Tooela and Grants Ville about forty miles west of Salt Lake City. This was in the Spring of 1858.

I was very much fatieged from my recent trip fealing duty bound to gow at every call. I in company with about 30 others Started in Search of the Indians and Stolen Stock. On our arival at Skull Valey we were atac and fired upon by them at Several diferent times during the trip. We did not return the fire as we were instructed not to do so by Pres Young only in self defence. We traveled about two hundred miles West on to the Desert but could not overtake the Indians and had to come home with out the Indians or Stock, and no one was hurt. We were gone about two weeks and had a very hard trip.[32]

On ariving at Grants Ville we learned that the Saints had all to Move South in conciquence of the Armey passing through the City.[33]

June 7th 1858. Messers Powell and McCullay Sent out as peace Commissioners by the Government, arived in Salt Lake City and made arangements

[31]Brigham Young dispatched the Blackfoot Mission under the command of Andrew Cunningham to build a way station between Great Salt Lake City and points north in October 1857. Roberts, *A Comprehensive History*, 4:247. Young was considering a move north should the U.S. Army reach Utah Territory, perhaps to the Bitterroot Valley, which Mormon missionaries had explored since 1855. Accordingly, he strengthened the Mormon settlement at Fort Limhi, a strategic point just west of Lemhi Pass through the Beaverhead Mountains (the Salmon River Mission). Indian attacks on Fort Limhi in February 1858 convinced Young to abandon the move north. See Bigler, *Forgotten Kingdom*, 97–98, 137–39, 142–45, 151–52, 186–87; Bigler, *Fort Limhi*.

[32]For reports of Indian attacks on this party, see "Another Murder by Indians," *Deseret News*, 14 April 1858, 4/1.

[33]For the move south, see Arrington, *Great Basin Kingdom*, 182–92.

with Governe Brigham Young, then Govener of the Territory of Utah, to let the armey pass through the City and pledged the faith of the Nation that the Soldiers Should not molest the People or their Property.

Fearing that they would not keep their word, knowing that the Nation never had protected or defended the People of God, the Saints began moving South from this City and all settlements North, comencing their exidus Some time in March previous to the arival of the Commissioners. When I arived in the City from the Indian expedition I with others were detached as guards to guard the City and Property left by the Saints also to watch the Armey as they passed through the City and in case they did not keep their word to destroy all property in the City and country around by Fire, So that the property of the Saints might not fall in the hands of our Enimies, as it had done before and to fight the Armey to the death in defence of God's people if Need bee.

June 26th 1858 the Armey passed through the City and was from nine O lock in the morning till six O clock in the evening passing through in a continuous trott, numbering in all including Camp followers, upwards of three [inserted "Some say 7"] thousand persons. They made no disturbance or trouble.[34]

June 30th the Saints began returning to their homes.

In July 1858 I went and brought my Familey back from Payson, where I had taken them Some Seventy miles South of the City.

On my return in the later part of July my Brother Nephi and I commenced carrying on the Harness and Saddl business.

May the 14th 1859 my Wife Bertha bear me a Daughter. She was named Hannah Bertha and blessed under the hands of Bishop [L W.?] Hardy and Brother Atwood of the 12th Ward Where we were then living.

In 1860 I bought a lott in the 12th Ward and commenced building a House which I compleated in 1861.

May 12th 1861. Saturday night my wife Bertha bear me a Son, blessed under my hands and named Jonithan Victor.

October 7th 1863. At the Jeneral Conference I with others wer Caled to gow to Dixe three hundred miles South to rais Cotton.[35]

---

[34]President Buchanan named Lazarus W. Powell and Ben McCulloch peace commissioners in April 1858. On the abortive Utah War, see Furniss, *The Mormon Conflict;* and Bigler and Bagley, *The Mormon Rebellion.* Capt. Albert Tracy described marching through the city, deserted except for "a picked few of [Brigham Young's] 'destroyers' of decidedly rough and sinister aspect, left as a police, and with orders to fire the city in case we offered to occupy it." "Journal of Capt. Albert Tracy." See also Arrington, *Great Basin Kingdom,* 170–94.

[35]On the Cotton Mission to southwestern Utah, which began in 1861, see Arrington, *Great Basin Kingdom,* 216–17.

August 7th 1863, Friday morning at twenty minutes past five O clock my wife Bertha bear me a Son blessed and named Thomas Owen.

In the fall of 1863 I sold my house and Lott preparitory to preforming my mission South and recived for pay a Small span of Mules and a Wagon. I Sent all my things South by parties gowing with the exception of such things as neaded on the journey.

November 7th 1863. I Married Wife Helen Emily Bone. She and my wife Bertha were Sealed to me over the Alter in the Endowment House by Wilford Woodruff one of the twelve Apostles.[36] Witnesses Heber C. Kimball first concillor to Pres Young and ———. In the evening when I went to See my wife Helen I found a note on the table addressed to me Saying She had gone to Montana with a Jentile and that She did not belive that the Serimony Married us and wished me not to follow her. I showed the Letter to Pres Young and he said let her gow and not follow her. I did not See her for over a week again. I was making all preparations to move South. She came to me on the street with Mrs. Twitchel and beged me to forgive her as what she had Said in the letter was all false. I consented to gow and see her as She requested We Settled our dificilties parshaly. Helen Emily Bone was the Daughter of Henry Bone and Mary Ann Corbishley and was born in Hobart Town Vandermans land Australia Jany 6th 1842.

On the 14th of November 1863 I started South with my Familey with the exception of my wife Helen who remained with her Father. I was taken sick with the chill the first night out and was so bad that my wife had to drive the team till we arived in Springvill fifty miles south. . . .[37]

November 14th 1864. I rented a House of Charles Crismon in the 14th Ward and commenced keeping House with my wife Helen for the first time Scince our marrige in concequence of her actions which were to Say the least not that of a Wife to a husband and when She was about to be confined She consented to live with me and her Father moved in to the above mentioned house.[38]

---

[36]It was common for Saints to receive sealings before they went on distant missions, since the endowments had to be performed by the proper authorities in Salt Lake City. In the long years while the Temple was under construction, sacred ordinances were performed in the Endowment House on Temple Square, which opened 5 May 1855. Alexander, *Things in Heaven and Earth*, 177. On the history of Mormon plural marriage and the campaign against it, see Hardy, *Solemn Covenant*. Woodruff sealed twenty-seven couples this day. Kenney, ed., *Wilford Woodruff's Journal*, 7 November 1863, 6:135.

[37]Hampton was released from the mission because of illness. See Brigham Young to B.H. [*sic*] Hampton, 13 July 1864, letterpress copy book, 234, in Selected Collections DVD.

[38]Charles Crismon opened the first gristmill in Utah; see Brooks, ed., *On the Mormon Frontier*, 343n15.

December 15th 1864. My Wife Helen bear me a Daughter at twenty minutes past three O clock P.M., Still born kiled in berth. Named Helen Louisa and interd in my Lot in Salt Lake City Cemetry.

In the Spring of 1865 My wife Bertha being dissatisfyed Started to California by Stage. I Sold all her household furniture to get money to pay her pasage and to keep her Sometime after her arivle in California. She left her four children with me.[39] I then moved my wife Helen in the house that Bertha had left to take care of the house and four Children. Bertha after gowing about two hundred miles returned loosing her pasege money and Spending the balance, She had to return. After her return She Wished me to take her back, I told her that I would leave the Matter with Pres Young and do as he said. Conciquently She and her Mother came & Met Pres Young in his Parlor in the Lyon house. She confessed that She had done rong and was willing to try and do better if I would take her back. Pres Young said he should not Say for me to take her back but Said if I felt like taking her back, and if Should bee the means of Saving her, it would prove a blessing to me. Conciquently I took her back with the determination of doing the best I could for her as I always had striven to do. I then moved my wife Helen back to the Crismon house.

The same sumer I desolved partnerShip with George Joiner.

September 11th 1865. My Brother Nephi died at Ferimorze Little's house where he had been lying sick for some time under the care of my sister Julia Ann, then third wife of Fermorze Little. He Nephi died of consumption and was buried in my Lot in Salt Lake City Cemetry. Just previous to his death his youngest Daughter died at Ogden Where his Family were living. Neph Married one Julia Keets a divorced wife of Frank Townsend on [blank] 18 and was the Father of [blank] Children by her [blank] Boys and [blank] Girls.

December 9th 1865. My Wife Bertha bear me a Daughter She was named Louisa Georgianna and was blessed under my hands just previous to her death, which accurd When She was near two years old.

February Second 1866. My Sister Julia Ann Little lost her Son Edwin by death. His remains was burried in Salt Lake City Cemetry.

---

[39]According to dissident Fanny Stenhouse, "the first wife of 'Brig.' Hampton" told her that "her husband whipped her because she would not consent to his stripping their home of everything that was either useful or handsome in order to furnish a house for his second wife. Finally, he shut her up while he took her entire parlour furniture away." Stenhouse, *An Englishwoman in Utah*, 328–29. B.Y.'s first wife was Bertha, but the complaint may be Helen's. Stenhouse's autobiography appeared in several different versions; the full-length 1873 edition, called *"Tell it All,"* pp. 528–29, tells the same story without naming the Hamptons. See Walker, "The Stenhouses."

February 9th 1866. Twenty minutes past one P.M. My Wife Helen bear me a Son he was named William Brigham and blessed under the hands of Bishop Hogland, Bro [Turnboss?] and my self in the 14th Ward.[40] During 1866 I bought a quarter of a Lot in the 15th Ward and built my wife Helen a house I also built a two Story Shop in the place of the one I previously built.

In 1866 My Sister Julia Ann Little lost her Son Lewis Hill by death, his remains were burried in Salt Lake City Cemetry.

In the Year 1867 My Sister Julia Ann Little lost her Son Leon Fermorze by death his remains was burried in Salt Lake City Cemetry.

July 4th 1867. I Started to Sweet Water Mine in Company with James [B?] and others by permission of Pres Young. We got drove out by Indians, Some of the Miners kiled and Skelped. We had a narrow escape with our lives and arived home the 28th of July. I Sold claims in the mines that I had located for two thousand dollars which proved a great blessing to me as I had not been able to do any work for over a year on account of ill health.[41]

The 6th of August I was Elected Constable for the Second precinct Salt Lake City.

September 1st 1867. My Sister Julia Ann Little died of Consumption. Interd in Salt Lake City Cemetry. She was Married to Fermorz Little [blank] 1858 as his third Wife and was the Mother of five Children for Boyes and one Girl two of hoom survive her namely Brigham Ferimorz and Faney.[42]

September 18th my Wife Helen Bear me a Daughter ten minutes past two P.M. She was Named Lilia Victoria. I think that she was not blessed as her Mother was dissatisfyed with the principals of the Gosple.

October 9th 1867. My Daughter Louisa Georgianna Died her remains interd in Salt Lake City Cemetry . . . She was blessed under my hands a fiew minutes before she died her Funeral sermon preached by Bishop Hogland.

In the later part of October 1867 My Mother and my half sister Vilate and her Husband. . . .[43]

January 8th 1870. My Wife Helen bear me a Son at 10 minutes past 6 O Clock A.M.

---

[40]Abraham L. Hoagland served as bishop of the Fourteenth Ward from 1851 until his death in February 1872. William Hampton later gave his mother's name as Helen "Emily Huntley (Boone) Hampton" and used Huntley as his middle name. See Hampton, WPA Interview with Walker Winslow.

[41]"H.J." wrote about the Sweetwater mine in an 18 July letter; "Correspondence," *Deseret News*, 7 August 1867, 3/2.

[42]A nephew of Brigham Young, Feramorz Little was his uncle's business manager, a prominent railroad investor, and mayor of Salt Lake City. See Alexander and Allen, *Mormons and Gentiles*, 91.

[43]Here four pages (87–90) are missing.

January 8th 1870. The Utah Central Railway was laid to the edge of the Square intended for the terminous. Same day I recived an invitation to a grand Celebration and Ball to take place in the Theatre on the compleation of the U.C. Ry. Monday January 10th 1870 the last Tye and Rail laid and last Spike driven by Pres Young in presence of Thousands of people (The Spike and hamer were made of Utah iron). After the last Spike was driven Canon were fired and Bands of Music plaid interspersed with Speaches and Toasts and in the evening by displays of Fire Works and the elluminating the City. The same evening I tended a Grand [Complimary?] Ball and Super in the Theatre in honor of the Completion of the U C. Ry. I took Miss Mary J R Robinson as partner 11th tended another Select Ball at the same place Took Miss [P?] Young as partner. 14th I tended a Military Ball at the Theatre. . . .[44]

Friday January 21st 1870.[45] Bro [Leboren?] and I blest and married my Son Franklin also administered to him for sickness Bro. Leboren mouth.

January 24th 1870. The Godbie etes Organized by voting in Wm S Godbie and W. T. Harrison as equal Councillors to the Coming Man that is to Lead their Church. They have recived Revelation as to he is but the man does not know it him self but God has promised to Reveal it to him, So they Say (Godbie & Harrison). The officers of the Church are to be designated by Revelation and then voted in by balet by the members of their Church. Eli B. Kelsey was designated and voted in as one of the Twelve. Henry Lawrence as Trustee for the Church. I was presant at this Meating and tended most of their meatings to report their doings. In a Subsiquent meating Godbie, Harrison, Lawrence, Kelsey, Salisbury and others berated Pres Young and the authorities of the Church and the Church its self and said it Should be broken in pieces and when the defiant speakers wer talking and said any thing against the authorities or Church of Jesus Christ of Laterday Saints the Congrigation or Mob more properly Shouted, Clapt their hands and Stampt their feet. They made a very Small ripel which soon Subsided, their organization broken up and the members are a Miserable pack of Apostates.[46]

---

[44]The Utah Central Railroad, built largely with LDS church funds, connected Salt Lake City to the new transcontinental line at Ogden. See Arrington, *Great Basin Kingdom*, 270–75. For the laying of the last rail, see "Monday's Celebration" in History of the Church, 10 January 1870, 25–44.

[45]Hampton's 16 January 1870 entry summarized "a letter from Cosin Robert" in which Robert Hampton reported "Plurality of wives drove Me from the Church," but said he had not joined any other faith.

[46]Mostly successful businessmen who shared an interest in spiritualism, the Godbeites or New Movement objected to Brigham Young's economic policies and resistance to mining. In November 1869 William S. Godbe and Elias L. T. Harrison issued a manifesto declaring the Church of Zion. For more, see Walker, *Wayward Saints*; Bigler, *Forgotten Kingdom*, 266–68, 276–79; and the Afterword. For contemporary coverage, see "A Special's 'Revelation,'" *Deseret News*, 16 February 1870, 7/1.

Tuesday January 25th 1870. Franklin the son of my Wife Helen Died at half past 4 OClock A.M. of Lung diseas. Funeral Sermon preached by Bro Jeter Clinton his remains wer buried in my Lot in the Cemetry.

February 17th 1870. I and some of the police at about 10 O clock at night had some dificulty with Some Soldiers in atempting to arrest them for hiting an Indian. There was Several shots fired on both sides and no one hurt. I got shot through my clothes the ball passing through my left coat pocket through the Seat of my pants and drawers and tore My Garments slightly but did not pass through. The ball then past out through my right Coat pocket leaving 17 ball holes in my cloths. We captured two of them on the Military resirvation. They had an examination and were bound over on eight hundred dollars Bonds to appear at the next term of the Probate Court.[47]

February 22d 1870. I atended an aniversey Ball given at the Theater in honor of Washingtons Birth day. I took My Wife Helen as partner for the evening.

The 23d I atended a complimentry Ball in the Theatre given by the Manigment of the Same and took Miss Mary Jane R. Robinson but did not remain long on account of My Wife Helen Coming to the Ball and raising a Squall.

February 27th 1870. I proposed Marrige to Miss Mary J.R. Robinson. She accepted and on March 11th 1870 We wer Married in the Endowment House D H Wells Second Councillor to Pres Young performing the Sealing Ordinance. Witnesses Andrew Burt Wm Hyde and Bro & Sister Miles.[48] Mary Jane Randolph Robinson the Daughter Robert Johnston Robinson and Melison Hannah Gothard was born in Sunderland County of Durham England Nov 1st 1848.

Wensday Morning July 6th 1870. My Wife Helen after repeated injury and insult from the day we wer married Atact me in the public Street, Scrached me and tore my cloths all because I went to her House to See the Children.

July 7 & 8 1870. Wife Mary and I tended a Ball in the Theatre. Pres Young was there and invited me to gow with him to Ogden, where he and others were gowing to hold a two days meating.

Friday July 8th 1870. I was cited before Bp Burton of the 15th Ward on

[47]For the near-shooting, see "Local and Other Matters," *Deseret News*, 23 February 1870, 5/1.

[48]It is sometimes difficult to tell to which "Burt" Hampton refers. Andrew Hill Burt was Salt Lake City's chief of police and was murdered in August 1883. Hampton usually calls him "marshal" or "Capt." Burt. His cousin Alexander Burt (usually "Alex Burt"), also from Dunfermline, Scotland, was also a policeman and a county jailer. Alexander's son Andrew D., or "A.D.," was a policeman and county jailer in the mid-1880s. Andrew Hill's son Andrew John Box Burt ("A. J. Burt") was also a policeman. Hampton also refers to "J. W." Burt, presumably Joseph William Box Burt, another son of Andrew Hill's.

Complaint of my Wife Helen. Adjourned till the 9th at 8 Oclock P.M. Again Adjourned till the 12th at 8 Oclock.[49]

Saturday 9th. Started for Ogden with Pres Young and Others on the Cars arived at Ogden Tabernacle at 10 O clock where the People were Asembled to meat up. Two meatings wher held that day. Pres Young with others occupying the time, also two Meatings. Sunday 6 O clock in the evening started home arived at half past 7 O clock.

Tuesday July 12th 1870. At 8 O clock I met Bishop Burton Councillors three Teachers and my Wife Helen. She failed to Sustain her Charge against me. She found all maner of fault with me and without cause and would not listen to the Council of the Bishop and Said She would distroy my property and insult me every opertunity on the Public Street untill I would treat her better and untill She got revenge.

July 18th. I Employed Snow & Hoag Comence Suit against My Wife Helen in the Probate Court for a Divorce On the advice of Pres Young, I had to advance $35.00 as costs and Attorneys fees. The Suit was afterwards desmissed at her request as she did not want to be Seperated from me.[50]

July 19th 1870. Governer Shaffer in response to a call for a public meeting to Speak he Said, "Fellow Citizens rest ashured you Shall my feeble efforts to put down this infernal Theocracy meaning the Church and Kingdom of God.[51]

August 27th 1870. Recived a notice from E. W. East County Clirk that I was Elected Constable for the 2d Precinct Salt Lake City at the August Election.[52]

August 29th 1870. I in conection with Alderman Jeter Clinton, City

[49]The LDS church developed an elaborate court system to handle a variety of disputes and issues among members, especially family and marital; the bishop's court is the lowest level. See Firmage and Mangrum, *Zion in the Courts*, 25–47; and Gordon, *The Mormon Question*, 94–95.

[50]Latter-day Saints were encouraged to keep disputes between members in the church courts, but they sometimes resorted to civil courts. Hampton's action suggests Helen had already apostatized. See Firmage and Mangrum, *Zion in the Courts*, 322–31. Hampton charged in his petition that "she has on several diferent [*sic*] occasions struck your petitioner, torn his clothes, pounded and beaten him with the broom, fist, and scratched with her hands, and otherwise conducted herself toward your petitioner so that they cannot live in peace and union together." *Brigham Hampton vs. Helen E. Hampton*, petition for divorce, Salt Lake County Probate Court Records, 18 July 1870.

[51]President Ulysses S. Grant appointed J. Wilson Shaffer territorial governor in January 1870. Although he was dying of tuberculosis, Shaffer was determined to enforce federal authority in Utah. See Bigler, *Forgotten Kingdom*, 283, 285.

[52]Hampton's commission is recorded in Lieutenant Governor Executive Record Books, vol. B, 5 September 1870, 328; his other law enforcement commissions are found throughout these records.

Marshal McAllister Chief of Police Andrew Burt and the rest of the Police and asistants, 22 in number, were arrested on a warant issued by Judg Stricklan of the 3rd District Court, Charging us with breaking up Paul Englbreths Saloon or Whiskey Shop, Which was Abated under a Writ of Abatement issued by Alderman Clinton. McAllister, Clinton, Hyde and Burt released on bonds of Ten Thousand Dollars Each, I and the balance on two thousand. Each [are?] to appear at next Siting of the Court on 12th of September.[53]

August 30th 1870. Judg Stricklan Swor in One hundred Deputy Marshals and orderd the United States Marshal Patrick to See that they are all well Armed And all on account of the City Authorities trying to make Some of their Cheats observe the City Ordinances.

September 2d 1870. We wer all arrested again on Complain of Paul Engelbreth to recover Damages for breaking up his Saloon and wer admited to bail in the sum of sixty Thousand Dollars.[54]

Sept. 5th. I filed Bonds and got my Commision as Constable from Acting Governer Mann.

September 14th 1870. Governer Shaffer issued a Procklimation forbidding the Malisha from Drilling and disbanding them.[55]

September 17th. Helen had me before the Teachers of the 15th Ward. They desided that I Should try and live with her again and See if she would keep her promises to treat Me as a Wife should do a Husband.

---

[53]A non-Mormon liquor dealer named Paul Englebrecht became involved in a licensing dispute with the city and continued to operate without a proper license. Justice of the Peace Jeter Clinton dispatched police to abate Englebrecht's store as a nuisance, and they broke open barrels and smashed bottles reportedly worth twenty thousand dollars. See "Abatement of a Liquor Establishment," *Deseret News*, 31 August 1870, 6/1; and *The People vs. Paul Englebreth* [*sic*], Salt Lake County Probate Court Civil and Criminal Case Files, 13 June 1870. The abatement had dramatic consequences. Federal district judges had recently ruled that the U.S. marshal (a federal appointee), not the territorial marshal (appointed by the Mormon-dominated territorial legislature), should impanel grand juries, and that probate courts had no criminal jurisdiction. Utah territorial supreme court chief justice James B. McKean, appointed in 1870, arrived determined to enforce anti-polygamy laws. McKean heard the suit by Englebrecht against Clinton and the police for malicious destruction of property. The case was appealed to the U.S. Supreme Court; meanwhile McKean launched other prosecutions described below. See Firmage and Mangrum, *Zion in the Courts*, 138, 141–48, 246–47; Englebrecht's lawyer's version in Baskin, *Reminiscences of Early Utah*, 32–35; Bigler, *Forgotten Kingdom*, 286–95. For a contemporary Mormon view of McKean, see a reprinted *Omaha Herald* editorial of 4 October 1871 in "The Utah Conspiracy," *Deseret News*, 11 October 1871, 8/3. For President John Taylor's summary view of McKean's campaign, see "Correspondence: Utah and the Mormons, Letter 5," *Deseret News*, 1 April 1874, 13/1.

[54]See "The Whiskey 'Ring': Its Moves," *Deseret News*, 7 September 1870, 6/4.

[55]When Nauvoo Legion commander Daniel H. Wells called a three-day muster, Governor Shaffer, as commander in chief, appointed Gen. Patrick Connor, who was former commander of Camp Douglas, commander of the territorial militia and forbade any musters except by his orders. This was the effective end to the thirty-year history of the Nauvoo Legion. See Bigler, *Forgotten Kingdom*, 285–88; Madsen, *Glory Hunter*, 190–92.

September 22d 1870. I and the rest of the Police were endited for breaking up Paul Engebreth Whiskey Shop. The Enditment charges unlawfull, willfull and Malisious distruction of Property.

October 23d 1870. The Criminal cases against the Poleice and I laid over till next ajourned term of Court. 28th Sival suits comenced against the Police and I by P Engebreth to recover damages for breaking up his Whiskey Shop.

October 31st 1870. Govener Shaffer Died at ten minutes to 6 O clock A.M. When he was taken to the Depot previous to Shiping East I was apointed to Clear the road in front of the Prosession. His Death was no cause of sorrow to the Saints for he was their most bitterenimey and I say Good Ridens to all Such Caracters the less of them in this world the better.[56]

November 4th 1870. The Jurry brought in a Verdict against the Police and I of Guilty and assessed the Damages at the Sum of $5966.25 We gave notice of an Apeal to the Supreme Court being refused a new tryal.[57]

November 10th 1870. I in company of A P. Kimball and others Started to E T City about 20 Miles West to Arrest some Male and Car Robers.[58] We arrested two Suspisious Caracters and in Surching for money that was suposed to have been thrown away by the two Robers Arrested the day before by A P Kimball and others. I found a packet of Greenback and a Bar of Gold all amounted to about five Thousand Dollars.[59]

November 17th 1870. Wm Hyde and I Started for Elco Nevada with Taylor a Mail Rober arived there next morning and returned on the 19th distance the round trip 630 Miles.

November 22d 1870. Wm Hyde, A P Kimball my self and others Started for Elco to give testimony before the Grand Jury against the Mail Robers.[60] Sunday 27th arived at home Same day went to Camp Douglas to See Andrew Burt and others imprisoned there for what was known as the Wooden Gun Rebelion. December 3d Burt and the rest were releist on $2200.00 Bail.[61]

[56]A somewhat kinder death notice appears in "Death of Governor Shaffer," *Deseret News*, 2 November 1870, 6/3.

[57]See "The Verdict in the Liquor Case," *Deseret News*, 9 November 1870, 5/4.

[58]Located in Tooele Valley at a mill established in 1849, E. T. City was named after Apostle Ezra T. Benson.

[59]"Capture of Train Robbers," *Deseret News*, 16 November 1870, 12/2.

[60]The *Deseret News* identified A. P. Kimball as Heber Parley Kimball, son of Heber Kimball. Ibid.

[61]Shaffer died on 31 October 1870. Less than a month later, on 21 November, between one hundred and three hundred militia men marched, some apparently with wooden guns. The territorial secretary had them arrested and sent to Camp Douglas; they were later released. For one version see Roberts, *A Comprehensive History*, 5:353–57; for the post, see Hibbard, "Fort Douglas 1862–1916." For testimony about the rebellion, see "That Rebellion—The Evidence in the Case," *Deseret News*, 30 November 1870, 1/1.

December 6th 1870. I, A P Kimball and others Started for Elco to give testimony against the Mail Robers. 8th left for home. Trial posponed till Second Monday in January.

December 9th 1870. I arived at home and found my Wife Mary in Bead having on the 8th been deliverd of a Daughter at half past 10 O clock A M.

January 2d 1871. W J Hooper and I Started by Cars for Ogden in Serch of McKay and Heath Mail Robers that had escaped from the City Jail. On ariving at Ogden found McKay and two other prisoners that had escaped with him. January 3d. Received a telegram from Captin Burt Stating that Heath had gone to Corine. We went to Corine and searched all that night and part of the next day and did not find him, returned home the evening of the 4th.[62]

January 9th 1871. I and others went to Elco arived on the 10th. 11 & 12 gave testimony. 13th Verdict of Guilty as charged against Taylor Baker and [Martil?] Same evening started home where we arived the morning of the 14th.

January 23d 1871. I Sold my House in the 15th Ward to Roan Edwards for two thousand Dollars, possession given the 20th of February.

January 30th 1871. I bought two houses and Lots in the 20th Ward One of George Smith for Seven hundred and fifty Dollars the other of Henry Lewis for five hundred and Seventy five Dollars. Same evening attended a Ball given by the Police in Social Hall. While there I recived a Notice from the High Council[63] which reads as follows

Salt Lake City
January 30th 1871

Mr. B.Y. Hampton
Dear Brother
Sister Helen Hampton has preferd a charge against you before the High Council for ill treting her and not complying with the Bishops Court of the 15th Ward. You are hereby notifyed to appear at the City Hall on Friday next at half past one O clock to answer Said charge. Very Respectfully
Your Brother,

John [N?] Pike Clerk

Thursday February 2d 1871 my Wife Mary took our Child to the 17th Ward for Meating and had her Blest under the hands of G B Wallace and George Morris and named Julia Randolph.

---

[62]See "Local and Other Matters: The Mail Robbers," *Deseret News*, 2 November 1870, 7/2.

[63]A council of high priests served as a kind of appellate court from the bishop's court. Firmage and Mangrum, *Zion in the Courts*, 30–34.

Friday February 3d 1871. I attended the High Council as per notice. Following is the decision of the High Council. My Decision is that Sister Helen E. Hampton Accept the terms Bro Hampton has to offer and do the best she can. Take the house Bro Hampton offers and make it as clean and comfortable as posible and when her husband visits her Welcome him treat him kindly and affectionetly. And Bro Hampton must do the best he can to make her happy and comfortable by providing for her visiting her and be to her a Husband. George B Wallace Act President of the High Council.

February 21st 1871. I moved my Wife Helen and her Children to the 20th Ward having previously taken Bertha's children from her (Helen) on account of her abuse of them and me when I went to See them and gave them to my Wife Mary to Care for. Who has been a good and kind Mother to them, which they all will testify to. And I Say God bless her for her Motherly care over them and her Wifley conduct towards me.

February 23d 1871. I gave a Deed for my place Sold in the 15th Ward to Proctor alias Edwards and recived two thousand dollars. Same day recived a deed from George Smith for his place in the 20th Ward and paid him Seven hundred and fifty dollars. 25th recived a deed from Henry Lewis for his place in the 20th Ward and paid him $575.00 28th Moved Mary and Children to 20th Ward.

March 11th 1871. I donated twenty five dollars in the School of the Prophets for the Emigration of the Poor Saints from the Old Country.[64]

March 25th 1871. I recived a Note from the High Council forbiding me disposing of any part or portion of the house and Lott that Helen lived in. The Notice Came to late for I had sold 4 rods South front of the East end of said Lot to Mrs [Wediboring?] for $200.00 dollars The Sale being made five days previous to receiving the Notice from the High Council. The Money was used to improve Helens house and make it more comfortable for her.

March 28th 1871. I went to Ogden in Search of a Foarger and a witness to a Rape case did not find them, returned home Same day.

April 17th. I requested the High Council to Divorce me and My Wife Helen on account of her conduct and accusations against me. Bro Wallace informed me that the High Council could do nothing with her in regard to a Divorce as she was determined to make me all the trouble she could.

[64]In 1867 Brigham Young resurrected the School of the Prophets, first established in 1832, in response to the capitalistic influx that the transcontinental railroad was expected to bring. The School was a sort of town meeting of all worthy male priesthood holders that helped implement a variety of official social and economic policies. See Arrington, *Great Basin Kingdom*, 245–51; Bigler, *Forgotten Kingdom*, 261–62; and Patrick, "The School of the Prophets."

May 29th 1871. I Started for Echo after an Indian that had Stolen a horse from John W. Young.[65] Got him and returned home the Same day.

June 1st 1871 was Pres Youngs 70th birth day. 3d I went to Ogden with him as his baudy guard where he held a two days meating. My wife Mary went with me and visited my Brother Eaderly. Sunday 4th returned home from Ogden. 5th Pres Young Said he wished that I could arange my business So that I could gow with him to Soda Springs.

August 7th 1871. At the County Election held in the City Hall, C.M. Halley a Son of Judg Halley created a disturbances and insulted people all day. He was chalinging for the Opisition which consisted of Federal Official Apostates and black Legs in Jeneral. In the afternoon I locked him up in the City Jail for about five minuts for his disorderly Conduct. The 11th he filed a complaint against Jeter Clinton, J. Y. Smith, Jonithan Needham and my self in the 3d District Court (James B McKean Judg). The Comencement of a Suit to recover damages for fals imprisonment in the Sum of Twenty five Thousand Dollars. Snow & Hoag Attorneys wer imployed to defend us who filed an answer to Halleys complaint denying the charge.[66]

September 6th 1871. Thomas Owen, my Son became 8 years Old and was Babtised By Mark [Linzey?], 7th Confermed under the hands of Bishop John Sharp and others.[67]

September 11th 1871. The 3d District Court met an open venira issued and put in the hands of US. Marshal Patrick. The Jurrors Summoned both Grand and Petit wear composed of Jentiles and Apostates, with the exception of George Q Cannon, James Townsend and H.B. Clowson who were not alowed to Sit on the Jurrys because of their Religious belief as Laterday Saints.

At this Term of the Court, what was known as the McKean Raid, That had been Runing for Some time, Almost reached its Zenith. Laws and Presi-dent wer Swept aside and Rulings made to Suit the times. Mormons were indited by Packed Grand Jurrors, Arrested and put in Prisons or released on Exorbitant Bonds And convicted on purgerd testimony of the worst Villans in the Country And found guilty by packed Jurrors composed of

---

[65]A son of Brigham Young.

[66]For the lawsuit by the "ill-mannered puppy" C.M. Hawley, Jr., see "Local and Other Matters: The Facts," *Deseret News*, 23 August 1871, 1/3. Cyrus Hawley, C.M.'s father, was a federal district judge.

[67]Born in Scotland, John Sharp led an overland company to Utah in 1850 and was a prominent religious and political leader in the territory for thirty-five years. He acted as Brigham Young's agent during and after the building of the transcontinental railroad and rose to be a director for the Union Pacific Railroad.

the Sworn Enimies of the Laterday Saints And Sentenced by the Judges to the full extent of the Law. For further particulars see Church History.[68]

Friday September 22d 1871. The Grand Jurry found bills of Inditements against Pres Brigham Young, D H Wells, Joseph A Young, Orson Hyde and Hosia Stout for Murder in the first degree, on the testimony of Bill Hickman and his palls in crime.[69] Friday Pres Young and others started to Grants Ville to hold a two days Meating. They had an Escort of about twenty Men. 24th I in company with the Police and others went to Meat Pres Young and partie on their return home. We met them at the point of the West Mountain. The company on their return numberd about Seventy five Men all well armed. We arrived in the City the Same evening.

September 25th 1871. I comenced Guarding Pres Young at his request. 27th went with him to the Warm Springs Bath House. 30th We went riding. October 2d Pres Young quite Sick. Same day at twenty five minutes to 6 O clock P.M. Pres Young came in to his office and was arrested by Marshal M.T. Patrick on a warrant issued out of the 3d District Court (James B McKean Judg) charging him with Lewd and Lacivious Cohabitation with Some 16 Women as his Wives.[70]

Same day D H Wells arrested by Marshal Patrick on Same charge as Pres Young Lewd and Lacivious Cohabitation.

October 4th 1871. Pres Young worse. 5th better and attended Special Conference in the Tabernacle I went with him afterwards I went to Court. 6th we went to Conference. 7th Georg Q. Cannon Arrested on the charge of Lewd and Lacivious Cohabitation with his wives. 7th and 8 I went with Pres Young to Conference. 8th Conference ajourned to the 6th of next April.

Monday October 9th 1871. Pres Young went to Court at 2 Oclock P.M. and gave bonds in the sum of Five Thousand Dollars, Wm Jennings and John Sharp his bondsmen. 8th & 9th the Great fire in Chicago 10,000 people homless. 10th Argument to Quash the Inditement against Pres Young, By

[68]Roberts, *A Comprehensive History*, 5:382–417; Tullidge, *The History of Salt Lake City*, 512-27.

[69]William A. Hickman claimed to have killed several men in 1857 on the orders of Brigham Young and other Mormon leaders. He confessed to Robert Baskin, whom Judge McKean named acting U.S. attorney in 1871, leading to the indictments and arrests described below. See Hickman and Beadle, ed., *Brigham's Destroying Angel*.

[70]The charge was based on a territorial statute rather than the federal Morrill Anti-Bigamy Act. Successful prosecutions of polygamy under Morrill only began after the 1874 Poland Act, which changed the method for selecting grand juries. See Alexander, "Federal Authority versus Polygamic Theocracy," 87–89. See "Plea in Abatement in the Case of the People vs. Brigham Young," *Deseret News*, 18 October 1871, 12/1. For the prosecuting attorney's view, see Baskin, *Reminiscences of Early Utah*, 54–57.

Fitch and [Mann?] [Hemsted?], and Kirkpatrick Snow, and Hoag A [Miner?], Legrand Young, and Hossie Stout Attorneys for defendant. For Prosicution R.N. Baskin U.S. Prosicuting Attorney and George R Maxwell.[71]

October 12th 1871. The motion to Quash the inditement against Pres Young overuled by Judge McKean. In the later part of his Opinion he Says It is therefore proper to Say that while the case at bar is called The People vs Brigham Young its other and real title is Federal Authority versus Polygamic Theocracy. The Government of the United States founded upon a Written Constitution finds within its Jurisdiction Another Government Claiming to Come from God. Imperium in Imperio—Whos policy and practices are in grave particulars at variance with its Own. The one Government Arrests the Other in the person of its Chief and arraigns it at the bar. A System is on trial in the person of Brigham Young. Let all concerned Keep this fact Steadily in view and let that Government rule Without a rival Which Shall prove to be in the right xxx and closed by saying The pending motion to Quash is overruled.[72]

October 12th and 13th. I was sick with the chills and feaver and remained at home. 14th I returned to guarding Pres Young. 16th I went with him to Court. He pled not guilty to the Inditement charging him with Lewd and Lacivious Cohabitation. D.H. Wells the same.

October 17th 1871. I went with Pres Young, D H Wells, George A Smith and others to Sandy Station 14 miles South on the Cars. We started at 3 O clock PM and returned in the evening at 7 O clock. 18th and 19th with Pres Young.

October 19th 1871. I was apointed Deputy City Marshal by J D T McAllister City Marshal. 20th went with Pres Young to Bath House. Same day The Thomas Hawkins case given to the Jurry. 20th A Virdict returned of guilty of the Charge of Adulterey with his Wives.[73] 21, 22 & 23 [October 1871] With Pres Young riding and walking Several places.

---

[71]Harvard-trained attorney Robert N. Baskin became a leader of the Liberal Party and the anti-polygamy campaign; he served as U.S. attorney for the third district court and later became Salt Lake mayor and chief justice of the Utah Supreme Court. George R. Maxwell, a youthful general famous as "the thunderbolt of Sheridan," served as land office registrar and U.S. marshal. Bigler, *Forgotten Kingdom*, passim; and Baskin, *Reminiscences of Early Utah*; for the lewd and lascivious indictment, see 54–58. John Gary Maxwell's recent *Gettysburg to Great Salt Lake* is a biography of Maxwell. Dr. Maxwell's biography of Baskin is forthcoming.

[72]Hampton probably copied those lines from "Editorials," *Deseret News*, 18 October 1871, 5/2; see also "Brigham Young on Trial," *Salt Lake Tribune*, 3 January 1872, 2/2.

[73]Hawkins married a second woman without his first wife's consent, a violation of "declared Mormon" practice. Judge McKean fined Hawkins five hundred dollars and sentenced him to three years in prison. See *Deseret News*, 25 October, 6/1; "District Court," 9/1; "The Hawkins' Case—The Accused Sentenced," 1 November 1871, 7/2; Tullidge, *The History of Salt Lake City*, 540–42, and Alexander, "Federal Authority versus Polygamic Theocracy," 92. Robert Baskin prosecuted Hawkins; see Baskin, *Reminiscences of Early Utah*, 39–44.

October 24th 1871. Pres Young orderd all the gates closed about his premises and office and Knon are permited to See him. About 9 O clock PM. Pres Young and George A Smith Started for St George about three hundred and fifty miles South to escape being arrested by the Dammible Court officials. I and ten others mounted on Horses and well armed went with them to the Point of the Mountain South where we met another escort, we then bid them good by and God bless you and Started back, arived home in the morning about daylight having ridden all night without getting out of our Saddles, Distance travled about 44 Miles. I was so badly used up that I had to lay in bead all that day and night. 26th went back to guard at Pres Young's office to prevent suspicion of his having left till he could get out of reach. Same day verdict renderd against Pres Young in the Mrs Cook case for $2,986 Dollars.[74] 27th at Pres Youngs. 28th the Judge sentenced Thomas Hawkins to pay a fine of Five hundred Dollars and three years imprisonment in the Penitentiary on a charge of Adultery for living with his Second Wife.

Saturday October 28th 1871. About 2 O clock P.M. M. T. Patrick US. Marshal and his Brother All Arrested D H Wells, Hosia Stout and Wm H Kimball on a warrant issued from the 3d District Court charging them with murder in the first degree.[75] All wer taken to Camp Duglas and placed in the custody of Jeneral Morrow. I went with them and remained all night. A guard of Soldiers was placed around the House day and night. 29th a great many of the Prisoners friends came to See them. I returned home about noon. 30th D H Wells was released on Fifty Thousand Dollars bail as he was Mayor of Salt Lake City and his Services were neaded to Keep quiet in the City. H. S Eldrege and William Jennings were Bro Welles Bondsmen.

December 13th 1871. Alexander Burt, G L Blithe, James Toms and John [Brazier?] were arrested on a Bench Warrant from the 3d District Court charging them with the Murder of Dr J King Robinson on October 22d 1866. 13 & 14 examination had Several witnesses examined. A Jentile by the name of Baker was the only one that knew any thing towards conviction. He identified James Toms, Blithe and Morris though Morris was not arrested nor had Baker ever Seen him but described him as he had been told by others.

[74]Sarah Ann Cooke was a Mormon who became a leader of the local anti-polygamy movement. After her husband's death, she became involved with a property dispute and successfully sued Brigham Young. See Van Wagenen, "Sister-Wives and Suffragists," 251–53; and Scott, "The Widow and the Lion of the Lord."

[75]They were charged with killing Richard Yates. See "Arrest of Mayor Wells," *Deseret News*, 1 November 1871, 6/1, and the discussion of the Yates murder in the Ann Gordge chapter of this volume.

Baker was hired by US. Marshals to Sware against these men. 18th One witness examined he did not know any thing to convict. Court ajourned to the 19th for more witnesses.[76]

The Hardest Looking Lot of Men I Ever Saw: A Prison Journal

Tuesday December 19th 1871. At 25 minutes past 10 O clock A M I was arrested on a bench Warrant issued out of the 3d District Court by J B McKean Judg, charging me with killing one Dr J King Robinson on the night of October 22d 1866. Deputy US. Marshal All Patrick and Samuel Paul arrested me. After my arrest John Brazier was discharged. 19, 20 & 21 investigation of our cases before crowded Court room of Spectators. Some 40 witnesses were examined pro and Con. The Same Day Helen visited me and said that I was at home sick on the night that Robinson was Kiled. The principal witnesses against us were Charles W Baker, a Jentile, and non resident and Thomas Butterword, a dirty apostate Mormon. They both Swore to most damnable lies. Baker was proven to have said he was swearing fals against us. Buterword Said in his testimony against me that Just before the Shooting he Saw a Man and Woman pass me on the Side walk and say *Good Night, Brig. Ham. Hampton,* and that was how he came to Know my name and Said that Just after the Shuting that Alex Burt and I ran past him, I ahead, both of us mufeled up and that he Butterword had Jumped over a pole fence in to Some ones lot and was squated behind a curant bush as we ran by and recognized me by my Shoes, had not seen me to know me up till that time nor for Several Months after the Shooting, altho I carried on the harness

[76]Late on 22 October 1866 a man seeking medical aid lured former army physician J. King Robinson from his home during the doctor's property dispute with Mormon city officials. Only 175 feet away and just west of Main Street and 300 South, Robinson was "barbarously murdered" in what Mormon insiders described as an intimidation attempt by the Salt Lake police that got out of hand; no one was ever convicted of the murder. See "Legal Ruling," *Deseret News*, 24 October 1866, 5/1; for the murder and investigation immediately following, see "Home Items: Murder," *Deseret News*, 31 October 1866, 5/1; "Close of the Inquest," 14 November 1866, 2/1; for the trial of suspects in December 1871, see *Salt Lake Tribune*, "The Robinson Murder Case," 16 December 1871, 3/1; "The Robinson Murder Case," 23 December 1871, 3/1; "Local and Other Matters: Court in Chambers," *Deseret News*, 27 December 1871, 7/2; for the insider's view, see Stenhouse, *Rocky Mountain Saints*, 616–19. Eveline Brooks Auerbach claimed her mother Fanny "was sure of one of the criminals but dared not tell." Ogden, ed., *Frontier Reminiscences of Eveline Brooks Auerbach*, 47. See also Bigler, *Forgotten Kingdom*, 248–58; Roberts, *A Comprehensive History*, 5:194–206; and the account by Robinson's friend and lawyer in Baskin, *Reminiscences of Early Utah*, 13–15. Someone composed a song about this murder. See Burt, "Ditties of Death in Deseret," 161–62. For Hampton's arrest, see "Local Matters: Arrested," *Salt Lake Tribune*, 14 December 1871, 3/1.

business for years on the Main Streets in the City. We proved that there was an Adobie wall for feet high at the time of the Shooting where Butterword said there was a pole fence and that it had been torn down and replace[d] with a pole fence. Baker said that he was at the Theater the night of the Shuting of Robinson and that Julia Dean Haynes was playing there and that he, Baker, got tired before the play was out and went up town to get some [Aislers?] and on his way home to the Colerado House he herd quarling on the corner of third South and East Temple streets and that he got behind a Six foot picket fence and listened to the quarling and saw the shuting but did not recognize any one. We proved that there was no Theatre that night and that Julia Dean Haynes was playing that Same night in a Theatre in Montana and that where Baker said there was a Six foot fence that there was only a three foot fence at the time of the Shuting and that it had been towrn down and replaced with a Six foot picket fence. Baker afterwards made an Affidavit before John T Cain, notrie public denying what he had testified to in Court and that Butterwood had told him, Baker, that he, Butterwood had sworn fals. And Baker further that they were hired by Deputy Marshals to Swear against us and were to recive $500.00 for each one convicted and $1000.00 for each one hung. The Baker Affidavit was Made January 3d 1872. . . . The Deputy Marshals concerned in the Baker and Buterwood Swearing were Sam Gilson, Ed Gilman Milt Orr.[77]

December 22d 1871. The argument in our case Closed, Thomas Fitch and C H Hemsted our Attorneys. Alex Burt discharged and afterward Arrested. I and J. L. Blyth, James Toms wer held without bail to wait the action of the Grand Jurry.[78] We are imprisoned in an uper room of the Freemens Hall near the City Hall where we have been Scince our Arrest Guarded by Deputy Marshals. We have to furnish our Selves with every thing we need and pay the guard for guarding us. Our Familes bring us our Meals. Hossia Stout and William Kimball are with us charged with Murder.

December 23d 1871. My Wife Mary came to See me and felt very bad. Same day and 24th a good many of our friend visited us. 25 Christmass we

[77]Baker's affidavit appeared in the *Salt Lake Tribune,* 26 January 1872. A Dr. Ormsby testified that Hampton was consumptive and that he believed he could not run a block. "Local and Other Matters: Court in Chamber," *Deseret News,* 27 December 1871, 7/2. On the actress Julia Dean Hayne, see Tullidge (who wrote plays for her), *History of Salt Lake City,* 752–55.

[78]For the testimony, see "The Mormon Murder Case," *Salt Lake Tribune,* 16 December 1871, 3/1; "The Mormon Murder Case," *Salt Lake Tribune,* 22 December 1871, 3/1; "The Robinson Murder Case," *Salt Lake Tribune,* 23 December 1871, 3/1.

had a good time. Our Families and friends visited us and brought every thing good to eat and drink. 26 Mary brought Willey Helen's Son to see me whom I had not seen for weeks nor his Sister Lilley as their Mother had locked them in the House and would not permit me to See them. . . .

In the evening of the 26 December 1871 Pres Young and partie returned home from the South having concluded to take their chances with the Court. 27th James Toms taken to Camp Duglas. Helen came and brought Willie and Lillie. At night I went home and saw Mary and returned to prison in the night unknown to the guard. 28th We aranged to pay Ed Gilman and [Cap?] [David] Evans, Dep Marshals $6.50 per day to guard us. In the evening I went to the Theatre had a private box where I could not be Seen. Acrost the Continent was plaid. 29th Mary came to See me. Evening Wm Kimball and I Went to the Theatre and saw one act. Then I went to Pres Young's office and Saw him. He looks and feals well. I also saw there George A Smith, Joseph A Young, O. P. Rockwell and R. T. Burton, all indicted for murder with the exception of Geo A Smith. None arrested as yet. . . . 31st Mary came to see me. Evening I went home and took a bath and returned to prison.

January 1st 1872. Hail the New Year. Every thing good brought us by our friends. Brass Grann Marshal Band came in the room and serinaded us. 6 O clock in the evening we and the Guard went to J C Littles to Super on his invitation.

January 2d 1872. Pres Young was Arrested by Patrick and Evans on a Warrant issued out of the 3d District Court charging him with murder in the first degree. At 2 O clock he went in court and was refused bail but was permited to remain in his own House and guarded by the Marshals. . . .[79] I and bro Blithe also went and had a private box where we could not be Seen. Just as we were Starting to the Theatre Bro W Woodruff one of the twelve Apostles viseted us.[80] 3d my Brother Eaderly and Bro George A Smith, Capt Hooper Deligate to Congress, George Q Cannon visited us.[81] Helen came to see me and brought the Children. 4th Mary visited me. D H Wells, Thomas Fitch, C H Hempsted and Ex [?] Morris visited us, the last three our Attorneys. In the evening I went home. 5th Mary came to See me

[79]"Brigham Young on Trial," *Salt Lake Tribune*, 3 January 1872, 2/2.

[80]Woodruff wrote that Hampton and the others "were in Prision under indiptment for Murder by the U.S. Judges Not Because they were guilty of any such Crime But to open the Ball of persecution against the Latter Day Saints." See Kenney, ed., *Wilford Woodruff's Journal*, 2 January 1872, 7:51.

[81]William H. Hooper was overwhelmingly elected delegate to Congress from Utah Territory and the state of Deseret in 1870; Bigler, *Forgotten Kingdom*, 278.

visited all day as usuel. Helen came and brought the Children and Captin Hooper visited us. Sunday 7th Some of the members of the Legislature visited us, evening I went home.

January 4th 1872. The 3d District Court Met and By Order Attorney Jeneral Ackerman at Washington, the Court was ajourned till the 2d Monday in March So as to give the Supreme Court of the United States time to enquire into the Conduct of the Courts and officers here. Same evening went to the Theatre with Mary had a private box provided by Pres Young. In fact he gave us prisoners the use of the West *Porcenium* Box whenever we wanted it. After Theater I went home with Mary. During the night there was an alarm that the Soldiers were agowing to try to take Pres Young to Camp Douglas. There was several hundred Men caled out to resist the Soldiers if they made the atempt. The men lay in wach all night in diferent Parts of the City. The most of them at the City Hall.

January 10th 1872. Thomas Butterwood one of the witnesses against us in the Robinson case was Arrested for passing Counterfit Money, held to bail in the Sum of $500.00 till next day. Sharp Walker an apostate went his bale.[82]

Same day Hemsted and Fitch visited us. 11th George A Smith visited us. Mary and Helen came to See me Same day. Butterwood had an examination before Judge Clinton, found guilty and held to wait the action of the Grand Jurry in bonds of One Thousand dollars.... 20th Grand Jurry found inditements against James Toms, James Blythe, Alexander Burt, and my self for Murder in the first degree for the aledged killing Dr Robinson. Alex Burt was Rearested and put in Jail with us. Same day Mary visited me and felt very bad. Helen commenced cuting up the fence as She has done before and a good many other dirty tricks....

January 20th 1872. Affidavit against Baker for purgery was made to day before Judg McKean in the Robinson case....

January 23d 1872. Judg McKean refused to issue a Warrant for the arrest of C W Baker. Application was made to Judg Halley for a warrant against Baker for purgery. Halley Said he would not Shrink from his duty. But requested that the application be made to Justice Clinton As it would cost him Halley his official head if he issued the writ. Halley said that it was an outrage that McKean did not issue the writ as it was his duty to do So

[82]Samuel Sharp Walker was one of the four Walker brothers who joined the Godbeite movement. See Bliss, *Merchants and Miners in Utah*. Butterword complained that the police harassed him because of his testimony; see Alexander, "Federal Authority versus Polygamic Theocracy," 93.

an Affidavit was made before Clinton and a Warrant issued. Same day Bro George Q Cannon visited us.

January 24th. C W Baker Arrested and brought before the Court. George R Maxwell, Bakers Attorney, waived examination as he, Maxwell, did not want the Testimony made public as it would implicate Several U S. Officials as well as him Self. Baker was held to wait the action of the Grand Jurry in the Sum of three thousand dollars. He could not procure bail and was turned over to Marshal Patrick and sent to Camp Duglass. There is no probibility of Baker being indited, for his affidavit was before the Grand Jurry and the names of Witnesses to prove his Making the afidavit. They Stole the Affidavit and did not indite Baker.[83] But indited us on his and Butterwoods Testimony. The Grand Jurry are all members of the ring with the U.S. Officials and determined to bring trouble upon the Saints if posible.[84] The Stolen affidavit returned when they found we had a certifyed copy of the Same. . . .

January 29th 1872. George C Bates U.S. prosicuting Attorney Telegraphed to his asistant to admit all persons held as U.S. Prisoners to reasonable Bail, As he had been so ordered to do by the Attorney Jeneral Williams at Washington. . . .

January 31st 1872. Judg McKean refused to admit any one to bail as we expected. He Said among other things that if we ware admited to bail that we would all be Linched, a nice excuse for not bailing us, done and Said to have its efect abrod and with the Government at Washington.[85]

February 1st 1872. Some Jentlemen from Rushey caled on us and give us $20[.]00 dollars. . . . 9th Mary and Helen came to See me. Same evening the 13th Ward Releaf Society gave us a Surprise party and super in Jail 10.

February 11th 1872. In the evening Hosia Stout and I went to Pres Young's office to See him. He felt well and told us to be patient and all will be well. . . .

Monday 12. The 10th Ward Brass Band and Bro Groves, Marshal Bond Came in to our Prison and Serinaded us it being an Election day to Adopt a New Constitution for the State of Deseret [*marginal note*: Should be March 18th for Election to adopt Constitution] and to ask Congress to admit us in to the Union as a State. . . .[86]

---

[83]See "Important Decision," *Salt Lake Tribune*, 27 January 1872, 2/3.

[84]Mormons often referred to their non-Mormon opponents as "the Ring" or "the *Tribune* Ring."

[85]McKean believed "it is not improbable that the irresponsible magistrate, called Judge 'Lynch,'" might act if he bailed out the prisoners. "Proceedings in the District Court," *Salt Lake Tribune*, 1 February 1872, 2/3.

[86]This was the fourth unsuccessful attempt at statehood. See Lyman, *Political Deliverance*, 17–18.

February 20th 1872. Thomas Fitch deliverd a Speach in the Convention in favor of admitting Utah in to the Union as a State 21st Mary visited me [in the] evening. I took her to the Theatre [and] after Theatre we went home.

March 3d 1872. The Convention ajourned *Sinidi* after adopting a Constitution for the futer State of Deseret. George Q Cannon, Thomas Fitch and Ex Secetary [Frank] Fuller, Elected Delegates to present the New Constitution to Congress.

Monday March 5th 1872. Helen went to Ed Gillman and Jack Neal (our Guard) and told them that Alex Burt and I wer home the night before and Said the next time I went home She would watch and have me arrested and Prosicuted for Lewd and Lacivious Conduct. She caled me every thing mean that she Could think of. The same evening She went to Mary and abused most Shamefully.

March 6th 1872. [Jew?] Charley that had been guarding us one week comenced threatning us with Camp Duglas if we did not pay him promptly and more than we had been paying the others. I gave him a good toung lashing and threatened him with a Congress Chair if he ever came back. He was discharged. A man named [Rourk?] put in his place. 12th Jack Neal one of our Guard Drunk and fell down stairs a thing which after happened as we jeneraly got the Guard drunk so we could get to gow to the Theater and home. March 13th 1872. A Dispach from A M. Bates (US. Prosicuting Attorney) in Washington Says that the Supream Court will overoul the Jurry System adopted by the Ring here as Illeagal, which will releas all Prisoners and make voyd all suits Prosicuted in McKeans Court.

March 20th 1872. In the Evening we were visited by a Suprise party consisting of some of our most respected Citizens Ladies and Jentlemen Mormons and Jentiles. Pres D H Well Wife and Children were present. After their arivile I went and brought Mary unbeknown to the Guard. The rest of the prisoners done the same or sent somone in their place. We had a good Super every thing that one could wish and a Jeneral good time. The party broke up at half past 12 Oclock. After partie out I went home with Mary.

March 21st 1872. A notice of our Surprise party in the papers. A good deal of ex citement among the Ring and Marshal Patrick Sencur he discharged John M Neal for allowing the Party. Allen put to Guard in in Neals place.[87]

March 22d 1872. I recived an anonimus Letter Stating that there was a

[87]The *Salt Lake Tribune* called it "The Prisoners' Ball"; 21 March 1872, 3.

plot on foot to bribe my wife Helen to Testify against me in the Robinson Case and others. About 10 Oclock Mary visited me. Shortly after Orders come from Marshal Patrick To send us all to Camp Douglas on account of the surprise party.[88] Same day at 4 Oclock PM. John L Blythe, Hosia Stout, Wm H Kimball, Alex Burt and my self arived at Camp Douglas and were put in prison with 18 other prisoners, the hardest looking lot of men I ever saw. We were Angles beside them both in looks and actions if apperances gows for any thing. We had hardly room to stand up the jail was so crouded. This is the first time in my life that I was compeled to look through iron grates.

Shortly after we were put in prison Brs DH Wells and HB Clowsun come up to See us and have us brought out of Jail and put in the Office of the Guard House including James Toms who had been up here in prison nearly three months. Bros Wells and Clowson went to See Jeneral Morrow who gave us a small room 9 by 12 feet with one small window hevely grated and the glass broken out. The room joined to and was a portion of the jail. At 6 O clock we Six in number were locked in this Small room the broken window proved a blessing to us as it was the only place we could get fresh air from. Some Slop caled Coffee and a Small peace of bread each constituted our Supers. When we made doun our bedes they coverd the entire floor. Saturday 23d at the firing of the canon our door was opned and we wer granted the privalege of prominading on a space of ground about two rods square with two sentries to guard us. At half past 9 Oclock AM we with 48 other prisoners were drawn up in line at guard mount for inspection which lasted about five minuts.

Sunday March 24th 1872. We had orders not to come out at Guard Mount with the rest of the prisoners which was quite a favor. The Oficer treated us with great respect as well as the Soldiers. Same day Mary visited me and a great many of our frins visited us. Storming all day. 25th George A Smith, B Young Jr and others visited us. 26th Mary and Children came to see me and many of our friends who brought us lots of good things to eat and drink To day a big Hospital Tent put up for us and orders that we be not locked up at night. . . .

April 1st 1872. To day I red in Mrs Stenhouses Book against the Mormons that My Wife Helen told her that she belived that I had something to do

[88]See "Removal of Prisoners" and Mrs. E.A. Faust to Marshal Patrick, 23 March 1872, in *Deseret News*, 27 March 1872, 12/4.

with throwing Human excrement on her, Mrs Stenhouse and Husband. . . .[89] 6th Cold and Rainy. Helen and her Children Came to see me in company with Bro Coulborn. They came in Wm S. Godbie's wagon. Helen came to see if I would give her Twenty four Dollars per month, The amount I had offered her before and she refused. I told her that I would Stand to the offer. She accepted, Then abused me most shamefully before every body and talkes of moving up to Camp to work for some officers. She stayed but a short time which was gratifying. Same day Bro Jones and others made their escape from a portion of the Jail that we were in. . . .

Monday April 15th 1872. At half past 8 O clock P.M. Orson P Arnold brought a copy of a dispach from Pres. Young which he had recived from Washington Stating that the Supream Court had reversed the Desision in the Engelbroth Case and declaird the Jurry to be ilegal and that all enditements found in Mc Keans Court were Illegal.[90] We sent the Dispatch to Jeneral Morrow, the comander at Camp Douglas. Also read it to the prisoners in the ajoining jail. There was quite a rejoycing among prisoners and our friends in hearing the news But the Ring felt as if there was Som thing rong in the Seats of their Pants.

Tuesday April 16th 1872. Earley this morning Bill Hickman Started for the City on Horse back in company with a Soldier. In a short time the Soldier returned with the Horses but no Bill Hickman, who feals very uneasy Scince the ruling of the Supream Court.[91]

Wednesday 17th. Mary and Brigham walked up and almost gave out, wind and snow so bad. Bro Georg A Smith, F Little and James Little and

[89]Shortly after the Stenhouses requested excommunication in 1870, four masked men assaulted them "with huge garden-syringes charged with the most disgusting filth" as they walked home. Fanny Stenhouse recognized one man's voice and had "every reason to believe" all were members of Salt Lake's police. One of their wives reported she accused her husband "and he had not denied it. It seems perhaps strange that any wife should act thus, but this poor woman had a great regard for me, but none at all for her husband who treated her most brutally." *"Tell It All,"* 579–82. Clarence Agramonte later charged that William G. Phillips had "showered filth on Mr. and Mrs. Stenhouse on Arsenal [now Capitol] Hill." "Loyal Indignation," *Salt Lake Tribune,* 12 July 1885, 4/2. Someone staged similar attacks on the homes of federal officials in September 1885. See "A Dastardly Deed," *Deseret News,* 16 September 1885, 9/1; and "The Object of the Outrage," *Deseret News,* 23 September 1885, 7/2.

[90]Notice of the decision appears in "The Englebrecht Case," *Salt Lake Tribune,* 16 April 1872, 2/1.

[91]Hickman's biographer agrees that the confessed murderer became increasingly worried about his safety. His *Brigham's Destroying Angel,* with its accusations that Brigham Young and others ordered murders, appeared on 5 February 1872, but the indictments, largely on Hickman's testimony, had been filed the previous November and were vacated with the *Clinton v. Englebrecht* decision in April 1872. Hickman left protective custody at Fort Douglas, returned to his home in Fairfield, sold out, and eventually moved to Wyoming. See Hilton, *"Wild Bill" Hickman,* 124–31.

other visited us. The Bros Little brought in some Ale. 18th Began made his escape at guard mount.

Thursday 18th of April 1872. Wm Hyde and Byron Groo brought a Dispach from Att Bates to asistant prosicuting Att High, ordering him to make application for the releas of all persons indited in McKeans Court. High then offerd to turn us over to the Territoral Marshel J D T McAllister who refused to recieve us saying that we had to be dicharge as we had been elegaly indited and imprisined. Many visiters to day.

Friday 19th. It is four months to day scince I was arrested. . . .

April 22d 1872. The 3D District Court met to day and ajourned till next monday, to avoyd if possible, releasing us from prison and prevent Pres Young from gowing to Confrence. Some visitors to day. 23d Mary walked up and a good many persons to see us.

Wensday 24th. Application made for A writ of Habescorpus before Elias Smith probate Judg for the Release of Pres Young. Z. Snow appearing for Aplicant. J S High and Gilchrist for the Government, who plead to the Jurisdiction of the Court Demurrer, enterd by Snow and sustained by the Court. Court ajourned till tomorrow.

April 25th 1872. Court met. Judg Elias Smith after hearing the testimony and arguments pro and con, Orderd that the prisoner Pres Brigham Young gow home with out horm or Molestation. Orson P Arnold brought in the news of Pres Youngs release. Same day Hosia Stout was permited to gow home. 26th Wm H Kimball released by Marshal Patrick. . . .

Saturday April 27th 1872. All Patrick deputy U.S. Marshal, came to Camp for those that remained in Jail, which were J S Blythe, James Toms, Alex Burt and Self. We wer taken to the U S. Marshal's office then to the Court room before Judge Hawley. After siting there an hour and a half we wer informed that the Probate Court was in session and had issued a Writ of Habis corpus which was in the hands of Marshal Patrick commanding him to bring us before the Probate Court. I then asked the Marshal what the delay ment, he said thare was two writs of Habiscorpus for us, one from the Probate and one from the 3D District Court.

I told him that I thought them was some Damned double Dealing going on. Shortly after Court was called to order and Maxwell and Gilchrist read the writ for our releas. I then enquired of Judg Halley the reason of those proceadings and at whos request the writ was granted and was informed that the writ was for our releas and that one Mr Walker had swor out the writ. I told the Judg that we new nothing of the matter and that we did not wish to be released on an application from such a Sourse As the parties interesting them selves in our behalf was our worst enimies and that we did not need any of their asistance or profesed friendship As we had plenty of friends and money and did not want any bill presented for services by such as was trying to releas us as we had not employed any of them and if they were doing it out of friendship that we did not want any of that and asked for time to inform our Attorney which was granted. The time set for next Monday at 10 Oclock. At my request we were taken back to Camp Douglas.[92]

Before we were brought down from Camp the Soldiers told us that there was agowing to be a row in the City to day And that all Officers and Soldiers was required to remain in Camp. Which we did not understand untill we found that there was two Writs issued for our release. The 3D District Court issued a writ after the Probate Court had Thinking it would rais a muss. It was the last resort of the Ring to rais a fuss. Thinking we would be releas-sed from their custoday by the Teritorial Marshal Mc Allister as we were Teritorial Prisoners. And then they would call on the Troops and cause a colision between them and the People. The Soldiers were held in rediness all day and two mounted Soldiers came down ahead of us in the morning. One was stationed at the U.S. Marshals office, where Govener Woods[93] was all the time we were in Court, To give orders for the troops to come down if we were demanded by the Territorial Marshal.

The same day when we returned to Camp Lutenant [Ornoss?] told us that the Offisers and Soldiers were orderd to remain in Camp to be ready at a moments warning an event which was looked for every moment while we were in the City. After ajournment of Court and while in the Marshals office I told the Govener, US. Marshal and a good many of the Ring that we Knew all their plans to rais a disturbance and that they were Damnedly foiled for we would not do as they wanted us to but that we would gow to Camp and if they did not chuse to take us that we would walk up and remain there and rot in prison before we would give them the least chance for a disturbane at our expence or the People.

---

[92]For the competing writs, see "Application by Hosea Stout et al. for Writ of Habeas Corpus," entry 5592, Salt Lake County Probate Court Civil and Criminal Case Files, 26 April 1872.

[93]Utah territorial governor George Woods.

Sunday April 28th 1872. Confrence met and ajourned to the 6th of next October. Pres Young outsmarted the Devel by ajourning Confrence. After this the Ring could Court untill he was released as a prisoner and atend confrence which he did. . . .

Monday April 29th 1872. We went to Court at 10 O clock AM Our Attorneys Hemsted and Fitch Moved to dismiss the Writ of Habis Corpus before the 3D district Court on the Grounds that the Writ was not asked for by us and that we did not desire its benefit from that court. Court ajourned till 2 Oclock to make up its ruling. At 2 O clock Halley gave a long ruling foren to the case and abused the Probate Court and US Marshal for releasing Pres Young At the close he granted us our request and dismissed the writ and remanded us back in to the hands of the US. Marshal and were taken back to Camp Douglas. Hosia Stout returned with us. Mary tended Court and we took diner at the Townsend House while wating for the Judg to Study up his ruling.

Tuesday April 30th 1872. The Herald contained the desision of the Supream Court at Washington in the Engelbroth case which came last night officialy signed At 10 O clock same day Judg [Obed F.] Strickland ordered that we and all Teritorial prisoners be turned over to the Territorial Marshal J. D. T. Mc Allister. Judg McKean held that the US. Marshal has the right to hold all Territorial as well as US. prisoners for the purpose of aiding the Ring in persicuting the Saints that is why we were in the hands of the US. Marshal and sent to Camp. Mary walked up to camp to see me [and] arived in time to ride down to the City with us. About 6 O clock PM we and all persons that was endited in McKeans Court was released encluding Bill Hickman together with some 15 or 16 others that was brought down from Camp at the same time we were. As soon as we were released I Mary and some others went to see Pres Young. It was a happy meating. We then went home. In the evening I went to Hellens to see the Children.

Always Have the Drop on Our Enimies and Strike the First Blow

The same evening Pres Young Sent an invitation for Mary and I to be at the 5 O clock Train in the morning to take a trip to Brigham City in company with all those of the Bretheren that had been rleased from prison and all those that had been hiding from the Hellhounds. May 1s at 5 O clock AM the train started Pres Young DH Wells George A Smith Some of the twelve and all the Bretheren that had been released from prisons and those that had been endited and their Wives and several Missoinary on their way to the States and Europ composed the Company filling three cars. We arived at Ogden at 7 O clock AM the Missonarys took the train for the east and the balence of us went on to Brigham City where we arived about 9 O clock AM. A good many people at the Depot to meat us we remained a few moments then returned to the Switch where the narrow gage connects with the Union Pacific Ry Where a larg number of Children and grown persons were assembled to have a May party and to greet us. There was several Bands in attendanc which discursed Sweet Music. Pres Young Smith Well and others addressed the assembley we then partook of a sumptuis repast and returned to the City at 730 PM.

Thursday May 2d 1872. CW Baker was released on a writ of Habis Corpus by Judg Strickland.[94] He also ruled doun the Liquor Laws and said that the Mayer and Aldermen had no wright to collect Licenses and Taxes. Same day Hawkins released from the pen and held under five thousand Dollars bonds which was given. Frday 3d I commenced my police duties again.

May 4th 1872. The Tribune published an Affidavit perporting to be made by Thomas one of our witnesses against Baker for purgery. The Affidavit charges A Burt, Wm Hyde and others with getting Baker to make Affidavits and leave the Country. It is an infamous thing. Thomas says it was forced out of him while in prison by threats from George R Maxwell and Sam Gilson and CW Halley Thomas will make an Affidavit to that efect and deny all his former Affidevit says.[95]

May 6th 1872. Sam Gilson was Arrested on the complaint of Thomas and held to bail in the sum of five thousand dollars for forcing Thomas while in Jail to make the above mentioned Affidavit. 7th Sam Gilson held on examination before S[amuel] W Richards a Justice of the Peace and was bound over to the Probate Court in the sum of three thousand dollars. Sharp Walker went his security.[96]

May 11th. I atended the door of the School of the Prophets As I had done before I was put in prison.

[94]See "The Baker Affidavit Case," *Salt Lake Tribune*, 3 May 1872, 3/2.

[95]For the first affidavit, see "Affidavit of John Thomas," *Salt Lake Tribune*, 4 May 1872, 3/2.

[96]See "Local and Other Matters," *Deseret News*, 8 May 1872, 16/1.

Friday June 7th 1872. I and wife Mary were invited by Pres Young to gow with him to Brigham City to attend a two days meating. We could not gow on account of me being very sick. In July I was nominated for constable in second precinc to be voted for in Augusts Election.

Saturday August 3rd 1872. The School of the Prophets dismissed till further Orders. In the evening the Maxwell Ratification was broken up by hises and groans from the croud As the Ring abused Pres Young and others. August 4th 1872, The Tribune has a very foul and fals artical against the Police and sais that I said we the Police would break up the Ratification meating for Maxwell. Which is fals in every particular. I told Fred Parris Editor of the Tribune that what was published in his paper about me was a lie and that any one that thought it was true was a lier at heart.[97]

August 5th 1872. I was Elected constable for the second precinct. This mornings Mining Journal says that the Police disturbed the Maxwell Ratifycition Meating and that Brigham Young Hamptin don all he could to break up the meating. Which is fals.[98]

August 6th 1872. I told one of the Editors of the Mirning Journal that what his paper said about the Police and I was false And told him that they could not get any more items from the Police record And thretened to cick him out of the City Hall if he did not leave which he done in short order.

August 29th 1872. Two Houses of Ill-fame were broken up by the Police Kate Flint and Cora Rubodo proprietors.[99] At night about twelve O clock a man named J. W. Watkin a pimp for prostitutes Being inraged becouse of the breaking of of Houses of ill-fame And his occupation being gon Attempted to Shuit Alex Burt and I in the back as we were pasing out of Zabriskies Saloon. John Cramer alias Dutch Jon caught the revolver and

[97]The Liberal Party was meeting to ratify its nominees, including George R. Maxwell, registrar of the Utah land office, for Congress. The *Tribune* reported "hissing, shouting, and yelling as none but Saints can do." Perhaps referring to Hampton and other policemen, Maxwell told the crowd "we thought we had buried the bloody arm that struck Robinson down," while R. N. Baskin said, "the men who had heretofore cut the throats of others all around the city were and are the men who are fit to do the work of their master [Brigham Young], which had been seen tonight." "A Loyal Mass Meeting Broken Up," *Salt Lake Tribune*, 5 August 1872, 3/3. The *Deseret News* regretted that there had been disturbances. See "That Ratification Meeting," *Deseret News*, 7 August 1872, 12/1. Maxwell lost to George Q. Cannon, the People's Party candidate, by a better than 10 to 1 margin and unsuccessfully contested the election. Bigler, *Forgotten Kingdom*, 296. Fred T. Perris was the general manager of the *Tribune*. See Malmquist, *The First 100 Years*, 28, 31.

[98]"How They Showed It," *Salt Lake Tribune*, 5 August 1872, 2/2.

[99]Other sources refer to the second woman as Cora Conway. See Nichols, *Prostitution, Polygamy, and Power*, 28–30.

saved us from being shot. We arrested Watkin and lodged him in Jail all night. Next day he was fined fifty dollars.[100]

September 2D 1872. I was released from police duty and commenced collecting Licenses for the City.

September 17th 1872. My wife Mary gave birth to a Daughter at 15 minuts to 10 O clock P.M.

October 3D 1872. Mary took the baby to fast meating and had it blessed under the hands of Bros Squires, Willard and Huffman and the name of Vilate Margarat given her.

October 8th 1872. I was served with a Subpeana from the 3d District Court to answer in a Suit in Chancery comenced by Paul Engelbroth (for the breaking of his saloon) against Salt Lake City D H Wells Mayor J D T McAllister City Marshal Andrew Burt Capt of Police and B Y Hampton Dept City Marshal.

October 1872. [Rehnke?] and Lutz Engineer Salt Lake City, D. H. Well Mayor, J D T McAllister City Marshal, A Burt Capt of Police and B Y Hampton Dept Marshal from prosicuting them further for Selling liquor without a license.

October 28th 1872. Kate Flint comenced suit in the 3d district Court against me and others for breaking up her House of illfame. The amount of damages claimed is $27513.00 being three times the value of the property claimed to be destroyed.[101]

December 11th 1872. I arrested C W Baker for Robing a man of $83.00 in money at the Theatre and December 28 he was found guilty of the charge and sentenced to two year in the penitentiary.[102] This is the kind of men the Government officials employ to sware against Mormons.

December 30th 1872. My son Brigham Young paid ten dollars tithing being the first money he had erned.

January 2d 1873. I was shown a badg to be worn by the Gentile Leag of Utah with the enitial letters G. L. U and a five point star in the midle and some word a crost the top which I have forgoten all worke in silk on blew silky Ribon about 1¼ inches wide and about 6 inches long being forked at the lower end. The person showing me the badg told me to be on my gard

[100]For the abatement and the shooting (the latter very similar to Hampton's version), see "Police Court" and "Attempted Assassination," *Deseret News*, 4 September 1872, 12/1–2.

[101]For Flint's successful suit (although she won a fraction of her claim), see *Flint v. Clinton et al.*, case no. 554 (3d dist. civil case files, 1877).

[102]See "Committed," *Deseret News*, 18 December 1872, 9/2.

and to tell Wm G Phillips to do the same as some members of the GLU had taken an oath in their meatings to Kill us by the 20th of the present month.[103]

January 4th 1873. I met a Lady Mrs McKay a Gentile in a party. She told me that she was the person that Sent the badg and warning which should be headed as she had recived the badg and information from one of the members of the Leage. We found the warning timley as we were wachd by the G.L.U and followed home many times after night. I had a guard gow home with me many times which prevented them from molesting me. They are such cowards that a half dozen dare not attac CH Grow and I which was tried one night. As we started for them they run in every direction.

February 27th 1873. Brs DH Well asked I and several of the police to gow and meat Pres Young who with others were returning from the South where they had been spending the winter. We started at 7 O clock AM in a Special Carr Bro Wells and others abord We met them at Draper [with] Pres Young and Jeneral Thomas L Cane and Families all well.[104] We arived in the City about 6 O clock PM. Bro Wm G Philips and I road in Pres Youngs cirrige with him from the Depot to his home.

Saturday March 15th 1873. I and Mary went to Ogden in Company with Pres Young and others to meat Deligate Wm H Hooper and George Q Cannon who were returning from Washington. They arived in Ogden a short time after us in good health and spirits. They returned to the City with us where we arived at 6 O clock P.M. We had two bands in attendance on the train.

March 17th. I went to Ogden to employ some persons to detect houses of ill fame in the City. I engaged two men Mary went with me and we made a visit to my Brother Eaderly. We returned home same evening.

March 18th. I went to Ogden and arrested one William Anderson for seduction and returned to the city the same evening.

June 18th 1873. Andrew Burt, Alex Burt and I went with Pres Young and

---

[103]On the Gentile League of Utah, see Roberts, *A Comprehensive History*, 5:372–78; and Tullidge, *The History of Salt Lake City*, 590–92. The chairman of the Liberal ratification meeting assured the crowd they had a GLU for protection, but Maxwell's biography pointed out problems with these reports. See "A Loyal Mass Meeting Broken Up," *Salt Lake Tribune*, 5 August 1872, 3/3; and Maxwell, *Gettysburg to Great Salt Lake*, 162–64.

[104]Thomas L. Kane was an influential Pennsylvania Democrat who had become sympathetic to Mormon interests; he helped convince President James K. Polk to enlist the Mormon Battalion in 1846 and played a crucial mediating role in the peaceful entry of the Utah Expedition in 1857. See Bigler, *Forgotten Kingdom*, 184–87. He and his wife Elizabeth spent the winter of 1872–73 with Young in southern Utah; Elizabeth later published a book about it. Kane, *Twelve Mormon Homes*.

others to Evinston a 125 miles East in a Special car to meat Pres George A Smith and others on their return from Jerusalem.

Saturday June 28th 1873. By request of Bro Andrew Burt I joine the same prare circle of which he was a member and over which A H Raligh presided.[105] We always meat Saturday evenings. . . .

February 6th 1874. I finished paying my wife Marys Emigration amounting to $6565.

February 15th 1874. I commenced to complete a list of my wife Marys dead relations preparition to being Baptised and Sealed for them.

March 17th 1874. Bro Andrews Burt and I went to Bishop Sharp and gave in our names to join the Holy Order of God as Pres Young had requested [those] that wished to join the United Order to hand in their names to the Bishop of their respected wards.[106]

March 19th 1874. I was sworn in as Deputy City Marshal by Robert Campble City Recorder and received a certificate of apointment from him.

April 23d 1874. I started for Topeka Kansas with a man suposed to be John F Bender Charged in conection with his wife son and Daughter of committing many murders for money In Lubot County Kansas. After riding three days and nights without sleep I arived at Topeka Kansas Sunday the 26th at half past 12 O clock PM.[107] Two men met me at the Depot by request of Governer Orsborn. They both identified the man I had in custodey as Bender. I then lodged Bender in Jail and the Sheriff gave me a recipt for Bender. I then went to the 5th Avenue Hotel where the Governer Borded and was interduced to him. I stoped at the same Hotel and was constantly interviewed by reporters for diferent papers throughout the country.

27th. I went to the Niew York and Niew Orleans Circus and Menagery the same that was in Salt Lake City last year. The manager and proprietoer

[105]Alonzo Hazeltine Raleigh was an early Mormon settler and longtime Salt Lake alderman. Tullidge, *The History of Salt Lake City,* 882–85.

[106]On this Mormon effort to practice communal economics, see "The United Order of Enoch," in Arrington, *Great Basin Kingdom,* 323–49.

[107]John Bender, his wife, son John, and daughter Kate (who may not have actually been related) allegedly robbed and murdered some twenty travelers at their tavern on the road between Fort Scott and Independence, Kansas. The case made national news; see, for example, "The Kansas Murders," *New York Times,* 13 May 1873, 1. For Hampton's prisoner being identified in Salt Lake City and Kansas, see "Old Man Bender in this City," *Deseret News,* 15 April 1874, 4/1; "Bender Positively Identified!" 29 April 1874, 7/4. Evidently the identifying witnesses were wrong, as no Bender was ever brought to trial. See Hardy, *Kate Bender.* A comic book version of the case by Rick Geary, *The Saga of the Bloody Benders,* appeared in 2007. The Benders have a considerable Internet presence.

Mr Cole invited me in without charge. The same day several men arived from Chery Vale nere where the Bender Tradgies had taken place. All identified Bender. 28th. I caled on the Attorney Jeneral of the State to enquire about my expenses as agent of the State and the Rewards that had been offerd. He sent me to the Govener and he in turn sent me to the Secretary of the State C A Morris. I went to the State House and saw the Secretory made my business known and made to him my return as agent of the State and with it filed the Sheriffs Certificate given me for Bender. Also filed my bill against the State Sworn to before a Notary public. The Secretary said that my bills would have to be sent to C.E. Ward County Attorney for the actions of the bord of County Commisioners.

April 29th 1874. I again visited the Governer to see if I could get my expences paid. Amounting to three hundred dollars and the Five hundred dollars reward he had offered for the arrest of Bender. He told me to meat him at the State Home at 10 O clock and he would arange maters with me. We met as per aggreement and after all that I could say and doo he told the Secertary to give me thirty dollars the amount I needed in conection with what I had to take me home. So I got bilked out of my expences and the reward muney. During the war She was caled the Bleading State of Kansas but her other and Proper name is the Bilking State of Kansas when she has any thing to do with Mormons. . . .

May 3d 1874. I arived at Green River at 7 A.M. for breackfast. At 1 30 PM I took diner at Evanston and at 8 40 P.M. I arived at home my expences for the round trip amounted to $330.00

May 8th 1874. Mother arived from Austin Nevad to make us a visit.[108]

May 9th. I attende a Confrence in which was taken a vote to sustain the New Order or to Sustain the Kingdom of God by sustaining home manufactorys home industries and trade with and sustain one another insted of patronizing and sustaining our enimies. Sumthing that I heartily endorse and have always endeverd to carry out in my life and hop I always may.

June 8th 1874 Mother started for home. I went as far as Ogden with her where she will remain a few days. Andrew Smith (who accompanied us) and I Arrested a man by the name Scott [Danall?] for robing Miss Belmont. 10th. I went to Bingham to subpeona witnesses in the same case.

---

[108]Julia moved to the mining center at Austin, Nevada, to be with her daughter Vilate and her husband. Hampton, Papers, 66.

June 11th 1874. In complyance with an order from the War Department forbiding the Mormon Authorities [from] Arresting Soldiers for breaking the City Ordinances, which Order was obtained at the request of General Morrow, Major Gordan at the head of a company of Cavelry armed and equiped as the law directs drew up in line in front of the City Hall at 12 O clock AM and orderd his men to dismount and load their carbines which was done. Then the Major as big as mortal man ever grew Armed with an order from General Morrow on the City Authorities demanding the imediate releas of a Soldier named Hacket confined in the City jail and if the demand was not complied with that Major Gordan was to breake the Jail and take him Hacket at all hazards. The Major came into the City Hall with three guards fully armed to demand the prisoner. He enquired for Judg Clinton or Captin Burt. I told him that they were not in at present. He asked me if I had charge of the Jail. I told him that I had not and if he would look through the Ground he might find the parties he was looking for. In reply he said with an oath that he would nock the Jail down. He took a portion of the soldiers to the jail in rear of the City Hall and commenced work by trying to batter down the Jail door which they failed in. They then forced the iron bars from the window and pulled the prisoner Hacket through. The Soldiers and Crowd comenced hooping and yelling like so many deamons and cep it up for some time through the streets of the City. This is the kind of treatment our Magnanimus Government and its Officer Show and give to the Laterday Saints. 12 and 13th. General Morrow tried to get the Mayor D H Wells to comprimize the matter and say no more about the occurance and here after when the soldiers violated the city ordinances to arrest and turn over to the military authorities without trial. The Mayor told the General that if the soldiers broke the peace they would be arrested fined and imprisoned as before and if the General wanted the soldiers in Camp he could pay their fines or break the Jail as he had done. The whole afair was telegraphed by the Mayor to the Secretary of War, The Attorney General, and Bro Geo Q Cannon deligate at Washington.[109]

July 11th I was nominated in caucus for constable for 4th pricinct.

July 16th 1874. My Wife Mary bear me a Son at 5 O clock AM.

August 3d 1874. Election. I was Elected Constable for the 4th precinct. Same day earley in the morning US Marshal George R Maxwell and several

[109] See "The Military Use Force," *Deseret News*, 17 June 1874, 9/1; and "The Civil the Higher Law," *Deseret News*, 24 June 1874, 9/3.

of his Deputies gathered around the Poles at the City Hall and comenced insulting and abusing people that did not belong to the Ring. And told the police that they had no business around there and that they the US Marshals would run things their own way during the Election which they tryed to do.

In the after noon one of the police Wm G Phillips arrested a person for disturbing the peace. Phillips was then arrested by Dep US. Marshals Wm P Apleby and [Fagan?] the first an apostate Mormon the other drunken Shoe maker.[110] Shortly after Phillips arrest[ed] Capt A Burt and Andrew Smith was arrested. Then came the rumer that the US Marshals designed arresting all the police. Then here some of their crowd got up a row and during the Malee the Pol boxes were to be seized and destroyed and thus defeat the Election of our officers.

In a little while Milt Ore a drunken US Deputy was arrested for disturbing the peace and put in the City jail. The Dep Appelby comenced yelling at the top of his voyce that he was a Deputy US. Marshal and warned every body to keep their hands of[f] of his sacred person. And demanded the releas of Ore ameaditly or there would be great trouble arise. In a short time a Writ of Habis corpus was issued by Judg McKean for Milts Ors releas.

Captain Andrew Burt went and told Mayor Wells that the Marshals and ruffs were trying their best to create a riot and get possession of the polin boxes. The Mayor come to the City Hall and while standing in the door way to the room where the voting was gowing on Ore and a lot of ruffs made a rush for the door where the mayor was standing. The Mayor undertook to stop them and have them gow in quiet. The Marshals then attempted to Arrest the Mayor for preventing people from voting. In the disturbance the Mayor had his coat nearly torn off his back by the mob. The police suceeded in getting the Mayor away from the Marshals and ruffs and closed the door to the polling room. The Mayor then went on to the front balcony of the City Hall and commanded the crowd to dispurs and said if they did not the police would dispurs them.

In the mean time Jeter Clinton Judg of the Election was arrested also Capt Burt my self and others of the police by Deputy US Marshal Smith. With the intention of getting us away from the City Hall so they could break up the Election. Judg Clinton refused to gow with the Marshal unless he was forced. Capt Burt told Smith that as soon as the Election was over and the Pole boxes

[110]William P. Appleby was the son of a prominent early LDS leader, William I. Appleby. He testified for George R. Maxwell to contest George Q. Cannon's election to Congress in 1873.

secure then we would gow with him and not till then. Burt told Smith that there was agowing to be a row and that we were agowing to stay and tend to it.

After the Mayors requested the crowd to dispurs Captain Burt appeared at the front door of the City Hall and told the crowd to listen to the Mayors request. When several Marshals an ruffs made a rush for him hallowing down with him [and] arrest him and Etz [etc.]. The ball then opened. Captin Burt, Phillip Ringwood, N V Jones my self and others commenced the work of cleaning the side walk which was done in short order. Several of the Marshals and their crowd beat a hasty retreat with soar and bleading heads and not one of the police were hurt. After that it was very quiet and the election went on without hinderance for the first time during the day.

After the close of the poles we that were under arrest namley Jeter Clinton, Andrew Burt, James Livingston, Charles Ringwood, Wm G Phillips, C H Grow, and B Y Hampton started with the Marshals to the Marshals Office. On the way there the mob crowded on to Judg Clinton and came near tramping him to the ground which they would have done if we prisoners had not broken away from the Marshals and rushed to his rescue. We got through the crowd and made them stand back at the musels of our revolvers and had to gow the balence of the way with our revolvers in hand to protect our selves.

The mob would have reinacted the Seans of Missouria and Illinoys if they dared they would have murdered us while we were prisoners. After we got in to the Marshals office the crowd could be hardly kept back.

The Governer got up in a wagon in the street and requested the crowd to gow home like good little boys and said that we would be attended to to the extent of the laws. We were released on our own reconizance of three hundred dollars till the 5th at 10 O clock.[111]

August 4th 1874. Mayor Wells was arrested for resisting the marshals the day befor and was held under bonds of one thousand dollars to appear

[111]The election was for territorial delegate to Congress. The Liberal (non-Mormon) candidate was the attorney Robert N. Baskin; the People's incumbent (Mormon) was George Q. Cannon. U.S. Marshal George Maxwell's (non-Mormon) deputies tangled with (Mormon) policemen as partisans challenged the voting credentials of each other's supporters. As noted above, Maxwell was a former candidate for the same office and an active Liberal; Mormons were certain that the U.S. marshals were trying to steal the election, which Cannon won comfortably. "Disgraceful Proceedings," *Deseret News*, 12 August 1874, 8:5; and "Local Matters," 19 August 1874, 1/3–4, agree with Hampton's version in most details. The *Tribune*, naturally, condemned the "plug-uglyism perpetrated during the day by a cowardly band of policemen." "The Election," *Salt Lake Tribune*, 4 August 1874, 4/2. See also Tullidge (who called the marshals' actions "'bayonet law,' enacted for the reconstruction of the South"), *The History of Salt Lake City*, 611–14, quote on 611; Roberts, *A Comprehensive History*, 5:377–80; and Bigler, *Forgotten Kingdom*, 300–301.

on the 5th. [August] 5th. We all appeared before Commissioner Dewey an Irishman. Cases ajurned to the 11th at which time our cases came up for hearing. The testimony against us did not amount to any thing but we proved that the marshals wer drunk and were the agressors. Judg Southerland and Snow wer our Attorneys [with] Carney & McBride for the government. Desision reserved till the 15th. At the ajournment of Court Andrew Burt Stephen Taylor and N V Jones wer arrested for resisting and assaulting the Marshals with intent to kill on the 3d of Aug and held to bail in the sum of five thousand dollars each.

August 15th 1874. Commisioner Terrney gave his decision. He released Andrew Burt and my self and held the others in bonds of five hundred dollars each to wait the action of the Grand Jurry. Mayor Wells case laid over till Thursday. Burt, Taylor and Jones case set for Monday.

August 17th 1874. The Tryals lasted all day and ajourned to the 18th. Same day Andrew Burt arrested for assautting B F Whittemore with intent of doing bodialy injoury.

August 18th 1874. Andrew Burt discharged. Taylor and Jones held under one thousand dollars bonds to wait the action of the Grand jurry. W W Brozzie and I went their bonds. Same day I recived my commision from the Govner as constable.

August 24th. Mayor Wells dischared after all their efirts to convict.

September 3d 1874. Mary took our son to first meeting and had [him] blessed under the hands of Bishop Sharp and Bros [Neary?] and Masen and named [him] Frank Robinson.

September 12th 1874. I attended a meating of the Niew Order in the Tabernacle on invitation of Pres Young.

Sept 14th 1874. I attended a meeting of the Order in the 20th Ward. 16th. I attended another meating of the Order and adopted the by laws and constitution. I and Family took 32 shares at five dollars per share.

October 6th 1874. The grand jurry organized under the Poland bill.[112] 7th. Thomas Rich one of the Grand jurrors endited for lude and lacivious

[112]The federal Poland Act of June 1874 stripped the Mormon-dominated probate courts of criminal and most civil jurisdiction and gave those cases to the federal district courts, with U.S. attorneys and marshals serving as federal court officers. The act created a new method of selecting grand and petit juries that would (in theory) prevent either side from dominating. See Bigler, *Forgotten Kingdom*, 299–300; and Firmage and Mangrum, *Zion in the Courts*, 148–49. For the selection of grand jurors, especially the court's questioning about their willingness to prosecute polygamists, see "Probable Excitation of Excitement," *Deseret News*, 7 October 1874, 8/1.

cohabitation his bonds place at $10000. He would not give bonds and was sent to the pen.

In the Month of October George Q Cannon was indited for marrying more than one wife charge Lewd and Lacivious condict.[113] During the same month George Reynolds was indited for bigomy bonds five hundred dollars.[114]

October 29th 1874. Pres Young and George A Smith started for Dixie. Capt Burt and A Smith went with them as far as Provo.

Oct 30th. When Burt and Smith were leaving them to return home Pres Young blessed them and all the Police boys and requested Bro Burt to tell the police that he sent his blessing to them and tell them to be good boys. And treat our enimies as the enimies of the Kingdom of God. And treat them kindly and let them see we did not stoop to as low and mean things as they And to take care of our selves and not get hurt or killed. But always have the drop on our enimies and strike the first blow.

November 4th 1874. I wife Mary and daughter Hannah Bertha were babtised and sealed on the alter in the Endowment Home for some of Marys and my dead relations. . . .

Febrary 19th 1875. I went south on Rail road Seventy five miles south by invitation of Pres D H Wells to meat Pres Young and others there was two car loads of us. We found Pres Young and party well and returned to the City at 35 minuts past 4 O clock PM. Hundreds of spectators were at the depot to meat Pres Young. He took of his hat and saluted the crowd and said God bless the good and those that live to work richesness.

July 22D 1875. The Firemen gave a grand ball in the theatre. Pres Young, D H Wells, Geo A Smith, several of the twelve, and gereal Smith [Col. John E. Smith] and two of his staf and many other representitive citizens made up the party including my self, wife Mary, and Daughter Hannah. I was one of the Floor managers. There was between six and seven hundred present.

March 11th 1875. Pres Young fined twenty five dollars and one days imprisonment in the penitentiary for not paying the $3,000 Attorneys fees in the case of Anna Eliza Young vs Britham Young being deamed in contempt of court. There was no contempt as the Attorneys on both sides aggreed to let

[113]The Mormon press joked that "Are you indicted?" was becoming a popular salutation. "Local and Other Matters," *Deseret News*, 21 October 1874, 8/5.

[114]Mormon leaders evidently chose George Reynolds, a secretary to Brigham Young, to test the constitutionality of the Morrill Anti-Bigamy Act of 1862, the first federal attempt to eradicate plural marriage. After two trials Reynolds was convicted and appealed to the U.S. Supreme Court, which upheld Morrill in 1879. See Firmage and Mangrum, *Zion in the Courts*, 151–59; and Baskin, *Reminiscences of Early Utah*, 61–72.

the case gow by defalt so as to take an appeal As they could not get it the question of an apeal any other ways. The Appeal was over rooled and a fine for contempt as above.

Pres Young was then taken to the pen in charge of AK Smith a Dep US. Marshal and remained the 24 hours and returned to the City about 2 O clock PM.

There were during the night of his imprisonment hundred of the Bretheren went out in the vacinity of the Pen and remained all night and till he returned.[115]

In the evening Capt Burt and I went out to see if every thing was all right and returned about 10 O clock PM. It was very stormy all day and night.

March 13th. I and others went to Ogden to meat Bro George Q Cannon our deligate returning from Washington. The train was 4 hours late which detained us till near midnight before we got home.

April 1st 1875.[116] I donated $25.00 toward building the St George Tempal. Same day George Reynolds was convicted of poligamy In 3D District Court.[117]

September 1st 1875. Bro George A smith died. I attended some of the time during his illness.

Oct 3d. U S Grant President of the United States visited Salt Lake City. Pres Young and others went to Ogden to meat him in a special train. 4th. U S Grant left for the East on Special train at 4 PM.[118]

October 29 or 30th 1875. Pres Young was arrested on an [order] from Judg [?] of the 3d Dist Court to inpris Pres Young untill he paid Ann Eliza $9500[.]00 Alimony. He is very sick and the Marshals are guarding him at his home.

---

[115]Ann Eliza Webb Dee married Brigham Young in 1868 and sought to divorce him in 1873. Ann's divorce case made a minor sensation; Judge McKean ruled that she was entitled to a hefty alimony. When Young refused to pay, he was jailed overnight. Granted a divorce in 1876, Ann wrote a book with a journalist and toured the Chautauqua circuit speaking against polygamy. Young, *Wife No. 19*. See also Arrington, *Brigham Young*, 334, 373; and Firmage and Mangrum, *Zion in the Courts*, 249–51, 335.

[116]During this unexplained and unusually long gap in Hampton's diary, from 1 April to 29 August 1875, the *Tribune* accused him and fellow policeman Nathaniel V. Jones of brutally beating a drunk. See "Police Brutality," 8 July 1875, 4/2; "Police Outrages," 9 July 1875, 4/4.

[117]On 29 August President Young invited Hampton and others "who hav assosiated themselves together for the purpos of building up the Kingdom of God" to a meeting in the old tabernacle. Hampton and his wife Mary attended the meeting on 31 August and "had a good meating which ajourned to Saturday the 11 of September." The Hamptons were among fifty or so persons, along with the First Presidency and the Quorum of the Twelve Apostles, who met to launch the United Order of Salt Lake City No. 1, the capital city's version of the United Order of Enoch. See Journal History, 31 August 1875.

[118]"Visit of President Grant," *Deseret News*, 6 October 1875, 8/2.

November 1st 1875. Pres Grant caled a meating of the Cabinet in conciquence of Pres Youngs Arrest and submited his case to the Attorney Jeneral of the United States.

November 17th 1875. Pres Young released on a writ of Habis corpus by Judg White.

December 4th 1875. I was ordained and set apart as one of the Presidents of the 33d Quorum of Seventies under the hands of H S Eldredge, Joseph Young and others.

December 9th 1875. I and some of my familey those herein named were Babtised in the Endowment home Covenanting to keep and observe all of the rules of the United Order. B Y Hampton Babtised by Andrew Burt and confirmed under the hands of Bros B F Neslin and W C Dunbar. Mary Jane Ranalph Robinson Hampton babtised by Bp. John Sharp and confirmed under the hands of W C Dunbar and B F Neslin. B Y Hampton Jr babtised by Andrew Burt and confirmed under the hands of Bros John Squires and W L N Allen. Hannah Bertha Hampton babtised by Bp John Sharp and confirmed under the hands of Bros B F Neslin and W C Dunbar. Jonithan V Hampton babtised by Andrew Burt and confirmed under the hands of John Squires and W L N Allen.

Dec 23d. Thomas Owen Hampton was babtised by Robert Patrick and confirmed under the hands of Bros Andrew Burt and J D T McAllister. By request of Bishop Sharp I assisted in confirming the Bretheren and Sisters that were rebabtised in the Endowment house December the 9th and 23d Feby 21st/76 appointed City Marshal.

March 1st 1876. An address to young girls appeard in the Womans Exponent writen by my wife Mary it being her first production.[119]

March 9th 1876. I assisted in confirming over a hundred persons from the 20th ward babtised in the Endowment house.

April 5th 1876. I went with Pres Young to Ogden to look at the new iron Bridge bult over the Weber River for the Utah Central Railway. We left Salt Lake City at 915 AM and returned 1 30 PM. Same day about 5 O clock P.M. 4 magazines on arsnell hill containing about 40 tons of powder exploded

[119]M. J. R. Hampton, "A Word To the Girls," *Woman's Exponent*, 1 March 1876, 1/1. Mary Hampton warned young women of the dangers they were in and counseled them to obey their parents. The *Woman's Exponent* was the semi-official organ of the LDS Relief Society. Under its long-time editor Emmeline B. Wells, the paper staunchly defended LDS interests, including plural marriage, while also advocating woman suffrage. See Bennion, "The *Woman's Exponent*."

killing two boys Hill and Richason blowing them to fragments but fiew peaces of them could be found. A woman and child was kiled and others injured and thousands of dollars worth of property destroyed principly in the wrecking of windows. Nearly all windows within a radius of a mile and a half of the explosion were broken. My house was considerably damaged being over a mile distant from the magazines.[120]

April 6 & 7. I assisted in holding an inquest in the bodies of the 4 persons kiled by the explosion. April 15th. A peace appeard in no 22 of the Exponent writen by my wife Mary entitled Honor thy Father and Mother.[121]

April 17th 1876. My son Brigham Young Hampton recived his endowments and was ordained an Elder under the hands of W J Smith and others.

April 19 1876. I went with Pres Young and others to Odgen to view the new bridge and dedicate a new Building erected by the releaf society of Ogden. We returned home the same evening.

May 13th 1876. My son Brigham Young was ordained a Seventy under the hands of Abinadi Pratt and others and admited a member of the 33d Quorum of Seventies.

June 15th 1876. I Wife Mary and three children went on an Excursion to Short Branch and on the lake in the boat caled the General Garfield. The company consisted of Joseph F Smith one of the quorum of the twelve and Family and several of the Families of the other members of the Quorum of the Twelve and many other good bretheren and sisters. Names of the committie that got up the excursion Andrew Burt, Henry Dinwoodey, A C Pyper, George Crismon, and B Y Hampton.

August 3d 1876. My wife Mary bear me a Daughter at 25 minuts past 7 O clock PM weid 10 lbs.

August 16th 1876. I assisted in confirming between 40 and 50 persons members of the 20th ward Babtised and rebabtised covinanting to keep the rules of the Niew Order.

August 16th 1876. 16 Navojoe indians arived from Arizona to hold a confrance with Pres Young. The counsil lasted about two hours. I was presant

---

[120]"The Explosion Yesterday," *Salt Lake Tribune*, 6 April 1876, 2/1–2. Four powder magazines belonging to ZCMI, the DuPont Company, and the Walker Brothers located north of today's Utah State Capitol exploded with devastating effect after two boys, Charles Richardson and Frank Hill, apparently used the DuPont magazine door for target practice. Hurtling rocks also killed a child, Joseph H. Raddon, and the pregnant Mary Jane Van Natta as she pumped water three-fourths of a mile to the west. For an excellent account, see Bashore, "The 1876 Arsenal Hill Explosion," 246–55.

[121]Mrs. M. J. R. Hampton, "Honor Thy Father and Mother," *Woman's Exponent*, 15 April 1876, 1/2.

during the counsil. When they had finished I took four of the indians home with me to super. Same day I receved my Commission from Governer Emery As constable of the 4th Precinct Having been Elected on the 7th of the same month at the regular Election.

September 7th 1876. I attended fast meating in the 20th ward and assisted in confirming also blessing children. Mary was presant with our babey which was blessed under my hands and others and named Blanch Melison.

September 29th 1876. At half past 12 O clock AM I started with A. K. Smith Deputy US. Marshal up Big Cottonwood Canyon to serve an injunction on C A Patten A government Official to prevent him from selling Bro D. H. Wellses lumber to pay stumpage. We arived at Silver Springs at 20 minuts to 6 O clock AM having travled some 30 miles and served the papers on Patten and partie who had several of our Bretheren under arrest for cutting timber for Bro Wells. Which course in is keeping with government officials when Mormons are interested. Patten disreguarded the Orders of the Court and sold the lumber and not any thing don with him for it.[122]

October 1st 1876. I attended Quorum meating and assisted in ordaining members in to the 33d Quorum of Seventies. A duty that I have been caled upon several times to perform is Ordaining Seventies and Elders.

October 28th 1876. My Brother Eaderlys son Alex died of Small pox and November 16th he lost his little daughter with the same desease and November 17th I sent him fifty dollars to help him in his bereavement.

February 8th 1877. I and Mary attended a Sociable at Mayor Littles. City Officers and City Council and their Families made up the party.

April 27th 1877. I and others went to York seventy five miles south on railroad to meat Pres Young on his return from Dixie we returned the same day. The Same day I was requested by Andrew Burt City Marshal to take charge of a guard to guard Pres Young Consisting of six men each night comencing with the first ward.

June 18th 1877. I wife Mary and daughter Hannah Bertha receved our Patriarcial blessings under the hands of John Smith the head patriarck of the Church.

July 5th 1877. I assested in confirming about fifty persons that were babtised in the Endowment House from the 20th ward.

Monday August 27th 1877. I attended Prare Circle in the Endowment House at 8 O clock P.M. in company with other prare circles. About 60

[122]For predictably opposite views of this issue, see "The Stumpage Affair," *Salt Lake Tribune,* 30 September 1876, 2/2; "Local and Other Matters: Stumpage," *Deseret News,* 4 October 1876, 1/1.

persons in all met and offered up prare in behalf of Pres Young who is very sick.

28th Pres Young was not expected to live. Circals caled on to meat every hour in turn in the Endowment House to pray for him.

29th [August 1877]. I went to Endowment House to pray with my circle for Pres Young reported that he is some better. At a quarter to 3 O clock PM I went to see Pres Young who was Moaning and apparantly in great pain. When I saw his suffering a spirit came over me to pray the Lord to ease his pain that he might die easey for I felt that he could not live from the first I saw him on Tuesday the 28th at 2 O clock.

I offired up a secret prare to the Lord while I was looking upon Pres Young in his sufering and as soon as I had said Amen John W Young and George Q Cannon requested the Bretheren present to neal and lay their hands upon him and pray for him as they should be led. R T Burton took the lead and was followed by George Q Cannon, John W Young and others. They were all posessed of the same spirit that I was as soon as I stept in to the room. Fir[st] they prayed the Lord to spare his life if consistant with his mind and will and if not to end him of his pain that he might die easey and depart in peace. As soon as we rose to our feet the hard breathing seased and he seamed perfectly easey and continued so untill he departed this life which happened one minute past 4 O clock PM August 29th 1877 Without a pain or strugle. A fiew moments previous to his death I wen to the Endowment house to meat with my prare Circle to pray for Pres Young. We were dressed and about to comence our services when David McKenzie came and told us that Pres Young was dead. We then prayed for his Familey and the Saints in jeneral. It was a sad time for us all.[123]

The same evening I sat up with and watched over Pres Youngs remains in company with Bros J R Winder, R V Morris and Alex Burt till 12 O clock at night at which time we were releved by A M Musser and George F Gibbs.

August 30th 1877. I watched over Pres Youngs remains till noon. Public places and many stores are closed there is a jeneral fealing of sadness with the Saints.

August 31st 1877. R T Burton, J R Winder, Andrew Burt, James Sharp and I was appointed by the Twelve and others as Marshals of the day during the funeral of Pres Young which was to take place September 2d at 12 O clock M.

[123]For descriptions of Young's death and funeral, see *Deseret News*, 5 September 1877, 8–9; and Tullidge, *The History of Salt Lake City*, 624–25.

I had charge of the guard at Pres Youngs residence for the last five months. Also at the tabernacal while he lay in state. The guard consisted of fifty men at a time changed every six hours. Thare was several thousand people vewed his remains Saturday and Sunday in the Tabernacle and several thousand that could not get the opertunity before service comenced which took place September 2d 1877 at 12 O clock. Thare was not less than twenty five thousand people at the funeral. After the services were over Pres Youngs remains were burried in his lot near his house. Peace to his ashes.

September 28th 1877. I attended the laying of the corner stone of the Assembley Hall on the Temple Block by the Quorum of the Twelve and other branches of the preisthood.

October 8th 1877. I paid for and recived 20 Shairs of the Cooperative tanery stock at $5.00 per shair total $ 100.00.

November 1st 1877. My son Brigham Young Hampton married Hannah E Dunbar at the Historians Office Bro D H Wells performing the Serimony. Mary and I and others presant.

February 20th 1878. I was apointed Deputy Sheriff for Salt Lake County by Theadore McKean Sheriff and attend the 3d district court in the absence of the United States Marshal. I gave bonds in the sum of two thousand dollars Andrew Burt and William Hyde my bondsmen.

June 18th. My wife Mary bear me a son at 10 minuts to 5 O clock AM. He weighed 11 lbs.

August 1st 1878. Mary took our son to first meating and had him blessed under of G C Riser and others and named Leon Brigham.

August 5th. Election I was elected constable for 4th precinct.

August 10th 1878. I recived my Commission from Governer Emery as constable.

November 6th 1878. John R Winder City Tax assessor and collector appointed me his deputy. I gave a thousand dollar bond F Armstrong and William Hyde my shurities.

December 21st 1878. I was taken sick with congestive chills which culminated in double pneumona and lung feaver. The Elders were sent for and administered to me. I continued to get wors [until] the Doctors Benedict and Anderson were sent fir. They examined me and said I could not live. My Brother Eaderly was telegraphed for and came. Sister Dunber was caled in. After two weeks of loving care and attention from my wife Mary night and day with the assistance of Sister Dunbar and my Brother Eaderly. And by the blessing of God through the Administrations of the Elders I was restored to consiousness and gradualy regained my health. At the end of six weeks I went to [town?].

May 4th 1879. Pres D H Wells was sentenced by Judg Emerson in the 3d District Court to pay a fine of one hundred dollars and two days imprisonment in the penitentiary for Contempt of court in refusing to describe the Garments worn by parties while the Sealing Ordinance was being performed in the Endowment House. The case on tryal was Owens vs Miles for Poligamy.[124] The same evening Bro Well was taken to the Pen by M Shaughnesy US. Marshal who refused to allow any one to accompany Bro Well. By a good deal of talk and perswasion which was not in very mild terms I and one or two others preswaded him to lett one of Bro Wellses sons gow and remain with him during his imprisonment.

Sunday May the 5th 18789. I and wife Mary went and saw Bro Wells in the Pen.

In the afternoon we went to the meating in the Tabernacle where a meating was caled by the authorities of the Church to meat in the council house directly after the Tabernacle meating closed. The object of the meating in the Council house was to get up a reception for Bro Wells and to gow to the Pen on the day of his releas and escort him in to the City. At that meating I was appointed one of the marshals of the day. On the 7th there was a grand turnout over ten thousand people in line of the prosesion and over twenty thousand spectators in the streets and in the line of march . . . fir particulars see Deseret News of May 7 & 8 1878.

May 19th 18789. I was summoned and appeard before Bishop John Sharp and council to answer charges preferd against me by my wife Helen. She made the same charge before Pres John Taylor and he refered them to the Bishop. The only part of the charges considerd was the charge of desertion, Divorced, and devision of property. The charge of desersion I pled guilty to this for I suport her and children but do not Bead and Board with her

[124]For the examination in *Owens v. Miles*, see "The Nasty Case," *Salt Lake Tribune*, 30 October 1878, 4/2; for the contempt charge against Wells, see "The Case of 'Contempt,'" *Deseret News*, 7 May 1879, 8/5, 9/1; "One More Judicial Outrage," *Deseret News*, 7 May 1879, 9/1–2. Carrie Owens refused to become John Miles's plural wife. Her case inspired non-Mormon women to create the Ladies' Anti-Polygamy Society, later the Woman's National Anti-Polygamy Society, which lobbied for anti-polygamy legislation. See Hayward, "Utah's Anti-Polygamy Society," 17–28; Iversen, *The Antipolygamy Controversy*, 28; and articles in the society's own newspaper, "The Ladies' Anti-Polygamy Society of Utah," *Anti-Polygamy Standard* 1:1 (April 1880), 1/1; and "The Woman's National Anti-Polygamy Society," 1:5 (Aug. 1880), 33/1.

because she is an apostate and I do not feal Justified in doing any other way than I have done. No decision give till I furnish the Bishop a shedule of my property which I done the next day.[125]

May 23d 18789. The Engelbroth case of which was a defendent was settled by the city fir $8000[.]00.[126]

July 1st 1879. Julia Ranolph was babtised in the Endowment House by Bro Worthing she being 8 years old. July 3d She was confirmed under the hands of Bro Lewi Richards and others. During the first part of July my son Thomas 6 was taken sick with a soar throat and chills which proved to be Diphtheria but he soon recovered.

July 21st 1879. Our little Daughter Blanch Melison was taken sick with the Diphtheria and died July 24th at half past 4 O clock AM and was burried at 5 O clock the same day without any funeral services with the exception of a dedicatory prare offerd up by Andrew Burt at the Grave. . . .

July 25th 1879. Our son Frank Robinson was taken sick with Diphtheara. During his sickness July 30th he was ordained an Elder under the hands of [T B?] Lewis I and others and on July 31st at 11.55 P.M he died in great agony and August 1st at 12 O clock M he was burried without any funeral service with the exception of a dedicatory prare offerd up at the grave by Bro H W. Fowler. . . .

July 28th 1879. Our Daughter Vilate Margaret took sick with the Depht-heara and died July 31st at 10 45 AM. Buried the same day at 6 O clock PM. No funeral services only dedicatory prare at the grave by Bro T B Lewis. . . .

August 2d 1879. Our daughter Julia Ranolph was taken Sick with the dephtheara and died August 6th at midnight just as the clock was striking 12. She was buried on the 7th at 2 O clock PM without funeral services. A dedicatory prare was offerd at the grave by Bro T B Lewis. . . .

All four of the above named Children were burried in my lot in the Salt Lake Cemetry. All that was posible for loving hearts and hands to do was done for them in their great suffering and sickness but without avail in checking the cursed diseas with whitch they wer atac or in saving their

[125]The *Tribune* used Helen's complaints to make general accusations against polygamy. Justice Jeter Clinton insulted her, treatment a *Tribune* reporter attributed to "being a discarded wife of a member of the police force." She asked the *Tribune* to publish what the reporter called "insults and contumely" from "her former sister Saints." "Ill-Treatment of a Child," *Salt Lake Tribune*, 4 April 1874, 4/5. Helen complained four days later that a gang of Mormon boys (including "a son of Mr. B. Y. Hampton") called her "a dirty rotten Gentile" and threw rocks at her children and her windows. One said he "would cut your throat if I could." "Mrs. Hampton Explains," *Salt Lake Tribune*, 8 April 1874, 4/2.

[126]Journal History, 23 and 24 May 1879.

lives. My prare is that their mother and brothers and sisters and I may so live and keep the commandments of God and our covinants with each other that we may be counted worthy when we shall have completed our Earthly existance to join and be assosiated with them throughout all Eternety.[127]

August 14th 1878 [1879]. Mary and I with our baby Leon the only child left us and who was very sick went to Ogden and stoped at my Bro Eaderleys. 16th We went to Brigham City and stoped with Bro John Burt. 17th Returned home. . . .[128]

August 23d 1878 [1879]. My daughter Hannah Bertha was taken down with the Depththeara and came near daing. In about three weeks she became convelesant.

Oct 9th 1879. My Sister Vilate and her doughter Allice arived from Austin Nevada on a visit to us.

June 19th 1880. At 915 O clock PM my wife Mary bear me a son weigh[ing] 11 lbs.

August 2d 1880. I was elected constable for 4th precinct of Salt Lake City at the regular Election.

August 5th 1880. We took the Baby to fast meating in the 20th ward and had him blessed under the hands of my self and others and named Ralph Robinson. Aug 10th. Appointed Deputy Sheriff.

February 12th 1880. I got permisson from President John Taylor and Joseph F. Smith (George Q Cannon not-concurring) to circulate a petition asking the City Corporation to purchas fifty thousand dollars worth of stock in the Utah Eastern Railway. 13–15 and 16th. I circulated said petition among the business men of the city and got 665 signers. On Sunday the 14th I sent to each ward in the city a copy of the petition to be signed. All the wards responded with the exception of the 10. 13. and 18. The number of Signers 850 making a total of 1515. On the 16 the petition was presented to the City Council and referd to the Commitie on ways and means. Subsiquently the

[127]Epidemics of diphtheria (or "croup") raged throughout the American West but were particularly devastating to the large families of Utah Territory: the Hamptons were not alone in losing multiple children in the space of a few days. The bacterial disease caused death by asphyxiation or heart failure and was so highly infectious that the Salt Lake Board of Health banned public funerals. For descriptions of the disease, see Steele, *Bleed, Blister and Purge*, 263–66.

[128]On 23 August 1879 Hampton received a letter from Andrew Burt "deeply sympthizing with you in the great losses which you have lately sustained," along with a gift of $150. Notables signing the letter included Mayor Little, Alderman John Sharp, tax collector John Winder, future Utah governor Heber Wells, and "A Salesman."

committie reported in favor of the city apropriating fifty thousand dollars for the Utah Eastern Railway as soon as their finances would allow of it.[129]

December 4th 1880. George Romney and I was appointed to preside over the Seventies in the 20 ward.

December 6th 1880. The U E Ry Co engaged me to canvass for the sale of stock in their road.

July 6th 1881. At a meating of the tax payers of the 20th ward I was elected a school trustee. Term of office 3 years.

October 1st 1881. I was appointed Specil agent by the County Court of Salt Lake Court to collect Liquor Licenses within the Corporate limits of Salt Lake City as the Liquor dealers refused to pay their Licences to the City and the City dads was afraid to prosicute them. I comenced with my detectives and cout [caught] as high as 22 a day. I then comenced prosicutions and git judgments against several. Then levied Executions and moved their goods and stored them away thereby closing up their Saloons. In a short time the liquor men comprimized and I collected of them $7,400.00 and paid it over to the County Treasuer. As Collector I give a bond to the County of $5,000[.]00 Frank Armstrong and George Crismon my surities.

About November 1st 1881 I was appointed a Teatcher in the 20th ward. T B Lewis was my companion Teacher to visit the Saints.

June 5th 1882. I was Elected one of the directors of the 20th ward institute and appointed one of the Editors of the Index.

July 13th 1882. My wife Mary bear me a daughter at 3 20 O clock AM.

September 6th 1882 she was blessed under the hands of T B Lewis and others in the 20th ward fast meating and named Mary Allice. In the later part of the 1882 I was appointed Treasurer fir the 20th ward institute.

January 1883. I was reelected one of the Board of directors and appointed treasurer of the 20th ward institute.

June 5th 1883. On the reorganizing of the Quorumes of Seventies I was removed from the 33d Quorum and placed in the 13th as one of the Presidents. The district comprises the 20 & 18 wards. In the fore part of July I was appointed as one of a committie to get up a concert in the Tabernacl for the 24th of July.

---

[129]The Utah Eastern Railroad was built from Coalville to Park City to transport cheap coal to Salt Lake. It was an enterprise of Zion's Central Board of Trade, an organization meant to coordinate cooperative LDS economic efforts after the United Order of Enoch proved a failure. See Arrington, *Great Basin Kingdom*, 342–48.

In August 1883 the City Council adopted my plan of numbering the homes in Salt Lake and I superintended the numbering of all the Houses in the City. Also got up the system of plating and recording as is now used by the city for recording house numbering.

January 3d 1884. I was reelected Treasurer fir the 20th ward Institute.

March 18th 1884. I had my right leg broke about 4 inches above the ankle joint by the breaking of a lader while triming treas. Dr Benedict was caled in to set it which he did and left it lying in a pillow without splints fir 13 days. During the time my leg got out of place nearly every day. My wife Mary and Son Brigham puled it in place several times. Twice I had Dr Pike come and pull it in place as I got to week to do it. March 31st my leg was set again by Dr Benedict and put in plaster of Paris. Bro C H Wilcken and my son Brigham held my leg part of the time while the Doctor was [w]raping it.[130] They give out and Gus King Benedicts assistant took me by the heal to hold my leg and mis placed the bones. I told him and the Doctor that they were not holding my leg right and they took no notice of what I said. Conciquently a botch job was made of it and I will in all probality be a cripal for life.

About two weeks after my leg was put in Plaster I was taken sick with the pneumonia and the Doctors gave me up but through the untiring efforts of my wife Mary night and day in nursing me And the administrations of the Elders my life was spaird. Joseph F Smith, Brigham Young, T B Lewis, and Wm Salmon were among the first to administer to me and from the time they laid hands on me I began to recover as Bro Joseph F Smith who was mouth at the time said I should.

September 2d 1884. My wife Mary bear me a daughter at 3 05 AM.

September 10th 1884. She was blessed under the hand of Bro T B Lewis and my self and given the name of *Irene*.

May 7th 1885. Our daughter Mary Allice broke her arm and was set by Dr Anderson.

May the 11th 1885. Bishop Sharp and Council desided that my wife Helen could have a divorce if she wanted it but not the house and lot and thousand dollars asked for in her complaint filed with the Bishop some fiew days previous to the decision.

---

[130] C. H. Wilcken (1830–1915) won the Iron Cross with the Prussian Army in Denmark. After deserting from the U.S. Army in October 1857, Wilcken cast his lot with the Saints and served with Hampton on the Salt Lake Police. He acted as bodyguard, driver, and nurse for a series of Mormon prophets. Seifrit, "Charles Henry Wilcken," 308–21.

May the 5th 1885. In the Deseret News a comunication from some person in Montina was published which said that Profesor Clayton had kept my wife Helen as a price mistres for 10 years and that about a month ago he had married her and were agowing to move North. I told Claiton of the communication in the News. He denide it and said they were not married. I did not use the smoothest language to him and forbid him gowing to my home any more. . . .[131]

November 13th 1884 [1885]. I started for San Francisco California where I arived on the 15th and purchased about $1500[.]00 worth of Holiday Goods from Feigenbaum & Co and durring the Holidays opened a store on Main Street at which time I disposed of the most of the goods. The balaece was afterwards sold at private sale.

The Work of Detecting Crime

Owing to the increas of Houses of ill fame and street walkers in Salt Lake City And the Mayor James Sharp and Marshal Wm G Phillips after repeated requests from the Citizens to do something to check the increas of the crimes above mentioned and nothing being done A Citizens Committie was formed to take the matter in hand and see if parties guilty of Lude and Lacivious conduct could not be detected and punished especialy the Government Office Holders that are prosicuting and persicuting the servants of God for keeping his laws of Marrige.[132]

About the first of May 1885 Francis Armstrong Chairman of said committie of which I was a member asked me if I could detect the Government Officials and others in their Hoardoms and Adultery and bring them to Justice if the money was furnished to do the work. I told him that I would do my best.

[131]The couple had married. "Professor" Joshua Elliott Clayton, a founder of the Scientific Society of Utah in 1885 and who was sometimes credited with opening the Tintic mining district, began work as a mining expert in the Georgia gold fields in 1842. Clayton arrived in California in 1850 and became a respected civil and mining engineer in San Francisco and successful speculator throughout the West. He invented the "Clayton & Veatch process" and helped lay out Aurora, Nevada, where he discovered the rich Real del Monte claim on Last Chance Hill in 1860. Mark Twain credited Clayton with extracting "about four times as much as any other mill in the camp" at his twelve-stamp mill, and Twain claimed Clayton had promised to teach him the process. Clemens, *Mark Twain's Letters*, 1:188n9, 194n3, 209, 216, 223. W.H. Hampton recalled his step-father fondly: Clayton "never went to school a day in his life and yet he was the best engineer, office and field, I have ever known. I learned more from him by accident than I did from the university by design." See Hampton, WPA Interview with Walker Winslow.

[132]For details, see Nichols, *Prostitution, Polygamy, and Power*, 32–36.

William Salmon and Andrew Smith were associated with me making a committie of three to superintend the work of detecting crime. We had about 25 men employed without pay consisting of Home Missionarys and others including the entire police force with the exception of two and the marshal who knew nothing of what was gowing on. The work of detecting was caried on about 5 or 6 months during which time the committie worked night and day and used the police and other guards as they were neaded without the knowledge of either the Mayor, Marshal or any of the City Officers.

The detecting was done by hiring woomen keeping Houses of ill-fame to rent us a room in their house in such position that it connected with several other rooms and by apitures in the doors and walls the beastile conduct of men and women gowing to such houses for illicit intercourse was viewed by guards placed in position for the purpos of witnessing against them.

There was about a hundred male persons detected in their filthy conduct including several Government Officials and men in high standing in the community also including a Babist Minister named Dewit and a Mrs Newcom the leader of the chior in the Babist church.[133] All bitter enimies of the Saints and oposed to plural marrige as practized by the Servants of God. 87 percent of those detected were Jentile married men 95 percent married men and 5 percent Mormons that were considered on the verg of aposticy for years past.

After we had employed a Mrs [A. J.] Field who was keeping a house of ill fame to permit our guard in her house. I on 29th of June 1885 started fir San Francisco Cali to employ detectives to help us on the work of detecting the L & L.

I remained in Sanfrancisco 8 days and employed Dan Goldstine and Mattie Woodard and returned home on Friday the 10 of July and sent money to Goldstine to help them to come here Mattie bilked Dan out of five hundred dollars and conciquently bilked us and did not filfill their engagement.

Some time in August we employed Faney Devenport to assist us in detecting the L & L. She kept a house of ill fame. The first Arrest of F.O.H. [Federal Office Holders] was Oscar Vandercook a Deputy US. Marshal. He was habes corpused by Judg Zane of the 3d dist court and the City Ordinance he was arrested under ruled down to sheald him from the Law. He was then arrested under the statutes and was habescorpused before Judg Zane who

[133]The Baptist minister was Rev. H. G. DeWitt. *Salt Lake City Directory, 1885.*

held the Law good. Vandercook then took an appeal to the Supream Court which ends all danger of his being punished.[134] Others were arrested and pled guilty and others found guilty who took appeals to the 3d District Court where on motion of C.S. Varian asistant prosicuting attorney Judg Zane desmised them without a hearing anything to save the F.O Hes.

When W H Yearian was arrested for lewd and lacivious conduct with Mrs Newcom the Supream Court of the Territory issued a writ restraining all officers from further prosicuting Yearian untill their august body had enquired into the matter which they did and after holding the case under advisement for a long time ruled down the Law that Zane sustained in the Vandercook case Judg Zane desenting.[135] Still the shealding hand of protection held over the F.O. Hes And any thing to convict the Laterday Saints in obeying the law of God by marrying more than one wife.

Before we commenced arresting the L & Ls Mrs Field and Devenport closed up their homes and went to Denver And wer brought back on warrants issued out of the 3d District Court by Judg Zane. (*Se margin note*) [Our committies with others held a Meatin All feard inditement and as none seamed anxious for the honors I volinteerd to take the whole responsibility on my self as the following will show.] They and I were indited for conspiracy and keeping houses of ill fame. There was 4 against me 2 for keeping houses of ill fame and 2 for conspiracy to keep houses of ill fame to catch the L & Ls in.

The following are the names of the Grand Jurrors that indited me and segrigated cohabitation cases against Mormons and would not indite keepers of houses of ill fame when the testimony was brought before them because they are all frequenters of such places.[136] Messrs. R. Evans. forman Wm A Pitt. James W Thompson. John C Lambert. Sam Levy. James Gibson. Wall

---

[134]For Vandercook's arrest, see "The Lascivious Charge," *Salt Lake Tribune,* 22 November 1885, 4/5. For Zane's denial of habeas corpus, see "Gleeful Fiends," *Salt Lake Tribune,* 12 December 1885, 2/2; and "The Vandercook Habeas Corpus," *Deseret News,* 16 December 1885, 13/2. For the dismissal of prosecutions, see "Floored Again," *Salt Lake Tribune,* 15 December 1885, 4/2. Affidavits against Vandercook and a half-dozen others, all signed by Hampton, are in Hampton's papers, along with an affidavit of 8 January 1886 by Justice of the Peace Adam Speirs listing seven defendants found guilty in his court and taking appeals to the third district court. B.Y. Hampton, Papers, folder 5. On federal Judge Charles S. Zane, see Alexander, "Charles S. Zane, Apostle of the New Era." U.S. Attorney Charles S. Varian recounted the case, along with earlier prosecutions of polygamists, in an April 1914 statement in Baskin, *Reminiscences of Early Utah,* 209–29.

[135]W.H. Yearian, a merchant, was arrested for alleged offenses committed on 7 October 1885. See "The Mormon Plot," *Salt Lake Tribune,* 24 November 1885, 4/2.

[136]Despite the presence of several other well-known brothels, only Hampton and his "detectives" were indicted. For the segregation of cohabitation cases, see the Lorenzo Snow case below.

Arnold. Samuel Green. Charles Denhalter. George Harrison. W F Raybold. Thomas Davis. J S Scott. J T Clockey. A Gebhardt. Some of the above were Mormons but not enugh to prevent or procure Inditements and are not guilty of Visiting baudy houses.

December 6th 1885. I was arrested by Deputies Marshal [Greaman?] and Smith on 4 more counts. My bondsmen was Wm H Rowe and S P Teasdel as I was held in $3600[.]00 by commissioner Wm McKay.[137]

December 8th 1885. I went in to Court and pled not guilty to the 4 inditements against me. For the purpos of packing a Jurry that would convict me the regular lawfull panel of Jurrors was desmissed and a jurry selected by Marshal E A Ireland from among the most rabid Jentiles Enimies of the Laterday Saints and friends of and associates of hoars and hoar masters and eavel doers in jeneral. My Attorneys Hoag and Burmaster and Sheaks managed to have the case gow over to the December Term of Court.

December 22d 1885. My tryal was commenced and the following named jurrors T J Alma, Forman, Jos P Keats, George S Ellis, Isaac Hazelgrove. Andrew C Brixen, C A Dahl, Fulton Haight, Chas W Lyman, J M Darling, Samuel Paul, John J Duke, and T E Harper. All selected from the other side and of the same caracter as above described and simpathy with the L & Ls.[138]

The above jurrors found me guilty as was expected on what little testimony that could be squeased out of Mrs Fields and the statement of M R Evans (forman of the Grand Jurry that indited me) As to my testimony before that body was a positiv Lie and he knew it and so did Varian and others of the Grand Jurreys contradicted him and all other witnesses but that did not amount to any thing. I must be convicted to save the F. O. Hes.

Wensday December 30th 1885. I was Sentenced by Judg Zane to one years imprisonment in the County Jail in conection with a long hourang from the Judg. I took an apeal to the Supream Court of the Territory and was refused but pending the appeal by Judg Zane.[139] I was taken in custody by Sheriff John Groesbeck and put in a well furnished room on the Second floor of the County Court House and furnished 3 meals a day at the expence

[137]The signed bonds for all three charges are in Hampton, Papers, folder 4.

[138]For the charges against Hampton and the madam Fanny Davenport, see *People vs. B.Y. Hampton*, Third District Territorial Criminal Case Files, case no. 286, 7 December 1885; and *People vs. Fanny Davenport and B.Y. Hampton*, Third District Territorial Criminal Case Files, case no. 288, 8 December 1885.

[139]For non-Mormon views of Hampton's trial, see "Brig Roasted!" *Salt Lake Tribune*, 23 December 1885, 4/2; "Brig's Christmas Gift," 25 December 1885, 4/2; and "Taken to Jail," 31 December 1885, 4/2. For the Mormon press's views, see "B.Y. Hampton's Trial," *Deseret News*, 30 December 1885, 1/2; "The Full Penalty," *Salt Lake Herald*, 31 December 1885, 8/2; and *Journal History*, 6 January 1886.

of one dollar a day to the County and treated as well as any one could wish being a prisoner.[140]

February 7 1886. As was expected the Supream Scoundrels (Court) confirmed the action of the lower court in my case. . . .

December 30th 1885. The following person visited me in prison. . . . (5 visiters)

December 31st 1885. . . . The County Court took diner in my room . . . (22 visiters).

January 1st 1886. The following named persons visited me during the month. Wife Mary. 19. visits. . . . Samuel Bateman [of the] Police under Inditement for cohabitation came to my room to hide from the Marshals .9. times and staid from .1. to .3. days each time. . . .[141] Faney Devenport 1. . . . McMuran in hiding 1. . . . No of visitirs in the month 110 No of visits 312.

January 6th 1886. I was taken to the City Hall to testify against J W Farrell for Lewd and Lacivious conduct. He was proven guilty took an appeal to the 3d District court and desmised without further tryal as he was on the list and belonged to the adulterous croud.

January 9th 1886. The Edmonds bill against the Saints and plural marrige passed the Senat by 38 votes for to 7 against. Names of 6 who volentary placed their names on the record without qualifications or excuse Senator Blair of Niew Hampshier, [Wilkinson Call] of Florida. Gibsen of Louisiana. *Hampton* of South Carolina. Morgan of Alabama and Vance of North Carolina. Hoar of Massachutes voted against the bill because it proposed to rob the Mormons of Utah of a vested right but with that provision expunged he would have voted to rob the whole Mormon people of all their vested rights.[142]

---

[140]As Hampton's diary entries make clear, he had a great deal of freedom to come and go. The *Tribune* complained from an early date about this lenient treatment. See "Brig. Hampton's Imprisonment," *Salt Lake Tribune*, 8 January 1886, 4/2. Hampton's long lists of visitors have been cut from this text, except for those of his wife Mary and a few others of special interest, and the monthly totals. Hampton's visitors often brought food or cigars and—in this era before strict adherence to the Word of Wisdom—bottles of beer, wine, porter, and brandy. On the latter, see "The Adoption of a New Interpretation of the Word of Wisdom," in Alexander, *Mormonism in Transition*.

[141]Federal officials purposely sought out LDS church leaders (Bateman was not among those) as subjects for anti-polygamy prosecutions. Most of them went "on the underground," moving among safe locations. The Mormon strategy was enormously disruptive but largely successful; among high-ranking authorities, only George Q. Cannon and Lorenzo Snow were caught. See Gordon, *The Mormon Question*, 158–60; and Bigler, *Forgotten Kingdom*, 327–30.

[142]Hampton means the Edmunds-Tucker Act. The first Edmunds Act, passed in early 1882, put teeth into the anti-polygamy effort by creating a new, more easily prosecuted offense of "cohabiting with more than one woman." It also contained provisions stripping polygamists of political rights and creating a new federal board to supervise elections. Edmunds-Tucker contained further restrictions, *(continued)*

January 14th 1886 Bro Hill brought me the following Letter

Presidents Office
Church of Jesus Christ of Latter Day Saints
Salt Lake City U.T. January 13th 1886

BY Hampton Esq
Co Court House City

Dear Brother

Your esteemed favor of the 10th inst has ben recived and perused with interest we are pleased to witness the spirit which you manifest under the somewhat trying circumstances in which you have been and are placed. We sincerely trust that your health will be preserved to you and that you will be sustained by the Spirit of God, and he able to maintain a chearful and equable demeanor.

You may rest assured that the Lord will control all these events for his Glory and the salvation of his people. So far as yourself and the brethren in your efforts to expose the hypocracy and wickedness of those who are persicuting us and who have been loud in their proffesions of morality, we have no doubt that your motives were good and the conciousness of this will sustain you.

With Love and praying the Lord to bless you

We are your Bretheren
John Taylor
George Q Cannon[143]

January 22d 1886. N V Jones and Frank M Treseaden who wer working on the detecting business in connection with me in finding out the moves of the marshals and Government officials against the Saints were arrested to day on charge of bribing one Franks a deputy US. Marshal. Treseadens bond was placed at $5000. and he was sent to the pen. Jonses bonds $10,000. which was given. The facts are that Franks was not a deputy marshal when he was approched to give us any information he had in reguard to the moves of the Marshals against the Mormons but was employed and acted as deputy marshal by Ireland.

January 23d 1886. Bro Henry Lunt President of Seeder [Cedar] Stake and patriarch caled upon me though not aquainted. Said that I should be blessed

including disincorporating the LDS church and the Perpetual Emigrating Fund and stripping women of the right to vote. See Bigler, *Forgotten Kingdom*, 317–18; and Firmage and Mangrum, *Zion in the Courts*, 161–97, 197–209. Robert Baskin lobbied for the bill. See Baskin, *Reminiscences of Early Utah*, 173–82.

[143]The original of this letter, with identical content but better spelling, is in Hampton, Papers, folder 4.

from this time on only acknowledg the hand of God in all things and that I was making money faster than ever before comparitively speaking on account of the course I had taken in detecting the lecherous scoundrels in their crimes for which I am now sufering imprisonment and said I should be blessed and asked God to bless me.

January 26th 1886. I went with A J Burt to see Faney Devenport.

Jany 31st 1886. I went to super at Bro S H Hills on his invitation.

February 1st 1886. The following named persons visited me during the month my wife Mary visited me 11 times. . . . S Sudbery mail carier for undergrounds 18. . . . No of visiters during the month 94 no of visits 273.

February 4th 1886. My birthday I am 50 years old to day and in jail. What next [?] Ralph and Leon gave me ten cents each for my birth day present. . . .

February 8th 1886. Marshal E A Ireland offerd a reward of $50000 for information that would to the arrest of George Q Cannon for cohabitation with his wives.

February Sunday 14th 1886. Rumerd that George Q Cannon was arrested at Humbolt Nevada.

February 15th 1886. Pres D H Wells now in England sent me his regards through his son H M Wells and said I had done a good work and to bear all things patiently and all would turn out right. Same day Jose E Taylor sent me his kind regards.

February 16th 1886. Rumerd that Geo Q Cannon had jumped the train at promintory [and] did not arive on train as expected.

February 16th 1886. A detachment of Soldiers went on special train to Promintory after Bro George Q Cannon. In this the Land of the Free and home of the brave Any thing will do for Mormons.

February 17th 1886. George Q Cannon arrived about half past 8 O clock AM badly brused and sore having falen from the Train. He was guarded by soldier[s] with loded carbines and a most wonderfull display of bravery over a Sick Mormon not able to rais his head. What would have been done if he had been well and hearty. It would have taken the whole American Armey to manage him. Well might the prophets say that in the last days that one servant of God would chase a thousand and that two would put Ten thousand to flight. Same day George Q Cannon was admitted to bail in the small sum of $45,00000 for a misdemeanor of cohabiting with his wives. John Sharp and Ferimorze Little went his bonds for $25,000 and H S.

Eldredge and Frank Armstrong went his bonds for $20,000 his trial set for the 17th of March.[144] In the evening I went home with A J Burt. Saw my family and Faney Devenport who met us at my house.

February 21st 1886. Jailor A J Burt took me a riding up city creek canon and we caled at Bro Sudberys and had *wine*.

February 22D 1886. I answerd a letter of R W Sloans who is on a mission in Ireland I also wrote a letter to Bro D H Wells who is presiding over the Eurepin Mission. Same evening at a Mining meating held in the County Court house the following named persons wer present L J Nutall Pres Taylors private secretary, George Reynolds, John Q Cannon, M W Taylor, and John Beck. Same evening the Cannon boys thumped prosicuting Att Dixon and were arrested.

February 23d 1886. Hugh Cannon was trid in the justices court before Judg George D Pyper for hiting Dixon. The Judg said before passing sentence that the custmary fine for such offences where the parties making the assalut were drunk was from 15 to 25 dollars but on account of his (Hugh Cannon) youth and being perfectly sober and as Mr Dixon had recived but slight injuries he would assess a fine against him (Hugh Cannon) of $35.00 and in default of payment would be committed to the county jail one day for each dollar fine. Hugh Cannon was brought to the County jail and put in my room. US. Deputy Marshal Franks came with A J Burt who brought Hugh to see where Hugh was put as he Franks had a warrant for his arrest on the same charge that he had just been fined for and while Franks went to hunt Sheriff Groesbeck N V Jones and I had Hugh Cannons fine paid and he told [him] to Scip which he did and when Franks returned with the Sheriff for Hugh and his bird had fled there was some tall swearing done by the two.[145]

---

[144]U.S. Marshal Ireland offered a five-hundred-dollar reward for Cannon's arrest, more than for President John Taylor. En route to Mormon colonies in Mexico, Cannon was arrested at Humbolt, Nevada. Ireland took charge of Cannon but, somewhere near Promontory, Cannon either lost his balance and fell (his version) or jumped from the car. Deputy Marshal Vandercook sent an infantry detail from Fort Douglas to escort the prisoner. The government set bail at forty-five thousand dollars for an offense with a maximum penalty of six months and a fine of three hundred dollars. See Roberts, *A Comprehensive History*, 6:126–32; and Bigler, *Forgotten Kingdom*, 329–30. Cannon's sons Abraham H. and Frank J. had "arranged a plan whereby we hoped to rescue Father from the hands of his enemies should he so desire.—Frank was to go out to meet the train, and was to be met at Corrinne by a party from Ogden who were to hold up the train while the prisoner was being removed." Cannon, Diary, 15 February 1886, 6:16–17.

[145]Hugh Cannon, another of George Q.'s sons, struck U.S. Attorney William H. Dickson because of intimate questions Dickson had asked Hugh's mother before the grand jury. While Hugh may have been sober, Frank and Angus Cannon were drunk when they "got mixed up in scuffles with Dickson, Erb, and others." See Cannon, Diary, 22 and 24 February 1886, 6:22, 26; and Malmquist, *The First 100 Years*, 100.

February 26th 1886. CH Wilcken took me to Bro George Q Cannons Home to see him. I was cordialy recived by bro Cannon and Family. He is very indignant over the beating he recived from the Government officials and soldiers. He was very much bruised but on the improve.

March 1st 1886. The following named persons visited me in prison during the month. My wife Mary visited me 13 times. . . . Total visiters for month 162. visits. 253.

March 2d 1886. FM Treaseden our Detective arrested on the charge of conspiracy to kill Franks Dixon and Ireland a put up job by the above three US. officials to make Treseden turn against NV Jones. Treseden had an examination before commissioner Sprague and was discharged. He was afterwards indited on the same charge the Deps are hunting for him.[146]

March 9th 1886. Members of the Legislators met in the court room of the County Court house. George Q Cannon, FM Lyman, HJ Grant and others presant at the meating. CH. Wilcken, Lihi Pratt, AJ Burt and I stood guard during the meating for fear of a Surprise from the Deps.

March 17th 1886. George Q Cannon did not appear in court to day the times set for his tryal his bonds was declared forfited. Same day D Backholts Little girls had a birth day party and sent me pies and cakes.

March 22d 1886 evening. I went home to se the sick baby found him almost well.

March 25th 1886. I recived a letter from Helen at the hands of my son William B in which she warns me to be carefull as it is rumerd that I gow home and take other liberties that will get me and the Sheriff in to trouble and hopes that I will take the warning kindly as she has not spoken to me for many Years and requests that I will destroy the Letter as soon as read.

March 26 1886. Deputies Franks and Smith raided NV Jones hous for FM Treseden who was in my room at the time. I notified him to gow out of the back door and through the block as the Deps might visit me to see if he was in. They did not come and Treseden got away all right.

March 31st 1886. A committie from the Grand Jurry visited the County Jail and came in my room and reported that I was very well fixed and was my own guard as I held the key to the door in my room. They feal very bad that I am not in their clutches and confined in a Dungon. Names of the committie F.M. Bishop, Milt. Barrett, and A.R. Carter.

[146]See "Wholesale Murder," *Salt Lake Tribune*, 4 March 1886, 2/2.

April 1st 1886. The following named Persons visited me during the month to wit. My wife Mary visited me during the month 16 times. . . . Total no of visitors for month 90 visits 223.

April 3d 1886. I went to the 3D District Court to have my bondsmen SP Teasdle and Wm H Rome released from their bond and the three other inditements aginst me pending tryal As I do not want to be in jail and under bonds as well. The case was argued by my Attorneys and taken under advisement by Judg Z. S. Zane and after several days deliberation on the grave subject he refused to releas my bondsmen. So much for being a Laterday Saint.

April 7th 1886. CH Wilcken took me to se Pres George Q Cannon at his house. We had a plesent time for about two hours.

April 10th 1886. Franklin D Richards one of the Twelv Apostles Sent me his regard and best wishes by NV Jones. In the evening NV Jones took me riding. We spent the evening at CH Crows.

April 11th 1886. Dep Sheriff AD Burt took me home to see my mother who is very sick.

April 12th 1886. Lew Nealey reported to us that FM Treseaden our detectiv had scipped. He is under $5000. bonds and we are responcible to his bondsmen for the amount. The court declaird Tresedens bonds forfited. Same day Lehi Pratt returned from running Fanney Devenport out of the country. Same day John Sharp and Ferimorze Little paid to the clirk of the 3D District $25,000.00 the amount of George Q Cannons bonds declard forfited by the Court. Which they were security for. They paid it against the wish and protest of George Q Cannon and others who wanted to test the validity of such exorbitant bonds. They Sharp and Little claimed that their Honors were at stake and they must pay the bond (Their Honors with the Tribune and the Enimies of the Saints are more to them Than the Honor of the Authorities of Gods Kingdom and all his Saints). Wait and see what will become of them if they do not repent.[147]

April 16th 1886. AD Burt took me home to see my Mother and to arrange with David Jones to buld me a cespool and sink.

April 16th 1886. Thomas Butterword the fellow that testifyed against me in the Robinson case One of the meanest and bigest liars on Earth was

[147]Feramorz Little had been Hampton's brother-in-law until his sister Julia died of tuberculosis in 1867. After pleading guilty to unlawful cohabitation in 1885, Sharp was stripped of his church offices and widely considered a traitor. See "A Mormon Bishop Deposed," *New York Times*, 5 September 1886, 6.

blown up and kiled by an explosion of jiant powder that he was warming at a fire in a mine in little Cottenwood, another person was badly injured at the same time by the name of McDonald.

April 25th 1886. J W Burt took me home to see Mother who is very sick Still.

April 27th 1886. Dep US. marshal Franks served a subpeona on me to appear in the 3D District Court in the case of the people vs Faney Devenport fir Keeping a hous of ill fame. I went to court. The case was ajourned till 2 O Clock. At 2 O clock I appeard in Court. The case ajourned till 10 O clock tomorrow. From Court I went home in charge of A D Burt to see Mother who is some better. My Brother Eaderly Wife and child Mrs Julie Delin and a Miss Farley had just arived from Ogden in a team to see Mother who was not expected to live long when word was sent them the day before I returned to jail and found Mary and Ralph wating for me.

April 28th 1886. I went to court at 10 O clock as a witness agaisnt Faney Devenport and as I was jointly indited with her in the same case. The case against me was desmised Court. Ajourned till 2 O clock at which time I was put on the stand to testify, which I refused to do on the grounds that the assistant prosicuting att C S Varian (who was then prosicuting the case against Faney) some time previous told the Court that I and others connected with me in detecting the Government Officials in their Hoardom shold not be believed under oath and etz and parties that we had tistifyd against in the justices court had been desmised by Judg Zane on the statement of Varian. . . .

April 29th 1886. Adam Poul started for San Francisco Call to arrest Frank M Treseden who had jumped his bonds.

May 1st 1886. The following named persons visited me in jail during the month to wit Wife Mary visited me 18 times during the month. . . . Total no of visitirs for month 74. Visits. 175.

May 1st 1886. I went to se my attorneys at their request as assistant prosicuting att Varian proposed to them to dismiss all cases against me and Faney Devenport if she would come in and recive sentences in the case just tried against her. I told them to say if they would dismiss the suit against her bondsmen as well then she would come in and recive sentence as they could not have her and the bond money both. Dixon & Varian say that they will have the bond money $150000. I told the attorneys to fight it to the last dich. We then run Faney out of the United States in to Canada out of the L & L reach.[148] Same day while on my way uptown I met M.R. Evans Forman of the Grand Jurry that indited me and the one that came in to Court when I was in tryal and told a positive lie as to my testmony before the grand jurry. I told him that if I owed the Deval a dozen liars and he wood not take him Evens for the debt he the Deval could gow to hell for his pay.

May 1st 1886. A C Brixen one of the Jurry that found me guilty beged my pardon. Said he had nothing against me personally and that he did not think I had outo have been found guilty but he could not stand out against the other eleven jurrors and the abuse of the Tribune so he had to vote against me. I forgave him and we meat as ever.

May 4th 1886. N V Jones recived a telegram from A M Paul saying that he had arrested F M Treseden in San Francisco. Same Day Govener Caleb W West arrived to take the place of Gov Eli H Murray removed.

May 7th 1886. Marshal Salomon brough me an invitation to the reception to be given the New Govener in the Theater this evening. I declined the honor and my wife and sister Vilate and Daughter Hannah went to the reception which was a grand afair. . . .

May 10th 1886. Frank Cannon sentenced to three months imprisonment in the county jail and a fine of a hundred and fifty dollars and costs for Hugh Cannon hiting Dixon.

May 10th 1886. The Supream Court of the United States desided that they had no jurisdiction in the cases against Lorenzo Snow one of the Apostles convicted of cohabiting with his wives (Three segregated convictions contrary to the evidence) and reversed their decision in the Cannon Case. A Subterfuge so as to leave the Mormons in the hands of the Ring and courts that they may be used up. Wait and se who will be used up first not the Mormons shure.[149]

May 11th 1886. C H Wilcken took me to Bro George Q Cannons House and he and I administerd to Sister Martha Cannon who was quite unwell.

May 14th 1886. Adam Paul just arrived with F.M. Treseden from San

---

[148]For testimony in the Davenport case, see "The Triumph of Unbridled Lust," *Deseret News*, 5 May 1886, 8/3.

[149]The Lorenzo Snow case tested the legal doctrine of segregation, or charging a husband with cohabitation for each period of time he spent with a plural wife. The U.S. Supreme Court dismissed Snow's appeal on the grounds that it did not possess jurisdiction to hear it, which also meant that the court went back to a previous cohabitation case, *Cannon v. United States* (1885), and vacated that decision as well. In a subsequent Snow appeal, however, the U.S. Supreme Court rejected the segregation principle. Firmage and Mangrum, *Zion in the Courts*, 178–83.

Francisco. Treseden says that he did not design jumping is bonds, but he don it all the same.

May 15th 1886. Three prisoners escaped from the county jail by taking up a flag[stone] and diging under the wall and came out on the lam. They made good their escape.

May 18th 1886. Bro Cleghorn sent me a bottle of Port wine by Wm Salmon.

May 23d 1886. O P Arnold took me a riding.

May 28th 1886. A petition was being sirculated among the business men of the city asking Govener West to pardon me.

May 31st 1886. A D Burt took me home to se the Famely. They had all gon to Hannahs to eat Ice cream we went to Hannahs and cream with them.

June 1st 1886. The following named persons visited in prison during the month. My Wife Mary visited me 15. times. . . . S Sudbery 1. and his Daughter Miss Marsha 1 and an other lady 1. caled at the gate in a carrige and we had a long talk both Ladies are on the underground. . . .[150] P H. Lannon 1. caled at the front gate in his Buggy. I told him in plain English what I thought of the Tribune of which he is managing agent. . . .[151] Total visitors in month 79 visits. 159.

June 4th 1886. A D Burt took me home Ralph had hurt him self and Irean sick. Same day Mayor Armstrong presented a petition to Governor West signed by 350 persons Mormons Jew and Jentiles business men of the City asking the Govener to pardon me.

June 6th 1886. The Tribune published the petition with all the names and the addess of my attorneys and a dirty peace agaisnt the Attorneys the Signers of the Petition and my self. Telling the Governer indirectly not to pardon me. I have no doubt but that he will follow in the path the Tribune points out.[152] The Deseret News did not even mention the petition and the Hearld had 4 lines saying the petition had been handed to the Govener some three or four days after it happened.

June 7th 1886. O P Arnold took me a riding after dark.

[150]Male polygamists were the main targets of antipolygamy legislation, but their wives faced the prospect that Congress could declare their marriages void and make their children illegitimate, with serious consequences for inheritance rights and public reputation. Some wives went into hiding to avoid testifying against their husbands. See James, " 'Between Two Fires.' "

[151]Patrick H. Lannan and C. C. Goodwin, already the *Tribune*'s editor, bought a four-fifths interest in the paper in 1883. Malmquist, *The First 100 Years*, 73–74.

[152]See "Working for Hampton," *Salt Lake Tribune*, 6 June 1886, 6/2. The petition has over four hundred names, including several businesses.

June 9th 1886. 4 Jentile Ladies brought some boquets of flowers to the prisoners. I recived theree for my share and wrote a toast to the 4 ladies which was published in the hearld the next morning as follows. Heres to the four ladies who brought boquets to the county jail May their paths through this life be strewn with flowers and in the life to come may they be crowned with the faithfull and sit down with Abraham Isaac and Jacob in Christs Kingdom.

June 17th 1886. J. M. Darling one of the jurrors that found me guilty offerd to sha[k]e hands with me. I told him that I could not give him my hand in friend ship to a person that would convict me on popular predguice and the [?] of the Tribune. He said he did not blam me. He said it was the hardest thing he ever done in his life to bring a verdict against me as he had always looked upone me as a personal friend and a jenteleman. I asked him on what testimony he convicted me. He said on my own and afterwards said that he belived that if I had been allowed to Carry out my plan in breaking up houses of ill fame it would be a good thing for the City as they were overrunning the town. That is the kind of Honorable Jentleman that sits on Jurries and convicts Mormons. Same day Frank Dyer the New US. Marshal takes the place of E. A. Ireland US. Marshal Removed. A scoundrel of the first magnitude and his sucessor will prove to be wors if posible.

June 22D 1886. Mary went to the lake with the 20th Ward Sunday school and took the four children and road in a boat on the lake and had a good time. In the evening A D Burt took me home to see them. I found them all well.

June 23d. J W Burt took me a riding in the evening.

June 27 1886. J B Stewart and Miss Dean caled on me in the evening and sung Nearer my God to the. Oho my Fathe though that cruelest and Home Sweet Home.

Tuesday June 29th 1886. My Wife Mary and Daughter Hannah caled on Governer West at the Wilke home to enquire if he designed pardoning me or not. He positivly refused to do any thing for me. They came to the jale to tell me the news with their Eyes streaming with tears and Mary felt so bad after returning home that she was taken Very sick and had to send for Dr. Anderson. Same evening A D Burt took me home to se my wife Mary. I found her some better but very sick. On my return I caled at the City Hall and sister Poley Burts.

June 29th 1886. I wrote the following Letter and mailed it to Governer West.

Salt Lake City June 29th 1886

To His Exelency Caleb W West Govener of Utah Territory

Dear Sir

My Wife and Daughter came to see me to day with with tears raining down their cheacks. On enquirey as to what was the matter they informed me that they had called on your Exelency to learn if you designed listning favorbly or not to the petition of a fiew of my friends asking you to pardon me for my alleged offence.

They have told me your reasons as best they could in their excitement for refusing to favorbly consider the petition. I fear you have been miss lead in regard to the matter.

Would you please give me your reasons for refusing to grant the prare of the petition.

Respectfully
B Y Hampton

PS. Address B Y Hampton 268 Second South St West

Up to August 1st 1886 the Govenor has not answerd my letter but the answer given my wife and daughter was that I was a bad man and none of [us] is safe if he is out.

July 1st 1886 The following named persons visited me during the month. My Wife Mary visited me in prison 17 times. . . . Total visiters for month 77 Total visits 158.

July 6th 1886. At 4 O Clock PM I in company with R S Burton, M E Weiler and John C Cutler went 13 miles over Jordan near Bingham Canyon to look at some land one mile wid and three miles long taken up by county offical and others. F Armstrong one of the owners promised to let me have Eighty Acres. We returned home at 9 O clock PM.

July 9th 1886. O P Arnold took me a riding. We caled at Bro C. H. Wilckens home and I went in and saw Sistr Wilcken and Bertha Wilcken. We then went to the Tithing Office and saw C H Wilcken and Samuel Sudberry and returned to prison between 11 & 12 O clock PM.

Friday July 16th 1886. I orderd the Deseret News stoped because it did not defend the signers of the petition to the Govener for my releas against the attacs of the Tribune and because they did not mention either the delivery of the petition to the Govener or his refusal to pardon me but if a hors Theaf or any one else is pardoned they News can give them at least a half colum of notice and when I have worked for the public good I do not think that the Deseret News treats me right and on this Rock we Split. Same day T E Taylor Manager of the Deseret News caled on me and I told him what I thought about the Deseret News treatment of me.

July 18th 1886. A D Burt took me home to see my Familey.

July 19th 1886. I took my wife Mary home in A D Burts Buggy. Same evening a primary was held in the county court house to Elect deligates to the County Convention to be held on the 24 inst.

Saturday July 24th 1886. The Convention met in the County Court house at 2 O clock PM. and used my room for committie purposes. A Ticket was mad up of good men by the Convention. Same day S Sudbery caled and asked me to gow to the Tithing Office this evening about 8 O clock also brought me the following which explains its self (if not I will).

Presidents Office
Church of Jesus Christ of Laterday Saints
Salt Lake UT July 23D 1886

James Jack Esq

Please pay Brigham Y. Hampton one hundred dollars on the General Tithing Office and charge donation account.

Your Brother
John Taylor

I supose the above came by reason of my asking C H Wilcken to ascertain if the Church (or any one in his knowledge) would loan me a thousand dollers on good security and mortgage as I had some debts that was pressing me and that I neaded means to keep my family the remainder of my imprisonment.

I wrote the following letter to Pres Tayler in recipt of the above Order.

Salt Lake City July 24th 1886

Pres John Taylor

Dear Brother

Your order of July 23d 186 On James Jack Esq for one hundred dollars to be drawn from the General Tithing Office in my favor and chargable to donation account has been recived this day at the hands of Bro Samuel Sudbery.

Which Order I herewith return with many thanks for your kindness and hope that you will take no offence as I most shurly do not mean any.

I have a balance of a Mortgage on some of my property amounting to five hundred dollars which must be paid and I would like to gett five hundred more to defray expenses while in prison which makes one thousand dollars that I nead.

If the Church or any one would lend me the ammount I will give any security in the way of Mortgage required and would take it as a great favor.

Your Brother in the Gosple
B.Y. Hampton

Same evening at 8 O clock I took AD Burts Buggy and went to the Tithing Office and saw S Sudbery D Bateman Bro Bennett City Marshal A Soloman and CH Wilcken who I gave the above letter to to deliver to Pres Taylor. We had considerable talk on my affairs and other things. I returned to prison a little after ten O clock PM.

July 25th 1886. I had AD Burts Horse & Buggy and took Mary a riding through the park and returned to prison about 10 O clock PM.

July 26th 1886. The High Council met in the County Court House A.J. Burt, AD Burt and Guard as several of the Council are in hiding from the deputies Bro Henry Dinwoodey is one of the Council and to day was released from the pen after six months Imprisonment. Council ajourned at 11 O clock PM.

July 29th 1886. I took Mary home in AD Burts Buggy.

July 30th 1886. I was sent for and went to Sister Polley Burts ajoining the City hall and saw Bro Samuel Bateman one of Pres Taylors guard who brought me word from Pres Taylor in reply to my letter of the 24th Inst. He Pres Taylor said that I must not Mortgage my house but that the Bretheren that I had been associated with should pay me the thousand dollars and arrange so that I could draw my full salary for the balance of my imprisonment and that he would pay one third of the thousand dollars if they the committie whom I was associated with would pay the balance. I returned to jail about 9 O clock PM and went acros the street to se Bro J W Fox Jr who is very sick.

The same evening General Logan arrived from the East and spoke in the Pavilion. Thousands of the Grand Armey of the Republic (GAR) arrived in the City the last fiew days and met in the pavilion.[153] Most all the speakers abused the Laterday Saints most shamefully both these passing through our City to California that know nothing of us only what they here from the scoundrels in our midst who are ploting our ruin and who abused us in the most vile manner possible in presence of the assembled thousands

[153]Illinois congressman, senator, and volunteer general John Alexander Logan had been the Republican vice-presidential candidate in 1884 due in part to his status as a Civil War hero and prominence in the GAR. The veterans were bound for the GAR's twentieth annual encampment at San Francisco.

of the G.A.R and requested the GAR to report their cursed lies when they return home that thereby they the Rule and Ruin cleck [clique] may prevail on Congress to pass laws to disfranchis us and give them the Rule and Ruin Ring the offices that they may [fob?] on the Spoiles robed from us.[154]

August 1st 1886. The following named persons visited me in prison during the month my wife Mary visited me 17 times. . . . no of visiters for month 85 no of visits 170.

Tuesday August 3d 1886. Our Son Leon Brigham was baptised in the Endowment House Font by Bro John Cotton being eight years old.

August 4th 1886. Mary and children went to [Granit?] by rail [and] had a good time.

Thursday August 5th 1886. Leon Brigham was confirmed at fast meating in 20th ward under the hands of George White (mouth) [blank] Scofield, W C. Dunbar, D Murdock, and Wm Miller.

August 6th 1886. I took Mary a riding in A D Burts buggy.

Aug 7th 1886. O P Arnold took me ariding.

Aug 11th 1886. I went home on A M Cummins Jr Horse. Returned at 10 PM.

August 15th 1886. A D Burt took me home in his buggy.

August 20th 1886. I took Mary home in A D Burts Buggy. Mother worse.

Aug 21s 1886. Mary took [Mamey?] to Dr Andersens and put under the influence of cloroform and her rectum being down was replaced. Same day A J Burt brought me Faney Davenports photo and a letter which she sent to me in his care.

Aug 22D 1886. A D Burt took me to the New County poor house and to Mrs Deckers who I went to see if she wished to trade her country property for property in the city. Same evening Burt took me home to see Mother who is very sick.

August 24th 1886. Jacob Moritz sent me a dozen bottles of bear.[155]

Aug 26th 1886. A M Musser gave me a pamphlet entitled Social Problems of to day or The Mormon Question by a Jentile.[156] He also gave me several pamphlets on the Mormon question when I first came here.

Aug 30th 1886. A D Burt took me home to see the folks.

Tuesday August 31st 1886. I went over Jordan with A D Burt to see a New

[154] See "The Grandest Yet!" *Salt Lake Tribune*, 31 July 1886, 4/5.

[155] Jacob Moritz was a prosperous local brewer.

[156] This was Dyer Daniel Lum's *Social Problems of Today: or, the Mormon Question in Its Economic Aspects . . . by a Gentile*, a sympathetic study published in 1886.

Road Scraper works. Presant Mayor Armstrong, Judg E A Smith, J. W. Fox Jr, J M Winder, C Livingston and several others.

Tuesday August 31st 1886. In the evening a little after 8 O clock PM and through the whole of the night and most of the next day Earth quakes were felt through most of the eastern states. People rushed from their Houses and Hotels in their night clothes and Charlstown South Carolina was almost intirely destroyed and many person kiled and wounded and about Ten million of property destroyed. The shock continued over two days.[157] See Newspapers of November 1st 1886.

Tuesday August 31st 1886. Over three hundred (Saints) Emigrants landed at Castle Gardens New York. Over one hundred were detained by Commissioner Starr and Stephenson as paupers and are to bee sent back to the old country so says dispaches. No wonder the Earth shakes at such injustice. Afterwards stated that 40 more or less were detained and sent to Wards Island a pauper prison. Subsiquently all with the exception of five ware released on bonds. The five were returned back to England some time in September. This the Great Government of the United States in their attempts to break up Mormonism *Fizzel* and Emigration will continue.[158]

Sept 1st 1886. The following named persons visited me during the month My wife Mary visited me 13 times. . . . Total visiters 84 total Visits 200.

Sept 3d 1886. Sheriff Burt took me to se August Wilcken who is very sick. We also visited C H Wilcken first wife and daughter.

Sept 4th 1886. The Margetts Estate Brewery sent me a dozen bottles of porter.

Sept 5th. John Q Cannon a son of George Q Cannon confessed to the crime of adultery and was cut off from the Church in the Old Tabernacle on the above date [with] A[ngus] M Cannon president of the Salt Lake Stake of Zion puting the motion. John Q Cannon was second counciler to Bishop Preston head Bishop of the Church.[159]

Sept 8th 1886. A D Burt took me to C R Savages where my wif mary and I had our likneses (photographs) taken.

---

[157]The 7.3-magnitude tremor that struck Charleston at 9:50 P.M. on 31 August 1886 was felt as far away as Boston and Bermuda. It killed some sixty people and remains South Carolina's most powerful earthquake.

[158]See "The Mormon Invasion," *Deseret News,* 1 September 1886, 6/2.

[159]For a highly amused version of this incident, see "John Q. Cannon Cut Off" and "The Latest Mormon Scandal," *Salt Lake Tribune,* 7 September 1886, 4/2–4. For a recent look at this perplexing romance, see Cannon, "The Tragic Matter of Louie Wells and John Q. Cannon," 126–90.

Sept 9th 1886. Lehi Pratt took me ariding behind a spanking team of Pres Taylors. We left the County Court House at 9 O clock PM travled 27 or 28 miles and returned at 12[.]15 O clock AM making the distance in 3¼ hours.

September 13th 1886. Mary paid balance due on [Pipper?] note amounting to five hundred dollars and had the mortgage canseled. Same day sister Rachel Grant sent her best wishes by my wife Mary.

September 16th 1886. J B Fletcher a Jentile came to se me as my wifes Helen Attorney to se if I was willing for her to have a divorce and to dead the house and lot where she lives to her children. I told him she could have a divorce if she wanted it but no money or property. The children if they would remain with me I would continue to care for them if not they would have to look out for them selves.

September 17th 1886. My son W B Hampton was arrested for theft [and was] taken before Commissioner Wm McKay and discharged. Proved to be a peace of shite wer he of the partie complaining.[160]

Sept 18th 1886. J B Fletcher caled to se if I would approve my wife Helen in getting a Divorce from the probate court. I told him no so long as she did not ask for any thing else.

Sept 19th 1886. Samuel Sudbery caled to say that August Wilcken wished to se me before he died which is expected any day.

Sept 19th 1886. A D Burt took me to see August Wilcken [as] he is slowly sinking and was glad to see me. Same evening A E Hyde took me ariding around the driving park.

Sept 23d 1886. Gardo House and Sister M Benetts residence searched by deputie Us Marshalls for pres Taylor a Water hall.[161] The same evening while thinking over the persicutions that were being heaped upon those that have obeyed the law of Celestial Marrage The following forcibly came to my mind. If I was President of the Church and the Lord wils I would send all poligamist on Missons. Sease to employ lawyers to defend poligamy and cohabitation cases and if any were arrested let them gow in to court and refuse to plead and let the Hel Hounds do their worst and call on the Bishops to collect means from those that have to spare and suport such missionarys and their families that were in nead and also make it a test of Fellowship of those that profess to be Saints that purchased goods of or

[160]See "Grand Jury," *Deseret News*, 22 September 1886, 12/1, which dismissed the incident as a family feud.

[161]The Gardo House was sometimes used as a residence and office by LDS presidents. Brimhall and Curtis, "The Gardo House," 173–201.

associated with the Enimies of the Church and Kingdom of God. All of which I think would be a good plan but I am not caled to run the Church.

Sept 25th 1886. Sister Hannah T King died.[162]

Sept 26th 1886. A.D. Burt took me home.

Sept 28th 1886. Mary and Ireen went to Sister Kings Funeral in the 13th Ward meating House at 2 O clock PM and went to the grave yard in a Hack I hired for the ocasion. Same day The Jury in the Jones and Treseden case brought in a verdict of guilty when the witnesses for the prosicution proved that Us Marshal Ireland US. Prosicution Attorney Dixon and several US. Deputy Marshals was the criminals and conspirators.[163] Earth Quakes shacks almost every day during the month in and about Charleston and divers other places. The warning voice of the Lord is being made manifest every day to the wicked but they will not head it.

In Tulidges history of Salt Lake City page 636 will be found the following. At a meatin of the Bretheren held Jany 29th 1839 in the State of Missouri On motion of Pres Brigham Young it was resolved that we this day enter in to a covenant to stand by and assist each other to the utmost of our abilities in removing from this State, (Missouri) and that we will never desert the poor who are worthy, till they shall be out of the reach of the exterminating order of General Clark, actin for and in the name of the State.

The covenant then mad was follows[:]

We whose names are hereunder written, do each for out selvs individually covenant to stand by and assist each other, to the utmost of our abilities, in removing from this state; and we do hereby acknowledge ourselvs firmly bound to the extent of all our available property, to be desposed of by a committee who shall be appointed for that purpose, for providing means for the removing of the poor and destitute who shall be considerd worthy, from this country, till there shall not be one left who desires to remove from the state: with this provision, that no individual shall be deprived of the right of the disposal of his own property for the above purpose, or of having the controle of it, or so much of it as shall be necessary for the removing of his own family, and to be entitled to the overplus after the work is effected; and furthermore said committee shall give recipts for all property, and an account of the expenditure of the same.

[162]As noted, Hannah Tapfield King was Hampton's mother-in-law while he was married to his first wife, Bertha.

[163]See "The Bribers Cinched," *Salt Lake Tribune,* 29 September 1886, 4/2.

This covenant was signed by the followg name[s:] John Smith, Brigham Young, John Taylor, Jonithan Hampton my Father, James Hampton my Uncle [and] afterwards a memb of the Mormon Batalion. Also 195 others.[164]

October 1st 1886. The following persons visited me in prison during the month my Wife Mary visited me 17 times.... Total visitors 75 Total visits 183.

Friday Oct 1st 1886. I borrowed one thousand Dollars from A J. Burt for one year or less at 10% Cent per annum giving my note and mortgage on hose and Lot in Security. Which I was compeled to do to suport my Family while in Jail up to the above date. Those that was in the detective business with me having good offices and good Saleries Seam to think I dont nead any thing. Their names I will give here after if they do not come to trial.

October 6th 1886. J B Fletch my wif Helens Attorney said Helen was agowing to se Dixon U.S. prosicuting Att about making me give her and children some means. Same day H B Clawson in interduced me to Mrs J B Whipple a Widder Lady and Matron of the Deseret Hospital. She is a dosey.

Oct 7th 1886. A. D. Burt took me to Becks hot Springs and we had a bath.

Sunday Oct 10th 1886. My daughter Hannah B. Burt had a son born about 8 O clock A.M.

Oct 11th 1886. I went with N V Jones up city creek 10 miles to meat Porter Brother to Locate a miner. They did not meat us. Snowed and rained considerable. We returned at 6 30 P.M.

October 13th 1886. A J Burt and J. H. Moyle County Sheriff and Attorney gave a Super in the County Court hous having recenty been elected to Office. Present A M Cannon, Jose E Taylor and about 20 others county and City Officials. Dismissed about 12 O clock at night.

Thursday Oct 14th 1886. I went with N V Jones up City Creek met Porter Bros and located what is to be a Gold and Silver mine. We located in 1500 feet each, I caled my Location the Cheaf Conspirator. We returned home at 6 O clock PM.

In the night O P Arnold brought Deputy US. Marshal E A Franks to my room in the court House. I made arangements with him to asertan if my wife Helen was married to Professor Clayton and to learn what she was doing against me with US prosicuting Att Dixon as she had made threats and Willey had not come for their monthley payment. I thought something was in the wind. Subsiquently I paid Franks $10.00 for his services which

[164]The document appears in Tullidge, *The History of Salt Lake City*, 636–37.

amounted to nothing as I found out all I wished to know about her before Franks made a move.

Saturday October 16th 1886. Helen, William & Lillie left the house [and] sold part of the houshold goods at Auction. Shipped some to Prof J. E. Clayton at Portland Oregon. Left some Furniture in the house and on Sunday thay all three followed their goods.

Oct 17th 1886. AD Burt took me to see my Daughter Hannah and to my own house to se the folks. Mary and Some of the children had gon to ward meating. Same day I wrote a Letter to Willie directing it to Portland Oregon telling them that I new all about their movements and said to them that if they ever wished to come back I would do the best I could by them.

Oct 25th 1886. AD Burt took me home to see the folks.

Oct 27th 1886. AD Burt took me ove[r] Jordon to their farm 10 miles from the City. On returning about noon I found John T Caine deligate to Congress and JR Winder wating to see me. Same evening AM Cannon Jr took me *ariding.*

Oct 30th 1886. AD Burt took me home.

November 1st 1886. The following named persons visited me during the month. My Wife Mary visited me 10 times. . . . Total visitors 59. Total visits 156.

Friday Nov 5th 1886. I wrote the following lette to Pres GQ Cannon.

Salt Lake City Nov 6th 1886

Dear Brother

On October 4th 186 I wrote a letter to Bro CH. Wilcken asking him to enquire if it would be wise or not to prosicute the L&Ls I assisted in detecting. Receiving no answer I take the liberty of asking you the question whether it is best to prosicute the L&Ls or not.

Scince I have been in prison I have erged the committie = (which in the commencement of the detecting work numberd something near a dozen who graduly withrew by seasing to take any interest further than saying Sickum and that has seased ever scince I have been in Prison) = now numbering three to prosicute the L&Ls but always met with first one excuse and then another. The first was hold on till Judg Zayne et al rules in the Yearian Newcom case. Second wait till the U S. Marshall Ireland is removed which will be soon. Third we are agowing to have a new Judge or Judges. Fourth wait till we have a niew Sheriff and prosicuting attorney for the County and then we will go for them. When asked again why not gow ahead the excuse is there is no use of waisting your powder. Wait till Just before the cases become outlawed. In that time there may be a change of Officers and then we will give it to them. If we wait till that time I cannot guess what the next excuse will be. So for as I am conserned I would like to have them the L & Ls prosicuted. I think if that was done there would be less chances of my being sent back to prison for another year or more. Then now G S. Erb, Sharp S. Walker and W. L. Pichard sent me word that if I did not dismiss all cases against the L & Ls that they would put me in jail and keep me there. So far they se that my being in Prison has the desired efect of keeping them from being prosicuted. And there is hardly a question in my mind but that they will put me back in Jail for another year which is a very *Expensive Luxery* for me to bear But then I am in the hands of my Bretheren that are Caled to preside over the Church and if they say hold on hold on it is with me without a murmer. If it does put me in jail for anothe year and if they say gow ahead gow ahead it is [all the same] with me. Jail or no Jail. So what is for the best good of all without the consideration of my self or Family is all I ask.

Your Brother in The Gosple
B.Y. Hampton

Tuesday Nov 16th 186 I received the following letter from Geo Q Cannon in reply to the above letter.

Presidents Office
Church of Jesus Christ of Laterday Day Saints
Salt Lake City U.T. Nov 1886

Dear Brother

I have received your favor of the 5th and have perused it with care. I never hear of you without having my fealings aroused at your situation. It seems that you are a scape goat to bear and carry off the sins and burdens of others. In your attempt to show up the corruptions of those who have been howling against the "Mormons" you have fallen a victim and have had to bear the brunt of their assaults. In this I have felt you were deserving of simpathy and not mear simpathy alone, but help to extricate you from your unpleasant position. It is not very encouraging to feel that because your feet have been ensnared by our enemies, you must be left to pull yourself out as best you can, or be left untill the snarers will choose to releas you.

I submited your letter to a friend.[165] He did not seem impressed with the feasibiliity of prosicuting the L & L as the Courts are now constituted. He asked at what time there cases would be outlawed. As I have forgotten our law on this point I could not answer. One thing is very clear to me, and that is, you should not be left where you are a day longer than is absolutely necessary or than can be helped. You feal willing I know, to endure whatever

[165]Hampton probably understood Cannon's "friend" to be President John Taylor.

you are required to do, even if you should have to remain as much longer, or more than that where you are. But why should you be required to do this? I do not think it would be right, if it can possibly be avoided, for you to be expected to make such a sacrifice unless greater results are to be accomplished than appears possible at presant. I am not disposed to advocate compromise with our enemies in any forms or for any cause, but while I am firm in my views respecting this, I am not in favor of you being kept in the gap and being made to suffer with no apparent good results. If I could see you, we could canvass the situation and perhaps find some opening for your relief.

It has struck me that it might be well for you to converse freely with Bishop H B Clawson. I have confidence in his Judgment and shrewdness, and he has been greatly blessed on the mission we have intrusted him with to Arizona. It is principally due to his efforts, under the blessing of the Lord that our bretheren were released from the Prison in Deetroit; and he has been very successful in other business confided to him. I shall write to him and ask him to call upon you.

Aney thing in my power to do for you, I will do with pleasure. Accept my kind regards, The Lord bless you

I am Your Brother
Geo Q Cannon. . . .

Nov 11th 1886. A.D. Burt took me home and to S.P. Teasdels Store to explain our Ordinance that I got up as amends on water rates which I wish the City Council to pass, When I left Bro Teasdle gave me a box of cigars which I sent to the Pen to Orson P Arnold who is serving out a sentance for cohab.

Saturday Nov 13th 1886. N.V. Jones and F M Treaseden was each sentenced by Judg Zane to three years in the Pen for a charge of bribery and according to the testimony they wer not guilty but Dixon and Ireland US prosicuting Attorny and US Marshall proved them selves guilty of Conspiracy by their own witnesses but then they are not Mormons.

Nov 17th 1886. Jos E Tayler & J W Fox Jr spent the evening with me.

Monday Nov 22D 1886. My Wife Mary fell and dislocated her left sholder. I went home with A D Burt and helped Dr Anderson put her under the influence of Cloroform and set her sholder. I remained home with her all night. She did not have any rest on account of Pain and the shock she sustained by reason of the axident.

Nov 24th 1886. A D Burt took me home. I found Mary better. Same night A M Cannon arrested and put under $10,000 bonds for cohab.[166]

[166] See "Angus Cannon Again," *Salt Lake Tribune*, 25 November 1886, 4/2.

Nov 25th 1886. Sister N V Jones brought me some fruit and cake. Evening a meating in my room to settle some matters between the two sister Burts wives of Andrew Burt. Poley Burt did not come not being notified. Present Sister Ann O Burt, A J Burt, J W Burt, Eliza Burt, Bp W L N Allen, A M Cannon and Jos E Tayler who spent the evening with me after the balance had gon.

December 1st 1886. The following named persons visited me during the month My Wif Mary visited me 14 times. . . . Total visitors 61 Total visits 140.

Total No of visitors for the year 1017. Total No of visits " " " 2429.

Decembe 1st 1886. I gave my note and a mortgage for one Thousand dollars to pay F. Davenport at the rate of 10 percent per anum. The committie not paying her as they aggreed with me.

Dec 8th 1886. I wrote a letter to Pres Geo Q Cannon giving a history of my detective work and the way I had been treated by those engaged with me.

December 14th 1886. I gave my Note for Ninety dollars payable in three months in favor of the General Tithing office in Settlement of my tithing for the curant year.

Thursday Dec 16th 1886. Bro E M Dalton of Parowan Shot and killed by deputy U.S. marshal Wm Thompson Jr who had a warrant for Daltons arrest for cohabitation. Dalton did not offer to run or resist when caled on to halt the caling to halt and the shuting by Thompson almost instantainous. Thus Mormons are treated by Government Officials.[167]

Monday Dec 20 1886. I get mesured for a suit of clothes at Cutler Bros. The County or some one besides my self to pay for them.

Thursday Dec 23d 1886. Brigham Young, C H Wilcken, J W Fox Ser and J W Fox Jr Spent the evening with me in prison.

December 25th 1886. I took diner with J W Fox Jr and wife it being Christmas.

December 28 1886. J Greenewald sent me a box of cigars.

Wedensday Dec 29th 1886. After diner I was released from prison having spent just one year in the County Jail for detecting Goverment Officials and others in their Hoardoms and Adulterie. My Bro Eaderly Wife and two children came from Ogden to meat and great me in my release from prison. My daughter Hannah Husband and children came and took super with us.

[167]See "Official Murder at Parowan" and "The Parowan Murder," *Deseret News*, 22 December 1886, 8/1, 12/2; "An Escaping Mormon Shot," *New York Times*, 17 December 1886, 2. A jury in Beaver acquitted Thompson of manslaughter, but many Mormons continued to see it as a case of murder. See Bigler, *Forgotten Kingdom*, 333–34; and Dix, "Unwilling Martyr."

December 31st 1886. I mad Affidavit against all persons caught in their Hoardums which I helped to detect just previous to and for which I was sent to prison, and while in prison no one would make the affidavits for fear of being sent to prison the same as I and now I cannot prosicute the L & Ls because those that were conected with me in the detective work are to say the least weak in the Knees.

On being released from Prison I resumed my duties as License Collector fro Salt Lake City Corporation.

All Broken Up

January 11th 1887. U S Marshal Dyer refused me a pass to the pen on account of my detecting the L & Ls. Jany 12 The Edmund Tucker bill passed the House under gag rool. Jany 20th. Mary & I attended a suprise party at Bishop Benets House.

Sunday Jany 30th. I Spoke about 10 minuts in the 20th ward meating house.

Tuesday Feby 2d. A Suprise party goten up by Bishop Bennett consisting of 35 or 40 persons visited my home we had a good time.

Monday Feby 7th 1887. The Supream Court at Washington reversed the desisions in Lorenzo Snow case and the segregating business in cohabitation cases by the Crusaders was stoped.

Tuesday Feby 8th 1887. 4 o clock P.M Bro Lorenzo Snow released from the pen on the desision of the supream Court. Same day I was Elected one of the 13 directors of the Eclesiastical organization of the 20th Ward.

Feby 11th. US Marshal & Posse Searched the Gardo House, Tithing Office & presidents office this morning and in the afternoon the Endowment house and did not find any one. Same day I met Bro Lorenzo Snow on the Cars and he said it was a fether in my cap Dyer refusing me a pass to the pen.

Feby 17th 1887. The Confrence committie Report on the Edmunds Tucker bill accepted and addopted in the House of Representatives 202 to 40. Feby 18th. Same bill passed senate 37 to 18.

Feby 28th 1887. I filed my bonds for $500.00 in county clerks office as one of the Ecleasiastic board of the 20th Ward.

March 3D 1887. The Edmunds Tucker bill became a Law by the President of the United States Grover Cleavland not having suficient back bone and honnor to veto the bill or sign it it became a law by [?]

March 13th. I spoke in the 20th Ward meating House a fiew minuts.

March 14th. I attend 20th Ward Ecleasiastic board meating and 13th Quorum of seventies and spoke a fiew minuts at the later.

President John Taylor

Dear Brother

I design gowing to Logan in the near futer to do some work for the dead and not wishing to forget the living I thought of taking another wife. If you think I am worthy of such a blessing Or if by remaining as I am I can do more good in the way of [wating?] and Etz. Just as you think best will please me.

Your Brother In the Gosple
B.Y. Hampton. . . .

Dear Brother

The business of which you wrote me on the 12th instant had better be deferred we think for three or four months.

With Kind Regards
Your Brother
John Taylor

Tuesday April 5th 1887. Mary and I were Baptized in the Endowment House font by [Peater?] Read. Thursday following in fast meating in 20th ward Mary was confirmed Wm H Naisbit mouth. I was confirmed same time and place George Romney mouth. I assisted in confirming one and bore my Testimony.[168]

Aprial 10th 1887. Mary and I started for Logan we staid all night at Ogden with Sister Delan Eaderly & wife came there to see us. 11th about 2 O clock PM we arrived at Logan and put up at sister Perrys and went to the Temple and gave in the names of those we were to be baptized for. I gave $20.00 to the Temple. 6 inches of snow fel through the day.

April 12. Mary & I were baptized for our dead. . . .

April 13. Commenced Endowment and sealings for the dead. See Endowment and sealing Record of same date and on to April 29th 187. I paid $13.00 for assistence in the Temple.

April 17th. Bro & Sister Phares Wells arrived from the City and put up at sister Perrys with us.

---

[168]Hampton did not identify whom he intended to marry (perhaps the widow Whipple who was a "dosey"?), but it seems likely that he or Mary changed his mind, hence the rebaptisms as a sign of commitment.

Thursday April 21st 1887. Bro Phares Wells asked me to have his sister Catherine Wells who is dead Sealed which I did. . . .

Sunday April 24th. We went to the Logan Tabernacl and I was caled upon to speak which I did for a fiew minuts. April 27. I sent a Box of Oranges and 5 lbs of candy to the Logan Temple workers. . . .

May 13th 1887. I attended a gathering at the City Hall. About 40 persons present at supper many of hoom were in hiding.

May 15 1887. After dark Lehi Pratt had a 3 or 4 months child by a plural wife burried in the Salt Lake Cemetry. I was present thus the saints have to do to elude the officers of Government who are prosicuting the saints for Obeying the law of God.

July 5th 1887. I was on motion of Heber J Grant appointed assessor and collector of Water Rates by the City council under the new water ordinance and have to give $5000[.]00 bonds though I had been doing the same thing year before.

July 25th 1887. Pres John Taylor died in exile at the residence of Bro [blank] in [blank].

27th. I was appointed one of the committee to arrange for the Funeral of Pres Taylor.[169]

July 29th 1887. Pres Taylor Funeral in the Tabernacle. After the Funeral I met in the Presidents office. Most of the Quorum of the twelve and many others in hiding.

Saturday July 30th 1887. The government of the United States commenced suit against the Church & P E Fund to desolve their charters and confiscate their surplus property which is claimed to be about 3 milion of money.[170]

Sept 30 1887. I met with the Quorum of the Twelve and took J F Smith home in my Buggy.

Oct 3d 1887. attended Eclziastic board meating in 20th ward.

Oct 9th 1887. Pres Woodruff & Erastus Snow appeard in the stand in the Tabernacle and spoke to the people.

Oct 11th 1887. I attended 13th Quorum of Seventie and spoke a fiew minuts.

[169]Taylor died in hiding at the home of Thomas F. Rouche in Kaysville on 25 July 1887. Many Latter-day Saints believed his death was hastened by anti-Mormon persecution. See Roberts, *A Comprehensive History*, 6:187–90.

[170]The Edmunds-Tucker Act dissolved the Perpetual Emigrating Fund Company, but federal officials found only about four hundred thousand dollars in promissory notes. See Firmage and Mangrum, *Zion in the Courts*, 241–42.

Oct 18th 1887. At 3 minuts to 8 O clock AM my Wife Mary gave birth to a fine Son.

November 12th 1887. We had to move our things (Temple clothing etz) from the Endowment House as the US Marshal Receiver in the Church suits for the Government had on Friday the 11th 1887 took possession of the Tithing Office and is expected to take possession of the Temple Block. The taking possession of the Tithing office by the US Recever was on the Same day that the 6 Anarchists were was [*sic*] hung at Chicago for agitating the doing of the very thing that the Government of the United States is doing with this people Confiscating their property without Warant of Law.[171]

November 15th 1887. Dyer US Receaver demand the Gardo House, Historian Office, Temple Block and all Church Books & Papers.

Nov 17. I attended Ecleziastic board meating in 20 Ward meating House.

November 23D 1887. Dyer took possession of the Presidents Office turning out the clerks and puting in two deputies in charge.

Dec 5th 1887. Sister Eliza R Snow Smith died and on the 7th The funeral was held the assebley Hall I was present & wife Mary.

December 12th 1887. I wrote a Letter to Pres Woodruff, Cannon & Smith Offring them the use of my Home whenever they chose come.

Friday 16th 1887. I met at the Presidents Office in Company with Mayor Armstrong, E A Smith, A Soloman, J W Fox Jr, A J Burt, & C H Wilcken to make a settlement of money due me on detective account which Armstrong Smith & Fox Jr aggreed to pay but left me to pay the a/c amounting to near two thousand dollars beside $900 paid J W Burt out of my Salery while in prison and over one hundred dollars court expences. Pres Woodruff Cannon & Smith required them to fulfill their contracts with me. Same day made arrangements to purches Sister Bennetts Home for $4500[.]00.

Dec 23D 1887. Evening at H M Wells. The Jordan Lake & Park Company of which I am a member gave a Corp super to Pres W Woodruff, Geo Q Cannon, Joseph F Smith, Bishop Whitney and Their own members.

---

[171]The Edmunds-Tucker Act authorized the federal government to escheat all LDS church–owned real estate not used exclusively for purposes of worship in excess of fifty thousand dollars. U.S. Marshal Frank H. Dyer was the first appointed receiver. He moved to escheat much property, including Temple Square, before church attorneys negotiated a list of approved properties pursuant to a case before the U.S. Supreme Court. See "Suits Against the Church" and "The P.E. Fund Company," *Deseret News*, 12 October 1887, 10/2, 11/1. The court upheld the seizure at the time, and the property was finally restored in 1896. See Roberts, *A Comprehensive History*, 6:193–201; Bigler, *Forgotten Kingdom*, 348–49; and Firmage and Mangrum, *Zion in the Courts*, 253–60.

Tuesday Decembe 20th 187 President Willford Woodruff, George Q Cannon & Joseph F Smith came to my house we gave them the use of two bead rooms parler & Dining room.[172]

Dec 29th. Heavy claps of thunder and snowing at the same time.

Dec 30 1887. Pres Woodruff Cannon and Smith went home will return on Tuesday evening. Same day I paid $180.00 Tithing for the year 187 and mary paid $100.00 Tithing for the year 1887.

Tuesday 3D 1888. Pres Woodruff Cannon & Smith returned.[173]

Jany 5th 1888. 920 Oclock AM we had our son blessed under the hands of Pres Wilford Woodruff, Geo Q Cannon, Joseph F. Smith and my self. Pres Woodruff *Mouth* The name given Mundell Robinson Hampton.

January 6th 1888. Pres Woodruff Cannon & Smith left my Home to gow to other quarters at 7 O clock PM. They with about 25 others prominent men and undergrounds met at the County Court House where a sumtious supper was prepard by E A Smith & others. Bros Cannon Smith & DH Wells & others spoke we had a good time.

Jany 19th 1888. I in company with 4 others took Pres Woodruff Cannon & Smith Slay Riding.

February 3D 1888. My Son JV Hampton daughter Blanch died Feby 5. Funeral held at my House. Bro George Romney conducted service. Bros George Bywater & OF Whitney preached funeral Sermons and Spoke splendidly. Blanch was born Oct 8th 1885.

Feby 11th. Donated $5.00 to 20th ward meating House.

Feby 17th 1888. A Suprise party of about sixty persons visited us and all had a good time.

March 31st 1888. Wife Mary & I donated $20.00 to Manti Temple to help furnish it.

May 2D 1888. The Supream Court granted NV Jones & FM Treaceden a new trial after being in the pen for 18 months and the lower courts refused to give them a niw trial as they were rongfully convicted in the first place.[174] I went with his familey to the pen to bring them home.

May 20th at 7.20. A.M. Started for Manti by rail to attend dedication of Temple arived same day about 5 Oclock P.M.

---

[172]Woodruff does not mention staying on 20 December but noted his stay with the Hamptons on 27 December. Kenney, ed., *Wilford Woodruff's Journal*, 27 December 1887, 8:473.

[173]Ibid., 3 January 1888, 8:479.

[174]"Territorial Supreme Court," *Deseret News*, 5 May 1888, 1/3.

May 21st. Attended dedications. I sat with the Seventies. The dedication was a grand afair. 22D,. Arived home I also donated ten dollars to the Temple.[175]

May 27th 1888. Apostle Erastus Snow died.

[May] 28 [1888]. I brought Preasdent Woodruff from his home to the office and assisted in aranging for funeral Services of Bro Snow. I was Selected one of six pall bearers. June 9th 1888. Took mail to first presidency. June 11th. Brought George Q Cannon his house to place of hiding.

June 22D 1888. My daughte Hannah Burt lost her son Frankie of Scarlet Feaver. 23D funeral.

July 10th 1888. Started to California by way of Portland Oregon. Took Wife Mary Sons Leon & Mundell. Paid for tickets $128.00. Arived at Portland by the way of the dalls and Columbia River at 7 oclock PM put up at St Charles Hotel. July 15th. Arived at San Francisco put up at International Hotel No 824 & 826 Kearney street. 16th Rented rooms at 40½ Gearey street and boarded at the Popular resturant oposite. Miss Zina V Hide roomed with us. 21st had a rid on one of the large boats on the bay for six hours trip and lunch free given by the NEA [National Education Association] to the School Tearches excursion of which we were members. Saturday 22D 1888. At 8.30 AM Started home leaving Family in San Francisco. July 23D. At 11 PM arived home.

Aug 4th 1888. Family arived home all well. Sunday 19. Took George Q Cannon to McDonals residence where he was hiding.

July 23D 1888. Our Son Ralph R. was Baptised in the Endowment house font by Joseph Keddington.

July 24th 1888. Met first presidency at City Hall and at[e] Ice cream with them.

Salt Lake City Sept 1st 1888

Elder B Y Hampton Dear Brother

This is to notify you that at the adjourned annual meeting of the members of the Church Association of Salt Lake Stake of Zion held this day at the Assembley Hall you were selected a member of that Organization by a unanimous vote.

Respectfully A W Carlson Sectz

---

[175]Built between 1877 and 1888, the Manti Temple cost about one million dollars, including large contributions of labor and materials under the United Order. Arrington, *Great Basin Kingdom*, 339–40.

I paid Tithing for the year 1888 $180.00 dollars. This year 1888 finished paying off Fancy Davenport Mortgage and Note for $1000.00 a long and ardorous task performed. Still leaving due me over $2000.00 dollars spent of my own money by reason of the Finance Committie (in the detecting of the lecherous gang that were pursicuting the Saints) failing to meat their obligations consiquently threw the burthon on me. Committie named on page 232.

[*Marginal note*: Later part of 1888 rented ground of B Young estate. . . .]

January 26th 1889. Sister Mary Ann Hadson died in 20th ward of pneumonia age 63 years and 5 months [and] was buried in my lot in City Cemetry. A friend in need is a friend in deed and such she was to us a constant attendant night and day [when] our four Children lost or died of Dipthera.

In the earley part of 1889 I donated $20.00 my wife Mary $5.00 and son Leon $1.00 to asist in building vestry to 20th ward meating house.

April 1889. Sold my 180 G Street to H M Wells for $1500[.]00.

May 6th 1889. Let Contract to Taylor Romney Armstrong Co to build me a two Story brick dwelling on my lot corner of G & 4th St for $3650.00. When completed cost $6500.00. Subsiquently Sold to Arthur Pratt for $10,000.00.

Oct 12th 1889. Started for Deseret [canal] in company with Pres Woodruff, Geo Q Cannon, A H Cannon, C H Wilchken, S Bateman, A Solomon and a Son of Pres Woodruffs in a special Train. Went over the land bought by us. Comenced Canall and other works also went hunting and returned home Oct 16th at 10 A M.[176]

The following named and their wives and sweet hearts were invited to be presant at the dedication of my niew house on the 9th day of December 1889. We gave a supper and dance. Sixty persons sat at table besides my familey. Pres George Q Cannon Offerd Dedicatory prare. Those presant with their wives were Pres W Woodruff, G Q Cannon, J F Smith, Apostle Brigham Young, Pres A M Cannon, Jos E Taylor, C W Penrose, L John Nuttall, W C Dunbar, J W Fox Jr, Bp G Romney, George F Gibbs, J F Simmons, J W Burt, C H Wilcken, Lehi Pratt, Marshal A Saloman, Sheriff A J Burt, O F Whitney, Samuel Bateman, George D Pyper, J J Daynes Invited and not present, J W Fox, J R Winder, John Picket, Geo Reynolds, F Armstrong, A M Wells, A F Turnbow.

---

[176]Abraham H. Cannon was president of the Deseret Canal Co. The trip was "to see our land there, to preach and to hunt ducks." Cannon, Diary, 12 October 1889, 11:136–37. See also Kenney, ed., *Wilford Woodruff's Journal*, 12 October 1889, 9:58.

Dec 16th 1889. I and all Members of the Hydraulic Canall Co arrested having a short time previous been Endited (by a liberal Grand Jurry Ex postmaster Lynch forman) for attempting to defraud Salt Lake City by selling them our stock and water rights at their own instance and request. All done for Election thunder as after Election was over we ware all dismissed. No cause of action.[177] I paid Tithing for the year 1889 $210. and my Wife Mary $50.

Sept 30th 1890. Daughter Mary Alice baptized in Tabernacle font by Joseph Keddington. Oct 2. Confirmed under hands of her Father & B Y Hampton & others. Tithing 1890 Self $100. Wife 74.10 Spring of 1890 leased ground of B Young estate on Commercial Avenue. . . .

Jany 3D 1891. Wife Mary gave birth to a dughter at 10 45 PM Saturday. Jany 17th 1891. My mother Julia Foster Hampton died at one oclock PM Saturday in her 80 year having been born Nov 18th 1811. Jany 20th. Funeral services in my house. Bp Whitney and Jos E Tayler preached funeral sermons. Buried in Salt Lake City Cemetry Lot 1 B 13 in plot M.[178]

February 16th 1891. Received Telegram from Ketcham Idaho informing me that my son Brigham Y Hampton was kiled on the evening of the 13th of February by a snow slide while gowing from mine to cabin also one Charles Shear. At 8 oclock of 16th my Son J V Hampton, Mrs Eliza [Heartenstein?], A. E Hyde and self started for Ketcham by rail. 17th at 6 PM arrived at Ketchum. On morning of 17th 22 men with 30 horses started for Bolder Creek through snow 3½ feet deep to get the bodies. 18th Sent Sons Familey home with him Sister Mrs [Hortenstein?] & my son J. V H. 19th bodies arrived started home with sons body at 4.50 PM. 20th at [?] two freight trains recked 1 man killed. After several hours wating reckage cleard at 340 PM then continued journey. Stoped at Pocatela all night 21st 5.40 AM. My son Thom O & A E Hyde over took me at 730 continued on journey arived home Saturday 5 10 PM. We took body to J E Taylor sexton. On my way home taken with chills all broken up was in bed several days. Could

---

[177]For the conspiracy charge against thirty-six defendants, mostly Salt Lake City elected officials, see *People vs. Francis Armstrong and others*, Third District Territorial Criminal Case Files, case no. 584, 27 September 1888; "Public Officers Arrested," *Deseret Weekly News*, 28 December 1889, 31/4. Hampton had been elected a canal company trustee; a majority of trustees voted to hire as their defense attorney William H. Dickson, the federal prosecutor who had convicted Hampton, over the latter's objections. See Cannon, Diary, 21 December 1889, 11:215. The company consistently lost money on their crops and real estate developments. See Cannon, Diary, 16 July 1890, 13:4; 9 October 1890, 13:135–36; 22 January 1891, 13:214.

[178]An obituary for Julia Foster (presumably based on information Hampton provided) mentions her marriage to Jonathan Hampton, but not her marriages to Thomas Cole or Brigham Young. "Death of Julia F. Hampton," *Deseret Weekly News*, 24 January 1891, 24/3.

not attend funeral of son which was held in 20th ward meating house Feby 22D 1891 at 11.30 A M. O F Whitney and C R Savage preached funeral sermon. Funeral well attended. My sons remains wer buried in City Cemetry lot 1 Block 13 in plot M. March 1st 1891. Son Thomas O Hampton Started home to Ketchum to work in his mine.

Thursday March 5th 1891 had baby blessed under hands W G Phillips & J F Smith & self and named Edna R. March 22d 191 Received the following

> Presidings BPs Ofc S L City Mon 27th 191
>
> The committee a arrangments of the Funeral of the late counsellor D H Wells (The Services to take place in the Tabernacle on Sunday next at 12 m) respectfully request you aid in making and carrying out the necessary arrangements and would therefore be pleased to have you meat with them at the Bishops Office Saturday morning (tomorrow) at 930 o clock.[179]

Just the Scape Goat They Wanted

Brigham Young Trust Cos Record of their making me *ther Scape Goat.*[180]

In earley part of 1888 I leased ground of Brigham Young Est at no 62 first south street E and built a two story brick building in same at a cost of $5,000. And in Spring of 1890 I leased som more ground on commercial avenew Nos 11–13 & 15 and put up a three story brick 40 × 80 ft at a cost of $17,000. The leases for both peaces of ground was made in my wife's name Mary J R R Hampton I acting as agent.[181] The above leases had no tax clauses in them. Afterwards when buildings had been built new leases were made out without our knollage or consent with property sewer sidewalks and street paving taxes clauses in and we with most of their tenants had to sign or have leases cancled. Of corse we all signed like little men. Thus ended the first act of justice.?

August 1st 1890. I leased the building no 11. 13 & 15 on Com Avenew to L. E. Bamberger for $4,000 per year payable quarterly in advance. When I heard that Bamberger was about to ~~let~~ release to Elice St Omer a ladie of

---

[179]"Your Brethren"—Robert T. Burton, Hiram B. Clawson, and John Winder—signed this note. On 29 October 1891 Hampton recorded that "Wife & I donated horse & Buggy to Salt Lake Temple price $175.00" (perhaps noted as an error. Inserted in the margin is "[erorr?] See pag 248."). He reported he had paid $200, his wife $100, for a "Year Total Tithing" of $300.

[180]The Brigham Young Trust Company was established to manage some of the late prophet's properties. Brigham Young Trust Company Records.

[181]Hampton is listed as a real estate agent with partner N. V. Jones in Hampton, Jones and Company. See *Salt Lake City Directory, 1890.*

easey virtue.[182] I went to Wm A Rasiter agent of B Young Est and told him what I feard Bamberger was about to do. Rasiters reply was Bro Hampton if you did not rent the premises for imoral purposes say nothing as we cannot do any thing about.

Subsiquently Elsie rented the first floor and basement to W H Hofenheimer. Then later on Hofeniheimer sub leased to B. K. Black & Co and still later on Elsie rented the uper part to one F. B. Gifford. In later part of 1891 Judg Zane instruckted the Grand Jurry to indicte all persons renting houses for purposes of prostitution. This scared the Brigham Young Trust Co which was composed mostly of the heirs of Pres Young and to hoom the Estate had been transferd to for management and as they had many houses occupied by prostitutes. Fear of inditement and their great respect for the good name of the late Pres B Young which must be protected at all hazards. Conciquently a meating of the branes (BYT CO) was caled and plans formed for escape and as I had been indited and served one year in the County Jail for detecting resorters to houses of ill fame Judg Zane and district Attorney Varian having had the honor of puting me where I could not disturb their kind and nearly every body both Gentiles and Mormons down on me for interfearing with the vested rights of the former, Conciquently I was just the Scape Goat they wanted and was sacrificed for their sins in the past. The atonment may stick for the past but I am a little afraid for the future. They may have to Slauter me again.

On the 4th day of November 1891 The Executive Committie of the B.Y.T. CO was sent to notify me that they were not pleased with the tennants in the two uper stories of my building on Com Avenew and that they would not receive any more ground rent from me untill thare was a change.

The three worthies of the Executive Committe were Spencer Clawson. Chairman (and alternate member of the high council Salt Lake Stake) L. G. Hardy member (and Bishop of 2D Ward City[)] and Heber Young (Son of B Young a nothing.[)] I went to a meating of the company shortly after the committies notice and asked for time to see Bamberger and make arangements if posible to cansel leases and get objectionable persons out but no time was given and George Q Cannon was president of the Company and presided at the time no quarters were given me.

---

[182]The madam went by "Elsie St. Omar"; for this incident, see Nichols, *Prostitution, Polygamy, and Power,* 89–90.

I then saw Bamberger we assisited all the parties that had cases they agreed to do any thing we wished. Elsey had just finishe papering painting and cleaning the premises at a cost of several hundred dollars and she said she would not stand in the way though it would be a big los to her and did not want to see me loos my property. She was a hundred times more considerate than my should be friends and I think in the day of Judgment She will out Shine many of the BYT co. We al belived it was a Scheam of the B.Y.T. CO to make a Scape Goat of me to Save their own honors ? and get possession of the property as it was bringing good rents. The sequel so proved.

Mr Bambergers Lease and all such leases were cancled to take efect Dec 1st 1890. The Cancelations wer made Nov 10th and immeadieatly placed on record in the office of County Recorder five days before the inditement was found against me. I had on several occasions refused to rent the premises for the purpose which the inditement charged.

At the time of my Inditement EB Wick & Emma White were Indited for leasing premises for same purpos as charged against me but no conexion with the BYT CO. The Grand Jurry that Indited us was composed of som of the worst element of the liberal gang (Mormon Eaters [Haters]) James Devine their foreman who has held position as Fire Cheaf most of this time scince and still holds his job A D 1900.

On March 26th 1892 District Attorney CS. Varian (who prosicuted hundreds of Mormons and Sent them to the Pen through Zanes Court and who sent me through the Same route to the County Jail for one year for detecting Government Officials and others of his kind frequenting houses of Ill fame). Moved that honorable? Zane court that the Inditements found against EB Wick, BY Hampton and Emma White who were alleged to have leased premises for improper purposes be wiped out and was so Orderd by the Court. Counsel added The Fact is these Gentlemen and Lady had nothing to do with the places whatever and it is a very Serious mistake. I belive the houses wer property located but these persons had nothing to do with them. On Reading this in the papers I wrote a note to CS Varian thanking him for doing me Justice once.[183]

With my name published abrod in the papers with such charges did not

[183]Emma Whiting was the woman indicted. As "Emma DeMarr," she had long been a successful Salt Lake madam, but she escaped prosecution in this case by the same loophole as Hampton: the "protection of landlords" proviso that excused a building's owner from prosecution if he/she did not know that a lessee was conducting a brothel. See Nichols, *Prostitution, Polygamy, and Power,* 89–90.

make me feal much like an Angle from above. I could not get any Settlement or Satisfaction out of the BYT co. Conditions continued building empty loosing rents and paying interest and taxes for months.

I then wrote Pres Woodruff asking if the BYT CO could be handled by Church authority for the course they wer persuing against me. No answer. In a fiew weeks I wrote again. No answer. After a long wait I went in person and enquired the Reason for no answer to my letters and was informed by Pres Woodruff that my letters had been referd to the Secretary of the BYT CO (might as well ask a thief to sit in Judgment on his own case) and that the Church could do nothing with Corporations as they were mixed up with Gentiles. I was quite vexed at the answers given and said if the Church cannot corect rongs I will se what Courts can do. In a fiew moments Spence Clawson came to my office in the Constitution building and proposed arbitration I chosing one BYT CO choosing one and they two choosing the third. I consented on the spur of the moment and knew my fate then as well as after. I Selected Orson Wosley at N V Jones sugestion and George Q Cannon chose the other two. I was in R W Young's (office he a member of the company and their attorney) when he telephoned George Q Cannon president of the company asking who he would have to arbitrate the case.[184] He selected Legrand Young ex attorney and member of the company also J R Winder second council to Bp Preston presiding Bp of the Church and J P Freeze a member of the high Council Salt Lake Stake Semmingly thinking he had the whole three to select. I objected to Legrand Young on account of his relation to the company and accepted Winder and Freeze. R W Young told me what was said through the telephone. I made the remark that George Q Cannon had told me that he had no influence with the Company yet he dictated the whole thing which rather netled R. W. Young.

The arbitration day came and there was much said about the honor of Pre Youngs name and how questionable and rong it was to rent houses for such purposes I all the time denying in Strong terms of having rented for any such purpose. The desision was as I predicted which I had in writing but mis laid so I cannot find it. In efect it was that B Y Hampton had no rights that the BYT CO had to respect and what else dare they say. The guns

[184]A grandson of the Mormon prophet, Richard Whitehead Young graduated from West Point in 1882 and Columbia University Law School two years later. He resigned his commission in 1888 and became a prominent attorney in Utah. Young commanded the Utah Light Artillery in the Philippines during the Spanish-American War and the 65th Infantry Brigade during World War I as a brigadier general.

were to big for them to face when self interest in such a big Stake. I forgive the Committie that did the Arbitrating but not the B.Y.T. CO.

Things continued as usule I loosing money every day untill Apostle B Young returned from presiding of the European mission. On meating him and George Q Cannon at Tempelton corner Bro Cannon remarked to Bro Young that I thought that he Cannon was my worst enemy on Earth. I said no but you know Bro Cannon that you have not treated me right. Bro Young was Vice President of the BYT CO also my friend and took hold of the case and in corse of time brought about a settlement with the assistance of Bro Geo Q Cannon. They proposing I say the least I would take for both peaces of property and the BYT CO Say the most they would give and if any diferance they Young & Cannon paying me the diferance I offerd to take $17,000. BYT CO Paid me $16,000. Ganing a diferance of $1,000. which was arranged by Cannon & Young giving me their individual notes for $500.00 each. When the notes became due I returned them to Bros Cannon & Young they promising to get the B.Y.T. CO to pay the $1,000. If they ever tried they did not accomplish any thing as I never received the money [*inserted above*: May 6th 1893 this settlement was made as above stated.] I was forced to a settlement with a loss in rents interest and [?] on both buildings No 62 first South E and No 11 13&15 Commercial Avenew in the Sum of $10,000. With the $1,000. unpaid makes a total loss of $11,000. Rather an expensive Scape Goat to bear others sins. As soon as my building 11 13 & 15 on Commercial Avenew fel in to their hands it was rented to Chinamen who carry on the business of Merchandising Gambling Opem dens prostitution and filth. And later on the BYT CO Employed a Gentile one A C Brixen to fit up their big three story brick building on corner of Commercial Street and Commercial avenew for any thing that might come along. Ada Willson a notorious Keeper of houses of Ill fame was rented a portion of the uper part of said building which was fited up to suit her fancy so it could be run on the Parisian Style and it is known all ove the country by travling men and tourists as the little Paris. Though it is the bigest house of its kind west of New York. Annother portion of the uper part is used as a gambling house with all kinds of games including whiskey and cigars. Etz and a portion of the lower flower is rented for a Gosple mission with free medical advice lodging 10 cts baths free and meals one cent a dish.[185] If Brixen could only get a Methodist Camp meating

[185]For Ada Wilson and her Palace brothel, see Nichols, *Prostitution, Polygamy, and Power,* 117.

on the roof the thing would be compleet. How we do honor the good name of our beloved and departed President Brigham Young and question and deplore the renting of houses for such purposes. Next.

During all this time and for many months before and after the BYT CO Raid on me their Rep Spence Clawson had one of the worst dives that has ever been in this or any other City and had been a great sorce of anoyance to the City officials. City Marshal Young told me that the building 62 & 62½ on Commercial street was owned or managed by Spence Clawson and that the uper story was occupied by three Japineas Prostitutes and one white woman a snake charmer. The ground floor had two French women. C.S. one Nigar hoar and a Chineas wash house all under one roof. I investigated Records and premises and found what the marshal and Police said to be true. I took the liberty of telling Spence Clawson of the grand assortment and up to date instituition he presided over. He made no denial and the dance went on till the building was about to fall and the inmates had to get [out] to save being injured. A nice man Spence Clawson to Judg others.

Following list of names composed the Brigham Young Trust Co during their raid on me in the interest of purity and honor of a good name (B.Y.T. CO).[186]

George Q Cannon — President
Brigham Young — Vice "
Spencer Clawson — Chairman of Executive Committie
L G Hardy — Member " " "
Heber Young — " " " "
Richard W Young — Secretary
Spencer Clawson — Treasurer
Joseph Don C Young — Oscar B Young
George W Thatcher — Wm A Rasiter
Hiram B Clawson — John Q Spencer
John W Young — Brigham ~~H~~ M Young
Phineas H Young — Charles S Burton
Isaac A Clayton — Charles O Card
Hyrum S Young — Albert C Young and

Jacob F Gates. 21 officers and directors appointed for 10 years Incorporated February 24th 1891. All relations. Any one reading over the above names

[186] The list of officers appears in Brigham Young Trust Company's records.

would say it cannot be posible that such men violate the law every day by renting houses to prostitutes Gambles Rum selles and Chineas in this AD 1900 but never the less it is true. The all mighty dollar is above the law and the good name of their benefactor Pres Brigham Young deseased.

I finished writing the above to day Saturday February 17th 1900. B.Y. Hampton *This 1901* = [*continued in margin* = The BYT CO have rented a portion of their building on cor of Commercial & Commercial avenew to Miss Elsie St Omer *The* woman that was in my house when They jumped me and held their hands up in holy horror at such thing. Every thing they have falsley charged me with they have been guilty of a hundred times over and all they Hav brought upon me finacialy and other wise will come home to them.]

[*Marginal note, page 248*: April 24th 192 my oldes son B Y H Jr Son died 25th. Funeral buried in my upper lot City Cemetry by his Father.]

June 13th 1901. Had my foot badly hurt by falling brick from 4th story of BYT cos building Commercial st.[187]

Oct 4th 1891. Our daughter Ireen was Baptised by George E Wosley in Tabernacle font.

Oct 5th 1891. Confirmed under hands of Bro [Towey?] & others in fast meating 20th Ward.

Tithing for 1892

March 8th 1892. Donated horse and buggy to Salt Lake Temple amt alowed $175.00. Placed to wifes credit $75. My cred $100. March 20th. Recived this Certificate Salt Lake City March 20th 1893.

> This Certifies that B Y Hampton is a member of the 20th Ward in the Salt Lake Stake of the Church of Jesus Christ of Laterday Saints in fellowship and as such we recommend him to be admitted to the Dedication Services of Salt Lake Temple.
>
> George Romney Bishop
> Angus M Cannon President of Stake

Friday March 24th 1893. At 12[.]30 O clock P.M. I was on recommendation of High Council Ordained a high Preast under hands of Angus M Cannon P[r]es of Stake and Elias Morris Pres of High Preasts Quorum. Some time in March I purchased a peice of ground in South Temple st [?] west & 1st west 33 ft by 12 rods deep and during the year built a 3 story brick with

[187]A careless workman dropped bricks from the roof that struck Hampton on the foot and shoulder; a few inches' difference might have killed him. Journal History, 13 June 1892, 5.

basement for Hotel purposes caled Hampton House which was opened Oct 6th 1893. Cost near $25,000.[188]

April 5th 1893. About 800 Gentiles wer permited to visit the Salt Lake Temple before dedication.

April 6th 1893. Salt Lake Temple dedicated at 10 oclock A.M. by First Presidency and all Quorums of the Preasthood. Dedicatory sermons lasted 30 days. 40 meatings wer held. A hundred thousand people attended during dedicatory services.

April 20th 1893. A meating of first presidency Qurom of the Twelve 7 presidents of seventies Presidents of Stakes and their councilers Presiding Bishop and Council and a fiew others in Temple which lasted from 10 AM to 6[:]30 P.M. Fasting & prare. Speaches and prare Circle in Celestial Room the bigest scince the days of Enoch. At about 4 PM The Lords Supper was addministerd 117 persons partook I among them. Wm Salmon and I were doorkeepers during the whole time of dedicating service and wore a Ribon badge with picture of Temple printed on it.

May 8th 1893. Wife Mary donated $34[.]00 to Temple an amount that was paid me for door keeper at Temple dedication and I wood not accept. Same day I donated $100. to Temple and paid $100. Tithing and my wife $25.

May 9th 1893. Received a note from Lorenzo Snow president of Temple saying I had been suggested as a worker in the Temple and was invited to meet at that building May 16th at 10 AM to councel on the subject. May 16th met in annex of Temple with several others and was acceped as a worker without pay indefinatly. May 20th at 1 PM Set apart as worker in Temple in anex under hands of George Q Cannon and Franklin D Richards and had a Rehersal.

May 23D 1893. Commenced work in the Temple in the various Ordinances administerd there. I worked in the Temple during the year 126 days.

Jany 13th 1894. Son Leon B was ordained a deacon by Wm A Martin in 17th Ward.

From Jany 23D to end of year worked in Temple as Ordinance worker 108 days.

February 26th 1895. At 1 PM Wife and I on invitation attended 87 anniversary of Pres Woodruffs Birth day in Temple.

---

[188]For the Hampton House at 140 W. South Temple Street, see *Salt Lake City Directory, 1894–95*, 1898; "Fire Insurance Map of Salt Lake City, 1898," sheet 001.

March 1st 1895. Wife & I attended a birth day reception in Temple of Pres Woodruff 88 birth day & wife I worked in Temple of and during a portion of the 1895 and attend Temple workers prayer Circle in Temple Friday afternoons after work was over.

Cost of Salt Lake Temple $3.469.118

Dec 2D 1895. Mundell R Hampton our Son Baptised by John T [Th?] in Tabernacle Font. Dec 5th Confirmed under hands of Bishop [Tirgen?] in 17th Ward fast meating.

Nov 10th 1896. Son Leon B went on a mission to southern States and was assigned to work in Missippi. He was 18 years old.

Sept 8th 1898. Funeral of President Willford Woodruff. Born March 1st 1807 at Farmington (Now Avon) Connecticut Baptized into the Church Dec 31st 1835 Ordained an Apostle April 26th 1839 Sustained as President of the Church April 7th 1889 Died Sept 2D 1898 in San Francisco California. *Se 1897 Record below.*[189]

Dec 9th 1898 Son Leon Returned home from his mission having spent a portion of the latter part of his mission 4 months in Illinois among my relitives he was away 25 months & one day having done a good work and greatly improved being a man and a good preacher.

February 23D 1897. The City Council gave my Wife contract for boarding City prisoners at 7½ cts per meal for two years which was a God send for us as we had lost home and every thing else. March 22 1897. My Wife was appointed matron of City Jail by City Council conpensation $20. per mo.[190]

January 9th 1899. Discharge granted in Bankupsy By Gudj Marshal which case I was forced to take having lost over $60,000.00 dollars in last five years not saving my house or any thing else being foolish enugh to give up all my possessions to my Creditors hoping to redeam some. As soon as I was in the closest quaters they closed in and sold me out $5,000. House went for 2.100, Lots that cost $1.400. Sold for $2.25. and the hotel Hampton Home that cost $25.000. went for $7.300. and so on through the chapters all done by my Bretheren.[191]

[189]For a full biography, see Alexander, *Things in Heaven and Earth.*

[190]For Mary as police matron, see *Salt Lake City Directory, 1899.*

[191]A series of lawsuits by his creditors, which also named Mary, forced the Hamptons into bankruptcy. See *S. J. Brown vs. Mary J. R. R. Hampton et al.*, Third District Civil Case Files, case no. 497, 10 October 1896; *Barton and Company vs. Mary J. R. Hampton et al.*, Third District Civil Case files, case no. 1149, 9 October 1897; *Ann O. Burt vs. Mary J. R. R. Hampton et al.*, Third District Civil Case files, case no. 1730, 2 February 1898; *Taylor Romney Armstrong Co. vs. B. Y. Hampton et al.*, Third District Civil Case files, case no. 2520, 5 April 1899. In each case the court decided against the Hamptons and ordered the sale of their mortgaged property to satisfy creditors.

Matron M. J. R. R. Hampton of the Salt Lake City Police
Mary J.R.R. Hampton was appointed matron of the Salt Lake City jail in 1898, bringing the family needed income.
Courtesy Utah State Historical Society.

Jany 31st 1899. Received from Pres Snow Nine hundred and Sixty Six dollars out of four thousand Six hundred paid out of my own pocket up to January first A D. 1900. I paid George Q Cannon $1.00. borrowed money Bro Preston $1.65. borrowed money which left me $7.000.

Feby 4th 1899. I am 63 years old. Feby 5th Sunday Wife and I attended fast meating in Temple at 10 oclock AM whitch we have done several times before. In the morning at 6 40 PM I started for St Louis to trade in the Stock Exchange with my little capital it being to small to do any business this side of there. 8th arived at St Louis and put up at Terminal hotel. A fearfull blizard was raging the worst ever known there. From 8th to 17th Thermometer range from 10 to 26 below zero. I could not get out of hotel to do any thing. My lungs got so bad that I started home on 17th at 9 AM and arived home on 19th at 4 PM.

Sat April 1st 1899. Edna R Hampton our daughter was baptised in Tabernacle font by Arthur F Burnes. Confirmed Sunday April 2 in 13th Ward meating House under hands of Hamilton G Park & others.

April 3. Wife & I attended a birth day reception in Temple in honor of Pres Lorenzo Snow on his 85 birth day. The Qurom of the Twelve wer present. All spoke including Pre Snow Counscil. The Temple workers wer presant lunchon was served and many songs and resitations renderd.

April 11th [1899]. Son Ralph R Started for [?] Canada on promise of $2.50 to $3.00 per day and if all works right will make his home thare. He is not 19 years old yet.

April 18th [1899]. Son Leon B Started for Same place with same intentions. He has just returned from a mission.

April 19th 1899. I started for Denver at 8.50 AM on account of being sick with Lagrip.[192] Arived in Denver 20th at 9 AM. Put up at St Elmo. 21 took room on 1346 Stout Street at $2.00 per week. May 4th 1899. Moved to 1538 California St $2.50 per week. June 13th arived home much improved in health and much less cash in pocket. July 15th Ralph R returned home from Canada insted of getting from $2.50 to 3.00 per day got $1.25 [?]. One third of time could not work. July 28 1899. Leon B Returned having same conditions as Ralph. We had to pay their way up and back as well as purchas their out fits all of which with my travels mad a big hoel in $7.00. During the early part of 1900 I wrote several letters to Pres Lorenzo Snow stating the amount I had expended in Detective workin for the Church besides a year in the County Jail in 1886 and asked them to lend me two thousand dollars to help me on my feet as I had lost all I had through detective work. No answer came to any of my letters. About the first of Jun 1900 I got my back up on account of the Slight and insult so I wrote another letter withdrawing all former propositions and requested that I be paid the amount of money expended and due me. Conciquently received a letter from Pres Snow requesting me to meet the first presidency on the 7th of June 1900. Pres Snow being Sick a committie was appointed by the first presidency to investigate my case consisting of Apostles John H Smith, Heber J Grant and John W Tayler also Wm W Salmon and Andrew Smith member of Same committie as I on detective work (of committee on detection I was chairman). June 8th. The Committie met with me in Temple gate house. I gave them a plain Statement of facts. They all aggreed that I had been grosly misstreated and that I should be paid my money and so reported to Pres Snow and on 16th of June 1900 I received from Pres Snow $3634,00 amount due me for Detective

[192] *La grippe* is the French term for influenza.

work.[193] I gave Wm W Salmon and Andrew Smith $100[.]00 each for their assistance and loned Wm W Salmon $150.00 without interest. June 19th 1900. Started for Denver on D & RG at 8.30 AM arived in Denver June 20th at 930 AM. Rented room at 701 14th Street at $13.00 per month. July 21st 1900. My Wife Mary arived in Denver on a visit to me and we had a good time while she staid. Wednesday August 8th 1900. My Wife Started hom on D&RG train. Visited our son Leon and his fiance at Clear Creek. Aug 26th 1900. I took train for home where I arived Monday. 27th September 26th 1900. Our Son Leon B Hampton married Miss Bessie Morse from Clear Creek Utah In Salt Lake Temple John R Winder Officiating. In the evening had a wedding Supper [with] 37 guests presant mostly our own family. The Bride and Groom received a good many nice presants.

October 1st 1900. At 9.45 AM Started for San Francisco. Arived on 2D [and] took room at 237 Gerry street at $3.00 per week. Cold and raining. Oct 3D. Wrote home for half rate Fare as I was sick and could not stand the weather. Same day visited my Sister Vilate and Niec Alace at Golden Gate. Oct 4th. Went to Clift House. Oct 5th. Went to Alices to diner Vilate dined with us also visited Julia Deloss who shortly after was run over an kiled. 6th 7 & 8. Visited Clift house. 8th. Recived letter from home with half rate order. Oct 9th at 8 AM Started home on No 4 Train. Oct 10th at 10 PM arived home. I paid 40 cts and wif $3.00 Tithing for 1900. Total $3.40.

This should have been written in furthe back

April 8th 1900. Found out my name was on black list for non payment of Tithing for year 1899. Put thare by N A Empy Bishop of 13th Ward. I asked him to place Opisite my name the reasons why I did not pay Tithing for 1899 and he flatly refused. April 20th 1900. I mad out a list of Tithing I had paid in years past amounting to $5,532.35 and sent it to Pres Lorenzow Snow in a letter asking him if Bishop Empy had persued a proper course against me. *No Answer.* I then went to Bishop Preston head Bishop of the Church who said it was an out rage. = (as did many others in the Quorum of the Twelve and other positions including Pres Snow Later on) = and told me to make out a Statement of Reasons why I did not pay Tithing for the year 1899 and present it to Bishop Empy and *Tell him* to have it placed opsite *my name on non Tithing Record* which I did and reads as follows.

[193] John Henry Smith, a counselor to President Joseph F. Smith, mentioned the discussions that led to payment in his diary. White, ed., *Church, State, and Politics*, 457–58. See also Journal History, 7, 14, 18 June 1900.

B Y Hampton Paid no Tithing for the year 1899 for the reason that he did not earn any thing that year but lost thousands of dollars and the last peice of property (They he and wife possessed). My Wife Mary and six Children paying their Tithing for 1899 amounting to $31.70 Which the Bishop Empy Refused to put opisite my name on Record or any other Statement. I then went to Pres Snow in person and told him the facts. He said it was an outrage and many others had been served the Same as me by varioius Bishop and that he Snow would have a list mad out of those rongly delt by and require the Bishops to make proper corections and thus it Stands to this 10th day of Nov 1901.[194]

December 1st 1900. I was Taken very Sick and confined to my bead on Sunday the 16th. My whole left side was paralized and I was unconcious for several hours. The Doctor White told my Wife and children to put me in bead as I never would raley again but I fooled them again as I have many times befor when the Doctors gave me up. In less than 24 hours I was free from the Stroke but Still Sick.

February 14th 1901. My Wife Mary Jane Randolph Robinson and I received our Second Anointings in Salt Lake Temple under hands of Brothers J.R. Winder. Madsen & John Nicholson.[195]

March 27th 1901. I.D. Haines our old friend died at Odgen. Wife and I went to funeral but was a day to soon and on July 6 Same Year his Son Harry D Haines died at Ogden. Wife and I attended his funeral.

April 12th 1901. George Q Cannon first Counseler to Pres Snow died at Monteray California. Funeral held in Tabernacle in Salt Lake City Wednesday April 17th. July 12th 1901. Son Ralph R Started for big horn Country by way of Denver. July 13th. Second Cousin Mrs Lidia Dalton daughter of Cosin Robert Hampton of [Papa?] Illinois visited us on her way to California. July 28th 1901. Son Leon B Hampton appointed presiding Elder over Clear Creek Coal mining district. Sept 26th 1901. Son Leon had a Daughter born unto him Named Phyllis Mary.

Oct 10th 1901. At 3.35 P.M Pres Lorenzow Snow president of the Church

[194]Hampton's papers contain an exchange of letters on this topic, the last a letter from the Presiding Bishop's Office telling him his name had been erased from the Non-Tithepayer's Record for 1899. Wm. Preston et al. to B.Y. Hampton, Salt Lake City, 15 January 1902, folder 2.

[195]The Second Anointing endowed participants as priests and kings or as priestesses and queens and ensured one's "calling and election" to the highest degree of LDS salvation. That the Hamptons received this exclusive temple rite was a mark of honor.

of Jesus Christ of Laterday Saints Died. Funeral Sunday Oct 13th in Tabernacle then taken to Brigham City his former residence and buried in the afternoon of same day.

Son Ralph R returned from big horn country in Sept 1901 and later part of Oct went to Clear Creek over one hundred miles South to work with and live at his bro Leons.

[This is the last entry in Hampton's diary. He died of a second stroke on 21 July 1902 and was buried in the Salt Lake City Cemetery.][196]

[196]See "B.Y. Hampton Dead," *Deseret Evening News,* 21 July 1902; "Was a Man of Highest Heroism," *Deseret Evening News,* 24 July 1902; "Died of Paralysis," *Salt Lake Herald,* 22 July 1902, 5/3; "Death of B.Y. Hampton," *Salt Lake Tribune,* 22 July 1902. His widow Mary died at age 84 in 1933 in Salt Lake. See Mary Hampton, Death Certificate, 12 January 1933, Entry 14055, Utah State Office of Vital Records.

Afterword

The United States Army's arrival in Utah in 1858 changed America's Rocky Mountain Zion forever. The gradual assertion of federal authority provided growing protection for dissenters and, perhaps more importantly, ended Utah's isolation. The coming of the Civil War inaugurated an era of dramatic change that requires a concluding assessment of how dissenters contributed to the slow and contentious transformation of theocratic Deseret into the famously patriotic state of Utah. The territory's last three decades saw missionaries, miners, and the military challenge and change its religious rulers, as well as the nature and extent of dissension in the Mormon West.

Deeply depressed by his setbacks during the Utah War, Brigham Young did not take the army's arrival lying down. He both promised the puppet governor, Alfred Cumming, to let unhappy citizens depart in peace and stepped up the harassment and intimidation of Saints whom he judged disloyal to the kingdom. Despite the wounded prophet's determination to keep dissenters isolated and under tight control, the people most desperate to escape did so. A band of "half-starved" apostates reached the army's camp at Camp Scott by mid-May 1858, where they "represented that the Church was torn by dissensions." Outsiders had a skewed perspective on life in Utah, but they credited the reports of disaffected Mormons who assured them "that the United States troops would never have met with any serious opposition in attempting to enter the Valley, and that if protection should be afforded to them by the troops, fully one-half the entire Mormon community would embrace the opportunity to flee from the moral and physical slavery in which they are held."[1]

[1] Simonton, "Letter from the Army of Utah," 1 June 1858, *San Francisco Evening Bulletin*, 21 July 1858, 3/2–4.

Half the population did not abandon Utah even with the support of the government. The most peripatetic plains traveler of his age, Father Pierre-Jean De Smet, hit the trail again in 1858 as a chaplain for the Utah Expedition. De Smet never made it all the way to Utah, but between Fort Kearny and the forks of the Platte, he met over a hundred families on their way to Kansas and Missouri. De Smet's report suggests that four to five hundred refugees had fled "that terrible sect of modern fanatics" who ruled Utah Territory:

> They appeared delighted at being fortunate enough to leave, safe and sound, the famous promised land of Utah; thanks to the influence of the new governor, and the presence of the United States troops. They told us that a great number of other families would follow them, so soon as they should be capable of doing so, and of procuring the necessary means for the journey. They confessed that they would have escaped long before, had they not been afraid of falling into the hands of the Danites, or Destroying Angels. These compose the body-guard of the Prophet; they are said to be entirely and blindly at his disposal, to carry out all his plans, meet all his wishes, and execute all his measures, which often involve robbery and murder. Before the arrival of the United States soldiers, woe to any one who manifested a desire to leave Utah, or abandon the sect: woe to him who dared to raise a voice against the actions of the Prophet,—they rarely escaped the poniards of these Destroying Angels, or rather incarnate demons."[2]

The confrontation Brigham Young provoked with the federal government and the long litany of failed prophecies that accompanied his determined defiance of its authority further undermined Mormon loyalties, especially outside of Utah. Experts disagree, but it appears that by 1859 about half the population of San Bernardino had refused to heed the call to return to Utah or had returned to California, where a significant number of lapsed Mormons soon joined them.[3] By early 1861 Walter Murray Gibson reported San Bernardino, an early Mormon outpost in southern California, had become "a pestersome nest of apostates."[4] The ratio was apparently higher in the region that soon became the state of Nevada: "As near as I could learn about two thirds of the old settlers of Carson Valey are apostate, and a great many in Calafornia, some say ¼ or ⅓ of the whole," missionary Phineas Cook reported in 1860. "They say I am sent out as a spy to hunt up the desenters."[5]

---

[2]De Smet to Reverend Father, 1 November 1859, in Chittenden and Richardson, eds., *Life, Letters and Travels*, 3:717, 727–28.

[3]Beattie and Beattie, *Heritage of the Valley*, 311–15. Lyman, *San Bernardino*, 414–15, makes a complicated argument to the contrary.

[4]Gibson to Brigham Young, 9 January 1861, LDS Archives.

[5]Cook to Brigham Young, 8 June 1860, LDS Archives.

The Law Is Not King in Utah

Not long after the army's arrival, Joseph Venables Vernon sent federal judge Delana R. Eckles "a written statement of our circumstances and sentiments, for your own discretional use, when you have to plead for the redemption and salvation of poor perishing Utah, before the highest functionaries in the land." Vernon had journeyed from Hull, England, to Utah in 1852 with the Deseret Manufacturing Company, John Taylor's ill-starred attempt to transport sugar-making machinery across the plains, which Mormon stalwart A. O. Smoot dubbed the "D— Miserable Company."[6] Since he had not "been guilty of swearing in the streets, of getting intoxicated, of fighting, and carousing," Brigham Young said Vernon was "almost entirely unknown, because he has lived his religion, kept the commandments of God, and minded his own business." The prophet praised him as a Saint who was "happy all the day long, and satisfied, without making an excitement among the people."[7] In the wake of the Utah War, Vernon changed his mind, as shown by the complaints he sent to "The Honorable Chief Judge Eckles" at "the earnest request of numerous friends." Standing a favorite Mormon epithet on its head, Vernon described Brigham Young as "an ignorant apostate" and charged "Brigham's apostates are conspirators against the people of the world."

J. V. Vernon to Delana R. Eckles, 25 September 1858, National Archives, RG 59, M12, State Department Territorial Papers, Utah Series.

. . . First. Brigham the Apostate still remains virtualy and actualy the governor of Utah. By the perfidious arts of low cunning Governor Cumming has been seduced and duped. He is now in Mormon captivity, the willing and obedient tool of an ignorant apostate. The men whom Brigham appointed have become the members elect of the Legislature, the official acts of the Governor are conformable to Brigham's dictum, and though unseen, all are made to serve his sovereign will.

Since they have got Mr. Cumming into their power they speak of him in the most contemptuous manner: The common slang spoken at the corner of every street is, "Brigham governs the Territory and old Cumming receives the salary," "We'll make the laws and then we'll make the old devil sign them, or we'll cut his dam throat," And by way of nickname, they give him the euphonious epithet of "Swill-Tub."

---

[6] Whitney, *History of Utah*, 4:487.

[7] 16 March 1856, *Journal of Discourses*, 3:255. Confusion exists between Vernon and his son John Venables Vernon, namesake of Vernon, Utah, who was reportedly killed by the Goshutes.

Second. In this state of things, neither life nor property nor business operations are safe one hour. The Danite murderers are growing bolder and bolder every hour, they obtrude in any society—in a house—at any time they choose, they ask questions and use threatening language. A Captain of Brigham's guard told one of his men a confidence the other day that a plot was laid and would be ready for execution as soon as the snow came sufficiently to stop ingress and egress through the Kanyon. Previous arrangements being made, and a given night being decided upon, every gentile and every disaffected Mormon should be murdered at one and the same hour of midnight, and at the same hour a body of Indians would be ready to stampede the animals belonging to the Army, and, under mask of Indian depredations, they would harass the army in mid winter till they were all killed off. This disclosure has produced dreadfull alarm, and the people would do anything to get away but poverty holds them still.

Third. These Brigham's apostates are conspirators against the people of the world—they are bound together by bloody oaths never to [stop?] till they have overthrown the United States Government and demobilized the civilization of all mankind—they laugh and sneer at President Buchanan and his cabinet and use language too vile for print—they hold Uncle Sam at defiance and say they can outwit him anyhow, and they swear destruction upon every gentile citizen of America.

Fourth. This lawless gang of conspirators murderers and thieves organized together in the form and under the deceptive name of the Mormon church must now be broken up, or Utah will be annihilated as a Territory—no travelling will be safe through any part of the Rocky mountains—the mormons will appear in another form—they will make common cause with the Indians, and be a scourge to the nations of this continent for ages to come.

Fifth. A wise vigourous and unwavering Territorial Government supported by an efficient army and sustained by Federal powers would be all sufficient to accomplish the Desideratum:—the Mormons who are the most terrible of all braggarts are the greatest of all cowards. Only be judicious and firm, and the work is done. Brigham trembles before men of talent and experience.

Sixth. All the expense of bringing armies and officers to establish the supremacy of the United States laws and government in Utah is gone for nothing—it amounts to nothing—for Brigham's power is as much felt in the Territory as it was before his successor was appointed, and the entire failure of all this expedition and expense is attributable wholey and solely to the puerile pusillanimity of Alfred Cumming who ought to have been the Governor but is not.

Seventh. If the Federal Government will establish their authority in these valleys—will sustain you and your associates in administering law—will protect us in our property and possessions, and conduct the Territory on purely American principles, then [we] wish to remain here and assist you in effecting the reformation; but no one will give evidence in a court of law untill a portion of the Army be located near each city for our protection.

If you do not return early in spring we intend to leave the Territory, our lives are in jeopardy every hour while we remain here. We have now discharged our duty, fully confident that you will discharge yours zealously and faithfully, and we leave the [balance?] with the government.

We remain Esteemed Sir
Very Respectfully yours for Self and friends
J. V. Vernon

P. S. If you publish this letter please *do not* publish my name.

Judge Eckles, who had arrived home in Indiana late in 1858, described conditions in Utah to Secretary of State Lewis Cass, whose department oversaw federal courts until the creation of the Department of Justice in 1871. "Brigham Young is and for the year past has been Governor *de facto* of Utah. Under present circumstances I am not prepared to say it could have been otherwise," Eckles wrote. "Such is the terror induced over the minds of men by his lawless bands of Destroying Angels that, whatever may be their inclinations, they are unwilling to resist his dictation." While he was in Utah, "the highest crimes known to the law continue to be perpetrated with impunity." Neither the Mormon people nor their officials showed the slightest desire "to aid the Courts in bringing Mormons to justice . . . in that distracted country." The army post at Camp Floyd was forty-four miles from the nearest court, and the Mormons wanted it even farther away. Judges Charles Sinclair and John Cradlebaugh could do nothing. Without support from Congress by spring, they would be compelled to report "that the experiment to maintain Civil government in Utah is a failure."

To show how Brigham Young governed by fear, Eckles sent Vernon's letter to Cass, calling him "the most eloquent man in Utah" and asserting that Vernon, "a leading monogamist," headed "the party of inhabitants called by the Mormons 'Apostates.'" The judge defended Alfred Cumming and other federal officials from Vernon's charges, but he agreed that the thoroughly disloyal Mormons would "interpose every obstacle in their power to the action of every Federal officer who refuses to obey their leaders dictation." The law, said the chief justice of Utah's federal court, "*is not King in Utah.*"[8]

[8]Eckles to Cass, 18 January 1859, National Archives RG 59, M12, State Department Territorial Papers, Utah Series.

Security against Marauders and Persecutors: An Army Escort

Even at the height of the passions that raged during 1857, Brigham Young had insisted he was happy to see dissenters leave Zion and even promised to help send them on their way: "I will pledge myself that if there is a man, woman, or child that wants to go back to the States, if they will pay their debts, and not steal anything, they can go; and if they are poor and honest, we will help them to go," he said while speaking before U.S. Army captain Stewart Van Vliet. "That has been my well-known position all the time."[9] Perhaps, but Young's pledge contained a long string of "ifs" that provided a host of justifications to let him limit dissenters' rights.

As the courts fought a futile battle to bring justice to Utah in 1859, Governor Cumming fought to be the only federal official in the territory with authority to call a *posse commitatus*.[10] Exhibiting his authority over the army and judges, at the request of families wanting to leave the territory, Cumming asked Gen. Albert Sidney Johnston to provide them with protection. Johnston agreed to use the troops intended to police the Humboldt River route to California to provide "complete protection by a special escort" for those who wanted to leave Utah. In mid-May 1859, the *Valley Tan*, Utah's first independent newspaper, announced a meeting to be held at a non-Mormon hotel the following Saturday for those who wanted to take advantage of "a military escort to conduct us beyond the lines of danger, on our road to California." "Come one, come all!" the invitation read. The next day, the *Deseret News* printed a similar announcement.[11]

Not surprisingly, these events prompted a response from Brigham Young. Some men and women, he complained "turn their backs upon every upright principle and practice; we wish that such persons would leave our society, for we do not feel willing to fellowship them." Apostle Pratt also wished, Young said:

> the miserable, dissatisfied spirits would leave, but they will not all go. . . . We do not particularly care whether they go or stay; they are at perfect liberty to please themselves in that matter, because it is their Constitutional right

[9] 13 September 1857, *Journal of Discourses*, 5:230.

[10] Ashton, *Federal Judiciary in Utah*, 18–19.

[11] "Attention, Emigrants!" *Valley Tan*, 17 May 1859, 2; "Now's the Time for Emigrants!" *Deseret News*, May 18, 1859, 1.

> to stay here, if they do not infringe upon the rights of others, and observe the laws of the land as strictly as we do. The principal reason why I do not wish them to go is because they will be constantly troubling me to assist them back again. . . . The person that forsakes the faith of our Lord Jesus Christ will find himself ruined for time and eternity. How are they looked upon who have received the spirit of the gospel and forsaken it? Heaven with all its shining hosts despises and pities them; they will not have them, and hell is ready to spew them out. With a few exceptions, they are despised by the good and wise among men, by the noble and ignoble, all despise them, and they are in a most miserable condition.[12]

Perhaps with these words in mind, General Johnston ordered Maj. Isaac Lynde to escort the "unusually large number of emigrants" projected to abandon Utah and the "considerable number of defenseless families, (principally women and children,) wishing to leave this Territory for California." The families had asked "that the strong arm of the government may be specially extended over them," seeking "security against marauders and persecutors, which the laws of the Territory and the sentiment of the community will not give." Other families would join Major Lynde near Salt Lake, along the road, and at a designated rendezvous on Bear River.[13] Major Lynde left Camp Floyd on 12 June 1858 with a company of 162 infantry and dragoons, rations for ninety days, and eight ox wagons of dissenters under his protection. "These emigrants avowed themselves to be seceders [*sic*] from the Mormon faith, and state that they had reason to fear molestation from the Mormons, and for that reasons they sought the protection of the troops," Lynde reported.[14]

The emigrant meeting in May had estimated that about forty families would go, but no single source reports how many emigrants actually left Utah with the army.[15] Among those who did leave were Joseph Venables Vernon, author of the eloquent letter to Judge Eckles, and Peter McAuslan, the Scottish convert whose story is told by Polly Aird in *Mormon Convert, Mormon Defector.*[16] Using the traditional estimate of four members to a family, about 160 souls, approximately the same number as the soldiers who

[12]Journal History, 22 May 1859, 2–4; *Deseret News,* 1 June 1859, 9:97.

[13]Porter to Lynde, 5 June 1859, "Report of the Secretary of War," 189–90.

[14]Lynde to Porter, 24 October 1859, ibid., 240.

[15]Bayliss and Jester to Cumming, 21 May 1859, ibid., 183.

[16]After arriving in California, Vernon went to San Francisco. In 1865 he and his second wife and daughter moved to Hawaii, where he died in 1873. Claudia Bushman, email to Polly Aird, 5 April 2010. McAuslan settled in the Sacramento Valley with his extended family and died there in 1908.

accompanied them, joined the escort.[17] Any number of variables, such as projecting how many dissenters joined along the road or using a larger family size in the estimate, could raise the estimated number to as many as four or five hundred. Yet whatever number one picks, relatively few people took advantage of the government's protection.

Why? "I will tell you the reason why we could not leave this blood-stained land," wrote Aaron Dewitt, a noted dissident who remained in Zion. Utah was "a thousand miles from the nearest town East, eight hundred miles to the nearest settlement West, and God only knows how far to any place north and south." In all this vast tract, "no white man dwelt. No civilization was known, none but the red men roamed the dreary solitudes." Such a journey required "considerable food, a good wagon and team, in fact, everything necessary for a three month's pilgrimage. Nor was it safe for a few men to go together, unless they were well-armed." Every bishop knew your business, Dewitt charged, "and was always on the lookout. If you started they would send men to drive off your stock, and thus you would be compelled to return. Then if you did not behave and act the hypocrite, the bishop would send the Danites to use you up and send you across lots to that bright brimstone home we read about. Thus you see it was almost impossible to get away."[18]

We Expected to Be All Killed: The Morrisites

The army's presence provides another reason why many who had lost their faith in Brigham Young stayed in Utah, for even under Alfred Cumming's compliant administration of justice, the army provided a counterweight to Mormon power. This ended in late July 1861, when the commander at Camp Floyd (now renamed Fort Crittenden), Philip St. George Cooke, blew up the munitions dump, presented the fort's flagpole to Young, and marched virtually every soldier in the territory back to fight in the Civil War. The army would return eighteen months later, but, as historian David L. Bigler noted, "events would take place during that time that would make this period among the most significant and revealing in the history of Utah Territory."[19] One of the most meaningful of these events would be the saga of the followers of Joseph Morris, yet another Mormon prophet.

---

[17]Aird, *Mormon Convert,* 255. For more details on the army escort, see Aird, "Escape from Zion."

[18]Dewitt to Mrs. Elizabeth Durrant, 31 January 1875, in Simmonds, "Aaron Dewitt." Dewitt's claim that bishops sent Danites to dispatch dissenters is open to dispute.

[19]Bigler, *Forgotten Kingdom,* 199.

Ann Gordge provided this volume's first account of the Morrisites ordeal, but the movement Joseph Morris launched during the late 1850s merits more attention. A Welsh coalminer and LDS convert, Morris came to Utah with his wife and daughter in 1853. Disturbed by polygamy and disheartened with the excesses of the Reformation, Morris began receiving his own revelations and what he called "impressions from the Lord." Assembling his followers in the Church of Jesus Christ of Saints Most High near Ogden at Kington Fort, he launched a program of consecrated communism, and prophesied the exact date of the Second Coming of Christ. At first ignored, the new prophet identified himself as the Seventh Angel of Revelation who was destined to rule the world. He unleashed a flood of revelations during 1860 and attracted as many as a thousand converts in Utah, while half a world away Jesse N. Smith reported a "Morrisite wave swept over the mission, producing the first apostate break in the ranks of the Danish mission."[20]

The old prophet could ignore the new prophet no longer. Jesus told Morris he had brought the army to Utah "that I might stay the murders" that Mormon leaders had committed: "They would shed innocent blood without feeling the least guilt upon their consciences," the Lord of Hosts complained. Morris knew the withdrawal of federal troops put him in danger, but the Lord assured him, "I will make a slaughter among your enemies."[21] The movement began to unravel in 1862, when the Morrisites arrested three dissenters who tried to reclaim their consecrated property. Pliant federal officials issued writs to release the prisoners and arrest Morris and his lieutenants. To enforce the order, on 13 June 1862 deputy marshal and Nauvoo Legion colonel Robert T. Burton led some 250 men with two artillery pieces to the bluffs overlooking Weber River and the poorly located Kington Fort. Burton sent a Morrisite herdboy with a note demanding the surrender of the prisoners and Joseph Morris. Tired of waiting, Burton fired two "warning shots" at the fort, where Morris and his flock had assembled to await a revelation. One shot smashed into the fort, killing two women and wounding a teenage girl. In the subsequent three-day battle, the Morrisites fought until their ammunition ran out, killing two Mormons.

On Sunday evening, 15 June 1862, Colonel Burton demanded the fort surrender and the Morrisites began to throw down their arms. "What happened next is highly conjectural," historian E.B. Long observed. As

---

[20]Long, *The Saints and the Union*, 90; and Launius and Thatcher, eds., *Differing Visions*, 201.

[21]Morris, *The "Spirit Prevails,"* 123–24.

is often the case, both sides provided their own version of the story. The Mormon account made what looks like a case of cold-blooded murder appear perfectly reasonable: what is undeniable is that Burton shot Morris and gunned down two women who objected. A posse member shot John Banks, former president of the British Mission's London Conference, in the neck. U.S. Attorney Sumner Howard later told the attorney general that Salt Lake City's Mormon coroner Dr. Jeter Clinton inserted a scalpel in Banks's wound, "turned the knife in the wound, unjointed the neck," and dispatched him. "Whatever the cause, gunshot, poison, or knife," David Bigler wrote, "John Banks was surely dead by morning." The victors put the bodies of Morris and Banks on display in Salt Lake's city hall, along with the dead prophet's scepters, tin crown, and almost a hundred prisoners. A March 1863 trial acquitted two Morrisites, convicted seven for second-degree murder, and fined the rest one hundred dollars. Practically every Gentile in Utah, along with one Mormon—William A. Hickman—signed petitions seeking clemency. Three days later, the territorial governor pardoned them all.[22]

British convert and 1853 overlander William H. Hill was one of about twenty Morrisites who left Utah soon after their June 1862 arraignment. The letter he sent home from California late that year appeared all over Britain.[23]

William H. Hill, "A Voice from the City of the Saints," *Birmingham (England) Daily Post*, 17 January 1863.

A convert to Mormonism, who left the neighbourhood of Bristol some ten years ago, to join the company of Saints in Utah, give[s] a doleful account of his "experiences" in that highly-favoured region. Writing to a friend, from California, he says:—One day in Salt Lake convinced me that the Mormons were not what they were represented to be. I soon found out that the wisest plan was to say nothing, for fear of having my throat cut, which hundreds have had for speaking too freely. During my stay in the country I made considerable property. I had eleven cows and other young stock, a pair of mules, and horses and sheep, and plenty of wheat and a good farm. I and my neighbours used to meet of a night, and talk of the doings of the Mormons and their dark deeds. We wished that something might take place to bring about a better state of things.

[22]Long, *The Saints and the Union*, 91–92; and Bigler, *Forgotten Kingdom*, 213–14.

[23]This widely reprinted letter appeared in the *Caledonian Mercury* in Edinburgh, Scotland, in the *Glasgow Herald*, and the *Manchester Guardian*. The *Brooklyn Eagle* published it in the United States on 6 February 1863. Val Holley discovered the letter and identified the author as William H. Hill. See Holley, "Slouching Towards Slaterville," 256–58.

Well, it so happened that, about two years ago, a man from Manchester, in England, arose and represented himself to be Brigham Young's superior, exposing Brigham Young with all his power, showing his deception, his fallacy in deceiving the people, which proved a good opportunity for myself and others to back him up. We rallied around the man to the number of about 300. Our wives and children numbered about 700. We all gathered to one place. They came from several hundred miles around. We met for every day for fourteen months, preaching, and exposing his villainy and corruption; such was our determination to withstand him to the death. Although threatened with extermination several times, we feared them not. Brigham used to send his reporters regularly all the time. We had some able speakers as ever stood before an audience—John Banks, of London; ___ Parsons [John Parson], of London; and Richard Cook, of Manchester. There is a man in London, sent there to gather the poor's money, to build a temple, when there has been money enough gathered to build a dozen temples. But, instead of building temples, old Brigham has built a monster theatre, and yet the foolish dupes won't believe the truth when it is told them.[24] Well, the man who is sent to London is a great cattle thief in Utah. When I first knew him, he had neither cow nor horse, and only one wife. Now, he has his seven wives, and claims other men's property. The time the soldiers came to Utah, some four years ago, this man played a prominent part, with the title of general. I was a ragamuffin soldier at that time. There were some men came in from California, with a large sum of money, to gamble with the soldiers. These men were taken prisoners, examined by the General, their money taken from them, their throats cut, and their bodies floated down the Jordan river. This is a small sample of the Mormons' dark deeds.[25]

Well, back to my old subject:—We continued to expose old Brigham until he would stand it no longer. He tried every way and means to starve us out: threatened his own party to cut them off it they ground any flour for us; counselled his Danite band to hover around us, and steal our cattle and horses, which they did, in open daylight, before our eyes; and threatened to shoot the first man that attempted to stop them. These Danites are murderers, always on hand to destroy and rob. Oftentimes they get killed by Brigham's order, if there is any danger that they will reveal any of Brigham's counsel. There were seven of them shot down in one day, for revealing to some of

[24]Brigham Young provided half the one hundred thousand dollars to build the Salt Lake Theatre, "The Cathedral in the Desert," which opened in March 1862. Whether Young used funds collected to build the Salt Lake Temple is unknown, but much of the financing came from profits he made selling government surplus from Camp Floyd, and, some say, from funds raised to build the Seventies Hall of Science.

[25]This is a garbled version of the murder of five Californians in the fall of 1857. For the facts, see Bigler, "The Aiken Party Executions." The general was Chauncey W. West, commander of Nauvoo Legion forces in northern Utah.

our men who it was counselled them to steal our cattle. Well, we worked old Brigham up to a warlike pitch. But this was too big a job. It looked like another Mountain Meadow massacre, where they killed 120 emigrants, and robbed them of their property. We happened to have three prisoners that we took, who had been stealing our cattle, and stole a wagon load of wheat, and threatened to shoot the driver. This proved a favourable opportunity for old Brigham Young to throw it on Uncle Sam's shoulders. He got Judge Kinney to draw up a writ for the release of these prisoners, which we refused, until our cattle and property were returned. Whereupon they sent up an armed force and four pieces of cannon—never came to offer us terms, but while we were met in an open bowery fired their cannon direct into our midst, killing three women. We immediately retired to our houses, they continuing to pour in upon us. We offered no resistance for two hours, until we expected to be all killed, when we took to arms, and withstood them for three days—about 60 to 1,000. They killed ten on our side. We fought them until our ammunition was all spent; after which we surrendered, when they rushed in upon us after we had hoisted a flag of truce. They came in like fiends of hell, and shot down two women and two men—John Banks, of London, and Joseph Morris, of Manchester. I was standing close to them when they were shot by a man titled Colonel Burton. Judge Kinney's orders were not to fire a shot, but Brigham Young's were to clear us right out. Well, we were taken prisoners of war, received a mock examination, and ordered to appear next March to receive another examination. But a great many will not be there; I shall not, for one. Well, they robbed me of all my means; but I managed to raise three yoke of cattle and a wagon, and now I am safe in California, away from the Mormons.[26]

Brotherly Love As Practiced in Utah: Causes of Disillusionment

As its leaders liked to point out, Mormonism was a hard row to hoe. The faithful thought they would find the Promised Land and have a role in building the Kingdom of God, but the harsh reality they encountered in Utah failed to match their expectations or their dreams. Like George A. Hicks, some who made the long and arduous journey to the new Rocky Mountain Zion did not believe the church leaders lived up to the tenets of the faith, and their disappointment led to their disaffection. An anonymous Scot from Dundee provided a telling account of what motivated their alienation.

[26]For more, see C. LeRoy Anderson's *Joseph Morris*, the best book on the subject.

"Mormonism as Seen by a Scotchman,"
Daily Union Vedette, 5 May 1864, 1/2–4; 4/1–2.
Reprinted from the *Dundee Advertiser*, 2 March 1864.

We make the following extracts from a letter written by a shrewd and honest townsman who has been resident in Utah to his friends at home. He speaks with all the energy of a convalescent from delusion, and some of his statements of fact are more forcible and graphic than suits our columns. We quote enough we trust to deter any victims of the wretched Mormon imposture among the poor of Dundee from quitting their country for the Sodom of the Salt Lake:—*Dundee* (Scot.,) *Advertiser*, March 2d.

You ask me what cause I had to leave Utah and the Mormon's faith? I will tell you. I had been led to believe that God had ordained that the "saints" in Utah, being far away from the "Gentiles," could in peace work out the most sublime purposes, which had for their object the calling together of all the children of men to enjoy liberty and brotherly love, or, in other words, to practice the religion of Jesus Christ. This was my expectation. It had been preached to us that in the land of the saints every saint was a brother, and that the strong, whether of mind or body, gave freely of his strength to the weak, and helped him to bear his burdens, and did their utmost to help the faithful in every good thing. But instead of this, every advantage is taken of the weakness of the weak. How can I get the most ease and honor out of others, returning to them the least of toil or self-denial? Is the question of questions in Utah as elsewhere. I had been told by elders in Dundee, and so have you, that when a Mormon had got his "endowments," he was a holy man because he had stood in holy places and heard the voice of God. All doubts as to the truth of the faith would be removed, and men could not help but be good and holy that had been "endowed," because all that could be given at the present time to man by the Holy Ghost was sure to be bestowed upon him in the "endowment rooms." Is it holiness to strip the simpleton of every farthing of money and clothes by telling him that money is useless in Zion, and then to laugh at his simplicity, which is often done? Is it holiness to say that the end justifies the means, and that the big men are the only judges of right and wrong, as is always done? Is it holy to have plenty and see your brethren bordering on starvation and not help them, on the hard-hearted plea that it is good to try their faith in this way, as is sometimes done? To have every one a spy upon another, not for the purpose of preventing him from over-reaching his brother, but that he might not breathe even to a friend of his crushed hopes, which might in time by accumulation get up such a revolution that would hurl the chiefs and prophets from their thrones, and show the poor and honest fanatics how they have been imposed upon? To break up letters at the Post-office, so that they might know all your communications with the outer world, and make it all but impossible to leave the territory if you were dissatisfied? This they moreover manage by discountenancing the use of money, and letting it be well understood that it is at the risk of your life that you leave Zion?

They counsel men to have no wealth but grain and stock which are too bulky to leave with; and to have no dealing with the Gentiles, for fear that they might get the means to leave before they got into their sworn meshes; and to get *double-wived,* so that they could not live in peace anywhere else. Is it holy to rouse the vanity of good-looking married women by telling them that they belong to a higher tribe in the Kingdom of Heaven than their husbands, in order that "endowed" elders might get them to leave their families and enter their harems? (Here several instances were given, with names and details.) Daniel H. Wells stood up in Salt Lake City and delivered a harangue to the workmen on public works, which perhaps you may have read in the *Deseret News.* That the workmen got the best of pay; that they got beef, mutton, poultry, pork, butter, eggs, flour, clothes; everything of the best—d—n money! while the poor hearers, cursing in their heart the abominable lie which was to go forth to be read by the brethren and sisters all over the world, were fain to get enough bread and molasses, yet durst not speak for fear of it getting to the ears of rouges who live in luxury, and would denounce them as grumblers and apostates in embryo (H. C. Kimball, Brigham's first counselor, told them that they might be glad of bread and water to dip it in, but of course that would not be printed).

When the United States soldiers came to Utah, brother Brigham sold them wood to put up barracks, and he got the gold for it. Some the brethren went to put up the building, and his godship all but damned the poor fellows, who wanted to get the means to cover their shivering bodies from the cold and something to fill their hungry bellies with. One exceedingly bold fellow coolly replied, "We were only working up the stuff that you sold them." One of our poor neighbors, without bread, asked the loan of some wheat from a big man called Haighton, who let him have it on condition that he pay him nine bushels for the six which he borrowed of him. He was to require the loan of it a very short time—a few weeks at most, and if the wheat was not of first class he was to require more. If I wished to buy a cow, my employer having one to sell, I am allowed a bushel of wheat as two dollars. Well, suppose I want a cow, and ask, "What is the value of your cow?" Thirty-five dollars says my employer. I have, say twenty bushels of wheat in his hands. I say, "Let me have five dollars and the cow." "Stop a little," says my employer, "what is the price of wheat in the city? I believe it is worth 75 or 80 cents there. I will allow city prices, but no more." So I have to pay more than forty bushels of wheat for my 35 dollar cow; and that is Utah brotherly love.

A young man in Salt Lake City was offered $25 a month from a Gentile merchant, and being a very religious person went to Brigham to get counsel about it. Brigham said, "You may work for me; I am as able to give $25 a month as he." The young man worked for Brigham until he wished to go somewhere else, then went to Brigham Young for his money, who gave him an order for $15 a month, at which the man demurred and said, "You promised me $25." "You are mistaken, my dear brother; I only said I was as able as the Gentile to give $25 a month; I did not say I would give it." This is a very saint-like action, is it not?

The high authorities ordered us (it was required of me) to prepare to remove the U.S. soldiers as midnight assassins. In a Council in which Brigham was present, I was informed by one who was also present, that it was reported some of the brethren were not willing to go down and live in the cotton country, as they wished to stay where they were. Brigham said, "If they don't go, skin them, skin them." That is the way they enforce obedience.

Some of the old mothers of Israel are extremely anxious to get married, or by proxy, to likely men. One went to Kimball and asked him to marry her. She was not to his taste, of course, so he told her to be gone for an old hag. But should they be very importunate, the Lord reveals to the big men to counsel (that is to command) some very pious young man to be a husband and protect the old lady; and should he not feel content it is told him that Hosea the Prophet was ordered by the Lord to marry a worse.

One of your old acquaintances married a young man, and he, poor fellow, had an old lady imposed upon him in this way by the Bishop of Farmington. Joseph W. Young, Brigham's nephew, got a leather bed to take across the plains for a woman on condition that she would pay the freightage. It was sometime before she was in a condition to pay it; but when she called for it (we saw the woman there) the rascal denied he ever saw it. But I need not cite instances of the abominable dishonesty and trickery of the main part of those in power. I have mentioned a few that I can vouch for the truth of; but some others that I know of would fill many sheets, and harrow up the feelings of the most obtuse by their painful and shameful character. But it may be said that the bad actions of fallible men are no refutation of "the sublime doctrines of Mormonism." No, but what guarantee is there for the truth of its mysteries when we find that a prophet so called, who tells his followers that he is God, can enrich himself off the poor and honest laborer; make them believe that good and evil can change places because he says so; that it is good to milk the gentiles and to slay men if he command it; to be midnight assassins and plunderers; to tell lies in order to convert men to his faith. But such strong meat as he calls it is not to be given to those who are considered to have stomachs too weak to digest it.

When I see men in authority act as I have seen the authorities act in Utah, I am thrown back on reason, common sense, and the good old doctrines taught by the founder of Christianity—viz: Do as you would be done by;

> forgive your enemies and pray for them that persecute you; and love one another. I have tried the practice of "endowed" men by this touchstone and found them wanting. By their fruit shall ye know them; and the fruit is this. All those in authority are rich, have the best looking-wives, and largest farms; the poor are at the mercy of the rich, and dare not complain; men's wives are to be "consecrated," and they have no power to leave Zion; men are not permitted to discuss anything that the chiefs object to, and no one is sure that his wife is his own if she is worth the attention of some Brother in higher authority. Men are afraid that their neighbors should know anything about their discontent, lest they tell the teachers; and men's wives are spies on their husbands. At the tything office in Salt Lake City, when such varieties as beef, pork, etc., are brought there, there a crush by the poor workers on the public works like the crush at a theater when a great star is to appear—in fact, a complete mob—but the servants of the big men are served first, and if there is not more than they want, the poor workers have to go without. The poor are degraded, and look like as many beggars in front of an almshouse. These are some of the fruits of brotherly love as practiced in Utah.[27]

Prove the Devil: Miners and Missionaries Transform Utah

The complaints the "shrewd and honest" Scotchman lodged against theocracy reflected the widespread concern among British converts about the increasing autocracy of Mormon society during the Civil War. Brigham Young faced a difficult situation both religiously and politically. On 6 April 1860 the eldest surviving son of "Joseph the Martyr" accepted the leadership of a non-polygamous and humane version of what came to be known as the Reorganized Church of Jesus Christ of Latter Day Saints. Three years later, Joseph Smith III sent missionaries to Utah in response to over five hundred letters from the Great Basin "urging young Joseph to send missionaries there," the *True Latter Day Saints' Herald* reported. The "Josephites," as they were called in Utah, expected "overwhelming results, perhaps even the downfall of Brigham Young's organization." They had reason to be optimistic: the reborn religion's emissaries had converted entire Mormon congregations in the Midwest, and many old Saints were deeply sympathetic.[28] "I was present when Bro. Joseph the prophet blessed little Joseph,

[27] The author devoted the balance of the letter to "some pictures of the effects of polygamy as we saw it."
[28] Launius, in Powell, *Utah History Encyclopedia*, 459.

and the power of God was manifest so we could not keep still; and I was also present when he blessed David, and the power of God was manifested again so we could not keep still; and if little Joseph is the man to lead the church, let him come on," testified old stalwart Stephen Hezekiah Goddard, who came west with the Pioneer Company in 1847.[29] Such recollections presented a serious challenge to President Young, who had long ago promised to step aside when the founding prophet's son came of age, but who now argued that Joseph Smith III's rejection of polygamy disqualified him from becoming the Lord's anointed.

While the rest of the nation was bathed in blood, Mormons maintained a detached neutrality in the conflict over slavery, but this did not prevent their leaders from repeatedly predicting the destruction of the Union.[30] With the arrival of the California Volunteers in October 1862, Young had some 750 federal troops and three cannons overlooking the Salt Lake Valley under the command of his avowed enemy, Col. P. Edward Connor. The federal officers soon established the territory's first daily newspaper, the *Union Vedette*, a sentinel that was in no way beholden to local religious authorities. Convinced a mining boom was the key to attracting non-Mormons to Utah, the officers encouraged their soldiers to explore and unlock Utah's vast mineral wealth, which they did with growing success.

Meanwhile, Edmund C. Briggs and Mormon Battalion veteran Alexander McCord arrived in Salt Lake City on 7 August 1863, seeking converts to the Reorganized church. Five days later, Brigham Young and some thirty associates met with Briggs, and the men immediately locked horns. Briggs "was met with a torrent of abuse; and denounced as a liar, thief, murderer, imposter, and apostate." Briggs received the attack coolly. President Young told Briggs he would not find a place to preach or live in Utah if he could prevent it—and further, that he would "not be responsible for his life on the streets for a single hour." His landlady evicted him the next morning, but Briggs soldiered on.[31]

Brigham Young's response to this dual military and sectarian challenge was to ridicule the government and restate his long-standing policy against prospecting for precious metals. He forbade cooperation with anyone representing

---

[29]Smith and Smith, *The History of the Reorganized Church*, 3:369.

[30]Alexander, *Utah*, 141.

[31]"Letter from Fort Bridger," *True Latter-Day-Saints' Herald*, 4:10, 15 November 1863, 145.

Joseph Smith III and excommunicated, intimidated, and attacked all who defied him. One man who refused to back down was veteran loyalist Charles Wesley Wandell, formerly a clerk in the historian's office at Nauvoo, correspondent for George Q. Cannon's *Western Standard*, and a founder of the Australian Mission. This talented and troubled man persuaded former Cedar City bishop Philip Klingensmith to describe his role in the notorious Mountain Meadows massacre. The gruesome details in Klingensmith's 1871 confession and Wandell's dogged pursuit of the facts cracked the case, deadlocked for fourteen years, wide open. Wandell, while serving as one of the young prophet's missionaries in Sydney, Australia, sent Joseph Smith III this account of his troubles in Utah. Less than six months later, Wandell would be dead of heart disease. The Reorganites who laid him to rest sang a hymn he wrote, "Weep, Weep Not for Me, Zion."[32]

WANDELL TO JOSEPH SMITH III, 25 SEPTEMBER 1874,
STEBBINS PAPERS, COMMUNITY OF CHRIST LIBRARY-ARCHIVES.

When I broke with Brigham Young in Utah, in 1864, a conspiracy was started against me; and he being master of all possible situations in that country and with an overwhelming force to back him up, and I unaided and alone, he, of course, could do as he pleased. As an example of the cruel and wicked persecution I received from his people, I will state that in the early days of Pioche city, a mining town situated less than 50 miles from the Mountain Meadow, some of his creatures caused the report to be circulated through the Utah teamsters hauling produce to that place that I had been engaged in the Mountain Meadows massacre! And so assiduously and cunningly was this calumny circulated, and kept up with such persistency, that many of the citizens of Lincoln County, Nevada, to-day no doubt believe it to be true. I was in California and had not seen Utah when that massacre occurred. At the time this calumny was first circulated I was a County officer for Lincoln County, and finally to defend myself from this calumny I wrote the "Argus" letters published in the Corrine Reporter. But the conspiracy succeeded in hedging up my way to make a living, and Brigham Young had prophesied that I should be poor.

What other crimes this conspiracy has charged me with I do not know. . . . I will here state a fact of quiet significance; and that is, that in Utah up to the time in 1864, of my break with Brigham Young, no charge had ever been preferred against me affecting my moral or Christian character, and no charge of any kind except that of prospecting for the precious metals!

---

[32]Newton, *Hero or Traitor*, 63.

It should likewise be borne in mind, that, in 1864, when I sent my letter to Brigham Young resigning my membership in his church, he had no right to make a charge against my moral character, without giving me due notice of the same, and a fair trial thereon where I could meet my accusers face to face. During my residence in Utah from January 1858 to July 1866 I never received a notice either verbal or written of any charges against me whatever, nor of any trial to be had in any case affecting me in any way whatever. While returning from a prospecting trip in 1864 I was unofficially informed that the H.P. [High Priests] Quorum had disfellowshipped me for prospecting!

I am aware that in writing the "Argus" letters, in which I held Brigham Young responsible for the Mountain Meadows massacre and for all the blood-atonement assassinations in Utah, I committed an offense against him which he will never forgive; but I have many hundreds of acquaintances in Utah who know me well; and it is only just and fair play to ask them to judge of me by what they know of me, and not suffer Brigham Young to altogether overwhelm me with calumnies and to destroy me simply because he thinks he can.

C.W. Wandell.

Reorganized elders Briggs and McCord faced repeated harassment throughout their year in Utah Territory. Brigham Young spread "scandalous reports" against "Brother Joseph" (Joseph Smith III) and secretly directed his own followers "not to harbor us in any manner, only as beggars, and to treat us with silent contempt, but don't tell them that it is the counsel, and that it came from me," Briggs charged. He had "not been able as yet to procure a single hall, or commodious house to hold meetings in, in all this city, or Territory." The tactics used against anyone who displayed the slightest sympathy for his message often verged on comical.[33]

Briggs spent thirty-six hours with Thomas Squires in Ogden Valley, but Squires "did not commit himself for or against me." Weber County bishop Chauncey West soon notified Squires to appear on 30 October 1863 and answer a charge against him. At the hearing, according to Briggs's telling, West said he had heard "that there are those here who are leaning towards young Josephism, and they are harboring those who have come here to teach Josephism." They had a right to believe as they pleased, West said, but he did not "feel to fellowship them as brethren and sisters." The bishop then got to the point: "Do you acknowledge Brigham Young as the one to lead

[33] *True Latter Day Saints' Herald*, 1864, 5:172–73.

the church? Do you believe in the right of Brigham Young as the legal successor of Joseph, and the Prophet and President of the Church?"

"May I ask a question?" Squires responded meekly. "What charges are preferred against me?" West refused to answer: "I am your bishop," he said, "and it is your duty to answer me, and I do not want any argument about it." Squires considered the questions out of order and refused to answer them. Bishop West turned to John Lewis and John Green, other suspects on his list, and got the same response. "Do the brethren here harbor men who are bitter enemies and are laying a plot to overthrow this people?" Bishop West asked. "I want the brethren to know I am a Brighamite to the backbone, and I will abide by Brigham's *counsel*, and his *counsel* at conference was to cut off all who *harbored* these d—d scamps in their houses. Bro. Brigham said don't you *harbor* these *infernal scamps, don't harbor them,* and now brethren, what shall we do with these brethren? Make a motion." Someone in the audience suggested Squires deserved another chance to answer West's questions. Squires replied, "Has anyone ever heard me speak against Bro. Brigham? If they have, let them say it now; I have always said that he was the president of this people." West then called the vote and Squires was cut off, along with Lewis and Green.

Briggs's undoubtedly biased report on the "high handed oppression of Brighamism" included a denunciation of "the monopoly that exists in the hands of the few" and Mormon leaders whose "greediness for gold seems to have no bounds." He ended with a clarion call for Utah "to witness the joys of gospel blessings and that peace in the Holy Ghost as was enjoyed in the days of the first Joseph" and to reject "the deep feelings of regret, remorse, shame, and sorrow, that are felt by the innocent-hearted ones of this Territory, who have been beguiled into this heathenish, soul-destroying, murderous, blasphemy, *polygamy*!"[34]

The reference to polygamy explained much of the appeal of the Reorganization's message in Utah, where the practice was a cause of resentment, conflict, and bitterness. "Several wagons with families of 'Josephites,'" *The New York Times* reported in early May 1864, "are now pilgrims back across the wearisome plains, still with a faith of a haven desired. Having failed to find at Salt Lake the paradise they anticipated, they now turn their eyes to the State of Illinois, in hopes to find a happy land there under the new leadership of the son and namesake of the original Mormon prophet."[35] In April the

[34]Smith and Smith, *The History of the Reorganized Church*, 3:368–73

[35]"Affairs in Utah," *The New York Times*, 28 May 1864, 9.

movement had over a hundred members in Salt Lake, while the Utah mission totaled over three hundred. When the two missionaries left in August 1864, the Lord's work "in this territory is onward with rapid strides to the spiritual observer," Briggs reported. All three of Joseph Smith's surviving sons later worked in the territory, and Joseph Smith III visited in 1876, 1885, and 1889, preaching to packed houses. The 1880 census counted 820 members of the Reorganized church in Utah, "and this did not take into account the many people who were converted from Mormonism and then quickly left the state." By 1890 more than a thousand Utah Mormons looked to Joseph Smith III, not Wilford Woodruff, as their prophet, seer, and revelator.[36]

If the Lord Won't Come, the Law Will: The Transcontinental Railroad

The Civil War and Abraham Lincoln's skillful management of "the Mormon problem" accelerated the transformation of Utah from a theocracy to an American democracy. The changes that the conflict wrought in the remote territory put LDS leaders in a bind: throughout the war, Brigham Young had to balance on a political tightrope as he focused increasingly on economics rather than matters of faith. Seeking to establish the independence of the Mormon kingdom and convinced that the war would make Deseret the most powerful force in the American West, he wanted to build a self-sustaining local economy firmly under his personal control. Meanwhile, the war brought an economic boom to Utah, and both Mormons and unbelievers made fortunes in freighting, merchandizing, and speculation. Sermons in the new tabernacle regularly denounced profiteering, even while the church and its leaders profited mightily. Mormon authorities sought to set prices for crops such as wheat, often to their personal benefit, while the army's substantial (and costly) presence created a free market they bitterly resented. Young and his fellow prophets issued a long series of unfortunate predictions: perhaps the most embarrassing was Young's pronouncement at the end of conference on 9 April 1865 that the Civil War would drag on for four more years. Upon leaving the meeting, the congregation learned that the telegraph had reported the surrender of the Army of Northern Virginia at Appomattox that morning.[37] The deep sorrow that swept Salt Lake with

[36]Launius, in Powell, *Utah History Encyclopedia*, 459. See also Shipley, "Voices of Dissent."

[37]"The Doctors Disagree," *Union Vedette*, 12 April 1865, 2/1.

Lincoln's assassination showed how much most of Utah's people had come to appreciate the folksy and wise president.

The Pacific Railroad Act of 1862 raised both hopes and fears in Utah. The small minority of Gentiles believed the railroad and the prospect of opening up Utah's vast mineral wealth would attract a substantial population to the territory that would be independent of Mormon control. Brigham Young had called for building a railroad to Utah since at least 1852 but feared that the influx of cheap goods and agricultural products would disrupt the local economy. The growing number of dissenters hoped it would bring a new order: "Now we have a railroad across the plains and settlements every little way and civilization is coming to Zion," Aaron Dewitt told his sister. "If the Lord won't come the law will, and if Jesus is not approaching, justice is."[38] The arrival of the railroad produced dramatic results, yet no one's dreams or nightmares came true. But for some, the railroad offered an escape.

Liberty (Missouri) Weekly Tribune, 25 June 1869.
From the *Corinne (Utah) Daily Reporter*.

Since the commencement of the work of building the great Pacific Railway high hopes have been entertained and cherished by a large number of men and women in Utah, known as dissenters and apostates from Mormonism, as inculcated by Brigham Young, that on its completion an avenue of escape would be open for them and they could make their way, undisturbed by the hirelings and cut throats of Brigham Young, from Utah to the States. The dissenters and apostates, we are assured, are by no means few, and it is openly stated that all who can rid themselves of what little property they still possess, will flee the Territory and return to the States.

Yesterday a party of dissenters and apostates, numbering about forty souls, all families, under the leadership of Mr. Warren Walling, late President of the Josephite wing of the Mormon Church, in Salt Lake City, arrived at the [Corinne] depot, opposite the city, the greater portion of them coming from Malad Valley, and the balance from Salt Lake City and vicinity. They chartered a car from the company, for which they paid $1,400, and have provided themselves with all the necessaries required on the trip. They purpose settling in Nebraska, on the Missouri river, near Omaha. From personal acquaintance with Mr. Walling and several others of the party, we can safely say they will make good, honest and industrious citizens of Nebraska, albeit they strongly adhere to their peculiar religion. This, we believe, is the first party of discontented Mormons taking their departure from Utah who go all the way by rail.

---

[38]Simmonds, "Aaron Dewitt." In 1875 Dewitt noted, "all who want can leave. But now the priests want us to go, and we wish to stay."

A Man May Be Honest Even in Hell: The Godbeites

Commerce was always one of Brigham Young's favorite subjects. The combative prophet often justified his draconian economic policies as a way to save the poor, whom he divided into three classes: "the Lord's poor, the devil's poor, and poor devils." Young made no secret of the broad mandate that he believed came with his high office: "You may say it is hard that I should dictate you in your temporal affairs. Is it not my privilege to dictate you?" he asked. "Is it not my privilege to give this people counsel to direct them so that their labors will build up the Kingdom of God instead of the kingdom of the devil?" Young admitted he knew many who felt it was none of his business where they traded, and he promised they would "never enter the celestial Kingdom of our Father and God." As Latter-day Saints, of course, they had the privilege "to do as you please. Just please yourselves; but when you do so, will you please bear the results and not whine over them."[39] The results, especially as the railroad drew closer and Young sought to impose control over every aspect of his followers' lives, were not pleasant.

For Brigham Young, cutting wages across the board was the place to start, wrote historian Harold Schindler. Young proposed reducing a laborer's pay to a dollar a day and sought to cut the four dollars that mechanics, masons, carpenters, and painters could make for a day's work to $1.50. The *Deseret News* "threatened to bring Chinese labor to Utah if 'working men did not come to terms.'" The proposal would affect life in Zion for decades, Schindler observed, for "it stirred the bold opposition of some of the most able and brilliant men in the community life of Utah."[40] The most prominent were British converts who shared an interest in spiritualism, including businessmen William S. Godbe and Elias L. T. Harrison and journalists Edward Tullidge and Henry W. Lawrence, Eli B. Kelsey, and T. B. H. and Fanny Stenhouse. Successful professionals and intellectuals, all had done valiant work in the service of their religion.

In October 1869 Harrison and Godbe published an appeal to the people and protest in their *Utah Magazine*, a forerunner of the *Salt Lake Tribune*, expressing their right to think, speak, and act, while agreeing to abide by the ecclesiastical law. The article, apparently the work of E. L. T. Harrison, soon appeared in the RLDS church's newspaper.

---

[39] 16 June 1867, *Journal of Discourses*, 12:57, 59.

[40] Schindler, "Hard Times Ahead," *Salt Lake Tribune*, 24 September 1995, B1.

"An Appeal to the People," *The Saints' Herald*, 1 December 1869, 16:338–40.

Since the date of writing my last editorial, a startling change has taken place in my situation, although not in my feelings or sentiments towards the members of our Church. For writing such articles as "Our Workmen's Wages," "The True Development of the Territory," "Steadying the Ark," etc., a charge has been preferred against me of apostacy, on the ground that I have no right to publicly discuss the wisdom of any measure or policy of the Priesthood and expect to retain a membership in the Church at the same time. For asserting my belief that the Gospel gives me the freedom to differ with the leaders of the church, and the privilege of stating my difference of opinion, provided I do it honestly and respectfully, I have been deprived of my membership in the Church—the doctrine being positively laid down on the occasion of my trial by President Brigham Young and Elder George Q. Cannon, that "*it is apostacy to honestly differ with the Priesthood in any of their measures.*"

If this definition of apostacy be correct, of course, I am an apostate, because it is true I do not see eye to eye with our ecclesiastical leaders on the subject of the reduction of our workmen's wages, the mineral development of the Territory, and similar matters.

I wish to give, in a brief way, a statement of the circumstances attending my expulsion, and the reasons by which I have been guided in the course I have taken, so that all my friends may judge for themselves. In doing this, I shall have to omit most of the preliminaries connected with the case, inasmuch as they occurred at the "School of the Prophets." Suffice it to say that, on Saturday, 16th October, an announcement that we had been violently denounced by President Young reached our ears, and the following Saturday we were publicly cited to appear before the High Council and "be tried for our standing."

On Monday we appeared before the High Council at the City Hall, which was densely packed with the authorities of the Church—no ordinary members, except those who appeared as witnesses, or were specially invited, being allowed to be present. The following is a brief synopsis of the trial, from minutes made on the spot.

After the charge of Apostacy had been preferred by Elder George Q. Cannon, on the ground of articles in the *Magazine* containing views on financial questions differing with those of the President, as well as on account of an expressed belief that members of the Church held not only a right to think but to express their ideas on such subjects, the question was put to Elder Cannon whether "it was apostacy to differ honestly with the measures of the President," to which he replied,—"It is apostacy to differ honestly with the measures of the President. A man may be honest even in hell." This idea President Wells confirmed by remarking that we "might as well ask the question whether a man had the right to differ honestly with the Almighty." Thus the doctrine was unqualifiedly asserted that the Almighty and the Priesthood, so far as its official dictates were concerned, were to be accepted as one and the same thing, on pain of excommunication from the Church.

William S. Godbe stated that his claim to conscientiously differ with the views of the leaders of the Church on certain questions, could not be apostacy, inasmuch as he had always believed that such were his rights. While he bore testimony to the divine mission of Joseph Smith, and to the appointment of Brigham Young as his successor in the Presidency of the Church, he denied his right to enforce unquestioning obedience upon all subjects secular and spiritual from its members. He believed the preservation of our unity was worth any price short of the concession of the right of thought and speech or any other true principle. That price he was not willing to pay even for unity. He claimed that he entertained none but the kindest feelings towards the Presidency and Priesthood severally, and trusted, however much they might object to his views, that they would at least concede to him honesty and purity of purpose.

E. L. T. Harrison then stated that if it was apostacy to differ conscientiously with the Priesthood of the Church, he must be considered an apostate, for he certainly did differ with them on some matters. The point upon which he most particularly differed, was their right to expel people from the Church because of a difference of opinion on matters of Church policy. He admitted that they had a right to demand of him implicit obedience to every gospel ordinance, as well as to every condition of a pure life. All that he claimed as his right was respectfully and temperately to discuss any difference of opinion he might entertain, without being cut off from the Church for so doing. . . .

It had been argued that we must passively and uninquiringly obey the Priesthood, because otherwise we could not build up Zion. He [Harrison] could not see this. A nation built up on such a principle could be no Zion. The only glory or beauty there could be in a Zion must result from its being composed of people all of whom acted intelligently in all their operations. Fifty thousand people acting in concert, building up excellent cities or doing anything else well, but doing it mechanically, because they were told, was no sight to be admired. A dozen persons, not operating half as perfectly as to the nature of their work, but doing what little they did intelligently, must be a far more delightful exhibition to God and intelligences.

These were his views. If they constituted apostacy, the Council must deal with him according to their laws. One thing, however, they could not do. They might cut him off from his brethren, but they should never cut his brethren off from his affections. He had been twenty years a member of this Church, and he intended to live and die with them, and no one should ever drive him from their midst. . . .

Typically, the church's First Presidency saw any action but unquestioned obedience as a threat to the faith's unity and safety. "I only want to cut their throats!" said George A. Smith in response to Godbe and Harrison. "Latter-day Saints do not fellowship a man who draws the sword to destroy them; do not fellowship a man who invites all hell to come here and cut our throats."[41] The authorities excommunicated the dissenters. In November 1869 Harrison and Godbe issued a manifesto proclaiming the Church of Zion, which became known as the Godbeites. The contributions of this "New Movement" included the creation of the Liberal Party, which contested elections with official LDS candidates, the liberalization of the church's ban on mining, founding the *Mormon Tribune,* which eventually became the *Salt Lake Tribune,* and raising the question of the role of individual conscience in Mormon life. For faithful Latter-day Saints, "the Godbeite revolt remains compelling because of its complexity and because many of its opposing ideals and contrasting virtues remain dilemmas to the present time."[42]

Dimensions of Disillusion in Deseret

From the time he assumed the "mantle of the prophet," Brigham Young was a divisive figure among the followers of Joseph Smith. Without a revelation, many apostles doubted that his position as president of the Quorum of the Twelve justified making him prophet, seer, and revelator in 1847. Others felt his devotion to the doctrine of plurality carried on a mistake that had helped make Joseph Smith a martyr and was now best buried and forgotten. Many simply did not like the man and preferred to follow less capable but perhaps more charismatic figures, such as James Strang, Lyman Wight, Alpheus Cutler, and William Smith, each of whom led LDS splinter groups. No one, however, questioned Young's commitment to Joseph Smith's revolutionary theology or to building the Kingdom of God. Again and again, Young would go to any lengths to carry on "the works of Joseph," causing consternation even among those who appreciated his competence and admired his forceful personality.

During the height of their power in the American West, the highest Mormon authorities openly admitted they had difficulty retaining their people's loyalty. "How many of the brethren that are brought here by the

[41]Arrington, *Brigham Young,* 359.
[42]Walker, *Wayward Saints,* 370.

Perpetual Emigrating Fund from England and other countries will keep the faith, and stay with the people of God, and do right?" Jedediah Grant asked in 1854. "I am afraid not more than half."[43] John Young, Brigham Young's older brother, testified in October 1857, "if there should one-half of the people apostatize and go away, the other half are pretty sure to stand. I heard brother Brigham say that, if there are not more than fifty that keep the faith and are united, the kingdom will be sure to stand."[44] God would never fail the Mormon people, Heber C. Kimball promised, but "we expect that many will apostatize, pitch over the dam, and go to wreck."[45]

Estimating the extent and nature of dissent in Utah Territory is a perilous task. With nothing more than anecdotal evidence—even the vast amount of available anecdotal evidence—calculating where the loyalties of Utah's population lay at any particular time is problematic. It is tempting to fall back on the generalization that historians of the American Revolution often use to gauge public sentiment: about one-third were rebels, about one-third were loyalists, and about a third did not care.

The research and analysis of Samuel A. Smith, an insightful and diligent young scholar, has replaced such idle speculation with hard data. While examining the 1880 federal census for Utah, "an extraordinarily comprehensive but little-analyzed record of the territory's population at a key point in Utah's adjustment to the end of isolation," Smith noticed marginal notations in the manuscript census schedules identifying an individual's religious sympathies. Smith discovered "Mormons in mining towns, non-Mormons in Mormon farm villages, and intricate mixtures of the two populations in Salt Lake and other cities," making it difficult to define rigid boundaries between Mormon and Gentile communities, especially when factoring in Utah's "increasing numbers of former Mormons—some in breakaway groups, others simply no longer active in Mormon religious life."[46]

Smith's analysis of the 142,745 Utah residents listed in the 1880 census found that 117,623, or 82.4 percent, were Mormons, while Gentiles numbered more than 14,000, almost 10 percent of the population. The *Deseret News* reported in 1882 that 120,283 of Utah's 143,963 residents, or 83.5 percent, were Mormons. The census identified 9,186 apostates, while the *Deseret News* counted

[43] 2 April 1854, *Journal of Discourses*, 2:148.

[44] 25 October 1857, *Journal of Discourses*, 5:370.

[45] 6 April 1857, *Journal of Discourses*, 5:19.

[46] Smith, "The Wasp in the Beehive," 6, 27.

6,988 "Apostates," 820 "Josephites," and 1,716 "Doubtfuls." The census data revealed that the "non-Mormon presence in Utah was extensive and diverse," with mining camps and railroad towns representing only one facet of the forces transforming the territory. The "large apostate population, distributed even more broadly across Utah's cities and towns," reflected that Utah now encompassed "a broadly defined continuum of transforming religious belief, political loyalty, and economic function." The census notations were often not legible or entirely unambiguous, and the vast majority identified as Mormon certainly represented a wide spectrum of belief and indifference, but these numbers provide a statistical snapshot of dissent in Mormon country.[47]

Nothing better supports Smith's analysis or illuminates the dynamics of dissent during Utah's last years as a theocratic territory than the story of "Monkey Town" at Monroe, "The Little Green Valley" in central Utah's Sevier County. Founded in 1871, the Mormon village was ripped apart three years later by Brigham Young's implementation of the United Order, a sweeping communal economic plan that proved to be one of the most disastrous policies of the prophet's entire career. This communalistic movement, also known as the Order of Enoch, followed the cooperative movement of the 1860s, which established church stores in every ward in the territory and let co-op members buy collectively and share the profits. The order proved far more radical, demanding, and divisive. When Monroe's intellectually curious religious leaders and cooperative managers, who had read Darwin, declined to join the order, the prophet's eldest son sacked them. The dissidents bought land south of town and created a separatist community. A local bard "wrote a batch of satirical verses about the descendants of monkeys living out there in Monkey Town, and the name attached itself to the region," sociologist Karl Sandberg wrote in a memoir of his hometown, which remained divided into "the Church culture and the Pool Hall culture." Monkey Town endures as "a monument to the Culture Wars of the 1870s, a tombstone of the original divisions in the town."[48]

Dissent in the Mormon Tradition

Many devout Mormon converts found Brigham Young's implementation of the Kingdom of God disillusioning and turned their backs on religion

[47]Ibid, 32, 43–44, 78; "The Mormon Problem," *Deseret News*, 6 September 1882, 6/2–4.

[48]Sandberg, "Getting Up a History of Monroe," 39–41, 43.

in general. "I have come to the conclusion that all religious denominations are the cogitations, surmisings and imaginations of the human mind, got up in a great many cases to give men power over their fellows for wealth, influence and power," John Duncan wrote in his memoirs. But when the old Scot died peacefully at his home in Heber City in June 1910, the local paper reported, "Mr. Duncan left the church a number of years ago, but during his separation as at all other times, he always bore his testimony that Joseph Smith was a prophet of God." Forty-four days before his death, Duncan was restored to the priesthood as a high priest. Apostle Francis W. Lyman asked that his passing "might be peaceful as the slumber of a little child." This prayer, the paper believed, was "fully answered in the painless death of Mr. Duncan."[49]

John Duncan's story will sound familiar to readers of the narratives collected in this volume, which testify to the range of experiences that both inspired and disheartened those who joined Joseph Smith's dynamic new religious movement. They merit respect and serious consideration. Yet as Roger Launius, one of the most perceptive writers on Mormonism's complicated past, observed:

> Dissent in the Mormon tradition has developed overwhelmingly negative connotations in our digested past. Always dissenters have been characterized in our history as misbegotten, woeful malcontents whose arguments were without foundation. Dissenters, because of flaws in their characters, were threats to the integrity of the gospel and deserving of expulsion. The institution was always judged to be sound, the dissenters themselves were defective. While this perspective has served as a defense mechanism for the various institutions of Mormondom from the beginning to the present, it is a deeply dangerous group attitude and must be altered in the institution's perception of its past.[50]

Mormon historical discourse needs a vocabulary of dissent that is more precise and equitable than simply branding people "apostates," whether the church excommunicates them or they simply leave. Apostate is a pejorative, used to marginalize and diminish those whose experiences lead them to part ways with the Mormon faith. The texts in this volume defy any such shallow dismissal. They range from straight-up apostates such as Ann Gordge, who wrote bitter attacks on the church, to the disaffected and "backouts" who simply gave up and left quietly, to reformers such as the Morrisites,

[49] Duncan, Autobiography, 30 May 1902; and "John Duncan Dead," *Wasatch Wave*, 10 June 1910, 2/2.
[50] Launius, "Mormon Memory," 22–23.

Josephites, or the Godbeites who tried to recreate an earlier and more innocent religion, to loyal dissenters such as George A. Hicks, and finally to the men and women like Brigham Young Hampton, who sacrificed so much for polygamy and loyally put their church's interests above their own but felt abandoned as the religion adapted and changed. The "apostate" epithet is best reserved for anti-church militants who lost faith, became embittered, and then preached or wrote hostile indictments of their former faith. Rather than becoming militant anti-Mormons, most became disaffected as a reaction to the policies of church leaders or the effects of their actions. Since the faith's highest authorities preached violence and covered up its consequences, many of them feared for their lives. Yet the range of experience of those who abandoned the Saints include those who never lost their love for the Mormon people or a longing for the ideal society they dreamed of building.

Historians should appreciate the moving narratives of forsaken faith so often chronicled in Mormon documents and value the range of adventures, beliefs, opinions, complaints, hopes, and fears expressed in these life histories. The stories they tell speak for themselves and should not be dismissed merely as the disgruntled complaints of traitors and turncoats. They should be taken on their own terms, whether they be wild fantasies or painfully accurate chronicles of deeply personal journeys. Such narratives can help historians of every persuasion create a more accurate, honest, entertaining, and ultimately humane interpretation of the Mormon experience.

Bibliography

Books and Pamphlets

Ahmanson, John. *Secret History: An Eyewitness Account of the Rise of Mormonism.* Translated by Gleason L. Archer. Chicago: Fieldstead Institute, 1984.

Aird, Polly. *Mormon Convert, Mormon Defector: A Scottish Immigrant in the American West, 1848–1861.* Norman, Okla: Arthur H. Clark Company, 2009.

Alder, Douglas, and Karl F. Brooks. *A History of Washington County: From Isolation to Destination.* S.L.C: Utah State Hist. Soc., 1996.

Aleshire, Peter. *The Fox and the Whirlwind: General Crook and Geronimo, A Paired Biography.* New York: John Wiley and Sons, 2000.

Alexander, Thomas G. *Mormonism in Transition: A History of the Latter-day Saints, 1890–1930.* Urbana: Univ. of Illinois Press, 1986.

———. *Things in Heaven and Earth: The Life and Times of Wilford Woodruff, a Mormon Prophet.* S.L.C: Signature Books, 1991.

———. *Utah: The Right Place.* S.L.C: Gibbs Smith, 1995. Revised and updated edition, 2003.

Alexander, Thomas G., and James B. Allen. *Mormons and Gentiles: A History of Salt Lake City.* Boulder, Colo: Pruett Publishing, 1984.

Allen, James B., and Glen M. Leonard. *The Story of the Latter-day Saints.* S.L.C: Deseret Book Company, 1992.

Allred, LaNora P. *Spanish Fork: City on the Rio de Aguas Calientes.* Spanish Fork, Utah: J-Mart Publishing Co., 1981.

Alter, J. Cecil. *Early Utah Journalism.* S.L.C: Utah State Hist. Soc., 1938.

Anderson, C. LeRoy. *Joseph Morris and the Saga of the Morrisites.* Logan: Utah State Univ. Press, 1988; "revisited," 2010.

Aquila, Richard, ed. *Wanted Dead or Alive: The American West in Popular Culture.* Urbana: Univ. of Illinois Press, 1996.

Arrington, Leonard J. *Brigham Young: American Moses.* New York: Alfred A. Knopf, 1985.

———. *Great Basin Kingdom: Economic History of the Latter-day Saints 1830–1900.* Cambridge: Harvard Univ. Press, 1958. Reprint, Lincoln: Univ. of Nebraska Press, 1958. New edition, Urbana: Univ. of Illinois Press, 2005.

———. *History of Idaho.* 2 vols. Moscow: Univ. of Idaho Press, 1994.

Arrington, Leonard J., and Davis Bitton. *The Mormon Experience: A History of the Latter-day Saints.* New York: Alfred A. Knopf, 1979. Second edition, Urbana: Univ. of Illinois Press, 1992.

Ashton, Clifford L. *The Federal Judiciary in Utah.* S.L.C: Utah Bar Foundation, 1988.

Backus, Anna Jean. *Mountain Meadows Witness: The Life and Times of Bishop Philip Klingensmith.* Spokane, Wash: Arthur H. Clark Company, 1995.

Bagley, Will. *Blood of the Prophets: Brigham Young and the Massacre at Mountain Meadows.* Norman: Univ. of Oklahoma Press, 2002.

———. *Frontiersman: Abner Blackburn's Narrative.* S.L.C: Univ. of Utah Press, 1992.

Bagley, Will, ed. *The Pioneer Camp of the Saints: The 1846 and 1847 Mormon Trail Journals of Thomas Bullock.* Spokane, Wash: The Arthur H. Clark Company, 1997.

Bain, David Haward. *Empire Express: Building the First Transcontinental Railroad.* New York: Penguin, 1999.

Bancroft, Hubert Howe. *History of Utah, 1540-1886.* San Francisco: The History Company, 1889.

Bangerter, Howard K., and Cory W. Bangerter. *Tragedy and Triumph: Your Guide to the Rescue of the 1856 Willie and Martin Handcart Companies.* Provo: McPrinting, 2004.

Barney, Ronald O. *One Side by Himself: The Life and Times of Lewis Barney, 1808–1894.* Logan: Utah State Univ. Press, 2001.

Baskin, R.N. *Reminiscences of Early Utah.* S.L.C: Tribune-Reporter Printing Company, 1914.

Beadle, J.H. *Life in Utah; Or, the Mysteries and Crimes of Mormonism.* Philadelphia: National Publishing Co., 1870.

Beadle, John Hanson, with Ovando Hollister and Murat Halstead. *Polygamy: Or, the Mysteries and Crimes of Mormonism.* Philadelphia: National Publishing Co., 1904.

Beattie, George William, and Helen Pruitt Beattie. *Heritage of the Valley: San Bernardino's First Century.* Oakland: Biobooks, 1951.

Bennett, John C. *The History of the Saints: or, An expose of Joe Smith and Mormonism.* Boston: Leland & Whiting; New York: Bradbury, Soden, & Co., 1842.

Bennett, Richard E. *Mormons at the Missouri, 1846–1852: "And Should We Die . . . ,"* Norman: Univ. of Oklahoma Press, 1987.

Bigler, David L. *Forgotten Kingdom: The Mormon Theocracy in the American West, 1847–1896.* Spokane, Wash: Arthur H. Clark Company, 1998.

———. *Fort Limhi: The Mormon Adventure in Oregon Territory, 1855–1858.* Spokane, Wash: Arthur H. Clark Company, 2003.

Bigler, David L., and Will Bagley, eds. *Army of Israel: Mormon Battalion Narratives.* Spokane, Wash: Arthur H. Clark Company, 2000.

———, eds. *Innocent Blood: Essential Narratives of the Mountain Meadows Massacre.* Norman, Okla: Arthur H. Clark Company, 2008.

———. *The Mormon Rebellion: American's First Civil War, 1857–1858.* Norman: Univ. of Oklahoma, 2011.

Bingham, Norman F., Lillian B. Belnap, and Lester S. Scoville, eds. *Sketch of the Life of Erastus Bingham and Family, Utah Pioneers of 1847.* Ogden, Utah: Intermountain Publishing Company, 1953.

Bishop, William, ed. *Mormonism Unveiled; Or, The Life and Confessions of the Late Mormon Bishop, John D. Lee*. St. Louis: Bryan, Brand & Co., 1877.

Bitton, Davis. *Historical Dictionary of Mormonism*. Second edition. Lanham, Md: Scarecrow Press, 2000.

Blackmar, Frank W., ed. *Kansas: A Cyclopedia of State History, Embracing Events, Institutions, Industries, Counties, Cities, Towns, Prominent Persons, Etc.* 3 vols. in 4. Chicago: Standard Pub. Co., 1912.

Bliss, Jonathan. *Merchants and Miners in Utah: The Walker Brothers and their Bank*. S.L.C: Western Epics, 1983.

Bowen, James Loren. *The Red Rider: Or, the White Queen of the Apaches: A Story of Wild Adventure*. New York: Beadle and Adams, 1877.

Bradley, Martha Sonntag. *A History of Beaver County*. Beaver, Utah: Beaver County Commission, 1999.

Brimley, Bliss J. *Book of Thomas Job*. Pleasant Grove, Utah: B. J. Brimley, 1988.

Brodie, Fawn. *No Man Knows My History: The Life of Joseph Smith the Mormon Prophet*. New York: Alfred A. Knopf, 1945. Second edition, 1973.

Brooks, Juanita. *Emma Lee*. Logan: Utah State Univ. Press, 1975. Second edition, 1984.

———. *John Doyle Lee: Zealot, Pioneer Builder, Scapegoat*. Glendale, Calif: Arthur H. Clark Company, 1961. Reprint, S.L.C: Howe Brothers, 1982. Logan: Utah State Univ. Press, 1992.

———, ed. *Journal of the Southern Indian Mission: Diary of Thomas D. Brown*. Logan: Utah State Univ. Press, 1972.

———. *Mountain Meadows Massacre*. Stanford: Stanford Univ. Press, 1950. Reprint, Norman: Univ. of Oklahoma Press, 1962 and 1991.

———, ed. *On the Mormon Frontier: The Diary of Hosea Stout*. 2 vols. S.L.C: Univ. of Utah Press, 1964.

———, ed. *Not by Bread Alone: The Journal of Martha Spence Heywood, 1850–1856*. S.L.C: Utah State Hist. Soc., 1978.

Brown, J. Robert. *Journal of a Trip across the Plains of the U.S. from Missouri to California in the Year 1856, Giving a Correct View of the Country, Anecdotes, Indian Stories, Mountaineers' Tales, Etc.* Columbus: For the Author, 1860.

Buerger, David John. *The Mysteries of Godliness: A History of Mormon Temple Worship*. San Francisco: Smith Research Associates, 1994; S.L.C: Signature Books, 1994.

Burlingame, Merrill G., and K. Ross Toole. *A History of Montana*. 3 vols. New York: Lewis Hist. Pub. Co., 1957.

Bushman, Claudia L., ed. *Mormon Sisters: Women in Early Utah*. Logan: Utah State Univ., 1997.

Bushman, Richard L. *Joseph Smith, Rough Stone Rolling: A Cultural Biography of Mormonism's Founder*. New York: Alfred A. Knopf, 2005.

Calloway, Colin G. *One Vast Winter Count: The Native American West before Lewis and Clark*. Lincoln: Univ. of Nebraska Press, 2003.

Carleton, J. H. *Mountain Meadows Massacre*. Spokane, Wash: Arthur H. Clark Company, 1995.

Carter, Kate B., ed. *Our Pioneer Heritage*. 20 vols. S.L.C: Daughters of Utah Pioneers, 1958–1977.

———, ed. *Heart Throbs of the West*. 12 vols. S.L.C: Daughters of Utah Pioneers, 1939–1951.

Cheney, Thomas E. *Mormon Songs from the Rocky Mountains*. Austin: Univ. of Texas Press, 1968.

Cheney, Thomas E., with Austin E. Fife and Juanita Brooks, eds. *Lore of Faith and Folly.* S.L.C: Univ. of Utah, 1971.

Chittenden, Hiram, and A. T. Richardson, eds. *Life, Letters and Travels of Father Pierre-Jean de Smet, S.J., 1801–1873. Missionary labors and adventures among the wild tribes of the North American Indians.* 4 vols. New York: F. P. Harper, 1905. Reprint, New York: Kraus Reprint Co., 1969.

Clark, D. W. *Travel and Adventure.* Ohio: Swormstedt and Poe, 1856.

Cleland, Robert Glass, and Juanita Brooks, eds. *A Mormon Chronicle: The Diaries of John D. Lee.* 2 vols. San Marino: The Huntington Library, 1955. Reprint with preface and introduction by Everett L. Cooley, S.L.C: Univ. of Utah Press, 1983.

Clemens, Samuel. *Mark Twain's Letters: Volume 1, 1853–1866.* 5 vols. Ed. by Edgar Marquess Branch, Michael B. Frank, and Kenneth M. Sanderson. Berkeley: Univ. of California Press, 1987.

Collier, Fred C., comp. *The Teachings of President Brigham Young, Vol. 3, 1852–1854,* S.L.C: Collier's Publishing Co., 1987.

Compton, Todd. *In Sacred Loneliness: The Plural Wives of Joseph Smith.* S.L.C: Signature Books, 2001.

Convis, Charles L., and Charles L. Convis, Jr. *Outlaw Tales of Nevada: True Stories of Nevada's Most Famous Robbers, Rustlers, and Bandits,* Guilford, Conn: Globe Pequot, 2006.

Cook, Lyndon W. *William Law.* Provo: Grandin Book Co., 1994.

———. *Nauvoo Marriages, Proxy Sealings, 1843–1846.* Provo: Grandin Book Co., 2004.

Cooley, Everett L., ed. *Diary of Brigham Young, 1857.* S.L.C: Tanner Trust Fund, Univ. of Utah Library, 1980.

Corrill, John. *A Brief History of the Church of Christ of Latter Day Saints, (Commonly Called Mormons;) Including an Account of Their Doctrine and Discipline; With the Reasons of the Author for Leaving the Church.* St. Louis: The author, 1839.

Coward, John M. *The Newspaper Indian: Native American Identity in the Press, 1820–90.* Urbana: Univ. of Illinois Press, 1999.

Cowdery, Oliver. *Defence in a Rehearsal of My Grounds for Separating Myself from the Latter Day Saints.* Norton, Ohio: Pressley's Job Office, 1839.

Cox, J. Randolph. *The Dime Novel Companion.* Westport, Conn: Greenwood Press, 2000.

Cronon, William, George Miles, and Jay Gitlin, eds. *Under an Open Sky: Rethinking America's Western Past.* New York: W. W. Norton, 1992.

Daynes, Kathryn M. *More Wives Than One: Transformation of the Mormon Marriage System, 1840–1910.* Urbana: Univ. of Illinois Press, 2001.

Debo, Angie. *Geronimo: The Man, His Time, His Place.* Norman: Univ. of Oklahoma Press, 1976.

Demos, John. *The Unredeemed Captive: A Family Story from Early America.* New York: Alfred A. Knopf, 1994.

Denton, Sally. *American Massacre: The Tragedy of Mountain Meadows, September 1857.* New York: Alfred A. Knopf, 2003.

Derry, Charles. "Autobiography of Elder Charles Derry." *Journal of History* 1:3–4 (July, October 1908): 259–91; 423–45. Reprinted as *Autobiography of Elder Charles Derry: The Apostle of Purity.* Independence, Mo: Price Publishing Company, 1997.

Derounian-Stodola, Kathryn Zabelle, and James Arthur Levernier. *The Indian Captivity Narrative, 1550–1900.* New York: Twayne Publishers, 1993.

Deseret News 1989–1990 Church Almanac. S.L.C: Deseret News, 1989.

Directory of Los Angeles, 1873. Los Angeles: King & Stratton, 1873.

Doctrine and Covenants of The Church of Jesus Christ of Latter-day Saints (D&C). S.L.C: Church of Jesus Christ of Latter-day Saints, 1988.

Ebersole, Gary L. *Captured by Texts: Puritan to Postmodern Images of Indian Captivity.* Charlottesville: Univ. Press of Virginia, 1995.

Ehat, Andrew F., and Lyndon W. Cook, eds. *The Words of Joseph Smith: The Contemporary Accounts of the Nauvoo Discourses of the Prophet Joseph.* Orem, Utah: Grandin Book Company, 1991.

Ekins, Roger, ed. *Defending Zion: George Q. Cannon and the California Mormon Newspaper Wars of 1856–1857.* Spokane, Wash: Arthur H. Clark Company, 2002.

Esshom, Frank. *Pioneers and Prominent Men of Utah.* S.L.C: Utah Pioneers Book Publishing Co., 1913.

Euler, Robert C., and Henry F. Dobyns. *The Hopi People.* Phoenix: Indian Tribal Series, 1971.

Faulring, Scott H., ed. *An American Prophet's Record: The Diaries and Journals of Joseph Smith.* S.L.C: Signature Books, 1989.

Fielding, Robert Kent. *The Unsolicited Chronicler: An Account of the Gunnison Massacre, Its Causes and Consequences, Utah Territory, 1847–1859.* Brookline, Mass: Paradigm Publications, 1993.

Fife, Alta, ed. *Exploring Western Americana.* Ann Arbor, Mich: U.M.I. Research Press, 1988.

Fife, Austin E., and Alta Fife. *Saints of Sage and Saddle: Folklore Among the Mormons.* Bloomington: Indiana Univ. Press, 1956.

Fire Insurance Map of Salt Lake City, 1898. New York: Sanborn-Perris Map Company, 1898.

Firmage, Edwin Brown, and Richard Collin Mangrum. *Zion in the Courts: A Legal History of the Church of Jesus Christ of Latter-day Saints, 1830–1900.* Urbana: Univ. of Illinois Press, 1988.

Flanders, Robert Bruce. *Nauvoo, Kingdom on the Mississippi.* Urbana: Univ. of Illinois Press, 1975.

Freeman, Judith. *Red Water.* New York: Pantheon, 2002.

Furniss, Norman F. *The Mormon Conflict, 1850–1859.* New Haven: Yale Univ. Press, 1960.

Geary, Rick. *The Saga of the Bloody Benders.* New York: ComicsLit: 2007.

Gibbon, Edward. *The History of the Decline and Fall of the Roman Empire.* London: W. Strahan and T. Cadell, 1782–1788. Revised edition, Philadelphia: Porter & Coates, 1845.

Gilmore, Leigh. *The Limits of Autobiography: Trauma and Testimony.* Ithaca: Cornell Univ. Press, 2001.

Givens, Terryl L. *The Viper on the Hearth: Mormons, Myths, and the Construction of Heresy.* New York: Oxford Univ. Press, 1997.

Gordon, Sarah Barringer. *The Mormon Question: Polygamy and Constitutional Conflict in Nineteenth Century America.* Chapel Hill: Univ. of North Carolina Press, 2002.

Gottfredson, Peter. *Indian Depredations in Utah.* 1919. Reprint, Tucson: Fenestra Books, 2002.

Green, Nelson Winch, ed. *Fifteen Years Among the Mormons: Being the Narrative of Mrs. Ettie V. Smith* [Mary E. Coray]. New York: H. Dayton, 1858, 1860.

Grimmett, Gerald. *The Ferry Woman: A Novel of the Mountain Meadows Massacre.* St. George, Utah: Cold Hill Press, 2004.

Hafen, LeRoy R., and Ann W. Hafen. *Handcarts to Zion: The Story of a Unique Western Migration, 1856–1860.* Lincoln: Univ. of Nebraska Press, 1960.

———. *Journals of Forty-Niners: Salt Lake to Los Angeles.* Lincoln: Univ. of Nebraska Press, 1998.

Hafen, Mary Ann. *Recollections of a Handcart Pioneer of 1860: A Woman's Life on the Mormon Frontier.* Lincoln: Univ. of Nebraska Press, 1983.

Haley, James L. *Apaches: A History and Culture Portrait.* Garden City, N.J: Doubleday and Co., 1981.

Hallwas, John E., and Roger D. Launius. *Cultures in Conflict: A Documentary History of the Mormon War in Illinois.* Logan: Utah State Univ. Press, 1995.

Hardy, Allison. *Kate Bender, The Kansas Murderess: The Horrible History of an Arch Killer.* Girard, Kans: Haldeman-Julius Publications, 1944.

Hardy, B. Carmon, ed. *Doing the Works of Abraham: Mormon Polygamy, Its Origin, Practice, and Demise.* Norman, Okla: Arthur H. Clark Company, 2007.

———. *Solemn Covenant: The Mormon Polygamous Passage.* Urbana: Univ. of Illinois Press, 1992.

Hartley, William G. *My Best for the Kingdom: History and Autobiography of John Lowe Butler, a Mormon Frontiersman.* S.L.C: Aspen Books, 1993.

Harwell, William S., ed. *Manuscript History of Brigham Young, 1847–1850.* S.L.C: Collier's Publishing Co., 1997.

Hazen, Craig James. *The Village Enlightenment in America: Popular Religion and Science in the Nineteenth Century.* Urbana: Univ. of Illinois Press, 2000.

Henrie, Manetta Prince. *Descendants of John Doyle Lee, 1812–1877.* Provo: M. P. Henrie, 1960.

Henrie, Samuel Nyal, ed. *Writings of John D. Lee.* Tucson: Hats Off, 2001. Second edition, Tucson: Fenestra, 2002.

Hickman, Bill, and J. H. Beadle, ed. *Brigham's Destroying Angel: Being the Life, Confession and Startling Disclosures of the Notorious Bill Hickman, Danite Chief of Utah.* New York: J. A. Crofutt, 1872.

Hilton, Hope A. *"Wild Bill" Hickman and the Mormon Frontier.* S.L.C: Signature Books, 1988.

Hirshon, Stanley. *The Lion of the Lord.* New York: Knopf, 1969.

Holzapfel, Richard Neitzel, and Susan Allen Myers. *The Utah Journey.* Layton, Utah: Gibbs Smith, 2009.

Homer, Michael W., ed. *On the Way to Somewhere Else: European Sojourners in the Mormon West, 1834–1930.* Spokane, Wash: Arthur H. Clark Company, 2006.

Huff, Emma N. *Memories that Live: Utah County Centennial History.* Provo: Daughters of Utah Pioneers, 1947.

Hulbert, Archer Butler, ed. *Letters of an Overland Mail Agent in Utah.* Worcester, Mass: The American Antiquarian Soc., 1929.

Hyde, John, Jr. *Mormonism: Its Leaders and Designs.* New York: W. P. Fetridge and Co., 1857.

Hyde, William. *Private Journal of William Hyde.* N.p: W. L. Woolf, 1964?

Ide's Helena City Directory for 1889. Helena, Mont: A. W. Ide, 1889.

Ingraham, Prentiss. *Pony Bob, The Reckless Rider of the Rockies: A True History of the Life of Robert H. Haslam,* New York: Beadle and Adams, 1885.

Iversen, Joan. *The Antipolygamy Controversy in U.S. Women's Movements, 1880–1925: A Debate on the American Home.* New York: Garland Publishing, 1997.

Iverson, Peter. *Diné: A History of the Navajos.* Albuquerque: Univ. of New Mexico Press, 2002.

Jenson, Andrew, comp. *Church Chronology.* S.L.C: Deseret News, 1899.

———. *Latter-day Saint Biographical Encyclopedia*. 4 vols. S.L.C: Andrew Jenson History Company, 1901.

Johnson, Melvin C. *Polygamy on the Pedernales: Lyman Wight's Mormon Villages in Antebellum Texas, 1845–1858*. Logan: Utah State Univ. Press, 2006.

Jolley, Bryant Manning. *Jolley Family Book*. Orem, Utah: Privately printed, 2005.

Journal of Discourses. 26 vols. Liverpool: Latter-day Saints Book Depot, 1854–86. Reprint, Schaan, Liechtenstein: Gastera Trust, 1955.

Kane, Elizabeth Wood. *Twelve Mormon Homes Visited in Succession on a Journey through Utah to Arizona*. Philadelphia: 1874. Reprint, S.L.C: Tanner Trust Fund, 1974.

Kelly, Charles, ed. *Journals of John D. Lee, 1846–47 and 1859*. S.L.C: Western Printing Co., 1938. Reprint, S.L.C: Univ. of Utah Press, 1984.

Kenney, Scott G. *Wilford Woodruff's Journal, 1838–1898*. Midvale, Utah: Signature Books, 1984.

Korns, Roderic, and Dale L. Morgan, eds. *West from Fort Bridger: The Pioneering of Immigrant Trails across Utah, 1846–1850*. Salt Lake City: Utah State Historical Society, 1951. Revised by Will Bagley and Harold Schindler. Logan: Utah State University Press, 1994.

LaCapra, Dominick. *Writing History, Writing Trauma*. Baltimore: Johns Hopkins Univ. Press, 2001.

Larson, Andrew Karl. *"I Was Called to Dixie": The Virgin River Basin: Unique Experiences in Mormon Pioneering*. S.L.C: Deseret News, 1961.

———. *Red Hills of November: A Pioneer Biography of Utah's Cotton Town*. S.L.C: Deseret News Press, 1957.

Larson, A. Karl, and Katharine Miles Larson, eds. *Diary of Charles Lowell Walker*. 2 vols. Logan: Utah State Univ. Press, 1980.

Larson, Gustive O. *The "Americanization" of Utah for Statehood*. San Marino, Calif: Henry E. Huntington Library, 1971.

Larson, Stan, ed. *Prisoner for Polygamy: The Memoirs and Letters of Rudger Clawson at the Utah Territorial Penitentiary 1884–87*. Urbana: Univ. of Illinois, 1993.

Launius, Roger D. *Zion's Camp: Expedition to Missouri, 1834*. Independence, Mo: Herald Publishing House, 1984.

Launius, Roger D., and Linda Thatcher, eds. *Differing Visions: Dissenters in Mormon History*. Urbana: Univ. of Illinois Press, 1994.

Leonard, Glen M. *Nauvoo: A Place of Peace, a People of Promise*. S.L.C: Deseret Book Co., 2002.

LeSueur, Stephen C. *The 1838 Mormon War in Missouri*. Columbia: Univ. of Missouri Press, 1987.

Lockley, Fred. *History of the Columbia River Valley, From The Dalles to the Sea*. 2 vols. Chicago: S. J. Clarke Publishing Co., 1928.

Lockwood, Jeffrey A. *Locust: The Devastating Rise and Mysterious Disappearance of the Insect that Shaped the American Frontier*. New York: Basic Books, 2004.

Long, E. B. *The Saints and the Union: Utah Territory during the Civil War*. Urbana: Univ. of Illinois Press, 1981.

Ludlow, Daniel, ed. *Encyclopedia of Mormonism*. 4 vols. New York: Macmillan Publishing Company, 1992.

Lum, Dyer Daniel. *Social Problems of Today: Or, the Mormon Question in Its Economic Aspects. A study of co-operation and arbitration in Mormondom, from the standpoint of a wage-worker. By a Gentile.* Port Jervis, N.Y: D.D. Lum & Co., 1886.

Lyman, Edward Leo. *Political Deliverance: The Mormon Quest for Utah Statehood.* Urbana: Univ. of Illinois Press, 1986.

———. *San Bernardino: The Rise and Fall of a California Community.* S.L.C: Signature Books, 1996.

MacKinnon, William P., ed. *At Sword's Point, Part 1: A Documentary History of the Utah War to 1858.* Norman, Okla: Arthur H. Clark Company, 2008.

Madsen, Brigham D. *Corinne: The Gentile Capital of Utah.* S.L.C: Utah State Hist. Soc., 1980.

———. *Glory Hunter: A Biography of Patrick Edward Connor.* S.L.C: Univ. of Utah Press, 1990.

———. *The Shoshoni Frontier and the Bear River Massacre.* S.L.C: Univ. of Utah Press, 1985.

Malmquist, O. N. *The First 100 Years: A History of the Salt Lake Tribune, 1871–1971.* S.L.C: Utah State Hist. Soc., 1971.

Manderscheid, Lorraine Richardson, ed. *Some Descendants of John Doyle Lee.* Bellevue, Wash: Family Research and Development, 1996.

Marquardt, H. Michael. *The Joseph Smith Revelations: Text and Commentary.* S.L.C: Signature Books, 1999.

Maxwell, John Gary. *Gettysburg to Great Salt Lake: George R. Maxwell, Civil War Hero and Federal Marshal among the Mormons.* Norman, Okla: Arthur H. Clark Company, 2010.

McConkie, Bruce R. *Mormon Doctrine.* S.L.C: Deseret Book, 1958. Second edition, 1966.

Merkley, Aird G., ed. *Monuments to Courage: A History of Beaver County.* Beaver, Utah: Daughters of Utah Pioneers, 1948.

Milner, Clyde A. II, Carol A. O'Conner, and Martha A. Sandweiss. *The Oxford History of the American West.* New York: Oxford Univ. Press, 1994.

Missouri General Assembly. *Document Containing the Correspondence, Orders, &c., in relation to the disturbances with the Mormons; and the evidence given before the Hon. Austin A. King, judge of the Fifth judicial circuit of the state of Missouri, at the Court-house in Richmond, in a criminal court of inquiry, begun November 12, 1838, on the trial of Joseph Smith, jr., and others, for high treason and other crimes against the state.* Fayette, Mo: Boon's Lick Democrat, 1841.

Moorman, Donald R., with Gene A. Sessions. *Camp Floyd and the Mormons.* S.L.C: Univ. of Utah Press, 1992.

Morgan, Dale L. *The State of Deseret.* Logan: Utah State Univ. Press and Utah Hist. Soc., 1987.

Moore, Beth. *Bones in the Well: The Haun's Mill Massacre.* Norman, Okla: Arthur H. Clark Company, 2007.

Morris, Joseph. *The "Spirit Prevails" Containing the Revelations, Articles and Letters Written by Joseph Morris.* San Francisco: George S. Dove & Co., 1886.

Mortimer, William James, comp. and ed. *How Beautiful Upon the Mountains: A Centennial History of Wasatch County.* S.L.C: Daughters of Utah Pioneers, 1963.

Mulder, William. *Homeward to Zion: The Mormon Migration from Scandinavia.* Minneapolis: Univ. of Minnesota Press, 1957. Anniversary edition, 2000.

Mulder, William, and A. Russell Mortensen, eds. *Among the Mormons: Historic Accounts by Contemporary Observers.* Lincoln: Univ. of Nebraska Press, 1958.

Newton, Marjorie. *Hero or Traitor: A Biographical Study of Charles Wesley Wandell*. Independence, Mo: Independence Press, 1992.

———. *Southern Cross Saints: The Mormons in Australia*. Laie, Hawaii: The Institute for Polynesian Studies, 1991.

Nichols, Jeffrey. *Prostitution, Polygamy, and Power: Salt Lake City, 1847–1918*. Urbana: Univ. of Illinois, 2002.

Ogden, Annegret S., ed. *Frontier Reminiscences of Eveline Brooks Auerbach*. Berkeley, Calif: Friends of the Bancroft Library, 1994.

Ortiz, Alfonso, ed. *Southwest*. Vol. 9 of *Handbook of North American Indians*. 20 vols. William C. Sturtevant, general editor. Washington, D.C: Smithsonian Institution, 1979.

Owens, Kenneth N., ed. *Gold Rush Saints: California Mormons and the Great Rush for Riches*. Spokane, Wash: Arthur H. Clark Company, 2004.

Palmer, Richard F., and Karl D. Butler. *Brigham Young: The New York Years*. Provo: Charles Redd Center for Western Studies, 1992.

Petersen, LaMar. *Hearts Made Glad: The Charges of Intemperance against Joseph Smith, the Mormon Prophet*. S.L.C: LaMar Petersen, 1975.

Peterson, John Alton. *Utah's Black Hawk War*. S.L.C: Univ. of Utah Press, 1998.

Peterson, Paul H. *The Mormon Reformation*. Provo: Joseph Fielding Smith Institute and BYU Studies, 2002.

Poll, Richard, Thomas G. Alexander, Eugene E. Campbell, and David E. Miller, eds. *Utah's History*. Provo: BYU, 1978.

Powell, Delna Swapp. *James McGaw Eleventh Pioneer Emigration Company 1852: Research of the James McGaw Pioneer Company to find relatives of the Levi Powell Family who were members of this Company*. Las Vegas: M. S. Bryson, 2002.

Pratt, Orson. *Prophetic Almanac for 1845*. New York: Prophet Office, 1844.

Pratt, Parley P. *Autobiography of Parley P. Pratt*. New York: Russell Brothers, 1874. S.L.C: Deseret Book Co., 1938, 1985.

Pratt, Parley P. *Proclamation of the Twelve Apostles of the Church of Jesus Christ of Latter-day Saints to All the Kings of the World, to the President of the United States of America; to the Governors of the Several States, and to the Rulers and People of All Nations*. New York: Pratt and Brannan, 1845.

Prince, Stephen L. *Gathering in Harmony: A Saga of Southern Utah Families, Their Roots and Pioneering Heritage, and the Tale of Antone Prince, Sheriff of Washington County*. Spokane, Wash: Arthur H. Clark Company, 2004.

Quinn, D. Michael. *The Mormon Hierarchy: Extensions of Power*. S.L.C: Signature Books, 1997.

———. *The Mormon Hierarchy: Origins of Power*. S.L.C: Signature Books, 1994.

———, ed. *The New Mormon History: Revisionist Essays on the Past*. S.L.C: Signature Books, 1992.

Roberts, Brigham H. *A Comprehensive History of the Church of Jesus Christ of Latter-day Saints*. 6 vols. S.L.C: Deseret News Press, 1930; Provo: BYU Press, 1965.

Roberts, David. *Devil's Gate: Brigham Young and the Mormon Handcart Tragedy*. New York: Simon and Schuster, 2008.

Schindler, Harold. *Orrin Porter Rockwell: Man of God, Son of Thunder*. S.L.C: Univ. of Utah Press, 1966. Second edition, 1983.

Schroeder, John W., and James R. Graff, comps. *Historic Helena: An Early-Day Photographic History of Montana's Scenic Capital City*. Helena, Mont: Thurber Printing Co., 1970.

Seegmiller, Janet Burton. *A History of Iron County*. S.L.C: Utah State Hist. Soc., 1998.

Shirts, Morris A., and Kathryn H. Shirts. *A Trial Furnace: Southern Utah's Iron Mission*. Provo: Brigham Young Univ. Press, 2001.

Slotkin, Richard. *Regeneration through Violence: The Mythology of the American Frontier, 1600–1860*. New York: Harper Perennial, 1973.

Smith, Henry Nash. *Virgin Land: The American West as Symbol and Myth*. Cambridge, Mass: Harvard Univ. Press, 1950. Reissued, 1970.

Smith, Joseph, Jr. *History of the Church of Jesus Christ of Latter-day Saints: Period I, History of Joseph Smith, the Prophet, by Himself*. Ed. by B. H. Roberts. 6 vols. S.L.C: Deseret News, 1902–1912.

Smith, Joseph III, and Heman Conoman Smith. *The History of the Reorganized Church of Jesus Christ of Latter Day Saints*. 7 vols. Independence, Mo: Herald House, 1967–1976.

Smoak, Gregory E. *Ghost Dances and Identity: Prophetic Religion and American Indian Ethnogenesis in the Nineteenth Century*. Berkeley: Univ. of California Press, 2006.

Steele, Volney, M.D. *Bleed, Blister and Purge: A History of Medicine on the American Frontier*. Missoula, Mont: Mountain Press, 2005.

Stegner, Wallace. *Mormon Country*. New York: Bonanza Books, 1942.

Stenhouse, Mrs. T. B. H. [Fanny]. *An Englishwoman in Utah: The Story of a Life's Experience in Mormonism*. London: Sampson Low, Marson, Searle, and Rivington, 1880.

———. *Exposé of Polygamy in Utah: A Lady's Life Among the Mormons*. New York: American News Co., 1872. Republished with introduction and edits by Linda Wilcox DeSimone, Logan: Utah State Univ. Press, 2008.

———. *A Lady's Life Among the Mormons*. New York: Russell Brothers, 1872.

———. *"Tell It All": The Story of a Life's Experience in Mormonism, an Autobiography*. Hartford, Conn: A. D. Worthington, 1873.

Stenhouse, T. B. H. *Rocky Mountain Saints: A Full and Complete History of the Mormons*. New York: D. Appleton and Co., 1873. S.L.C: Shepard Book Co., 1904.

Stewart, Polly, Steve Siporin, C. W. Sullivan III, and Suzi Jones, eds. *Worldviews and the American West: The Life of the Place Itself*. Logan: Utah State Univ. Press, 2000.

Stott, Clifford L. *Search for Sanctuary: Brigham Young and the White Mountain Expedition*. S.L.C: Univ. of Utah Press, 1984.

Toelken, J. Barre. *The Dynamics of Folklore*. Boston: Houghton Mifflin, 1979. Revised and expanded edition, Logan: Utah State Univ. Press, 1996.

Topping, Gary. *Leonard J. Arrington: A Historian's Life*. Norman, Okla: Arthur H. Clark Company, 2008.

Tullidge, Edward W. *The History of Salt Lake City and Its Founders*. S.L.C: Edward W. Tullidge, 1886.

Turley, Richard E., ed. *Selected Collections from the Archives of the Church of Jesus Christ of Latter-day Saints*. Provo: BYU Press, 2002.

Turley, Richard E., Jr., and Ronald W. Walker, eds. *Mountain Meadows Massacre: The Andrew Jenson and David H. Morris Collections*. Provo: BYU Studies, 2009.

Turner, Lynne Slater. *Emigrating Journals of the Willie and Martin Handcart Companies and the Hunt and Hodgett Wagon Trains.* 1996.

Twain, Mark. *Letters from the Earth.* Ed. by Bernard DeVoto. Preface by Henry Nash Smith. New York: Harper & Row, 1962.

Tyler, Daniel. *A Concise History of the Mormon Battalion in the Mexican War, 1846–1847.* S.L.C., 1881, reprint, Glorieta, N.Mex: The Rio Grande Press, Inc., 1980.

Underwood, Grant. *The Millenarian World of Early Mormonism.* Urbana: Univ. of Illinois Press, 1993.

Ure, James. *Leaving the Fold: Candid Conversations With Inactive Mormons.* S.L.C: Signature Books, 1999.

Utley, Robert. *Billy the Kid: A Short and Violent Life.* Lincoln and London: Univ. of Nebraska Press, 1989.

Van Buren County Hist. Soc., comp. *History of Bonaparte.* Bonaparte, Iowa: The Record-Republican, 1967.

Waite, Catherine V. *The Mormon Prophet and His Harem; Or, An Authentic History of Brigham Young, His Numerous Wives and Children.* Chicago: Riverside Press, 1866.

Walker, Ronald W. *Wayward Saints: The Godbeites and Brigham Young.* Urbana: Univ. of Illinois Press, 1998.

Walker, Ronald W., and Doris R. Dant, eds. *Nearly Everything Imaginable: The Everyday Life of Utah's Mormon Pioneers.* Provo: BYU Press, 1999.

Walker, Ronald W., Richard E. Turley, Jr., and Glen M. Leonard. *Massacre at Mountain Meadows: An American Tragedy.* New York: Oxford Univ. Press, 2008.

Wallis, Michael. *Billy the Kid: The Endless Ride.* New York: W. W. Norton, 2007.

Ward, Maurine Carr, ed. *Winter Quarters: The 1846–1848 Life Writings of Mary Haskin Parker Richards.* Logan: Utah State Univ. Press, 1996.

Weddle, Jerry. *Antrim Is My Stepfather's Name.* Phoenix: Arizona Hist. Soc., 1993.

West, Elliott. *The Contested Plains: Indians, Goldseekers, and the Rush to Colorado.* Lawrence: Univ. Press of Kansas, 1998.

Westergren, Bruce, ed. *From Historian to Dissident: The Book of John Whitmer.* S.L.C: Signature Books/Smith Research Associates, 1995.

Whipple, Maurine. *The Giant Joshua.* New York: Houghton Mifflin, 1941. Reprint, S.L.C: Western Epics, 1976.

White, Jean Bickmore, ed. *Church, State, and Politics: The Diaries of John Henry Smith.* S.L.C: Signature Books, 1990.

Whitley, Colleen, ed. *Brigham Young's Homes.* Logan: Utah State Univ. Press, 2002.

Whitney, Orson F. *History of Utah.* 4 vols. Salt Lake City: George Q. Cannon & Sons Co., Publishers, 1892–1904.

Whittaker, Frederick. *Dick Darling, the Pony Expressman: A Tale of the Old Salt Lake Trail.* New York: Beadle and Adams, 1874, 1884.

Willett, Edward. *The White Apache: Or, the Lifted Trail: A Tale of the Mid Ranges.* New York: Beadle and Co., 1871.

Young, Ann Eliza. *Wife No. 19: Or, The Story of a Life in Bondage.* Hartford, Conn: Dustin, Gilman, 1875.

Youngberg, Florence C., ed. *Conquerors of the West: Stalwart Mormon Pioneers.* 4 vols. Scottsdale, Ariz: Agreka Books, 1999.

Articles and Book Chapters

Aird, Polly. "Escape from Zion: The United States Army Escort of Mormon Apostates, 1859." *Nevada Hist. Soc. Qtly.* 44:3 (Fall 2001): 196–237.

———. Letter to the Editor. *Journal of Mormon History* 34:2 (Winter 2008): vi–vii.

———. " 'You Nasty Apostates, Clear Out': Reasons for Disaffection in the Late 1850s." *Journal of Mormon History* 30:2 (Fall 2004): 129–207.

Alexander, Thomas G. "Charles S. Zane, Apostle of the New Era." *Utah Hist. Qtly.* 34:4 (Fall 1966): 290–314.

———. "Federal Authority versus Polygamic Theocracy: James B. McKean and the Mormons, 1870–1875." *Dialogue* 1:3 (Autumn 1966): 85–100.

Allen, Barbara. "The Heroic Ride in Western Popular Historical Tradition." *Western Hist. Qtly.* 19:4 (Nov. 1988): 397–412.

Allen, James B. " 'We Were Willing Because We Were Obliged To': The Mormons, Their Religion, and Why They Left Nauvoo." In *The Iowa Mormon Trail: Legacy of Faith and Courage,* ed. by Susan Easton Black and William G. Hartley, 3–20. Orem, Utah: Helix Publishing, 1997.

Alley, John R., Jr. "Utah Supreme Court Justice William M. McCarty." *Utah Hist. Qtly.* 65:4 (Fall 1997): 372–83.

Alter, J. Cecil, and Robert J. Dwyer, eds. "The Utah War: Journal of Capt. Albert Tracy." *Utah Hist. Qtly.* 13:1–4 (1945): 1–128.

Aquila, Richard. "Introduction: The Pop Culture West." In *Wanted Dead or Alive: The American West in Popular Culture,* ed. by Richard Aquila, 1–16. Urbana: Univ. of Illinois Press, 1996.

Arrington, Leonard J. "Crusade against Theocracy: The Reminiscence of Judge Jacob Smith Boreman of Utah, 1872–1877." *Huntington Library Qtly.* 24 (November 1960): 1–46.

———. "The Settlement of the Brigham Young Estate, 1877–1879." *Pacific Hist. Review* 21:1 (February 1952): 1–20.

——— and Jon Haupt. "Intolerable Zion: The Image of Mormonism in Nineteenth Century American Literature." *Western Humanities Review* 22:3 (Summer 1968): 243–60.

Aveson, Robert. "Reminiscences of the Long Journey from England to 'The Valley' in the Sixties." *Deseret Evening News,* 3 January 1920, sec. 4, p. 6.

Bagley, Will. " 'One Long Funeral March': A Revisionist's View of the Mormon Handcart Disasters." *Journal of Mormon History* 35:1 (Winter 2009): 50–115.

Barnes, Jane. "Joseph Smith: Lost and Found." *Dialogue: A Journal of Mormon Thought* 41:1 (March 2008): 147–57.

Bashore, Melvin L. "The 1876 Arsenal Hill Explosion." *Utah Hist. Qtly.* 52:3 (Summer 1984): 246–55.

Beecher, Maureen Ursenbach, ed. "All Things Move in Order in the City: The Nauvoo Diary of Zina Diantha Huntington Jacobs." *byu Studies* 19:3 (Spring 1979): 285–320.

———. "Eliza R. Snow." In *Mormon Sisters: Women in Early Utah,* ed. by Claudia L. Bushman, 25–41. Logan: Utah State Univ., 1997.

———. "The 'Leading Sisters': A Female Hierarchy in Nineteenth Century Mormon Society." *Journal of Mormon History* 9 (1982): 25–39.

Beeton, Beverly. "Teach Them to Till the Soil: An Experiment with Indian Farms, 1850–1862." *American Indian Qtly.* 3:4 (Winter 1977–78): 299–320.

Bennion, Sherilyn Cox. "The *Woman's Exponent*: Forty-Two Years of Speaking for Women." *Utah Hist. Qtly.* 44:3 (Summer 1976): 222–39.

Bergera, Gary James. "Buckeye's Laments: Two Early Insider Exposés of Mormon Polygamy and Their Authorship." *Journal of the Illinois State Hist. Soc.* 96:4 (Winter 2003): 350–90.

Bigler, David L. "The Aiken Party Executions and the Utah War, 1857–1858." *Western Hist. Qtly.* 38:4 (Winter 2007): 457–76.

———. "Garland Hurt, the American Friend of the Utahs." *Utah Hist. Qtly.* 62:2 (Spring 1994): 149–70.

Bitton, Davis. "'I'd Rather Have Some Roasting Ears': The Peregrinations of George Armstrong Hicks." *Utah Hist. Qtly.* 68:3 (Summer 2000), 196–222.

Bold, Christine. "Malaeska's Revenge; or, The Dime Novel Tradition in Popular Fiction." In *Wanted Dead or Alive: The American West in Popular Culture,* ed. by Richard Aquila, 21–42. Urbana: Univ. of Illinois Press, 1996.

Brady, Margaret K. "In Her Own Words: Women's Frontier Friendships." In *Worldviews and the American West: The Life of the Place Itself,* ed. by Polly Stewart, Steve Siporin, C.W. Sullivan III, and Suzi Jones, 62–78. Logan: Utah State Univ. Press, 2000.

Brimhall, Sandra Dawn, and Mark D. Curtis. "The Gardo House." In *Brigham Young's Homes,* ed. by Colleen Whitley, 173–201. Logan: Utah State Univ. Press, 2002.

Burt, Olive Woolley. "Ditties of Death in Deseret." In *Lore of Faith and Folly,* ed. by Thomas E. Cheney, Austin E. Fife and Juanita Brooks, 162–63. S.L.C: Univ. of Utah, 1971.

———. "Murder Ballads of Mormondom." *Western Folklore* 18:2 (April 1959): 141–56.

Campbell, Eugene E., and Bruce L. Campbell. "Divorce among Mormon Polygamists: Extent and Explanations." In *The New Mormon History: Revisionist Essays on the Past,* ed. by D. Michael Quinn. S.L.C: Signature Books, 1992, 181–200.

Cannon, Kenneth. "The Tragic Matter of Louie Wells and John Q. Cannon." *Journal of Mormon History* 35:2 (Spring 2009): 126–90.

Christy, Howard A. "'Open Hand and Mailed Fist': Mormon-Indian Relations in Utah, 1847–52." *Utah Hist. Qtly.* 46 (Summer 1978): 216–35.

———. "The Walker War: Defense and Conciliation as Strategy." *Utah Hist. Qtly.* 47:4 (Fall 1979): 395–420.

Connelly, John C. "Hopi Social Organization." In *Southwest,* ed. by Alfonso Ortiz, 539–63. Vol. 9 of *Handbook of North American Indians.* 20 vols. William C. Sturtevant, general editor. Washington, D.C: Smithsonian Institution, 1979.

Davis, David Brion. "Some Themes of Counter-Subversion: An Analysis of Anti-Masonic, Anti-Catholic, and Anti-Mormon Literature." *Mississippi Valley Hist. Review* 47 (1960): 205–24.

DeVoto, Bernard. "Sin Comes to Ogden." In *Among the Mormons: Historic Accounts by Contemporary Observers,* ed. by William Mulder and A. Russell Mortensen, 451–52. Lincoln: Univ. of Nebraska Press, 1958.

Dix, Fae Decker. "Unwilling Martyr: The Death of Young Ed Dalton." *Utah Hist. Qtly.* 41:2 (Spring 1973): 162–77.

Dixon, W. Randall. "The Beehive and Lion Houses." In *Brigham Young's Homes,* ed. by Colleen Whitley, 124–31. Logan: Utah State Univ. Press, 2002.

Dushku, Judith Rasmussen. "Feminists." In *Mormon Sisters: Women in Early Utah,* ed. by Claudia L. Bushman, 177–79. Logan: Utah State Univ., 1997.

Fairchild, D.S. "History of Medicine in Iowa." *Journal of the Iowa State Medical Soc.,* 1927.

Fife, Austin E. "A Ballad of the Mountain Meadows Massacre." *Western Folklore* 12:4 (Oct. 1953): 229–41.

———. "Birthmarks and Psychic Imprinting of Babies in Utah Folk Medicine." In *Exploring Western Americana,* ed. by Alta Fife, 121–30. Ann Arbor, Mich: U.M.I. Research Press, 1988.

Gardner, Martin R. "Mormonism and Capital Punishment: A Doctrinal Perspective, Past and Present." *Dialogue* 12:1 (Spring 1979): 9–26.

Godfrey, Audrey M. "Housewives, Hussies, and Heroines, or the Women of Johnston's Army." *Utah Hist. Qtly.* 54:2 (Spring 1986): 157–78.

Godrey, Kenneth W. "Crime and Punishment in Mormon Nauvoo, 1839–1846." *BYU Studies* 32:1–2 (Winter and Spring 1992): 195–227.

Goodson, Stephanie Smith. "Plural Wives." In *Mormon Sisters: Women in Early Utah,* ed. by Claudia L. Bushman, 89–112. Logan: Utah State Univ., 1997.

Hartley, William G. "From Men to Boys: LDS Aaronic Priesthood Offices, 1829–1996." *Journal of Mormon History* 22:1 (Spring 1996): 80–136.

Hay, John. "The Mormon Prophet's Tragedy." *Atlantic Monthly* (December 1869): 671–78.

Hiles, Norma Derry. "Charles Derry: A Palimpsestic View." *John Whitmer Hist. Assoc. Journal* 4 (1984): 22–29.

Holley, Val. "Slouching Towards Slaterville: Joseph Morris's Wide Swath in Weber County." *Utah Hist. Qtly.* 76 (Summer 2008): 247–64.

Homer, Michael W. "The Judiciary and the Common Law in Utah Territory, 1851–61," *Dialogue: A Journal of Mormon Thought* 21:1 (Spring 1988): 97–108.

Iverson, Joan Smyth. "Feminist Implications of Mormon Polygyny." *Feminist Studies* 10:3 (Fall 1984): 505–22.

Ivins, Stanley S. "Notes on Mormon Polygamy." In *The New Mormon History: Revisionist Essays on the Past,* ed. by D. Michael Quinn, 169–80. S.L.C: Signature Books, 1992.

James, Kimberly Jensen. "'Between Two Fires': Women on the 'Underground.'" *Journal of Mormon History* 8 (1981): 49–61.

Jenson, Andrew, comp. "History of Las Vegas Mission." *Nevada State Hist. Soc. Papers,* 5 (1925–26): 119–284.

"John Middleton." In *Generations of Websters,* comp. by Amy L. Van Cott and Allen W. Leigh. Cedar City, Utah: Thomas Webster Family Organization, 1960.

Johnson, Jeffery Ogden. "Determining and Defining 'Wife': The Brigham Young Households." *Dialogue* 20:3 (Fall 1987): 57–70.

"Journal of Capt. Albert Tracy." *Utah Historical Quarterly* 13 (1945): 1–119.

Larson, Gustive O. "The Mormon Reformation." *Utah Hist. Qtly.* 26 (January 1958): 45–63.

———. "Orrin Porter Rockwell—The Modern Samson." In *Lore of Faith and Folly*, ed. by Thomas E. Cheney, Austin E. Fife and Juanita Brooks, 179–90. S.L.C: Univ. of Utah, 1971.

Launius, Roger D. "Mormon Memory, Mormon Myth, and Mormon History." *Journal of Mormon History* 21 (Spring 1995): 1–24.

———. "The Reorganized Church of Jesus Christ of Latter Day Saints in Utah." In *Utah History Encyclopedia*, ed. by Allan Kent Powell. S.L.C: Univ. of Utah Press, 1994, 459–61.

Limerick, Patricia Nelson. "Making the Most of Words: Verbal Activity and Western America." In *Under an Open Sky: Rethinking America's Western Past*, ed. by William Cronon, George Miles, Jay Gitlin, 167–84. New York: W. W. Norton & Co., 1992.

MacKinnon, William P. "'Lonely Bones': Leadership and Utah War Violence." *Journal of Mormon History* 33:1 (Spring 2007): 121–78.

Parshall, Ardis E. "'Pursue, Retake & Punish': The 1857 Santa Clara Ambush." *Utah Hist. Qtly.* 73 (Winter 2005): 64–86.

Rankin, Charles E. "Savage Journalists and Civilized Indians: A Different View." *Journalist History*, 21:3 (Autumn 1995): 102–11.

———. "Type and Stereotype: Frederic E. Lockley, Pioneer Journalist." In *Frontier and Region: Essays in Honor of Martin Ridge*, ed. by Robert C. Ritchie and Paul Andrew Hutton, 57–81. San Marino, Calif: Huntington Library Press, 1997.

Roberts, Allen Dale. "Profile of Apostasy: Who Are the Bad Guys, Really?" *Dialogue: A Journal of Mormon Thought* 31:4 (Winter 1998): 143–62.

Sandberg, Karl C. "Getting Up a History of Monroe: The Long Shadow of the United Order." *Sunstone Magazine* 104 (December 1996): 37–45.

Sanders, Ken. "A Thirst in the Desert: Utah's Early Settlers Like a Drink Now and Again." *Salt Lake Magazine* (December 2008).

"Saved from the Mormons." *The Galaxy: A Magazine of Entertaining Reading*. 14:5–6 (November–December 1872).

Scott, Patricia Lynn. "The Widow and the Lion of the Lord: Sarah Ann Cooke vs. Brigham Young." *Journal of Mormon History* 30:1 (Spring 2004): 189–212.

Seifrit, William C. "Charles Henry Wilcken, An Undervalued Saint." *Utah Hist. Qtly.* 55 (Fall 1987): 308–21.

Shepard, Bill. "Stealing at Mormon Nauvoo." *John Whitmer Hist. Assoc. Journal* 23 (2003): 91–110.

Shirts, Morris A. "The Iron Mission." In *Utah History Encyclopedia*, ed. by Allan Kent Powell. S.L.C: Univ. of Utah Press, 1994.

Simmonds, A. J. "Aaron Dewitt, the Man, His Times, and His Letter." *Saints Alive Journal* (Fall 1987). Digital copy at http://www.saintsalive.com/mormonism/murder.html [17 April 2008].

Toelken, J. Barre. "The Ballad of the 'Mountain Meadows Massacre.'" *Western Folklore* 18:2 (April 1959): 169–72.

Tullidge, Edward W. "History of Spanish Fork." *Tullidge's Qtly. Magazine* 3:2–3 (April, July 1884): two-part series.

Van Wagoner, Richard S. "The Making of a Mormon Myth: The 1844 Transfiguration of Brigham Young." *Dialogue* 28:4 (Winter 1995): 1–24.

Verdoia, Ken. "Genesis of a Newspaper War." *Salt Lake: Magazine of the Intermountain West* 14:1 (February 2003): 64.

Walker, Ronald W. "Golden Memories: Remembering a Life in a Mormon Village." In *Nearly Everything Imaginable: The Everyday Life of Utah's Mormon Pioneers*, ed. by Ronald W. Walker and Doris R. Dant, 50–53. Provo: BYU Press, 1999.

———. "The Stenhouses and the Making of a Mormon Image." *Journal of Mormon History* 1 (1974): 51–72.

White, Richard. "Outlaw Gangs of the Middle Border: American Social Bandits," *Western Hist. Qtly.* 12:4 (Oct. 1981): 387–408.

Wilson, William A. "Folklore of Dixie: Past and Present." The Twenty-second Annual Juanita Brooks Lecture. St. George, Utah: Dixie State College, 2005.

Newspapers

Anti-Polygamy Standard (Salt Lake City)
Birmingham Daily Post (Birmingham, England)
Corinne Reporter (Corinne, Utah)
Daily Nevada State Journal (Reno, Nevada)
Deer Lodge New North-West (Deer Lodge, Montana)
Deseret News and Deseret Weekly News (Salt Lake City)
Helena Herald (Helena, Montana)
Millennial Star (Liverpool, England)
Nauvoo Expositor (Nauvoo, Illinois)
The New-York Prophet
New York Times
New York Tribune
Ohio Star (Ravenna, Ohio)
Salt Lake Herald
Salt Lake Tribune
San Francisco Evening Bulletin
Territorial Enquirer (Provo, Utah)
Times and Seasons (Nauvoo, Illinois)
Union Vedette (Salt Lake City)
Valley Tan (Salt Lake City)
Warsaw Message (Warsaw, Illinois)
Warsaw Signal (Warsaw, Illinois)

Theses and Dissertations

Britsch, Ralph L. "Early Latter-day Saint Missions to South and East Asia." Ph.D. diss., Claremont Graduate School, 1967.

Brooks, Karl. "Amos Milton Musser." M.A. thesis, BYU, 1962.

Hayward, Barbara. "Utah's Anti-Polygamy Society, 1878–1884." M.A. thesis, BYU, 1980.

Hibbard, Charles G. "Fort Douglas, 1862–1916: Pivotal Link on the Western Frontier." Ph.D. diss., Univ. of Utah, 1980.

Patrick, John R. "The School of the Prophets: Its Development and Influence in Utah Territory." M.A. thesis, BYU, 1970.

Petrik, Paula. "The Bonanza Town: Women and Family on the Rocky Mountain Mining Frontier, Helena, Montana, 1865–1900." Ph.D. diss., State Univ. of New York at Binghampton, 1982.

Saunders, Richard L. "Francis Gladden Bishop and Gladdenism: A Study in the Culture of a Mormon Dissenter and his Movement." Masters thesis, Utah State University, 1989. Digital copy at http://scholarship.utm.edu/9/ [13 May 2010].

Shipley, Richard Lyle. "Voices of Dissent: The History of the Reorganized Church of Jesus Christ of Latter Day Saints in Utah, 1863–1900." M.A. thesis, Utah State Univ., 1969.

Smith, Samuel A. "The Wasp in the Beehive: Non-Mormon Presence in 1880s Utah." M.A. thesis, Pennsylvania State Univ., 2008.

Van Wagenen, Lola. "Sister-Wives and Suffragists: Polygamy and the Politics of Woman Suffrage 1870–1896." Ph.D. diss., New York Univ., 1994.

Manuscript, Archival, and Digital Sources

Arthur, Christopher. The Autobiography of Christopher J. Arthur. MSS A-25-1. Utah State Hist. Soc.

Ashworth, William B. Autobiography of William B. Ashworth. MSS A-27-1. Utah State Hist. Soc.

Ballantyne, Richard. Journal, 29 May to 8 August 1848. LDS Archives.

Barton, Eliza Jane. Autobiographical sketch. LDS Archives.

Bishop, Lee Fuson. Unpublished Introduction to Ann Gordge Autobiography, Bishop Variant. Property of Sharen L. Moon, 1993.

Booth, Charles. Journal, 1854–1855. LDS Archives.

Brigham Young Letterpress Copybook Transcriptions. LDS Archives.

Brigham Young Trust Company Records. File no. 853. Corporation Files, Salt Lake County Clerk. Utah State Archives.

Brooks, Juanita. History of Washington County. MSS A4218. Utah State Hist. Soc.

Bullock, Thomas. 1848 Journal. MS 1385:5. LDS Archives.

Cannon, Abraham Hoagland. Diary. MS 3. Special Collections. Marriott Library, Univ. of Utah.

Case, Hamet Hubbard. 1859 Correspondence and Laramie to Oregon: Notes by the Way. MSS P-B 207, Bancroft Library.

Census of Wales, 1841. Family History Library, S.L.C.

Church Historian's Office. Journal 1844–1879. LDS Archives.

Church in Wales. Parish Church of Dale. Bishop's Transcripts, 1799–1878. Microfilm 1238692 item no. 5. LDS Family History Library, S.L.C.

Cox, DeLaun Mills. History. Works Progress Administration, St. George, Utah, Federal Writer's Project, 1935. M 270. Special Collections, Washington County Library, Utah.

Cramer, Thomas J. B. Overland Journey from Kansas to California, 1859. WA MSS 115. Beinecke Library, Yale Univ.

Dowdle, Absalom Porter. Autobiography. LDS Archives.

Duncan, John. Journal and Autobiography, Typescript, MS 18145. LDS Archives.

Emery, Henry. "Journal of Henry 'Harry' Emery." Edited by Karen Emery, 2001. Digital copy at Ancestry.com.

Farnham, Augustus. Missionary Journal. LDS Archives.

Frost, Burr. Diary. LDS Archives.

Gardner, Robert. Biography and Journal. BX 8670.1 .G176b. BYU Library.

General Minutes of the Australasian Mission. LDS Archives.

Gibbons, Andrew Smith. Diaries, 1858, 1877–1878. MSS A 1533. Utah State Hist. Soc.

Hamblin, Jacob. Diary, 1854–1857. MSS A 567-1. Utah State Hist. Soc.

Hampton, Brigham Young. Papers. LDS Archives.

Hampton, William Huntley. Interview with Walker Winslow, 9 December 1938. Accession W13901, Federal Writers' Project, Works Progress Administration, Library of Congress. http://lcweb2.loc.gov/wpa/29080112.html [2 May 2010].

Hicks, Frances, and Maud H. Lewis, comp. Life History of George A. Hicks. Daughters of Utah Pioneers.

Hicks, George Armstrong. Broadside for play, *Celestial Marriage*. 792 H529c 1886. BYU Library.

———. History of Spanish Fork. MSS 284. BYU Library.

———. Scrapbook 1887–1925. MS 8805. LDS Archives.

———. Stephen Markham Biographical Sketch. MSS SC 418. BYU Library.

History of the Church, 1839–circa 1882. LDS Archives.

Journal History of the Church of Jesus Christ of Latter-day Saints. LDS Archives.

Kimball, J. Golden. Diary. MS 662. Special Collections, Marriott Library, Univ. of Utah.

King, Hannah Tapfield. Journals. LDS Archives.

Knox, William. Diary. LDS Archives.

Lee, Ann Gordge. Autobiography. MSS SC 1706. BYU Library.

———. Autobiography, Bishop variant. Property of Sharen L. Moon, copies in possession of the editors.

Lee, John Doyle. Papers of John Doyle Lee, 1841–1877. Henry E. Huntington Library, San Marino, Calif.

Lee, Rachel. Diary. HM 26338. Henry E. Huntington Library, San Marino, Calif.

Lewis, Blanche Moore. Caroline Hicks. http://freepages.genealogy.rootsweb.ancestry.com/~pioneervoices/chicks.htm [2 April 2010].

Lieutenant Governor [Utah] Executive Record Books, Series 242, Utah State Hist. Soc.

Lockley, Frederic. Recollections of Territorial Utah. Fred Lockley Papers, Typescript. MSS C0199. Dept. of Rare Books and Special Collections, Princeton Univ.

Lyman, Amasa M. Journal. In Juanita Brooks Papers. B-103, box 16. Utah State Hist. Soc.

McCall, Kenneth. Biography of Joseph Smith Thompson. Kansas City Public Library.

Mormon Pioneer Overland Travel, 1847–1868. Search engine at http://www.lds.org/churchhistory/library/pioneercompanysearch.

Musser, Amos Milton. Diary. MS 8140. LDS Archives.

New Harmony, Utah, Ward Record. MSS A110. Utah State Hist. Soc.

Pace, James. Autobiography and Diary, 1811–1888. BX 8670 .M82 vol.13. BYU Library.

Record of Fiftieth Quorum of Seventies, Spanish Fork, Utah. LDS Archives.

Register of the Ann Gordge Lee Autobiography. MSS SC 1706. BYU Library.

"Report of the Secretary of War, Dec. 1, 1859." *Message from the President of the United States to the Two Houses of Congress*, 36th Congress, 1st Session, House of Representatives. Washington, D.C: George W. Bowman, 1860. Serial Set 1024.

Rogers, Isaac, to Lester P. Rogers. Fort Hall, 11 July 1848. MS 3987. LDS Archives.

Rogers, Sadie, ed. East Millard Pioneers, Death Notices as Published in the *Progress*, 1913–1937. Typescript, 1938. Family History Library.

Salt Lake City Council. Minutes. Salt Lake City Recorder's Office. Copy in Family History Library, S.L.C.

Salt Lake County. Probate Court Civil and Criminal Case Files, 1852–1887, Series 373. Utah State Archives.

Salt Lake Stake Minutes, 1847–48. LR 604 109. LDS Archives.

Second District Court, Minute Book. Series 5319. Utah State Archives.

Siegfried, Mary H., comp. List of Known Dead Buried in Old Mormon Cemetery Nauvoo, Hancock County, Illinois. 1941. Family History Library, S.L.C.

Sievers, Ruth Bishop. Affidavit. Twin Falls, Idaho, 26 July 1988. Copy in the possession of the editors.

Stebbins, Henry A. Papers. P24, Community of Christ Library-Archives, Independence, Missouri.

Squires, John Fell. Autobiographical Sketch. LDS Archives.

Tanner, Thomas. Autobiographical Sketches. LDS Archives.

Third District Civil Case Files, 1896–ongoing. Series 1622. Utah State Archives.

Third District Territorial Civil Case Files, 1851–1896. Series 9802. Utah State Archives.

Third District Territorial Criminal Case Files, 1882–1896. Series 6836. Utah State Archives.

United States Federal Census, 1860, 1870, 1880, 1900.

Utah County Military District 1850–1866. Utah Territorial Militia Muster Rolls, 1849–1870. LDS Archives.

Utah History Suite, Edition 3. Provo: Historical Views, 2001.

Utah State Archives. "Supreme Court." Agency History #868. http://archives.utah.gov/research/agencyhistories/868.html [2 April 2010].

Utah State Office of Vital Records and Statistics Death Certificates, Series 81448. Utah State Archives.

Wilson, John S. Overland Journey to California from West Virginia, 1859–1860. WA MSS S-795. Beinecke Library, Yale Univ.

Wray, Clayton. The Story of the Second Murder in Iron County, Utah: Olive Olivia Curtis Coombs. MSS A 5562. Utah State Hist. Soc.

Index

This index uses the following abbreviations: AG for Ann Gordge, BY for Brigham Young, BYH for Brigham Young Hampton, JDL for John Doyle Lee, and MMM for the Mountain Meadows massacre. Counties specified after place-names are all in Utah unless another state is named. References to illustrations appear in italic type.

The Editors

A native of San Francisco and resident of Seattle, Polly Aird attended Wellesley College and graduated Phi Beta Kappa from Stanford University with Distinction in History. She worked as a scientific editor for the National Academy of Sciences in Washington, D.C., and for the Lunar and Planetary Laboratory at the University of Arizona. She later managed communications for the computer science division of The Boeing Company. While researching the lives of her Scottish great-grandparents, she learned they had been early LDS converts who left the faith. Ms. Aird has written award-winning articles for the *Journal of Mormon History*, the *Utah Historical Quarterly*, *Dialogue*, and the *Nevada State Historical Quarterly*. Her *Mormon Convert, Mormon Defector: A Scottish Immigrant in the American West* (2009) won the Best Biography Award from the Mormon History Association and was a finalist for the Western Writers of America's Spur Award.

Jeff Nichols graduated from the State University of New York at Geneseo and served for nine years as an officer in the U.S. Navy. He studied with the late Dean May and earned his Ph.D. in history at the University of Utah and now teaches Environmental History, Latin American History, Vietnam and America, and American Women's History at Westminster College in Salt Lake City. His *Prostitution, Polygamy, and Power: Salt Lake City, 1847–1918*, won the Mormon History Association's Best First Book Award. His interests extend to theater, and he has appeared in several Westminster Players productions.

Will Bagley is general editor of the Arthur H. Clark Company's documentary history series KINGDOM IN THE WEST: *The Mormons and the American Frontier*. He has written and edited more than twenty books on overland emigration, frontier violence, railroads, mining, and the Mormons, and he has won best-book awards from the Western History Association and the

Denver Public Library, as well as the Western Writers of America Spur Award. Mr. Bagley's most recent books are *So Rugged and Mountainous: Blazing the Oregon and California Trails, 1812–1848*, the first of four volumes of the series *Overland West: The Story of the Oregon and California Trails*, and *The Mormon Rebellion: America's First Civil War, 1857–1858*, with David L. Bigler.

Kingdom in the West Series

The role of the Church of Jesus Christ of Latter-day Saints in the settlement of the American West has been a subject of controversy and fascination for 150 years. Kingdom in the West: The Mormons and the American Frontier explores the story of the Mormon people and their part in the wider history of the American West.

1. *The Pioneer Camp of the Saints: The 1846 and 1847 Mormon Trail Journals of Thomas Bullock*, edited by Will Bagley. 1997.
2. *Forgotten Kingdom: The Mormon Theocracy in the American West, 1847–1896*, by David L. Bigler. 1998.
3. *Scoundrel's Tale: The Samuel Brannan Papers*, edited by Bagley. 1999.
4. *Army of Israel: Mormon Battalion Narratives*, edited by Bigler and Bagley. 2000.
5. *Defending Zion: George Q. Cannon and the Mormon California Newspaper Wars of 1856–1857*, edited by Roger Ekins. 2002.
6. *Fort Limhi: The Mormon Adventure in Oregon Territory, 1855–1858*, edited by Bigler. 2003.
7. *Gold Rush Saints: California Mormons and the Great Rush for Riches*, edited by Kenneth N. Owens. 2004.
8. *On the Way to Somewhere Else: European Sojourners in the Mormon West, 1834–1930*, edited by Michael W. Homer. 2006.
9. *Doing the Works of Abraham: A Documentary History of Mormon Polygamy*, edited by B. Carmon Hardy. 2007.

10–11. *At Sword's Point, A Documentary History of the Utah War, 1857–1858*, edited by William MacKinnon. Two volumes, 2008 and 2013.

12. *Innocent Blood: Essential Narratives of the Mountain Meadows Massacre*, edited by Bigler and Bagley. 2009.
13. *Playing with Shadows: Voices of Dissent in the Mormon West*, edited by Polly Aird, Jeff Nichols, and Will Bagley.

Subsequent volumes will include studies of Mormon-Indian relations, the Mormon-related works of Dale Morgan, and the trail to southern California from Salt Lake.

Series subscriptions are welcomed. Manuscript proposals of a documentary nature may also be submitted. Address inquiries to the publisher:

The Arthur H. Clark Company
2800 Venture Drive
Norman, Oklahoma 73069-8218
(405) 325-5609